Hoover Institution Publications 106

Lenin and the Comintern

Lenin and the Comintern

VOLUME I

Branko Lazitch

and

Milorad M. Drachkovitch

Hoover Institution Press
Stanford University
Stanford, California

Hoover Institution Publications 106
Standard Book Number 8179—1061—1
Library of Congress Card Number 74—157886
Printed in the United States of America
© 1972 by the Board of Trustees of the
Leland Stanford Junior University

Contents

Preface

Every researcher who delves into the history of the international Communist movement knows that all the documents of the Communist International are in Moscow, integrated into the central archives of the Communist Party of the Soviet Union at the Institute of Marxism-Leninism. It is less well known that Deposit No. 2 of these archives is entirely devoted to Lenin, including his activities in the Comintern; that Deposit No. 17 holds documents concerning the Central Committee of the Russian Communist Party and its role within the Comintern; and that Deposit No. 495 contains the records of the Executive Committee, the Presidium, and the Secretariat of the Comintern. On the other hand, every researcher also knows that access to these archives has always been barred to non-Soviet scholars, and that even Soviet scholars have only rarely been allowed to quote from the hitherto unpublished sources in these archives. Even the "fraternal parties" who have asked Moscow for documents pertaining to their own history have usually failed in their efforts, with only few exceptions. One of these took place in the winter of 1957, when Tito received from Khrushchev a part of the Comintern archives dealing with the Communist Party of Yugoslavia; but it contained only documents which the Yugoslav party had once sent to the Comintern, and no materials concerning the role of the Comintern, its directing bodies, and the emissaries it sent at different times to the Yugoslav party. That situation remains unchanged today, more than half a century after the founding of the Comintern and more than a quarter of a century after its official dissolution; nor is there evidence to suggest that access will be increased in the near future. There is, in fact, a danger that substantial parts of the archives may be destroyed. By the terms of a special decision taken in 1967 by the Central Committee of the Russian Communist Party ("Rules Concerning the Deposits of the Archives of the Communist Party of the Soviet Union"), only three categories of documents are guaranteed against any act of destruction: those concerning the life and activities of Lenin and members of his family; those concerning the history of the party before and after its victory in the October Revolution, including the year 1923; and materials pertaining to the organs of the party and the actions of partisans during the Great Patriotic War of 1941-45. All other deposits, including the archives that record Comintern history as well as those which deal with events during the Stalinist era, are potentially subject to destruction under the following stipulation: "Documents belonging to the deposits of archives of the CPSU can be destroyed only after examination and approval of the elimination lists by a party archive commission of expertise and control." (See *Partiinaia zhizn*, Moscow, No. 20, October 1967, p. 55.)

With the Comintern archives inaccessible, there remain two possible sources of documentation for a history of the Comintern under Lenin. The first source is the literature on the Comintern published in the East and the West. Probably the richest repository of that literature in the Western world is the Hoover Institution on War, Revolution and Peace at Stanford University. But that source, excellent as it is, is an inadequate basis for a whole history of the organization, for the simple reason that the Comintern was secretive by its very nature, and its public documents were often issued to conceal rather than to reveal the meaning of its activities. To limit one's research to the published literature by and concerning the Communist International would be to leave in obscurity what the Comintern itself wanted kept secret or only partially known. Thus confined in his research, one could not treat amply such an essential aspect of the Comintern as its first apparatus (which is the subject of the longest chapter of this volume). Nor could he provide satisfying coverage of certain paramount events, such as the role of the Comintern in the March 1921 action in Germany or the part it took in splitting the main Socialist parties in Europe. And what is more important, he could not begin to approach in an enlightened way the fundamental problem studied in the two volumes of this history: the relations between the headquarters in Moscow and the national sections of the Third International.

For all these reasons the authors have tried to supplement available library sources by using as their second source a large amount of archival material that emanated from the two most important foreign sections of the Comintern under Lenin—the German and

x

French communist parties. For the first time, in the West or the East, it has been possible to draw from some unpublished confidential documents—for example, the minutes of several of the Comintern Executive Committee and Presidium meetings in the period 1921 to 1924—and from important correspondence between the leaders of the Comintern and the chiefs of the German and French sections. Relying whenever it seemed appropriate upon published memoirs of numerous leaders of the Comintern or other personal documents, we have made all possible use of these confidential documents stemming from leading bodies—the Presidium and the Executive Committee of the Comintern, and the Central Committee and the Politburo of both the French and German sections. Once in possession of these materials, we had to apply the method of scientific deduction to the task of forming conclusions. Like paleontologists who have tried to reconstruct the form of a prehistoric animal with the help of a few fossils, or biologists who must establish a blood composition on the basis of a few drops of blood, we have sought to reconstruct the life of the Comintern with the help of substantial yet partial archives—first for the volume now offered to the public and then for the second volume, which will cover events until the time of Lenin's death in January 1924. Because coverage of the first volume ends with the spring of 1921 whereas the major part of the available archives concerns the period between 1921 and 1924, more of this archival material was used in preparing the second volume than the first.

To the essential elements represented by the unpublished official documents of the Comintern we have added data from some other sources hitherto unused, such as the manuscript memoirs of certain important Communists (for example, those of Karl Steinhardt-Gruber, whose name is closely linked to the foundation of the Comintern, or Albert Treint, a member of the directorate of the French Communist Party and later its secretary-general) or the reminiscences of other important persons as disclosed to the authors in personal interviews (as with Pierre Pascal, who attended the first Comintern congress, and M. Goldenberg, a delegate to the Second Congress of the Communist International). The most precious help of all was graciously given by Mr. Boris Souvarine, who was the French Communist Party representative to the Comintern and who without interruption was a member of the

Executive Committee, the Secretariat, and the Presidium of the Executive Committee of the Comintern from 1921 to 1924. Mr. Souvarine was associated with this research project from the beginning. Not only did he lend the benefits of his own first-hand experience to the project; he also placed at our unrestricted disposal the numerous French party and Comintern archives from the times when he held high official positions in both organizations.

This work on the Comintern under Lenin is intended neither as a history of the Comintern's national sections nor as a social and political history of the times in which the Comintern put down its roots. It is an account of the role of the Comintern in the life of its most important sections. Even in analyzing an event such as the March 1921 action in Germany, our objective was to determine the role the Comintern played in that event and to examine the relations between Moscow and the German Communist Party, not to describe the unfolding of the action itself. By the same token, many aspects of the social and political history of Leninist times properly fall beyond the scope of this project.

This work has benefited from many sources of financial, moral, and intellectual support. The Relm Foundation granted generous initial financial aid for the entire project. Many members of the Hoover Institution's staff helped in different ways: the authors are particularly grateful to Professor Wiktor Sukiennicki, whose numerous special studies on the different aspects of the Comintern's early history yielded much valuable information, and to Mr. Bertram D. Wolfe, who read large parts of the manuscript and offered many useful critical remarks. Special thanks are due also the Library for Political Studies in New York City and to its director, Mr. Joseph Buttinger, who kindly authorized extensive use of the unpublished materials from the Paul Levi Archives. We are grateful to Mr. Robert Addis, who so competently translated large portions of the manuscript from French into English, and to Mr. Gene Tanke for his final editorial help. We wish also to thank Mrs. Olga Stael for painstakingly checking the footnotes and typing and retyping the manuscript, and Miss Ludmila Sidoroff for her substantial help in preparing the index. But although many people have helped in the production of this work, the authors alone bear the responsibility for its contents.

Finally, we should like to refer readers to *A Biographical Dictionary of the Comintern*, prepared by Branko Lazitch and published by the Hoover Institution Press. This dictionary, which summarizes the political careers of more than 700 persons who played active roles in the Comintern, seems to us an indispensable supplement to the present two-volume history of the Comintern under Lenin.

B. L.
M. M. D.

Lenin and the Comintern

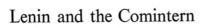

—1—

Proletarian Internationalism During World War I

"The war has devastated Socialism as it has devastated the world."
This statement by a French Socialist leader accurately suggests the
situation of the Second International throughout World War I. The
guns of August 1914 shattered the unity of the international Socialist movement; the overwhelming majority of Socialist leaders,
as well as the rank and file in both belligerent camps, quickly
succumbed to patriotic fever and subordinated the claims of internationalist proletarian class struggle to the requirements of national defense and national solidarity. In the Entente countries the
leaders justified their attitudes by invoking the principle of legiti-
mate national defense. In the countries of the Central Powers
many Socialists upheld their conduct by quoting the imprecations
of Marx and even more of Engels and Bebel against Russian tsarism as the principal reactionary force in Europe.* Everywhere the
Socialists insisted that they had not changed their basic ideological
and political views, and expressed the hope that after the war the
Socialist International would again become a workable instrument.
As the war progressed, and millions in all lands wearied of a war of
apparently endless stalemate, this "defensist" current weakened
somewhat, but it remained the dominant Socialist force in some
countries and a strong one in others.

*"On November 17, 1885, when Engels wrote Bebel of his hope that the
armies of the civilized lands of Western Europe might refuse 'to kill each
other off for the sake of the lousy Balkan peoples,' he added an additional
thought . . . : 'If it [the slaughter]must come, then I only hope that my old
injury doesn't prevent me, at the right moment, from mounting my horse
again.' . . . Bebel shared the hope and the patriotism of his teacher. . . . In
1891 under solemn circumstances, at the Erfurt Congress of his party, . . .
Bebel told the delegates: 'If Russia, the refuge of cruelty and barbarism, the
enemy of all human culture, attacks Germany in order to partition and destroy her . . . then we are as much interested, and more so, than those who
stand today at the head of Germany, and we will fight against the attack."
Bertram D. Wolfe, *Marxism. One Hundred Years in the Life of a Doctrine.*
New York, 1965, pp. 72-73.

To the left of the "defensists" stood the minority of Socialist internationalists who were preoccupied above all with how to stop the war. (In neutral countries such as Italy and Switzerland these represented a majority within the Socialist movement.) They adhered to the spirit and letter of Marxist internationalism, as codified in the resolutions of the Second International's prewar congresses. Clearly a minority at the outset but representing a growing political force everywhere, the internationalists also believed in restoring a unified Socialist movement cleansed of the nationalist aberration. Peace was in their eyes the precondition for the revolution they continued to profess.

To the left of the internationalists stood the smallest, scattered group of Socialists, those who advocated taking advantage of the conditions of war to promote Socialist revolution, and who proclaimed the Second International beyond redemption. International proletarian revolution and the building of a new International was the basic slogan of this group; the leader of Russian Bolshevism, Vladimir Ilich Lenin, became its most ardent spokesman. Even in this group the openness of Lenin's avowed defeatism made him unique.

LENIN TAKES THE STAND

The Russian revolutionary movement, inside and outside Russia, was divided on the question of the war, just as the Socialist movement was in other countries. In Russia "the patriotic bacchanal did not leave the masses of workers untouched: not a few of those who had been striking yesterday joined the ranks of patriotic demonstrators today. Among the Social Democrats themselves confusion reigned."[1] The tiny parliamentary representation of Marxist revolutionary groups, the seven Mensheviks and five Bolsheviks, agreed on a joint declaration on the war, drafted by the Mensheviks, which at the Duma session of July 26 (August 8) was read by the Menshevik deputy V. I. Khaustov as expressing the stand of the Social Democratic fraction of the Duma. The declaration denounced the war in vehement terms and attributed responsibility for it to "the ruling classes of all the countries now at war"; but it also contained a sentence which stated that "the proletariat, a constant defender of the freedom and interests of the people, will at any time fulfill its duty and will defend the cultural treasures of the people from all attacks, wherever they originate—whether from abroad or inside the country."* To compound the ambiguity of their stand on the war, the Menshevik and Bolshevik deputies did not vote either for or against war credits, having walked out of the Assembly.

In Russian Social Democratic émigré circles the war created even greater divisions. "Among the Russian Socialist émigrés abroad, especially in the countries of the Entente, the great majority stood under the influence of the ideology of 'Defense of the Fatherland.'" [2] The pioneer of Russian Marxism, Georgi Plekhanov, became an ardent "defensist" and supporter of the movement to volunteer for service in the French army. Prominent Bolsheviks such as N.V. Kuznetsov (Sapozhkov), secretary of the Bolshevik center in Paris, and former Bolsheviks such as G.A. Aleksinsky, deputy to the second state Duma, followed the same patriotic trend. However, the leading Mensheviks abroad, Y. Martov and P.B. Axelrod, opposed the war as internationalists and emphasized the speediest establishment of peace as the imperative of the proletarian struggle.

To this whirlwind of conflicting opinions, emotions, and attitudes, Lenin was soon to add his voice. On September 6, 1914, a day after his release from Austrian internment in Galicia, he attended a small Bolshevik meeting in Bern, Switzerland, at which he presented seven theses on "the tasks of revolutionary Social Democracy in the European war." One of the theses assailed "the betrayal of Socialism by a majority of the leaders of the Second International" and proclaimed "an ideological and political collapse of that International." Theses six and seven unambiguously rejected any idea of "defensism," stating that "by far the lesser

*Quoted in F. I. Kalinychev, *Gosudarstvenaiia Duma v Rosii*, Moscow, 1957, p. 595. One of the signers of the declaration, Bolshevik deputy A. Badayev, remarked in his memoirs that despite its anti-war character, "our declaration did not contain a clear and precise characterization of the war or of the position of the working class and did not give a well-defined revolutionary lead." *The Bolsheviks in the Tsarist Duma*, New York, 1932, p. 200. In Bertram D. Wolfe's view, "the Declaration . . . was pure Menshevism, pure Kautskyism, and Kautsky, as Lenin was to write to the first follower to whom he could send a letter after the war broke out, 'is now the most harmful of them all.'" *An Ideology in Power. Reflections on the Russian Revolution*. New York, 1969, p. 101.

evil would be the defeat of the Tsar's armies" and that there existed "the necessity of turning the weapons not against the brother wage-slaves of other countries, but against the reaction of the bourgeois governments and parties in each country."[3] The same theses were rearranged into a manifesto, "The War and Russian Social Democracy," issued in October in the name of the Central Committee of the Russian Social Democratic Labor Party and printed on November 1 in the party organ *Sotsial-Demokrat*. The key sentence of the manifesto advocated "turning the present imperialist war into civil war," and doing so with different stages of revolutionary endeavor in various belligerent countries—in less-developed Russia the task was to establish a democratic republic, but in all the more advanced countries it was to bring about a Socialist revolution.[4]

The same issue of *Sotsial-Demokrat* (November 1) contained another of Lenin's articles, entitled "The Position and Tasks of the Socialist International," in which the idea of establishing a Third International to replace the defunct Second was mentioned for the first time: "The Second International is dead, overcome by opportunism. Down with opportunism, and long live the Third International, purged not only of 'turncoats' . . . but of opportunism as well . . . To the Third International falls the task of organizing the proletarian forces for a revolutionary onslaught against the capitalist governments, for civil war against the bourgeoisie of all countries, for the capture of political power, for the triumph of socialism."[5]

A copy of the October Manifesto was sent through a courier to Russia, and a Bolshevik Party secret conference was convened in November to discuss it. The meeting, held near Petrograd, in the zone where military justice ruled, was reported to the police by an agent high in the councils of Bolshevism, and its participants were arrested. The trial of the arrested Bolshevik deputies and other party leaders which was held in mid-February 1915 (and at which Alexander Kerensky defended the accused) revealed that Lenin's views were not unanimously shared, as he himself wrote on March 29, 1915: "[The trial of the Russian Social Democratic Workers faction has proved that] this advance contingent of revolutionary Social Democracy in Russia failed to display sufficient firmness at the trial. . . . To attempt to prove one's solidarity with the social-patriot Mr. Yordansky, as Rosenfeld [L.B. Kamenev] did, or one's disagreement with the Central Committee, is a wrong method, one that is inexcusable from the standpoint of a revolutionary Social Democrat."[6] The court verdict which exiled the Bolshevik leaders to Siberia prevented their disagreement with Lenin from becoming a political rift, but the episode indicated that Lenin's "defeatism" did not suit the dispositions of even his closest followers in Russia.

The picture abroad could not have satisfied Lenin either. Unity among the Russian internationalists could not be achieved; Trotsky openly criticized the slogan that Russia's defeat would be the "lesser evil," and his opinion was shared by prominent Bolsheviks, including N.I. Bukharin and N.V. Krylenko. Lenin, of course, was not swayed by their objections and at another Bolshevik conference in Bern (February 27 to March 4, 1915), he not only reiterated but sharpened his position. The resolution of the conference reaffirmed that "the defeat of Russia under all conditions appears to be the lesser evil," and castigated as "profoundly erroneous" the thought that "a democratic peace is possible without a number of revolutions." The transformation of the imperialist war into civil war was called "the only correct proletarian slogan." The "opportunism" of the Second International was called a "direct betrayal of Socialism," and the Socialist "centrism" of Karl Kautsky was singled out as a particularly harmful and hypocritical form of opportunism.* Moreover, part of the resolution entitled "The Third International" declared that "it would be a harmful illusion to hope to restore a real Socialist International without a complete organizational separation from opportunists."[7] The Bern resolution in fact contained the basic ideas which Lenin and his tiny

---

*Lenin's fury had been concentrated from the beginning on the "betrayal" of German Social Democracy, with a particular vehemence directed against Karl Kautsky, whom in a letter dated October 17, 1914, Lenin termed as "more hypocritical, more revolting, and more harmful than anyone else." *Polnoe sobranie sochinenii*, 5th ed., vol. 49, Moscow, 1964, p. 16. Lenin's anti-Kautsky virulence may be explained above all because Kautsky was not vulnerable to attack as a "social-chauvinist" since he opposed the war, but favored a reunification of the Socialist International at the war's end and a common drive for peace.

group of followers would develop in endless variations during the
ensuing years and which would finally result in the creation of the
Third International.

While trying, with little success, to persuade quarreling groups of
Russian Socialist émigrés and dissenting Bolsheviks of the rightness
of his political and tactical views, Lenin was also busy influencing
those Socialist circles in different countries which at least rejected
"defensist" postures and resented the impotence of the Second
International. The best forums for this effort were provided by a
series of international Socialist conferences held in neutral Switzerland.

The first of these conferences was convened on the initiative of
Swiss Social Democrats, who met with representatives of the Italian Socialist Party in Lugano on September 27, 1914. A copy of
the Bolshevik theses on war was sent to Lugano, but despite its
denunciation of the war the conference advocated a pacifist solution ("an early cessation of the massacre of the peoples") and not
the Bolshevik revolutionary solution.[8] Six months later, on March
26-28, 1915, the International Conference of Socialist Women,
called by Clara Zetkin, secretary of the International Socialist
Women's Bureau, was held in Bern. The delegates, from several
European countries and from both belligerent camps, represented
essentially left Socialist tendencies, but here again not civil war
but struggle for peace was approved, and pacifist slogans were
proclaimed most appropriate to achieve militant Socialist unity.
This position was espoused by Clara Zetkin but rejected by Lenin.
On the eve of the Bern conference he wrote to Alexandra Kollontai (who had just joined the Bolsheviks but did not yet agree with
the slogan of civil war): "The thing I fear most at the present time
is indiscriminate unity, which, I am convinced, is most dangerous
and harmful to the proletariat."[9] Lenin's views at the Bern conference were presented by Inessa Armand and supported by a Polish
delegate. Still, in the words of Lenin's wife, Nadezhda Krupskaya,
"We remained alone. On all sides our 'splitting' policy was denounced. . . . The goody-goody pacifism of the English and the
Dutch did not advance international action a single step."[10]

Similar results were obtained from the International Youth Conference held at Bern on April 4-6. To the draft resolution of the majority of the conference, which called for "an immediate end to the war," the Bolshevik delegates Armand and Yegorov countered with a resolution which advocated launching revolutionary mass actions against the imperialist war and transforming it into a civil war. The Bolsheviks also attacked every shade of opportunism and social chauvinism in the Socialist movement, including "centrism." The conference rejected the Bolshevik draft by 13 votes to 3. (A Polish delegate was the only non-Russian to support it.)[11]

These two Bern conferences, which brought together representatives of the anti-war movement among European Socialists, reflected a situation that would prevail, with only slight alterations, until the end of the war: the scattered Socialist opposition to the war began to assume organized shape on an international level, but from the outset the internationalists were split into two clear-cut factions—the pacifist majority and the Bolshevik-led minority. The two larger conferences which later convened in Switzerland at Zimmerwald and Kienthal, and which epitomized what came to be called the Zimmerwald movement, made this point explicit. They also offered an opportunity for Lenin to advance his ideas on a broader front.

In May 1915 the Executive Committee of the Italian Socialist Party proposed an international conference to be attended by all Socialist parties and groups which rejected the concept of civil peace and were ready for international action against the war on the basis of the proletarian class struggle. In order to prepare such a conference seven persons met in Bern on July 11, 1915: Robert Grimm of the Swiss Socialist Party; Angelica Balabanova and Oddino Morgari of the Italian Socialist Party; Grigori Zinoviev representing the Russian Bolsheviks; P. B. Axelrod representing the Mensheviks; Adolf Warski (Warszawski) of the Main Presidium of the Social Democratic Party of Poland and Lithuania; and Henryk Walecki of the left wing of the Polish Socialist Party. In view of the fact that three of the participants at this preliminary meeting—Balabanova, Warski, and Walecki—were eventually to rise to the highest positions in the Comintern, it is significant that Zinoviev received no support for his proposals to narrow the list of

conference participants by drawing from only the most radical
Socialist groups and to put on the conference agenda an item
concerning the creation of a Third International.*

In the meantime, during the summer of 1915, Lenin and Zinoviev were busy writing a pamphlet entitled *Socialism and War*.
Lenin was also corresponding with friends in different countries
urging them to arrange for reliable leftists to attend the forthcoming conference, or to have them send their proxies to Lenin.
The pamphlet itself, translated into French and English, contained
some very precise ideas which merit close attention. The first
chapter concentrated on the issue of "social chauvinism" or Socialist "defensism,"which was called a betrayal of Socialism and of
the text and spirit of the resolutions of the congresses of the
Second International. The most derogatory epithets were again
reserved for Karl Kautsky, and passing reference was made to the
"different forms of Kautskyism" to be found in the writings of
Leon Trotsky, the Dutch Socialist radical Henriette Roland-Holst,
and the Bulgaro-Rumanian Socialist Christian Rakovsky. In the
third chapter Lenin and Zinoviev assailed all attempts to reconstruct the Second International, and stated that the Italian-Swiss
Socialist conference in Lugano and the Women's and Youth conferences in Bern, despite good intentions, had "entirely failed."
They then heaped compliments on the German leftist splinter
groups and their magazines *Lichtstrahlen* and *Die Internationale*
and fully endorsed their statement that "the Kautskyist 'center'
was more harmful to the cause of Marxism than open social chauvinism." Here, however, Lenin and Zinoviev made an observation
which revealed what would later become one of the trademarks of
their operational techniques in the Comintern, namely the use of
the united front in certain phases of political maneuvering:

> Generally speaking, our attitude towards the vacillating elements in the
> International is of tremendous importance. Those elements, namely

---

*Reporting to his party about the Bern preliminary conference and his unsuc-
cessful attempts to influence the other participants, Zinoviev warned with
displeasure that "it is clear that the so-called conference of the Left will in
reality be a conference of 'conciliators' of the 'Center' with social chauvinists.
It is clear that no one cares seriously about the calling of the so-called Left
conference." *Leninskii sbornik*, vol. 14, pp. 161-64. English text in Olga Hess
Gankin and H. H. Fisher, *The Bolsheviks and the World War*, Stanford, 1940,
pp. 312-15.

Socialists of a *pacifist* shade, exist both in the neutral and in some belligerent countries (in England, for instance, the Independent Labour Party). These elements can be our fellow travelers. It is necessary to get closer to them with the aim of fighting the social-chauvinists. But we must remember that they are *only* fellow travelers; that as far as the main and fundamental problems are concerned, when the International is reconstructed, those same elements will go, not with us, but against us, with Kautsky, Scheidemann, Vandervelde, Sembat.

Lenin and Zinoviev enumerated next those small groups of genuine revolutionary Social Democrats in Germany, Russia, Scandinavia, in the Balkans (the Bulgarian "Tesniaks"), in Italy, in England (part of the British Socialist Party), in France, and in Holland ("Tribunists"). At the end of the third chapter they became very specific:

It is quite obvious that in order to create an *international* Marxist organization, the separate countries must be ready to create independent local Marxist parties. Germany, the home of the oldest and strongest labor movements, is of decisive importance. The near future will show whether conditions have already become ripe for the creation of a new Marxist International. If so, our party will gladly join such a Third International, purged of opportunism and chauvinism. If not, it will mean that a more or less protracted period of evolution is required before this task of purging is completed. Our party will then be the extreme opposition inside the old International pending a time when the basis for an International Association of Workers resting on the basis of revolutionary Marxism will have been created in the various countries.*

The Zimmerwald conference (September 5-8, 1915) offered to Lenin his first opportunity to take personal leadership in a complicated political battle, which he eagerly approached with three objectives in mind: to forge a coherent international nucleus of like-minded revolutionaries; to influence as much as possible the other participants who were not likely to subscribe to his political line; and to widen the rift between the internationalists in attendance and the absent "defensist" socialists. The heterogeneity of the conference facilitated Lenin's task. Out of 38 delegates he

---

*The full text of this pamphlet is reproduced in *Collected Works of V. I. Lenin*, vol. XVIII ("The Imperialist War"), New York, 1930, pp. 214-58. Emphasis in the text. It is interesting to note that Lenin and Zinoviev were willing to remain within the Second International as its extreme opposition until the Germans were ready to found a new International.

could count on eight to support him on the basic issues. They
were, besides himself and Zinoviev: Ian Berzin (Winter), representing the Lettish Social Democrats; Karl Radek, representing the
left wing of the Polish Socialist Party; Zeth Höglund and Ture
Nerman, representing the Social Democratic youth organizations
of Sweden and Norway; Fritz Platten, a Swiss Social Democrat;
and Julian Borchardt from Berlin, editor of the left-Socialist magazine *Lichtstrahlen*.[12] When its own draft of the conference resolution was voted on (and rejected by 19 votes to 12), this hard core
of the "Zimmerwald Left" was temporarily joined by four other
delegates: Henriette Roland-Holst of the Dutch left-Socialist magazine *De Internationale*, Leon Trotsky of the Russian Social Democrat paper *Nashe slovo*, and Victor Chernoff and Marc Natanson,
representing the Russian Social Revolutionary Party. The non-
Leninist majority of the conference was composed of most of the
German delegation, the French, the Russian Mensheviks, and some
of the Poles and the Italians. In between wavered a few conference
"centrists"—Trotsky, Grimm, Balabanova, and Roland-Holst.
Nuances aside, the basic division of the conference was described
by Zinoviev in the following way: "The conference proved ... to be
rather diversified in its composition. Besides convinced Marxists
there were sentimental socialists, elements which vacillated toward
the center, comrades who had not settled their accounts with
pacifism, adherents of reformism and syndicalism whom at present
life pushes in a different direction than formerly, etc."[13]

The essential points on which the majority of the conference
and the left disagreed were two: First, the majority emphasized
that "in no way should the suspicion be aroused that this conference wishes to bring about a breach and form a new International." Second, the majority proclaimed that "only through a continuous, ever-increasing collaboration of all the proletarian forces
can that influence which will force the rulers to cease this horrible
massacre of the people be attained."[14] The manifesto of the conference, accepted largely in the form drafted by Trotsky, was
essentially a Socialist-internationalist-pacifist document. It bitterly
criticized pursuit of the imperialist war and blamed the official
Socialist parties as well as the International Socialist Bureau for
failing in their duties; but its main emphasis was put on "the

struggle for liberty, for brotherhood of nations, for Socialism," and on taking up the fight "for a peace without annexations or war indemnities."[15] Although he signed the manifesto, Lenin in a separate statement (co-signed by Zinoviev, Radek, Nerman, Höglund, and Berzin) objected that it contained "no clear characterization of the means of combating the war."[16]

The two main political currents of the Zimmerwald movement, while continuing their anti-war cooperation, also took organizational steps which accentuated their disagreements. The Zimmerwald conference decided to establish in Bern an official International Socialist Committee (ISC) composed of Oddino Morgari, Angelica Balabanova, and the Swiss Charles Naine and Robert Grimm, a group which reflected the internationalist-pacifist majority of the conference. At the same time, as a sort of a non-official counterpart, the Left set up its own bureau consisting of Lenin, Zinoviev, and Radek. Evaluating the work done in Zimmerwald, Lenin made several important distinctions. He emphasized that the ideological struggle at the conference was waged "between a solid group of internationalists, revolutionary Marxists, and the vacillating near-Kautskyists," and criticized again the "timorousness" of the conference's manifesto. On the other hand, he stressed as a positive achievement that "we succeeded in introducing [into the manifesto] a number of the fundamental ideas of revolutionary Marxism," so that it became "a step forward toward a real struggle against opportunism." He then argued in favor of working together with the vacillating internationalist elements, on the condition that the Bolsheviks retain full freedom of action and criticism: "It would be bad military tactics to refuse to move together with the growing international movement of protest against social chauvinism because this movement is slow, takes 'only' one step forward, is ready and willing to take a step backward tomorrow, to make peace with the old International Socialist Bureau."[17]

To consolidate and extend the gains achieved in Zimmerwald, Lenin used the same method he had been employing between 1905 and 1912 in Russian Social Democrat politics: while remaining in the main movement, he organized his own, the left's organizational nucleus, which issued as its organ, in Zurich, the *Internationale Flugblätter*, and later a review, *Vorbote*, as distinguished from the *Bulletin* of the International Socialist Committee. Moreover, in different countries—Germany, Switzerland, Sweden, Norway, Holland, the United States—periodicals spreading the ideas of the Zimmerwald Left began to appear.

During the latter part of 1915 and throughout 1916 the Bolsheviks abroad engaged in battles on several fronts, with differing degrees of success. On the one hand, Lenin sometimes furiously disagreed and debated with "the Bolsheviks of the former *Vpered* group (Lunacharsky, Manuilsky, and others) on the national question and with the Bukharin-Piatakov group on the defeat of one's own government, the right of self-determination, and the minimum program in general."[18] He accused Bukharin of being "devilishly unstable in politics,"[19] and came close to breaking with Radek.* In the spring of 1916 he also criticized the tactical programs of the German, Dutch, and Polish lefts, and in the pages of the *Sbornik Sotsial-Demokrata* "analyzed and attacked the attitude of Radek and [Rosa] Luxemburg on defense of the fatherland and the right of self-determination, the attitude of the Dutch, Polish, Scandinavian, and Swiss lefts on disarmament, and the position of Bukharin on the state."[20] On the other hand, while these quarrels jolted the already tiny ranks of the revolutionary left and further augmented Lenin's reputation as an incurable splitter, the Zimmerwald Left made slow but notable progress on two fronts. It contributed to the widening of the gap between the International Socialist Committee and the International Socialist Bureau (whose secretary, Camille Huysmans, tried without success to reestablish ties between the European Socialist parties on the basis of a mutual "amnesty"), and it strengthened its own influence within the larger Zimmerwald movement. These trends were visible at a meeting of the enlarged International Socialist Committee in Bern (February 5-10, 1916), which convoked the second Zimmerwald conference. Zinoviev, co-opted into the membership of the ISC, described the meeting as a step forward "away from the

*Besides disagreements on some theoretical problems, Radek shortly before the Zimmerwald conference did not see eye to eye with Lenin on one central issue, as he wrote in his autobiography: "I believed that the road to civil war was yet very long, that it was impermissible to raise the question of splitting." *Granat*, Entsiklopedicheskii slovar Russkogo bibliograficheskogo instituta, 7th edition, Moscow, n.d., vol. 41, part II, p. 157.

marshland of Ledebour, who dictated his will at Zimmerwald,"* particularly because of the more radical wording of the meeting's address and the fact that it denounced the idea of mutual Socialist amnesty.

According to Zinoviev, the second Zimmerwald conference, held in Bern and Kienthal (April 24-30, 1916), was another step forward for the Zimmerwald Left. Numerically, its progress was hardly noticeable: out of 44 delegates, the leftists could count on twelve—three Bolsheviks, three Poles, three Swiss, a German, an Italian, and a Serb.† However, the non-leftist majority was heterogeneous, and the multitude of groups and wavering positions permitted the left to exercise greater influence than its numbers would otherwise have allowed. The central issue at the conference turned around the problem of the Zimmerwald movement's attitude and relations with the International Socialist Bureau, which was trying, after transferring its seat from Brussels to the Hague, to reestablish international Socialist contacts in anticipation of renewed postwar cooperation. The Kienthal gathering was highly disunited on the question of how to cope with the Bureau. The majority, though critical of the Second International and the Bureau itself, was inclined to cooperate with it; the left was adamantly opposed to any kind of cooperation. After no less than six resolutions were offered to solve that problem, a compromise resolution was passed. It repeated criticisms of the Bureau and refused to take part in the calling of its plenary meeting, but it expressed willingness to attend such a meeting if the ISC could first work out a program of joint action. The resolution recognized "irreconcilable antagonisms" within the Second International but ruled out any plans "to decree and create artificially a new International."[21]

Contre le courant, vol. II, Paris, 1927, p. 73. According to Zinoviev, "within the Zimmerwald bloc, there exist many non-Marxist, non-revolutionary elements. The influential groups of that bloc have more sympathy for Ledebour [a German left-wing internationalist-pacifist Socialist leader] and his groups, than for Liebknecht; they have more sympathy for Martov and Axelrod than for us." *Ibid.*

†Even these twelve delegates were not all iron-clad leftists. According to Zinoviev, the Italian leftist Serrati "drew near to the Zimmerwald Left"; the Serbian Social Democrat Kaclerović "joined, though not entirely, the left"; of the Swiss, he said that "two or three . . . were in agreement with us." *Contre le courant*, II, p. 79.

The final result of the Kienthal conference was ambiguous. On the one hand, Zinoviev's "step forward" was accomplished by the very fact that some of the Bolshevik theses and much of its radical phraseology were accepted as trademarks of the entire Zimmerwald movement. On the other hand, the movement as such, particularly in the organizational sense, was unwilling to serve the Bolsheviks' main purpose, which was to cut all ties with the Second International. Zinoviev himself recognized this, and wrote bluntly on June 10, 1916: "The influence of the Left has become much stronger than at the first Zimmerwald. The prejudices against the Left have weakened. Still, may one say that the die has been cast, that the Zimmerwaldists have pledged their word to break with the official 'Socialists,' that Zimmerwald *has become* an embryo of the Third International? No, in good conscience that cannot be said. All one may assert at the present moment is that there is more chance now than after Zimmerwald that the entire affair will turn in favor of the revolutionaries, in favor of Socialism."[22]

Zinoviev's caution was justified. Immediately after Kienthal, half of the ISC voted in favor of attending an international conference of Socialists from neutral countries, sponsored by Camille Huysmans, secretary of the International Socialist Bureau. "This means," complained Zinoviev, "that given the slightest opportunity of being seduced, half of the Zimmerwaldists will submit readily to the seduction."[23]

No one was more aware of the Zimmerwald-Kienthal ambiguities than Lenin; he was more convinced than ever that only he himself was theoretically and tactically correct, and he became increasingly skeptical that working within the Zimmerwald movement would bring political dividends. A series of polemical post-Kienthal articles indicated that on basic problems of theory and practice he was in disagreement with some of the most prominent Western and Russian leftists, including Bolsheviks. In August 1916 he wrote a sharp critical review of "The Pamphlet by Junius," a tract against the war and the official German Social Democratic Party published in January 1916 by Rosa Luxemburg (under the pen name "Junius"). Compared with the earlier writings of the magazine *Internationale*, he said, it represented a "definite step backward." His basic complaint was that on the theoretical level the Junius brochure was wrong to reject national self-determination and to dismiss the possibility of national wars in the epoch of imperialism; even worse, he said, was Junius' failure to attack Kautsky's opportunism, which indicated that "Junius has not completely rid himself of the 'environment' of the German Social Democrats, even the Lefts, who are afraid of a split, who are afraid to follow revolutionary slogans to their logical conclusions."[24] He emphasized that the only correct attitude was expressed in the Bolshevik September-November 1914 manifesto on war and the March 1915 Bern resolutions.

In October 1916 Lenin made a much stronger attack on a Bolshevik, "P. Kievsky" (the pen name of G. Piatakov); he said Kievsky's interpretation of imperialism would spread "the most hopeless theoretical confusion among the workers" and revive "a number of the old errors of the old 'Economists'."[25] At about the same time Lenin wrote another lengthy polemical article, "The Discussion of Self-Determination Summed Up," in which he pronounced himself in "fundamental disagreement" with the Dutch and Polish Socialist leftists who rejected the right of self-determination of nations under socialism.[26] Also in October he criticized the Scandinavian, Dutch, and Swiss Left Socialists for favoring the slogan of disarmament in the struggle for peace.[27]

If Lenin did not dominate the Zimmerwald Left in the realm of ideology and tactics, neither was he its undisputed political and moral authority, with the last and decisive word. In January 1916 when the review *Vorbote* appeared in Bern as the organ of the Zimmerwald Left, Lenin and Zinoviev were supposed to be both publishers and regular contributors, on an equal footing with the Roland-Holst and Trotsky group. But to Lenin's great surprise he was evicted from the editorial board. He complained of this in a letter to Henriette Roland-Holst dated January 21, 1916.[28] In another letter to her dated March 8, he said he had lost his editorial rights on the *Vorbote* and had been demoted to simple "contributor."[29] The following month, during the Kienthal conference, Lenin was threatened with isolation within the Zimmerwald Left. He wrote in a letter to Zinoviev dated May 21 (and first published in 1934): "You know that at Kienthal Radek wanted to build up a majority against us among the left, at the meeting of the left . . . and that an *ultimatum* was required to force him to recognize the *independence* of our Central Committee."[30] In the meantime the

second and last issue of *Vorbote* had appeared, and Lenin wrote to
A.G. Shliapnikov on May 23: "You may not know that Radek
pushed us out of the *Vorbote* editorial board. It was initially
agreed that there would be a joint editorial board composed of
two groups: (1) the Dutch (maybe plus Trotsky) and (2) us (i.e.,
Radek, *Grigori, and me*). This condition gave us equal rights on
the editorial board. Radek intrigued for months, and got the 'mis-
sus' (Roland-Holst) to *cancel* this plan. We were demoted to the
position of contributors. It's a fact!"[31]

In this quarrel with other members of the Zimmerwald Left,
Lenin could not even rely entirely on Zinoviev. As he explained in
a letter to Inessa Armand, dated November 30, 1916 (and published for the first time in 1949): "I had an argument last spring with
Grigori, who had no understanding at all of the political situation
at that time, and [he] reproached me for breaking with the Zimmerwald Left. This is nonsense."[32] After Lenin's death Zinoviev
confirmed Lenin's version of the *Vorbote* eviction but preferred
not to mention his own disagreements with him.[33] He confirmed,
however, that "during the years 1915 and 1916, we were an insignificant minority which tried to establish international ties and
keep contact with the Russian movement."[34]

In spite of his own earlier views on the necessity of influencing
the non-Bolshevik elements within the Zimmerwald movement,
Lenin grew impatient with his non-leftist partners there. Thus in
January 1917 he wrote a violent article (published for the first
time in 1924) in which he stated: "We openly expose the Zimmerwald right wing, which has deserted to the side of bourgeois-
reformist pacifism. We openly expose the betrayal of Zimmerwald
by R. Grimm, and we demand that a conference be convened to
remove him from his post on the International Socialist
Committee."[35]

Though disappointed with the Zimmerwald movement in general, Lenin increasingly hoped that a split was maturing in the
Socialist ranks of all countries and that this would strengthen the
Zimmerwald Left. In a speech at the congress of the Social Democratic Party of Switzerland, on November 4, 1916, he claimed to
see leftward trends in the Socialist parties of Germany (around
Karl Liebknecht and Otto Rühle), France (through the creation of
the Committee for the Re-establishment of International Con-

nections), Russia, England, and the United States.[36] He could in fact look with some satisfaction on the growth of revolutionary organizing and propaganda activities in several countries since September 1915, when the Bolsheviks had initiated them in Switzerland on a miniscule budget.* In Switzerland Fritz Platten, the popular Socialist leader in Zurich, and Willi Münzenberg, the secretary of the International Socialist Youth League, sided with Lenin against the internationalist-pacifist majority of the Swiss Socialists. Zeth Höglund in Sweden and Ture Nerman in Norway eagerly spread Lenin's ideas in the Socialist parties of their countries and later led pro-Zimmerwald splinter groups. The U.S.A. was visited in the winter of 1916-17 by Bukharin, Berzin, and Kollontai, who were instrumental in persuading the Boston Socialist Propaganda League† (and its periodical *The Internationalist*) to adopt the Zimmerwald Left platform in January of 1917.

But these were really no more than isolated endeavors which did little to sway most Socialist leaders and party members, who were still in the majority "defensist"-minded or evolving in the direction of pacifism instead of revolutionary defeatism. Lenin himself, an embattled political refugee in Switzerland, continued to preach the gospel of the coming revolution, but even he doubted that it would happen in his lifetime. In January 1917 he said gloomily in a lecture (whose text was first published in *Pravda* in January

*In his autobiography Karl Radek wrote: "The fighting funds of this organization [the Zimmerwald Left]were gathered as follows: Vladimir Ilich contributed from the Bolsheviks 20 francs, Borchardt from the German leftists 20 francs, and I from Hanecki's pocket in the name of the Polish Social Democrats 10 francs. In this manner the future Communist International had at its disposal for the conquest of the world fifty francs." *Granat*, vol. 41, part II, p. 160.

†The key personality of the Boston Socialist Propaganda League was Louis Fraina, a leading figure of the future American Communist movement. Until the outbreak of the February 1917 revolution in Russia, however, Fraina was particularly influenced by the ideas of Rosa Luxemburg and the Dutch left-wing Socialist Sebald Justius Rutgers. The influence of the aforementioned Russian visitors increased after the 1917 events in Russia, when everything that was happening there attracted a growing attention. These observations were communicated to the authors of this volume by Bertram D. Wolfe, who at that time was in close touch with Fraina and was an editor of a left-wing paper *Class Struggle*, along with John Reed, Louis Fraina, Jay Lovestone, Ludwig Lore, Nikolai Bukharin, Alexandra Kollontai, and Leon Trotsky. The Russians left for home soon after the journal was founded.

1925): "We of the older generation may not live to see the decisive battles of this coming revolution."[37] Gloom and intransigeance fit each other well, as his wife was later to remark: "Never, I think, was Vladimir Ilich in a more irreconcilable mood than during the last months of 1916 and the early months of 1917."[38] Then, with the sudden storm of the Russian February revolution, the outlook changed overnight. Once a refugee scribbler of angry pamphlets—"the Grand Inquisitor of the International, who fortunately lacks the power to carry out its [Bolshevik] ideas," as a political opponent comfortably called him in 1916[39]—Lenin was now heading home, a prophet seeking the power to make his dreams a reality.

BREAKING WITH THE ZIMMERWALD MOVEMENT

After the fall of the Tsarist regime in Russia, the desire for peace grew stronger among Socialists everywhere; in Russia, however, "defensism" and internationalist pacifism were splitting even further the ranks of the various Socialist parties and groups, complicating the already complex situation at the unstable top, where the Provisional Government and the emerging hierarchy of Soviets of Workers' and Soldiers' Deputies competed for political preeminence. On the issue of war and peace, the Provisional Government intended to pursue the war against Germany and remain faithful to the alliance with the Entente powers; the Petrograd Soviet advocated a more ambiguous stand, combining certain pacifist, Zimmerwaldian principles with the "revolutionary defensism" advocated by the Social Revolutionaries and the majority of Mensheviks. In a "Call to the Peoples of the World" issued on March 27, 1917, the Petrograd Soviet proclaimed that re-establishing and strengthening of the unity of workers of all countries was essential.[40]

It is paradoxical that while similar aspirations sprang up among Socialists everywhere, few could agree on the means of promoting a Socialist unity which could help bring the war to an end. A first initiative was taken by the Socialists of the neutral countries, the Danes and the Dutch, who decided to call a plenary meeting of the International to discuss the international situation. On April 22, at the request of the Dutch, the Secretary of the International Socialist Bureau, Camille Huysmans, issued a letter to all the national sections of the International inviting them to send representatives to a conference in Stockholm on May 15. The invitation included both majority and minority Socialists of the belligerent states; the invitation was brought to Russia by a Danish Social Democrat, Frederich Borgbjerg. The hostility which the French and British Socialists showed toward the Huysmans initiative made the Stockholm meeting impossible, but a Dutch-Scandinavian Committee was established on May 3 in order to pursue the original idea.

A second initiative to convoke an international Socialist conference came from the Petrograd Soviet, which sent a telegram on May 7 inviting the minority (pacifist-internationalist) Socialists in Great Britain, France, Italy, Switzerland, and Sweden to send delegates to Russia to confer informally with the Soviet. Finally, on May 10, the Zimmerwald Socialist Committee (which under the influence of events in Russia decided to move its seat from Bern to Stockholm) issued a circular letter inviting twenty political parties and groups, beginning with the Petrograd Soviet, to a third Zimmerwald conference to be held in Stockholm on May 31 (though the date was soon reset for the beginning of September).

As these various initiatives were unfolding, Lenin was campaigning in Russia for breaking with the International Socialist Committee and splitting the Zimmerwald movement. In a speech delivered on April 17, 1917, the day after his arrival to Petrograd, at a caucus of the Bolshevik members of the All-Russian Conference of the Soviets of Workers' and Soldiers' Deputies, he put forward as the tenth of his "April theses" the task of "rebuilding the International" by "taking the initiative in creating a revolutionary International, an International against the social-chauvinists and against the 'Center'."[41] Commenting on that thesis, Lenin insisted that "the Left-Zimmerwald movement exists in all countries of the world" and that "the masses must realize that Socialism has been split throughout the world." He added: "I hear that in Russia there is a movement towards unity, unity with the defensists. This is a betrayal of Socialism. I think that it is better to stand alone, like Liebknecht: one against one hundred and ten."[42]

Everyone in Petrograd, friend and foe alike, seemed to disagree with Lenin's position. Plekhanov called the April theses "ravings."[43] A friend of Kerensky's, Vladimir Stankevich, noted

in his diary: "A man who is talking such nonsense is not dangerous."[44] And the Bolshevik Kamenev published in *Pravda* on April
21 an article entitled "Our Differences," in which he stated that
Lenin's theses "represent the *personal* opinion of comrade Lenin,"
and that Lenin's general line appeared to be unacceptable to the
party.[45] In this he agreed with Radek, and the predominant majority of Bolsheviks, who believed that a break with the Zimmerwaldists would be "premature."[46]

Lenin was not moved   by such criticism and wrote a special
pamphlet on the subject prior to the Seventh Bolshevik Party
Conference which convened April 24-29 (May 7-12). He distinguished three groups within the international Socialist and labor
movement: social-chauvinists, who advocated national defense in
any imperialist war; centrists, who vacillated between social-
chauvinism and real internationalism (for example, Kautsky,
Haase, and Ledebour in Germany, Longuet and Pressemane in
France, Philip Snowden and Ramsay MacDonald in England,
Morris Hillquit in the United States, Turati, Treves, Modigliani,
and others in Italy, Robert Grimm in Switzerland, Victor Adler in
Austria, Axelrod, Martov, Chkheidze, Tsereteli, and others in
Russia); and finally the real internationalists, the Zimmerwald
Left. Karl Liebknecht, together with Otto Rühle, was singled out
as the outstanding representative of the Zimmerwald Left in Germany, and then followed a list of the others belonging to the same
trend in other countries: Loriot and Guilbeaux in France (Guilbeaux published a revue in Geneva); in England some members of
the British Socialist Party and the Independent Labour Party; in
the United States the Socialist Labor Party, as well as those
around the paper *The Internationalist*; in Holland the "Tribunists"
(Anton Pannekoek, Hermann Gorter, David Wijnkoop, and Henriette Roland-Holst, who though a centrist at Zimmerwald had now
joined the Bolshevik ranks); in Sweden the party of the youth or
the left already active in Zimmerwald; in Bulgaria the "narrow"
socialists; in Italy Lazzari, the secretary of the party, and Serrati,
the director of its central organ, *Avanti*; in Poland two groups,
Radek and Hanecki and then Rosa Luxemburg and Jogiches-
Tyszko; and in Switzerland and Austria various groups of genuine
revolutionaries.

After this enumeration Lenin concentrated his attacks on the Kautskyian center, emphasizing that "we Russians do not as yet know that the Zimmerwald majority are really Kautskyians." He continued:

> We can stand no longer this Zimmerwaldian mire. We must not, on account of the Zimmerwald "Kautskyians," remain more or less allied with the chauvinist International of the Plekhanovs and Scheidemanns. We must break with this International immediately. We ought to remain in Zimmerwald only to gather information.
>
> It is precisely we who must found, right now, without delay, a new, revolutionary, proletarian International, or rather, not to fear to acknowledge publicly that this new International is already established and working . . . .
>
> "To wait" for international conferences and congresses is simply to betray internationalism . . . . Let us not "wait," rather let our party found at once a third International. . . .[47]

Lenin's impatience was not shared by his party comrades, as the April national conference was to prove. Even during the Petrograd metropolitan conference of the Bolshevik party, which met a few days before the national meeting, Lenin's "theses" were criticized in the speeches by M. Tomsky, V.V. Kossior, and M.I. Kalinin. Kalinin in particular, stressing his status as an "old Bolshevik," remarked that what was new in Lenin's theses was not right, and hinted that he disapproved of "the comrades who came from abroad."[48]   At the national party conference, the first legal and open Bolshevik conference in the party's history, disagreements with Lenin were manifest on several issues. After Lenin's introductory report "On the Current Movement (the War and the Provisional Government)," Feliks Dzerzhinsky took the floor on a point of order and said: "From private talks, it is obvious that many people disagree in principle with the theses of the reporter. I suggest that we listen to reports presenting another point of view on the current movement, that we hear comrades who, together with us, have practically lived through the revolution and who have found that it has developed in a somewhat different direction than the one described by the reporter."[49]   Following this proposal, two co-reporters, Kamenev and Milyutin, analyzed the Russian domestic situation from a different angle.

The action on the last item on the agenda of the conference, "The Situation in the International and the Tasks of the Bolshevik Party," again showed the split between Lenin and the other party leaders. On the issue of an immediate break with Zimmerwald, Lenin was opposed by the entire conference and deserted even by Zinoviev. Zinoviev made a report to the conference and offered a draft resolution in which, while repeating all the former objections to reconstituting the old International through "mutual amnesty," he proposed to remain in the "Zimmerwald bloc,"to support there the tactics of the Zimmerwald Left and to "take immediate steps for setting up the Third International." Zinoviev was against Lenin's proposal to remain in Zimmerwald "only to gather information," because "we were the active people there, 'the initiators.'" He also suggested accepting the invitation of the International Socialist Committee to attend the third Zimmerwald conference and recommended the naming of proper representatives. The main difference between Zinoviev and Lenin lay in Zinoviev's belief that the Bolsheviks should not hastily isolate themselves. As he explained: "In order to build the International, it is necessary to do so internationally: we can take the initiative, but to organize, to decide, we must act internationally. The final break with the Zimmerwaldians we must make *together* with our like-minded comrades in Zimmerwald. I would consider it extremely premature to state that we are leaving Zimmerwald now. We are taking the initiative to build the Third International, but we should not break before we reach an agreement with the Left parties of Zimmerwald, and before every worker understands why we break."[50] Put to a vote, Lenin's proposal to add to the draft resolution, "We are staying [in Zimmerwald] for information's sake only," was defeated, and all those present, except Lenin, voted for Zinoviev's resolution.

Lenin's isolation with regard to the tactics to be employed by the Bolsheviks vis-à-vis the Zimmerwald movement, significant as it was, did not make invalid his strategic principle that an independent, Third International should be established. Moreover, the April conference unanimously rejected the Borgbjerg proposal for a peace conference (on the ground that Borgbjerg was "directly or indirectly" an agent of German imperialism). A few weeks later, on May 25, the Bolshevik Central Committee declined to partici- pate in the conference planned by the Petrograd Soviet, arguing that such a meeting would include "quasi-Socialist ministers who have deserted to the side of the bourgeoisie."[51] Even further co- operation with the Zimmerwaldists was narrowed in the sense that the Bolshevik representatives were to leave the third Zimmerwald conference "should the conference express itself in favor of any rapprochement or of any discussion of affairs together with the social-chauvinists."[52]

Russian domestic developments, and the establishment in May of a coalition government including some Zimmerwaldists, worked in favor of Lenin's intransigeance and supported his argument that no cooperation with "ministerialists" should be tolerated on any level, Russian or international. In a postscript to his pamphlet "The Tasks of the Proletariat in Our Revolution," written on June 10, Lenin exultantly claimed that the May 25 decision of the party's Central Committee "rectified the mistake" made at the April conference. "Let us hope," he added, "that the rest of the mistake will be rectified, as soon as we call a conference of all the 'Lefts' ('the third tendency,' 'Internationalist in fact.')"[53]

Lenin's position was also strengthened by the rapprochement between the Dutch-Scandinavian Committee and the Russian Soviets, as well as by the explosion of the "Grimm affair"—a complicated series of incidents which forced Robert Grimm to resign from the International Socialist Committee—and put the leadership of the ISC temporarily in the hands of three Scandi- navian Socialist Leftists (Höglund, Carleson, and Nerman) and Angelica Balabanova. But this was not enough to satisfy Lenin, who saw the Zimmerwald movement as unredeemable even under leftist leadership. In a letter to Radek dated June 17, he called Zinoviev's proposal to capture the Zimmerwald International "an extremely opportunist and harmful tactic," and closed his argu- ment in this way:

"To capture" Zimmerwald? This is to take *upon oneself* the dead weight of the Italian party (Kautskyites and pacifists), the Swiss Greu- lich and company, the American Socialist Party (still worse!), different Pelusos, Longuetists, etc., etc.

This would be to throw overboard all our principles, to forget everything that we have written and said against the center, to get involved and to disgrace ourselves.

No, if the left Swedes take Zimmerwald into their hands and if they want to get involved, we must put an ultimatum before *them: either* they declare at the next Zimmerwald conference that Zimmerwald is dissolved and the Third International established *or* we shall leave. One way or another, it is necessary to bury the poisonous ("Grimm," it is Grimm's) Zimmerwald and establish the *true* Third International consisting *only* of leftists, *only against Kautskyites.* Better a small fish than a big cockroach.[54]

Whatever role Lenin's "ultimatum" to the new ISC could have played, the post-Grimm Zimmerwald leadership maintained a more pronounced leftist course and on July 11 officially declined to take part in the preparatory work for the projected Stockholm general Socialist conference (which in fact never took place). In the same period the "July disorders" in Petrograd forced many Bolshevik leaders underground and temporarily paralyzed party work. In the absence of Lenin and Zinoviev, the Sixth Congress of the Bolshevik party (July-August), held semi-legally in Petrograd, dropped discussion of the International from its agenda. Disagreements still existed within the Bolshevik leadership on the question of participating in international Socialist conferences. On August 30, from his hiding place in Finland, Lenin sent a furious letter to the bureau of the Bolshevik Central Committee abroad (in Stockholm) in which he called Kamenev's position in favor of participating in the Stockholm conference, still planned by the Dutch-Scandinavian Committee, "the height of folly and baseness." While lambasting the "social-chauvinist Zimmerwald gang," Lenin pleaded again for independent Bolshevik action:

We are making a gigantic and unpardonable mistake by delaying or postponing the calling of a conference of the Left for founding the Third International. We are now duty bound to call such a conference, while Zimmerwald is hesitating so scandalously or is compelled to be inactive, and while there is still a legal (almost legal) Internationalist Party in Russia of more than 200,000 (240,000) members (a Party which exists nowhere else in the world in wartime). It would be simply criminal if we were *too late* to do this (the Bolshevik Party in Russia is being daily driven further underground). Money will be found for the conference. There is a possibility of bringing out several numbers of its bulletin. There is a center for it in Stockholm. There is French support ("Demain") and English support (the Socialist *Labor* Party of America-their delegate is Reinstein). I have no idea what sort of a fellow he is: according to the newspapers he welcomed the unifying congress of the Mensheviks, which means he is suspect. The other day he was in Petersburg and will probably go to Stockholm). However, *apart from* the Socialist *Labor* Party of America, there is also English support: Tom Mann in England, and the minorities in the British Socialist Party, and the Scottish Socialists, and the International in America.

It would be criminal to postpone the calling of a left conference now. It would be immeasurably stupid to "wait" for a "large" number of participants, and to be embarrassed by the fact that at present there are "few," for at present such a conference would be a force in the realm of *ideas*, quite independent of the number of participants, whereas later it might be *silenced*.

The Bolsheviks within Polish Social Democracy, the Dutch, the "Arbeiter Politik" and "Demain"—this is a sufficiently large *nucleus*. If one were to act energetically, several Danes (Trier and others who have left the party of that scoundrel Stauning) could be added to it. Also there are some young Swedish people (against whom *we* are committing a sin, because we are *not leading* them and they *ought to be led*), some Bulgarians, the left from Austria (Franz Koritschoner), some friends of Loriot in France, some members of the Left in Switzerland ("The Youth International") and in Italy, as well as those aforenamed elements in the Anglo-American movement. . . .

Such a conference must be convened immediately. Its temporary bureau should be established. Its appeal and draft resolutions should be printed in three languages for distribution to the parties. Once again I repeat: I am deeply convinced that if we do not do this *at once*, we shall make our own work in the future infinitely more difficult, and it will enormously help the "amnesty" of the traitors of Socialism.[55]

Two striking characteristics distinguish this letter: there is no mention of the German Spartacists within the nucleus of groups which Lenin thought should build the Third International; and for the first time, there is insistence on the decisive role to be played by the Bolsheviks in taking the initiative to establish the new

International. Despite Lenin's admonitions, however, the third Zimmerwald conference opened at Stockholm on September 5. Attendance was smaller than at Kienthal or Zimmerwald: only 34 delegates from ten countries were present (Germany, Russia, Poland, Norway, Sweden, Finland, Rumania, Austria, Switzerland, and the United States). In addition, some Danish, Bulgarian, and Serbian Socialists were in touch with the conference. As on the previous occasions it was a heterogeneous meeting, though this time the leftist elements, led by Radek, had the support of the majority. There was no unanimity on the question of a general Socialist conference, and publication of the conference's manifesto was delayed owing to disagreements at the top about the desirability of issuing it immediately. (It called for an international general strike in support of the Russian workers and the launching of a general working-class struggle for peace.)

Lenin's total contempt for the work and decisions of the third Zimmerwald conference was clearly expressed in a brief note, "On the Zimmerwald Question," written in the first half of September, during the conference itself. "It is now particularly clear," Lenin wrote, "that it was a mistake *not* to leave it. . . . We must leave Zimmerwald *immediately*. . . . When we leave rotten Zimmerwald, we must decide immediately, at the plenary session of September 16, 1917, *to call a conference of the Left*, the Stockholm representatives [V. Vorovsky and N. Semashko] to be entrusted with the task. For what has happened is this, that having committed a folly, having remained in Zimmerwald, our party, the only party of internationalists in the world having as many as seventeen papers, etc., *plays the game of conciliation* with the German and Italian Martovs and Tseretelis."[5][6]

The idea that it was the immediate duty of the Bolsheviks to take the initiative and establish the Third International did not leave Lenin's mind in the weeks to come. In an article written on October 19-21, he emphasized that "outside of Russia there is at present not a country in the world where there is comparative freedom for internationalists to meet." Still, he saw one obstacle ahead: "The establishment of the Third International ought not of course be understood formally. Not until the proletarian revolution has triumphed in at least one country, or until the war has come to an end, may we hope for a speedy and successful movement towards the convoking of a *great* conference of revolutionary internationalist parties of various countries; nor for their consent to a formal adoption of a new program."[57]

A few weeks later, the Bolshevik coup in Petrograd fulfilled Lenin's precondition for holding the conference at which the Third International would be born, but over fifteen months passed before such a meeting was held. The delay followed not because of lack of will but because the Bolshevik exercise of power raised unexpected questions, including the form which the new international revolutionary movement should assume.

FROM OCTOBER TO BREST-LITOVSK

Once in power, Lenin's major foreign policy preoccupation was the issue of peace, but not peace in the usual Socialist sense. The peace he intended to offer was to serve two essential purposes: to win widespread popularity for the Bolshevik cause at home, and to trigger social revolution abroad.

There existed in fact a close relationship between Lenin's domestic actions and his analysis of the international situation. A month before the actual seizure of power in Petrograd Lenin wrote, "the workers' revolution against the war is irresistibly growing everywhere, and it can be spurred on, not by phrases about peace (with which the workers and peasants have been deceived by *all* the imperialist governments including our own Kerensky government), but by a break with the capitalists and by the offer of peace."[58] A few days later, discussing whether the Bolsheviks could retain state power, Lenin's answer was that the key to victory was Bolshevik resoluteness to take power and retain it "until the triumph of the world Socialist revolution."[59] Two weeks before the Petrograd coup, Lenin argued at a meeting of the Bolshevik Central Committee that "the international situation is such that we must take the initiative."[60] A week after this, at another Central Committee session, he insisted that "certain objective data of the international situation" showed that by acting immediately "the Bolsheviks would have all proletarian Europe on their side."[61] On this and other occasions, Lenin pointed to the mutiny in the German fleet in August 1917 and the frequency of workers' outbursts in Italy, Germany, and Austria as confirmation of the maturing revolutionary crisis everywhere.

Bolshevik victory transformed Lenin's pre-revolution arguments into tools of state policy. A day after the seizure of power, at the Second All-Russian Congress of Soviets on October 26, the solemn "Peace Decree" drafted by Lenin offered "immediate peace without annexations . . . and without indemnities" to all the belligerent peoples and their governments, and declared the willingness of the new Soviet government to abolish secret diplomacy, and to publish all secret treaties concluded by the previous provisional government. The decree called particularly upon the "proletarian heroism" of the British, French, and German workers, who "have rendered the greatest service to the cause of progress and Socialism by their great examples," and requested their help "to conclude peace successfully and at the same time emancipate the laboring and exploited masses of our population from all forms of slavery and all forms of exploitation."[62] According to John Reed, during a highly emotional debate at the same congress, "One spoke of the 'coming World-Revolution of which we are the advance guard'; another of 'the new age of brotherhood, when all the peoples will become one great family.'"* But of all the speakers at the congress, Leon Trotsky, the new People's Commissar of Foreign Affairs, made the most direct and dramatic statement: "We are putting all our hope on this, that our revolution will solve the European revolution. If the peoples of Europe do not arise and crush imperialism, we shall be crushed—that is beyond doubt. Either the Russian revolution will raise the whirlwind of struggle in the West, or the capitalism of all countries will stifle our struggle."[63]

This opinion was fully shared at that time by Lenin himself, who on November 7 stated in a speech (after mentioning that "the lower strata of the proletariat in Germany are prepared to respond to our call in defiance of the will of their leaders"): "We believe in the revolution in the West. We know that it is inevitable, but it cannot, of course, be made to order. . . . . We cannot decree a

*Ten Days that Shook the World, New York, 1960, p. 177. In John Reed's account of Lenin's speech at the same occasion, Lenin exclaimed: "But we hope that revolution will soon break out in all belligerent countries; that is why we address ourselves especially to the workers of France, England, and Germany. . . . The revolution of November 6 and 7 has opened the era of the Social Revolution." Ibid., p. 176. A few days later, on November 13, Reed reported that Lenin and Trotsky sent through him the following message to the revolutionary proletariat of the world: "Comrades! Greetings from the first proletarian republic of the world. We call you to arms for the international social revolution." The Liberator, New York, March 1918, p. 21.

revolution, but we can help it along. We shall conduct organized fraternization in the trenches and help the peoples of the West to start an invincible Socialist revolution."[64] A month later, on December 14, at the request of the Swedish left-wing Social Democrat Höglund, Lenin wrote an article (first published in German in May 1918 in the organ of the International Alliance of Socialist Youth Organizations) in which he said: "The Socialist revolution that has begun in Russia is . . . only the beginning of the world Socialist revolution. Peace and bread, the overthrow of the bourgeoisie, revolutionary means for the healing of war wounds, the complete victory of Socialism—such are the aims of the struggle."[65]

Three specific means were devised by Lenin to encourage the incipient revolutionary process abroad: peace negotiations with Germany and her allies; propaganda abroad; and political recruiting and training of non-Russians, mainly the prisoners of war, living at the time on Russian soil. The armistice negotiations with Germany (announced on November 23 and actually begun on December 2 at Brest-Litovsk) were conceived from the outset as a revolutionary weapon. On December 12 Trotsky did not mince words in explaining it:

> We are conducting these negotiations [at Brest-Litovsk] . . . so as to accelerate the rising of the working masses against the imperialist cliques. We are ready to support this uprising with all the forces at our command. . . . We do not doubt for a moment that, in consequence of the present war, the workingmen of Europe will repeat the fight of the Russian proletariat, a month sooner or later, on more powerful economic foundations and in a more perfect political form. . . . Our whole policy is built on the expectation of this revolution. The peace-program, as submitted to us, can be fully accomplished only by overthrowing the capitalist governments.*

---

*In the preface to Trotsky's pamphlet *What is a Peace Program?*, Petrograd, February 1918, pp. 2-4. "Almost in the very hour of the opening of the Brest-Litovsk peace conference . . . Trotsky announced in Petrograd that 'yesterday a freight car full of propaganda for peace and socialism was dispatched to Germany.' 'Although we are negotiating peace with Germany,' declared the Foreign Commissar, 'we continue to speak our usual revolutionary tongue.' " Louis Fisher, *The Soviets in World Affairs*, London, 1930, vol. 1, p. 32.

At the same time a decree of the Council of People's Commissars, issued on December 13, and published in *Pravda* three days later, announced that the Council "deems it necessary to come to the assistance of the left International wing of the labor movement of all countries, by all possible means, including funds, whether the said countries are at war with Russia, or allied to Russia, or occupying a neutral position. For this purpose the Council of People's Commissars resolves: that the sum of two million rubles shall be placed at the disposal of the foreign representatives of the Commissariat of Foreign Affairs for the needs of the Revolutionary Internationalist Movement."[66]

The Commissariat's personnel functioned to serve these intentions. The former distinction between "foreigners" and "nationals" was in some measure discarded on all administrative levels of Soviet foreign policy planning and execution. Revolutionaries of many nationalities were given highly responsible posts in the Soviet hierarchy. This state of affairs was graphically described by John Reed in an article devoted to the Commissariat of Foreign Affairs:

Upstairs functions disjointedly the Bureau of the Press, with an army of translators, under the erratic direction of Comrade Radek, of Austria and other places—a violent young Jew. Next door is the newly founded Department of International Propaganda, presided over by Boris Reinstein, American citizen and incorrigible mainstay of the Socialist Labor Party of the U.S.A.—an excessively mild-mannered little man who burns with a steady revolutionary ardor. Under him are formed committees of the various peoples—German, Hungarian, Rumanian, South-Slavic, English-speaking—engaged in propagating the ideas of the Russian Revolution abroad. . . .

Every week the "diplomatic couriers" of the People's Commissariat leave Smolny for the capitals of Europe, with trunk-loads of this material, bent on stirring up revolution.[67]

During the first months of its existence, the Commissariat of Foreign Affairs devoted itself chiefly to revolutionary propaganda, mostly among the soldiers of the Central Powers, both in the field and in Russian captivity. Daily papers in German, Hungarian, Bohemian, Rumanian, and Serbo-Croatian were issued, and emissaries were sent out to visit the prisoner-of-war camps in Russia and Siberia, where they were to encourage the formation of Socialist organizations.[68] On January 22, 1918, in a conference held at the Commissariat, it was decided to centralize work among prisoners of war by placing it under the supervision of the Department of International Revolutionary Propaganda of the People's Commissariat of Foreign Affairs.[69] Along with the propaganda work went the first efforts to build on Russian soil national military units which would be incorporated into a Soviet international army. As a symbol of the identification between the new Soviet state and the international revolutionary movement, the opening session of the Third All-Russian Congress of the Soviets, on January 23, was attended by alleged representatives of several foreign countries, who publicly affirmed their complete solidarity with the Soviet government and its policy. *Izvestia* wrote: "The eyes of the toilers of the whole world are directed on Russia: her victory is their victory, her defeat is their defeat—so unanimously have said the Socialists of Rumania, America, Norway, and Switzerland."[70]

The completely changed situation in which the Bolsheviks found themselves during that euphoric period between October 1917 and February 1918 helped determine their views about establishing a Third International. While there is no evidence that Lenin personally considered, at that time, any plan for immediately founding the new International, other prominent Bolsheviks envisioned the founding of such an International coinciding with the coming world revolution and assuming the form of international Soviets. According to the contemporary Bolshevik press, by the end of January 1918 the general situation in Europe was particularly favorable for an immediate revolution. On January 19 *Izvestiia* published two letters: "The Mole of Revolution is Working Well," and "The World Revolution is Coming." In the first letter it was said: "After Great Russia, the Ukraine; after the Ukraine, the Don; after the Don, Finland. After Russia, Austria and Hungary, after them France and England, and finally Germany. The mole of revolution is working everywhere." The second letter asserted: "The establishment of the Soviets of the Workers' Deputies in Vienna and Berlin proves clearly that the masses are starting to speak 'Russian.' And this gives a guarantee that the movement will reach the 'Russian' finale." On the next day, January 20, under the heading "The World Revolution Becomes a Fact," *Izvestiia* wrote: "Should the Russian Revolution remain isolated, the danger would exist that she would be crucified on the cross of world imperialism. The Russian workers and peasants realized this, and that is why they appealed for assistance to their comrades in other countries. This appeal has finally been heard. The proletarians of Austro-Hungary and Germany are hurrying to the assistance of the Russian Revolution. . . . The victory of the world revolution is just around the corner."

Three days later *Izvestiia* published an official appeal by the Petrograd Soviet of Workers' and Soldiers' Deputies to the Soviets in Vienna and Berlin. In this appeal, signed by Zinoviev, it was said that "the Soviets are the new organization which has been brought forth by the socialist revolution in all countries . . . the workers' movement in France as well as in Italy and England is pregnant with them. . . . An international Congress of the Soviets, that is the goal which has been put on the agenda of history."[71] In this optimistic atmosphere a theoretical discussion was started in *Pravda* on the post-revolutionary social and political organization of a world-wide Socialist society. On January 16, E. Preobrazhensky published an article entitled "Toward New Shores," in which he endorsed the idea of an international conference of the Soviets of Workers' Deputies and commented: "The outlines and the structure of that third Revolutionary International, which our party has always advocated, stand out now with complete clarity. [It will not unite just] a handful of isolated small groups and persons from various countries, as the social-patriots were sneeringly assuring our workers. . . . The locomotives of history rush us to the creation of the International of *revolutionary Soviets*." Preobrazhensky's idea was welcomed by Béla Kun, who in another *Pravda* article, "The International of the Future," published on January 21, analyzed the First and Second Internationals and concluded that in contrast the Third International should assume the form of "Soviets of Workers' and Peasants' Deputies, as organs of proletarian dictatorships, consolidating all proletarian and semi-proletarian elements in every country. These will be organizations of world dictatorship of the proletariat and represent all economic and political interests of the toiling masses." This would lead to "Internationalism in the form of a federated republic of Soviets of the proletariat of all countries finally freed from the national oppression of imperialism."

The problem of building a new International was approached not only theoretically. In December 1917 the Swedish leftists Höglund and Kilbom had come to Petrograd to discuss with Bolshevik leaders the convening of a Zimmerwaldist conference. In response, the All-Russian Central Executive Committee of Soviets (VTsIK) held a preliminary meeting in Petrograd on January 24, 1918, to plan a new Left-Internationalist conference. The following persons were in attendance: Höglund and Grimlund, of the Swedish Marxist Left; Nissen, a leftist Norwegian Social Democrat; the Russian Left Social Revolutionaries Natanson and Ustinov; Stalin, representing the Bolsheviks (this was the first appearance of Stalin at a conference connected with the establishment of the Third International); Dolecki from the Social Democratic party of Poland and Lithuania; Bujor of the Rumanian Social Democrats; a Yugoslav Social Democrat, Radošević; Reinstein of the American Socialist Labor Party; and individual representatives of the British Socialist Party and the Armenian and Czech Social Democrats.

The restricted scope of the meeting, and the absence of the most prominent Bolsheviks, indicated that it was not aimed at accomplishing much beyond discussing the ways and means of convening a larger International Socialist conference. The resolution of the gathering stressed that two conditions should be fulfilled by parties or groups wishing to qualify for participation in a future conference: they should "stand on the path of the revolutionary struggle against their own governments for an immediate peace" and should provide "assistance to the Russian October Revolution and Soviet power."[72] It was also decided that a delegation of the VTsIK composed of Natanson (Bobrov), Ustinov, and Kollontai would go abroad in order to establish relations with revolutionary internationalists in other countries. *Izvestiia* listed the following persons and groups abroad with whom "the Russian Revolution will come to an understanding": Liebknecht's partisans and the Independent Socialists in Germany; the followers of Friedrich Adler in Austria and [William] MacLaine in Great Britain; and the French minority Socialists and the Italians.[73]

Bolshevik hopes of provoking uprisings in the territories of the Central Powers came to naught by early February, and the strategy of procrastinating with peace negotiations at Brest-Litovsk failed also. Trotsky's formula of "no war and no peace" proved unworkable because of the German military decision to follow up the break in negotiations with the Bolsheviks by a new advance into Russia. Faced with the danger of a German invasion the Bolshevik leadership split into three camps. The largest, in the beginning, was led by Bukharin and heatedly advocated resistance and the waging of a revolutionary war; Lenin and others favored concessions and an immediate offer of peace to Germany; and Trotsky remained in the middle with his "no war and no peace" formula. Lenin's attitude in the Brest-Litovsk crisis was of decisive importance, and though his arguments prevailed in the end it was only after a dramatic confrontation within the party leadership. In part this resembled the clash which occurred in 1907 when Lenin, opposing other prominent Bolsheviks, argued in favor of participating in the Duma and was furiously attacked for his "opportunism." But in 1907 participation or non-participation in parliamentary work could only favor or harm the party tactically, whereas now, a decade later, the entire fate of the revolution depended on the decision of how to face the danger of a German invasion.

On January 8, 1918, Lenin had presented 21 theses "On the History of the Question of the Unfortunate Peace" at a meeting of leading Petrograd party functionaries. He still maintained at that time that it was "beyond doubt" that the Socialist revolution in Europe "must come," and that one should drag out peace negotiations "so as to give other peoples a chance to join us." At the same time, however, he acknowledged "the incredible chaos" characterizing the Russian military situation and stated bluntly that "the peasant majority of our army would at the present juncture unreservedly declare itself in favor of peace with annexations and not in favor of an immediate revolutionary war." Under these conditions the only correct solution would be to make every concession to the Germans that would allow the Bolsheviks to maintain power in Russia proper, so that "the socialist revolution can be most firmly and reliably ensured the possibility of consolidating itself, or, at least, of maintaining itself in one country until it is joined by other countries."[74] The formation of the Soviet of Workers' Deputies in Berlin and Vienna, in the middle of January, kindled new hope in Lenin that the revolution in Germany might have begun, and on January 21 he added a twenty-second thesis recommending further delaying at the peace negotiations.

The events of the ensuing weeks destroyed all hopes for a revolt in Germany, and instead German troops were marching eastward. The Bolshevik Central Committee convened on February 18 and once more Lenin remained with a minority and the waging of a revolutionary war against the Germans was approved. Then, on the question of whether to sue for peace should no revolution occur in Germany, Trotsky sided with Lenin and a bare majority of six to five voted in favor of immediate peace. The speech Lenin made before the final vote indicated the alarm with which he viewed the situation. He complained that "while playing with war we have been surrendering the revolution to the Germans."* He warned his comrades that "Ioffe [the Bolshevik representative at the Brest-Litovsk negotiations] wrote from Brest that there was no sign of a revolution in Germany." "If the Germans said that they wanted to overthrow Bolshevik power, we would naturally have to fight," exclaimed Lenin. But since that was not the case, territorial concessions were a lesser evil: "The revolution will not be lost if we give up Finland, Livonia, and Estonia."[7][5]

Indeed, the Brest-Litovsk peace treaty, signed on March 3, cost the new Soviet regime a considerable part of its territory, but it preserved Bolshevik power in Petrograd, which was more important than a party crisis and a temporary foreign political humiliation. During the Brest-Litovsk crisis Lenin appraised the situation realistically and was ready to make a temporary retreat, conceding all that was necessary at a desperate moment to preserve a position which would permit recovery in Russia and hasten the revolution in Europe. He reckoned on coming military and political events to nullify the treaty, and he was right in his expectations. The unfolding of these events, however, was not the result of the proletarian revolution in Europe which Lenin prophesied, but of the victory of the Entente powers, which Lenin did not desire and which indeed he had made more difficult, first by staging his coup

*Polnoe sobranie sochinenii, 5th edition, vol. 35, Moscow, 1962, p. 336. A few days later, on February 23, Lenin again bitterly assailed the "phrase-mongering" of his Bolshevik opponents and threatened to resign: "I personally, of course, would not remain for a second either in the government or in the Central Committee of our Party if the policy of phrase-making were to gain the upper hand." *Ibid.*, p. 367.

in Petrograd in November 1917, and then by concluding the Brest-Litovsk treaty in March 1918.

"MANEUVERING, WAITING, AND RETREAT"

Maximal concessions on everything but the essential position (maintenance of Bolshevik power) and total "defensism" if that position were threatened—these were the two guiding principles of Lenin's policy in the aftermath of Brest-Litovsk. Being obliged to sign what he called the "unfortunate, immeasurably severe, infinitely humiliating peace"[76] (which he often compared with the 1807 Tilsit peace that Napoleon imposed on Prussia) did not quash Lenin's faith in the eventual revolution in Europe. In his report to the extraordinary Seventh Congress of the Bolshevik party, on March 7, 1918, he stated again that "there would doubtless be no hope for the ultimate victory of our revolution if it were to remain alone, if there were no revolutionary movements in other countries. . . . Our salvation from all these difficulties is an all-European revolution. . . . It is an absolute truth that without a German revolution we are doomed." But he refused to be pessimistic about the future: "We shall overcome our split, our crisis, however severe the disease may be, because an immeasurably more reliable ally will come to our assistance—the world revolution."[77] A week later, speaking about the ratification of the peace treaty at the Fourth All-Russian Congress of Soviets, Lenin again emphasized that "we shall wait until the international Socialist proletariat comes to our aid and shall then begin a second Socialist revolution that will be world-wide in its scope."[78]

The conclusion of the Brest-Litovsk peace treaty had profound consequences for the Soviet side in three areas: diplomacy, military matters, and agitation-propaganda work among prisoners of war in Russia. In the field of diplomacy—for which the Bolsheviks initially had nothing but contempt and which they believed the spread of the revolution would annihilate altogether*—it became necessary to build the usual structure of diplomatic representation

---

*Trotsky describes in his autobiography how he initially viewed his functions as People's Commissar of Foreign Affairs: "I will issue a few revolutionary proclamations to the peoples of the world and then close the shop." *Moia zhizn*, Berlin, 1930, vol. II, p. 64.

abroad, in order to defend the interests of the new Soviet state in the traditional sense and to promote revolutionary unrest in the countries of the "imperialist" enemies of both belligerent camps. Under instructions from Trotsky, and then from his successor as Commissar of Foreign Affairs, Grigori Vasilevich Chicherin (who replaced Trotsky in the spring of 1918), a series of prominent Bolsheviks were nominated to perform the duties of ambassador-revolutionary in several capitals: Maksim Maksimovich Litvinov in London, Adolf Abramovich Ioffe in Berlin, Vatslav Vatslavovich Vorovsky in Scandinavia, Ian Antonovich Berzin in Switzerland.

The work of the Commissariat abroad was hindered by the small number of official Soviet diplomatic outposts in Europe, but many more unofficial agents carried on the work. According to John Reed, "By September 1918, the [Soviet] Ministry of Foreign Affairs had on its payroll 68 agents in Austria-Hungary, and more than that in Germany, as well as others in France, Switzerland, and Italy."[79] Lenin himself was in constant communication with the Soviet representatives abroad, and he openly spelled out their revolutionary duties without making any distinction between their party and government functions. Convinced that the revolutionary movement was maturing everywhere, Lenin instructed them to spend money unsparingly to foster social upheavals. He wrote to Angelica Balabanova in Stockholm: "The work you are doing is of the utmost importance and I implore you to go on with it. We look to you for our most effective support. Do not consider the cost. Spend millions, tens of millions, if necessary. There is plenty of money at our disposal."*

The case of Adolf Ioffe's ambassadorship in Berlin is particularly significant in this respect. While in Berlin (between April and November 1918) Ioffe had a free hand in financing revolutionary propaganda and supplying funds for the purchase of arms. His embassy was depicted by Lenin as "that one 'burning' house on the streets of Berlin [which] would set all Germany alight."[80] Lenin became irritated by what seemed to him Ioffe's inefficiency,

---

*A. Balabanova, *My Life as a Rebel*, New York, 1938, pp. 174-75. A little further on Balabanova adds: "Large sums of money began to arrive, ostensibly to finance the work of Zimmerwald, but most of which, as I soon discovered, was to be paid out to agents who were creating 'Bolshevik' movements and newspapers throughout the world." *Ibid.*, p. 175.

and scolded him in a note dated October 18, 1918: "We should
play the role of a center in the struggle of ideas on an international
scale, but we do nothing!! We should publish a hundred times
more. There is enough money. Translators can be hired. And we
do nothing! This is scandalous."[81]

Lenin's impatience notwithstanding, Ioffe did his best in trying
to subvert the government to which he was accredited, as he admitted in *Izvestiia* after his return from Germany. Replying to
charges of interference in internal German affairs, Ioffe said "[I]
helped as far as it lay in my power [to promote] the victory of the
German revolution." He even declared that his aid to the revolution was greater than charged: "It was not 105,000 marks, but
several hundred thousand marks, that was handed to Minister
Barth* for the purchase of arms."[82] A sympathetic observer, at
that time, has vividly described these and similar aspects of Ioffe's
ambassadorship in Germany:

> Ioffe's functions were not merely diplomatic. He was a revolutionist.
> He wanted to precipitate an insurrection against the government to
> which he was accredited and to which, presumably, he was persona
> grata. Acting in perfect bad faith—he admitted it in January 1919—he
> worked assiduously against the Imperial Government. More than ten
> Left Social Democratic newspapers were directed and supported by the
> Soviet Embassy in the German capital. The embassy bought informa-
> tion from officials in various German ministries and passed it on to
> radical leaders for use in Reichstag speeches, in workers' meetings, and

*In his book of reminiscences about the German revolution of 1918, Emil
Barth dealt briefly with Ioffe's allegations. He admitted having received
money "from the German comrades, " but denied any direct contact with
Ioffe. He called Ioffe's public statements "the greatest imaginable stupidity"
and added "I do not believe that there exists another . . . person that would
brag about the misuse of extraterritoriality." *Aus der Werkstatt der deutschen
Revolution*, Berlin, 1920, p. 86. In another story about his clandestine work
in Germany, Ioffe stated that "the money intended for the purchase of arms
was passed on by me not directly to Herr Barth, a newcomer to the workers'
movement, who in any case inspired me with little confidence. As intermediaries I had, of course, to make use of comrades with greater claims to my
confidence, who enjoyed a better reputation in the workers' movement. But
apart from all this, the people's delegate Herr Barth knew perfectly well that
several hundreds of thousands of marks which, according to his own admission, he received from German comrades, were in the last analysis provided
by me." *Izvestiia*, December 17, 1918. Quoted in *Soviet Documents on Foreign Policy*, selected and edited by Jane Degras, London, 1951, p. 127.

in the press. Anti-war and anti-government literature was sent to all parts of the country and to the front. Tons of literature were printed and clandestinely distributed by Ioffe's office. "It is necessary to emphasize most categorically," Ioffe wrote in an almost unknown memorandum, "that in the preparation of the German revolution, the Russian Embassy worked all the time in close contact with the German Socialists." Leaders of the German Independents discussed most matters of revolutionary tactics with Ioffe, who was an experienced conspirator. In a radio message dated December 15, 1918, broadcast by Ioffe to the revolutionary Soviets of Germany, he admitted having paid 100,000 marks for the purchase of arms for the revolutionists and announced that he had established in Germany a 10,000,000-ruble fund for the support of the revolution, which was entrusted to Oskar Kohn, a Socialist deputy. [83]

In Switzerland also, large sums of money were put at the disposal of ambassador Berzin to foster revolutionary propaganda, as appears from Lenin's letters and telegrams during the second half of 1918, when the end of the war approached and the Bolshevik leader thought he perceived the outlines of the international revolution. On August 3 he wrote to Berzin: "For God's sake don't save the money [sent] for publishing purposes (in German, French, Italian, English), [use] it fast, fast."[84] Eleven days later, in a brief letter dated August 14, Lenin twice repeated the same directive: "Don't save the money."[85] On October 15, just before the collapse of the Central Powers and in response to Berzin's report announcing the outbreak of revolutions in the countries of the Entente, Lenin again insisted on the necessity of intensifying the propaganda in four languages, and stated: "There is enough money where you are . . . I shall give even more without asking for a receipt. Let me know how much. We should publish a hundred times more, in four languages. These leaflets should have 4, 8, 16, 32 pages."[86] On November 1, just before the armistice in Europe and complications in Switzerland which brought the expulsion of the Soviet ambassador from Bern, Lenin repeated his directive to Berzin: "Able comrades shall visit you. Don't spare money, especially that destined for propaganda in France."[87]

Despite the revolutionary functions of Soviet embassies abroad, Soviet diplomacy after Brest-Litovsk was marked by what Lenin on several occasions during the spring of 1918 called "maneuvering, waiting, and retreat."[88] That was also the period when the initially undistinguishable activities of "state" and "party" began to assume separate identities as indicated by Y.M. Sverdlov, chairman of the seventh Bolshevik party congress: "We shall no longer be able in our capacity as a government, as the Soviet power, to carry on that widespread international agitation which we have hitherto conducted. This does not mean that we shall engage in such agitation one single jot less. But we shall now have regularly to carry on this agitation not in the name of the Sovnarkom [government], but in the name of the Central Committee of our Party."[89]

After the "heavy defeat of the revolution"[90] at Brest-Litovsk, urgent emphasis was placed upon building a new revolutionary army. On February 23, when Lenin threatened to resign if his peace policy were rejected by the party, he declared: "We shall set about preparing a revolutionary army, not by phrases and exclamations... *but by organizational work*, by deeds, by the creation of a proper, powerful army of the whole people."[91] The resolution of the Fourth All-Russian Congress of Soviets, which ratified the Brest-Litovsk treaty, proclaimed it "the unconditional duty of all working people to muster all forces to re-establish and improve the defense potential of our country, to re-establish its military strength on the basis of a socialist militia and the universal military training of all adolescents and adults of both sexes."[92] How important that crash program of building a new army was may be seen from Lenin's letter of October 3, 1918, to a joint session of the All-Russian Central Executive Committee, the Moscow Soviet, and representatives of factory committees and trade unions. Lenin wrote: "We decided to have an army of one million men by the spring; now we need an army of three million. We can have it. *And we shall have it.*"[93]

Lenin conceived the new Red Army as an international army for worldwide civil war. The very decree of January 28 on the "Workers-Peasants Red Army" defined it not as a national army of the Russian state but as an international army of the world proletariat. According to the text of the oath, approved by VTsIK on April 22, its soldiers were to swear fidelity to the "toiling classes of Russia" and "of the whole world." In several of his speeches to

Red Army soldiers Lenin stressed its international character. For example, on August 2, on the eve of the departure to the front of the Warsaw revolutionary regiment, composed of volunteers of several nationalities besides the Poles, Lenin said: "It is your great privilege to uphold sacred ideas arms in hand, and to make international brotherhood of nations a reality by fighting together with your frontline enemies of yesterday—Germans, Austrians, and Magyars. And, comrades, I am confident that if you muster all your military forces and set up a mighty international Red Army, and hurl these iron battalions against the exploiters and oppressors, making your battle cry 'Victory or Death'—no imperialist force will be able to hold us!"*

Internationalist work was also pursued inside Soviet Russia during the spring of 1918, on two different levels: among the war prisoners and through the People's Commissariat of Nationality Affairs, headed by Stalin. On April 15, the first All-Russian Congress of Prisoners-of-War Internationalists took place in Moscow, with some 400 delegates speaking in the name of 500,000 POWs of different nationalities. A 21-man Central Executive Committee was elected for the new organization, called the International Revolutionary Organization of Socialists, Workers, and Peasants. A manifesto to the homeward-bound prisoners was issued by the congress appealing to them to be pioneers in the international social revolution of the proletariat and to be ready for an armed insurrection. The chairman concluded the congress with the words: "Hail, the Third International! Hail, the World Revolution!"[9][4]

Despite political difficulties resulting from German protests about Bolshevik agitation among war prisoners, the Bolsheviks did not renounce their internationalist revolutionary propaganda. Continuing the January-February theoretical discussion on the Third International, *Izvestiia* published on March 24 an unsigned letter

---

Polnoe sobranie sochinenii, 5th ed., vol. 37, p. 26. English version in *Collected Works*, vol. 28, p. 40. Jacques Sadoul, a member of a French military mission to Russia and sympathetic to the Bolsheviks, noted on April 28: "On the Russian front, French officers have also established the presence within the Russian regiments of German and Austrian prisoners, who were very bravely fulfilling their duty as internationalists, as citizens of the world, against the tyranny of their 'countries' governments and against their compatriots." *Notes sur la révolution bolchévique,* Paris, 1920, p. 325.

in which it was stated that establishment of the new International was "the only way of saving the Russian Revolution, of bridling imperialism in general, and German imperialism in particular, and of organizing the world proletariat's struggle for Socialism." May Day slogans hailed the "World-wide Soviet Republic," the "Third Communist International," and denounced "counter-revolutionary appeasers in all countries."[95] Domestic Bolshevik propaganda at this time presented the idea of the Third International as a sort of panacea for all difficulties.

Similar internationalist work was performed by the People's Commissariat of Nationality Affairs. In April and May German and Czechoslovak departments were established, organizing respectively Russian citizens of German and Czech origin. On July 27 *Pravda* reported that the Commissariat already had thirteen different national departments; by the end of 1918 the number rose to twenty. Some of them played an important role after the German defeat in November 1918 and in the founding of the Third International in March 1919.

The emerging separation of state and party functions dictated transforming political indoctrination of prisoners of war to party organs. To accomplish this, foreign Communist sections were organized around the Bolshevik Central Committee: Hungarian and Rumanian at first, and then Yugoslav, Czechoslovak, and German.[96] In May of 1918 they assumed a new organizational form: the Federation of Foreign Groups of the Russian Communist Party (Bolsheviks), under the chairmanship of Béla Kun. The Federation, working throughout Russian territory, had many political duties (propaganda and indoctrination) as well as military duties (fighting against the White Guard and counter-revolutionaries). The official report of the Federation, issued at the end of August 1918, described its task as "the unification of all foreign Communists, members of the Russian Communist Party, for their inclusion in the Third Communist International, and for the common struggle against the Social Democratic appeasers."[97]

GREAT HOPES AND GRAVE PERILS

Expecting the pendulum of events to swing in favor of the Bolshevik cause on a global scale, Lenin impatiently watched the unfolding of the last stage of the war crisis in Europe. Before 1914, as an exile in the West, he had anxiously awaited the smallest news from · Russia and literally threw himself on any militant arriving from there; now, installed in Petrograd but cut off from Europe, he was looking for any sign of an impending revolution abroad, and from any source: a foreign newspaper, an incoming messenger, or a foreign communist group working in Russia. In late August of 1918 Lenin received a delegation of Finnish Communists, headed by Kuusinen and Sirola, who informed him of the progress of their congress, just under way in Moscow. (On August 29 the Communist Party of Finland was formally founded.) On October 20 Lenin obtained the first issue of the newspaper *The Third International*, the organ of the French Communist group in Soviet Russia, and in a speech he made on November 6 he quoted from it. He got hold of a copy of the Spartacist paper *Die Rote Fahne*, launched in Germany on November 9 and quoted from it in a speech made on December 14. A few days later he received more issues of the same paper and the first copy of the Austrian Communist newspaper *Der Weckruf*, and these inspired him to write an article on "democracy" and dictatorship on December 23. At this time, very few foreign Communists could reach Russia, and anyone who succeeded could easily see Lenin—such as the Dutchman S. J. Rutgers, who came from the United States via Japan and on September 25 discussed with Lenin the situation of the Socialist movement in those countries.[98]

It was only natural that in the fall of 1918 Lenin's special attention was concentrated on Germany. The defeat of the German Empire nullified the Brest-Litovsk peace stipulations, and once again aroused Bolshevik hopes that the international proletarian revolution was around the corner. While in July and August domestic civil war and foreign intervention threatened the very existence of the Soviet regime, the anticipation of events in Germany and elsewhere in the fall came as a harbinger of salvation. On October 1, 1918 upon hearing the first news from Germany, Lenin wrote a note to Sverdlov and Trotsky saying: "Things have so 'accelerated' in Germany that we must not fall behind either. But today we are already behind. . . . The international revolution has come so close in *one week* that it has to be reckoned with as an event in the *next few days*. . . . We are all ready to die to help the German workers advance the revolution which has begun in Germany. . . . We must have *by the spring* an army of three millions to help the international workers' revolution."[99]

Ill after an abortive attempt on his life, Lenin was unable to attend the conference of the VTsIK and Moscow Soviet on October 3, and he sent a letter saying: "The crisis in Germany has only begun. It will inevitably end in the transfer of political power to the German proletariat. . . . The time is approaching when circumstances may require us to come to the aid of the German people, who are struggling for liberation from their own imperialism, against British and French imperialism. . . . . Let us . . . multiply our efforts in creating a proletarian Red Army."[100] On October 18, addressing himself to the Spartacist group in Germany, he wrote: "The decisive hour is at hand: the rapidly maturing German revolution calls on the Spartacus group to play the most important role, and we all firmly hope that before long the German socialist proletarian republic will inflict a decisive blow on world imperialism."[101]

Lenin's enthusiasm for the revolution in Germany was enhanced by another of his growing convictions, and this conviction was destined to become an article of the Bolshevik creed: the Russian revolution was to be viewed not only as a predecessor of the European revolution but as its model. This was made explicit in his pamphlet *The Proletarian Revolution and the Renegade Kautsky* (begun on October 9 and finished on November 10), in which he stated: "Bolshevism *has created* the ideological and tactical foundations of a Third International, of a really proletarian and Communist International, which will take into consideration both the gains of the tranquil epoch and the experience of the *epoch of revolution, which has begun.*"[102] The impact of Bolshevism, in Lenin's eyes, was universal—"not only the general European, but the world proletarian revolution is maturing before the eyes of all"—which brought him to conclude that "Bolshevism *can serve as a model of tactics for all.*"[103]

In such a frame of mind it was not hard for Lenin to feel an arrival of a revolutionary tide in countries other than Germany. On October 9 he hailed "the impending proletarian revolution in Europe—in Austria, Italy, Germany, France, and even in Brit-

ain."[104] In early November 1918, when revolution was proclaimed in Germany, Lenin's optimism reached its zenith, as attested by
his wife, N. Krupskaya: "On November 8, 9, 10, and 11, Vladimir
Ilich gave his entire attention to the German revolution. He made
speech after speech. His face was alight with joy, as on May 1,
1917. The days of the first anniversary of the October Revolution
were the happiest of Vladimir Ilich's life."[105] One of those
speeches, delivered on November 8, 1918, to the Sixth All-Russian
Congress of Soviets, faithfully reflects the euphoric state in which
Lenin peremptorily asserted that revolution was already aborning
in many of the countries of Europe:

> When we took power in October we were nothing more in Europe than
> a single spark. True, sparks began to fly, and they flew from us. This is
> our greatest achievement, but even so, these were isolated sparks. Now
> most countries within the sphere of German-Austrian imperialism are
> aflame (Bulgaria, Austria, and Hungary). We know that from Bulgaria
> the revolution has spread to Serbia. We know how these worker-peasant
> revolutions passed through Austria and reached Germany. Several coun-
> tries are enveloped in the flames of workers' revolution. In this respect
> our efforts and sacrifices have been justified. . . . We have never been so
> near to world proletarian revolution as we are now.[106]

The list of revolutions did not stop there, for on December 4
Lenin wrote to Serrati: "We all hope that a proletarian revolution
will soon begin in Italy, and other Entente countries."[107] Likewise, addressing the third workers' cooperative congress, on
December 9, Lenin stated that "Britain, France, America, and
Spain have been infected with the same disease and are fired with
the same flame as Germany, the flame of the universal and worldwide struggle of the working class against imperialism."[108] If one
enumerates again the countries which Lenin at that time believed
to be prone to immediate revolutionary upheavals—Germany,
Austria, Hungary, the Balkans, France, Italy, Great Britain, Spain,
America—one may see how poorly he was informed about the real
situation in these countries and why he was in such haste to establish the new International.

Parallel with Lenin's wishful thinking about the internationaliz-
ing of the proletarian revolution, Stalin's "small international" was

feverishly put to work: several "national commissars" had organized "independent workers' and peasants' governments" in the Ukraine, Estonia, Latvia, Byelorussia, Lithuania, and even Poland. The "independent" armies were at the disposal of these "governments" and between December 1918 and February 1919 several "independent" Soviet republics appeared in east-central Europe, supposedly to serve as links between the Russian and the German revolutions. Scores of highly trained agitators (such as Radek) were sent from Russia to Germany and other central European countries to help in the revolutionary process. At a Moscow workers' meeting on November 27, Lenin visualized the spreading of Soviets everywhere, "from Austria and Germany to Holland and Switzerland, countries with the oldest democratic culture."[109] And at the Second All-Russian Trade Union Congress, on January 20, 1919, he announced: "the Soviet movement has ceased to be a Russian form of power of the proletariat; it has become the policy of the international proletariat in its struggle for power. It has become the second step in the world-wide development of the socialist revolution. The first step was the Paris Commune."[110]

Still, in spite of all these revolutionary exhortations Lenin was aware how precarious the general Bolshevik situation was: "Never before," he said on October 22, "have we been so near the world workers' revolution, and. . . never have we been in such a perilous position."[111] Cut off from the outside world, and relying more on his revolutionary expectations than on prosaic facts, Lenin was only dimly aware that by the end of 1918 many forces were beginning to complicate the unfolding of the revolutionary process elsewhere: the revolution in Germany did not end in victory for Liebknecht, there were no signs of revolution in either Central or Western Europe, and Soviet representatives, official and unofficial alike, were being expelled from the countries to which they were accredited (as was the case with Litvinov and Berzin) or arrested or kept in confinement (as in the case of Radek in Germany and Manuilsky in France). Moreover, "imperialist" enemies were on all sides encircling Russia. In typical Leninist fashion, the Soviet government was ready by early February to make concessions to the Entente powers[112] while at the same time the Bolshevik party was busily preparing to found the Third International. The very uncertainty of the situation, and in particular Lenin's realization that "Europe's greatest misfortune and danger is that it has *no* revolutionary party,"[113] prompted him to put into effect what he had preached since the fall of 1914.

The Founding of the Comintern

Without Lenin the Russian Bolshevik Party would not have been what it was, nor would the events of October 1917 have unfolded as they did. And without a Leninist party and a Leninist revolution, any Communist International, had one seen the light of day, would have been a political entity of an entirely different stamp. Zinoviev thus seems to have been perfectly justified when he wrote on the occasion of Lenin's death: "Inasmuch as in a thing like the Communist International one may speak about the role of an individual, one may consider it Lenin's creation."[1]

The founding of the Communist International, however, was not a single, improvised act but the outcome of a long process, which Lenin initiated. He provided the driving idea; launched it as a slogan; translated it into action. Just as he had publicly suggested as early as the autumn of 1914 that the Party abandon the name "Social Democratic" in favor of "Communist" but the change was not made until 1918, so he had also cried in September of 1914 "Long live the Third International," but only after his victory in Russia, five years later, was he actually able to found that new organization. Lenin's main decisions throughout his career were motivated by either his historical perspective or tactical considerations. The decision to establish the Communist International was motivated by both. The historical prospect was the imminence of the Socialist-Communist revolution in Europe; the tactical consideration was the absolute need to have a ready alternative to the international Socialist conference scheduled to convene in Switzerland in February 1919.

Lenin's behavior at that time was predicated upon an extremely simple, clear perspective, based upon an unshakable conviction: the splitting within the Socialist movement in Russia between the revolutionaries (Bolsheviks) and the reformers (Mensheviks) was to be repeated within the international workers' movement; likewise, what had happened in Russia during 1917 (the fall of the Tsarist regime, the democratic revolution, the collapse of the ensuing liberal regime and of the Socialist government, and the ultimate advent of Communism) was all going to happen in the immediate future throughout Europe as well. Hence the revolutionary events in Europe presented a triple challenge: to defeat opportunist and reformist Socialism, to found a new revolutionary International; and to bring about the triumph of the revolution—three goals which, from late 1918 to 1920, Lenin did not doubt for an instant were imperative and on the verge of being achieved. The order of priorities to be given to these three objectives—affecting the Party, the International, and the Revolution—was for Lenin a mere matter of technique, detail, and circumstance. Logically, the creation of the Communist parties in Europe should have preceded the founding of the Communist International (as Rosa Luxemburg and Leo Jogiches were to point out), but in terms of the actual possibilities open to the Bolsheviks the opposite was the easier course. If Lenin was unable single-handedly to bring about immediate formation of Communist parties in the leading countries of Europe, he certainly was able, in Moscow, to impose the founding of the Communist International. Thus, though lacking Communist parties in Europe, one would at least have a Communist International ready when the Revolution unfurled its banners.

The formal propaganda and organizational activities for establishing the Third International were renewed in Moscow, after a break of some months, near the end of 1918. On November 28, a meeting of the Communists "who used to live in England and America and speak English" took place and an "Anglo-American Communist Group" was organized. The task of the group was to launch "agitation and propaganda among the English and American POWs [from the interventionist troops in Russia], and to look for ways and means of sending revolutionary literature to England, America, etc."[2] Big internationalist mass meetings were organized in Moscow on December 5 and in Petrograd on December 19; at both, speakers of different nationalities forecast the imminence of proletarian revolutions not only in Europe but also in Asia.[3]

Since December 1918 a tactical consideration had been added to this short-term historical prospect of the imminent outbreak of revolution in Europe: the urgent need to create a ready alternative to the international Socialist conference scheduled to convene in Switzerland. The British Labourites had issued a call to all the Socialist parties proposing that they organize an international conference; it was to meet in Lausanne on January 6, 1919, but was postponed until January 27 and ultimately did not begin until February 3, in Bern. On December 24, in reply to their invitation, the Central Committee of the Bolshevik Party sent a telegram, published the next day in *Pravda*, calling upon all the revolutionary and internationalist elements in the European Socialist movement to boycott this "conference of enemies of the working class disguised as Socialists," pointing out that "the Third International, in charge of the world revolution, already exists."[4] It was during those very days that Lenin finally decided to set up the Communist International. Indeed, he could not sit calmly by and do nothing while his revolutionary International, which he had been the first to advocate back in 1914 and which he considered to have been in existence since the takeover of power in Russia, was outdistanced by the Second International, that "corpse" he had so often proclaimed dead since 1914 and whose leaders, in his eyes, were a pack of traitors.

At the very time the Bolsheviks announced their condemnation of the upcoming Socialist conference, Lenin had his first opportunity since assuming power in Russia to converse in person with an emissary of the Spartacus League, who was not a simple courier (as Herta Gordon had been in the summer of 1918), but a member of its governing body, Dr. Eduard Fuchs, attorney. Their meeting, and even Fuchs's visit to Soviet Russia, were mentioned neither in the Soviet nor in the Spartacist press, because Dr. Fuchs's activities as one of the party's leaders were being kept secret. Not until 1925 did the Soviet press publish the message that this Spartacist emissary had brought from Rosa Luxemburg, and the name of the messenger was not revealed until 1963: "Sometime after December 25 [1918], Lenin had a talk with the member of the Central Council of the Spartacus League, E. Fuchs. Fuchs transmitted to Lenin a short note from Rosa Luxemburg."[5]

The note from her, dated December 20, 1918, was indeed brief. It made no reference to any common Spartacist-Bolshevik undertakings, particularly as regarded the possible future founding of a new International. And—a characteristic detail—among the greetings from others that she conveyed to him, she omitted the name of Leo Jogiches, the Spartacist leader who had known Lenin best and longest: "Am availing myself of my uncle's [Eduard Fuchs] trip to send you warm greetings from our family, Karl, Franz, and others. Please God that our wishes come true in the coming year. Wishing you all the best. Uncle will tell you all about us. In the meantime, handshakes and greetings."[6]

Shortly after this talk, while Fuchs was preparing to return via Scandinavia to Berlin, Lenin decided to convene a conference for the purpose of founding the new International. He expressed his intention to Chicherin in a detailed note on December 27 or 28, 1918; he stressed in the very first sentence: "We *urgently* need (with ratification by the Central Committee before the Spartacist leaves) to set up an international socialist conference for the founding of the Third International."[7] In his note Lenin set forth most of the points he considered important. First, the place: preferably Berlin, in which case the conference would be public; or in Holland, in which case it would be secret. In any event, Moscow was not then envisaged. Next, the date: February 1, 1919—that is, approximately the date of the Socialist conference in Bern, in order not to be outdone by the Social-Democrats and not give them the advantage of being the only ones to have organized an international conference. Then the essence of the program: the International's "platform" was to be drawn partly from the theory and practice of Bolshevism, partly from the program of the German Communists as formulated in *Was will der Spartakusbund?* ("What Does the Spartacus League Want?"). Bukharin was to be in charge of this project. Lenin stipulated that to be invited to this conference the parties and groupings would have to: (1) separate themselves from the "social-patriots"; (2) rally to the Socialist revolution and dictatorship of the proletariat; (3) adopt the principle of power in the hands of Soviets and not restrict themselves to bourgeois parliamentarianism. He specified that the Bolsheviks should not require of all members of the Third International that they call themselves "Communists," but that they merely be willing to discuss the question of changing the names "Social-Democrat" and "Socialist" to "Communist," while promising never in any way to fasten upon the Third International the old "Zimmerwaldian" label.

The list of parties and groupings that Lenin drew up showed the Communist parties in the following order of precedence: Spartacus League (Germany), Finland, German Austria, Hungary, Holland, Russia, and so on. The list went on to name other supporters such as the narrow Socialists of Bulgaria, the Rumanian Social Democratic Party, the Norwegian Social Democratic Party, the Italian Socialist Party, as well as various leftist groups such as, for example, the group that had formed around Fernand Loriot in France. In short, the entire skeletal structure of the future congress of the International was there, just as it was to be publicly defined four weeks later in the January 24 letter of invitation. Lenin entrusted to Chicherin and Bukharin the task of putting his draft into final form: "I ask that you get on with this job *immediately* and that you and Bukharin draw up the *plan* on the basis of all these points. *Reply immediately, no matter how briefly*."[8] There is no doubt whatever that Chicherin carried out Lenin's order so that Fuchs, when he left, could bear a message to that effect to the leadership of the Spartacus League.

As for Lenin, he continued to shape his decisions to the facts surrounding the German Communist movement. Just as the arrival of a Spartacist leader had prompted him to decree the immediate founding of the Third International, the assassination on January 15, 1919, of the two Spartacist chiefs, Rosa Luxemburg and Karl Liebknecht, would move him to transform the confidential message of late December 1918 to the Spartacus League, concerning the founding congress of the Third International, into a public letter of invitation to all Leftist parties and groupings—but with one essential change. The congress would convene in Moscow instead of Berlin. On January 19, 1919, Lenin addressed a meeting organized in Moscow in memory of Rosa Luxemburg and Karl Liebknecht, and on January 21 he presided over a session, attended by several Russian and foreign Communists, devoted to the convening of that congress and to the wording of the letter of invitation, published in *Pravda* and *Izvestiia* on January 24. Always keen to sense and take into account the slightest change in power relationships, both within his own camp and in that of his partners or adversaries, Lenin could not fail to draw certain practical conclusions from the defeat suffered by the Spartacus League in January 1919, followed by the death of Rosa Luxemburg. By January 21, 1919, the power relationship between the Bolshevik Party and the Spartacus League was no longer what it had been at the end of December 1918.

The meeting of January 21, 1919, which Lenin attended and presided over, was reported on ten years later by two of the participants, both of whose versions were at some points inaccurate. Boris Reinstein, who worked under Chicherin at the Soviet Commissariat of Foreign Affairs, and who without any mandate whatever was proclaimed "American delegate," recounted: "As the new year approached, a little meeting was held, attended by the representatives of the Central Committee of the Russian Communist Party and by several comrades who had worked specially on that project. They drew up an appeal to the revolutionary proletarian organizations of all countries, inviting them to dispatch representatives secretly to Moscow for March 1, 1919, to discuss the founding of the Communist International. Naturally, I was happy to sign the appeal in the name of the Socialist Labor Party of America."*

The second account came from another employee of Chicherin's, J. Fineberg, who figured as British representative in these preparations for the congress. He is closer to being right about the date of the meeting (January 1919) but commits other errors, probably deliberate. Fineberg cuts this meeting down to only four participants, still considered party-liners as of 1929: Lenin, Chicherin, Sirola (the Finn), and himself. He left out the others present and then added his own signature to the manifesto, writing in 1929: "Although I had no mandate from my party, the British Socialist Party, to pledge it to the formation of the new International, nevertheless I signed the manifesto in the name of the

*B. Reinstein, "Auf dem Wege zum 1. Kongress der Komintern," *Die Kommunistische Internationale*, Nos. 9, 10, 11, March 13, 1929, p. 671. This recollection of the past contains two material errors. First, the date is wrong, because the meeting held for the signing of the international appeal did not take place just prior to the New Year (there may have been some other meeting at that time for the purpose of drawing up the message that Fuchs was to carry back to Berlin, which Reinstein may have attended as an employee of Chicherin's). Secondly, the date of March 1 was not mentioned in the appeal.

party, in the conviction that it would approve my action."* The fact is that his signature does not appear on it. But his account of the purpose of the meeting and the part played by Lenin is fairly accurate: "The workers were to be exhorted once and for all to break with that organization of traitors [the Second International] and rally to the banner of a new international organization that was leading them in the battle successfully begun by the Russian proletariat to bring down the bourgeoisie. It was in this sense, more or less, that Lenin set forth the reasons that had prompted him to call this meeting. He laid before us the draft of a manifesto to the workers of the world, proposing to have it signed by the representatives of the Russian party and those of like-minded foreign parties then in Moscow. After a brief discussion, Lenin's proposal was adopted."[9]

Following that small Kremlin conference on January 21, six days before the date set for the opening of the Bern conference, the news of the imminent establishment of a "new revolutionary international" was announced by the Soviet press and broadcast by radio and telegraph to the world on January 24. The document, entitled "On the First Congress of the Communist International," was signed by nine persons in the name of eight parties: Lenin and Trotsky for the Bolsheviks; Karski (Julian Marchlewski) for the foreign bureau of the Communist Workers' Party of Poland; Rudnyánszky for the foreign bureau of the Hungarian Communist Party; Duda for the foreign bureau of the Communist Party of German Austria; Rosin for the Russian bureau of the Central Committee of the Latvian Communist Party; Sirola for the Central Committee of the Communist Party of Finland; Rakovsky for the Executive Committee of the Balkan Revolutionary Social-Democratic Federation; and Reinstein for the Socialist Labor Party of North America. The invitation to attend the founding congress of the new International was addressed to 39 "parties, groups, and trends," 33 of them in Europe (including Great Britain), 4 in the United States, one in Australia, and one in Asia

*J. Fineberg, "Erinnerungen an die Gründung der Kommunistischen Internationale," *Die Kommunistische Internationale*, Nos. 9, 10, 11, March 13, 1929, p. 686. This text was written at a time when history à la Stalin was being tailored in various ways, one of which was simply to deny any role played by former leaders subsequently branded "anti-Party" and to write in roles for those who had adhered to the new line.

("Socialist groups in Tokyo and Yokohama, represented by comrade Katayama"). No Turks, Chinese, Indians, or Persians were invited, despite the participation of their representatives in the preparatory international mass meetings in Moscow and Petrograd in December.

The text of the invitational document resembled closely Lenin's note to Chicherin of the previous month. The fourteenth of its fifteen points stipulated that "the congress must establish a common fighting organ for the purpose of maintaining permanent coordination and systematic leadership of the movement, a center of the Communist International, subordinating the interests of the movement in each country to the common interest of the international revolution."[10] Simultaneously with the issuance of the invitation, Lenin published on January 24 a "Letter to the Workers of Europe and America." In it he identified the widespread appearance of Soviets with the birth of the Third International, and even affirmed: "Its exact shape remains to be determined, but actually the Third International already exists now."[11] Likewise, on January 24 and 25, at the Second All-Russian Trade Union Congress, the matter of establishing a new International was debated and the resolution adopted by the congress stressed that "the congress, in its desire to establish a genuinely proletarian International, welcomes the Russian Communist Party Central Committee's initiative in calling an international Communist congress."[12] Several days later, the letter of the Russian Communist Party's Central Committee regarding the convening of its Eighth Congress, published on February 2, listed as point three on the agenda the founding of the Communist International.

Once the basic decision was reached, everything else followed smoothly and on February 25, 1919, the Spartacist delegate Hugo Eberlein was already in Moscow, where under his assumed name, Albert, he spoke at the plenary session of the Moscow Soviet. On the next day "Lenin gave orders that the delegates to the first congress of the Comintern were to be housed and fed in the Kremlin."[13] At the same time he roughed out the points that he wanted included in the congress agenda and sent the draft to Chicherin, who acted promptly, as Jacques Sadoul confirmed in his diary: "On February 28, around midnight, I got a telephone call from Chicherin reminding me that an international Commu-

nist conference was to convene two days later, that the French
Communist group in Moscow was to send a delegate, and that by
ten o'clock the next morning I was to hand in a report on the
bankruptcy of bourgeois democracy in France. When I took him
that report, Lenin told me the agenda."[14] In verification of
Sadoul, the official Soviet history of Lenin's works notes that at
the end of February and on March 1 or 2 he did "elaborate the
theses 'On bourgeois democracy and the dictatorship of the proletariat,' did outline and draft them, and wrote the final text."[15]
During those few days Chicherin was busy verifying the mandates
of the delegates and heading up the Mandate Committee when the
congress started. Various duties were assumed by his assistants and
by the assorted foreign refugees employed at the Commissariat,
who were suddenly promoted to the status of delegates of the
foreign Socialist parties and groups.

Concerning the circumstances surrounding the birth of the
Comintern, Henri Guilbeaux, one of the best informed of the
foreign Communists in 1919, was later to write: "The close relationship between the Commissariat of Foreign Affairs and the
Third International was amply demonstrated by the presence of
Chicherin and Vorovsky, the respective People's Commissar and
Assistant Commissar of Foreign Affairs."[16] Another foreigner
present at this founding congress was Arthur Ransome, who would
note in his diary the role and presence of Karakhan and Litvinov
at the congress, while a third foreigner in Moscow at the time,
Marcel Body, a Communist like Guilbeaux, would say about the
crowd of Chicherin's employees: "The great majority at this first
congress were Russian delegates and foreign representatives who,
in one form or another, worked at the Commissariat of Foreign
Affairs, itself heavily represented by Chicherin, Karakhan, Rakovsky, Angelica Balabanova, Berzin, and all the heads of the different
foreign sections."[17]

OPPOSITION FROM THE SPARTACUS LEAGUE

In the period immediately preceding the founding of the Communist International, Lenin had a basic obstacle to surmount: he
attached fundamental importance to having the Spartacus League

as a founding member of the Third International, but the League staunchly opposed the idea of the International being founded at that time. During the troubled weeks at the end of 1918 and the beginning of 1919, the Spartacus League and Germany in general were as important in Lenin's eyes as the Bolshevik Party and Soviet Russia, perhaps even more so. On January 12, 1919, when he sat down to draft his "Letter to the Workers of Europe and America," he started it by asserting that "when the Spartacus League took the name 'German Communist Party,' then the *founding* of the really, truly proletarian, internationalist, revolutionary Third International, the *Communist International*, became a *fact*."[18]

When Lenin made this statement, he did not yet know that the leaders of the Spartacus League, especially Rosa Luxemburg, its brain, and Leo Jogiches, its chief organizer, were expressing in its inner councils more subtly shaded opinions on all aspects of the Communist movement in Germany and Europe. When Karl Radek arrived in Berlin on the eve of the congress convened to establish the German Communist Party, he learned from Rosa Luxemburg that she had had to convince Jogiches of the need for founding another revolutionary party outside the Independent Socialist Party, a step which Jogiches regarded as premature. Hugo Eberlein revealed that several days later at this congress, held during the last two days of December 1918, the party leadership was divided over what the new party should be called: "We wanted to name it the Communist Party. Rosa Luxemburg and Jogiches were ardently opposed to this. They wanted it to be called the Socialist Party. The argument dragged on late into the night. When a vote was taken, Rosa Luxemburg was in the minority. The vote was four to three. Paul Levi had abstained; he did not care what the party was called. It was decided that the Spartacus group would be known thereafter as the Communist Party of Germany. The congress ratified this decision."[19]

Rosa Luxemburg's arguments (as summarized by Eberlein five years later) even then touched upon the relations of the Spartacus League with the Bolsheviks, and upon the matter of a new Communist International:

The Russian Communist Party is still alone in the International. The parties of the Second International will fight it mercilessly. The duty of the Communists is to snatch Western Europe's Socialist parties away from the Second International to form a new revolutionary International. The (Russian) Communist Party will never succeed in this by itself. The gulf is deep between it and the Western Socialist parties, particularly those of France, England, and America. It is for us revolutionary Germans to supply the hyphen between Eastern Europe's revolutionaries and the still reformist Socialists of the West. We can perform that function better as a Socialist party. But if we present ourselves as a Communist party, our connection with the Russians will make our job harder in the West.[20]

Several days after the congress that established the German Communist Party, and after the return of Dr. Fuchs from Moscow—during the first week of January 1919, before the armed clashes in Berlin that began on Monday, January 6—the Spartacists had to decide who to send as their delegate to the Moscow meeting concerning the new International and what position they should take with regard to the meeting.

On the first point, the choice of Rosa Luxemburg and Leo Jogiches was Hugo Eberlein. Rosa Luxemburg explained her choice to Eberlein, who reports it thus: "It was out of the question that either she or Karl Liebknecht would attend, for neither could leave Berlin. Rosa felt also that the German Communist Party should be represented at that conference by a German comrade whose political judgment had not been affected by prior disputes involving Russian comrades (she was alluding to the differences of opinion which she and Jogiches had had with the Bolsheviks). She proposed that I go."[21] Paul Levi's explanation given to Y.S. Reich—"Thomas" (a prominent Comintern functionary) of the choice of Eberlein, though of a different tenor, sheds further light: "Paul Levi confided to me later (after breaking with the Communist International) that Jogiches had told him why he chose Eberlein: because he was known to be narrow-minded, indeed obtuse, but stubborn and tenacious, which made Jogiches feel sure that the people in Moscow would not succeed in swaying him."[22]

As to what attitude the Spartacists should adopt, the views of Rosa Luxemburg and Jogiches showed themselves, once more, to be different from those of Lenin, as had often been the case for nearly fifteen years. Only this time the power relationship between Lenin on the one hand and Rosa Luxemburg and Jogiches on the other operated overwhelmingly in Lenin's favor; that had not been true earlier. Rosa Luxemburg's opinion, as expounded to Eberlein, was summarized by him as follows: "The Bolsheviks will probably propose the immediate establishment of an International, even if there are only a few delegates present. The need for a Communist International is absolutely obvious, but founding it now would be premature. The Communist International should be definitively established only when, in the course of the revolutionary mass movement gripping nearly all the countries of Europe, Communist parties have sprung up. And, in particular, it would be necessary also to select the moment of its founding so as to speed up the process of detaching the revolutionary masses from the Independent (Socialist) Party."[23]

In the days that followed, revolutionary clashes erupted in Berlin. Rosa Luxemburg and Karl Liebknecht were assassinated on January 15. The German party's decapitated and diminished leadership needed time to ponder and talk over the proposed founding of the new International. Eberlein reports:

> Shattered by the pain of the irreparable loss of our leaders, we did not dream of engaging at that moment in any serious political discussions. Then a meeting was held on Kochstrasse, attended by Jogiches, Karski, Pieck, Levi, and Eberlein (Meyer was in jail). I disclosed to the comrades my last conversation with Rosa. Leo Jogiches, whose viewpoint was the same as hers, explained it once again. It was decided that I would be the delegate, and that my absolutely imperative mandate would be to reflect the opinion of Rosa and Leo. A few days later there was another meeting, which I did not attend. Ernst Meyer was there. Several days after that, I left for Moscow.[24]

Arriving in Moscow after many vicissitudes, Eberlein participated in three very different conversations. The most important, of course, was the one he had with Lenin. Lenin, despite the distance and lack of communication, had correctly divined Rosa Luxemburg's thoughts, just as she had guessed his about the immediate founding of the International. Eberlein relates:

On arriving in Moscow, I first had a personal interview with Lenin. I gave him a detailed report on the situation in Western Europe.... When I told him the opinion of Rosa Luxemburg and of the Spartacist governing body about the founding of the Communist International, he showed no surprise and said that he had foreseen their position.... Yes [he said], these arguments [of Rosa Luxemburg] did have a certain value from the tactical standpoint, but it was necessary to proceed immediately with the founding anyway.... Then he added (and I quote him here verbatim): "But I consider it extremely difficult to get on with the founding without the approval of the German Communist Party."[25]

After this conversation Lenin realized that the final obstacle to his proclaiming the immediate establishment of the Third International was indeed a serious one, but still he did not consider himself beaten. In the twenty years of his political experience he had acquired a real technique for rallying to his point of view activists and leaders who the day before had still been against him. His powers of persuasion and a course of events that appeared to prove him right had combined to surround him with men who, now his closest collaborators, had but recently been in total disagreement with him. So it was with Trotsky, who during his exile had frequently disagreed with Lenin over a period of some thirteen years; with Zinoviev, opposing Lenin at the crucial moment on November 7, 1917; with Balabanova and Rakovsky, who but yesterday in the Zimmerwald movement were in conflict with him; and with Jacques Sadoul, who in 1917 had come to Russia as envoy of Albert Thomas, the "social-patriot" French minister.

So the first thing Lenin did—tending to believe that good and loyal militants, especially those of proletarian background, were "savable" and could be persuaded—was to put pressure on Eberlein. The result was a series of conversations with some of the most important Bolshevik leaders, which Eberlein has described: "In our discussions, which for the most part took place in Lenin's office, the question was immediately brought up as to whether the conference was going to preside over the founding of the International. I was the only one who spoke out against the idea, as my party had instructed me to. The Russian comrades—especially Trotsky, Bukharin, and Rakovsky—tried to convince me of the need for immediate action.... They demolished my arguments, one by one. Lenin finally decreed that, if the German party persisted in its view, the founding of the International would be postponed."*

Eberlein had been in Moscow since February 25, so these discussions took place during the last few days of that month. The upshot was that Lenin appeared to abandon his original intention because of the German Communist Party's opposition. This was the first and the last time in the realm of the new International that he would swerve from his own policy because of disagreement from a foreign Communist party. Indeed, even this renunciation was merely tactical and would not even last a week. Lenin had been wrong in believing that he could change Eberlein's mind. Jogiches had judged his envoy better. Eberlein exercised his imperative mandate to oppose the immediate founding of the International, an attitude which forced the Bolshevik leaders to give way, as Zinoviev had to concede a few days later in his remarks to the Eighth Bolshevik Congress: "After studying the situation, the Central Committee of our Party deemed it inarguably necessary that we immediately set up the Third International. But it was our opinion also that, since the German Communists were against this, stating their opposition in the form of an ultimatum, we could not allow the slightest strain in our relations with the German Spartacists."[26] That ultimatum did not go down well with Lenin, though he did not show this immediately, for he seemed to give in. The resentment that it aroused in the Bolshevik leaders was not directed against Eberlein personally but against the spirit of the Spartacus League as shaped by Rosa Luxemburg and Leo Jogiches. Ernst Meyer, who came with the German delegation to the Second Congress of the Comintern more than a year later, would report on this to the Fifth Spartacist Congress: "The Russian comrades are also dissatisfied with the attitude of the German Party, because last year, at the founding congress of the International, comrade Eberlein as the delegate of our governing body spoke out against

*H. Eberlein, "Souvenirs sur la fondation de l'Internationale communiste," *La Correspondance Internationale*, February 27, 1924, p. 154. In his version of 1929, Eberlein mentioned only Bukharin, the two others, Trotsky and Rakovsky, having already been expelled from the Bolshevik Party. On the other hand, it is disputable whether Rakovsky took part in these debates, since according to the minutes of the congress he returned from the Ukraine only on the second day, March 3.

founding the Third International just then. He announced on that occasion, as Jogiches had no doubt instructed him, that he would walk out of the congress if it resolved to set up the Third International."[27]

In any case, on March 1, 1919, Lenin seemed to bow to the ultimatum of the Spartacist delegate. When that same day, early in the morning, Jacques Sadoul came to bring him his report on the bankruptcy of bourgeois democracy in France, he noted in his diary afterwards: "When I brought him my report, Lenin told me the agenda. I knew that he wanted to transform this conference into a congress that would found a new International. But he struck me as not yet too confident about how this proposal would be received by the European delegates."[28] Indeed, far from being confident about its reception—not by the European delegates, as Sadoul wrote, but by Eberlein, the only important European delegate—Lenin showed by two actions that very day that he was taking due account of the Spartacist delegate's categorical opposition. First, he read through and edited the theses on the Communist International drafted by Zinoviev in preparation for the forthcoming Eighth Bolshevik Congress. The Lenin-approved version appeared on March 2 in *Pravda* and *Izvestiia*. On that day, in the late afternoon, the international communist conference was to begin. The Zinoviev theses, revised by Lenin, now indicated that the head of the Russian party and the future president of the International expected the Communist International to be created *after* the Eighth Bolshevik Congress, scheduled to begin its work on March 18—which proves that the final wording of those theses reflected the Spartacist ultimatum, for Article XII stated:

The international "Socialist" conference at Bern, which tried to revive the corpse of the Second International, is in fact only a tool in the hands of the imperialist "League of Nations." As a counterweight to that international organization of exploiters and their lackeys, the Eighth Congress of the Russian Communist Party takes the decision to found *an international workers' association, the Communist International. . . .* The hour has struck for the creation of a true Communist International, which in the near future will lead a suffering humanity toward a World League of Soviet Republics and to the destruction of every government in the old sense of the term.[29]

The second action that Lenin took on March 1, in the evening, was a decision adopted at a closed meeting of the most important Russian and foreign Communist leaders, who on the following day were to inaugurate the international conference. The minutes of that meeting—attended by Lenin, Zinoviev, Rakovsky, Bukharin, Eberlein, and Sirola—made Lenin's position clear from the very first: "Since the conference will not be called upon to establish the Third International, it will be devoted to working out the platform, election of officers, and publication of a rallying appeal. It will be known as the International Communist Conference. Initially it will be held in secret. What happens after that remains open."[30] So on the eve of the opening of the congress, Lenin, the master of Soviet Russia, appeared to bow to the will of Rosa Luxemburg, now dead, and of Leo Jogiches, who would be assassinated a few days later. But with Lenin, yielding today for a tactical reason did not mean that he would not press forward again tomorrow if a more favorable opportunity arose. Since 1903 he had participated in many congresses and conferences. He knew he could come about in midstream and reverse an initial decision if he rode the current right, could play the persuader, and take advantage of some new development (even if he had to bring it about). He had a plan in the back of his mind for this international congress too, a fact noted by Eberlein at the end of their first conversation, during which the latter had voiced unshakable opposition: "He [Lenin] proposed that the matter of the founding of the Communist International not be brought up until the end of the session."[31]

AN IMPROVISED CONGRESS

Lenin opened this international meeting on March 2 at ten minutes after six in the evening, an hour later than had been decided upon the night before. From the first instant he began twisting the decision of the previous evening which stipulated that the meeting would be an international *conference*. He proclaimed: "By order of the Central Committee of the Communist Party of Russia, I declare this first international Communist *Congress* to be in session."[32] These words were addressed to a very small number of Soviet and foreign Communists assembled in the Kremlin in a little hall known as the Mitrofanevski, formerly a part of the Tsarist Palace of Justice.* Indeed, there was an enormous difference between the thirty-nine Leftist revolutionary parties, groups, and other entities which were listed in the letter of January 24, 1919, and were invited to send representatives to the first international communist congress, and the mere thirty-four individuals who were present, most of them suddenly promoted to the status of delegates with voting or advisory rights.

The technical and material difficulties then confronting Europe, and Russia's isolation, made it impossible for most of the invited foreign delegations to get to Moscow at all—quite apart from the fact that some of them, for various ideological and tactical reasons, preferred not to go. But even among those who would have consented to be represented, some received the invitation much too late, as reported by one of the subsequent founders of the British Communist Party, Tom Bell: "As a matter of historical fact it should be stated here that the Socialist Labour Party was included in the groups invited to the first congress of the Communist International. But this was only learned through the New York *Weekly People* a month after the congress was over, otherwise efforts would have been made to be represented."[33]

Here Lenin used one of those procedures he had so widely employed in the course of his battles within Russia's Socialist movement prior to the November revolution: lacking duly authorized representatives, he preferred more or less imaginary delegates (and their votes at the congress) to none at all. The leaders of different factions in the Social Democratic movement had often castigated him for fabricating delegates, organizations, and even parties. Rosa Luxemburg, for example, writing in the Danish Socialist newspaper *Sozialdemokrat* on October 20, 1913, had protested Lenin's misuse of the seal of the Social Democratic Party of Poland and Lithuania in his attempts to obtain financial aid from the Danish Socialists. She did not mince words in denouncing

---

*In Bolshevik circles this place was known as the Hall of the Revolutionary Tribunal, owing to the fact that the first death sentence by a revolutionary tribunal was pronounced there against Admiral Shchastny on June 21, 1918 (five days after the official restoration of the death penalty).

"this [Lenin] faction, which even in Russia has been striving for years to split the workers' movement and which systematically and unscrupulously promotes factional strife, and has now set up a fictitious 'central committee' [for Poland and Lithuania] which no one recognizes, this faction which resolutely blocks every attempt at unity, and so leads the Russian party to the brink of ruin."[34]

What Lenin was doing then abroad, and had been doing on a restricted scale in émigré circles, he would do again later, as master of Russia, on a worldwide scale. A good illustration of his methods was the selection of the "delegates" to the first international Communist congress. Out of the thirty-four delegates to the congress, only four of them were persons not then residing in Russia: two Scandinavians (Stange, the Norwegian representative, and Grimlund, the Swedish delegate, in neither of whose countries a Communist party existed) and two others, specially delegated to attend the congress, in whose respective countries a Communist party did exist, Max Albert (pseudonym of Hugo Eberlein) from Germany and Gruber (pseudonym of Karl Steinhardt) from Austria. All the others, domiciled in Soviet Russia, found themselves vested with the right to represent the various countries in which they had formerly lived and the parties in which they had once been active. This was the case with all the countries named on the official roll of the congress: Hungary (Rudnyánszky), Switzerland (Platten), United States of America (Reinstein), Bulgaria and Rumania (Rakovsky), Poland (Unszlicht), Finland (Sirola, Manner, Kuusinen, the two Rahja brothers), Latvia (Gailis), Lithuania (Gedris), Estonia (Pögelman), France (Guilbeaux and Sadoul), Czechoslovakia (Handlíř), Bulgaria (Djorov), Yugoslavia (Milkić), Great Britain (Fineberg), Holland (Rutgers), China (Lao Hsiuchao), Korea (Kain), Turkey (M. Subhi), and finally the Zimmerwald Committee (Balabanova). Some of these individuals were delegates of national Communist groups affiliated with the Bolshevik Federation of Foreign Communist Groups. But the effective membership of these foreign groups was also very small, ranging from about ten in the French group to ninety (in December 1918) in the Hungarian and one hundred twelve in the Yugoslav.[35]

Another index of how representative the delegates to this first congress really were is the genuineness and validity of their mandates. Most, if not virtually all, of these foreigners had received no authorization whatever to represent the movements whose delegates they purported to be. Lenin used these foreigners living in Russia as he had previously used the Bolshevik militants in the party's service. Before 1917—at the congresses or conferences in Stockholm, Prague, Poronino, and elsewhere—he would find ways to have this or that person named delegate from the Ukraine, from Georgia, Poland, or Lithuania. Now in Moscow he was deciding that so and so would be the delegate of a large country like France, Great Britain, or the United States, and he would bestow upon that person as many mandates as he pleased. But if the method was the same, Lenin's situation certainly was not. Before 1917, as a simple political refugee heading a minority faction in the Russian Social-Democratic movement, he found it difficult to muzzle the opposition from Socialism's leading spokesmen such as Rosa Luxemburg, who in October 1912, on behalf of the Social Democrats of Poland and Lithuania, wrote to the International Socialist Bureau in Brussels with reference to a circular of Lenin's aimed at splitting the Polish-Lithuanian Socialist movement: "Lenin's piece of writing is the latest scandal in this comrade's series of scandals. Heretofore they occurred in the Russian movement; now Lenin is starting to transfer them to the International. Quite apart from the fact that Lenin's circular constitutes uncalled-for and unqualified meddling by him in the internal affairs of another party, the point that we want to nail down here is that Lenin, with his writings, is misusing the International Socialist Bureau to promote the divisive ambitions of a mad fanaticism, and tries to make of it a tool for political humbug."[36] But when Lenin, now in power, used and abused in 1919 those same methods that Rosa Luxemburg had condemned in 1912, he did so as one able to translate his thoughts into action no longer just within Russian territory but on the scale of the European continent. A brief look at the "delegates" to that first Comintern congress tells the story:

E. Rudnyánszky: Awarded three votes by the Mandate Committee, he attended as representative of the Hungarian Communist Party, yet at the time of the congress he had absolutely no contact with that party.

Otto Grimlund: The representative of Sweden's Social Democratic Left, he was the only one at the congress (besides the Austrian, Gruber) who could say in his speech: "The [Central] Committee of our party has gladly accepted the invitation to take part in the founding of the Third International, a logical out-growth of the Zimmerwald movement. . . . I have been instructed to vote for the founding of the Third International."[37]

Emil Stange: The representative from Norway, likewise award-ed three votes, in his speech on the first day of the congress, he had to confess: "At the time of my departure from Christiania, it [the Party leadership] had not seen the invitation to this congress. That is why I cannot take any position with regard to the new Communist International without first consulting my colleagues of the Central Committee."*

Fritz Platten: A resident of Soviet Russia, in January 1918 he had been wounded while shielding Lenin against an attempt upon his life. The Mandate Committee ruled that he had been "unable to bring written credentials with him," but that did not prevent it from awarding him three votes and appointing him one of the chairmen of the congress.

Boris Reinstein: He left the United States in June 1917 to attend the third Zimmerwald conference in Stockholm and went over to Bolshevism only after its victory at Petrograd. In De-cember 1917 he was put in charge of the International Revolution-ary Propaganda Section at the Commissariat of Foreign Affairs, and in April 1918 he became a member of the Russian Bolshevik Party. He had no authorization or instructions to represent the Socialist Labor Party of North America, nor to sign the January 24 appeal, nor to act as cofounder of the Comintern. Nevertheless, the Mandate Committee awarded him five votes, as many as were given to the Bolshevik Party and to the Spartacus League.

Christian Rakovsky: The head of the Bolshevik government of the Ukraine, he would within several days be elected to the Cen-tral Committee of the Russian Communist Party. Of Bulgarian

*Pervyi kongress Kominterna, Moscow, 1933, p. 35. Lenin had spoken with Stange on February 20, on the eve of the final arrangements for convening the first international Communist congress. Obviously it was easier to pin the "delegate" label on foreign militants already settled in Soviet Russia than on a Socialist militant only there on a visit. Similarly, it was easier for Stange to decline bestowal of the Lenin mandate than for the other foreigners, en-sconced in Russia. Anyway, Stange left Moscow on March 3, the second day of the congress, and was not present for the proclaiming of the Communist International. (Concerning his departure, see ibid., p. 53.)

origin and a militant in the Rumanian Socialist movement before 1917, he had no mandate from any Balkan party, yet he declared in the first sentence of his address to the congress that he was "speaking in the name of the Balkan Federation, founded in 1915 and consisting of the Rumanian, Serbian, and Greek parties and the Bulgarian 'Tesniaks'."

Józef Unszlicht: Representing the Polish Communist Party, and at that time head of the "Tsentroplenbe" (Central Bureau for War Prisoners), a Soviet agency, also War Commissar in the Soviet government at Wilno, he was awarded three votes for Poland on the strength of the "full powers" bestowed upon him —according to the minutes—by a telegram from Ioffe at Wilno.*

The Finnish delegation, second in size only to the Bolshevik Party's contingent, consisted solely of exiles who had been living in Soviet Russia since 1918.

Stoian Djorov: Representing the Bulgarian Communist group, he was given a consultative vote at the congress. He probably held the record for the longest stay in Russia: he had settled there at the beginning of the century; in 1908 he joined the Bolshevik wing of the Russian Social Democratic Labor Party in Odessa, and in 1919 was in charge of the Bulgarian section within the Federation of Foreign Communist Groups.

The three Baltic delegates, who also lived in Soviet Russia, pre-

*Unszlicht's participation at the founding congress of the Comintern remains clouded in mystery. According to his official biography, in February 1919 he was appointed War Commissar of the Soviet Republic of Lithuania and Byelorussia, and in early March was elected to the Central Committee of that party at its congress of unification—and this at the exact moment that his name was appearing in the minutes of the Comintern congress as the delegate of the Polish Communist Party! That biography has no word about his being at the founding congress of the Comintern, nor about his name's not being on the list of participants at the Eighth Bolshevik Party Congress, held from March 18 to 23. Cf. Unszlicht's biography in *Voprosy istorii KPSS*, no. 7, July 1964, pp. 84-88. On the other hand, at the beginning of 1969, half a century after the event, Unszlicht's speech, given at the March 4, 1919 session in favor of the immediate founding of the Communist International, was published for the first time. However, neither the official German Comintern edition of the congress's minutes, printed in 1920, nor a more complete Russian edition of 1933, contain any trace of that intervention by Unszlicht. Cf. text of his speech in *Z pola walki*, Warsaw, no. 2, February 1969; also in *Voprosy istorii KPSS*, no. 4, 1969, p. 78.

sented curious credentials. Karl Gailis, claiming to speak for Latvia, based his alleged mandate (according to the official minutes) on a telegram in code sent from Riga by P. Stuchka, head of the Soviet administration in Riga, in which city the Sixth Congress of the Latvian Communist Party was being held at the same time as the Moscow congress. The case of Hans Pögelman, the Estonian representative, was similar except for the explanation of where his mandate came from. He had been a member of the Soviet government of Estonia until it collapsed in January 1918, when the Communist government and Central Committee had fled to the safety of the Russian town of Luga, where they were then busy organizing a national conference in exile, to open on March 20. As for the delegate from the third Baltic country, his situation was much the same: the same telegram from Ioffe that had authorized Unszlicht to speak for Poland conferred upon Kazimir Gedris authority to represent Lithuania and Byelorussia, whose joint Communist congress was scheduled to be in session from March 2 to 6, again at the same time as the Moscow congress.

The remainder of the European delegates had no mandates of any kind, not even fictitious ones. An example was Ilija Milkić, a representative for Yugoslavia. As he would admit a year later at the Comintern's Second Congress, "When at the first congress of the Third International I spoke in the name of the Serbian proletariat, and of the Yugoslav proletariat in general, I had no formal mandate from our party, which had had no opportunity to send me one."[38] The same was true of J. Fineberg, the announced British representative.

Finally, there were four other delegates who figured in the congress proceedings—Henri Guilbeaux, Gustav Klinger, Lea Katscher, and K. Petin, Lenin's creations pure and simple. Guilbeaux arrived on the afternoon of March 5, talked with Lenin that same night, addressed the congress the next day, and was awarded five votes, as many as given to the Bolsheviks and the Spartacists.* He was declared the delegate of the Zimmerwald Left in France, though actually he had no mandate at all. In fact, Lenin was rewarding

*In a later edition of the minutes of that first congress, published in 1933, the number of votes assigned to Guilbeaux was reduced to one.

a loyal friend, one who had been at his side before 1917. He knew, moreover, that the head of the pro-Bolshevik Zimmerwald Left in France, Fernand Loriot, out of solidarity would not repudiate Guilbeaux's fictitious mandate. When in April 1919, at the SFIO congress in Paris, the Socialist deputy Mayéras attacked Guilbeaux, disputing his right to represent French Socialists in Moscow (he had not even belonged to the Socialist Party prior to 1914), Loriot cut him short, explaining that Guilbeaux had had a "limited mandate."

A similar procedure was applied in the selection of a second Swiss delegate, a woman, Lea Katscher, who subsequently took no further part in the Swiss Communist movement she was supposed to be representing at this congress. Y. S. Reich (Thomas), one of the organizers of the congress, explained her presence thus: "But a rumor was circulating that he [Platten] had his own opinion. That is why the committee of three organizers was visited one day by Chicherin, who asked to see comrade Katscher, a kind of adventuress who had played at opposition within the women's movement in Switzerland and who had arrived in Russia with Platten— without any mandate, of course. On top of which, she had a bad reputation. Platten was shocked, but in vain. Lenin insisted, and Katscher was admitted to the conference."[39]

The case of Gustav Klinger was no less odd. The same Y. S. Reich (Thomas), describes the role that was played by Klinger, who was named one of the four chairmen of the congress, alongside Lenin, Eberlein, and Platten: "To counteract any impression that the whole of the German Communist Party was against formation of the Communist International, a second delegate was kept in reserve, one Klinger, a Volga German, who had no connection whatever with the German Communist Party. After the matter was ironed out with Eberlein, Klinger did not attend in any capacity as representative of the German Communist Party but was allowed to vote on behalf of the Communists from the German settlements along the Volga."[40]

Finally, there was a certain K. Petin, a member of the "Austrian delegation" along with Gruber. At the Vienna conference on February 9, 1919, it had been decided to send just one representative to Moscow, and that was Steinhardt (Gruber).

Nevertheless, two representatives showed up at the congress–for purposes that would not become clear until the day after it was over. Petin (whose name was wrongly given in the first editions of the minutes of the congress as K. Fatin) disappeared completely after the congress. He had been utterly unknown in the Austrian Communist movement. In fact, he was of Latvian origin, had belonged to the Russian Bolshevik Party only since 1918, and later became a leader of the Volga Commune, established by the local German population. For reasons unknown, in February 1919 he happened to be in Vienna and became the traveling companion of Steinhardt, who in his memoirs says of him only that he was "a returnee who spoke a little Russian."[41]

Apart from these fictitious delegates constituting the bulk of the listed participants, there were some who were not named on the official roll. One was Alexandra Kollontai, who translated Guilbeaux's speech. Another was Y. S. Reich (Thomas), who took part in the preparations for the congress as well as in the congress itself. Then there was Pierre Pascal, the second representative of the French Communist group, as is seen from the photograph of the congress participants and from his memoirs, published on the fifth anniversary of the founding of the Comintern in its official organ. Missing from the list, too, were some of the contingent from the Commissariat of Foreign Affairs such as Litvinov and Karakhan, as noted in the diary of Arthur Ransome, an English journalist who was permitted to enter the congress hall on March 3. The name of Josef Stalin does appear, though his presence was not noticed by Ransome, Sadoul, or Guilbeaux, and he is not seen in the official congress photograph, in which Lenin, Trotsky, Zinoviev, Bukharin, and several other Bolshevik leaders are clearly recognizable. On the other hand, the names of some of those who appeared in the official photograph of the congress (such as Kamenev, Enukidze and Steklov) are nowhere mentioned in the texts pertaining to the congress.* Likewise, the attendance of

*An amusing if somewhat grotesque detail with regard to that photograph of "delegates" to the congress, is that it includes a certain Kantorovich, whose sole role in Soviet Russia and in the International Communist movement was his service as personal secretary-valet to Chicherin! (This person, easily spotted on the photograph, was identified by Pierre Pascal, a delegate to the congress and close collaborator of Chicherin, and by Marcel Body, secretary of the French Communist group in Moscow in 1919.)

some other Bolsheviks was revealed only half a century later. Such was the case of Borodin, whose biographer wrote: "After having taken part at the first congress of the Communist International, Borodin traveled in 1919 through several countries, a bearer of Comintern messages."[42] This was also the case of the wife of Dzerzhinsky, who noted in her memoirs: "Beforehand, between March 2 and 6, the first congress of the Comintern convened, which I also attended."[43]

Lastly, there were two of the delegates who did not make it to the congress. One was Eugen Leviné, the second Spartacist delegate chosen by Rosa Luxemburg (he had been born in Russia), who, after leaving with Eberlein, was arrested en route a short time later. The other was László Rudas, a delegate of the Hungarian Communist Party, who reached Moscow shortly after the congress ended but did have an opportunity to take part in some of the first meetings of the Comintern's Executive Committee.

So the true facts about the delegates named on that list of thirty-four persons were far different from the official story. The overwhelming majority of these people belonged directly or indirectly to the Bolshevik Party, were Bolshevik militants conveniently transformed into "representatives" of other parties. In addition to the seven official members of the Russian Communist Party delegation (Lenin, Trotsky, Zinoviev, Stalin, Bukharin, and the two advisory delegates, Ossinsky-Obolensky and Vorovsky), most of the European delegates were members of the Bolshevik Party. This was true of those "representing" the Ukraine (Skrypnik and Gopner), Hungary (Rudnyánszky), Poland (Unszlicht), the Balkan Federation (Rakovsky), the Baltic countries (Gailis, Pögelman, and Gedris), the Volga Germans (Klinger), the Americans (Reinstein), and the Zimmerwald Committee (Balabanova). In fact, when the Eighth Congress of the Bolshevik Party opened, a few days after the founding of the Comintern, numerous "delegates" of foreign Communist parties who had attended the Comintern congress simply became delegates of the Bolshevik Party, having either deliberative (such as Gailis, Gedris, J. Rahja, Sirola) or consultative votes (Klinger and Rudnyánszky). They had joined the Bolshevik Party between 1903 and 1917. The Asian delegates—

some having full voting rights, others there in an advisory capacity—all belonged to the Bolshevik Party. Thus, with some three or four exceptions, this allegedly international Communist congress, that became the founding congress of the Communist International, was actually a gathering of Bolshevik Party members to whom Lenin had assigned certain titles and roles.

This improvisation of the roster of international delegates was matched by the impromptu character of the congress proceedings. At first the sessions took place with no journalists present. A little later one Western journalist, Arthur Ransome, attended. The debates, moreover, were not taken down in shorthand, which enabled Eberlein ten years later to assert that the report of his position on the immediate establishment of the International did not entirely correspond to what he had actually said at the time: "This report cannot lay claim to full correctness . . . Unfortunately there are no typewritten reports. But the printed report fails to give my personal statement that I was fully agreed with the conference, and that, had I a free hand, I should have voted for the immediate establishment of the Communist International."[44] The minutes of the congress were written afterwards, which explains their gaps and contradictions (even between the official editions of 1921 and 1933) and also the differences between what they report and the gist of other documents. Concerning the makeup of the congress presidium, for example, the minutes name Lenin, Albert, Platten, and Klinger, whereas Sadoul, a delegate to the congress, noted in his diary: "The congress lasted four days. The presiding office, headed by Lenin, consisted of Zinoviev, Buhkarin, Platten, Eberlein, and Gruber."[45]

The same improvisation was evident in the working out of the documents of the congress. The preparatory conference of March 1 had commissioned Zinoviev, Bukharin, and Platten to draft the manifesto of the congress, but when Trotsky joined the group he immediately took over the drafting, as he had done in 1915 at Zimmerwald and would do during the subsequent Comintern congresses. A few days after the founding of the Communist International, its newly appointed president, Zinoviev, reported to the Eighth Congress of the Bolshevik Party and admitted the haphazard manner in which the work of the First Comintern Congress had been accomplished: "A note is presented: why were the statutes [of the Comintern] not worked out? The congress enjoined the Executive Committee to prepare a draft of statutes and to submit it to a commission for discussion. It goes without saying that this is not an easy task. In general we have not yet solved the organizational problems; I recognize this frankly, and they cannot be resolved here. This is a problem for the future." [46]

So this founding congress, prepared for too hastily, was also poorly organized. But this did not greatly concern Lenin. He and his Bolshevik colleagues engineered the congress through maneuver and bluff, as they had done in the past and would do again the following year, using the same methods to fabricate delegates for a congress of Eastern peoples at Baku. To Lenin it was a time-tested weapon of political warfare. Deceit was permissible in pursuit of the sacred aim, when one was sure that events were going to prove one right. From the standpoint of his Marxist voluntarism, it was not necessary to wait for history, like the Social Democrats before 1914, or submit passively to it, like the working class foundering in reformist trade-unionism during that same period. No, what was needed was to anticipate history, then force men and push events into conformity with the anticipated. It is in this light that Lenin's techniques at that first international Communist congress must be viewed.

It is certainly rare in political history, and still more in the history of the international labor movement, that a meeting so sparsely attended and so unrepresentative could take a decision so far-reaching in its political and historic impact as that of the establishment of the Third International. But Lenin founded a Communist International not because of an assemblage in Moscow but because of what he believed was going to happen in Europe: mass Communist parties would emerge and the revolution would break out. In the days that followed the founding of the International, revolutions did indeed break out in Europe (Hungary, Bavaria), and the months to come would see Europe's large Socialist parties (the Italian, French, and German Independents) drift toward the Communist International, which by 1920, at the time of its Second Congress, had become, as Lenin put it, "fashionable." In March 1919 Lenin moved ahead of events by unfurling the banner of the Third International, to which very few then flocked. But soon afterward events began to occur—or so he thought—as he had foreseen, justifying his decision *a posteriori*.

LENIN'S DECISIVE MOVE

The opening of the congress was characterized by two particularly striking facts, about two individuals. One was Lenin's own role. The other was the exceptional importance of the Spartacus League delegate Hugo Eberlein. Neither would be true of subsequent congresses. This was the first and last time that Lenin would attend every session of a congress of the International and preside over all of them. He opened the first session on March 2, presided over it, then presided over the four ensuing ones between March 3 and March 6, and then made the closing speech. He wrote the resolution on bourgeois democracy and the dictatorship of the proletariat, as well as the article devoted to the founding of the International on March 5.

This was also the first and last time that a foreign Communist party—here the German Communist Party—would play an official role (genuine or not) superior to that of the Russian party. At this first congress it was Eberlein, the German delegate, who had the place of honor. Five years later he would write: "I was the only one there able to speak for a Communist party, apart from the Russian party."[47] Being the sole representative of the only important Communist party in Europe, he was to be heaped with titles and functions as no foreign Communist ever would again at a congress in Moscow. His party was listed at the head of the parties present at the congress, ahead even of the Russian party. The preliminary conference on March 1 had ruled that German was to be the official language, but that "Russian will be permitted too." At the first session of the congress Zinoviev hailed German as "the language of international Socialism." Eberlein headed the list of reporting speakers assigned to describe to the congress, at its first session on March 2, the state of the movement in the different countries, taking precedence over even Zinoviev, the Russian speaker. The next day, March 3, he was the first to address the assemblage on the subject of the International's platform, ahead even of Bukharin, its real author, and another honor befell him too, as he himself wrote: "In keeping with Lenin's assessment of the importance of the Spartacus League, I was elected to all the committees and to the chairmanship of the conference."[48]

Apart from the reports of numerous speakers on the revolutionary movement in their respective countries, which contained little that was either true or new about what was really happening there, and aside from the theses, resolutions, manifestoes, and the International's platform (all merely propaganda), this first congress dealt with only one important substantive issue: Should or should not a new International be set up immediately? Such a discussion should have been superfluous after the decision taken by the preliminary conference on March 1, but it suited Lenin's purpose perfectly.

At the start of the first session on March 2, after Lenin's opening address, Platten, the co-chairman of the meeting, undertook to inform the congress of the decision taken the night before by the preliminary conference: "According to one opinion, the assemblage should constitute itself the Third International. Another view, represented chiefly by a delegate from abroad, was that it would be wiser to characterize these sessions as merely a Communist conference and to postpone until later the business of establishing the Third International. . . . The proposal was made to regard our present meeting as a conference whose job it would be to convene, in the near future, a true congress that would proclaim the founding of the Third International."[49] Platten was immediately followed by Zinoviev, who explained in the name of the Bolshevik Central Committee the reason for the very conditional Bolshevik support of the decision taken by the preliminary conference: "Our Party is of the opinion that it is high time to found officially the Third International. And we would have proposed founding it here and now, at this first meeting. But since our friends from Germany, the German Communist Party, continue to insist that this meeting be only a conference, we deem it necessary, for the moment, to support that position. We declare, however, that we shall pursue our agitation for the earliest possible founding of the Third International as a formal organization."[50]

So the support of the Bolsheviks left the door open. Lenin was momentarily backing down—without saying for how long—while reserving the right to plead the cause anew at the first favorable opportunity. Immediately after the statement by Zinoviev, followed by one from Kuusinen merely reaffirming the Bolshevik viewpoint, the international conference took the same decision as adopted at the preliminary meeting the previous evening, namely that this assemblage would be considered an international Communist conference and not a congress for founding a new International.

Yet this same issue, seemingly settled at the start of the congress, popped up again the very next day, at the session of March 3, which began at noon. The item on the agenda was the platform of the new International, and the first speaker, Eberlein, started with a brief explanation of why the Spartacists believed any immediate founding of a new International to be tactically inopportune. He devoted the bulk of his speech to the item on the agenda, the platform. Bukharin, who followed him, likewise spoke only of that, as did the next speaker, Rutgers. But the speaker after that, Otto Kuusinen, instead of addressing himself to the platform, set out to refute Eberlein's arguments as to the prematureness of establishing a Third International then: "The situation is ripe," he said, "world revolution has already begun, and that is why we must set up the Revolutionary International now."[51] As he put it, this new International already existed: "because as of now we actually have a Third International, namely in great revolutionary Russia. You know, comrades, that for more than a year now revolutionary Russia has indeed constituted the new International."[52]

The spontaneity of Kuusinen's statement appears suspect. Only the night before he had subscribed to the viewpoint expressed by Zinoviev on behalf of the Bolshevik Central Committee, and now today he was returning to the attack. It seems improbable that he would have dared to flout the agenda in this fashion had he not been covered (or, more likely, pushed) by the Bolshevik delegation to the congress, more specifically by Lenin himself or his alter ego, Zinoviev. Moreover, Kuusinen's argumentation bore an authentic Bolshevik stamp, so much so that his statement that a Communist

International did in fact exist from the moment that Communist Russia came into being is found again in the exegesis delivered by Zinoviev on March 18 to the Bolshevik congress: "'It [the Third International] was born on that day when the working class won in Russia its brilliant victory under the standard of international- ism.'"[53]

From the Kuusinen episode on, the story told by the minutes of the congress becomes equivocal. According to these minutes, after Kuusinen the podium was mounted by Gruber (Steinhardt), who began his speech: "We, the delegates from German Austria, can find no words to express our joy at being here among you. We just arrived an hour ago, after incredible difficulties and a journey of seventeen days."[54] This statement was made, according to the official minutes, in the late afternoon of March 3, yet Arthur Ransome, present since the start of the session, which had begun at noon, noted in his diary that the Austrian delegate had been there at that time. But—and it is here that we encounter the cru- cial and most controversial point in the proceedings of the congress—the story of the effect produced by that speech and the direct consequences of it has evoked far deeper questions and doubts than the exact time of Gruber's arrival.

There are five different and contradictory versions of the effect had by his appearance on the podium. The first is that of the official minutes, which mention nothing special. Gruber's speech was a report of the political situation in Austria, of the treachery of the Social Democrats and the vigorous action of the Communist Party, but it contained no plea for the founding of a Communist International, and indeed did not allude to the issue at all. Accord- ing to this same source, the March 3 session ended after his speech, and the third session began the next morning, March 4. On that day a proposal was submitted calling for the immediate founding of a Third International. It bore the signatures of four so-called foreign delegates (Gruber, Grimlund, Rakovsky, and Rudnyánszky) but it had not been signed by any of the Bolshevik delegation. The reading of this proposal sparked a lively debate in which, along with other speakers assailing Eberlein's arguments, Gruber took part. Zinoviev, Balabanova, J. Rahja, Rakovsky, Sadoul, Gruber, and Fineberg took the podium in that order. In his remarks Gruber polemized with Eberlein, expressing himself in favor of immediate establishment of the International, as other speakers did, but there was nothing exceptional about his speech, nor did it have any great effect.

Unlike that first version, the second version comes to us from the International's best-informed sources, people such as its first secretary, Vorovsky, who shared that duty with Balabanova. This version introduces a major correction, emphasizing the profound moral and psychological impact of Gruber's speech upon arriving at the congress. Under a pen name, Vorovsky wrote in an article in *Pravda* shortly after the International was founded: "At the conference of the Communist International there was a rare and memorable moment, one that has deeply etched itself into the minds and hearts of those present. It was when the delegate from German Austria mounted the podium. . . . It was impossible to listen without profound emotion to the unembellished tale of this Austrian comrade, who told with such enthusiasm how his hope of reaching Moscow had sustained his strength along the way, how Red Moscow indeed seemed to him the Promised Land."[5] [5]

A third version was recounted on the fifth anniversary of the Comintern's founding, by its president, Zinoviev, who on that occasion inserted two elements not found in either of the preceding ones. First, he asserted that the Bolshevik delegation had co-signed the motion made to set up the International then. Secondly, he said that it was the arrival of the "Austrian delegation" (and not just Gruber's speech) that had tipped the scales in favor of establishing the Comintern immediately:

On March 4, 1919, the Russian delegates, in accord with those of the Communist Parties of German Austria, the Left Social Democratic Party of Sweden, the revolutionary Social Democratic Federation of the Balkans, and the Communist Party of Hungary, submitted a motion calling for immediate establishment of the Third International. This move had been preceded by long discussions. . . . We thought first of confining ourselves to a temporary organizing committee that would convene a new congress, and of not proceeding to set up the new International just then. At that moment [on March 4th] the delegation from Austria arrived. The comrades had had an unusually difficult journey. Two of them traveled almost the whole way on railroad-car buffers, disguised as prisoners of war. They brought along a mood of revolutionary decisiveness. They smelled of the powder of battle, of the

battles then igniting in so many countries. They stood up on our
side. . . . Their speeches also had an effect on the delegate of the
German Communist Party. A vote was taken. The Communist International was proclaimed unanimously—except for the abstention of the
German delegate.[56]

Boris Reinstein's account, five years later, highlighted only Gruber's role, making no mention of "Austrian delegates" or of the
"private discussions" referred to by Zinoviev: "It was above all
Gruber [Steinhardt], the delegate from Vienna, who with his vigorous remarks on the second day at the evening session, helped to
clear the atmosphere. . . . That speech, coupled with the formal
motion made by several comrades that the Third International be
set up immediately, altered the course that the congress had followed up to then."[57]

The fourth version depicts an even closer link between Gruber's
speech and the founding of the International, but adds a role played
by Lenin personally (or Zinoviev, which is the same thing). We
find it in the report that Y. S. Reich (Thomas) made to Boris Nicolaevsky:

The arrival of Gruber-Steinhardt livened things up. . . . Wearing a shag-
gy beard and a ragged soldier's greatcoat (with one whole flap torn off),
he marched straight up to the podium. "I am the delegate of the Austrian Communists!" he announced, immediately taking out a knife and
slashing open his greatcoat, from which he drew forth his mandate. He
addressed the assemblage, relating almost in tears what he had had to
endure in crossing the lines of the Ukrainian front. It really made one
shudder. As he was finishing, someone seated at the table of the presidium whispered to him "Shout 'Long live the congress of the Communist
International!'" which the Austrian thereupon did. . . . Balabanova then
gave her report on the work of the Zimmerwald committee, after which
she moved, seconded by Rakovsky, that the Zimmerwald group be dissolved. At this juncture someone—Lenin or Zinoviev—proposed that a
decision be taken to set up a Communist International and to designate
this present conference as its first congress. Some of the delegates,
tipped off in advance, instantly shouted their acclaim. All present
jumped to their feet, lifted their hands and sang the International.
Eberlein, swept up in the torrent, raised his hand too. Taking advantage
of the opportunity, the chairman declared the motion unanimously
adopted.[58]

Finally, there is a fifth version, again supplied by active participants in the congress, but this one says nothing about any part
played by Gruber's speech, emphasizing instead the decisive role
of Lenin. One of the witnesses was Gruber (Steinhardt) himself,
who reports in his memoirs that he delivered his first speech at
that first congress on the evening of March 2 (the official minutes
place it on March 3 and Zinoviev on March 4). His words triggered
no discussion favoring the immediate founding of a Third International, nor was there any resolution calling for implementation
of such an idea. It was not until two days later that Lenin himself
made the big decision, which he communicated to Steinhardt personally before announcing it to the congress:

> Before the start of the morning session on March 4, Lenin called me
> aside for a little talk. . . . On my arrival, I had delivered to the confer-
> ence presidium a copy of the resolution of our own party congress
> calling for the founding of a Third International. Lenin informed me
> that an identical resolution was on the agenda of the opening confer-
> ence session. The motion made by the Russian delegation was defeated
> because of the objections of the German delegate, Eberlein. . . . Lenin
> told me of his intention to bring the Austrian resolution up for discus-
> sion at the start of the afternoon session. He said that he would justify
> debating my motion out of turn by reporting that a major delegation
> had been unable to get to the conference on time. . . . Meanwhile I had
> prepared the necessary draft, which was signed by Lenin, Grimlund
> (from Sweden), Rakovsky (from the Ukraine) and by me. The confer-
> ence acceded to Lenin's proposal. I made a brief speech in support of
> my motion, which, when the vote came, passed unanimously—except
> for Eberlein, who abstained.[59]

Apart from his role at the first congress, Steinhardt never claimed to have contributed significantly to the founding of the Comintern. He did not even mention the subject at the Second Congress,
or during his trip afterwards to Southern Russia and the Crimea, as
we know from R. Thal-Goldenberg, who was among those traveling with him.

Eberlein, the most important foreign delegate at the congress, in
his own recollections of the founding of the Comintern (first on
the occasion of its fifth anniversary, then on that of its tenth),
made no reference at all to any part played by the Austrian del-

egate.* This silence concerning Gruber's role is reinforced by the testimony of other participants, who attribute the actual birth of the International primarily to the midwifery of Lenin. In the chapter of his diary entitled *Les Séances* ("The Sessions"), Jacques Sadoul takes no note of any impact of the Gruber speech but does describe in glowing terms the talents as a tactician that Lenin displayed at the Moscow congress:

> Twenty years of furious struggle in the forefront of the Russian Social Democratic Party; uninterrupted leadership of its Bolshevik faction, conceived, nurtured, then ushered by him to its present apotheosis; experiences in the ways of international congresses; an awesome knowledge of the human heart and mind; an unparallelled political flair; bulldog tenacity strangely combined with a natural propensity to expediency—he seems to venerate the will to power in all of its forms, and the leisurely force of guile as well as the quick might of battle—all of this and many other qualities, which I have many times analyzed before, make of Lenin, notwithstanding his legendary reputation as a sectarian and fanatic, an inspired opportunist—intransigent when it is opportune to be so—craftiest of the jousters at a congress session, most dazzling among the schemers in the back rooms.[60]

To what could all of these encomia, which Sadoul heaps upon Lenin for his deportment at the congress, possibly refer if not to that decisive matter of the proclaiming of the Communist International? The recollections of the other Frenchman present at the congress, Pierre Pascal, likewise published in the official organ of the Communist International on its fifth anniversary, speak only of Lenin as the architect of the International: "I saw Lenin on the day of triumph, the day on which that dream to which he had devoted a lifetime of thought, toil, and struggle, finally came true. It was early March 1919, with the founding of the Third International. . . . His efforts had been crowned with success. In the few words that I heard him speak I perceived that joy of creation

*H. Eberlein, *La Correspondance Internationale*, February 27, 1924, p. 154. Eberlein made the obvious error of attributing the decision to set up the International to three important events that happened, according to him, between March 2 and 6, 1919, namely the proclaiming of the Soviet Republic of Hungary (which actually did not take place until March 21), the proclaiming of the Soviet Republic of Bavaria (which did not occur until April 7), and the murder of Leo Jogiches (which did not take place until March 10).

known to one who has undertaken a colossal task with awesome responsibilities."*

Notwithstanding these five different versions of how the decision to set up immediately a Communist International was brought about, the official document certifying the birth of the Comintern reads as follows:

> The representatives of the Communist Party of German Austria, the left-wing Social Democratic Party of Sweden, the Balkan Social Democratic Revolutionary Labor Federation, and the Communist Party of Hungary, propose the foundation of the Communist International:
>
> (1) The necessity of the struggle for the dictatorship of the proletariat demands the existence of a consolidated international organization of all Communist elements.
>
> (2) The foundation of the Third International is all the more a duty since at the present moment in Bern, and afterwards perhaps in other places, the attempt will be made to restore the old, opportunist International and to gather together all the irresolute, indeterminate elements of the proletariat. Consequently it is necessary to draw a sharp line of demarcation between the revolutionary proletarian and the treacherous Socialist elements.
>
> (3) If the Third International is not founded by the present Moscow conference the impression may be given that there is no unity among the Communist parties; that, of course, would weaken our position and would increase the confusion among the vacillating elements of the proletariat in all countries.
>
> (4) The foundation of the Third International is consequently an unconditional historical necessity, and it must be accomplished by the international communist conference held in Moscow.[61]

This root decision of the Moscow congress, in Lenin's eyes, opened up a dual short-run historical prospect. One result would be that the leadership of Europe's revolutionary movement would

---

*P. Pascal, *La Correspondance Internationale*, February 6, 1924, p. 85. By 1967 the sole survivor of those who had participated in this founding congress—two of the women, Gopner and Balabanova, having died in 1966—Professor Pascal has confirmed the view that Lenin's was the decisive role in the creation of the International, adding: "The Austrian delegate had no influence at all on the actual decision to found the Communist International." (Stated by Pascal in a discussion with Branko Lazitch on November 7, 1966.)

thereupon fall to the Russians, but only briefly. When Zinoviev, named president of the International, delivered his analysis to the Eighth Bolshevik Congress, as Lenin's faithful spokesman he declared: "We can say that at the founding of the Third International hegemony in the domain of ideas belonged unreservedly to the Russian Communist Party, and I know of nothing that one can be prouder of. . . . The Executive Committee of the Third International . . . must for the moment be based in Russia. We have declared this a temporary situation, adding that we would be happy to be able to transfer as soon as possible the head office of the Third International and of its Executive Committee to another capital, to Paris for instance."[62] Lenin in turn was to write in April of 1919, and would publish in the first issue of the Comintern's official organ, to come out in May, his article "The Third International and Its Place in History," in which he would stress the temporary nature of Russian hegemony in the international labor movement, placing it in historical perspective: "For only a short time, naturally, hegemony within the revolutionary proletarian International has passed to the Russians, just as at different periods during the nineteenth century it belonged to the British, then to the French, and then to the Germans."[63]

The second ingredient of that same short-run historical prospect was that world revolution had already started, in the West if not throughout the world. Lenin repeated his certainty of this at every opportunity on the occasion of the International's founding. Closing the congress on March 6, he concluded with the words: "The victory of the proletarian revolution throughout the world is assured. The hour for the founding of an international Soviet republic is near."[64] His article on the founding of the Comintern, published that same day, ended with the same profession of faith: "The founding of the Third, the Communist International, is the prelude to an international Soviet republic, to the world victory of Communism."[65] Again that same day, at a meeting devoted to the establishment of the International, Lenin voiced the same conviction a third time: "The comrades present in this room have watched the founding of the first Soviet republic. They witness today the creation of the Third International, the Communist International. They will all see the establishment of a World Federative Republic of Soviets."[66]

Even before the proclaiming of the Soviet Republic of Hungary on March 21, and of that of Bavaria on April 7, Lenin was expecting the revolutionary tidal wave. In his report on the party program to the Eighth Bolshevik Congress on March 19, he declared revolution to be imminent in Poland, reasoning by analogy from what had happened in Russia, which he deemed applicable to other countries: "Among the Poles, self-determination of the proletariat is on the march. Here are the latest figures on the makeup of the Warsaw Council of Workers' Deputies: Polish social traitors 333, communists 297. By our revolutionary calendar this shows that their October is not far off. They are now having their August, or even September, 1917."[67] Shortly afterwards, when Soviet Hungary came into being, Lenin in a note to Karakhan wrote: "We must hold out yet a few months and our victory will be assured."[68]

The Communist defeat in Hungary, like the ones before it in Bavaria and Berlin, did not shake his certainty. He considered them merely temporary setbacks, foreign versions of the Bolshevik reverses at Petrograd in July and August of 1917, a prelude to triumph in October. Thus in the August 1919 issue of the Comintern's official journal he wrote: "Now, the transformation of the imperialist war into civil war has become a fact in a number of countries, not only in Russia but also in Finland, in Hungary, in Germany, and even in neutral Switzerland, and that civil war is maturing is seen, felt, and sensed in all advanced countries without exception."[69] (The expression "all advanced countries" clearly indicates that at this time Lenin excluded from that process the backward and colonial countries.)

This deep conviction of Lenin's without which he would not have pressed for immediate founding of the International at all costs, was shared by Zinoviev, who had become titular head of the new International. In the course of the debates at the Moscow congress he had said to Eberlein: "In Germany you have a party on the march toward power, and within a few months a proletarian government will be set up in Germany."[70] In the first issue of the Comintern's official journal he exulted: "At the time of this writing, the Third International has as its main basis three soviet republics—in Russia, Hungary, and Bavaria. No one will be surprised, however, if by the time these lines appear in print, we shall have not merely three, but six and more soviet republics. Europe is hurrying toward the proletarian revolution at a break-neck pace. . . . . The victory of Communism throughout Germany is now inevitable. . . . In a year's time we shall begin to forget that Europe had ever fought for Communism, because by that time all Europe will be Communist."[71]

This euphoric spirit gushed from many of the contributions to that first issue of *Communist International*, published in May 1919. László Rudas, the delegate of the Hungarian Communist Party, who did not arrive in Moscow until after the congress was over, wrote on the subject of Soviet Hungary: "The proletariat has confidence in the ultimate triumph of the revolution throughout the world."[72] The delegate of the Austrian Communist Party, Steinhardt, committed his country to imminent revolution: "Already the Soviets of Hungary have fraternally joined the Russian Soviets. And the revolutionary forces of the proletariat of the former Danube Monarchy will soon follow their great pioneers."[73] Jacques Sadoul affirmed for his part: "Revolution is progressing in France."[74] And the second French speaker at the congress just ended, Henri Guilbeaux, concluded his article on revolution in France with the conditioned prediction: "The armed French proletariat must create a Red Army for the defense and completion of the revolution. Later, this army—when its task at home is finally achieved—will prove the reliable protector of the Belgian proletariat and the proletariat of Romanic Switzerland, where the bourgeoisie is still very powerful. Leaning on the Russian Federative Soviet Republic, the French Republic of Councils will be invincible; and if a similar movement spreads in all countries which have not yet succeeded in overthrowing their class governments—undoubtful symptoms whereof already appear—then the European Republic of Councils will be proclaimed in Europe."[75]

The Comintern and the Communist Revolutions
of 1918-1919

With the exception of the Baltic countries, which experienced short-lived Communist regimes owing to the action of the Bolshevik Party and the Red Army, the Communists tried to seize or retain power at five points in Europe: in Finland and Berlin, before creation of the Comintern; and in Hungary, Bavaria, and Vienna, shortly after its birth. Not all of these attempts belong directly to the history of the Communist International, for some of them took place before it came into being, but they were indirectly linked to its history in that they influenced its political orientation, tactics, and organization. Without the five revolutions or putsches of 1918-19 the Communist International would undoubtedly have existed, but the climate of the years 1918-20 would not have been so euphoric, for the prospects would have seemed less bright.

In 1918-19 the Bolshevik conviction that Communist victory was imminent in the West was founded on a belief in two types of revolution—one type known as bourgeois, democratic, or nationalist, and another type known as proletarian, Socialist, or Communist. It was revolutions of the first type which in 1918 racked the defeated Central Powers, resulting in the overthrow of the traditional monarchies in Germany, Austria, and Turkey, in the introduction of parliamentary government into certain countries, and in the creation of a number of new states. To the Bolsheviks this was but a phase, a first step, necessary but temporary, which would precede the true and ultimate revolution: Communist revolution. The Bolsheviks had believed firmly in this inevitable schedule even before those revolutions, so that when they occurred, the certainty of Lenin and his colleagues was reinforced. Events had proved them right.

The failure of those revolutions did not upset the Bolsheviks. For them revolutionary setbacks were lessons to be learned from, and were regarded as a spur to new endeavor. "Without the 'dress rehearsal' of 1905, the 1917 revolution, bourgeois in February and proletarian in October, would have been impossible," wrote Lenin.[1] What mattered to him, after the formal birth of the Comintern, was to subject to the analytic method of criticism and self-criticism the key problems raised by all these revolutions or putsches: the role of the Communist party in the revolution; the attitude to be adopted toward Social Democrats; the position to be taken toward parliamentarism and syndicalism; solutions for the agrarian question and the problem of nationalism. Bolshevism being a science of revolution, and the Russian Bolsheviks, unlike foreign revolutionaries, being the only ones who had known how to achieve victory and maintain power, it followed that the Bolshevik theses concerning the main items on the agenda must prevail, for only they had been sanctioned by success. Thus it was that the experience gained in the five revolutions of 1918-19 served as a kind of negative backdrop for elaboration of the general line of the Comintern, which was to preoccupy its Second Congress in the summer of 1920.

THE REVOLUTION IN FINLAND

The first revolution in Europe claiming to be Socialist erupted in Finland. On January 15 (28), 1918, the Red Guard took Helsinki, and on the following day a Council of People's Delegates was formed, consisting of fourteen members and presided over by Kullervo Manner, former President of the Finnish Diet. On March 1, 1918, the Socialist Workers' Republic of Finland, as the regime officially called itself, concluded a treaty of friendship with Soviet Russia "to strengthen the friendship and brotherhood between these two free republics," as the preamble stressed. Lenin was overjoyed at this revolution, the more so as he had predicted it two days in advance, declaring to the Special All-Russian Congress of Railway Workers: "We now see that a workers' revolution is expected any day in Finland, that same Finland which for twelve years, since 1905, has enjoyed complete internal freedom and has had the elective right to democratic institutions."[2]

When the predicted occurred, Lenin hailed "the conflagration of proletarian insurrection" in Finland, and prophesied its outbreak in Rumania.[3] And since the Soviet government at the time was making no effort to conceal its wish to see revolution spread, and its intention to help spread it, Trotsky—in his dual capacity as Commissar of Foreign Affairs and head of the Soviet delegation conducting the peace negotiations with Imperial Germany—sent off a telegram from Brest-Litovsk expressing solidarity with revolutionary Socialist Finland, which was to do battle against the troops of that same Imperial Germany.[4] In his report to the Seventh Bolshevik Party Congress on March 7, Lenin expressed his hope for an early German and world revolution, promising meanwhile to help with the Finnish revolution.[5] The next day, in his report on the Bolshevik Party's new program, he singled out Finland as a country with a new type of proletarian power.

A few weeks later, however, in May, Marshal Mannerheim with the aid of German troops brought down Finland's Socialist regime, and most of its leaders—Manner, who headed the revolutionary government, Yrjö Sirola, minister of foreign affairs, Edward Gylling, minister of finance, Eero Haapalainen, minister of war and commander-in-chief of the Red Army, Otto W. Kuusinen, minister of education, the Rahja brothers, and others—had to seek refuge in Soviet Russia, where they subjected their revolution to criticism and self-criticism. Arriving in Russia after such a fiasco, these leaders were hard put to explain their behavior, as Manner revealed later: "I met Comrade Lenin for the third time at the beginning of May 1918, in his office in the Kremlin. Our revolutionary struggle in Finland, which had lasted three months, was over. We had been beaten. We saw and felt that we had made some very big mistakes. We ourselves had been defeated in spirit. On our return from Finland, Comrade Kuusinen and I went to see Comrade Lenin. We walked along pensively, with aching soul and conscience, like men who had fallen down on the job. The question flashed through my mind: What will the Old Boy say to us now? Will he flatten us with his big hammer? "[6]

To judge from Manner's account, Lenin did not receive the two harshly. He said to them: "You mustn't lose your courage or be depressed, prepare yourselves to do a better job next time."[7] But Manner does not disclose in his memoirs, published in a collection in 1934, that Lenin did not confine himself to these amiable generalities. The Finnish leaders were required to deliver themselves of a self-critique, an institution unknown to the Second International and which only made its appearance in the international Communist movement. The essence of this self-critique was contained in a brochure, written by Kuusinen, completed in October 1918 and published under the aegis of the Communist International.*

The nub of the Kuusinen *mea culpa* was his confession that the Finnish Communist revolution had preceded the existence of the Finnish Communist Party—a major infraction of the Bolshevik credo. Actually, unlike the Baltic Socialists and those of Poland and the other nations of the old Tsarist empire who got dragged into the battles between the Bolsheviks and Mensheviks within Russia's Social Democratic Party, the Finnish Socialists had managed to stay aloof. The difference was considerable. Among the former, one found declared Mensheviks lumped together with confirmed Bolsheviks; among the Finns there were only Social Democrats. When the February 1917 revolution erupted, Lenin in the name of the Bolsheviks demanded an immediate break with the Zimmerwald movement internationally and a merciless fight against ministerialism internally. Finland's Social Democratic Party took the reverse position: "It is very characteristic," wrote Kuusinen, "that at the party congress held in June [1917] (at which in passing we aligned ourselves with the Zimmerwaldists), not a voice was raised to demand that any Socialists entering a coalition government be thrown out of the party."[8]

The absence of a revolutionary party would have been forgivable if there had at least been some convinced revolutionaries, but those too were lacking, according to Kuusinen: "We did not believe in revolution; placed no hope in it and did not aspire to it. In that respect we were model Social Democrats."[9] Hence, in Bolshevik eyes, defeat was inevitable. That a revolution led by authentic

*Initially Kuusinen was not reckoned among the leading figures of the Finnish Soviet Republic, as were Manner, Sirola, and Haapalainen, but soon he was one up on them all. He became the one man most trusted by the Russians, who, under the Bolshevik method, contrived to have or plant within every workers' movement a faction loyal to them, and within every faction a man who was theirs. In the case of Finland that man was Kuusinen, which explains how he came to have a more important role than other Finns in the Comintern's central apparatus.

revolutionaries might in the end fail was documented history; but for a revolution to succeed without being led by true revolutionaries was impossible.

This original error begat many others, committed by and during that short-lived Socialist republic. Lenin had been teaching the Bolsheviks that a revolution must be seriously and minutely prepared, as seen from the letters that he sent from his hideaway in Finland during the weeks preceding the October 1917 coup. The Finnish leaders did just the opposite: "In November [1917]," wrote Kuusinen, "we had decided, however, to avoid revolution, partly because we did not wish to jeopardize our democratic gains, partly also because we hoped, by adroit parliamentary maneuvers, to escape the whirlwind of history." [10] Whereas Lenin saw in parliamentarism merely a tool for Communists to use when battling within legal bounds, Finland's future commissars had seen it as an end in itself: "The deceptive luster of democratic parliamentarism had completely dazzled us. . . . In the revolution of the winter of 1918 the Finnish Social Democrats had no thought of transgressing the limits of the representative system." [11] In Lenin's view, the general strike had to be followed by decisive revolutionary action, but the Finnish leaders had deemed otherwise: "The general strike gripped the entire country. Our Revolutionary Central Committee debated the question of taking the offensive. We, misnamed Marxists, wanted no part of any revolutionary act." [12] Lenin held that a revolution in the name of the working class must produce a dictatorship of the proletariat, while in Finland the revolution had proclaimed as its goal the defense of the democratic system: "But what was the watchword, the war cry, of that revolution? The power of the working class? No, the movement's watchword was still the same democratic order, but this time such an order that could not be destroyed." [13] Finally, whereas Lenin had been teaching since 1905 that a revolutionary army must learn how to retreat in good order, the Finnish revolutionists offered the spectacle of a headlong rout. This was stressed in another brochure, published by the Communist International in 1919: "But this retreat was a failure. The order given for it was not very strictly obeyed. . . . The whole of the front did not realize the true situation until too late. So that instead of an organized military retreat which, as was hoped, might have saved tens of thousands of revolutionary fighters, it was a bloody débâcle, with desperate hand-to-hand combat." [14]

All these lessons, learned and published after establishment of the Communist International, were later augmented by other observations in conformity with the Bolshevik viewpoint. Thus on the tenth anniversary of the Finnish revolution one of its leaders, Sirola, denounced the error made with regard to the peasants: "The vacillation of the Finnish Social Democrats in this matter resulted in a large part of the working peasantry being forced to side with its class enemies. Certain of our Communist sections [of the Communist International] have not yet fully grasped this lesson. . . . [15] The mistakes made in the Finnish revolution are not a uniquely Finnish phenomenon. It is to be feared that they will be repeated in any proletarian revolution. This is why the revolutionary proletariat in all capitalist countries should study and carefully analyze the lessons taught us by the Finnish revolution." [16]

As for the Finnish Communists who had taken refuge in Soviet Russia, they accomplished after the fact what they should have done before it. At their conference in Moscow in August 1918 they formally broke with the Social Democrats and reformist Syndicalists. But it was too late. The Finnish revolution, which had its "July 1917" in January of 1918, was never to have its "October." Instead, it simply faded away. The founding of the Finnish Communist Party at that August 1918 conference after the revolution was merely a repeat of what had happened with the Bolsheviks in 1912 at Prague before the revolution.

REVOLUTIONARY STIRRINGS IN BERLIN

In the weeks preceding the founding of the Comintern and during the days immediately following, Germany and especially Berlin were the theater of actual revolutionary battles. They were triggered on Sunday, January 5, 1919. Crowds of Communists poured into the streets of Berlin and took over several buildings, one being that of *Vorwärts*, the official organ of the governing Socialist Party. The next day, armed clashes occurred, and the fighting went on until January 11, ending in defeat. On January 15, Rosa Luxemburg and Karl Liebknecht were assassinated. Snuffed out in the capital, the revolutionary movement continued to flicker on in a few of the German provinces (Rhineland-Westphalia, Saxony, Württemberg, Central Germany) but it was everywhere harshly suppressed by the Socialist government. It surfaced again in Berlin on March 3, while the congress that founded the Comintern was in session in Moscow. The German capital was gripped by a general strike, which two days later turned into armed conflict, again ending in defeat. The strike ceased on March 8, the fighting on March 10, the day on which Leo Jogiches was murdered.

These eruptions brought cheer and hope to Lenin, Trotsky, and the other Bolshevik leaders, isolated from the outside world in Petrograd and Moscow. Unlike Finland, which was only a little country, the scene of this new revolutionary ferment was Berlin, capital of one of Europe's most important countries. The Bolsheviks saw in this a living confirmation of those objective general laws of revolution which they believed that they had discovered and were the first to apply. They equated the fall of the German monarchy in November 1918 with that of the Russian monarchy in February-March 1917, the attempt to overthrow the Berlin Socialist government in January 1919 with what had happened at Petrograd in July 1917. The failure in Berlin in no way diminished their certainty, for the parallel in Petrograd had failed initially too. From words that Trotsky wrote the day after Rosa Luxemburg and Karl Liebknecht were assassinated, one sees with what complete confidence he envisaged future events in Germany: "What happened at Petrograd was an exact duplicate of what later occurred in the streets of Berlin, in January 1919. We at the time never doubted for a moment that those July days were but the prelude to our victory. In Germany, where the first revolutionary explosion occurred in November 1918, the events parallelling our July were already unfolding in early January. The German proletariat is accomplishing its revolution on a tighter schedule. Where we need four months, they have needed but two. And there can be no doubt that this same rate will be maintained to the end. From the German July to the German October may not be a period of four months, as it was with us, but perhaps no more than two." [17]

Though this indeed was the dominant view in Petrograd and Moscow, it was not remotely shared by the Communist leaders in Berlin. Unlike the abortive Finnish revolution, the Berlin move-

ment did not lack leaders. First, it was headed by a nucleus of
experienced Spartacists, three individuals who had come through
long years of hard revolutionary fighting: Karl Liebknecht, Rosa
Luxemburg, and Leo Jogiches. Secondly, they had at hand an
authentic representative of the Bolsheviks, Karl Radek, a man who
at the time probably knew best of all both the prevailing situation
and the leaders of Europe's two main Communist parties, the
Bolshevik Party and the Spartacus League. Of these four who
dominated the German party, particularly in Berlin in January
1919, three had had close connections with the revolutionary
movement in Tsarist Russia: Rosa Luxemburg, Jogiches, and
Radek. On the eve of the event they all had the same attitude
toward the attempted Berlin revolution—skepticism and opposition. Only Liebknecht, the least versed in Russian and Bolshevik
affairs, indulged himself in a little more optimism.

According to the basic primer of Communist revolutionary
action, as taught by Lenin, the seizure and maintenance of power
depended on two inseparable factors: the existence of a revolutionary party organized to abet the struggle for power; and the
ability of that party to exert a decisive influence on the majority
of the working class—or at least on the majority of its most representative segment, such as workers' councils (called in Russian
soviets)—in a country's most important city. But as soon as Radek
reached Berlin in mid-December 1918, he realized that these two
essential preconditions had not remotely been met.

At the editorial office of *Rote Fahne*, where he had his first
conversation with Liebknecht, Rosa Luxemburg, Paul Levi, and
August Thalheimer, Radek recognized immediately how precarious were the ties of the German Communists to the masses of
working people: "There was no Spartacist faction at all in the
Congress of Councils. . . . 'And what about the Berlin Workers'
and Soldiers' Council?' 'We had no organized group there
either. . . .' 'And how large an organization *do* we have in
Berlin?' I asked. 'We are in the process of mustering our forces.'
When the revolution started [in November 1918], we had no
more than fifty men in Berlin."[18] This situation prompted Radek
first to oppose the revolutionary action in January 1919, then to
write openly that same year before leaving Germany: "In Germany, when the revolution broke out, the revolutionary party was

more of a theoretical direction than a party, a mind without a body." [19]

The founding congress of the German Communist Party, which opened on December 30, 1918, and which Radek attended as "member from the Soviet Republic of Russia and one of the six emissaries from the Russian Government to the German revolutionary workers," [20] confirmed his initial gloomy impressions. If the preceding week had revealed to him that the working masses were not yet ripe for a proletarian revolution, he was now to become aware that the Communist party itself was not yet equal to the job either: "The party congress made blatantly clear how young and inexperienced the party was. Any contact with the masses was extremely feeble. The congress took an ironical attitude toward negotiating with the independent left. I did not have the feeling that this could, or should, be called a party." [21]

The German Communist Party's general lack of political maturity was particularly evident in its attitude toward parliamentarism and the trade union movement. According to Lenin, a Communist party should not systematically oppose every form of parliamentary activity, just as it should not fall victim to the "parliamentary cretinism" of the Social Democrats. Now, at the founding congress of the German Communist Party, the second item on the agenda was the matter of the attitude they should adopt with regard to the National Assembly that was to convene. The reporter on the question was Paul Levi, who pleaded for Communist participation, vigorously supported by Rosa Luxemburg. Otto Rühle, the second Socialist deputy in the Reichstag who had voted against the war credits in 1915 (the first having been Liebknecht), was against such participation, and several other speakers agreed with him, among them two young militants soon to distinguish themselves in the Soviet Republic of Bavaria, Eugen Leviné and Max Levien. In the final vote those opposed prevailed, 62 to 23. On the trade union question the left Communists again prevailed, despite an opposing speech by Rosa Luxemburg, but there was no vote.

So German Communism was afflicted at birth with that infantile disease known as "leftism." More serious still, whereas in Europe a year later Lenin did his best to cure this illness, and was largely successful, in Germany on the eve of 1919 circumstances did not permit of that therapy. Lenin's voice did not reach that far, and the opinions of German leaders like Rosa Luxemburg, Leo Jogiches, and Paul Levi were overruled. The full gravity of the situation became evident in the first days of 1919, when the leaders, outvoted by the militants, were dragged into a revolutionary episode of which they disapproved.

The inefficiency and lack of coordination on the part of the Communists in Berlin struck Radek, who noted: "The masses seized buildings that had no importance, like that of the newspaper *Vorwärts*. . . . Liebknecht lost contact both with me and with the Central Committee. In all the commotion he had dropped out of sight, and was sitting somewhere in the Bötzow brewery with the representatives of the independent workers."[22] From these deliberations between Liebknecht—who was accompanied by Wilhelm Pieck, another member of the Central Committee—and Berlin's independent Socialists and workers' representatives (*Obleute*) emerged a manifesto, dated January 6 and signed by Georg Ledebour, Liebknecht, and Schulze, proclaiming nothing less than the overthrow of the Ebert-Scheidemann government: "The Ebert-Scheidemann government has made itself impossible. We, the undersigned Revolutionary Committee representing the revolutionary Socialist workers and soldiers (Independent Social Democratic Party and Communist Party), do declare it deposed. The undersigned Revolutionary Committee have temporarily assumed the functions of government."[23]

This decision appeared to emanate from the Communist Party leadership, for another manifesto of the German Communist Party, dated January 8, called upon the workers to form a Red Guard and disarm the counterrevolutionaries. Actually, the January 6 manifesto had been signed by Liebknecht without the Central Committee of the Communist Party having any knowledge of it. Radek noted this in his memoirs, and Pieck confirmed the fact:

The Central Committee of the German Communist Party could not be informed about these meetings, and it was not possible either to notify them immediately of the decisions reached. Thus it was not learned until later consultation with the Central Committee that, while they did assent to the fight against the government's policies, they did not sanction the goal, namely taking over the government. . . . The Central Committee of the German Communist Party held a meeting on January 8, at which Jogiches and Rosa Luxemburg very severely criticized the way the affair had been handled, and it was categorically demanded that Liebknecht and I resign from the Revolutionary Committee. Liebknecht found that a very hard thing to do.*

The next day, January 9, Radek addressed a letter to the Central Committee of the German Communist Party advising against any attempt to seize power:

In this situation an attempt by the proletariat to seize power is unthinkable. If the government should fall into your hands through a coup d'état, within a few days it would be cut off and strangled from the provinces. . . . You have enough vision to see that the fight would be a hopeless one. Your own members, Comrades Levi and Duncker, have told me that you are aware of this. . . . In July 1917, though we then were stronger than you are now, we did our utmost to restrain the masses, and, when that did not succeed, we stepped in ruthlessly and saved them from imminent disaster. [24]

So, unlike the Finnish revolution, whose leaders subjected it to "self-criticism" ex post facto, the January 1919 revolutionary episode in Berlin had the benefit of a witness from Moscow who criticized it on the spot. His gloomy appraisal of it concerned not only Germany. On February 10, 1919, a month after the January fiasco and two days before his arrest in Berlin, Radek reaffirmed his doubts about the imminence of any revolution in Europe: "Today, as I write this letter, one naturally cannot tell how soon revolution will come. As I have often written in the Russian press, and as I told you in my lectures, I am convinced that the development of revolution in Western Europe will be slow because of the strength and organization of the bourgeoisie and because the pro-

---

*W. Pieck, "Erinnerungen an die Novemberrevolution und die Gründung der KPD," in *Vorwärts und nicht vergessen—Erlebnisse aktiver Teilnehmer der Novemberrevolution 1918/1919*, Berlin, 1958, p. 71. In his last address to the Central Committee of the German Communist Party on May 4, 1921, Paul Levi, directing his remarks at Pieck personally, recalled the dramatic atmosphere of that meeting: "You remember how obstinate Karl Liebknecht was, and you remember how it was Leo Jogiches who proposed that right then while the fighting was going on, a biting statement be published in *Rote Fahne*, disowning Karl Liebknecht, announcing simply that 'Karl Liebknecht no longer represents the Spartacus League vis-à-vis those in charge of the revolution.' You know, too, what a dim view Rosa Luxemburg took of Karl's behavior, and how severe her criticism was." *Was ist das Verbrechen? Die Märzaktion oder die Kritik daran?* Berlin, 1921, pp. 33-34.

letariat lacks revolutionary allies, such as the peasants were in
Russia."[25] In September 1919, in a brochure published under a
pseudonym, Radek restated this opinion: "So even though the
*situation in Germany is very revolutionary, and even though the
class contradictions continue to worsen to the point of absolute
irreconcilability, we must expect that the revolutionary crisis will
drag on.*"*

The Radek outlook, forged on the scene, was in marked contrast to the Lenin vision cherished in distant Moscow. This would
be brought home to Radek when, in January 1920, he left Berlin
and returned to Russia. Lenin and Zinoviev would spend the
better part of 1920 waiting for the revolution which they believed
imminent in Europe, particularly in Germany. Not until after a
turning point, in 1921, would Radek be free to write in the official organ of the Comintern what he had been saying back in
1919 and 1920: "Seizing power was as yet impossible. Ninety-nine
percent of the [German] proletarian masses were utterly incapable
of serving as a power base. Most of them followed the Social
Democratic banner; but even the revolutionary minority was confused and vague."[26]

THE BAVARIAN SOVIET REPUBLIC

In addition to the revolutionary episode of January 1919 in the
capital of Germany another occurred three months later in
Munich, the capital of Bavaria. But this time the revolutionaries
did not confine themselves to proclaiming the overthrow of the
majority Socialist government; they actually overthrew it and held
power briefly. In Munich as in Berlin, the Communist movement
was led by individuals who had been involved in revolutionary

*Arnold Struthahn, *Die Entwicklung der deutschen Revolution und die Auf-
gaben der Kommunistischen Partei*, Stuttgart, 1919, p. 17. Emphasis in the
text. While imprisoned Radek maintained contact with the leaders of the
German Communist Party; the impression he obtained of what was going on
reinforced his convictions: "I forbade the leaders of the German party, who
lived illegally and were persecuted by the police, to visit me in the prison. I
maintained contact with them by correspondence, and saw that the Party had
no leadership. . . . Comrade Broński, who succeeded in paying me a visit in
jail, fully shared my opinion that the first wave of the revolution was declining. . . . " Karl Radek, "November—Eine kleine Seite aus meinen Erinnerung-
en," in *Archiv für Sozialgeschichte*, Hannover, 1962, vol. II, pp. 155-56.

activity in Tsarist Russia, the important difference being that the Berlin leaders—Karl Radek, Leo Jogiches and Rosa Luxemburg—had been against the January 1919 enterprise, while those in Munich—Dr. Eugen Leviné and Max Levien—were the authors of the Soviet Republic proclaimed there on April 13, 1919. Since the political situation in that city was highly complex and explosive, and regarded as full of lessons for the Comintern, the behavior of the Communists in Bavaria must be described in broad outline.

In early March 1919, Eugen Leviné, a Russian-born naturalized German educated in Germany and already a prominent militant in the German Communist Party, was sent to Bavaria by the party's new leader, Paul Levi. His mission was to take in hand the party newspaper, *Münchner Rote Fahne,* though it was understood that actually he would assume leadership of the entire party. He was given precise instructions as to the line to be followed on the stormy Bavarian political scene: "It must be understood that any occasion for military action by government troops must be strictly avoided. In all frankness and with every emphasis the workers must be told that they should forgo any kind of armed action, even when a local or momentary success might be possible." [27]

What struck Leviné on his arrival in Munich was the weakness of the Communist party there, and above all its political disorientation. "The party organization was still extremely feeble," noted his wife, to whom Leviné confided: "My friends here are the merest children, unblemished by any experience. A vast confusion reigns." [28] Some party members were in sympathy with the policies of the assassinated Socialist leader, Kurt Eisner, or with the anarchists. The main problem facing the Bavarian Communist Party was what position to take concerning the firm intention of the independent Socialists, anarchists, and even certain majority Socialists to proclaim establishment of a Soviet Republic in Munich. Leviné opposed the idea from the beginning, and when such a republic was proclaimed nevertheless on April 7, the Communist attitude toward it was extremely critical and hostile. They had no confidence whatever in the coalition leadership of the new regime. They denounced it as a creation of petty bureaucrats living in a dream world, realizing that the situation was far from ripe for a Soviet-type government. Leviné did not mince words: "Proclaiming a Soviet Republic at this juncture is a disaster. We don't even have any party here yet. Everything is still being built. The necessary preconditions are lacking: no factory councils, no workers' councils, insufficient influence among the troops for the successful conduct of such a struggle." [29]

At the same time, since the republic had become a reality in Munich at least, the Communists saw in it "unlimited opportunities for action." [30] Leviné explained thus what the communist party was to do under the circumstances: "We shall work feverishly to bring about a real Soviet republic. We shall educate the proletariat, organize it into factory councils and Communist groups. We shall carry the class struggle to the countryside, shall agitate among the soldiers and arm ourselves for the moment when it shall be granted us to fight and triumph for the Soviet Republic." [31]

Disappointed by the Communist refusal to join it, the new Soviet regime trumpeted its revolutionary will nonetheless and set out to play a major role in the international chessboard. One of its leaders, Erich Mühsam, a kind of anarcho-Communist and admirer of Lenin's, explained that the Bavarian revolutionaries, impressed by what was happening in Hungary and anticipating revolutionary putsches in Brunswick and Thuringia, believed that they should take advantage of the situation to push Austria too into the camp of Soviet republics: "That will destroy the influence of the [Otto] Bauers and [Friedrich] Adlers, and a bridge will have been built. If at the same time islands are created in Brunswick and Central Germany, that advance will signal revolution throughout Germany, and the authority of Ebert, Scheidemann, and Noske will crumble. So in the establishment of a Soviet republic in Bavaria I saw an event of great moment for world revolution." [32]

The new minister of foreign affairs of the Bavarian republic, Dr. Franz Lipp, a Socialist journalist, sent an enthusiastic telegram in this same vein to Moscow, reporting that "the proletariat of Upper Bavaria [was] happily united," and that the Socialists, independents, and Communists stood "welded together solid as a rock, in union with the peasantry." [33] On hearing the news from Bavaria, but not knowing quite what to make of it, Lenin sent two telegrams to Béla Kun. The first, dated 7 April, 1:45 P.M., was very short: "Lenin requests you greet Bavarian Soviet Republic, requests detailed information as soon as possible, especially regarding socialization of Bavarian land." [34] The second telegram followed thirteen hours later (on April 8 at 2:15 A.M.), again mainly requesting information: "We request you to give us details on the revolution that took place in Bavaria. We do not know anything except a short radiogram from the Bavarian Soviet government. We request to be informed as to how events are shaping up and whether the new order is completely and entirely the master. . . . How do things stand in Bavaria with the agrarian program of the Soviet government? " [35] Zinoviev, as chairman of the Executive Committee of the Communist International, telegraphed to the Bavarians his "warm greetings" and expressed his conviction that the time was not far off "when all of Germany will be a Soviet republic." Chicherin too sent a wire to Lipp, asking in particular for information on the relationship between the Munich Communists, independent Socialists, and the "Scheidemänner." He confessed that "we have no information at all about what is really going on there." [36]

Despite its grandiose designs, the Bavarian Soviet Republic did not take root. It lasted but six days. "It was a week of raucous and at times ridiculous confusion. Regulations, pronouncements, proclamations, orders and counterorders were drafted, printed, and distributed in hectic tempo. . . . In six days . . . it [the Republic] brought only disorder and appropriately acquired the title of 'Pseudo Soviet Republic' (*Scheinräterepublik*). The title was bestowed by the Communist party; it was appropriate not because the KPD refused to participate in the government, but because there was in reality no government at all." [37] On April 13, Palm Sunday, a putsch was attempted against the regime in Munich. It failed, but was mainly responsible for impelling the Communist party to take control of the government.

In deciding to guide the destinies of this second Bavarian Soviet Republic Leviné again disobeyed Paul Levi's instructions. In fact, at the very moment that the new Bavarian republic was being proclaimed, the Central Committee of the Communist Party, forced to go underground, was in Leipzig. It was there that the appeal of Munich's Communist leaders reached Levi, also their request that he come to the new red capital. Levi refused, dubious from the outset about the seriousness of the enterprise. However, he "sent two members of the central committee to Munich, with explicit instructions to 'liquidate the putsch.' The Communist Party's central committee demanded that the Communists themselves liquidate the Soviet republic and return to their positions as of the end of March and the beginning of April. The leaders of the Bavarian party organization, rejecting Levi's orders, were able to convince one of the delegates of the rightness of their own policies, and the latter remained to work at the battlefield of the Bavarian revolution." [38]

The job of Leviné and of the Bavarian Communist Party was made the more difficult by his agreement to collaborate with the independent Socialists, who held the majority in Munich's Factory and Soldiers' Council and in the new fifteen-member Action Committee, whose membership was soon increased to thirty. Belonging to its four-member Executive Committee, Leviné and Max Levien sat at the pinnacle of the pyramid of this new regime. In reality their situation was untenable, for everything militated against them: the inexperience of their own party, the heterogeneous makeup of the new governing team, the economic and military situation of their isolated republic.

Despite these difficulties the new regime steered from the outset a more precise, more methodically revolutionary, in fact a more "Bolshevik" course. Leviné's conception of the essential task of the new republic was in important respects authentically Leninist: "The Soviet republic is a dictatorship of the proletariat in that the proletariat assumes full power, not only to bring about freedom and practice brotherhood and justice, but to suppress the bourgeoisie, to keep the middle class down ... The middle class must simply disappear, also the bureaucracy, police, and courts." [39] In a speech delivered before a meeting of the Factory Councils after three days in power, Leviné enumerated the steps that the regime had taken: confiscation of the banks, now under the control of commissars; arming of the proletariat (according to him, the main task); expropriation of the lands of wealthy peasants which they themselves were not working, with a promise of further action on behalf of the small peasant and farm laborer; establishment of a number of special commissions for such purposes as dissemination of propaganda, conduct of military affairs, communications, and socialization of the economy; and finally a commission to combat counterrevolution, which had started arresting political suspects and taking hostages. The general strike continued in support of the regime, and the middle-class sections of Munich were searched for surplus food. Leviné advised his listeners to flood the city with a sea of red flags, promising to distribute texts of revolutionary songs. [40]

The new republic's foreign policy was in keeping with its internal dictatorship of the proletariat. The first message from the Executive Council, telegraphed to Moscow, proclaimed: "The Executive Council of the new, truly proletarian Soviet republic greets the Russian and Hungarian working class and their Soviet republics. The Munich working class will harness its forces to the service of that great historic mission which its brave Russian and Hungarian brothers have set out upon.... Long live World Revolution! " [41] In an article published on April 21 entitled "On the Eve of Proletarian Revolution in Vienna," Leviné expressed his hopes: "Communism is on the march—in Vienna, Graz, and German Austria too. Vienna sits between Munich and Budapest. Today we extend our hand to our brothers in Hungary over Vienna's head. A symbol. When will our brothers in Austria become the third member and give their hand to us? Communism is on the march! " [42] The next day, addressing a crowd from the balcony of the Wittelsbach Palace on the occasion of the halting of the general strike, Leviné shouted to them: "The proletarian revolution has come from the East. The East is where happiness is, where the sun has risen. We thank our Russian brothers, who, as the first to rise up and, with their enormous strength and immeasurable willingness to sacrifice, take the mighty task upon their shoulders, were the first to assail the ranks of capitalism and storm the citadel of capital. We have followed them; others will follow us! " [43]

The news of establishment of a second Bavarian Soviet republic received an enthusiastic welcome in several quarters in Soviet Russia. On April 15 the executive committee of the Latvian Workers' Council wired its hearty congratulations to the Bavarian government. In a telegram to Béla Kun (of unknown date), Zinoviev, in the name of the Comintern, once again expressed his "unshakable conviction" that events in Bavaria proved that "the time is not far off when the entire German Reich will be a Soviet republic. It is quite clear to the Communist International that those in the key positions are now engaged in the struggle, and that the immediate fate of proletarian revolution throughout Europe depends on you." [44] The Comintern leaders' awakened interest in Bavaria was also manifested in their dispatch of a secret emissary to Munich. Having learned their lesson from Radek's arrest in Berlin, they sent their agent to the Bavarian capital in strictest secrecy. The role that he played there remains a mystery, except that he arrived before April 13 and was introduced into the small circle of Communist militants under the assumed name of A. Albrecht.*

As for Lenin himself, he allowed two weeks to elapse before sending, on April 27, his "wholehearted greetings" to the Bavarian Soviet Republic. His message, in fact, was a precise catalogue of the radical measures that he deemed urgent in Bavaria. Before getting down to cases, he asked: "What measures have you taken to fight the bourgeois executioners, the Scheidemänner & Co.? " There followed a long list of what amounted to political, economic, and policing suggestions: create Workers' and Servants' Councils in the different sections of Munich; arm the workers and disarm the bourgeoisie; confiscate factories within Munich and the capitalist farms on its outskirts; double or triple the wages of farm workers and unskilled laborers; order a six-hour working day; immediately resettle the workers in comfortable middle-class apartments; seize all banks and take hostages from among the bourgeoisie; provide larger food rations for workers than for the bourgeoisie; levy an emergency tax on the bourgeoisie; and so on. "The most urgent and extensive implementation of these and similar measures . . . should strengthen your position," Lenin argued. [45]

The striking parallel between these measures proposed by Lenin and those already taken by Leviné remained purely symbolic, for on the very day on which Lenin sent his message the Bavarian Communists suffered a decisive political defeat. Their relations with the independent Socialists, ambiguous from the start, came to a breaking point, which ended in a vote of no confidence in the

---

*The real name of this emissary was A. Abramovich, about whose political career more will be said in the next chapter. He did not reveal his identity in Munich, and left the Bavarian capital for Berlin during the night of April 30-May 1.

Executive Committee by the Factory and Soldiers' Councils, which forced Leviné and Levien to resign. The charges against the Communist leaders bore upon a whole series of political and economic problems concerning which they were accused of intransigeance and incompetence. But the charge that probably carried the most weight was that they were foreign agents. In its April 29 issue the regime's official newspaper explained in these terms the main reason for the vote of censure against the Communist chiefs: "We agree with the Russians on the basic idea of a proletarian Soviet republic, but in carrying out that idea—and consequently in all individual practical measures—we must conduct a Bavarian, not a Russian policy." The ouster of the Communists was also presented as a precondition for an end to the civil war and acceptance of the Soviet republic by the peasants and some of the middle class. [46]

Having lost their political power to the independent Socialists, the Bavarian Communists saw no other road but that of offering military resistance to the forces of the Free Corps advancing on Munich in the name of the government of the Bavarian Free State, based at Bamberg and headed by the majority Socialist Johannes Hoffmann. With the independent Socialists busy seeking a reconciliation with Hoffmann, the Bavarian Red Army, commanded by a twenty-six year-old sailor, Rudolf Egelhofer, decided to fight on alone. The battle was brief, its outcome obvious in advance. Ironically, on May 1, the very same day that the Communist resistance collapsed in Munich, Lenin was shouting in his speech in Moscow's Red Square that "the liberated working class is celebrating its anniversary freely and openly not only in Soviet Russia, but also in Soviet Hungary and Soviet Bavaria." [47]

The Communist débâcle in Bavaria elicited markedly differing interpretations from the several principal leaders of the German Communist Party. One of them, Ernst Meyer, setting himself up as Leviné's systematic defender, declared in one article that the Soviet Republic of Bavaria had pursued "a policy which, from the proletarian revolutionary standpoint, can only be called classical." [48] In another article he argued that Leviné's political ideas on the need to dismantle the bourgeois governmental apparatus matched those of Lenin, and that the Bavarian Communists had correctly understood the decisive role that the Communist party must play in the revolution. "Leviné's behavior," wrote Meyer, "constitutes one of the most glorious pages in our party's traditions."[49] A similar opinion was expressed by Paul Frölich, who published a pamphlet on the events in Bavaria under the pseudonym of Paul Werner, though he did advance some strong criticisms too. Like Meyer, Frölich, who came to Munich in the name of the German Communist Party's Central Committee as soon as the Soviet regime had collapsed, absolved the conduct of the Communists in this vein: "That was the signal for the best part of the workers and troops to enter the fray. The party leadership, which had planned initially to exploit the situation only for propaganda purposes, now took charge of the battle. It led to victory. . . . There was no turning back anymore. The most essential precondition was fulfilled: victorious action by the masses. A Soviet republic was now the only thing possible. We placed ourselves unreservedly at the disposal of the working class."[50]

Mixed with this moral support of the Communist action were other thoughts of Frölich's presenting the political behavior of the Bavarian Communists in a different light. He conceded, for instance, that the Communist organizing ability was extremely weak: "Our organizing experience, and any experience we had at the job of governing, barely extended beyond Munich and its outskirts. One reason was that our party at that time, even in Bavaria, was still very loosely structured, was confined to individual cities, and had as yet no inner cohesion. One could see that this weakness in our party was at the same time a weakness of the Soviet regime."[51]

The conclusion that Frölich drew from this observation agreed with the key tenet of the Bolshevik creed: "The most important thing that we learned from our brief governing experience was this: without a firm party organization a government is powerless, cannot implement its program."[52] He conceded also—another lesson preached by Lenin—that the independent Socialists, allied with the Communists at the start of the revolution, were unstable partners, ready to desert at the critical moment. Frölich attributed this to their social background: "In the long run it became clearer and clearer that the USPD represented the petty-bourgeois elements in the working class. It shared their timidity and pettiness. It used every device of small-minded demagogy and sought gradu-

ally to dismantle our positions."[53] Finally, on the agrarian question, a major concern of Lenin's, Frölich stressed the utter failure
of the Bavarian Communists to win over the peasants to their
cause: "The communist revolution cannot expect any help or
understanding from the agricultural workers either. . . . In Bavaria
the farm population is not revolutionary; it is if anything counterrevolutionary."[54]

Unlike Meyer and Frölich, Paul Levi severely criticized the
Communist behavior in Bavaria. Arguing with Frölich, he insisted
that "the masses are still far removed from fully sharing our viewpoint, otherwise our goal would already be achieved. They still
often travel roads different from those we prefer." For this key
reason, Levi himself categorically opposed the April 13 action:
"The Bavarian Soviet Republic of April 13 was just as impossible
as the one of April 6, and the 'victorious action' at the large
industrial concerns of Maffei, Krupp, and so on was no adequate
basis, no 'essential precondition,' for a Bavarian Soviet Republic."
He went on to accuse the Munich Soviet republic of having failed,
on the one hand, to evoke any echo within Germany, while on the
other of having raised false hopes in Russia and Soviet Hungary:

> The Munich comrades, however, failed to take yet another factor into
> account. For us in Germany the painful outcome of the Munich affair,
> apart from the terrible losses of our best fellow fighters, was not a
> major setback. The German revolutionary labor movement suffered lit-
> tle from the events in Munich. Incomprehensibly, however, those events
> apparently generated illusions abroad—we mean particularly in Russia
> and Hungary—concerning the possibilities created by them within Ger-
> many, and their significance for Germany, illusions which could have
> no basis in the actual condition of the over-all German revolutionary
> movement, and which might prove highly dangerous for Hungary, Aus-
> tria, and even for Russia.[55]

All these criticisms of the German Communist leaders were
taken into consideration by the Comintern, for which the events
in Bavaria constituted but one more proof of how essential it was
to make certain basic precepts obligatory for all Communist parties. This was done at the Comintern's second congress, where
discussion of the main problems—the role of the party, the attitude to adopt toward revolutionary allies, the agrarian question—

were closely tied to the experience gained from the two Bavarian Soviet republics. As to the strictly Communist aspect of the events in Munich, Paul Levi, peering through the usual Bolshevik lenses, compared the episode to the days of July 1917 in Petrograd.[56] A July not followed by an October.

THE COMINTERN AND SOVIET HUNGARY

Of all the revolutionary actions that occurred in Europe during 1918-19, the one in Hungary remains the best known in the history of the Communist movement. True, it was not the most important. The events in Germany in 1919 marked a turning point in the history of the German and European proletariat, while those in Hungary were but an episode. Nevertheless, to the Bolsheviks, Soviet Hungary was the nearest and most useful of the political undertakings of the period. First of all, it was the only revolution in Europe staged by a team which had gone through the Bolshevik school and come straight from Soviet Russia.* Also, the Hungarian revolution had one exceptional feature, unique for its time: it was born suddenly and without violence on March 21, 1919, through the uniting of the Hungarian Social Democratic Party with the Communist Party on a revolutionary Marxist platform. Hungary's "Mensheviks" and "Bolsheviks" thus merged to run a dictatorship of the proletariat domestically and align themselves with Soviet Russia externally. Finally, the Hungarian revolution did not collapse before it came to power, as happened in Berlin, or two weeks afterwards, as did the second Bavarian Soviet government. In Hungary in 1919 the Communists held power for 133 days, from March 21 to August 1.

Born 15 days after the founding of the Communist International, Soviet Hungary was in touch with Lenin by radio the next day. On that occasion, as on all others deemed important, it was not Zinoviev, the president of the International, who was addressed,

*The Hungarian group in the Russian Communist (Bolshevik) Party, consisting of some Hungarian prisoners of war led by Béla Kun, was formally established in Russia on March 24, 1918. Seven months later, on November 4, at a conference in Moscow, the group changed its name to Communist Party of Hungary. Twelve days after that, Béla Kun and a picked handful of his followers were back in Budapest. Cf. Rudolf L. Tökés, *Béla Kun and the Hungarian Soviet Republic*, New York, 1967, pp. 68, 79, 49.

but Lenin, the head of the Bolshevik Party and the Russian government. On March 22, Lenin ordered maintenance of continuous radio contact with the Hungarian government. The proclaiming of a Soviet regime in the country filled him and his colleagues with boundless joy, for it seemed to prove their fundamental thesis that a European revolution was only days away. On March 23, from the rostrum of the Eighth Bolshevik Party Congress, Lenin declared flatly: "We are certain that *this will be the last difficult half-year*. Our conviction is greatly strengthened by the news we announced to the congress the other day of the success of the proletarian revolution in Hungary." [57] To the government in Budapest the congress sent a telegram, signed by Lenin and Zinoviev, stating: "The eighth congress of the Russian Communist Party sends fervent greetings to the Hungarian Soviet Republic. Our congress is convinced that the time is not far off when Communism will triumph throughout the world. The working class of Russia is making every effort to help you. The world proletariat, watching your struggle with intense interest, will not permit the imperialists to raise their hand against your new Soviet Republic. Long live the World Communist Republic! "[58]

The many words of encouragement heaped by Moscow on Budapest were not just empty ceremonial phrases; in Bolshevik eyes, the Hungarian mirror reflected the image of the immediate future of all Europe. In an article published in the first issue of the new official Comintern organ, Zinoviev gloated: "When the Hungarian bourgeoisie turned in their resignation, this was no isolated phenomenon. It was the most unmistakable sign of the times. Historically, the entire European bourgeoisie is now resigning." [59] On April 18, Trotsky said much the same in an article entitled "Spring of Decision": "The history of mankind has known single weeks in which great issues were decided. No sooner had the enthusiasm over the newly established Soviet Republic in Hungary started to abate a little when the proletariat of Bavaria seized power and held out the hand of fraternal solidarity to the Russian and Hungarian Soviet Republics. The workers of Austria are rushing by the hundreds and thousands to Budapest to volunteer for Hungary's red army." [60]

Bolshevik enthusiasm was due not only to the fact that a Soviet regime had been established in Hungary but also to a very delicate feature of that regime: the union of Socialists with Communists. Lenin questioned Kun about this several times. The latter did his best to reassure the Bolshevik leader. Writing to Lenin on April 22, he reasoned: "And, quite frankly, I would say that even strictly from the standpoint of principle it would be hard to find any fault with the manner in which we acted. The agreement we achieved on the basis of this platform definitely covers both principle and tactic, which is why it has resulted in genuine unity. The rightist elements have been kicked out of the party; the old trade-union bureaucrats are gradually being sifted out."[61] In Moscow on May 27 Lenin talked with Tibor Szamuely, the Hungarian Soviet Republic's Deputy People's Commissar for War, after which, that same day, he wrote a long message to the Hungarian workers lavishly praising them for what had been accomplished in Hungary: "The news that we are receiving from the Hungarian Soviet leaders fills us with joy and enthusiasm. Hungary has had a Soviet government for only a little over two months, yet in organizing the Hungarian proletariat it already seems to have outdistanced us. . . . You have set the world an even brighter example than Soviet Russia through your ability to unite, at a single stroke, all Socialists on a platform of genuine proletarian dictatorship."[62]

Since Lenin had given his blessing to this merger of the parties on the Hungarian left, the Communist International could only go along. In June 1919 the Comintern's official organ published an article by Jenő Varga, People's Commissar of Finance, a Socialist who had become a leader in the new Socialist-Communist Party, in which he defended the unification: "Today total harmony reigns within the Hungarian proletariat. . . . The leaders of the former Social Democratic Party now work in unison with the Communists to strengthen the dictatorship [of the proletariat]."[63] The Comintern Executive Committee stamped its own approval on the Hungarian experiment, declaring in a letter to the congress of the new party: "The actions of the Hungarian government of soviets and Hungarian Communist Party during the first month of your dictatorship will remain forever a model of proletarian fearlessness and Communist foresight and wisdom."[64]

As in the case of Germany in January 1919, from March to June of that year Moscow was seething with optimism over Hungary. The sentiment was not shared, however, by all European

Communists, including those in Hungary. Within a day or two after a Soviet government was set up in Budapest, Béla Kun confided his uneasiness to his comrades: "It has all gone too smoothly. I simply couldn't sleep. I lay awake the whole night trying to think where we could have gone wrong, because there must be something wrong somewhere. The whole thing was too easy. Sooner or later we'll find the flaw. I am only afraid that it may be too late." [65] But if Kun was still wondering where the flaw was, Paul Levi put his finger squarely on it two days after the Communist takeover in Budapest, when he wrote:

> Despite the great power and magnitude of the events, we must not lose sight of the historical setting in which it all occurred. It must be said that the new revolution in Hungary, which has replaced bourgeois democracy with a soviet-type government, is not the fruit of a victory won in battle by the Hungarian proletariat over the Hungarian bourgeoisie and landed aristocracy. It is not the result of a struggle in which the bourgeoisie was beaten by the proletariat but a simple consequence of the fact that the Hungarian bourgeoisie—and there is no other way to put it—simply laid down and died. . . .

> But is the Hungarian proletariat really mature enough? We see only one thing. That revolution, too, started with the "uniting of all Socialists." There, too, all the scum who betrayed the Hungarian proletariat, as Ebert and Scheidemann did the German, are now falling all over themselves in support of the Soviet republic and proletarian dictatorship. That is the danger hanging over the Hungarian revolution, one which we must publicize and warn against in the interest of our brothers in Hungary, and in the interest of the German movement. [66]

Karl Radek, in prison at the time, was not free to express himself. As soon as he did have an opportunity, several months later, he said much the same thing: "As it turned out, agreeing to the proposed unification of the two parties was a fatal error." [67]

In December 1919, held by Austrian authorities in the fortress of Karlstein, Kun still defended as necessary the uniting of the Communists and Socialists: "Why did we unite with the nonrevolutionary Social Democrats at the start of the revolution? One must remember that our party was small, with relatively few members, and could never have done the job by itself." [68]

The merging of the Communists and Social Democrats was judged differently in Moscow after the collapse of the Hungarian

Soviet regime. Then, ex post facto, it was termed a capital error. From the Bolshevik perspective, only one simple obvious conclusion could be drawn from the events in Hungary; it was because the Communists (Bolsheviks) and Social Democrats (Mensheviks) had merged that the revolution was crushed, this outcome being plainly the work of the Socialist traitors. On August 11, 1919, before any direct knowledge of the situation in Hungary had reached him, Zinoviev stated flatly: "We must understand that the old established Social Democratic parties are our mortal foe. That is what the events in Hungary have taught us."[69] A short time later Lenin, in this same vein, charged with "objective" treason even those Socialists who had gone along with the unification in complete sincerity:

> There can be no doubt that some of the Hungarian Socialists went over to Béla Kun *sincerely*, and were quite *sincere* in proclaiming themselves Communists. But that does not alter the essential fact that a person who "sincerely" proclaims himself a Communist, yet, when the chips are down, shilly-shallies and plays the coward instead of sticking to a ruthlessly hard, unswervingly determined, superbly courageous and heroic policy (the only course consistent with acknowledging the dictatorship of the proletariat)—such a person, with his weakness of character, vacillation, and chicken-heartedness, is as much of a betrayer as a dyed-in-the-wool traitor.[70]

This definition thereupon became law, for in the introduction to the "Conditions for the Admission of Parties to the Communist International," authored by Lenin, and submitted to and adopted by the Comintern's Second Congress, it was written: "No Communist shall forget the lessons learned from what happened to the Hungarian Soviet Republic. The Communists' merger with the reformists cost the Hungarian proletariat dearly." This interpretation became mandatory and was subsequently adopted even by the former Hungarian commissars, who were not of that opinion during their rule in Hungary or in the time immediately after. The old explanations were banished forever, and in the report of the Hungarian Communist Party, presented on the eve of the Second Comintern Congress, Mátyás Rákosi, Deputy People's Commissar for Commerce in the then defunct regime, joined the chorus: "We were not long in seeing that, despite the merger, the Social Demo-

crats took advantage of every opportunity to undermine the dictatorship." [71]

The former Social Democrats, even those who had joined the
Communist Party, were no longer permitted to doubt, much less
refute, this compulsory explanation. Even to hint that the Socialists may have been necessary for the Communists to come to
power was heresy. But Béla Kun stuck to that opinion even after
the fall of the Hungarian republic, adding that he himself had
definitely needed their assistance, not only to seize power, but
above all to get out of jail.* Similarly, the parallel thesis holding
that it was Social Democratic treachery that had cleared the way
for the Horthy regime also became official dogma, thus ceasing to
be a safe subject for debate; this eliminated the painful need to
take into account or even admit the excesses of the Béla Kun
government and its possible contribution to the creation and
strengthening of the Horthy reaction.† In a word, from the Soviet
experience in Hungary the Comintern leaders, which is to say the
Bolshevik Party chiefs, culled whatever suited their arguments and
helped to shore up their own theses.

A further illustration of this was the Hungarian Soviet regime's
agrarian policy. That government did not follow the example of
the Bolsheviks, who had distributed land to the peasants, but proceeded directly to nationalize it, a fact on which Béla Kun congratulated himself at the party congress on June 12, 1919: "A
happy confluence of circumstances has enabled us to see to it that
socialized production has not remained a figment of utopianism in
our country, for most of our agricultural land is already being
farmed collectively." [72] After the fall of the Communist regime,

---

*On February 21, Béla Kun and 68 other prominent Communists were arrest-
ed on charges of conspiring against public order and inciting to riot. Exactly a
month later the imprisoned Communists walked out of their cells and formed
a coalition government with the majority Socialists, and the Hungarian Soviet
Republic was born. Cf. R. L. Tökés, *Béla Kun and the Hungarian Soviet
Republic*, pp. 122-23.

†József Haubrich, a former Socialist and one of the signatories of the agreement establishing the United Socialist-Communist Party, who had served as
first People's Commissar for Economic Affairs, then for the Army, said four
years later in a conversation with an Austrian Communist whom he had met
in Moscow: "If I had not gone along with the stupidities of Béla Kun and
supported them, there would be no Horthy in Hungary today." From the
memoirs of Lucien Laurat (manuscript in the possession of the authors).

Kun upheld this view as long as he remained in Austria. In an interview that he granted on December 21, 1919, to a radical American journalist, he asserted: "The peasants as a whole approved the Communist program for land tenure and utilization. One should note in this connection that in our country, unlike Russia, the land was not divided up."[73] Since this conflicted with Bolshevik doctrine, Kun ultimately had to change his tune and claim just the opposite. In an article written ten years later on the events of 1919, he revised his former views: "From those two circumstances flowed the two fundamental errors made in the Hungarian revolution: merging with the Social Democratic Party, and the doctrinaire un-Bolshevik approach to the problem of the peasants, an approach which deprived the proletarian revolution and its most progressive class, the proletariat, of an essential revolutionary reserve force, the peasantry. Those two mistakes were fatal."[74]

It was certainly true that the Hungarian peasants did not support the Communist regime, a fact which the Bolsheviks found useful in defending their own views on the agrarian question. But it was equally true that the great majority of the revolution's "most progressive class, the proletariat," did not support the regime either. Jenő Varga minced no words on the subject when, several months after its collapse, he wrote: "Because they lacked any revolutionary training, and since there was no organized Communist party, the Hungarian workers weren't the least bit interested in making sacrifices for their [Communist] government, that is, for the future of Socialism. They demanded immediate improvement of their standard of living. Because this was impossible, they deserted the ideal of a dictatorship of the proletariat."[75]

It was true also that "revolution" was far too strong a word to describe the Communist takeover in Hungary in March 1919. The Communists did not fight their way to power; it was handed to them. This crucial fact was pointed out by Paul Levi at the time and acknowledged by two of the leaders of the Hungarian Communist regime after its demise. In January 1920, while interned at Karlstein near Vienna, Kun and Varga both did some writing on Hungary's recent Soviet episode. Kun wrote a pamphlet, Varga a book, in which they were explicit on this point. According to Kun, "proclaiming a dictatorship of the proletariat on March 21 was not the result of an initiative by a revolutionary Communist party. It was simply the inevitable outgrowth of the existing situation which made the whole thing possible, a situation characterized by the cowardice and temporary disorientation of the forces in the labor movement that were against the revolution." [76] Varga put it: "In Hungary, strictly speaking, there was no proletarian revolution. Really by quite legal means, the power just passed overnight into proletarian hands." [77]

While it was true, as Kun said, that "the evolving international situation did more than any revolutionary activity by the proletarian masses in Hungary" [78] to propel the Communists into power, their own appraisal of the international situation, formed while they were in jail in Budapest, was every bit as unrealistic as that of Lenin and Zinoviev, the only difference being that their illusions brought about their downfall. Several months after the collapse of Soviet Hungary one of its leaders, signing himself M. Gabor, wrote an article in the official Comintern journal entitled "A Report on the Fall of Soviet Power in Hungary," in which he made no bones about admitting that "the Communists' chief motives for taking power were the following: (1) the hope for an actual military union of the Russian and Hungarian Red Armies in joint defense of the social revolution and workers' and peasants' power; (2) the hope for active support from the international proletariat against an attack by international capitalism on Soviet Hungary. These hopes were not realized." [79] Russia's Red Army was not moved to Hungary's borders, and the working class of the Entente countries, called upon to stage a general strike on July 21 as an expression of solidarity with Soviet Hungary and a protest against any armed intervention there, failed to respond.

So these two key ingredients of the Soviet episode in Hungary were quickly forgotten by the Comintern, which retained from it only those "lessons" deemed useful for its own propaganda and convenient formulations. By the next year, just before the Comintern's Second Congress, there was hardly anyone left but Paul Levi, the head of the German Communist Party and a future chairman of that congress, who dared to discuss openly the Hungarian revolution and what had really been learned from it—particularly the two key questions as to whether its defeat was predictable from the situation as it existed on March 22, and whether it was the duty of Communists to acquiesce in a policy obviously marked for disaster. Levi for his part answered yes to the first and no to the second, concluding: "I must confess that I no longer remember what or whether I used to think about defeats. Since the fighting in Berlin in January and March of 1919, and since the collapse of the ventures in Munich and Hungary, my faith in the wonder-working qualities of defeat has been shaken."[80]

At the Comintern's Second Congress, however, the agenda was jammed with items to be discussed, including even the use of Esperanto, but an analysis of the revolutionary failures of 1919 was not scheduled. The silence was a clear announcement that Lenin wished everyone to forget all about them, fateful though they proved to be for Communism in Central Europe.

CAPRICE VIENNOIS: THE BETTELHEIM "PUTSCH"

Of all the revolutionary attempts undertaken by the Communists in 1919, there was only one for which the Comintern disclaimed all responsibility, rapidly consigning it to oblivion: the June "putsch" in Vienna, led by Dr. Ernő Bettelheim. It was a fiasco so complete that the Comintern thought best to disown it totally and condemn it before trying to erase it from people's minds.

Fiasco or not, it was part and parcel of the revolutionary psychosis so much in vogue in the spring of 1919. When Béla Kun and his followers came to power in Budapest, they were sure that their victory was a precursor, if not to world or European revolution, at least to revolution in the countries immediately neighboring them. Since the Communist takeover had proved so easy in Hungary, there was no reason not to attempt the same exploit in the nations bordering Hungary—all in the name of world revolution. On this subject Béla Szántó, the People's Commissar for National Defense, wrote: "The Hungarian proletariat, having been given a chance to seize power, shouldered, in so doing, the revolutionary duty to promote and speed up world revolution, to strengthen, encourage, and urge onward the proletariat of other countries in their revolutions. That was our revolutionary duty."[81]

It was in this spirit that the Béla Kun regime sought to advance the revolutionary cause in the adjacent countries, specifically Yugoslavia, Czechoslovakia, and above all, Austria. Yugoslav Communist Party secretary Filip Filipović went to Budapest to talk with Béla Kun before the latter's rise to power. After establishment of the Communist regime a member of the Hungarian Communist Party central committee, Iván Matuzovits, who was of Yugoslav origin, organized a Yugoslav Red Guard in Budapest. In the Yugoslav province of Baranya an attempt was made to proclaim a "Soviet Republic of Baranya." On July 21 there was a Communist putsch in the town of Varaždin in Northern Croatia. In Zagreb, the capital of Croatia, the authorities uncovered "the Diamantstein affair" (named after the agent who carried the funds from Budapest to Zagreb). Filip Filipović and several other members of the Yugoslav Communist Party central committee were arrested. Though the Hungarian Red Army was unable to cross the Yugoslav border, it did succeed in advancing into Slovakia, which on June 16, 1919, resulted in the creation of a "Soviet Republic of Slovakia," under the leadership of Antonin Janoušek, former head of the Czechoslovak section of the Hungarian Socialist [Communist] Party and a close collaborator of Béla Kun's. But by July 4, after the Hungarian troops withdrew, the "Soviet republic" was finished. Its revolutionary government fled to Miškolc, a town in northeast Hungary.

The country most "worked on" by the Béla Kun regime was Austria, selected as the ground most suitable for expansion of the Hungarian revolution. Béla Kun himself freely admitted this on June 19 in his report on the Hungarian Soviet Republic's foreign policy: "Revolution in Germany and Austria is objectively inevitable for economic reasons alone, not even counting the revolutionary activity of the proletariat, or the fact that powerful new forces—the establishment of Soviet republics in Russia and Hungary—are influencing the course of their social revolution." [82] At the very moment at which he was giving this speech, an attempt was made to promote that "objectively inevitable" revolution through the agency of Dr. Bettelheim, aided by the "powerful new force" of the Hungarian Soviet Republic.

The episode can be divided into two stages. In the first, the actors were largely in agreement. In the second, after the fiasco, disagreement opened an abyss between Dr. Bettelheim and Moscow. In the first, the events ran as follows. On May 1, 1919, an Austrian Communist leader, Karl Toman, was in Budapest telling people that revolution was imminent in his country and demanding assistance from the Hungarian Communist regime, which was cheerfully promised. In mid-May a second delegation came to Budapest on the same mission, whereupon it was decided to send Dr. Ernő Bettelheim, a Budapest lawyer and a member of the central committee of the Hungarian Communist Party in February-March 1919, to Vienna to lay the groundwork for, and then execute, a takeover by the Communists. His authority was unlimited—as were, for all intents and purposes, the funds placed at his disposal. Bettelheim related afterwards: "The source of my authority is indicated by its nature and scope. It was completely unlimited, and specifically provided that I was to reorganize the Austrian party, even at the cost of smashing it, if I found that the existing organizational forms were impeding the work or rendering it impossible. It was the express wish of my principals that a Soviet republic be proclaimed in Austria. And I so informed the Austrian party." [83] As for the money at his disposal, he said nothing about it publicly in defending himself after the fiasco, but Karl Radek, who was first to criticize the action, reported openly: "Dr. Bettelheim let loose on Vienna a legion of agitators who spread thousand-Krone bills around like grease, to lubricate the putsch wheels." [84] One of the Austrian Communist militants of the time, Otto Machl (Lucien Laurat), who participated in the Bettelheim venture, tells in his memoirs where the money came from: "Bank notes were flowing like water. Béla Kun had sent in tons of them, specially counterfeited for the occasion. After the dismemberment of Austria-Hungary, the new little countries that succeeded it had hastily stamped their own names on the old bills as a first step in creating national currencies of their own. Austria had not yet done this, and since the bank notes of the Monarchy were printed in both Vienna and Budapest, Béla Kun had printed up in Budapest enough Austro-Hungarian money to finance the Vienna putsch."*

*L. Laurat, "Le Parti communiste autrichien," in *Contributions à l'histoire du Comintern*, Geneva, 1965, p. 78. Otto Bauer, leader of the Austrian Socialist Party's left wing, corroborates this statement: "The Hungarian embassy [in Vienna] became a center for agitation. A large amount of money flowed in from Hungary to the Austrian Communist Party." *Die österreichische Revolution*, Vienna, 1923, p. 138.

Arriving in Vienna around the middle of May, Bettelheim judged the situation to be as "ripe" for a Communist takeover as that of Budapest had been prior to March 21: "I got to Vienna in May 1919. The situation was the same as that of Hungary at the time the dictatorship of the proletariat was proclaimed." [85] So he pronounced the situation objectively ready for revolution. The disintegration of the social and political forces in Austria had advanced to the point where even Radek, in criticizing the putsch, would later say: "Seizing power through a putsch would have been possible in view of the weakness of the Austrian government." As for the "subjective" situation, that is, the strength of the Communist Party, Bettelheim found it very different at the base than at the summit. At the base it had gained in numbers and morale as a result of the events in Hungary and Bavaria, which both bordered on Austria. "From March to May 1919 the party membership jumped from ten to fifty thousand, the highest figure ever, and never again attained in the interwar period." [86] Bettelheim judged the party leadership, on the other hand, to be woefully unequal to the task. So, armed with his unlimited authority, a week later on the night of May 26, at a meeting of the expanded central committee, which now consisted of about fifty people, elected in February 1919, he replaced the whole crew of them with a four-man directorate. Two of the old central committee members not included in it were Elfriede Eisler-Friedländer (later known as Ruth Fischer) and Joseph Strasser. Two members of the new directorate, Toman and Melcher, had been prisoners of war in Soviet Russia. A third, Franz Koritschoner, had been one of the founders of the Austrian Communist Party. The fourth, Johannes Wertheim was leader of the International Federation of Revolutionary Socialists.

From then on, preparations went forward for a Communist takeover in Vienna, and the last strategy meeting before the scheduled uprising was held on June 12. Except for Melcher, who ostentatiously left the room, the others present approved, and by dawn it was unanimously decided: "The counterrevolutionary government must be booted out by armed force, and a Communist Party dictatorship proclaimed in the name of the proletariat. For this purpose, an armed demonstration by the proletariat and military must be arranged for June 15." Bettelheim added: "Budapest was informed of the whole plan." [87]

But the plan, alas, was a dead flop. On June 13 the Socialist government announced that the scheduled reduction in the size of the militia, demanded by the Allied Armistice Commission and being used by the putschists as a pretext for their announced demonstration on June 15, was to be postponed. At the same time the Vienna Workers' Council, after hearing a report by Friedrich Adler, decided by an overwhelming majority (235 to 27) to disapprove the armed demonstrations set for that date. In spite of this warning, preparations for an uprising to establish a Communist dictatorship continued. So on the next day, June 14, the Council issued another proclamation: "The workers of Vienna overwhelmingly reject any irresponsible insurrection, and will therefore refrain from participating in the present Communist action." [88] The Communists had some internal problems, too. Ousted party leaders, like Elfriede Friedländer, and those dissatisfied with the party policies, like Melcher, worked actively against the project. And the police were not asleep either. On June 14 they arrested some one hundred Communist militants who had assembled for a last-minute meeting. The takeover had to be called off. But since it was now too late to notify everybody, nearly five thousand persons turned out in Vienna to demonstrate on behalf of the hundred or so jailed the night before. In the resulting brawls some two dozen were wounded, twenty killed.

It was only after the plan failed that the disagreements arose concerning what had happened and why, and about the nature of Bettelheim's authority and instructions. That his authority was great is obvious from the fact that he became "boss" of the Austrian Communist Party overnight, and was able to clean out its leadership and push the whole organization into preparing for an insurrection. But debate has raged about the source of his authority. Speaking for the Comintern, first Radek and then Zinoviev declared that Bettelheim had been picked for the job by Soviet Hungary, not by the Communist International. On his side, Radek wrote: "Dr. Bettelheim came to Vienna in mid-May as a Hungarian emissary. He also represented himself as an authorized agent of the Communist International, which supposedly had given him the mission of setting up an Austrian Soviet republic as soon as possible. . . . The truth is, however, that Dr. Bettelheim's 'mandate from Moscow' was either the figment of a young comrade's imagination, one who knew nothing about Communism, or a piece of trickery by a political adventurer." [89] In his report of the Executive Committee presented to the second world congress, Zinoviev said much the same: "A complicated situation was produced within the ranks of our party in Austria when our Hungarian comrades unfortunately sent there a certain Bettelheim as their representative. Incidentally, that individual had no authority or instructions from, or to act for, the Communist International. All reports to the effect that he was our man in Vienna are utterly false." [90]

A year later, writing in the Viennese journal *Kommunismus*, Bettelheim got in his licks. He denied playing the role attributed to him by Radek and Zinoviev, namely, that of a purely Hungarian representative: "I was not the emissary of the Hungarian Revolutionary Ruling Council, for no government can assign anyone a mission like that. Nor was I sent by the Hungarian party, because, since the proclaiming of the Hungarian Soviet Republic and dissolution of the Hungarian Communist Party, I belonged to no party or any other group. For reasons of principle, I did not join the new 'Socialist party,' so the latter would hardly have given me any assignments or made me its representative. The Austrian party knew all about this." [91] Of his authority and instructions from the Communist International, Bettelheim wrote: "Then we have the statement that I did not get my instructions from the Communist International directly. I never said I did, merely that they were given to me by the Communist International's representative. I told the Austrian party so at the time. . . . When Comrade Zinoviev declares that I was not a representative of the International, he is not disowning me but either the International itself or its representative who gave me the instructions." [92]

Though he refused to divulge the name of that Comintern representative in Budapest in May 1919, what he did reveal about the source and nature of his instructions was in curious contrast to the Comintern's obvious eagerness to hush up the affair as quickly as possible. The fact that Bettelheim had enjoyed the support of Franz Koritschoner, the only Austrian Communist whom Lenin had known since before his victory in Russia, suggests that he was probably telling the truth and that his authority and instructions had indeed been relayed to him by a highly placed individual, for "Comrade Koritschoner was a firmly convinced proponent of the insurrectionary tactic advocated by Bettelheim, whom he did introduce everywhere as the representative of the Third International."[93] The credibility of Bettelheim's version is further strengthened when one compares the Vienna fiasco with other later attempted putsches during the reign of Zinoviev, such as the one in Central Germany in March 1921, and the strong-arm play in Tallinn, Estonia, in 1924. The procedure in these latter cases was similar to that followed in Vienna, as was the manner in which the planners ran for cover after the plan failed. The iron rule was that, whenever a scheme flopped, Moscow was never remotely to be linked to it. Blaming Zinoviev or his emissaries was inconceivable (and, of course, forbidden). The announced responsibility for the miscarriage was usually fastened on those haplessly there on the scene, whether they had actually participated (as Bettelheim had in Vienna) or had abstained and even condemned the action (as Paul Levi had in Germany). The guilty party was never the true ultimate source of the initiating command (Moscow) or even the implementing agent (Moscow's emissary); guilty, however, was anyone who violated "party discipline" by revealing in public who was really at the bottom of the affair. That was the Bettelheim sin.

His lengthy brief, published in August and September of 1921, merely drew angry retaliation from Moscow against both himself and *Kommunismus*, the journal that ran his articles. It was shut down by order of the Comintern, and on March 17, 1922, the Comintern's Executive Committee heard a report from the committee on the Hungarian question, delivered by Radek, Bettelheim's original accuser.[94] One of the decisions taken was to expel Bettelheim, which was opposed by Jenő Landler, head of the anti-Béla Kun wing of the Hungarian Communist Party in exile. But Bettelheim was beyond salvation.

PERSPECTIVES FROM MOSCOW AND BERLIN

In September 1914 Lenin had proclaimed the Second International dead and argued the need to establish a Third International. Few people paid much attention to him at the time. But in March 1919 his Third International was born and fast became a political

force. Since 1914-15 he had been calling for a break not only
with the Socialists of the right but with those of the center also, a
break which at that period almost nobody, beginning with the
German Spartacists, was willing to accept. But from 1919-20 on,
this long-standing demand started to become a reality within the
European labor movement. In November 1917 Lenin had proclaimed that the Bolshevik takeover in Russia was only part one of
an inevitable revolution throughout Europe. So when initially
there were some so-called bourgeois and national uprisings in Central and Eastern Europe, followed in 1918-19 by the first attempted Communist revolutions, he fervently believed that events once
again would unfold according to his predictions. When Soviet-type
revolutions broke out in countries adjacent to or near Soviet
Russia, as in Finland and Hungary, Lenin's reaction was twofold:
on the one hand, faithful to his internationalist spirit, he wanted
to help them politically and militarily; on the other hand, he saw
in these events a genuine beginning of a wider European revolution, a prediction that he made often enough at that time. There
existed, however, a distinction in what Lenin could do in these
two different situations: survival of actual Soviet revolutions required his direct and immediate help; revolutionary outbreaks in
more distant Western countries could only be hoped for and promoted indirectly by propaganda and financial support. Thus, when
the objective circumstances prevented Lenin from rescuing his geographically closest followers, he quickly lost his illusions about the
fate of revolutions in Finland and Hungary; it took him longer,
however, to lose his illusions about the revolutionary chances in
more distant countries, with whose local conditions he was not
well acquainted.

When the Bolshevik Party's Seventh Congress convened in
March 1918, and Lenin had to fight off the adversaries of his
Treaty of Brest-Litovsk, the Communist left, which opposed his
position, was already citing what they termed Bolshevik betrayal of
the Finnish revolution as proof that Lenin had ceased to aid the
revolution in other countries. Lenin answered this argument on
March 8 in his speech ending the discussion of the report on war
and peace: "The allegation that we betrayed Finland is sheer childishness. The fact that we retreated before the advancing Germans
in the nick of time helped the Finns!... We did not betray the

Finns or the Ukrainians."[95] Several days later, on March 14, at the
special congress of Russian Soviets, he shouted: "They claim we've
betrayed Finland and the Ukraine. What shamelessness! But
events have cut us off from Finland, with whom we had a tacit
understanding since before the revolution, and with whom we
have now concluded a formal accord."[96]

In the following year, 1919, Lenin took the same attitude
toward Soviet Hungary, but in two steps. The first was his impul-
sive readiness to give immediate military assistance, the second was
his realization that such assistance was beyond his means. On April
21 in a telegram to Vatsetis, commander of the Soviet troops, he
had urged as a most pressing task "the establishment of the most
reliable possible railroad link with Soviet Hungary."[97] At the end
of July, Béla Kun sent an urgent plea for Russian help against
foreign military intervention in Hungary, accusing Rakovsky and
Chicherin of bad faith in that regard; in reply, Lenin assured him
that he was mistaken about them, but promised no aid—"We are
aware of Hungary's difficult and dangerous situation, and we are
doing our best. But immediate aid is sometimes physically impossible."[98] It took Lenin several months to realize that revolutionary Russia was in no position to assist Hungary militarily. It
had taken him less time to grasp that the same was true of Finland. While a few months was enough for him to comprehend the
limits of Soviet Russia's military capabilities, it was not enough
for him to digest the corollary, namely that the chances of revolution in Europe were just as poor as Russia's chances of helping to
bring it about.

It was at this key level that Communist perspectives differed so
grossly in Moscow and Berlin. Lenin, Trotsky, and Zinoviev believed revolution in Europe a certainty; the two leading Communists in Berlin, Karl Radek and Paul Levi, were convinced of the
opposite. To the Moscow Communists the revolutionary wave
appeared to be rising; Radek and Levi, who were on the scene,
could see that it was ebbing. When in the summer of 1919
Europe's last Communist republic, in Hungary, was crushed,
Lenin's faith in a revolution in the West continued unabated. In
November, at the Second All-Russian Congress of the Communist
Organizations of Eastern Peoples, he said:

You are aware that the class struggle in Germany has now intensified, that it is getting closer and closer to civil war, to a battle by the German proletariat against Germany's imperialists, who, despite their republican camouflage, have remained imperialists to the core. Everyone knows that the social revolution is moving forward day by day, hour by hour, in Western Europe, and even in America and England. . . . It goes without saying that only the proletariat of all the world's advanced countries can win final victory. We Russians are beginning the work which will strengthen the English, French or German proletariat.[99]

The very month in which Lenin spoke thus in Moscow, Karl Radek, in jail in Berlin, had a pamphlet published in which he expressed an opposing view of the chances of any international revolution: "In Russia the struggle for political power lasted eight months. In Germany it has been going on for over a year, and, unless the signs deceive us, it will take a while longer. . . . In any case, opposing the government with armed force would now be fruitless."[100] A few days later, in a message to the second congress of the German Communist Party, which had started on October 20, Radek admitted: "World revolution is a very slow process, in the course of which one has to expect more than one setback."[101] At that same congress the party chief, Paul Levi, in his report on the general political picture, said: "The proletariat's over-all situation is clear. It has suffered defeat after defeat, and step by step counterrevolution is rising."[102]

Since the Berlin perspective differed so drastically from Moscow's on the chances of international revolution, it was natural that it should also differ on the matter of relations between Soviet Russia and the capitalist world. To his party's Eighth Congress on March 18, 1919, Lenin said: "We live not only in one country but in a system of countries, and for the Soviet Republic to exist for long side by side with imperialist nations is impossible. One of the two systems will ultimately triumph over the other. But before that happens, there is bound to be a series of terrible conflicts between them."[103] Yet that same year, in Berlin, Radek wrote: "These are lessons that a thinking Communist can learn about foreign policy from the two years that the Soviet Republic has existed. They prove that a country governed by the proletariat does not have to depend on the immediate victory of world revolution or go down in ruins. They show that it is possible to live in peace with the capitalist nations, which of course must first be convinced, through bitter battles, that doing away with a country ruled by the proletariat is not so easy." [104]

Lenin was to suffer again in 1920 his disappointments of 1919. Soviet efforts to help revolution along in other countries, this time in Poland and Germany, failed. The real or imagined attempts at revolution—in Italy, Poland, Germany, and Czechoslovakia—came to nothing. Only then, by the end of 1920 and in early 1921, did he reluctantly begin to read the handwriting on the wall and start rethinking the future.

—4—

The Initial Apparatus of the Comintern

The Bolsheviks' claim that the Third International was born on the day on which their party took power in Russia was no mere phrase but the actual truth. Although it had no name, official leadership, constituting congress, statutes, or formal members, this de facto International was nevertheless zealously active in the international labor movement. Its work was divided into two complementary functions: preparing for the founding of the new International, and substituting for it until its official birth.

To accomplish this double task, Lenin had at his disposal but a single instrument (created the day after November 7, 1917) partially capable of operating abroad: the Commissariat of Foreign Affairs, known by its Russian abbreviation Narkomindel, since the Federation of Foreign Communist Groups under the Bolshevik Central Committee necessarily had to confine its activities to Russia alone. In the months that followed the November coup, months marked by uncertainty about the Bolshevik hold on power and by operational improvisation and lack of personnel, Lenin had little choice but to use the Narkomindel as his principal weapon in the international labor movement. Bourgeois governments had always used diplomacy as a cover for espionage; why should the world's first revolutionary government be deprived of its use as a cover for revolution? And since Lenin and his comrades firmly believed at the time that revolution was imminent in Europe, at least in some of the important countries, the revolutionary Russian government would not have to resort to hypocrisy, as bourgeois governments did about their espionage, nor conceal its revolutionary activity, there being no need to keep up appearances with regimes about to be swept away by revolution: "The October Revolution was hardly a month old when the People's Commissariat for Foreign Affairs addressed a circular note to the allied and neutral missions in Petrograd. The note, dated December 3, 1917, defined the basis upon which the new Soviet state envisaged its relations with the international revolutionary movement. It read in part: 'The Soviet power considers diplomatic relations necessary not only with governments, but also with revolutionary- socialist parties seeking the overthrow of existing governments.'" [1]

In conformity with that note, the new rulers sent as envoys to the different European countries the very Bolsheviks who had been championing the cause of revolution in those same countries. In Sweden, Vatslav Vorovsky, a member of the Bolshevik Party's Foreign Bureau in Stockholm after the February 1917 revolution, suddenly, after the October revolution, became the Soviet Government's diplomatic representative. Maxim Litvinov, the Bolshevik representative in England during the war, was appointed the Lenin government's emissary to that country. Ian Berzin, who had participated in the international Socialist Zimmerwald conference, returned in 1918 as chief of the Soviet Government's diplomatic mission to Switzerland. Finally, after heading the first Soviet delegation to the Brest-Litovsk negotiations, with the prime objective not of concluding a lasting peace but of engaging in "revolutionary agitation," Adolf Ioffe reappeared as the Soviet Government's diplomatic representative to the same German government that he was planning to topple. If other countries of Europe were not similarly favored, it was only because their government would not allow representatives of the Lenin government to set foot on their soil.

Once installed as diplomatic agents, these Bolsheviks began, or rather resumed, their political labors, which consisted primarily of giving every possible aid to the first partisans of Communism in those countries. In Sweden, Vorovsky maintained direct close collaboration with Karl Höglund and Frederick Ström, Swedish Communist spokesmen who served as liaison men between Moscow and various Communist groups in the West. In Great Britain, Litvinov, named the Soviet Government's diplomatic representative on January 3, 1918, wasted little of his time at the Court of Saint James; he preferred to spend it giving not so diplomatic instructions to Communism's first British adherents, as one of them, Thomas Bell, has written: "One Thursday in February 1918, I got a letter from Arthur MacManus urging me to join him in London for an important meeting with Litvinov, then acting as Soviet representative, to be arranged for the weekend. . . . Our conversation with Litvinov turned on the general situation and the Bolsheviks' achievements, the position of our movement in Great Britain, and the attitude of our Party to the Russian revolution."[2] Berzin was also busy in Bern with the affairs of the future International, as attested by several letters of Lenin's dating from June to October 1918, in which four names closely linked to the beginnings of the Comintern frequently recur: Guilbeaux, Gorter, Platten, and Herzog. Berzin himself would confirm this in the opening lines of his report to the All-Russian Central Executive Committee on his return to Soviet Russia: "We were admitted [to Switzerland] only on condition that we would conduct no revolutionary propaganda there. We had to accept that condition, get there and start to work. An abnormal situation was created: We, representatives of the Russia of workers and peasants, had to establish relations not with the Swiss working class but with the bourgeois government. Even so, we went on with our job of revolutionary propaganda."[3]

In Berlin, Ioffe was similarly engaged. He both conducted revolutionary propaganda and gave political and financial aid to revolutionary elements. He made no secret of this on his return to Soviet Russia, declaring proudly in the official organ of the Soviet government: "I too helped, as far as it lay in my power, in the victory of the German revolution."[4] This assertion was supported by Wilhelm Dittmann, one of the three Independent-Socialist ministers in the German government at the end of 1918 and one of his party's four delegates to the Comintern's Second Congress, who would state that "Ioffe did act in the interests of German and world revolution."[5] Moreover, these Soviet ambassadors to Europe were in frequent touch with Lenin, who in his letters demanded that they perform duties more akin to revolutionary *agitprop* (agitation and propaganda) than to diplomacy.[6] Another feature of these early diplomatic missions was that the personnel were recruited without regard to nationality. All that was asked was that they serve and advance the cause of Communism. Thus in Switzerland in 1918 the Soviets' so-called diplomatic mission included Berzin, of Baltic descent, S. Bratman, a Pole, Y.S. Reich, a Polish Jew, N. M. Liubarsky, a Russian, and A. Balabanova (under the cover of the Red Cross mission), of Russian birth but long an Italian citizen.

Diplomatic missions were not the only cover that Lenin used for Communist activities within the international Socialist movement; other means were needed, the more so because in November 1918 Ioffe and Berzin with their respective entourages were expelled from Berlin and Bern, and Vorovsky too was back in Soviet Russia by the beginning of 1919. Another form of camouflage brought into play during 1918 and early 1919 was the Red Cross, whose Russian-led missions had the ostensible job of repatriating prisoners of war and Russian citizens. The names of the individuals comprising those missions tell the whole story. In Vienna, Dr. J. Bermann, who had been president of the commission for the repatriation of Russian war prisoners since January 1918, was at least as interested in the Austrian Communists as in the Russian prisoners. Detected by the police and accused of having provided the sum of 200,000 crowns for the launching of the Communist paper *Weckruf*, he was expelled from Austria in January 1919. In Switzerland there was Angelica Balabanova, ensconced in Zurich as a representative of the Soviet Red Cross. In France were the two leading Bolshevik specialists (aside from Trotsky) in the labor-movement affairs of that country, Inessa Armand and Dmitri Manuilsky; a Soviet diplomatic note dated January 12, 1919, announced the arrival in France of these two Red Cross "delegates," whose real purpose was later explained in Inessa Armand's official biography: "In February 1919 an important new mission, with Dmitri Zakharovich Manuilsky and Inessa Armand, went to France as part of the Red Cross delegation. Their job was to help repatriate soldiers of the Russian expeditionary force stranded in France after the end of World War One, and to tell them the truth about Soviet Russia. It was also essential to get a better idea of the French labor and revolutionary movement."[7] This little team, however, did not succeed in its mission. From the moment it disembarked at Boulogne-sur-Mer, it was kept under such close surveillance by the French authorities that it was unable to make contact with the elements in France favoring the founding of a new International.

In Germany the Soviet government entrusted the job of looking after Russian prisoners of war to the German Spartacist Eduard Fuchs, whose political mission to Moscow and conversation with Lenin in December 1918 were mentioned earlier (see Chapter

Two). "At the end of the war the Soviet government appointed Fuchs to set up an organization for the care of Russian war prisoners in Germany, making him the overall supervisor of the German camps for Russian POWs. He went to Russia in connection with repatriation of the Russian war prisoners, helping at the same time with repatriation of German prisoners of war."[8] Actually, as we saw, the Fuchs trip to Soviet Russia was to serve as an important link in the chain of events that would culminate in the founding of the Communist International, a fact that would not be made public until much later.

Largely cut off from its offshoots abroad, the Narkomindel had leisure at home to build up an international Communist apparatus until the creation of the Communist International itself. As an intimate of Lenin's was to put it: "Besides, prior to establishment of the Communist International, there existed at the Commissariat of Foreign Affairs a propaganda bureau, which was, so to speak, its embryo."[9] It was Radek who in December 1917 headed this international propaganda bureau, where another future leader of the Comintern, Béla Kun, also came to work, more or less replacing Radek, who left to take part in the negotiations at Brest-Litovsk.[10] After the Brest peace was concluded, Radek resumed his job, this time as chief of the bureau for Central Europe (hence mainly Germany). Working in that section were other foreign Communists from among Lenin's earliest followers, men such as J. Fineberg and B. Reinstein, whose role in the founding of the Comintern has been noted.

Of this period another of the pioneers of the Communist International, M. N. Roy, would later say: "In those days the Soviet Foreign Commissariat and the Communist International worked in close collaboration."[11] Their overlapping of functions was reflected in the alternating tasks assigned to the Narkomindel and Comintern, and in the parallel jobs held simultaneously by many of the Bolshevik leaders at the time. In 1919 Christian Rakovsky headed the Ukrainian Soviet government and was in charge of the Comintern's southern branch, born shortly after the founding of the Comintern and with headquarters in the same office in which Rakovsky functioned as chief of the government. The number two spot in the hierarchy of this southern branch was occupied by Angelica Balabanova, who at that juncture was entitled both Secretary of the Communist International and Minister of Foreign Affairs in the Ukrainian government. Sometimes the same individual would shift virtually overnight from the Narkomindel to the Comintern. Thus in 1918 Julian Marchlewski (Karski) left Berlin as part of Ioffe's diplomatic mission but returned to Germany in early 1919 as a secret emissary of the Comintern. In 1920 he was the Polish representative at the Comintern's Second Congress and head of the Byalistok provisional government. In 1921 he was a member of the delegation sent by the Soviet government to negotiate with Finland, and after that he left on a so-called diplomatic mission for the Far East. On his return, he participated in the July 1922 deliberations of the Comintern's Executive Committee on the Far East. The same thing happened with another Polish Communist, Mieczysław Broński, who in 1919 and early 1920 lived in Germany as a representative of the Comintern but at the end of 1920 appeared in Vienna as Soviet ambassador to Austria.

These expedients of 1918 and the beginning of 1919, adopted so that Moscow could keep an eye on Europe, were to give way, after the founding of the Comintern, to more systematic procedures designed to assure a permanent presence of Moscow's emissaries in the leading countries of the capitalist world.

CREATION OF THE GOVERNING AGENCIES OF THE COMINTERN

The official act of establishment of the Communist International in March 1919 was not followed immediately by any concerted worldwide political activity. Propaganda took precedence over organization. This departure from the principles of Bolshevism, which was primarily concerned with ways of translating revolutionary ideas into political realities, was an outgrowth of several circumstances. First, the Communist parties supposedly comprising the Comintern either did not exist at all or did not yet have any mass membership. As for the Comintern, its first governing body consisted of a handful of men of no particular stature or achievement, as one of its members, Y.S. Reich (Thomas), was later to admit: "The agencies of the Communist International's Secretariat were all set up, but were running empty, so to speak. They had no foreign contacts or correspondence, and no information from abroad. . . . All the important militants had been assigned to other jobs, which left only the second-raters, who lolled around, with nothing to do, in the vast halls of the once privately owned Hotel Mirbach."[12]

Moreover, unlike the Secretariat, based in Moscow, the President of the International, Zinoviev, continued to live in Petrograd and came to Moscow only once a week. As chairman of the Petrograd Soviet, he was faced with a particularly difficult situation during the Yudenich offensive against that city. He himself later conceded at the Comintern's Second Congress: "What was the Communist International when it was founded in March 1919? Nothing but a figment of propaganda. And it continued to be only that for the entire [first] year of its existence."[13]

Unlike the subsequent congresses, which regularly dealt with aspects of the organization of the Comintern and of its sections, the founding congress passed but a single resolution of an "organizational" nature, which entrusted the running of the new International to two bodies: an Executive Committee, known as the ECCI, and a Bureau, popularly referred to from 1919 to 1921 as "the Little Bureau." That same resolution stipulated that the ECCI was to include "a representative of the Communist parties of the most important countries," listed as Russia, Germany, Austria, Hungary, the Balkan Federation, Switzerland, and Scandinavia.[14]

This decision remained a dead letter, as Zinoviev admitted: "So, in addition to the Russian party, six other parties were immediately supposed to dispatch representatives to serve on the Executive Committee. Matters were such, however, that very few of these parties could keep permanent representatives in Russia, where the Executive Committee was to sit."[15] Actually, not a single foreign representative came from any country with a mandate from his party to serve on the ECCI, as is clear from Zinoviev's further explanations. The German Communist Party was unable to be represented on the ECCI between the First and Second Congresses. The Austrian delegate K. Steinhardt returned to Moscow on the eve of the Second Congress. The Scandinavians participated fleetingly. The Balkan Federation representative did not show up until the spring of 1920. The Swiss Communists had no one left after Platten's departure. Indeed, there was only the Hungarian representative, Endre Rudnyánszky, a former prisoner of war who had never returned to Hungary, and who was helped out for a while by his fellow countryman, László Rudas, who had arrived from Budapest the day after the founding of the Comintern. Zinoviev has supplied an exact definition of the body governing the Comintern during the first sixteen months of its existence: "The executive could not function as a centralized entity. It was a Russian institution. That is what we now want to change."[16]

In his report to the Comintern's Second Congress, Zinoviev named those members of the Bolshevik Party's Central Committee delegated by the Party to serve on the ECCI: "From the Communist Party of Russia the following comrades belonged to the Executive Committee of the Communist International: Balabanova, Berzin, Bukharin, Karakhan, Klinger, Litvinov, Zinoviev, Vorovsky, and others. Comrade Lenin and other comrades also attended the most important meetings as delegates of the Russian Communist Party."[17] Operating within this circle was a still tighter circle comprising the Bureau of the Comintern (the future Presidium of the ECCI), led by Zinoviev as President of the International, with Berzin, Vorovsky, Balabanova, and Radek (after the latter's return from Germany in 1920) as Secretaries of the International.

These two entities, the Executive Committee and the "Little Bureau," constituted the Comintern's official governing bodies, but they were not so in fact. All the important decisions made for the Comintern, as well as for the Soviet Government, emanated from the only effective source of Communist power: the Politbureau of the Bolshevik Party.Balabanova, unfamiliar with Bolshevik methods, was to learn this in her job as Secretary of the Comintern: "I was surprised to find that the topics of discussion at our executive meetings had so little relation to the work we had been elected to do. (Later, when I discovered that our meetings were mere formalities and that real authority rested with a secret Party committee, I was to understand the reason for this.)"[18] This dependence of the Executive Committee and Presidium on the Bolshevik Party Politbureau (hence actually on Lenin himself), neither specified nor hinted at in any Comintern statute, was to become the cornerstone of the entire Comintern edifice. Initially, between the First and Second Comintern Congresses, this dependence was most apparent through the fact that the membership of the Presidium, Secretariat, and Executive Committee of the Comintern consisted solely of Bolsheviks, who were obliged to implement automatically the decisions of their own Politbureau. Later on, those three governing entities would contain some foreign Communists, able and willing to express disagreement since they were not bound by Bolshevik discipline.

Some of the members of this first Bolshevik crew that ran the Comintern held their positions very briefly, while others stayed on until the end of their careers at the Bolshevik Party pinnacle. To the first category belonged those who gave up their jobs as high Comintern functionaries to devote themselves thenceforward exclusively to Soviet diplomacy, men like Karakhan, Vorovsky, and Litvinov. Berzin still figured in the Bolshevik delegation to the Second Comintern Congress, but by then he was no longer Secretary of the ECCI. Klinger did belong to the ECCI on that occasion, but after the congress he disappeared from the Comintern leadership. Another elimination signaled the first purge at the Comintern summit; its victim was Angelica Balabanova. Having joined the Bolshevik Party only in the second half of 1917, she saw herself appointed Secretary of the Comintern on the day after it was founded, by decision of the Bolshevik Party's Central Committee— that is, by Lenin personally, who in that first team to run the Comintern needed at least one known personality from the international labor movement. Balabanova filled the bill very nicely, having been much in view in the Second International, a key figure in the Zimmerwald movement and a prominent militant in the Italian Socialist Party, the only mass Socialist party in Western Europe that welcomed the creation of the Third International and voted to join the new organization. But even by 1920, before the Comintern's Second Congress, she was removed from her job as Secretary of the Executive Committee, after being shipped off to Kiev in 1919 to busy herself with the Southern Bureau; and this elimination, quite apart from the personal animosity that existed between her and Zinoviev, was in itself symbolic. Of those running the Comintern, the last to join the Bolshevik Party was the first to be expelled.

Thus, through various eliminations from that original Comintern team, by the time of the Second Congress there remained only three leaders as true mandatories of the Bolshevik Party and real bosses of the Comintern: Zinoviev, Bukharin, and Radek. Nearly ten years later Trotsky would write about them, when they were ousted from the Comintern leadership and he himself was in exile: "Under Lenin, *immediate* supervision of the affairs of the International had been entrusted to Zinoviev, Radek, and Bukharin. In deciding matters of any importance, Lenin and the author of these lines participated. Needless to say, on all basic questions involving the International, Lenin called the tune."[19]

The top man in this triumvirate, in title and in fact, was Zinoviev, in title because he had been named President of the Communist International to start with, in fact because he wielded power in Lenin's name. Lenin had picked Zinoviev to be his alter ego in the Comintern because of the exceptional services that he had rendered to Lenin's cause. He had supported Lenin faithfully for more than ten years in the Bolshevik Central Committee. He had undergone his baptism of fire at Lenin's side at the Zimmerwald and Kienthal conferences. He had belonged to the Bolshevik Party's first Politbureau, formed in October 1917, and was chairman of the Soviet of Petrograd, capital of the October Revolution. The fact of his having suffered a revolutionary lapse on the eve of November 7, 1917—a memory still fresh in 1919—and of having nevertheless been restored by Lenin to his high party functions, increased his indebtedness to Lenin and guaranteed his total obedience. For all these reasons, in the early days of the Comintern, in 1919-20, Zinoviev was strictly the mouthpiece and errand boy for Lenin.

Bukharin, a recent member of the Bolshevik Party's Central Committee, elected for the first time at its Sixth Congress in July-August 1917, also had to seek pardon for his Left deviation in 1918, which for the first time had put Lenin in the minority within the Central Committee of his own party. Like Zinoviev, Bukharin had vast knowledge of the international Socialist movement. He had spent time in Central Europe, Scandinavia, and North America. Taking a lively interest in matters of theory and ideology, he had just the right qualities for waging massive battle against the Social Democratic theoreticians in Germany, Austria, and elsewhere.

Radek, the third member of this triumvirate, unlike Bukharin, did not lean toward theory and ideology but rather toward a journalism of propaganda and polemic. He was the only one of the three who had not come out of the Bolshevik Party and the Russian Socialist movement proper; over the previous fifteen years he had been active successively in three Socialist movements, the Polish, the German, and the Russian. A member of the Zimmerwald Left at the international Socialist conferences in Switzerland in 1915 and 1916, associated with the secretariat of that Left along with Lenin and Zinoviev, he did not join the Bolshevik Party until 1917, becoming a member of its Foreign Bureau (with Vorovsky) at Stockholm in the summer of that year.

SUBORDINATE PERSONNEL AT COMINTERN HEADQUARTERS

In the beginning, the Comintern lacked personnel at every level, both at the top and in the lower echelons. The few Old Guard Bolsheviks had to share the governing functions in party, state, and Comintern with the 1917 Bolsheviks, but personnel still had to be found for the lower-level political, technical, and administrative chores. The lower down one went in the hierarchy, the greater the number one found of recent-vintage Bolsheviks. Thus, to publish the official organ of the new organization, the journal *Communist International*, the first issue of which appeared two months after the formal founding of the Comintern, the choice fell on V. O. Liechtenstadt-Mazin, who had spent ten years in Tsarist prisons but did not join the Bolshevik Party until early 1919: "When in March 1919 it was suggested to him that he become Secretary of the Petersburg Section of the Bureau of the Communist International, so as to edit and manage publication of the journal, he took on the job with youthful zeal."[20] A similar case was that of V. Kibalchich (Victor Serge), a former anarchist who prior to the October Revolution had had no connection with either the Bolshevik Party or the Russian Social Democratic movement; he was put in charge of the French edition of the journal.

The journal's first issue contained an article entitled "The Latest News from Germany," signed by James Gordon, which led the reader to assume, on the basis of information allegedly received directly from there, that revolution was imminent in that country, while the second issue included an article entitled "Letter from France," signed by A. Victor, prophesying the same event there also. In fact, the first article had sprung from the pen of Y.S. Reich (Thomas) and the second had been written by Victor Serge.

These two men had been assigned the task of getting out the journal's first two issues; lacking original material, they invented fictional correspondents in Germany and France, where they themselves had long since ceased to live.

These first issues of the journal were printed and published in Petrograd, where Zinoviev spent most of his time, while the Comintern's official headquarters continued to be in Moscow. This separation rendered the functioning of the Comintern's initial governing body still more complicated and haphazard. Marcel Body, secretary of the French Communist group in Moscow, has described its beginnings in the following way:

> It was first in Moscow, shortly after the first congress of the Communist International, that I started frequenting its headquarters, located in a private hotel, on Denezhnyi Pereulok, which used to house the German Embassy, in the room in which Count Mirbach was assassinated. I must say that I did not see any activity at all there for months. . . . In Petrograd the first offices of the International were established at the Smol'nyi during March or April 1919, when they began to recruit Russian and foreign personnel for the publications, which under Zinoviev's direction were to inaugurate the Comintern's public activities. . . . To head the different publishing services in Petrograd, Zinoviev had appointed Kobetsky, who knew several languages including German. Kingisepp, an energetic and capable woman, worked under him on the German edition of the pamphlets and journal. Victor Serge handled the French editions all by himself until I arrived in Petrograd in December 1919. . . . The editor of the English editions at the Smol'nyi was Fineberg (Feinberg), who was among the delegates to the International's first congress, at which, as a department head in the Narkomindel, he had been selected to serve as one of the foreign delegates.[21]

BASIC STRUCTURE OF THE COMINTERN

The Bolshevik success in Russia, having confirmed Lenin's theses on the role of the Communist Party in the capture of power and in the revolution that would follow, rendered logical and acceptable the argument that the Lenin formula must be extended from the Bolshevik Party to the Communist International, from the Russian revolution to world revolution.

Consequently, the first organizational steps taken at the Comintern's founding congress were a carbon copy of the Bolshevik

Party setup. Thus the Comintern's Executive Committee, which met at more or less regular intervals, matched the Bolshevik Party's Central Committee, and the Comintern's Bureau (or "Little Bureau"), known after 1921 as the Presidium of the Executive Committee, corresponded to the Politbureau of the Bolshevik Party's Central Committee. The Secretariat of the Comintern's Executive Committee was the equivalent of the Secretariat of the Bolshevik Party's Central Committee, and the Comintern's Control Commission had the same functions as the Bolshevik Party's Control Commission. All these governing entities derived their authority from a theoretically supreme congress, which in Lenin's time assembled faithfully once a year, one for the Bolshevik Party and one for the Communist International. Just as one convened a national conference in the interval between two Bolshevik Party congresses, an enlarged plenum of the Executive Committee would be convened between two Comintern congresses. The Communist International was to have from the outset its secret web radiating out from Moscow, just as earlier the Bolshevik Party had had its secret web radiating from abroad into Tsarist Russia. This web hung from two pillars: the professional revolutionaries in the service of the leadership, and the secret funds which supported their activities; this was true first within the Bolshevik Party and then within the Comintern. The subdivisions which the Bolshevik Party had created within its governing body (Agitprop, Orgbureau) would be mirrored in the Comintern setup, a setup very different from what one found in the Socialist International.

Since the Communist Party was not to be a party like any other, and since the Communist International was not supposed to be like the Socialist International, this fundamental idea had to be drilled into all who joined. The mission of the Bolsheviks was to spread that truth to the new converts all over the world ready to follow Moscow's lead. Translated from terms of belief into terms of method, this meant that Moscow, from the beginning, had the right to intervene in the affairs of foreign parties, a point of which Zinoviev made no secret in the report he prepared for the Second World Congress: "[The Executive Committee]... deems it not only admissible but obligatory to 'meddle' in the work of parties that belong or wish to belong to the Communist International."[22]

Because of the fact that during the interval between the First and Second Congresses there were hardly any Communist parties in the West or in other continents, and because Soviet Russia was virtually cut off from the outside world by blockade and civil war, the Bolshevik blueprint could not immediately be used in many places. But wherever the Executive Committee (i.e., the Bolshevik nucleus) could intervene and impose its pattern, it did so.

Two cases in particular, cited in the Zinoviev report, serve to illustrate this. It was the Executive Committee of the Comintern that assumed the right to appoint a new Central Committee for the Finnish Communist Party, whose leaders had taken refuge in Soviet Russia. Since this established a precedent, Zinoviev explained the Comintern's action as being in compliance with a request from the Finns themselves, and he added that the Executive Committee was conscious of its great responsibility. The second case involved the Communist movement in the United States, where two different parties had formed, each claiming the sanction of the International. In this situation the Comintern introduced a method subsequently often used: it summoned representatives of the two parties to Comintern headquarters and imposed Moscow's "unity" decision upon them.

Soviet soil thus served in three ways to promote the international Communist cause. First, certain Communist parties of countries neighboring Russia were founded in Soviet Russia. This was true of the Finnish Communist Party, established in August of 1918, and of other Communist parties of regions formerly a part of the Tsarist Russian empire.* Secondly, reversing a historical process, the Bolshevik Party, which before the war had held its own congresses abroad, now enabled some of the new Communist parties to organize their congresses in Soviet Russia. This would be the case with the Polish Communist Party in the twenties, and even with Asian revolutionaries. Thus the Sixth Congress of the

---

*During the years 1918-19 the Communists native to these regions worked in organizations forming a part of the Russian Bolshevik Party. That this situation later changed, is attested by a letter dated June 7, 1920, which the Estonian Communist Party addressed to the Bolshevik Party's Central Committee: "It is now necessary to set up an Estonian Communist Party that will be autonomous, like all the parties in the International." *Ocherki istorii Komunisticheskoi partii Estonii,* Tallin, 1961, p. 405.

Chinese Communist Party took place in Moscow in the summer of 1928. Finally, in other instances the Bolshevik Party did its utmost to set up first in Russia certain foreign Communist groups which it would then send as militants back to their own countries to establish Communist parties. Later, in 1921, the Comintern began opening several specialized schools with the aim of forming new directing cadres for the Communist parties of the entire world.

FIRST COMINTERN EMISSARIES

One of the most important and least known aspects of the Comintern's history is its secret activities. Among these, the practice of sending emissaries abroad assumed from the first prime importance, which it retained as long as the Comintern officially existed. In the beginning, these envoys were discussed openly. At the Second Comintern Congress in July of 1920 article nine of its statutes was amended to read: "The representatives of the Executive Committee shall carry out their political assignments in closest contact with the Party headquarters in the country in question."[23] In his report to that congress Zinoviev named some of the countries visited by Comintern emissaries (Germany, Austria, France, the United States, Italy, Sweden, Norway, Bulgaria), but he did not name the emissaries themselves.

The more developed this emissary system became, the less it was mentioned in official Comintern publications. A rule was adopted to make no further mention of the activities of Comintern agents in capitalist countries.* Thus the difference between the official, "surface" history of the Comintern and its actual overall history (including the secret domain) is best illustrated in the doings of these emissaries. If we were to confine ourselves to a

---

*This rule survived the demise of the Comintern, for more than a quarter of a century after its dissolution the Communist parties in the West still keep secret the names and roles of the former Comintern emissaries to their respective countries, and all Soviet publications continue to preserve this silence. Thus, for instance, the fifth (and most recent) edition of Lenin's complete works does not even mention in the biographies appended to its volumes that individuals such as M. G. Broński or N. M. Liubarsky were Comintern emissaries.

study of the Comintern's official documents we would find no
more than a few pages on the subject, whereas an entire volume
would be needed to unravel the emissaries' role and to illuminate
their historical significance.

The dispatching of these revolutionary *missi dominici* accorded
both with Lenin's ideas and with the circumstances of the moment. It was in line with his ideas in that the knowledge and
experience gained by the Bolsheviks in Russia had to be spread
abroad, and that this could only be done in sending to foreign
countries men who had served the Bolshevik cause and who enjoyed Lenin's full confidence. It fitted the prevailing circumstances because in the civil war raging in Russia during 1919-20
and in the revolutionary war that Lenin and the Comintern had
declared upon the capitalist world, Lenin served as commander-in-
chief of the main revolutionary army (the Russian Communist
Party), which was temporarily cut off from its advanced detachments in the West (the Communist parties and groups). Hence the
emissaries were to reestablish the broken liaison and act as agents
of the commander-in-chief.

This coordination between "the general staff of the world revolution" (as the Executive Committee of the Comintern sometimes
referred to itself on festive occasions) and its detachments elsewhere could hardly be achieved by having representatives of the
West come to Soviet Russia, for the simple reason that the numerous material obstacles and unfamiliarity with the ways of clandes-
tinity in Western Europe would have made this enterprise most
difficult. The fact is that during the early months of the Communist International's existence very few European Communists visited Soviet Russia, and those who did visit did not represent much
of anybody. So throughout 1919 Lenin kept an eye out for any
foreign militants arriving in Moscow. Berzin, the Comintern secretary at the time, wrote:

> In the winter of 1919-1920, when I was secretary of the Executive
> Committee of the Communist International, not infrequently did I have
> occasion to bring to Vladimir Ilich foreign comrades who used to come
> to Moscow. However, compared with later years, such guests did not
> arrive too often. Intervention and blockade continued, and we were
> almost completely cut off from the outer world; contacts with the
> foreign Communist parties could only be arranged by "illegal" means

and were consequently inadequate. But then, every foreign Communist who succeeded in breaking through the ring of hostile capitalist encirclement was for us a very welcome and dear guest.[24]

Since Lenin lacked information concerning Communist activities in Europe, and since the Comintern's first partisans in Europe were not yet receiving political or material aid from the world's first Communist power, ways had to be found to establish reliable contacts with the outside world despite blockade and foreign intervention. That was the job of the special emissaries. Lenin took particular interest in these emissaries, whom he knew personally and whom he saw and talked with before they left for the West. This was the case in the autumn of 1919 when he received Y.S. Reich on the eve of his departure for Berlin, and S. J. Rutgers before he left for Amsterdam. His note to Chicherin of January 4, 1920, first published in 1961, revealed that Lenin knew by heart the names of many of these emissaries, just as he had previously memorized the names of his trusted agents working for the Bolshevik cause within Russia while he was residing in the West.

That same January 4, after he received a bundle of political literature from Litvinov, who was on a diplomatic mission to Copenhagen, and after expressing his disappointment at its meager contents, Lenin ordered that Litvinov and all members of the Bolshevik Party abroad, as well as every "bureau" and "agency" in foreign countries, keep sending in this political documentation incessantly and in large amounts. The note, a copy of which was sent to Klinger, the Secretary of the Comintern and then head of its administrative services, also bore the names "Abramovich, Kopp, Rutgers, Broński, Liubarsky, Reich, Ström, Höglund, Kilbom, Rothstein, etc." The "etc." signified that Lenin had more names in mind when he dictated the note.

The first on his list, A. E. Abramovich, was a man whom he had known and trusted since before the 1917 revolution. A member of the Bolshevik faction from the time he first joined the Russian Social Democratic Labor Party in 1908 and a political émigré after 1911, Abramovich spent the war years in Switzerland, where as a simple party militant he performed secondary tasks. He left Switzerland on the same train with Lenin and Zinoviev, returned to Western Europe shortly after the founding of the Comintern, and was entrusted with a series of missions in different countries under varying pseudonyms. In April 1919, during the period of the Bavarian Soviet Republic, he was in Munich under the assumed name of Albrecht. After the collapse of that republic he went to Berlin; a confidential letter written in mid-1919 by Paul Levi and dispatched by courier to Zinoviev reports that "Comrades Zürcher and Abramovich have been extremely helpful to us, and we would definitely like to keep them here." [25] When the Comintern's Secretariat for Western Europe was established in Berlin in October or November of 1919, Abramovich was still in Germany, where he signed an appeal in the name of that secretariat under the pseudonym of Albrecht. In February 1920 he was picked up by the German police but managed to be released after a short detention. After that, it was dangerous for him to work in Germany, and he went on to France and Switzerland, making trips also to Italy and Austria. He left for Russia to take part in the Comintern's Second Congress, taking with him Alfred Rosmer, who became one of the five presidents of that congress. Abramovich attended as a member of the French delegation, after which he returned to the West. Under the assumed name of Alexander, which he had used at the end of his stay in Germany, and then under that of Zalewski, in which name he held a passport, he took an active part in the preparations for the Socialist congress at Tours, which he attended. His assignment in France was to split the Socialist Party and in Switzerland to bring about a fusion of the small Communist Party, founded in German Switzerland in 1919, and the left wing of the Socialist Party. He accomplished both these tasks satisfactorily, but several days after the congress at Tours he was compromised in a politico-financial affair. In January 1921 he was arrested over a matter involving checks and then expelled from France. Having thus burned his fingers in Europe's principal countries, he returned to work at Comintern headquarters,* where he remained active until 1930, carrying out occasional missions to one place or another, one of them probably to China. He had the rare good fortune to survive the Stalin purges and was still alive in 1961. [26]

*According to Bertram D. Wolfe, Abramovich—Zalewski's secret work involved forging of passports for delegates and emissaries, disposing of confiscated jewels, transport of funds and other confidential clandestine work.

The second person on Lenin's list was V. L. Kopp. Unlike Abramovich, Kopp, who had been active in the Russian Social Democratic movement since 1898, declared himself successively "non-factional," then as a Menshevik, then as a follower of Trotsky; he did not join the Bolshevik Party until 1917. Again, unlike Abramovich, who performed his tasks as emissary according to the rules of Bolshevik clandestine activity (using false identity papers for display to "bourgeois" authorities and an assumed name within the Communist apparatus), Kopp employed a governmental cover. Attached to Ioffe's diplomatic mission and expelled with him in November 1918, he returned to Germany in 1919 in connection with the repatriation of the Russian war prisoners in that country. Unlike Inessa Armand and Dmitri Manuilsky, who failed in using that cover to establish themselves in France, Kopp was successful in Germany, where in April 1920 he signed an agreement with the German government concerning the exchange of military and civilian prisoners between the two countries. At the same time, he used his cover to carry on the work of the Comintern. A little later, after 1921, he was assigned to the diplomatic corps, as were many of the other leading figures in the initial Comintern organization, and one of the jobs he held was that of ambassador to Japan.

S. J. Rutgers, a Dutchman, third on the list of Comintern emissaries drawn up by Lenin, was given the assignment of setting up a branch of the Comintern in Amsterdam. Among Lenin's trusted men, Rutgers was the only one who had been neither a professional revolutionary, like those who came from Russia to Western Europe, nor even a professional politician, as was the case with the Scandinavians. This largely explains why his mission soon ended in failure and why he was the only one, of all those who Lenin named, to renounce political activity. After 1921, having returned to Soviet Russia, Rutgers went back to being an engineer, a profession which he continued to practice there until 1938, when he returned to the Netherlands.

Next on Lenin's list was a militant from the Polish Socialist movement, Mieczysław Broński, who had been living in Switzerland long before 1914 and who took part in the Kienthal conference of 1916, where he adopted a position very close to Lenin's. In 1917, after the Bolshevik victory, he went to Russia, where he held important jobs in the economic field, one being that of Assistant Commissar for Commerce and Industry. But in the spring of 1919, when the bad news came from Germany and the decapitated leadership of the German Communist Party was forced to operate underground, Broński was sent to Berlin as emissary for the Comintern. He worked there under the assumed name of Zürcher, after the Swiss city in which he had lived, and also under the name of M. Braun, with which he signed an article published in 1920 in *Communist International*. He took part in the international Communist conference in Frankfurt am Main in 1919, assisted Y.S. Reich in setting up the Comintern's Secretariat for Western Europe in Berlin, and cooperated with Paul Levi and other leaders of the German Communist Party until just after the Kapp-Lüttwitz putsch in March of 1920. Shortly afterward he was withdrawn from the Comintern's secret section and made a diplomat. That same year he became Soviet ambassador to Vienna.

N. M. Liubarsky, the next man on Lenin's list, was active in the Russian Social Democratic movement first within Russia and then, after 1908, in exile. He was closer to Plekhanov than to Lenin. Returning to Russia in 1917 and joining up with the Bolsheviks, he was sent in 1918 on a diplomatic mission to Switzerland. Expelled from that country, he returned to Moscow to help set up the Comintern organization. He soon left again on a secret mission to Italy, where he had lived as a Socialist émigré before 1914. Very active and influential in the ruling circle of the Italian Socialist Party, which had already proclaimed its adherence to the new International, Liubarsky went under the assumed name of Niccolini; his confidential reports to the Comintern leaders were signed with the pseudonym that he used within the Russian movement, "Carlo." After the split in the Italian Socialist Party and the founding of the Communist Party in 1921, he went to carry out a similar assignment in Czechoslovakia, after which, in 1922, he returned to Moscow to be attached to the Comintern's Executive Committee. He was later transferred to the Commissariat of Foreign Affairs.

Listed next by Lenin was Y.S. Reich, who arrived around October or November of 1919 in Berlin, where he established the Comintern's Secretariat for Western Europe, which was to keep him busy until April 1925. Of all the emissaries named by Lenin, Reich, who after the spring of 1920 went under the assumed name of "Comrade Thomas," had the mission covering the largest geographical area and longest span of time. He was the only one to set up and run an actual branch of the Comintern, encompassing a number of European Communist parties, starting with that of Germany. Unlike Abramovich, Rutgers, Broński, and Liubarsky, who were through with their secret assignments after a year or two, "Comrade Thomas" was to stay on the job for many years. He was also the only one of all the emissaries listed in Lenin's note to leave behind an account of his activities in Berlin from 1919 to 1921.*

The last person named on Lenin's list, apart from the three Scandinavians, who operated in Stockholm, a center devoted more to simple liaison than to political leadership, was F.A. Rothstein, a Russian Socialist militant who had been living as an émigré in England since 1890. In 1920 he was assigned the task of hastening the founding of a British Communist party. Lenin had known him since the beginning of the century and appointed him his "ambassador" to the British labor movement. In a letter published for the first time in 1965, Lenin wrote to him on July 15, 1920: "With regard to your trip to Russia, I vacillate. You are very important to the cause in London. . . . I believe that your playing a leading role in the Anglo Saxon movement (both with your pen and secretly) will be particularly helpful. It is of the utmost importance to get them back in line over there."[27] When Rothstein finally returned to Soviet Russia, he gave up his secret job for the Comintern and went into the diplomatic service.

Lenin's note, written in January of 1920, obviously did not name all of the Comintern emissaries who had secret missions in the West in 1919 and 1920. One must add to the list the names of other confidential emissaries who performed similar tasks: Felix Wolf, A. Guralsky, Vladimir Degot, A. M. Heller, L. B. Sunitsa, M. Borodin, and the one secret Comintern delegate who did not

---

*See the account of "Comrade Thomas" (with an introduction by Boris Nicolaevsky) in *Contributions à l'histoire du Comintern*, Geneva, 1965. He used three other assumed names: James, J. Gordon, and Rubinstein, the latter being the surname of his wife's family.

come out of the Russian Socialist movement but who had nevertheless known and worked with Lenin and Zinoviev before November 7, 1917, the Bulgarian S. Mineff.

The first two of those emissaries, Felix Wolf and A. Guralsky,
had missions involving Germany and the German Communist
Party. A young German employed as a clerk in a Russian bank,
Wolf was interned during World War I. It was in Siberia, before the
1917 revolution, that he first joined a Bolshevik organization. In
1918, after the Bolshevik victory, he was a member of the agitprop team assigned the task of spreading defeatist propaganda
among the German troops. At the end of 1918 he left for Germany in the company of Karl Radek and Friesland (E. Reuter).
His real name was Krebs, which he had translated into its Russian
equivalent, Rakov, but he called himself Felix Wolf when he returned to Germany, where he appeared at the founding congress
of the German Communist Party but was not arrested shortly after
it as Radek was. Wolf reported regularly to the Comintern on the
German Communist movement, sometimes working outside the
official party leadership and Berlin Secretariat of the Comintern,
as, for example, in maintaining contact between the Comintern
leaders and the KAPD* during 1920. He was actually a secret
member, if not of the Central Committee of the German Communist Party at least of its pro-Soviet faction, as is evident from
Radek's correspondence of early 1921, addressed simultaneously
to Wolf and to the German Communist Party leaders, Brandler,
Thalheimer, Frölich, Meyer, and Böttcher.[28] Wolf concerned himself especially with the organizational links between the German
Communist Party and the Comintern, as indicated by Radek's
reply of April 1, 1921, to a letter from Wolf: "As for the organizational matters discussed by Felix in his last letter, such as the
information service, the threesome, I shall now take all of that up
with Grigori [Zinoviev]."[29]

---

*Kommunistische Arbeiterpartei Deutschlands. Founded as a rival to the Ger-
man Communist Party in April of 1920. A typical "left-wing" communist
group with strong anarcho-syndicalist features, it never became a major political force but gave considerable trouble to the official German Communist
Party. It sent delegates to the Second and Third Comintern congresses, but it
was not accepted as a full-fledged Comintern section. It was criticized by
Lenin at the Third Congress, and by 1923 it was virtually extinct.

A. Guralsky, whose real name was Abraham Heifetz, was in Germany in the early months of 1920. M. N. Roy met him on a trip to Chemnitz, where both of them were looking for the Saxon Communist leader, Heinrich Brandler, and did not describe him in very flattering terms: "I had traveled from Berlin together with Guralsky, who had recently come from Moscow as a representative of the Communist International. Borodin introduced him to me as such. But he preferred to pass as a German under the assumed name of Kleine. He was a poor substitute for Borodin, in personal appearance as well as intellectually." [30] This same "Kleine" appeared in France in 1924 under the assumed name of "Lepetit" and continued to shuttle back and forth between the two countries.

Among the Comintern emissaries active in Europe but not mentioned on Lenin's list was Vladimir Degot, a man of impeccable revolutionary credentials. A member of the Russian Social Democratic Labor Party since 1904, a Bolshevik from the beginning, he was one of the pupils at Lenin's short-lived political school in Paris in 1908. Later, during the war, he was one of Lenin's trusted men among the Russian emigrants in Paris. After the founding of the Comintern, he belonged to its foreign center in Odessa until he was sent as an emissary to Italy and France. Arriving in Italy on the eve of the important Socialist Party Congress at Bologna in October 1919, he immediately established contact with the leaders of the extreme Left, with whom he collaborated closely in the months that followed. In March 1920 Degot left for Paris, where he met the leaders of the Committee for the Third International: Fernand Loriot, Raymond Lefebvre, Pierre Monatte, and Boris Souvarine. After that he went, via Berlin, to the Comintern's Second Congress. Arriving after it was over, he was received by Lenin, who questioned him at length about the Communist movement in France and Italy. The only one in this gaggle of Comintern emissaries to have published his memoirs, Degot returned to Italy in the autumn of 1920 for a stay of several months, during which he made three trips to Berlin, to the headquarters of the Comintern's Secretariat for Western Europe. From Italy he went to Paris, after which he again showed up in Italy in early 1921 just as the Communist party was being established there. On returning to France, he was arrested in Nice in May 1921 and expelled from the country.

A. M. Heller, a Russian Social Democratic militant, had lived in political exile in Italy prior to the 1917 revolution. A functionary of the Bolshevik Party in Turkmenistan, in March 1920 he was assigned to the Italian delegation to the Second Comintern Congress as a representative of the Bolshevik Central Committee. Later he was sent to Italy to present the Comintern viewpoint to the Italian Communist leaders. Using the assumed name "Chiarini," he also supplied Lenin and Zinoviev with information on the state of the Communist movement in that country.

L. B. Sunitsa, a member of the Russian Social Democratic Labor Party since 1905, lived as a political émigré in Germany and Austria from 1913 to 1918. Under the offical cover of providing aid to Russian war prisoners in Austria, he succeeded in establishing contact with the elements of the extreme Left in that country. He helped them in their work, and at the founding congress of the Austrian Communist Party he spoke on behalf of the Bolshevik Party. But by the time of the establishment of the Comintern he was no longer in Austria.

The only Comintern emissary who had not come out of the Russian Socialist movement was the Bulgarian, S. Mineff, a medical student during World War I in French Switzerland and a delegate of the Bulgarian Socialist Youth (narrow Socialist party) to the International Socialist Youth Conference in 1915 at Bern. Associated with the Bolshevik group in Geneva and a contributor to the journal *Demain*, Mineff belonged in 1916-17 to the small international circle that had been won over to Lenin's ideas. He entered the Comintern's secret service in 1919 and managed to be the only one who remained in it throughout the entire existence of the Comintern, spending the next twenty years going from country to country, changing his pseudonyms, showing up in one place under the name of Lorenzo Vanini, in another as Dr. Chavaroche, Lebedev, or Stepanov. In early 1919-20 he carried out his mission in France under the name of L. Vanini, the pseudonym under which he attended the Second Comintern Congress as part of the French delegation.

The only one of the Comintern emissaries to have traveled outside the European continent between the First and the Second Comintern congresses was Mikhail Borodin. A Social Democratic militant in Tsarist Russia up to 1906 and close to the Bolsheviks, he emigrated to the United States where he lived in Chicago and did not return to Russia until after the 1917 revolution. Early in 1919 he was sent by the Comintern on a political-financial mission which took him to New York as a representative of the Russian Red Cross, after which he went on to Mexico under the assumed name of Brantwein, where he played a role in the founding of the country's Communist party and established contact with M. N. Roy. After Mexico, at the end of 1919 he appeared in Spain, where he met with Socialist leaders and Anarcho-Syndicalists, as reported by J. Maurín, one of the leading militants of revolutionary Syndicalism in that country and later the founder and theoretician of the Partido Obrero de Unificación Marxista (P.O.U.M.):

> Speaking no Spanish, Borodin had with him as secretary and interpreter a Mexican named Manuel Ramirez,* who knew English. In Madrid, Borodin got in touch with representatives of the groups who were in favor of the Socialist Party's joining the Communist International. In his talks with the Communist leaders he had promised "fraternal aid" to the Communist Party as soon as it was established. ... He did not stay long in Spain. In the second half of January 1920 he had to go to Amsterdam, where a Communist conference was scheduled in which he was to take part. But his secretary, Ramirez, remained in Spain as emissary of the Communist International. [31]

Borodin attended the Amsterdam conference and then left for Berlin, where he was busy in the Secretariat for Western Europe during the spring of 1920. He finally went back to Moscow and immediately went to work at Comintern headquarters, where his first job was helping with preparations for the Second Congress and translating into English Lenin's book *"Left-Wing" Communism, an Infantile Disorder*. During 1920-21 he attended the meetings of the Comintern Executive Committee, before being sent on a mission to Great Britain (and later on a most important mission to China).

The criteria governing the selection of these first emissaries were relatively simple. Firstly, all had lived in the West before the

---

*The same Ramirez attended the founding congress of the Profintern in July 1921. In 1923-24 Ramirez, who had learned something of labor organization as a cigar-maker in Tampa, Florida, was the secretary of the Communist Party of Mexico.

Bolshevik Revolution and spoke one or more of the main Western languages: German, French, English, or Italian. This knowledge of the language of a country was supplemented by knowledge of the country itself. As for the emissaries from the peripheral regions of the old Tsarist Russian empire, they all spoke German as well as their own native languages, hence could participate in revolutionary activities in Germany readily and effectively. With the exception of Degot, they were not originally workers and became the Comintern's first professional revolutionaries. Their livelihood was assured by the Comintern organization. Secondly, apart from Abramovich and Degot, there were no militants among them who had belonged to the Bolshevik Party before 1917. All were Socialists who had rallied to Lenin's Bolshevism after 1917. Some were former Mensheviks (like Liubarsky), others former "Bundists" (like Guralsky) or ex-militants who had retired from revolutionary activity in Russia (like Borodin), while still others were foreigners won over to Communism in Russia (like Felix Wolf and Y.S. Reich, to whose names would be added in 1920-21 those of many Hungarians like Béla Kun and Mátyás Rákosi). [32]

There was a very simple explanation for this. The Bolsheviks, not having been very numerous prior to 1917, after their victory of November 7 had moved into highly responsible jobs in the apparatus of the Party and state, and of the Red Army, which left few of them available for work abroad. Moreover, since these initial missions involved a certain risk—such as arrest and detention, whether prolonged as in the case of Radek or brief as in the case of Degot and Abramovich—it was deemed wiser to keep the old Bolsheviks in Russia in positions of authority and send the new ones out into enemy territory. Thus was created a somewhat bizarre situation: these brand-new Bolsheviks were supposed to press for a split with the Socialist movement, to which they themselves had recently belonged, and were assigned the task of "Bolshevizing" the Socialist Left in the West, although they themselves had not long before refused to accept Bolshevik postulates.

Another paradox was in evidence during the first sixteen months of the Comintern's existence, from March 1919 to July 1920: nothing was said in any of its published releases about these emissaries, yet that omission did not prevent them from acquiring a special privileged status everywhere in the West. The domain of their activities became very broad, both in the matter of their relations with the Comintern and with the leadership of the Communist movements in the countries to which they had come to carry out Moscow's orders. The range of those activities varied, and their consequences were many and often decisive for local Communist movements.

First there was the job of keeping Zinoviev and Lenin informed about what was happening within the movement in a given country, with special attention paid to the revolutionary worth of its leaders and their loyalty to the Comintern. This work sometimes consisted in simple helping with documentation, as when Lenin in 1920 requested Heller to dig him up some quotations needed for his attack on Filippo Turati, and later on Claudio Treves.[33] But this reporting task took on major political importance when the emissary's written or oral reports to Moscow were accepted by Lenin and Zinoviev as the basis of their reasoning and decisions. Giuseppe Berti, the secretary for the Italian Communist youth in the early days of the movement, uses the example of his own country to illustrate the importance, during the first half of 1920, of the selective and partial information transmitted by Liubarsky, which Moscow took to be complete and objective: "Lenin's same critical line, in his little book *L'Estremismo* [*"Left-Wing" Communism*], with regard to the various trends among Italian Socialists, with regard to Serrati on the one hand, Bordiga on the other . . ., his utter silence, in that same note of his on Italy, concerning the group putting out the journal *L'Ordine Nuovo* [*The New Order*]. . ., then his very favorable judgment of them barely two or three months after publication of *L'Estremismo* . . . show what great practical importance the reports of the Comintern emissaries had assumed."[34]

In 1919 and 1920, when Lenin had more confidence in these emissaries than in the local Communists, and when the emissaries were in more or less regular touch with Moscow while the foreign Communist leaders mostly were not, any deterioration in the personal relations between the man from Moscow and a national Communist leader was enough to produce direct repercussions in the political sphere. The emissary could depict the country's Communist leader in the most unflattering light possible, which is exactly what happened in Italy, as attested by Berti himself (and later corroborated by Paul Levi in a statement on this same problem of the relations between the Italian leader and the Russian representative): "For a while, Niccolini [Liubarsky] lived right in Serrati's house, and his personal relations with him—at first good, then bad— finally started to be reflected in his reports to the Executive Committee of the Comintern on the Italian political situation and on the situation within the Italian Socialist Party." [35]

Then there was the job of political supervision and direction of the Communist nucleus in the country in which the emissary was carrying on his activities. While his powers of decision were vast, his responsibilities with respect to the local Communist movement were nil. Arriving with an official mandate, the emissaries were in contact with a small number of the country's Communist leaders but had nothing to do with the party rank and file. Consequently, they were not subject to the obligations that weighed upon the local Communist leaders. The emissary was not obliged to account for his actions to any group or agency within the party, nor was he subject to its control as the local leaders were. It was a one-way street. The first echelon was the national leadership, who were answerable to the emissary from Moscow (but not vice versa); the second echelon was the emissary himself, answerable to Lenin and Zinoviev (but never vice versa). The national leaders were not permitted to know the contents of the emissary's reports to Moscow, nor the full text of the directives that Moscow sent to the emissary.

The multiple activities of the emissaries were of interest to the local leadership in that they taught the latter certain elementary rules of Bolshevism, such as the rudiments of clandestine operation, promotion of factionalism within organizations still in the hands of the Socialists, the strengthening of one's own faction within the Communist ranks, the penetration of the ranks of adversaries, the Communist attitude toward Syndicalism, parliamentarianism, party centralism, and so on. It is certain that Moscow's first emissaries did have knowledge of these matters, even if most of them had not acquired it as members of the Bolshevik Party. It is no less certain that Europe's first Communist leaders (with the exception of the German Spartacists) were complete strangers to these concepts, a deficiency which they had to rectify as soon as possible, since these very rules were destined to form an integral part of the life of the Comintern.

In view of Europe's political situation in 1919-20, the emissaries from Moscow were to be primarily concerned with the problem of the relations between Socialists, in the usual sense of the word, and the new Communist sympathizers. Their next job was to lay down the political line for the Communist faction already functioning within the Socialist Party as a whole. Thus, in Italy in October 1919, Degot formed such a Communist faction within the Socialist Party, though it was an affiliate member of the Comintern. Two of his principal lieutenants were Nicola Bombacci, secretary of the Socialist Party, and Egidio Gennari, a former party secretary, while the party's real leader, Giacinto Serrati, was pushed aside. At the Bologna Socialist congress, Degot drew up a declaration in the name of the Comintern, which was read to the congress by Bombacci and released to the press over the opposition of Serrati, as Degot has reported: "Through Bombacci the matter of the declaration was submitted to the Party's Central Committee, and it was only on orders from the latter that Serrati published it." [36]

Within the French Socialist Party, another Comintern emissary, "Lorenzo Vanini," who attended the Strasbourg Congress in February 1920, worked in close cooperation with two of the leaders of the Committee for the Third International, F. Loriot and B. Souvarine. After the congress, he took them to Germany to make their first contact with the Comintern's Secretariat for Western Europe in Berlin. [37] A little later, in December 1920, a third Comintern emissary, Abramovich, was present at the congress in Tours, where he kept close watch on the doings of the Communist group that brought about the Socialist split. Other Moscow emissaries were present at the founding of the party in other countries, too, whether before establishment of the Comintern (like Radek in Berlin, or Sunitsa in Vienna) or afterwards (like Borodin in Mexico in September of 1919, when he delivered a message in the name of the Comintern.) [38]

Once a Communist party had joined the Comintern, the emissary posted to it participated personally in the work of its governing body, as in Germany, for instance, where Marchlewski,

Broński, and "Thomas" attended the meetings of the German Communist Party's Central Committee, a fact which Thomas reports in his memoirs in these terms:

> In my capacity as the "eye of Moscow," that is as emissary of the Executive Committee of the Communist International and of the Central Committee of the Russian Communist Party, I regularly attended the meetings of the German Communist Party's Central Committee. . . . I sent regular reports to the Central Committee [of the Russian Communist Party], in which I frankly described the situation within the German Communist Party and included information about some of its militants. . . . These reports were considered to be highly secret. Since they were to be read only by Lenin, Zinoviev, and the members of the Little Bureau of the International, I deemed it not only my right but my duty to speak openly and conceal nothing. [39]

The major decisions governing the life of the Comintern's most important sections were often determined by the will of an emissary imposing his viewpoint through the simple fact that he represented the authority of Moscow. Two eloquent examples of this come to mind. The first involved Italy toward the end of 1919 and the beginning of 1920, when before the leadership of the Communist faction within the Socialist Party, composed of two Russians and two Italians, the Italian Bombacci addressed the Russian Degot, "in a voice trembling with emotion": "Comrade, you alone can save the situation. The former head of the government, Nitti, has proposed to us Socialists in utmost secrecy that we participate in a parliamentary coup d'état that will proclaim a democratic republic and remove the king. Serrati is in agreement. Tomorrow the question will be definitely decided at the Party's Central Committee meeting. I am very eager to know your opinion so that I may announce it to the meeting." [40] This, according to his own memoirs, is what Degot replied: "In the name of the Comintern you can tell the Party's Central Committee that any participation in this coup d'état is a betrayal of the working class, which is unthinkable. Such 'revolutions' obscure the revolutionary class consciousness of the working masses, and in this situation it matters little who sits on the throne, Nitti or the king." [41] And Degot added: "This view, as I later learned, prevailed with the Party's Central Committee." [42] While no attempt will be made here to assess the value of Nitti's proposal, the future was soon to show that, notwithstanding Degot's position, it mattered very much who headed the government, for if Nitti had ruled in place of the king, and if, instead of the splitting of the Italian Socialist movement, a united Socialist bloc had supported that democratic republic, Fascism could not have been imposed so easily less than two years later.

The second case involved Germany, also in 1920, when the German Communist Party was divided over whether to let the KAPD into the Comintern as a fellow-traveler party, a problem which was resolved as follows, according to Paul Levi, the party chairman: "I wish to say further that this decision [to admit the KAPD] was not worked out by a member of the Central Committee, but by the representative of the Executive Committee, who in that capacity expressed his opinion concerning the solution. The Central Committee declared itself in agreement."[43]

There was an enormous discrepancy between the decisive role played in 1919 and 1920 by the first Comintern emissaries and the humble roles that they had played until then within the Russian revolutionary movement. In the autumn of 1918, Y. S. Reich (Thomas) was a simple functionary at the Soviet embassy in Bern, in charge of putting out the official bulletin *Russische Nachrichten* (*Russian News*). A year later he was head of the Comintern's Secretariat for Western Europe, which kept watch over the German Communist Party, the most important Communist Party in Europe, and submitted confidential reports about such top-ranking Communists as Paul Levi. In the autumn of 1918 Liubarsky, too, was a functionary at the same embassy. A year later, he was playing an influential role in Europe's first mass Socialist Party to have joined the Comintern, the Italian party, and his reports shaped the attitude of Lenin and Zinoviev in their growing hostility toward Serrati. Abramovich and Degot, low-level Bolshevik militants in 1919-20, emerged in France and Italy as key personalities in the relations between Moscow and the Communist leadership of those countries.

The fact that these emissaries were suddenly thrust so high up in the hierarchy would not have been so serious if they had had the talents and abilities needed to play their new roles. But many of them did not. As regards Abramovich, for example, all who knew him were unanimous in calling his intellectual and political abilities mediocre. Alfred Rosmer's opinion of "Ivan," whom he described as a simple Comintern "courier," actually referred to Abramovich: "While I could understand that Moscow might wish to use as couriers only people who were safe and sure, what I saw of this second- or even third-level Bolshevik made a disagreeable impression on me." [44] G. Berti, who, unlike Rosmer, never broke with the Comintern, likewise judged harshly the Comintern's first two emissaries to Italy, with whom he collaborated: "But otherwise these people were mediocre (sometimes very mediocre), as in 1920, the decisive year in the crisis of the Italian labor movement, when the Communist International was represented in Italy mainly by Niccolini (Liubarsky) and Chiarini (Cain Haller)." [45] *

The situation grew complicated when within a country a conflict broke out among these emissaries and ultimately involved the local Communist leaders. In 1919 and 1920, prior to the Second Comintern Congress, such conflicts were not uncommon. Thus, in Germany the Communist extreme left, which Lenin was getting ready to condemn, had the support of a Russian emissary. From prison, Radek reacted vigorously against that attitude: "Comrade Zaks-Gladnev, who was then working in Germany, strayed off to these left-communist positions and mixed them all up. I immediately set about writing a pamphlet on the development of the German revolution and tasks of the Communist Party." [46] In mid-1919 Paul Levi informed Zinoviev of these brawls among the Soviet emissaries, who supported conflicting trends in the German revolutionary movement: "Repeatedly here recently we have had to witness some very disagreeable spats among the Russian comrades, in which we ourselves took no active part. We have sent you a special letter and telegram concerning this." [47]

In Italy, too, discord flared between Liubarsky and Degot. Degot had worked from the beginning (since the autumn of 1919) with the Communist nucleus in the Italian Socialist Party (Bom-

*Berti's way of spelling "Chiarini's" real name—Cain Haller—is at odds with the brief biography as printed in Lenin's *Polnoe sobranie sochinenii* (5th edition, vol. 51, Moscow, 1965, p. 490), where the name appears as A. M. Heller. We have used the Soviet spelling in this work. In his book *Antonio Gramsci and the Origins of Italian Communism* (Stanford, 1967, p. 262) John M. Cammett writes: "Professor Giuseppe Berti has recently informed me that Chiarini's real name was Chaim Heller. . . ."

bacci and Gennari) and also with Amadeo Bordiga and his group, while Liubarsky initially was very close to Serrati; both Moscow emissaries were completely ignorant of the activities of the *Ordine Nuovo* group in Turin. Degot relates in his memoirs how he chanced upon that journal in early 1920 and had Antonio Gramsci come to Rome to establish contact with this Turin Communist group. When in late 1919 publication was started of a review entitled *Communismo—Rivista della Terza Internationale*, Liubarsky ("Niccolini") published in it a polemic against the conceptions of the workers' councils and factory committees as set forth in *Ordine Nuovo*.[48] Shortly thereafter, having now established contact with Gramsci, Degot sent his first favorable report about the *Ordine Nuovo* to Zinoviev and Lenin. Since relations between Serrati and Liubarsky deteriorated after April 1920, Liubarsky started to work with Gramsci and his group.

Sometimes it happened that the Comintern emissaries on the spot supported the viewpoint of the national party leadership on one or another matter and not that of Lenin and Zinoviev, who were not in direct touch with the country. This was the case when the German Communist Party, opposing Lenin's intention to let the KAPD into the Comintern as a fellow-traveler party, was supported by the Comintern emissary. Before his break with the Comintern, Paul Levi gave this account, veiling with the pseudonym of "Schulz" the identity of the head of the Russian delegation in Berlin: "And Schulz himself said that, 'We Russians that are here shall send a joint letter to Moscow urging them not to admit the KAPD for anything in the world.' The next day Schulz was arrested, and three days later came the news of their admission."[49]

If the initial situation gave rise to disagreements between the emissaries active in the same country, even though nearly all of them were of Russian origin and subject to Bolshevik discipline (which was still little known and not practiced by the Communists in the West), there was all the more reason for conflict between these first emissaries and the European leaders of the Communist movement. The cause was everywhere the same. These special Moscow envoys, armed with their mandates from Lenin and Zinoviev, behaved like lords and masters toward the local Communist chiefs, who for their part showed little inclination to submit automatically to the emissaries. After all they knew their country and their movement. Shortly before November 7, 1917, several of these Western leaders had occasion to meet with Lenin personally in Switzerland (among them P. Levi, F. Loriot, and G. Serrati), and Lenin certainly did not behave toward them as his underlings were now doing. These first conflicts, initially kept secret, prefigured what was to happen in 1921, when they would surface in the Communist press. In two cases, first secretly and then publicly, a veritable "class struggle" broke out within the Comintern between the Moscow emissaries, who behaved like representatives of the Communist ruling class, and the Western Communist chiefs, who had no wish to be treated like a subject class. In France two of the first Comintern emissaries, Abramovich and Vanini, had been the subject of complaints addressed to Moscow by Fernand Loriot and the Committee for the Third International, as Boris Souvarine has reported: "Both were recalled to Moscow when Loriot and I so requested after having disagreements with them. We were not going to take orders or submit to pressure. We wanted nothing more than to work with the Moscow envoys, but we refused to let them have the final say." [50] The Abramovich case degenerated into a scandal after his check affair and subsequent arrest in January 1921. Even after he was expelled from France, ten months after his arrest, Emile Bestel came to Moscow as a representative of the French Communist Party and demanded on December 2, 1921, of the Executive Committee Presidium that an inquiry be held into the Abramovich matter: "Concerning the Zalewski case, the Directing Committee of the French Party has requested an investigation in order to obtain from the Executive Committee a precise statement regarding Zalewski's position and responsibilities." [51] The request was granted, and on December 8 the Comintern Secretariat informed the *comité directeur* ("Directing Committee") of the French Communist Party: "In response to the French Party's request for an inquiry into the Zalewski case, the Executive Committee has appointed a special board, to include the two French representatives to the Executive Committee, which will examine Zalewski so as to permit this matter to be settled once and for all." [52]

A serious conflict also developed in Berlin between Paul Levi and the head of the Secretariat for Western Europe, "Thomas," as well as between Serrati and Liubarsky in Italy. Both times the cause was the same: reaction of the German and Italian leaders against the operational methods that Moscow was using behind their backs. In both cases the pretext was the same: these leaders had learned in Moscow of the confidential reports in which the emissaries had discussed them in derogatory terms. As to the conflict between Levi and Thomas, the latter reported what had just happened at the Second Comintern Congress:

> [Levi] was at Comintern headquarters in an office of Radek's, the latter having become one of the secretaries of the Third International. I never found out what they were talking about. I know only that Radek opened a drawer and said that he had there my secret reports on the German Communist Party. I even believe that Radek read him a passage from one of them. Then, without closing the drawer again, he went out. Left to himself, Levi picked up the reports and started to read them. Among them were those that described the members of the Central Committee of the German Communist Party and in particular Levi himself, reports which had especially interested Lenin and which he had requested me to continue sending. . . . . At the first meeting of the German Communist Party's Central Committee, Levi gave a detailed report on his trip to Moscow, adding that he must end his report on a personal note. He then brought up my reports. . . . He concluded by demanding that I be censured and that a request be sent to the Communist International and to the Central Committee of the Russian Communist Party that I be recalled to Moscow.[53]

There followed a big argument involving Lenin (who, according to Thomas, defended him but was furious at Radek), Zinoviev, Clara Zetkin, and Levi himself. In the end, Thomas was not recalled nor even prevented from participating in the Central Committee meetings, but Levi was not likely to forget the incident.

A few months later, Levi had occasion to draw Zinoviev's attention to an identical case, this time involving Serrati and "Comrade Carlo": "Extremely severe personal tension exists between Serrati and Carlo. The tension stems from the fact that Comrade Serrati, as has been true of other comrades, while in Moscow got to see some reports concerning Italy which Comrade Carlo had sent in and Serrati says that they were a far cry from the political and human relationship of trust that had existed between him and Comrade Carlo up to the time of his trip to Russia."[54]

Exposed to the double danger of conflict with the local Communist leaders and discovery by the "class enemy" (the police), the first Comintern emissaries dared not tarry long in any one country, except for Thomas in Berlin. This same element of instability characterized the beginnings of even the Comintern organization itself. As regards the construction of its secret network, whose mechanism was still being "warmed up," a few breakdowns were more or less inevitable and some of the emissaries fell into the hands of the police. That was to happen less often in the future, when the secret network was better perfected and the police less able to discover the emissaries. The first emissaries' uncertain stay in their assigned countries was also a sign that Moscow had not yet established its authority over the local Communist chiefs, who in 1919-20 could still get away with disagreeing with the Moscow envoys, protesting their behavior to Moscow, and demanding their recall sometimes with success—luxuries that were to grow rarer and rarer and disappear altogether in the not too distant future.

THE WESTERN EUROPEAN SECRETARIAT (W.E.S.): BACKGROUND

Lenin and his collaborators rarely swung from one extreme to the other in their assessment of events as quickly as they did in 1919, from over-optimism concerning the imminence of revolution in Europe to profound pessimism about their ability to stay in power in Russia. On the day after the creation of the Comintern they were prophesying the early spread of revolution through Europe, but several months later, after the revolutions in Bavaria and Hungary had been crushed and no others immediately followed, the revolutionary horizon had clouded over. Moreover, no mass Communist parties had been formed anywhere in Europe. But one fact towered above all others: Communist Russia itself was in the throes of civil war and menaced by what was called the intervention of the fourteen powers. Elena Stasova, the secretary of the Bolshevik Party's Central Committee at the time, wrote: "1919 was a very difficult year. The offensive of the fourteen powers against the Soviet republic created a situation so dangerous that the Party might be obliged to go underground if the forces of internal counterrevolution and the foreign interventionists temporarily got the upper hand. So it was necessary to make up pass-ports for all the members of the Central Committee, for Lenin in particular. We also had to assure that the Party would have materi-al means at its disposal." [55]

The month of October 1919 was especially full of dangers for the Lenin regime at two key points, Petrograd and Moscow. Yu-denich's offensive against the former capital had advanced to the point where Krasnoe Selo was taken, and the Bolsheviks had to rush Trotsky to the Petrograd front to relieve Zinoviev, who had panicked. Lenin deemed it entirely possible that the city would have to be abandoned to the Whites. On the other hand, Denikin's offensive against Moscow was forcing him to envisage evacuation of the new capital too, as Rutgers reported: "On October 14, 1919, the day of my departure, at 3:00 in the morning, Lenin called me in for a final talk. Denikin was just then threatening Orel, and all during our conversation Lenin was in touch with the front over a direct line. He was constantly called to the telephone. The situation that night was very serious and turbulent, and Lenin told me that, if Tula were taken, Moscow would fall too. His words to me were, 'If on your way you hear that Tula has been taken, you can tell our foreign comrades that we shall probably have to fall back to the Urals.' " [56]

Despite these dramatic interludes, Lenin never for a moment forgot about the international Communist movement and under-took two initiatives to breathe life into the Comintern in Europe and establish the first regular ties between Communists in the West and the Bolsheviks of Russia. Thus, October 1919 saw the birth of two branches of the Comintern in Europe, the Secretariat for Western Europe or W.E.S. (the abbreviation of its German name *Westeuropäisches Sekretariat*) in Berlin and the Western Bureau in Amsterdam. It was Lenin, too, who selected the trusted emissary who was to go to Berlin, Y. S. Reich–"Thomas" and the one to go to Amsterdam, S. J. Rutgers. The two left Russia almost at the same time after discussing with Lenin the tasks that they were to accomplish in Europe.

The Comintern was like an iceberg, its visible portion immeas-urably smaller and less important than its huge hidden part. The creation and operation of the Western European Secretariat illus-trate perfectly the nature of the Comintern's secret life from its beginnings. Even before officially and publicly instructing foreign Communists, at the Second World Congress in 1920, to combine their legal and illegal operations, the Bolsheviks furnished them a graphic example in the organization and functioning of the Western European Secretariat. Knowledge of its existence was to be restricted to the inner circle, that is, neither the public nor even the Communist press was to be informed. There were to be no written traces of this secretariat, and the error would not be made of trying to bureaucratize or institutionalize it. Even official Communist literature scarcely mentioned the existence and certainly never the activities of the Western European Secretariat. During the years from 1919 through 1921 the German Communist Party published, far and away, more material than any other Communist party in Europe. It held more congresses than any other (there were no less than seven in the period from December 1918 to August 1921), but it is difficult to find in that material so much as a whisper about the Western European Secretariat, except in a speech by Clara Zetkin at the German Party's Third Congress in February 1920 and in a brief debate at the Fourth Congress in April 1920. During 1920 and especially 1921 the German question was the top item on the Comintern agenda, but its many directives, circulars, and manifestoes contained no mention of the Western European Secretariat. In the voluminous proceedings of the Comintern's Second Congress, held in 1920, it is referred to only twice, the first time in a rather critical remark made by Louis Fraina, a delegate from the United States, and the second time by Paul Levi, in a single allusion. The role of silence was strictly observed, even by the leaders who broke, as Levi did in 1921. In his two pamphlets against the "March action" in which he took the Moscow emissaries to task, he made no reference to the W.E.S., to which he was intimately connected.

Here, then, from the very year of the Comintern's founding, we have one of the first traps that have been laid for the historian of that organization. Since the official communist literature of the period does not speak of the W.E.S., the historian is led to ignore it, while in truth the mere fact that something is not mentioned in Comintern texts does not remotely signify that it did not exist. It is therefore not surprising that the Western historiography on the

Comintern and German Communist Party, based on the official public literature, has almost completely ignored this institution.*

ESTABLISHMENT AND MAKEUP OF THE W.E.S.

In the summer of 1919, when Y.S. Reich was having trouble finding material to publish in the second and subsequent issues of the Comintern organ, he was suddenly summoned by the head of the Bolshevik Party and Soviet government: "Lenin called me at night to come to his house and told me straight out 'You have to go to Germany.'"[57] But it was not until six or eight weeks later that Reich was finally able to leave for Germany, where he arrived probably around the end of October or the beginning of November 1919, supplied with false papers, as Radek recounts in his memoirs: "He came to see me in jail, posing as the correspondent

---

*The volume *Der deutsche Kommunismus. Dokumente*, edited by Hermann Weber (Cologne-Berlin, 1963), which with its 650 pages and 200 separate texts currently represents the most detailed work on the subject, does not once mention the W.E.S. In the most voluminous of all collections of documents concerning the Comintern, *The Communist International, 1919-1943. Documents.* Volume I, 1919-22 (London, 1956), selected and edited by Jane Degras, in over 460 pages of texts and comments the editor devotes only two brief sentences to that Secretariat, and there are but two furtive references in the reprinted Comintern documents. However, it would be a serious error in historical judgment and interpretation to conclude merely because there are few writings about the W.E.S. that it was of little or no importance in the history of the Comintern. Yet that is what E. H. Carr, author of one of the most voluminous works on the history of Soviet Russia, has done. He devotes no more than a single page to the W.E.S., and he lists the sources in which he found those initials: a manifesto published in the periodical *Kommunisticheskii Internatsional*; a footnote in a book by Ruth Fischer (which is incorrect, moreover); a speech by Clara Zetkin at the Third Congress of the German Communist Party; and an allusion by a speaker at the Second Comintern Congress. The evidence being neither great nor accurate, he promptly draws from it several shaky conclusions: "The main function of the Secretariat was to publish information about the progress and achievements of the Soviet regime in Russia. But it seems to have had little contact with Moscow, except for the receipt of official Comintern documents, and to have enjoyed no political status or importance." (*The Bolshevik Revolution, 1917-1923*, New York, 1961, vol. 3, pp. 135-136.) The author, moreover, presents "Thomas" as "a Bavarian Communist"; obviously he has confused Y. S. Reich-"Thomas" of the W.E.S. with Otto Thomas, who in 1919 edited in Munich the Communist newspaper *Neue Zeitung*.

of some nonexistent Jewish newspaper. . . . When the guard went out, Thomas told me who he was and explained in detail what he proposed to do. Initially I looked upon his plans with mistrust, discovering only later what enormous energy and organizational talent this man possessed." [58]

Y.S. Reich's first job—he would not become known as Thomas until a few months later—was to put together a team to run the W.E.S. both politically and administratively (conspiratorially and financially). Since the Comintern itself did not yet have any administrative structure with clearly defined functions and a scale of official titles, this W.E.S. team was born of an improvised mixture of cliquishness and the personal prestige enjoyed by certain of the Communist leaders. Its members were drawn from the only two sources available, the most trusted of the top German Communists and the Moscow emissaries sent to Western Europe. To the first category belonged three of the most prominent of the German Communist Party leaders: Paul Levi, titular and actual head of the Party after the assassinations of Rosa Luxemburg, Karl Liebknecht, and Leo Jogiches; August Thalheimer, chief Party theoretician and a member of its governing body since the founding congress; and Clara Zetkin, much respected in the German Party because of her past and her age. As for the emissaries from Moscow, they were quite numerous in 1919-20. Some of them, such as Abramovich ("Albrecht") and Borodin, did not stay long in Berlin, while others, such as Broński, Guralsky, and Wolf, worked there for fairly lengthy periods. A number of other professional revolutionaries, who had become Comintern emissaries or collaborators of the W.E.S., showed up in Berlin from time to time: for example, Degot, on his way back from Italy; Mineff (Vanini), coming in from France; Voja Vujović, a Serbian Communist student active in France and elsewhere; Karl Frank, an Austrian Communist who installed himself in Berlin and worked for the W.E.S. On the German side, two other important figures were associated with the W.E.S. from the outset: Willi Münzenberg, who had been in touch with Lenin since the closing period of Lenin's wartime stay in Switzerland and who returned to Berlin and founded the Communist Youth International, and Dr. Eduard Fuchs, a lawyer reputed to be a great art connoisseur and the author of books on the problem of mores in society. Fuchs played a major role in the secret section of the German Communist Party and in the W.E.S., but of that there are even fewer written traces than of the W.E.S. itself. In fact, as "Thomas" reports, Dr. Fuchs was treasurer of the W.E.S. from the very beginning. He served as liaison man between important foreign Communists, such as Borodin and Roy, and the German Communist leaders. He took part in the Second Comintern Congress in 1920, though his name does not appear on the official list of the delegates (yet two interruptions by him at the July 29 session are mentioned in the minutes of the congress, and we have the testimony of W. Bringolf, who made the trip to and from Moscow with him). He sat on the Directing Committee (Zentrale) of the German Communist Party, as proved by a letter from J. T. Murphy, an important British Communist, dated December 14, 1920, in which Fuchs and Felix Wolf appear on the list.[59] This entrusting of important functions to secret party members and publicly non-party "men of confidence"—a practice inherited from Bolshevism—had perhaps its first perfect illustration in Western Europe with the case of Dr. Fuchs, but it was later to become an integral part of the Comintern's operating procedure.

Notwithstanding the participation of several eminent German Communists in the W.E.S., there is not the slightest doubt that that entity was created at the wish of the Russians and was an instrument serving them within the framework of the international Communist movement. This is why, whenever any discord erupted between the German Communist leaders and the W.E.S., the first reaction of the Germans was to criticize the latter as a Russian agency grafted onto the German Communist organization—which is what the KAPD did at its founding congress on April 4 and 5, 1920, in Berlin, when the speaker on the first item of the agenda, "Our Attitude Toward the Third International," expressed himself in these terms: "How did the Western European Secretariat come into being? Representatives were sent from Moscow to tell us of the Russian experience so that we might profit from it. . . . We who were in a position to observe the doings of these persons at close hand were often astonished at how little they knew of the realities and true situation in Germany, and at how little they bothered to familiarize themselves with the German scene."[60]

THE POLITICAL ROLE OF THE W.E.S. IN GERMANY

When Reich (Thomas) came to set up a branch of the Comintern in Berlin, west of the line from Warsaw to Vienna there existed in Europe but a single Communist party, that of Germany, decapitated by the death of its three leaders. That party itself would collapse after the events starting in January 1919, which exposed it to attacks from the police, as evidenced by the following scraps of information from the weeks preceding Thomas's arrival. The national party conference, meeting secretly in Frankfurt am Main on August 16 and 17, 1919, could take no decisions because the delegates were no longer elected in accordance with the bylaws; on September 17 the criminal police confiscated the party's principal cash assets and arrested several militants present at the time, Rosi Wolfstein among them; the party Zentrale, always underground, was transferred to Eisenach, and late in October it was established at Frankfurt am Main, after the conclusion of the Second Party Congress in Heidelberg. It was at this moment that Reich arrived and recorded his first impression: "I reached Berlin at the end of autumn in 1919. There was no Communist organization there worthy of the name. The arrests have created havoc." [61]

Having come with a mandate from Lenin and Zinoviev, like the two others who had preceded him, Broński and Wolf, the first job of the new Moscow emissary was to straighten out the situation in the German party. Henceforth these three emissaries were to participate in directing the affairs of the German Communist Party and take part in the meetings of its governing body on a level with the German members. They had, however, the enormous advantage of having the same powers of decision as the German members but not the same obligations, they being responsible not to the German Communist organization, as were the German members (who might not be reelected), but to the Comintern leaders in Moscow. These directing members of the W.E.S. took part in the wider party meetings, such as the Second Party Congress at Heidelberg on October 20-24, 1919, when the split with the Left occurred, and a representative of the Third International (probably

Broński, for Reich had not yet arrived) on two occasions attacked the ideas of Fritz Wolffheim, the faction leader of the Left opposition, which was about to leave the German Communist Party. [62]

The split that took place at Heidelberg automatically complicated the task of the Comintern delegation to Berlin, for henceforth there would be two Communist parties in that country, the KPD (Spartacists) and the KAPD (Communist Workers' Party of Germany). That would soon ignite a controversy between the Comintern's Executive Committee (actually Lenin, Radek, and Zinoviev), who wanted to let that party in as a "fellow-traveler," and Paul Levi, who was opposed to this. During 1920 this matter evolved into a veritable test of strength between the German Communist leadership and the Russian leaders of the Comintern, who were desirous of winning back the numerous militants who had left the German Communist Party at the Heidelberg congress. On learning of the split, Lenin expressed regret at the loss of all those Communists. Radek, who was on the scene in Berlin, did not succeed in alerting Lenin to this impending development because his letter was unforeseeably delayed in the mails. But Lenin and Radek, when the latter got back to Moscow, set about trying to attract the KAPD into the Comintern, and when they did get it admitted as a fellow-traveling member, opposition was expressed simultaneously by the leaders of the German Communist Party and those of the left wing of the Independent Socialist Party (USPD) who were ready to join the Comintern, as Zinoviev informed the Executive Committee at a meeting in November 1920: "The KAPD has applied to the Communist International for admission as a sympathizing or fellow-traveling party with the right to participate in deliberations and to vote, and it is my opinion that, in the event that this party does not take part in the unifying congress, we are obliged to accept its application. I must add that the Central Committees of the two parties, that is, of the German Communist Party and of the new independent Left-Socialist party, have directed me to convey a message to the Executive Committee expressing their disagreement with our viewpoint. I consider that attitude mistaken." [63]

The Executive Committee disregarded this double opposition of the German Communist Party and the left wing of the USPD, which were to merge into a single party in December 1920.

Throughout 1920 the Comintern maintained contact with the KAPD, after the Second World Congress as well as before, through the W.E.S. The more these two national groups permitted themselves to express disagreement with the Executive Committee, the more that entity's shadow in Berlin, the W.E.S., had to follow the line laid down by Moscow. The Executive Committee, or more precisely the Bolshevik crew in charge, would succeed in staying in touch with the KAPD without letting the German Communist Party leaders know about it, just as later on, in the autumn of 1920, it would admit the KAPD to the Comintern over the German Communist Party's opposition. But both times that party registered a protest, which did not remain secret. Thus, at the Fourth Congress of the German Communist Party in April 1920, the question was raised as to the strange fact that the German Communist Party representative in the W.E.S. was not kept informed about important matters already known to the KAPD, even though the latter was not a member of the Comintern. To that, Fritz Heckert, in the name of the Zentrale, would reply that there were ties between the KAPD and the W.E.S. outside the framework of the German Communist Party: "In part the W.E.S. is located where the KAPD has a suboffice, and the latter is better informed concerning various W.E.S. affairs than we ourselves. Moreover, a comrade employed by the W.E.S. holds a leading position in the KAPD."[64] As for the decision of the Executive Committee to admit the KAPD delegation to the Second World Congress before securing acceptance of the KAPD as a fellow-traveling member party, Paul Levi did not hesitate to express his displeasure: "Criticism from comrades so experienced as the Russians are is extremely valuable to us, and no one is going to turn a deaf ear to them. But I do think, too, that it is our duty to speak openly of certain matters that have not been to our liking."[65]

So the W.E.S. had its troubles in getting the two feuding groups, the KPD and KAPD, to accept and abide by Moscow's directives. But during the year from the end of 1919 to the end of 1920 there was yet a third movement that came out in favor of the Comintern, namely the left wing of the USPD. Where the KAPD was concerned, it was a matter of holding on to its militants for the Comintern even if they were already lost to the German Communist Party. As for the left wing of the USPD, the goal was to win it over to both the Comintern and the German Communist Party by merging it with the latter. The German Communist Party leaders had to be handled with kid gloves while Moscow was affecting the rapprochement with the KAPD so strenuously opposed by Paul Levi and his friends, for their help would be necessary in bringing in the left wing of the USPD, a step which Levi had been advocating since the end of 1919.

Shortly after it was set up, the W.E.S. began talks with the USPD. After its national congress, held in Leipzig in 1919, at which the existence of two factions, one pro-Soviet, the other anti-Soviet, was the dominant fact, on December 13 the USPD sent a letter to the Communist International inviting it to "a conference at which all the revolutionary parties will discuss the makeup of an International ready to fight." In its reply of January 15, 1920, the W.E.S. turned this proposal down; its policy was not to promote any international grouping outside the already existing Comintern but to bring about a split in the USPD and draw away most of its members: "So the issue here is not that of bringing different parties together in a new International but of deciding whether the USPD wants to join the Third International, and for that no international negotiations are necessary. Talks between the USPD and the Third International are all that is needed." [66]

Negotiations between the W.E.S., acting for Moscow, and the USPD leadership were indeed begun, but again the official leaders of the German Communist Party and their representatives at the W.E.S. were not informed about all that went on. This gave rise to a lively exchange at the Fourth Congress of the German Communist Party in April 1920, when a delegate asked a question about the secret negotiations between Moscow and the USPD being carried on through the W.E.S. without informing the German Communist Party representatives assigned to the W.E.S. That question was recorded in the minutes in an indirect form: "Wolf-Hamburg asked whether the reply from the Executive Committee in Moscow to the USPD had not long since been received by the Western European Secretariat and why it had not yet been published. He inquired further whether at a meeting of the Western European Secretariat it had not been expressly decided not to publish the reply because it too severely criticized the USPD." [67] The answers given by several of the German Communist Party leaders were embarrassed and contradictory. Thalheimer (referred to in the minutes as "representative of the party Zentrale at the W.E.S.") declared that "the facts are completely unknown to me," while Eberlein asserted that "the Executive Committee's reply was disclosed to us at noon yesterday by the Western European Secretariat."[68] For her part, Clara Zetkin (referred to as "representative of the party Zentrale at the W.E.S.") pleaded ignorance: "I find that until now we have had no knowledge of the answer." Paul Levi (also referred to as "representative of the party Zentrale at the W.E.S.") said in turn: "I know nothing of the affair other than that the USPD said that the reply has been received."[69] But at the end of the congress Levi returned to the incident, which he sought to dismiss with the statement: "The only concrete fact that emerges is that the Secretary withheld a letter from us for a while. The rest seems to be idle gossip."[70]

The contacts between the W.E.S. and the USPD were maintained in the months that followed, eventuating first in the dispatch of a USPD delegation to the Second Comintern Congress and then to the USPD congress at Halle in October 1920, where most of the participants went over to Communism.

THE W.E.S. AND THE COMMUNIST YOUTH INTERNATIONAL

Apart from these three movements on the extreme German Left, which claimed support from and allegiance to the Comintern, and with which the W.E.S. had its political problems, there existed in Berlin during 1919 and 1920 a fourth organization of a different nature, the Communist Youth International, known in Russian as the Kommunisticheskii Internatsional Molodezhi (KIM). It was established at a congress in Berlin held November 20-26, 1919, the very moment at which the W.E.S. was coming into being. From the beginning, indeed even at the founding congress, a divergence of views separated Willi Münzenberg, the founder of the KIM, and Lazar Shatskin, the Soviet Youth representative. "While Münzenberg was of the opinion that the youth organization must remain largely independent, Shatskin held that it must be absolutely subordinated."[71] A compromise was worked out, and though Münzenberg was a member of the team that ran the W.E.S., relations between the KIM and W.E.S. remained strained, as would be demonstrated at the first plenary session of the Bureau of the KIM, held June 9-13, 1920.

That meeting had brought together in Berlin a small group of militants all, except for Münzenberg, at the start of revolutionary careers which would take them to the summit of the KIM hierarchy. Apart from Münzenberg, there were future titular and actual leaders of the KIM, men like Voja Vujović (who used the pseudonym Wolf), representing Yugoslavia, Luigi Polano, representing the Italian Communist Youth, Richard Schüller from Austria, and S. Bamatter from Switzerland. In all, delegates of Communist (or still formally called Socialist) youth groups from thirteen countries were in attendance. The W.E.S. was officially represented by two delegates, one who went under the assumed name of Albrecht (Abramovich-Zalewski), the other under the assumed name of Felix (Felix Wolf).

Even in his introductory report on the work of the KIM's Executive Committee, Münzenberg minced no words in his criticism of the W.E.S.: "The work of the Executive Committee was severely impeded by the incredible indifference displayed toward the youth movement by the Western European headquarters of the Communist International, the Western European Secretariat. They repeatedly refused to forward our letters and other items that we sent, or to receive and forward such to us." [72] That Münzenberg was not alone in his attitude can be seen from a condensed version of the official minutes: "Comrade Albrecht of the Western European Secretariat asked to what extent the complaints about lack of support from that quarter were justified. Comrade Schüller from Vienna criticized primarily the activities and policy of the Secretariat in the first months after the congress. . . . Comrade Viktor* spoke about the relationship of the Youth International to the W.E.S., citing for comparison the close cooperation between the party and the youth in Russia. Finally, a controversy developed between the representative of the W.E.S. and members of the

*Viktor was the pseudonym of Joseph Greifenberger, who attended the founding congress of the Communist Youth International in Berlin as a delegate of the Union of Communist Youth of Lithuania and Byelorussia. Cf. article "Les victimes du fascisme lithuanien" in *L'Internationale Communiste*, January 15, 1927.

Executive Committee about the quality of the cooperation hitherto." [73]

The next day, June 10, Albrecht presented his report on the political situation, setting forth the Moscow viewpoint concerning the items on the agenda, particularly those up for debate at the Second Congress of the Communist International: the still uncomprehended role of the dictatorship of the proletariat; the "burning question" of tactics in the work of the different Communist parties; the problem of purging them; the proper attitude toward bourgeois parliamentarianism. It was certainly noticed by his listeners that at the end of his report he stressed "the iron necessity for centralizing the parties." [74]

Though he secured the support of Clara Zetkin in the discussion, Albrecht saw himself criticized by Münzenberg, who declared his disagreement on various points with the International and its Berlin Secretariat: "The tactic used by individual agencies of the Communist International against the centrists was not always a particularly felicitous one. . . . On the question of parliamentarism, a resolution will have to be drawn up in Moscow that defines in principle the participation of the Communist parties but leaves it to the individual parties to make their own decisions in specific cases in accordance with the political and revolutionary situation in their respective countries." [75]

Münzenberg had certainly leveled against the W.E.S. accusations more detailed than was desired to have reproduced in the minutes, judging from the fact that Albrecht and Clara Zetkin immediately took the floor to reply to them, especially to his charge that a mass action scheduled for November 7, 1919, had been sabotaged. Albrecht was evasive in his answer, declaring that on November 7 the W.E.S. was not yet in existence, a statement which elicited some ironic exclamations from the audience. The next speaker, who took the floor in the name of the Communist Youth leadership, Richard Schüller, displayed open hostility toward the W.E.S.: "Complaints about the W.E.S. are quite general, and the situation will definitely have to be changed." The Swedish delegate demanded that the activities of the W.E.S. be "thoroughly investigated" by the Communist International. [76]

This controversy, as it was termed in the official minutes, was characteristic of the state of mind of the pioneers of European Communism. While entirely in accord with the cause of the Bolshevik Revolution, they did not believe that Moscow, or its branch office in Berlin, was competent to make the decisions alone for this or that country and determine what tactics should be followed without taking into account the local situation and the opinion of the Communist national leaders.

POLITICAL ACTIVITY OF THE W.E.S. IN WESTERN EUROPE

From its inception the W.E.S. went well beyond the confines of strictly German affairs and was politically and organizationally active in several other countries of Western Europe. In February 1920 Clara Zetkin was able to present to the Third Congress of the German Communist Party a resolution in the name of the party Zentrale which stressed in these terms the importance of the work already done by the W.E.S.: "The party congress deems it advisable that the Western European Secretariat continue its work in the same manner as hitherto. It expects, above all, that the Western European Secretariat will further develop its relations with France, Italy, England, Switzerland, Scandinavia, and the Danube and Balkan countries, in order to establish live international contacts. . . . The congress declares that the activities of the Western European Secretariat to date have demonstrated that it serves a useful purpose." [77]

Within this framework a restricted initial conference of Europe's Communist leaders was held from November 26 to 29, 1919 in Frankfurt am Main; it was patterned after the secret meetings the Bolsheviks had held before October 1917. It was not publicly announced, nor were the subjects discussed or the site of the conference revealed in the press. Radek, still in Germany but under police surveillance (albeit not very strict surveillance, since he was able to cultivate many contacts both in person and by mail), wrote to Paul Levi on October 15, 1919, concerning the preparations for that international conference: "As far as our conference is concerned, B. said that he or P. should present a report on our situation . . . Since I am authorized to represent the Central Committee of the Russian Communist Party abroad, I can submit it. It would deal with (1) victory of the Entente; (2) the situation in Central Europe; (3) in the Near East; (4) in the Far East; (5) two years of Russian revolution plus one year of the German and Austrian; (6) the economic situation of the Entente countries and of world revolution; (7) tactical conclusions; (8) joint action. I shall have the manuscript ready by November 1." [78]

A few days later Y. S. Reich arrived in Berlin and got in touch with Radek. From there he went to Frankfurt am Main to open and preside over the conference, which brought together: Clara Zetkin, already attached to the W.E.S.; Karl Frank, an Austrian who became a member of the W.E.S. staff; Mieczysław Broński (to whom Radek had referred as B.), also attached to the W.E.S.; Valeriu Marcu, a young Rumanian Communist and friend of Münzenberg's, declared to represent the Balkans; and Sylvia Pankhurst, representing Great Britain.*

According to the brief description that Y.S. Reich has given of the conference, its main purpose was informational. The delegates submitted their reports concerning the countries and regions in which they worked, and Reich spoke on organizational problems in general. He announced the establishment of the W.E.S. in Berlin and the inauguration of the German, French, and English editions of the journal *Communist International*. He also promised material aid to the affiliated groups. A statement of the aims of the W.E.S., drawn up by August Thalheimer, was discussed and adopted, [79] as well as a resolution on Russia and a message of friendship and support to Lenin. "Support of Russia was the main problem facing the conference, also the activities of the Western European Secretariat." [80]

Apart from organizing the Frankfurt conference, the W.E.S. had another mission during early 1920: to complete preparations for the Comintern's Second World Congress on the ideological level

*The French Communist group from the Committee for the Third International was invited to the Frankfurt conference but could not make it. Two of the leaders on that Committee, Fernand Loriot and Boris Souvarine, left for Germany three months later and went to Berlin, where they met Vujović, Borodin, and Zalewski. Loriot and Souvarine had occasion to make the acquaintance of the representatives from the offices in Berlin ("Lorenzo Vanini") and Amsterdam (Henriette Roland-Holst) at the SFIO congress in Strasbourg at the end of February 1920.

and to assure maximum participation by militants from all over Europe. It worked mainly at the second task. As for the political preparations, the W.E.S. set about elaborating some "theses" on a number of problems that were to be discussed at the congress. Thalheimer, the only member of the W.E.S. essentially concerned with questions of ideology, politics, and economics, in January 1920 drew up "the theses on tactics of the Third International in the struggle for dictatorship of the proletariat," which the German edition of the Comintern organ presented with this explanation: "They are now submitted for international discussion. These guiding principles have been formulated by Russian and German Communists working in close cooperation."[81]

As for cooperation between the Russian and German Communists, the Thalheimer "theses" were a rehash of several ideas put forward by Radek, specifically in a pamphlet published shortly before by the W.E.S. As regards international discussion, there was none. These "theses," presented in the German edition of *Communist International* as a tactical platform for submission to the Second Congress, appeared in the Russian edition of that same journal, just as the congress was getting started, under a far more modest description: "We publish this document from the Western European Bureau as material for discussion."[82] But since Lenin by now had drawn up his own "theses" on the "main tasks of the Communist International," the Thalheimer "theses" were not discussed much less resuscitated by Lenin. This was characteristic, for it coincided with the moment when the W.E.S. was beginning to lose its political importance, though retaining its administrative function. Even so, Thomas himself remained high up in the Comintern hierarchy. As late as March of 1922, while he was in Moscow, he took part in the meetings of the Comintern's supreme governing body, the Presidium of the Executive Committee.[83]

THE ADMINISTRATIVE ROLE OF THE W.E.S.

There were two distinct periods in the life of the W.E.S. During the first, which extended from its founding until mid-1920, it played an important political role; during the second it was more and more taken up with its purely administrative functions. In the beginning, some of the business of the Comintern was handled by the W.E.S., whose multiple activities were in sharp contrast to the relative idleness of the Comintern offices in Moscow and Petrograd. During that time, the political and military situation being what it was, the Communist movement in Western Europe, though still virtually in an embryonic state, displayed both ideological and organizational autonomy. Whenever that autonomy resulted in leanings contrary to Moscow's ideas, as happened in Amsterdam and Vienna, the Executive Committee did not hesitate simply to abolish the offending entities. Where no "deviationist" tendencies were in evidence, as in the case of the W.E.S., Moscow would soon succeed in snatching away all political authority and in confining the agency to essentially administrative duties.

From its inception, the W.E.S. had of necessity to set up a team of technicians, couriers, and liaison personnel, whose job it was to transmit or carry out instructions either from Moscow to Berlin or from Berlin to some other place in Europe. The head of this administrative setup was a personage from Soviet Russia, Slivkin, who in 1919—at the time of the proclamation of the Lithuanian Soviet Republic headed by Vikenti Mickievicz-Kapsukas (another future Comintern dignitary)—was named Commissar for Supply.* He appeared in Berlin in 1920 and took charge of organizing communications between the W.E.S. and Moscow, a task which he accomplished quickly and well by a method described in essentially the same terms by all who benefited at the time, such as Thomas on his trip to Russia in 1920, and Victor Serge in 1921, who wrote: "We were a dozen delegates and agents of the International, discreetly and sometimes openly accompanied by a diplomatic courier, Slivkin, a big merry fellow in charge of every imaginable kind of smuggling and who had bribed all the police, customs agents, and border guards along our route." [84]

To play its role effectively, the W.E.S. had to follow from the outset the Bolshevik rules about working legally and illegally at

---

*Proletarskaia revoliutsiia, the official journal for the history of the Bolshevik party, wrote about Slivkin in 1922: "An odious individual in the pleiad of those who succeeded in sneaking in behind Soviet power and Party." No. 8, 1922, p. 84, footnote.

the same time. False papers, false identities, the use of diplomatic and nonpolitical covers, conspiratorial domiciles where hunted militants could take shelter, liaison plans ensuring contact and conversations between underground agents, the use of a middle-class false front as regards residence, dress, and style of life so as not to attract the police attention—all this came into being for the first time in Western Europe thanks to that Comintern branch installed in Berlin. The W.E.S. became all the more valuable because in addition to its illegal operations it set up a publishing house in Germany to reprint there everything that the Comintern put out in Moscow, thus becoming the principal center for dissemination of Communist propaganda in Western Europe. For this exploit Radek paid homage to Thomas: "Publication of all these writings did not become possible until comrade Thomas appeared in Berlin and, though illegally there himself, set up a marvelous legal Comintern publishing house." [85]

Three elements were necessary for the W.E.S. to erect its international apparatus: militants skilled in clandestine work, technical means of communication, and funds to finance the enterprise. As for the militants, all from Soviet Russia, they carried out either strictly political missions (like Reich, Wolf, Guralsky, Vanini, Abramovich) or had technical or administrative duties such as serving as couriers, for which women were often used to maintain liaison between Berlin and the various other capitals of Western Europe. Among these were Orlova, Antonova, Jeanne (the assumed name of Helen Unszlicht, the sister of Józef Unszlicht), and Stanislava (the wife of a Franco-Russian-Polish Socialist militant, Dr. Jacques Goldenberg)—all of course supplied with false papers. As for means of communication, the W.E.S. maintained channels to Moscow that were parallel to but independent of those of the German Communist Party, which in turn had its own radio link with Moscow and on certain occasions sent its own secret couriers (like Dr. Eduard Fuchs, Herta Gordon, and Alfred Kurella). The breadth of Thomas's organizing ingenuity was demonstrated in 1920 when he succeeded in renting two airplanes and a boat to carry delegates to the Second Comintern Congress, not to mention the false papers, diplomatic passports, and so forth, which they all had. As regards funds, Thomas had from the outset the necessary means with which to finance Communist propaganda, subsidize the German Communist Party and neighboring parties, and cover the travel expenses of the Western European Communist militants.*

THE BUREAU IN AMSTERDAM

Significantly, Lenin chose Y.S. Reich (Thomas) to go to Berlin to establish the Comintern Secretariat for Western Europe there, and several days later chose S. J. Rutgers to go to Amsterdam to open a Comintern bureau in that city—in other words, two Western European Communists living in Soviet Russia, and not European Communists living in Western Europe. Undoubtedly there were prominent local Communist personalities capable of handling such an affair, as in Germany Paul Levi or Clara Zetkin, whom Lenin had known for a long time and who already enjoyed a certain prestige and authority within that country's Communist movement, in which Thomas was virtually unknown. The same was true in Holland, where Henriette Roland-Holst and Hermann Gorter were much better-known political figures than Rutgers, who had been away from the country many years. But, at least in Lenin's eyes, Thomas and Rutgers had a conclusive advantage over the others: they had lived in Soviet Russia in Bolshevik surroundings and had participated in the founding of the Comintern. Just as in 1912 he had preferred to send a militant from his own entourage, Kamenev, to head the Bolshevik parliamentary group in St. Petersburg, Lenin had more confidence in those Western Europeans who had become Bolsheviks in Russia than in the militants in Western Europe, even if they had been among those close to him before November 7, as Levi and Gorter had been.

There was another similarity in the appointments of Thomas and Rutgers. On the eve of their departure both were received by Lenin for a private talk about what they were to do. To his emissaries leaving Moscow for Western Europe, Lenin spoke as he once had to his Bolshevik agents leaving Paris or Geneva for Russia. Certain practical aspects of this kind of work were always on his

---

*The financial side of the W.E.S. activities, as well as of the entire supreme apparatus of the Comintern, is discussed in the second volume of this work, in the chapter entitled "Development of the Secret Apparatus of the Comintern."

mind: the money required to run the apparatus and spread propaganda; the method of reaching one's destination; the addresses of trusted persons whom one should contact. This latter point especially remained etched in Rutgers' memory: "During our conversation he gave me numerous instructions, also addresses abroad which might be useful. I recall that he gave me the addresses of Paul Levi, Fuchs, and Broński-Warszawski* in Berlin, Franz Koritschoner and the late professor Karl Grünberg in Austria, Liubarsky in Italy, etc." [86] Lenin also prepared a short message for the Dutch Communists which reflected his two main ideas at the time. The first made plain that he was not deceiving himself about the critical times through which revolutionary Russia was passing: "Our situation is very difficult because of the offensive of fourteen countries. We are doing our utmost." [87] The second expressed his unshakeable conviction that, notwithstanding Russia's temporary crisis, the cause of international Communism would triumph: "The victory of world proletarian revolution is inevitable, in spite of everything." [88]

It seems probable that Lenin, in obedience to one of Bolshevism's fundamental rules of clandestine work, which required that all sectors be partitioned off so as to minimize the danger of police detection and repression, did not inform Thomas about Rutgers' mission nor Rutgers that Thomas had already left, though the two had similar if not identical assignments. Neither Thomas in his memoirs nor Rutgers in his makes the slightest allusion to the matter. A statement by Clara Zetkin supports this hypothesis. According to her, when he left Moscow, Rutgers was unaware of what was going on elsewhere and learned only en route "that such a thing as the Western European Secretariat already existed and was in business." [89] Another reason for Lenin's not mentioning to either the duality of their labors was his wish to avoid "jurisdictional" disputes, which indeed were to develop almost immediately. Assigned the job of setting up the Amsterdam Bureau, Rutgers had brought with him, too, the decision of the Comintern's Executive Committee as to the desired makeup of its staff: "Berzin, then secretary of the Executive Committee, had picked out for the

---

*Rutgers was confusing here the two prominent Polish Communist militants Mieczyław Broński (who at that time lived in Berlin) and Adolf Warski-Warszawski.

Amsterdam Bureau five Dutch Communists well-known to Moscow: Wijnkoop, Van Ravesteyn, Gorter, Pannekoek, and Madame Roland-Holst."[90] But it would overestimate Moscow's authority to assume it great enough to end the political divisions between those five personages. The Bureau's staff never did have the desired makeup because of the profound disagreement between the two "ultra-left" Communist intellectuals, Gorter and Pannekoek, on the one hand, and two other Communists, both politicians, in charge of the Communist newspaper *De Tribune*, Wijnkoop and Van Ravesteyn. The latter explains the situation in his history of the Communist movement in Holland: "It goes without saying that the editors of the *Tribune* refused to serve on a Bureau with that composition. They feared being outvoted by the two 'radicals,' whose opinions and tactics they disapproved of, since Madame Holst would probably side with them on the important issues."[91] In November 1919, when Rutgers arrived in Amsterdam, he found these two rival groups in pitched battle. The conflict, according to him, was about the prospects for revolution in Europe. Gorter and Pannekoek considered it imminent; Van Ravesteyn did not.* Owing to the conflict, the staff of the Amsterdam Bureau was cut to three: Wijnkoop as president or manager, Rutgers as secretary general, and Henriette Roland-Holst as a simple member.

So, from the beginning, this suboffice was unable to implement the Comintern's instructions with regard to the makeup of its staff. This first failure was soon followed by two others. First, the Bureau did not succeed in establishing contact with Moscow; second, it did not adhere to the Bolshevik rule about simultaneous legal and illegal operations. This double dereliction was the more serious as the Western European Secretariat had accomplished both tasks.

*According to Van Ravesteyn, the origins of the conflict went far back, specifically to the alleged pro-German attitude of Gorter and Pannekoek during World War I. See Rutgers, "Vstrechi s Leninym," *Istorik Marksist*, no. 2-3, Moscow, 1935, pp. 91-92, and Van Ravesteyn, *De Wording van het Communisme in Nederland, 1907-1925*, Amsterdam, 1948, pp. 188, 206. One should add that Gorter fired the same charge back at Van Ravesteyn, accusing him of being pro-Entente during World War I. See *Réponse à Lénine sur "La maladie infantile du communisme,"* Paris, 1930, p. 95.

Contact with Moscow was the raison d'être of the new Bureau, for Lenin and his colleagues certainly had no intention of creating an independent center in Western Europe but only one for liaison with Moscow.* Actually, though the Bureau started operating in January 1920, and the international Amsterdam conference that it organized took place from February 3 to 6, contact with Moscow was not established until the end of April. Meanwhile the W.E.S. was in communication with Moscow and did not wish to bring the Amsterdam Bureau into the picture. Not until April 26 did Rutgers inform Boris Souvarine, secretary of the Committee for the Third International in France: "It is possible at present to communicate with Moscow through Stockholm. . . . The Stockholm comrades are asking us to establish communication with you by courier via Belgium. There is a German channel in Stockholm that could be used by several other countries." [92] But nothing came of any of this, as a few days later Moscow abolished the Amsterdam Bureau. That is why Rutgers was later to write that "unfortunately, it was administratively impossible to maintain contact with Moscow." [93]

The Dutch leaders were not experienced in clandestine operations either, for the simple reason that they had never engaged in any before. In this respect the difference between the two Comintern branches in Berlin and Amsterdam was striking. As much as secret operations were rigorously practiced in the former, they were neglected in the latter. A whole secret setup existed in Berlin, supplying false papers for militants in danger, sending couriers to Moscow on diplomatic passports, providing clandestine lodging for foreign communists, and so forth. Nothing of the kind existed in Amsterdam, not even embryonically. No less marked was the difference between the international conference at Frankfurt and the corresponding one held two months later in Amsterdam. The W.E.S. conference in Frankfurt was kept secret not only during its sessions but afterwards too, and except for Sylvia Pankhurst in her

---

*The decision of the Amsterdam conference indicates this clearly: "After discussion it was resolved that 1) the Bureau shall bear the name 'International Sub-Bureau of the Communist International' and shall act in concert with Moscow." *Bulletin du Bureau auxiliaire d'Amsterdam de l'Internationale Communiste*, No. 2, Amsterdam, March 1920, p. 5.

newspaper in England and Clara Zetkin at the German Communist Party congress, no one breathed a word about it. In Amsterdam the conference organizers housed nearly all the foreign delegates in a well-known hotel, and they all ate together in an equally well-known restaurant. The police knew exactly where the conference was being held and kept track of its proceedings, as the *Bulletin* conceded and Rutgers himself admitted several months later, after the Bureau had been abolished: "As for the conference in Amsterdam, it has been definitely proved that an electric light, etc., was installed in a wardrobe in the meeting hall so that the revolutionary meetings could be spied upon. During one discussion by the Union of Revolutionary Intellectuals, some Dutch comrades dragged two police spies out of that wardrobe (sic!)."[94] Moreover it was Borodin, the only Russian militant present, who discovered the listening device, as later recounted by another participant, J. T. Murphy: "Mikhail Borodin, who arrived the day after it [the conference] had begun, discovered them [Dutch policemen] in an adjoining room with a dictaphone apparatus connected to the conference room."[95] That it should be Borodin who made the discovery is not surprising. He was the only one there who in his career as a militant had had experience in illegal operations and was familiar with police methods.

THE AMSTERDAM CONFERENCE

One of the prime tasks assigned to Rutgers in Moscow was organizing a meeting of those in Western Europe who supported the Third International. Since at the end of 1919 and in early 1920 it was still not possible to bring them to Russia they had to be assembled where they were, in Western Europe, as the Bureau's *Bulletin* made clear: "In the course of November 1919 Comrade Rutgers returned from Russia with orders from the Executive Committee of the Third International to open a bureau in Amsterdam, the makeup of whose staff was designated by the Committee. This suboffice was to have as its main tasks: (1) to establish a center for Communist propaganda with a bulletin and other publications in three languages; (2) to enter into relations with the different Communist groups and parties in Western Europe and

America; (3) to organize an early international Communist conference." [96]

The staff of the Amsterdam Bureau quickly got in touch with Communist leaders in several countries, making trips for that purpose to England, France, Belgium, and Switzerland. Since at the end of January 1920 three British and two American militants happened to be in Amsterdam, the office decided, as the same *Bulletin* reports, "to take advantage of the presence of the British and American comrades to hold a conference in Amsterdam," which started on February 3, 1920.

The Dutch group, as was to be expected, was the most strongly represented, both by the left wing (Gorter and Pannekoek) and by the Bureau staff itself, Wijnkoop, Rutgers, and Henriette Roland-Holst. From England came four militants representing various schools of thought. Of the four, two were to play an important role in the initial phase of British Communism, Sylvia Pankhurst and J. T. Murphy. Two were there from the United States, Jacob Nosovitsky, an undercover agent in the service of the American police (and probably of Britain's Scotland Yard also), and Louis Fraina, who was soon the butt of accusations and even under investigation because of his alleged suspicious behavior both politically and financially. From Germany there was only one duly appointed delegate, who represented the Bremen opposition in the German Communist Party, later to become the KAPD. Two delegates from the Belgian Communist group attended. One of them, E. Van Overstraeten, would later found the Belgian Communist Party. The *Bulletin* noted also that "a Dutch comrade who had participated in the Hungarian revolution, a representative of the revolutionary movement in the Dutch East Indies, and a Chinese comrade took part in the conference, though having no formal mandate." [97] Finally, "toward the end of the conference German and Swiss delegates arrived but could not take part in the regular discussion."* From the list of delegates published in the Amsterdam Bureau's *Bulletin* only one name was missing, that of Mikhail

---

***Bulletin du Bureau auxiliaire d'Amsterdam de l'Internationale Communiste*, No. 2, March 1920, p. 5. "The Swiss Communist Party was represented there by J. Herzog." Jules Humbert-Droz, *Mon évolution du tolstoisme au communisme, 1891-1921*, Neuchâtel, 1969, p. 345.

Borodin, who went from there first to Berlin, then to Moscow. Finally, the conference received several "letters of friendly support," as the *Bulletin* called them, one from the future founder of the Spanish Communist Party, Merino-Gracia, the other from two leading figures on the French Committee for the Third International, Fernand Loriot and Boris Souvarine.

In terms of the number of militants attending, the Amsterdam conference was more representative than the one at Frankfurt held shortly before under W.E.S. auspices. If it had no lasting impact and was survived by the Amsterdam Bureau for only three months, that was because of its political orientation, which led to disagreements with Moscow and friction with the W.E.S. As for the ideological content of the conference, it is amply revealed in the "Documents on the International Conference at Amsterdam."* The rather crowded agenda contained a number of items on which there was obvious agreement—such as, for instance, action against foreign intervention in Russia, antimilitarism, support of the Red Army, and so on. But there were several other items on which the position taken by the Amsterdam conference conflicted with Lenin's views, particularly the policies adopted on parliamentarianism, trade unions, and whether Communists should join the British Labour Party.

The theses on parliamentarianism drawn up by the Amsterdam Bureau, and the "Explanations of the Theses," directly repudiated Moscow's ideas:

> In a circular letter dated September 1, 1919, and addressed to the groups belonging to the Third International, the Secretary of the Executive Committee, Zinoviev, sets forth at some length the attitude that Communists should adopt toward parliaments and the importance of parliamentarianism for the working class. . . . But this line laid down by the Moscow Secretariat is now no longer a sufficient guide in any and every actual situation. . . . We wish to assert, and we are convinced that in this all Communists agree with us, that there can be cases in which it is necessary to boycott parliamentary action. . . . It is not within the

---

*The first issue of the *Bulletin* published the theses prepared for the Amsterdam conference, the second published the documents and the proceedings. This did not prevent E. H. Carr from writing that "No official record of the conference exists." (*The Bolshevik Revolution, 1919-1923*, vol. III, p. 170,n).

province of an international congress to decree whether this or that country is in a revolutionary state. The Communists within each country should decide that for themselves. [98]

The theses on syndicalism were "presented and defended with nice intellectual vigor by the American comrade L. Fraina," the official minutes report, and were adopted unanimously. But the minutes overlooked a fact somewhat more important than Fraina's intellectual vigor, namely, that his ideas did not square with Lenin's on the role of Communists in trade unions, the concept of the Communist cell being completely foreign to these Western militants both politically and in the trade-union context. Also, the conference came out against the British Communists' joining the Labour Party, and since the resolution did not seem sufficiently explicit, shortly afterwards the Bureau, over the signature of its three staff members, sent a message to British Communists stating that "we strongly appeal to our English friends to unite on the basis of no affiliation with the Labour Party." [99] This was diametrically opposed to the policy about to be formulated by the Comintern at Lenin's direct instance.

THE AMSTERDAM BUREAU'S INTERNATIONAL ACTIVITIES AND ITS CONFLICT WITH THE W.E.S.

The Amsterdam Bureau was to concern itself simultaneously with disseminating propaganda and organizing the Communist groups in Western Europe. Apart from publication of two issues of the *Bulletin*, the propaganda effort boiled down mainly to the writing of manifestoes and appeals in support of the Soviet and Communist cause. But with the appearance of the first issues of the *Bulletin*, Henriette Roland-Holst stressed the unlikelihood of Europe's working masses' being triggered into action by such appeals (assuming that they ever heard them): "The masses in all of Central, Southern, and Western Europe must learn to act together, as the masses within a single country learned to do in the preceding period. The first efforts in that direction—on July 21 and November 7, 1919—were miserable failures both through the treachery and flabbiness of the leaders, those men of the 'happy medium' in

France and England, and through the lack of will and drive on the part of the masses."[100]

The members of the Bureau, mainly Henriette Roland-Holst during her trips around Europe, maintained cooperation between Amsterdam and the left-wing Communists in three countries right up to the moment that Lenin was about to write his denunciatory book *"Left-Wing" Communism*. . . Once again Lenin and the Dutch Bureau were at loggerheads. In one of the three countries, Great Britain, the Bureau was egging on leftists who were refusing to join the Labour Party. In another, Switzerland, the ideas of the Bureau were shared by the Communist group of Jakob Herzog, who in February 1920 dispatched a report on the situation of the Communist movement there in which he violently attacked Fritz Platten, the former secretary of the Swiss Socialist Party: "The Platten group is made up of people who have no scruples about accepting paltry little government jobs. . . . Anyway, no one hears anything more about them; they apparently have fallen asleep. Another thing, these people always seem to prefer working with right-wing Socialists than with us."[101]   Barely a year earlier this same Platten had had the honor of presiding, alongside Lenin, over the founding congress of the Communist International. Finally, in Belgium the group of Socialist Young Guard that broke with the Belgian (Socialist) Workers' Party also had strong leanings toward left-wing Communism.*

Only in France did the Amsterdam Bureau establish ties with the Committee for the Third International, which was not in the left-wing Communist camp. The official organ of that group, *Bulletin Communiste*, the first issue of which appeared on March 1, 1920, published several appeals and manifestoes of the Amsterdam Bureau as well as a few articles by Dutch Communists, just as it cooperated closely with Roland-Holst, who had come as a foreign delegate to the Strasbourg congress of the Socialist Party, held from February 25 to 29, 1920. She gave a moving speech there in favor of joining the Third International, and had a debating duel with Jean Longuet; the greeting from the Communist Interna-

---

*"When Van Overstraeten left Belgium to attend the Second Congress of the Comintern, he and his party were completely committed to the 'left-wing' position." James W. Hulse, *The Forming of the Communist International*. Stanford, 1964, p. 168.

tional, which she read, carried the double signature of the Berlin Western European Secretariat and the Amsterdam Bureau.

Encouraging leftist tendencies among Communists in the West was not the only sin of the Amsterdam Bureau. To this "tactical deviation" was added an organizational one. The Bureau took it upon itself to set up another branch of the Comintern, this time for America, and even proceeded to allot spheres of influence on the basis of that decision, taken at the February meeting: "The American Communist Party is requested to do what is necessary to establish a sub-bureau for the two Americas and to organize a pan-American conference based on the preparations already made in Mexico. The Western European Secretariat in Berlin will be asked to serve as secretariat for Central Europe, to consist of delegates from Germany, the Danube countries, the Balkan states, and Poland. The secretariat for Central Europe will maintain communication with those countries as well as with Moscow and Amsterdam. It will constitute a section of the Amsterdam Bureau." [102] In a word, the Western European Secretariat, conceived and staffed by Lenin, was transformed into a Central European secretariat, suddenly subordinate to the Amsterdam Bureau. This decision, reflecting a total ignorance of Bolshevik organizational concepts, was naturally opposed by the W.E.S., which took good care to have it nullified.

On the first page of its first issue, the Amsterdam Bureau's *Bulletin*, under the signature of Roland-Holst, reported that the Bureau was in constant touch with the W.E.S., but the Amsterdam conference, meeting several days later, made clear that the relationship was far from cordial. First of all, the W.E.S. had no representative present for the opening of the conference, and when at the end a delegation did arrive from Berlin, it immediately opposed the decisions that had been taken there: "The members of the Executive Committee (Wijnkoop, Roland-Holst, and Rutgers), as well as a British delegate and the American delegate, did succeed in having a few conversations with the comrades who had come from Germany, among whom were two delegates from the Communist Party's Central Committee, a delegate from the Western European Secretariat and Russian Communist Party, and one from the Youth International. The discussion bore solely on the staffing of the Amsterdam Bureau, the present staff being unacceptable to the comrades in question. There were long hours of argument with no final agreement." [103]

To avoid an out-and-out break, the Amsterdam and Berlin representatives decided to carry on with their respective tasks for another three months, then to call a new international Communist conference to settle the dispute. In arranging this compromise it was the Berlin representatives who behaved like true Bolsheviks and the Amsterdamers like innocents, for in the three months that followed the doom of the Amsterdam Bureau was sealed.

On returning from Amsterdam the German delegation—consisting of Clara Zetkin and Paul Frölich of the German Communist Party, Willi Münzenberg from the Communist Youth International, and a representative of the W.E.S. under the assumed name of "Posener" (probably Broński borrowing the name from the Polish town of Poznan)—made no attempt to conceal their disapproval of the work and decisions of the Amsterdam Bureau. Clara Zetkin was instructed to raise the matter at the German Communist Party's Third Congress, scheduled to start on February 25. There she analyzed, one after another, every aspect of the Amsterdam Bureau's activities. She accused it of not having passed on to the delegations and foreign parties the theses drawn up in Berlin and sent to Amsterdam with precise instructions that they be disseminated to all European Communist groups with which the Dutch center was in contact. She insisted that the Amsterdam conference had represented no one, citing the absence of delegations from most of Europe: Germany, France, Italy, Scandinavia, Austria, Poland, the Balkans. She called it a "rump conference," asserting that "from just the practical and technical standpoint, I know of no conference that was so poorly, indeed so frivolously, prepared for and run as that one." [104] But above all she assailed the pretension of the Amsterdam Bureau in attempting to set itself up as the guiding center for all of Europe, and she told of the controversy about this during the German delegation's stay in Amsterdam: "Also, we most emphatically opposed having the headquarters of the main Bureau in Amsterdam. . . We demanded that it be in Germany. . . We stuck to our guns, insisting that the headquarters belonged in Germany, the country that was now the heart of the revolution in Western Europe." [105] In conclusion, she submitted to the congress a resolution expressing the W.E.S. viewpoint, which summarized all the complaints enumerated in her speech and condemned the pretensions of the Amsterdam Bureau. It was adopted.

But Berlin did not content itself with verbal condemnation. It took practical steps also, the first being to withhold financial aid from the Amsterdam Bureau. On this point the Amsterdam conference had expressed itself as follows: "If Moscow makes sufficient funds available, decisions will be made as to their distribution and use." [106] Now, Moscow *did* make sufficient funds available, but they had been in Berlin for several months, whence they did not flow on to Amsterdam, whereupon the Amsterdam *Bulletin* ceased to appear. This was confirmed in a report by the three secretaries of the French Committee for the Third International: "The Amsterdam Bureau not only never spent Lenin's 'twenty billion rubles' but never saw a farthing of it. Moreover, after putting out two issues of its *Bulletin*, it had to suspend publication for want of funds." [107]

WHERE TO PUT COMINTERN HEADQUARTERS?

In the interval between the end of the First Comintern Congress in March 1919 and the opening of the Second Congress in July 1920, the situation of both Soviet Russia and the European Communist movement changed. In 1919 Soviet Russia was virtually cut off from the outside world, and its leaders were expecting revolution to break out in Western Europe at any moment. By the spring of 1920, on the eve of the Second Congress, Soviet Russia had been able to establish certain ties with the outside world, and if the Bolshevik leaders still believed that revolution was coming to Western Europe, they no longer saw it as quite so imminent as they had the year before. Besides, they were now counting as much, if not more, on Russia's Red Army as on the European labor movement.

This altered perspective was to change the behavior of the Bolshevik leaders. In 1919, at the time of the Comintern's founding and during the first months of its existence, they had deemed it possible to establish Comintern headquarters in some city other than Moscow, particularly Berlin, and they set up several branches, with political functions, in Western Europe. By 1920 they were refusing to even consider transferring Comintern headquarters outside Russia (though they still agreed to discuss the matter at the Second World Congress), in the same way that they were cancelling the political functions of the Bureaus established in the West. By 1921 not a single voice was raised to bring up the question of Comintern headquarters or of the political Bureaus abroad. The stages of this evolution deserve closer study.

In August 1919 the first issue of the journal *Die Kommunistische Internationale*, the organ of the Executive Committee of the Comintern, which began to appear in Germany even before the W.E.S. existed, was published in Berlin. The issue carried the documentation on the First Comintern Congress, including the decision to found the Comintern, with the explanation that "generally the delegates were of the opinion that the Bureau's headquarters belonged in Berlin. But since this would only be possible after establishment of a German Soviet Republic, for the time being the headquarters would be in Moscow."[108] This information did not appear in the Russian, German, and French editions of the first issue of the journal *The Communist International*, likewise devoted to that founding congress and published simultaneously in Russia; and there was not a word about it in the minutes of the congress, printed somewhat later. It is unlikely that the German Communist Party or Hugo Eberlein, its representative at the congress, could have invented this "general opinion" favoring Berlin as site for Comintern headquarters. It is more likely that the Bolshevik leaders soon changed their minds and decided to bury in silence what they had previously approved.

A few months later, at the time of the Second Comintern Congress, the question as to where the Executive Committee should be based was again raised, on the initiative of two prominent delegates, Wijnkoop from the Amsterdam Bureau and Paul Levi from the W.E.S. in Berlin. While the two Comintern branches were on opposite sides of virtually all other issues, their spokesmen were in agreement on this one. During the discussion of the proposed statutes Wijnkoop made a particular point of section 8, which defined the role to be played by the party in the country to be permanent host to Comintern headquarters. He deduced from it two different possibilities and practical consequences. The first was that the headquarters would stay in Moscow, but in that case, as he saw it, they would no longer have a truly international character: "Seemingly we are setting up an international Executive

Committee, but actually that is not the case. What we have here instead is an expanded Russian Executive Committee. . . . If the Congress believes that the headquarters cannot be moved to another place, then we do not at this time have a truly international Executive Committee, and we must content ourselves with a Russian one." [109] The other possibility was to transfer the headquarters to Western Europe: "I have suggested that the headquarters be moved outside of Russia, and I think that this should be discussed here. I have suggested Italy or Norway as host country because I believe the labor movement in those countries is now strong enough to be able to bring together a truly international Executive Committee. Comrade Levi has proposed that the headquarters be in Germany; I am as much in favor of Germany as of Norway or Italy." [110]

Levi, for his part, approached the problem differently. He did not raise the question as to where the Executive Committee should be based but sought rather to impose two restrictions on its operations in Moscow. He demanded first a statutory stipulation that the Communist Party of the country hosting the Executive Committee should have no more than five members on it. He then pointed out that, by force of circumstances, foreign delegates coming to Moscow to serve on the Executive Committee would be receiving their information solely from Russian sources, which would be less true if the headquarters were in some other country.

Wijnkoop and Levi were opposed by the American delegate, Louis Fraina, who was solidly against having Comintern headquarters in Berlin: "It is nonsense to suggest transferring the Executive Committee to Berlin. We had the Western European Secretariat in Berlin, and its outlook was limited, narrow, to a certain extent nationalistic and not internationalist." The Dutch-German objections were dealt the coup de grâce, however, by Zinoviev, who at the close of debate on the question ridiculed Wijnkoop without touching on the problem he had raised: "Comrade Wijnkoop has proposed here that we transfer the headquarters perhaps to Norway. We can draw up various plans and projects and could locate a few exotic republics. I must note, though, that here in section 8, as elsewhere in the statutes, not a word is said about Russia. . . . Wijnkoop says the Executive Committee would be an expanded Russian committee. Well, I say that maybe it will be an expanded Dutch committee." [111]

After that, Berlin was to have no further chance of being host
to the Executive Committee, or even of holding its own with
Moscow in the Comintern hierarchy, for as time went on the
failure of the Communist revolution in Germany became ever
more apparent, while the success of the one in Russia became ever
more solid. Nevertheless, while Berlin lost ground vis-à-vis Moscow,
it gained ground vis-à-vis Amsterdam and the other ephemeral
Comintern branches. Escaping dissolution of its Western European
Secretariat, Berlin found itself entrusted by Moscow with other
administrative and political Comintern business, which strengthened its relatively privileged position. Thus, when at the end of the
Third World Congress in 1921 the International Control Commission of the Comintern was about to be formed, the Little Bureau
(Presidium) of the Executive Committee decided on July 16 that
it would be based in Berlin and that its chairman would be Clara
Zetkin.[112] That same year the editorial offices of *Inprecor*, the second official organ of the Comintern, were established in Berlin. A
few months later Moscow entrusted to Berlin yet a third operation. At its meeting of March 6, 1922, the Presidium of the Executive Committee ruled that "it is deemed necessary to transfer the
Women's Secretariat to Berlin."[113]

DISSOLUTION OF THE AMSTERDAM BUREAU

In his report prepared for the Second World Congress, Zinoviev
explained in these terms the creation and the number of foreign
Bureaus of the Comintern: "At the very start of its activities the
Executive Committee concluded that, in view of the blockade of
Soviet Russia and of the state of siege imposed upon the Communists by the bourgeoisie, it was absolutely necessary for us to have
suboffices of the Executive Committee in a number of countries,
and such offices were established in Scandinavia, Central Europe,
the Balkans, Holland, and Southern Russia."[114]

Of all those suboffices, the one in Amsterdam was the shortest-
lived. It opened for business in January 1920 and was dissolved by
Moscow at the end of April. The chronological correlation be-
tween these two facts was anything but fortuitous: in April 1920,
Lenin brought out his book *"Left-Wing" Communism—an Infantile
Disorder,* in which he criticized this "deviation" so widespread in
Western Europe, and on April 30, by decision of the Little Bureau

(Presidium), the Amsterdam office was closed down. A radiogram was dispatched immediately, and the next issue of *Communist International* carried the communiqué: "Unfortunately that Bureau, on several matters of the highest importance, deviated from the line laid down by the Executive Committee of the Communist International. The Executive Committee has been therefore obliged to revoke the authority granted by it to that group of Dutch comrades. The following resolution has been adopted unanimously."[115]

Thus, Moscow made a radical decision without hearing the accused or leaving even the ghost of a chance of appealing the verdict. If that procedure, so typically Bolshevik, was entirely normal for the Little Bureau, comprised at that time almost solely of Russians, it was not seen as normal by the European Communist movement, as yet unaccustomed to such methods. Barely a month after this telegraphed dissolution of the Amsterdam Bureau, the act came up for discussion at the June 1920 meeting of the International Communist Youth Bureau in Berlin, at which an Italian delegate, Montagnana, declared: "As to the Amsterdam Bureau, it must be said that we approve the reasons for, but not the manner of its dissolution."[116] That other objections were raised within the International to the way in which Moscow had dealt with the Amsterdam Bureau is attested by the long explanation which the Executive Committee felt obliged to include in its report prepared for the Second Comintern Congress. After charging that the Amsterdam Bureau had overstepped its authority from the outset and taken positions contrary to those of Moscow on important matters such as syndicalism, parliamentarianism, and the KAPD, the document went on to explain: "The Executive Committee was confronted with the choice of either letting matters drift and standing by doing nothing while confusion in the ranks of the Communist International increased, or of promptly closing down the Dutch Bureau, which had exceeded its authority. The Executive Committee chose the latter course, and is convinced that the Second Congress will ratify that choice."[117]

The Second Congress was not, however, invited to pass judgment on the appropriateness of that dissolution, which had become an irreversibly accomplished fact. So nothing more was said at it about the Bureau, except for a remark by Paul Levi, who contrasted the W.E.S. position that the British Socialist Party should stay on in the Labour Party, and that of the Amsterdam Bureau which was against that tactic.[118] The only concession made to the defunct Bureau was that neither it nor its *Bulletin* was condemned by name in the resolution that was passed concerning the main tasks of the Communist International—but only at the last minute, after a vote by the committee, was explicit censure of the Dutch group stricken from the original text that Lenin had written.[119]

LIQUIDATION OF THE OTHER COMINTERN BUREAUS

Another Comintern Bureau was liquidated in 1920, but not for reasons of "tactical deviation," the sin committed in Amsterdam. This time it was the Comintern's Southern Bureau, operating out of Kiev. On the birth of that Bureau, Marcel Body, who belonged to it, wrote in his memoirs: "During the First Congress of the Communist International it had been decided to form a Southern Bureau, staffed by Rakovsky and Angelica Balabanova, whose activities would radiate from the Ukraine out over the Balkan countries and Austrian territories with Slavic populations. Invited to become a member of this Bureau by Rakovsky and Balabanova, Sadoul accepted, and it was agreed that I would leave with him."[120] As was true of virtually all Comintern activities during 1919 and early 1920, in Kiev no real or apparent distinction was made between the Communist activities under the aegis of the Comintern and those sponsored by the Ukrainian Soviet Government. Rakovsky was in charge of both, and Sadoul was lodged with him.

It was probably out of Kiev that Rakovsky succeeded in establishing some contacts with Rumanian Communists (one of whom, Bujor, belonged to the Southern Bureau) and with Bulgarian Communists. Sadoul tried to do the same in France and did manage to send a courier, Boris Pokitonov, who carried messages to the Committee for the Third International during the Socialist Congress at Strasbourg in February 1920. It was the first and probably the last time that the three Bureaus—Berlin, Amsterdam, and Kiev—were represented at the congress of a Socialist Party in Western Europe. When the Polish Army marched on Kiev in 1920, the members of the Southern Bureau fell back to Moscow. After the Ukraine was reconquered that same year, the Kiev Bureau was not revived. This, then, was the second on Zinoviev's list, in his report to the Second World Congress, that were no longer in existence at the time.

In the latter half of 1920 the Stockholm Bureau was also closed down. Merely an administrative way-station, it had never been one of the Comintern's political centers. During the nearly total isolation of Soviet Russia from 1918 into 1920, until the Comintern's Second World Congress, Stockholm was a center for indirect liaison between Moscow and Western Europe. Here again, Lenin drew upon the Bolshevik past. In 1917, before gaining power in Petrograd, he had given Radek, Vorovsky, and Hanecki the job of setting up and running a Bolshevik Bureau in Stockholm; after gaining power, and after the founding of the Comintern, he had assigned to three Swedish left-Socialists won over to the Communist revolution—Ström, Höglund, and Kilbom—the task of forming a Comintern center in that city for establishment of liaison with the movement in Europe. It was the first of the three, Frederick Ström, who actually did most of the work. Between 1918 and 1920 he was simultaneously managing editor of the daily *Folkets Dagblad Politiken* and official representative of the Commissariat of Foreign Affairs of Soviet Russia. This afforded him a cover and at the same time a chance to keep in touch with Moscow and make contacts among Communist circles in Europe. From Stockholm, Ström corresponded with the Comintern's trusted agents in other parts of Europe, men like Rutgers in Amsterdam, Loriot in Paris, and Kopp in Berlin. In a letter dated April 6, 1920, he stressed that "we are now in direct touch with Moscow three times a week."* The Stockholm center closed down for essentially the same administrative reasons that had produced it. With liaison established, since the Second Comintern Congress, between Mos-

---

*Annie Kriegel, *Aux origines du communisme français, 1914-1920* (Origins of French Communism, 1914-1920), vol. II, Paris 1964, p. 560. It was almost at this same time, in the spring of 1920, that the Stockholm center undertook to organize a conference of Finnish Communist militants, some of them coming from Soviet Russia with Otto Kuusinen, others from their hiding places in their own country, among them Arvo Tuominen, who supplies this detail: "The secret liaison between Petrograd and Stockholm was very fast, the leaders of the Finnish Communist Party having at their disposal for the trip not only motor launches but a veritable ship belonging to the Comintern, which made it from Stockholm to Petrograd in little better than a day." *Skärans Och Hammarens Väg* (The Road of the Sickle and the Hammer), Helsingfors, 1958, p. 181.

cow and the rest of Europe, there was no longer any need to detour via Stockholm.

While liquidation of the Stockholm Bureau had no ideological or tactical motive behind it, this was not true of the Bureau in Vienna, which Zinoviev's report had vaguely referred to as "Balkan." The Austrian capital sheltered many of the leaders of Soviet Hungary, who had taken refuge there after the collapse of their regime in the summer of 1919. On February 1, 1920, Austrian and Hungarian Communists (among them Béla Kun) had launched a weekly magazine, *Kommunismus*. Gerhart Eisler and Karl Frank, prominent Austrian leaders, and László Rudas and György Lukácz, on the Hungarian side, were frequent contributors. From its inception the journal took "leftist" positions, which Lenin was in the process of vigorously criticizing. He even wrote a short but pointed article about the journal, in which he attacked the ideas of Lukácz, not hesitating to brand as "stupid" the anti-parliamentarianism of Béla Kun. [121] This condemnation was confirmed several weeks later, at the Second Comintern Congress, in a resolution on the main tasks of the Communist International (written by Lenin), which named that journal as the organ of the Communist International's Vienna Bureau for Eastern Europe. [122] Even so, the journal continued to appear after the Second Congress and to champion leftist positions. It was not until July 23, 1921, shortly after the Third World Congress, that the Little Bureau of the Executive Committee decided that *Kommunismus* would have to cease publication. [123] The death blow to the Vienna branch of the Comintern came several months later when the Presidium of the Executive Committee, at its meeting of March 8, 1922, declared laconically: "The Vienna Bureau is liquidated." [124]

Two other agencies of the Comintern met the same fate. The first was the Communist Youth International, based in Berlin. As will be seen later, that organization had displayed a hint of independence vis-à-vis Moscow. On July 23, 1921, the same day that the Little Bureau of the Executive Committee closed down the Vienna journal *Kommunismus*, it made a decision about the Youth International: "The Little Bureau deems it politically necessary to transfer the headquarters of the Youth International to Moscow." [125] Less than three months later the same Presidium made another decision, again aimed at a centralization of power, decreeing that "the Pan-American Bureau is dissolved."[126]

So this left only the W.E.S. still in business,* with much reduced administrative duties. Thus ended the decentralization which, initially, the Comintern encouraged and supported, and which had given a particular stamp to Communism in Europe. During that period the European Communist movement was not strong in terms of numbers, but quite varied in its ideas and rather independent with respect to the Soviet Union. After the Second World Congress, Moscow did its utmost to reverse that situation. The Communist movement became numerically stronger (notably through the creation of unified Communist Parties in Germany, France, and Czechoslovakia), but it showed less variety of thought and had much less freedom in its dealings with Moscow.

---

*On the liquidation of Middle Eastern and Far Eastern Comintern auxiliary bureaus, see the last pages of Chapter Nine.

The Communist International's Power of Attraction

The Third International was to be different in all respects from the Second, starting with the manner of its birth. The Second had appeared at the end of a social and political process that had taken many years, while the Third was born shortly after a violent historic event: the Bolshevik victory at Petrograd. Indeed, the creation of the Second International had been the outcome of a development spanning nearly twenty years: from the fall of the Paris Commune and the Hague congress of the First International, in 1871-72, to the Paris congress of 1889, where the Second International came into being. During that period Western Europe experienced three great social and political changes. Its economic expansion had increased the size of the industrial proletariat; the concentration of workers in the factories and large cities had stimulated development of the trade-union movement; and Socialist parties were established in the different countries, preceded or accompanied by the spread of Marxist thought, thanks to Friedrich Engels and a galaxy of Socialist popularizers. Only at the end of this process was it possible for a Socialist Workers' International to be born.

The Third International came into being by the reverse route. In founding it, Lenin started where the Second International had left off, and in pressing for the creation of national parties, he carried on what the Second International had begun. In place of evolution from below, he preferred the opposite, in keeping with the fundamental difference between reformist democratic Western Socialism and revolutionary authoritarian Russian Bolshevism.

From his very first move toward founding the Communist International, Lenin was faced with a double problem. How was an International to be created when the Communist parties supposed to comprise it did not yet exist? How were Communist parties to be established in the West and elsewhere when there were virtually no Communists anywhere in the Bolshevik sense of the term? This seemingly insoluble double problem was nevertheless resolved by Lenin in record time. On March 4, 1919, without even waiting for the birth of Communist parties in Europe, he proclaimed the existence of a Communist International. However, by late 1920, Moscow had succeeded in splitting several large Socialist parties and bringing suddenly into being a number of mass Communist parties in Europe. Lenin's method was obviously the reverse of what Europe's Social Democrats had used, and it conflicted with the view of these matters held by the sole Western revolutionary movement, the German Spartacists, inspired by Rosa Luxemburg. Her plan arose from the respect for mass movement. Her sequence was: first win the masses already supporting Socialism in the Second International and arouse the fighting spirit. Second, gain an understanding of the great discontented but unorganized masses and then found the Communist parties, after which it would be possible to create a genuinely revolutionary International. That is why she hesitated, even at the end of 1918, to break with the Independent Socialists in order to form a mere splinter communist party, and several weeks later came out flatly against the idea of the immediate setting up of a Communist International before the battle for the soul of the masses had been fought and won.

Lenin's approach of creation of an organization by fiat from above was certainly not democratic—from its inception Bolshevism rejected the concept of a so-called formal democracy—but it proved to be very effective. This was so not because of the persuasiveness of Lenin's arguments but because of a wide-spread fascination with the Bolshevik successes in seizing power in 1917 and consolidating it in 1920. Where the Social Democrats had taken some ten years to move by organic growth from the founding of great national parties to the establishment of the Second International, Lenin needed little more than a year to leap from the founding of his International to the formation of at least a few significant national parties. It is true, of course, that when Lenin founded the Communist International in March 1919 the delegates there to ratify the act were mere pawns having no genuine mandate, and there were no Communist parties in practically any of the Western countries. Yet it is also true that by the end of the next year the Communist International had grown into an organization with powerful support in many important European countries, though other parties he split unnecessarily and left in shambles.

During 1919 and up to the last days of 1920 Lenin was convinced that events would fall out as he had predicted. "Objectively" he was certain of this. The laws of history according to Marx (as interpreted by Lenin) had decreed the imminent collapse of capitalism. He was also "subjectively" certain of it, for the revolutionary method and organization that had won him victory in Russia could do the same in Europe. From this happy confluence of the "objective" and the "subjective," revolution would surely blossom forth everywhere. The "objective" being assured by the inexorable laws of history, he had only to worry about the "subjective," which is why he founded the Communist International and pressed for creation of Communist parties in Europe.

But this historically appointed conjuncture of the "objective" revolutionary situation with the "subjective" revolutionary factors, accidentally achieved by the strains of total war, the unexpected downfall of the Tsar, and the gentle (or incapable, however one may look at it) rule of the Provisional Government in the Russia of 1917, was not duplicated in the Europe of the postwar years. When the "objective" revolutionary situation was (or seemed) right, as in 1918-19 and the first half of 1920, the "subjective" factors weren't—that is, no Communist party equal to the job of revolution existed in Europe. Conversely, when by the end of 1920 and in early 1921 there were Communist parties in many countries of Central and Western Europe, the "objective" situation had ceased to be revolutionary, even in Lenin's eyes. Seeing the handwriting on the wall, he had to make his first big strategic shift.

The truth is that, when troubles unprecedented before or after descended upon the Europe of 1918-19—with age-old empires collapsing, with mass upheavals even in countries that had stayed out of the war and had a long history of domestic tranquility, such as Holland and Switzerland, with massive strikes gripping even victorious countries like France and England, with socio-political earthquakes in Eastern and Central Europe, and so on—there was little tendency anywhere to embrace Bolshevism or the Communist International. Lenin's key political weapon, the existence of revolutionary Russia in the hands of a Communist party, and his key ideological weapon, his appropriation of Marxism and the imposing of his Russian version as the sole authentic one, were not yet fully operational in 1918 and 1919. Soviet Russia was cut off from the outside world, and many Socialists were still wondering whether it could survive civil war, foreign invasion, and blockade. As for equating Marxism with Bolshevism, leading Marxist thinkers like Karl Kautsky, Rudolf Hilferding, and Otto Bauer thought it was pure and simple theft, and it was regarded as dubious no less by Rosa Luxemburg.

But in politics survival in power counts for more than debating skill, and the year 1920, marked by decisive Bolshevik victories in the civil war and the fluctuating advance against Poland, saw the rise of a strong suspicion that Soviet Russia might not, after all, suffer the fate of the Paris Commune or of Béla Kun's Hungary, but would perhaps live on to play a major role in the international labor movement and world politics. Coincidentally, the Leninist version of Marxism started to be taken seriously and with a few reservations came to be widely accepted by a number of Europe's left Socialist leaders.

From then on, Lenin's old prediction of world-wide duplication of that phenomenon regarded by many as uniquely Russian, namely the break between Bolshevism and Menshevism culminating in the creation of two distinct hostile parties, began to come true, whereupon Bolshevism ceased to be purely Russian and became quasi-international. Rarely in modern times, and never in the history of the labor movement, had the position of an individual undergone so radical a change, from a political weakness verging on oblivion to a strength so great as to be virtual omnipotence. Before the November 7 revolution, and even for a while afterwards, Lenin was ignored or spurned by nearly all of Europe's Socialists. But once he had consolidated his victory in Russia, he became the polestar of revolutionaries throughout the world. The triumphant revolution in Soviet Russia indeed did open up the world to Lenin and his Bolshevism. The prestige of the first revolution proclaiming itself both Socialist and proletarian, which abolished by law private ownership of the means of production and even promised a society without class inequalities, coupled with

the absence of any successful revolution in industrial Europe after
more than a half century of Socialist dreams, combined to produce a fact of long-lasting historic significance: Russian Communism and Communism per se became inseparable. Russian Communism was the father, international Communism the child. Of
course, when we say "Russian Communism," it would be more
accurate simply to say Lenin, for he was the builder of those three
historic revolutionary structures: the Bolshevik party, Soviet
Russia, and the Communist International.

The habit of equating Russian Communism with Communism
per se was to become firmly ingrained during the lifetime of the
Communist International, whose doings would always be principally governed by what was happening in Soviet Russia. Before the
Bolshevik revolution, and even for a whole year after it, not a
single Bolshevik-type party existed anywhere outside Russia. Even
the two dissident Socialist parties on the extreme left of Europe's
Socialist movement, De Tribune in Holland and the Tesniaks in
Bulgaria, did not share Lenin's views either before 1914 or during
the war. When in April 1917 a new Socialist party was founded in
Germany, the USPD, its thinking was far removed from Lenin's,
and the chief ideologues representing its three trends—Bernstein,
Kautsky, and Rosa Luxemburg—in varying degrees and for different reasons were downright hostile to his ideas. The only big Socialist party in Europe, Italy's, which because of that country's
special situation could afford to come out and openly oppose the
war, had nothing in common either with Lenin and his Bolshevik
party.

Lenin's ideas during his exile in Switzerland had not caught on
with Europe's Socialists, and his numerous manifestoes and appeals even after he had come to power in Petrograd did not result
in the expected immediate fraternization among the soldiers across
the trenches, nor did they transform the imperialist war into a civil
war or bring to life a single mass communist movement inside or
outside any of the existing Socialist parties. But the continued
survival of Soviet Russia and its successes in the civil war and the
war against Poland, plus the many contacts it established with the
Socialist movement in Europe, gave powerful impetus to the creation of Communist parties everywhere in Europe, and not long
afterwards on other continents too.

The fact that the Communist Party of Soviet Russia was the only one in the International to have staged a revolution and stayed in power—and could use the resources available to men in power—created an imbalance. It increased with each passing year and was characterized by the existence within the Comintern of a "strongman," the Russian party, and a weakling, the combined foreign parties. This imbalance was translated into a de facto monopoly. The foreign Communist parties were born *after* the seizure of power by the Bolsheviks, and since no foreign Communist party could exist *without* the permission of the Bolsheviks and the International (to say nothing of existing *against* their will), Moscow was to gain a monopoly on Communism through the growing ascendancy of the Comintern apparatus over the national sections and through the political and moral prestige of the Bolshevik revolution and the persuasiveness of power among simple militants. There could be no Communist movement independent of Moscow, only dissident Communists "beyond the pale" or non-Communist labor movements. Moscow was to sense this fundamental drift much sooner than were the national Communist leaders of Lenin's day. The result was twofold. Conscious of holding the upper hand, Moscow did not hesitate to break with fractious foreign Communist leaders, whereas some of them did continue for a time trying to "have Communism" without Moscow, not yet aware of the futility of the attempt.

Having become the Mecca or Rome of the Communist world, Moscow needed its Mohammed or Pope to give its power the seal of completeness. The role automatically devolved on Lenin, not because he grabbed it (as Stalin and Mao Tse-tung later did), but because circumstances forced it on him. As the Bolsheviks from the beginning had equated Russian Communism with Communism per se and Soviet Russia with the Communist International, so Marxism was now equated with Communism. As there could be no Communist movement outside the International, there could be no Marxist theory outside the Bolshevik version. Anyone seeking a Communism outside the Communist International was a renegade, as was anyone looking for a Marxism without the Communist International's stamp of approval.

These Bolshevik "equations" did not gain acceptance overnight. In the beginning, most Socialists, taking their Socialism from

Marx, realized that the Bolshevik revolution had been waged in the *name* of Marx but not *according* to Marx, in the *name* of the working class but not *by* the working class, and that the Bolsheviks were arbitrarily equating their own party with both Marxism and the proletariat. Immediately after the Bolshevik revolution the prevailing view among Marxist thinkers—whether German, Austro-German, Russian, or French—was that Marxism essentially lay outside Bolshevism. Communism next was regarded as but one version of Marxism. Finally, after Communism had proven for a number of years its ability to survive, and with the Social Democrats still floundering in their parliamentary pragmatism, the Communists wound up being considered the main if not the only true representatives of Marxism.

This practice of equating Bolshevism with Marxism was accompanied by a shrinkage of Marxist thought, just as later the identification of Leninism with Stalinism would impoverish Lenin's thought. Lenin as Marxist took from Marx what pleased him. Thus it was, for instance, that Marx's offhand remark, thrown in on several occasions, about a "dictatorship of the proletariat" was seized upon by Lenin and made the cornerstone of his entire edifice. The same use was later to be made of Lenin himself, when those claiming to follow his teachings would merely borrow from him whatever suited their particular purposes, like his casual aside about "socialism in one country," dropped at the end of one of his articles written in 1915.*

THE SOCIALIST MILITANTS COME RUNNING

Well before Lenin's victory in Russia, Marxism was saddled with a double ambiguity. Theoretically there were two Marxisms, a reformist (or revisionist) one and a revolutionary (or orthodox)

---

*This article, entitled "The United States of Europe Slogan," published on August 23, 1915, in the Bolshevik organ *Sotsial-Demokrat*, used the formula of the possibility of the victory of Socialism in one country in a very conditional way, qualifying what such a limited proletarian victory would mean: "The victorious proletariat of that country . . . would rise against the rest of the capitalist world, attracting the oppressed classes of other countries, raising among them revolts against the capitalists, launching, in case of necessity, armed forces against the exploiting classes and their states." *Polnoe sobranie sochinenii*, 5th edition, vol. 26, Moscow 1961, pp. 354-55.

version. Actually there was a left wing of some sort in many Socialist parties, and some had already split apart. Lenin was to catalyze that ideological and revolutionary Left and consummate the break between the two Marxisms, which until then had cohabited in most parties and in the only existing Workers' International. He did not accomplish this through the force of his ideas—amply developed before October 1917 but still unknown to most Socialists—but through the weight of his October victory. Those on the Left of Europe's Socialist movement, while disagreeing with Lenin, rallied to his support after his triumph in Russia. This was so of the two Socialist groups within formerly Tsarist Russia, the Finnish and Polish, and of three European movements outside Russia—the Spartacists in Germany, the Tesniaks in Bulgaria, and the Tribunists in Holland. (The case of the Norwegian Labor Party, which in April 1919 joined the Comintern as a whole, and of the Swedish Left-Wing Socialist Party, which did the same in June of 1919, is different because it did not last long: the splits among the Swedes in 1921 and 1924 brought about a break of many leaders and militants from the Comintern; a great majority of the Norwegians left the Comintern in 1923.)

Finland, very near Petrograd and a center of Lenin's revolutionary activities, had a well-established Socialist movement with no commitment whatever to Lenin's ideas. At the very moment that the Bolshevik revolution was winning in Petrograd, the Finnish Socialists (according to Otto Kuusinen, one of their leaders) were completely "spellbound by the fata morgana of democracy," hoping to achieve Socialism "through parliamentary debate," and, what was more, "were deluded into trying to avoid Socialist revolution, to circumvent that intermediate stage between capitalism and socialism—the dictatorship of the proletariat—a historical reality that *will* not be circumvented."[1] It was not until after the failure of the Finnish revolution, when many Finnish Socialist leaders chose exile in Soviet Russia, that they founded a Communist party with a program embodying Lenin's principles: armed insurrection, dictatorship of the proletariat, split with their "Mensheviks" or "Rightists," destruction of the bourgeois state apparatus, confiscation of all capitalist property, and all the rest.

In Poland after 1905 the Social-Democratic leaders were quite familiar with Lenin's ideas, which they roundly rejected. This was true of Rosa Luxemburg, who wrote articles against Bolshevism, and of Leo Jogiches, who fought Lenin within both the Polish and the Russian movements, and of other leaders like Warski, Dzerzhinsky, and Marchlewski. But after the Bolshevik victory the latter three rallied to Lenin's cause and became high dignitaries of the Comintern and Soviet state.

As for the Socialist movement outside formerly Tsarist Russia, Germany's Spartacists did not share Lenin's views and did not vote with him at Zimmerwald or Kienthal, yet after his victory and the death of Rosa Luxemburg they joined the Comintern and played important roles in it. The representatives of the other two leftist parties in Europe's Socialist movement present at Zimmerwald, Henriette Roland-Holst for the Dutch and Vasil Kolarov for the Bulgarians, did not side with Lenin either, nor did Angelica Balabanova, who was to become the first secretary of the Communist International, nor Christian Rakovsky, later first president of the Soviet government of the Ukraine, nor Leon Trotsky, who in 1917 became Lenin's right arm. Trotsky was the only one of all those at Zimmerwald who joined up with Lenin before the November 1917 victory. Of all the others on the left of Europe's Socialist movement it could be said as the Bulgarian leader, Khristo Kabakchiev, noted about the Tesniaks: "The October revolution completely changed the attitude of the Tesniaks toward the Bolsheviks, whose victory in the civil war finished shoring up the Tesniak faith in Bolshevism and Soviet power."[2]

The Bolshevik victory, not on the night of November 7, 1917, but their final victory two or three years later, as Kabakchiev pointed out, marked a change of course not only for the ex-Socialists who then went over to Lenin, but for Lenin too, who welcomed them with open arms. Contrary to the reports spread about him by his foes in the Socialist movement prior to 1917, he was not merely an implacable splitter who enjoyed schism for its own sake. He was also, especially in times of action requiring great combined strength, a wily strategist ready to accept help and obedience from any and all who had vilified him yesterday so long as they were with him today. As late as February 1917 Lenin could still call Trotsky a "swine" in a letter to Alexandra Kollontai, and a few days later, writing to Inessa Armand, could declare that Trotsky was always the same, ready to hedge and cheat, pretending to be a leftist while actually being a rightist.[3] A few months later, in August 1917, Lenin named this same Trotsky to the Central Committee of the Bolshevik Party, and three months after that, in October, recognized his ability to carry out the decision to seize power in Petrograd. In 1916 and early 1917, in his letters, Lenin castigated Radek, yet in May-June 1917 made him a Bolshevik Party representative in Stockholm, in 1918 Soviet representative in Germany, and in 1920 Secretary of the Communist International. In October 1917 he could fulminate against the "treachery" of Zinoviev, but the next day make him chairman of the Petrograd Soviet and in March 1919 president of the Communist International. In short, Lenin was always willing to forget the past as soon as the sinner was ready to toe the Lenin line.

He showed the same attitude in the International. At the Bern Youth Conference in 1915 its chairman, Willi Münzenberg, did not fully agree with Lenin, but in 1919 he was allowed to found and head the Communist Youth International. Clara Zetkin, the chairwoman of the International Women's Conference, also held in Bern in 1915, did not accept Lenin's ideas; in 1916, writing in the German Socialist newspaper *Gleichheit*, she denounced the Zimmerwald Left and Bolshevik sectarianism, which made Lenin furious.[4] Yet she later became a leading light in the Comintern, and on her visits to Moscow in 1920, 1921, and 1922 was the object of Lenin's most special attentions. The secretary of the Swiss Socialist Party and member of the Zimmerwald Left, Fritz Platten, was characterized by Lenin as late as February 1917 as "a man without character, if not worse."[5] The very next month, however, he entrusted to this same Platten the immensely delicate task of arranging with the German embassy in Bern for the trip of the Russian revolutionaries across Germany, and picked him to sit at his side as co-chairman of the Comintern's founding congress. At the end of 1916 Lenin was crossing verbal swords with Boris Souvarine. Their respective views on the war and Socialist action in general were then quite far apart, and remained so for a while after the Bolshevik victory, with Souvarine not hesitating to write: "One fears that with Lenin and his friends the 'dictatorship of the proletariat' means a dictatorship of the Bolsheviks and their chief, which could prove disastrous for the Russian working class, hence for the world proletariat."[6] When several months later Souvarine became secretary of the Committee for the Third International and in 1921 came to Moscow as a representative of the French Communist Party, the Comintern did not object and Lenin himself supported passage of a motion electing Souvarine to two of the Comintern's top executive bodies, the Presidium and Executive Committee (against the advice of Béla Kun). In December 1916 Lenin wrote that the ideas of Jules Humbert-Droz were a "hopeless porridge" and "idiot pacifism,"[7] yet when this same militant founded the Swiss Communist Party and in 1921 became secretary of the Communist International, Lenin made no objection. In February 1918 he complained of "this French captain [Jacques] Sadoul, whose mouth is with the Bolsheviks but whose head and soul are with French imperialism."[8] A year later, in March 1919, Captain Sadoul was named delegate to the Comintern's founding congress and took part in its Executive Committee meetings at Lenin's very side.

As with individual militants, Lenin could bring himself to forget the past behavior of an entire party. The Italian Socialist Party, for instance, never once supported his views at the Zimmerwald or Kienthal conferences. But that did not prevent him from getting them into the Third International in 1919; they were the first big Socialist party in Western Europe to vote to join the Comintern.

Like Lenin, the Comintern was no more reluctant in 1919-20 than the Bolshevik party had been in 1917-18 to welcome people from outside the Socialist movement and with no Marxist background. Going straight to Bolshevism and the Third International without the "original sin" of first being screened through a Socialist party and having prior knowledge of European Marxism had certain advantages in Bolshevik eyes, for the less one had been exposed to non-Bolshevik Socialism the easier it was for the Bolsheviks to implant their own views. The more a field had been sown with the seed of true Marxist theory and cultivated by trade unions and the labor movement, the harder it was for the Bolsheviks to impose themselves. They preferred to start on virgin ground. And in lieu of Marxist theory and a trade-union organization and labor party, they had two other magnets to attract militants to their fold. One was the fascination of the "Socialist revolution," the other the hatred of the "imperialist war."

The role played by these two issues was highly important in Russia at the end of the war. The sequence of events there proved that the precondition for a revolution's success was a militant support for the cause by people who until recently had been unaware of its existence. The cause here was Lenin's Bolshevism. In Soviet Russia not only hundreds of thousands of soldiers, workers, and peasants, but also foreigners who chanced to be in the country were converted to Russian Communism and subsequently took part in the Communist movements of their respective homelands and in the Comintern. Most typical of these were the ex-prisoners of war from the Austro-Hungarian army who joined first the Bolshevik revolution, then the Comintern. In that crowd of ex-prisoners there was only one man who was internationally known as a left-Socialist militant and a Marxist theoretician, Otto Bauer; and he rejected Bolshevism from the outset and back in Vienna in 1919 he wrote a critical pamphlet on the Bolshevik experiment. It was many of the other prisoners, unknown within the Socialist movements of their countries before the war, in most cases not even members of a Socialist party, who rallied to Bolshevism. The best known were the Hungarians Béla Kun, Endre Rudnyánszky, Tibor Szamuely, Ferenc Jancsik, József Rabinovits, Ernő Pór, Mátyás Rákosi, Károly Vántus, Sándor Kellner, and Ernő Seidler, all of whom became leaders in the Hungarian party or Comintern (or both), and a number of whom gained a certain fame through the existence of Soviet Hungary in 1919 and through later events in Russia, the Comintern, and Hungary.

The same phenomenon existed in Austria, the one difference being that the Austrian Communist Party never became as celebrated as the Hungarian since power was never thrust into its hands, nor did it come within reach of it. Moreover, in its way stood a strong left-Socialist Party with notable Marxist theoreticians in its ranks. Most of the Communist leaders in Austria had been prisoners of war in Russia: Karl Toman, one of the founders of the Austrian Communist Party; L. Forst-Feigelstock, its first treasurer; Gilbert Melcher, in 1920 appointed military commander of the first German regiment created for the eventuality of a Soviet victory in Poland and a subsequent entry of the Red Army into Germany; Johann Koplenig, secretary general then chairman

of the party; and Gottlieb Fiala, a member of the Executive Committee of the party and Executive Committee of the Comintern
(like Koplenig). Two of the founders of the party in Czechoslovakia, Alois Muna and Břetislav Hula, likewise served their Communist apprenticeship in the Bolshevik revolution. The same was true
of Vladimir Čopić, the future secretary of the Yugoslav Communist Party, and of Ernst Friesland (Reuter), the future secretary of
the German Communist Party. Other foreigners in Russia during
the period of the Communist revolution also became leading
figures in their parties or the Comintern, men like the Americans
John Reed and Robert Minor, who had come to Russia as journalists. From France, there were Jacques Sadoul and Suzanne Girault,
who had come to Russia as a teacher and governess, from Persia
Sultan-Zade and from Turkey Mustafa Subhi, not to mention the
many Chinese and Koreans integrated into the Comintern's Far
Eastern activities after the First Congress, such as Chü Chiu-pai,
who came to Russia as a newspaperman in 1920 and seven years
later became the secretary general of the Chinese Communist
Party.

Along with journalists and war prisoners, another category that
spread Bolshevism to other lands was made up of veteran Socialists
impatient of their party's "immobilism," and those with old personal or family attachments to the revolutionary movement in
Russia (for example, Rosa Luxemburg, Leo Jogiches, Karl Liebknecht, Max Levien, Eugen Leviné, Arkadi Maslow). This power of
attraction increased and, if not in 1917-18, at least by 1919-20
had started to act upon Socialist militants in Western Europe, as
L.- O. Frossard, one of those affected by it, has written:

> Assailed by a world of enemies and half starving, amid anarchy and
> turmoil, Russia was struggling to build that land of justice and har-
> mony that we had all dreamed of. Outlawed and hated everywhere else,
> there Socialism was triumphant. What the Socialists of every country
> had been wishing for, wanting, preparing for, waiting for in vain the
> Socialists of Russia, driven by an implacable will, were achieving. Over
> the ancient empire of the Tsars waved the red flag of the International.
> No more exploitation of man by man! Capitalism had at last been
> throttled, floored, dispossessed! Thus everything conspired to make
> the Russia of the Soviets the center of the Socialist world. All
> turned toward her . . . her prodigious radiation warmed Socialist

hearts. Onward! Mankind was not doomed, for over Russia a new day was dawning! As in all the great crises of history, tormented souls were in search of a mystique, which now they had found. Henceforth Moscow was to be for them "the pinnacle of religion." [9]

The ideal seemingly being achieved in Soviet Russia was in total contrast to the war that had devastated Europe. Before these militants (most of them young) embraced the cause of Bolshevik Russia they had already felt attracted to Socialism, not because of its doctrine but out of disgust and hatred of the war, as Frossard emphasized: "Only their hatred of the war brought these young recruits to us. They reached us filled with a terrible bitterness, built up over the tragic years. The war had cruelly marked them, and the odor of death still clung to their martyred flesh. The spirit of revolt was awake in them. Returning from the immense massacre mutilated and battered, they hungered for quick revenge. They blamed the system that had made them suffer, and were ready to overthrow it." [10] So it was enough to be sickened by that slaughter, to be out of sympathy with the old Socialist leaders who had rallied to the support of the existing governments, whether in the name of the "sacred union" in France or of the Burgfriede in Germany, to be automatically on the road to joining up with the Communist International. The political motives and psychological forces that drove these militants into the arms of Communism and the Third International had almost nothing in common with the political motives and psychological forces that had moved an earlier generation, during the period of prolonged peace from 1871 to 1914, to join the Social Democrats and the Second International. This different political origin of the militants in the Communist International was to have an important influence on the future affairs of the Communist movement in Europe.

MASS SUPPORT OF THE COMMUNIST INTERNATIONAL

Just as it was Europe's former Socialist militants who were the first to join the Communist International, it was natural that the first mass leaning toward Communism should originate in existing working-class organizations, namely the Socialist and Labor parties and to a much smaller extent the trade unions, less interested by nature in a "new social order" and more interested in improving their status in the society in which they actually lived. In fact the number of workers belonging to trade unions had roughly tripled, and the membership of the Socialist parties had doubled, between 1913 and 1919. Thus the number of trade-union members in Germany had jumped from 4,513,000 to 11,900,000; in Great Britain from 4,173,000 to 8,024,000; in France from 1,027,000 to 2,500,000; in Italy from 972,000 to 1,800,000; in Belgium from 200,000 to 715,000; in Austria from 260,000 to 803,000; and in Switzerland from 60,000 to 180,000. The increase in Socialist party memberships was no less spectacular. With a membership of 1,430,000 in 1913, the British Labour Party had 4,000,000 by 1919. The French Socialists went from 100,000 in 1914 to 180,000 in 1919. In 1912 the German Social Democratic Party numbered 970,000 while by 1920 the Socialist Party of Germany had 1,180,000 and the USPD had another 893,000 members.

How did these two kinds of mass working-class organizations react to the call to join forces with the Communist International? First of all, it is important to remember that in 1919-20 there existed in Europe a strong current of sympathy for the defense of Soviet Russia. In Great Britain the trade unions and Labour Party spearheaded a move against the Allied military intervention in Russia. But the mere fact of wishing to defend the Communist revolution in Russia did not mean that one was ready to attempt the same thing at home, or even to found a local Communist party. And even among those who did want to found such a party, few indeed were those who conceived of it as a mere extension of Russian Bolshevism on Western European territory.

Generally speaking, the numbers rallying to the Communist International were in inverse proportion to the numerical strength of the organizations in question. The numerically strongest organizations, the trade unions, saw a smaller proportion of their members opt for Bolshevism than did the numerically weaker Socialist parties. The Communists succeeded everywhere in splitting the latter, sometimes gaining a majority, sometimes setting up a sizable faction. On the contrary they were not as successful among the trade unions, for the Communist militants in them represented only a tiny fraction of the membership, tolerated by the leaders of some unions and discriminated against by the leaders of others.

The numerical strength of the Communist movement in each of the Western countries depended on the respective contributions from these two sources, the trade unions and the Socialist parties. The more the Communist parties benefited from a support of the Socialist and trade-union organizations, the more deeply the Communist parties could take root in a country. Conversely, the less a split propelled Socialist and trade-union militants into the Communist fold, the less the new Communist party could thrive and wax. Nowhere in Europe did it prove possible to set up a mass Communist party where the Socialists and trade-union organizations remained impervious to Communism. In only two European countries in 1919 did the trade-union organizations and Socialist parties, closely interlinked, rally to the Communist International. One was Italy, where the Socialist Party decided to join the International on March 19, 1919, and the other was Norway, where the Labor Party did the same on April 8. Everywhere else the Communists would attempt to split the Socialist parties, which with more or less success they proved able to do, though they did not succeed in the trade unions, whose leadership put up more resistance and whose rank and file showed less interest in utopian schemes, especially as they became more and more aware of how badly workingmen fared in the New Russia. In other words, the more actual workers an organization had as members—and in every country the trade unions were numerically stronger than the Socialist parties—the harder it was for the Communists to split the organization. Conversely, the more nonworkers an organization had in its membership (such as the Socialist parties, whose membership contained many rural folk with some intellectuals and semi-intellectuals at the top), the easier it was for the Communists to split it.

In the countries in which the Communists were unable to reach the masses either through the Socialist party or the trade unions— as in England, Belgium, and Austria—the Communist party was condemned to remain a splinter group of no political importance. But even in the countries in which they did succeed in splitting the Socialist parties to their own advantage—as in France, Czechoslovakia, and Germany (in the USPD)—they were unable to duplicate the feat in the trade unions. In France at the end of December 1920, at Tours, the majority of the SFIO voted to join the Communist International, but at the end of July 1921, in Lille, the majority of the trade unions (CGT) voted against joining the Red Trade Union International. In Czechoslovakia the majority of Socialists went over to the Communist party and joined the International, but the majority of organized labor did not follow suit and join the Red Trade Union International. In October 1920 at Halle, Germany, the majority of a large Socialist party, the USPD, voted to join the Communist International, yet in the German trade unions the Communists always remained a weak minority.

Unlike the trade unions and the Socialist parties, the majority of the youth in the Socialist and labor movements went over to Communism. The leading figures at the First International Conference of Socialist Youth held in Stuttgart in August 1907, immediately after the congress of the Second International, with one exception, all became Communist militants. The organizer and one of the two chairmen of that conference was Karl Liebknecht, later a founder of the German Communist Party, and the secretary of the conference was Hermann Remmele, a subsequent leader in the German Communist Party and the Comintern. At the conference reports were presented by four militants: Hendrik de Man, Karl Liebknecht, Henriette Roland-Holst, and Gyula Alpári. All of them but de Man went over to Communism in 1918. In November 1912, at the same time as the extraordinary congress of the Socialist International at Basle, an international conference of Socialist Youth was held. A few years later the representatives of nine out of the fourteen delegations were among the founders of the Communist parties in their respective countries. Moreover, nearly all were associated with the work of the Comintern's leading organs: Kabakchiev (Bulgaria), Höglund (a delegate for three Scandinavian countries), Manner (Finland), Lévy (France), Wijnkoop (Holland), Dobrogeanu-Gherea (Rumania), T. Nerman (Sweden), and Münzenberg (Switzerland). In Sweden the pre-1914 leaders of Socialist Youth, Karl Zeth Höglund, Frederick Ström and Karl Kilbom, were within the Comintern hierarchy from the beginning. The same was true in the case of Antonín Zapotocký and Karel Kreibich, both of whom were pre-war Socialist youth militants, one in the Czech and the other in the Sudeten Social Democratic movement; they became founders of the Czechoslovak Communist party and its representatives in the Communist International. In Italy, the future founder of the Communist party, Amadeo Bordiga, was active in the Socialist youth movement before 1914, and in September 1917 was chosen by the congress of the Federation of Young Socialists to be the editor of its paper *Avanguardia*. The youth who became politically active only after August 4, 1914, were attracted by the Communist International to an even greater extent, and participated in a decisive way, first, in the establishment of individual Communist parties and then in Comintern work. Such was the case of Franz Koritschoner and Richard Schüller in Austria, of Jakob Herzog and Emil Arnold in Switzerland, of Eduard Van Overstraeten in Belgium.

The drive for new members launched by the Comintern in 1919 was more effective among the Socialist youth than among the Socialist parties. Thus in France in April 1920 at the National Conference of Socialist Youth held in Troyes, a large majority of the delegates voted against any immediate joining of the Communist International, but in September of that same year, at a new national conference in Paris, a sizable majority voted in favor of joining. This change of mind preceded by several months a similar development in the SFIO, which in February 1920 at the Strasbourg congress refused to join the Communist International but voted by a large majority to join it in December of that same year at Tours.

This leftist tendency on the part of Socialist youth became all the more characteristic as in many countries the Socialist youth and Socialist party split over the issue of the International. The youth favored joining it; the party was opposed. This was the case in Sweden, where the official Socialist party by proposing to invoke sanctions against some of the youth leaders, particularly Höglund and Kilbom, accelerated the creation (in May 1917) of the Left Social Democratic Party, which was represented at the founding congress of the Communist International, and was praised by Zinoviev at the Comintern's Second Congress in these terms: "We must acknowledge the services which the Left Social Democrats of Sweden have rendered to the Communist International. It is a movement that has grown up out of the Youth movement." [11] Even in this party the youth was ahead of the official leadership in joining the Comintern, the youth proclaiming its membership in May 1919, the party itself not until the following month. In Denmark in May 1919 the majority of members of the Socialist youth voted in favor of an organizational separation from the Social-Democratic party; in October of the same year another referendum voted to sever all ties with official Social Democracy and approved the immediate creation of a Left Socialist party, which soon joined the Comintern, while the Social Democratic Party remained adamantly opposed to it. The same generational break occurred in Norway: in April 1919 the entire Norwegian Labor party decided to adhere to the Comintern, but when in 1923 a conflict arose with Moscow, the majority of the youth remained faithful to the Comintern while the majority of the party broke with Moscow.

The same situation prevailed in Slovakia. In September 1920 the Congress of Socialist Youth (among whose moving spirits were Mihály Farkas, future secretary general of the Communist Youth International, and Viliam Široký, future prime minister of the Czechoslovak Communist government) unanimously voted to join the Communist International. When the Congress of Slovakia's Social Democrats met on September 19, it came out in favor of the ideas of the Communist International, but not unanimously, because the party leader Derer and his followers walked out. This same break between the Socialist youth and the Socialist party occurred in Spain. In December 1919 the Federation of Socialist Youth decided to join the Communist Youth International (which represented a final break with the Socialist party), and in March 1920 that Federation transformed itself into the Workers' Communist Party and adhered to the Comintern, while in April 1921 the majority of the Socialist party voted against joining the International. The result was that the young element broke away with the minority favorable to the Comintern, almost all of them winding up in the Communist camp. The same thing happened in Italy in January 1921, with the difference that in 1919 the Socialist party in its totality decided to affiliate itself with the Comintern, but when an ideological cleavage began to divide the party into two camps—the Socialists, followers of either Serrati or Turati, and the Communists, belonging to either the *Ordine Nuovo* group or the group animated by Bordiga—the majority of the party remained faithful to the Socialists while most of the Socialist youth opted for the Communist currents. At the Leghorn congress in January 1921, the majority of the Socialist party voted for Serrati and refused to do the bidding of the Comintern, while the majority of the Socialist youth delegates pronounced itself against Serrati and for the Communist party and the Comintern. A few days after the Leghorn congress, on January 27, the Federation of Socialist Youth assembled at its congress in Florence, and decided by a near-unanimous vote (35,000 out of 43,000) to join the Communist party; at the same congress Giuseppe Berti, the spokesman for the Bordiga tendency, was elected secretary of the new Federation of Communist Youth.

The break between the Socialist youth and their Socialist elders occurred in other countries, too, from Switzerland to the Balkans. In Switzerland in January 1920, the leadership of the Federation of Socialist Youth announced complete independence with respect to any political party; to this the Socialist party responded by expelling the Federation from its ranks. In Rumania, where in May 1921 the Communist party was established, the overwhelming majority of Socialist youth joined it. Nearly everywhere the "old" and the "young" no longer spoke the same language. When the young revolted against the war and its consequences, and thereby against the policies of the official Social Democratic parties during the war, their attitudes were not shared by the Social-Democratic leaders. And when these "elders" repudiated Russian Communism and were loath to join the Communist International, their arguments had little influence on the young. As for the International itself, its leaders in Moscow perceived from the outset the important role that youth could play in broadening the movement toward Communism and building up a sound Communist movement. The first written directive sent by Trotsky to the Communist Party of France in the name of the Comintern's Executive Committee, on July 26, 1921, contained the admonition: "We have to recruit new militants, particularly among the Communist youth." [12] From the birth of the Communist International, therefore, age was a dividing line between those militants who stayed with the Socialist parties and those who went over to Communism. Among the former, anyone under thirty was an exception, among the latter anyone over thirty.*

The professions or occupations of these young pioneers of Communism exhibited one constant: working-class people were rare, the overwhelming majority consisting of intellectuals and semi-intellectuals, with journalists, teachers, and lawyers predominating. At the founding congress of the French Communist Party in Tours, of the twenty-four members comprising the Directing Committee two were workers, while there were a number of journalists (like Amédée Dunois, Boris Souvarine, Paul Vaillant-Couturier, Victor Méric, and Paul Louis) and teachers (like Louis-Oscar Frossard, Marcel Cachin, Albert Treint, and Antoine Ker). In the German Communist Party, of the twelve members comprising the Zentrale that was elected at the founding congress ten were intellectuals, and six of these doctors of law or philosophy. The same was largely true of the other Communist parties at the time of their founding, in the Balkan countries, such as Yugoslavia, Bulgaria, or Rumania, those of Western Europe such as Italy and Spain, or Central and Eastern Europe such as Hungary and Poland. When the Second Congress of the International assembled in July and August of 1920, it was striking to note the very small proportion of workers in this group claiming the right to speak for the working class of the world. To complete the paradox, the

*In Italy, opposing Giacinto Serrati, born in 1874, and Costantino Lazzari, born in 1857 (like Filippo Turati), were two Communist nuclei, one in Naples under Amadeo Bordiga, born in 1889, and the other in Turin with Antonio Gramsci, born in 1891, Angelo Tasca, born in 1892, and Umberto Terracini, born in 1895. In France, on the one side there were Marcel Sembat, born in 1862, Albert Thomas, born in 1878, Paul Renaudel, born in 1871, and Jean Longuet, born in 1876, opposed by Raymond Lefebvre, born in 1891, Boris Souvarine, born in 1895, and Paul Vaillant-Couturier, born in 1892—Fernand Loriot and Charles Rappoport being rare exceptions, having reached the age of 50. In 1920 Léon Blum, a spokesman for the Committee of Socialist Resistance, was 48 and Boris Souvarine, who played the same role within the Committee for the Third International, was 25. In Germany, Philipp Scheidemann had been born in 1865, Friedrich Ebert in 1870, but Paul Levi in 1883, Heinrich Brandler in 1881, August Thalheimer in 1884, with Clara Zetkin the exception here. In Belgium, Emile Vandervelde had been born in 1866 and Camille Huysmans in 1871, while Van Overstraeten had been born in 1890, and Joseph Jacquemotte in 1883. In Austria, Karl Renner had been born in 1870, Friedrich Adler in 1879, and Otto Bauer in 1881, while Franz Koritschoner was born in 1891, the other founders of the Austrian party being still younger, as for example Paul Friedländer and Elfriede Eisler-Friedländer.

militants of working-class origin who had come to the congress belonged in the main to two trends or currents outside of Bolshevism—either Anarcho-Syndicalism and Revolutionary Syndicalism on the one hand, or Reformist Syndicalism on the other—whereas the nonworker militants, mostly intellectuals, were the very ones who had already opted for the Communist International. J. T. Murphy, a delegate of the British Shop Stewards' Committees, who was to become prominent in the British Communist Party and the Comintern, on the point of being won over to Communism was struck by this as regards the congress presidium: "In fact, I do not think a single one of the leaders of the congress was of the working class. I remarked on this to Radek, who quickly retorted by asking if Lenin was any the worse for belonging to the same social group. I agreed that he wasn't and ventured to doubt whether so high a proportion as were on the platform could be regarded as of the same caliber as Lenin." [13]

A strategist of the first order, Lenin was perfectly well aware that the support of these young intellectuals was not in itself enough, but he believed that it could be used as a tool to bring the masses over to Communism and the International. He had in mind two categories of "masses": those which were partly under the influence of the Social Democrats and the "trade-union aristocracy," and those which remained outside of these two mainstreams of Western working-class organization. Hence Lenin and the Comintern appealed to the Revolutionary Syndicalists and Anarcho-Syndicalists on the one hand, and on the other to the non-organized toiling masses, industrial as well as farm laborers.

This non-orthodox social and political background (non-orthodox from the viewpoint of classical Marxism) of many new Communist adherents was particularly striking in Germany. When at the founding congress of the German Communist Party in December 1918, the party leaders Rosa Luxemburg, Leo Jogiches, Karl Liebknecht, and Paul Levi were outvoted on the issue of tactics, in his confidential report to the Executive Committee of the Comintern at its Second Congress Levi attributed their defeat to the fact that when the Communist Party of Germany was founded it "included within it a large number of groups which, as regards revolutionary development, had sprung up haphazardly all over the country and mostly lacked any clear political ideology," which he characterized as "politically unorganized elements."[14] When the German Communist Party started to implant itself methodically throughout the country, after 1920-21, it gained ascendancy over two other workers' parties, the SPD and the USPD, only in central Germany, of which Trotsky wrote: "The proletarians of central Germany, the workers in the mining regions, have represented in recent times, even during the war, one of the most retarded sections of the German working class. In their majority they followed not the Social Democrats but the patriotic, bourgeois, and clerical cliques, and remained devoted to the Emperor, and so on and so forth."[15]

In some other countries, as in France when the Communist Party was founded there, a special source of Communist mass strength was the peasantry. The SFIO federations of the central and west-central parts of the country, mainly peasant like the Departments of Dordogne, Creuse, Corrèze, Cher, and Allier, came out almost unanimously for joining the Third International. These federations were not made up, strictly speaking, of the peasant proletariat (farm laborers) but essentially of small landowners. In other Departments, where there was no such unanimous support for the Third International, the breakdown of the votes within the federations showed the city dwellers voting against joining, the rural people voting in favor. This was true in the Department of Var, whose spokesman at the congress in Tours said in his report: "The urban sections came out mostly for the Longuet-Paul Faure motion. It was Toulon, the Department's most strongly labor-oriented town, that gave a majority to that motion. . . . The older sections of Var came out almost unanimously for adoption of the Blum or Longuet motions. It was the newer sections, particularly some of the recently created rural ones, that voted to adopt the Cachin-Frossard motion."[16]

This phenomenon, observed in the south of France, was in evidence in the north also, as the same delegate reported: "In the Lower Seine the countryside is for the Third International, as everywhere else, but we have to find out why in certain of the cities, even though they are Socialist, the majority do not favor it. As an example, I cite the case of Le Havre, whose splendid revolutionary spirit you know."[17] This split was to be characteristic of the labor movement in France in the years ahead, as Secretary-

General of the French Communist Party L.-O. Frossard noted in June 1922 in his statement to the enlarged Executive Committee of the Comintern: "Generally speaking, the Communist idea is marking time and in some instances is even in retreat in the urban areas, though it continues to make progress in the rural ones." [18]

THE SUPPORT OF THE REVOLUTIONARY SYNDICALISTS

While the Second International was the only existing organization acting in the name of Marxism and addressing itself to the working class, its reformist practice often contradicted its revolutionary phraseology, yet on two points the spirit and the letter of Marxism were observed. First, since Marx had already battled Bakunin at the First International, and as the London congress of the Second International in 1896 had voted to expel the anarchists, the Social Democrats had completely broken with the Anarcho-Syndicalists. They could either ignore or fight each other, but not cooperate. Secondly, Marxism being a theory and practice designed for the working class, the Social Democrats addressed themselves mainly, if not exclusively, to the industrial proletariat. And when Russia's Social Revolutionary Party oriented its action primarily toward the peasants and not the industrial workers, it was allowed into the Second International but nobody in it or in the International considered it Marxist.

On these two planes, Lenin would be practicing revisionism, without admitting it. Unlike Bernstein and other Marxists who freely acknowledged that they were revisionists, Lenin was so in fact while continuing to proclaim his doctrinal orthodoxy. Unlike the Russian Socialist Revolutionaries who directed their appeal to the peasant masses without reference to Marxism, Lenin addressed himself to these same masses but claimed at the same time that he was being true to Marxism. The paradox was only apparent, for Lenin was acting not as an ideologue but as a strategist. A political strategist, in order to carry out any revolutionary plans, must have at his disposal some masses ready to fight, just as a military strategist must have troops. As soon as Lenin perceived that the Revolutionary Syndicalist and Anarcho-Syndicalist movements in the West could bring new militants to the cause of the Communist International, he had a ready explanation for this which he included in his polemical arsenal as ammunition against the Social Democrats. Here is how he justified opening the doors of the Communist International to the Anarchists and Revolutionary Syndicalists in his *"Left-Wing" Communism, an Infantile Disorder*: "Anarchism was often a sort of punishment for the opportunist sins of the working-class movement. The two monstrosities were mutually complementary. And the fact that in Russia, notwithstanding that its population is more petty-bourgeois than that of the European countries, anarchism exercised a comparatively insignificant influence during both revolutions (1905 and 1917) and during the preparatory periods of those revolutions, must undoubtedly be partly placed to the credit of Bolshevism, which has always waged a most ruthless and uncompromising struggle against opportunism."[19] Lenin failed to add, however—for the obvious reason that it would have been tactically inopportune to recall these facts just as he was about to bring the Anarcho-Syndicalists into the Comintern—that Bolshevism, too, was a pitiless foe of anarchism. During the 1905 revolution, when the anarchists asked to be represented in the Petrograd Soviet, Lenin opposed their admission. Immediately after the 1917 revolution, Lenin temporarily accepted help from anarchist elements, though later he waged a veritable war of extermination against them, including the armed movement of Nestor Makhno in the Ukraine. Even in 1921, when Europe's Revolutionary Syndicalists were supporting the Communist International, Lenin continued to hurl thunderbolts against the "anarchist and Syndicalist deviation" within Russia's Communist Party. His target was a "workers' opposition" composed of Old Bolsheviks like Shliapnikov and Miasnikov, who having always followed Lenin were now becoming guilty of anarchist and Syndicalist deviation—simply because they became critical of Lenin's policies. On the other hand, many of Europe's true Anarcho-Syndicalist leaders, unfamiliar with Lenin's political ideas and opposed to the very thought of an organized political party, were deemed worthy, in 1920 and 1921, of being invited to Moscow to join the International. Here again, the contradiction in Lenin's attitude was only apparent. When he condemned the Bolshevik opposition for Syndicalist and anarchist deviation, he was acting within the confines of Soviet Russia, where his regime refused to tolerate any opposition whatever; but when he welcomed the anarchists and Syndicalists from capitalist Europe, his target was the Western world where he was preparing to assault the established order and needed all the allies he could get, including the anarchists and Revolutionary Syndicalists.

At the beginning of 1920, in the official organ of the Communist International, Lenin congratulated himself on the fact that the old enmity between Socialism and anarchism was being toned down, with the anarchists aligning themselves with Communism and not with the Second International. The following year Lenin continued to stress this anarchist support of Communism, writing in his *Letter to the German Communists*: "Throughout the world anarchism is splitting into two camps, pro-Soviet and anti-Soviet, for and against the dictatorship of the proletariat. This is not a new development but dates from the beginning of the imperialist war of 1914-18."[20] Aside from the fictitious claim that the anarchists took pro- and anti-Soviet positions in 1914, when Soviet power did not exist and nobody was talking about a dictatorship of the proletariat, it is true that a cleavage did occur in anarchist ranks. But here as elsewhere the attractive force of Bolshevism did not stem from its doctrine but from a confluence of events. Seen from the doctrinal standpoint, Bolshevism as defined in its 1919 program was the exact opposite of what the anarchists stood for, not to mention the organizational obstacle, where in the matter of centralism and discipline the Communist party was worse than anything that anarchism had ever fought. But seen in the context of prevailing political fashions, Bolshevism practiced what anarchism preached, namely, destruction of the bourgeois state and its apparatus plus extermination of the official Social-Democratic movement and the trade-union bureaucracy.

In 1919 the first nuclei of Revolutionary Syndicalism to come over to the Comintern were in France, with the group clustered around the newspaper *La vie ouvrière* (Worker's Life). This process was triggered in France sooner than elsewhere because Alfred Rosmer and the founder of the group, Pierre Monatte, had become friendly with Trotsky during the latter's exile in France early in World War I. In its first issue, *La vie ouvrière* published an article by Rosmer entitled "For the Third International,"[21] and in subsequent issues support of the Third International remained a fixed policy. Its director, Pierre Monatte, joined the Committee for the Third International, becoming one of its three secretaries. A short time later the leader of the Revolutionary Syndicalists in Italy, Armando Borghi, secretary of the Italian Syndical Union, wrote for the Comintern press and was in Moscow for the Second World Congress. In 1920 an eminent representative of German anarchism, Erich Mühsam, embraced the cause of the Communist International. In British Anarcho-Syndicalism, too, there were to be important defections to the Communist International, like that of James Larkin, an Irish workingmen leader, who would take part in the Comintern's Second Congress.

There were also some movements with anarchist or Syndicalist-revolutionary tendencies, such as the Shop Stewards' and Workers' Committees in Great Britain, several of whose militants attended the Second World Congress and later played an important role in the British Communist movement, men like William Gallacher and J. T. Murphy. The same happened in the United States with the militant organization known as the Industrial Workers of the World (IWW), some of whose leaders went to Soviet Russia and stayed there, such as George Andreychine and William D. Haywood, while others went as official delegates to the founding congress of the Red Trade Union International, one of these being George Williams.

In all these cases the militants of Revolutionary Syndicalism showed a tendency to identify their pacifism and antimilitarism with Lenin's opposition to the imperialist war, unaware of his idea in favor of turning it into a continuation as a worldwide civil war. They also imagined the Soviet system in Russia to constitute the exercise of power of, by, and for the workers, a belief made possible by their ignorance of the monopoly role of the Bolshevik Party in Soviet affairs. Thus what a publication of the IWW said on "Soviet rule" in September 1919 could be taken as an ideological justification for all Revolutionary Syndicalists and Anarcho-Syndicalists to support the cause of the Comintern: "Once the power is in the hands of the Soviets, the evolution toward industrial democracy is as swift as lightning. . . . In industrial organization the divine force of life received a form of expression which is full and complete. It is open, direct, free. The Bolsheviki also knew this. Hence 'all power to the Soviets! ' . . . The Soviets in Russia, like the Industrial Workers of the World organizations, are but instruments with which the workers do things themselves for themselves." [22]

The attractive force of Russian Communism consisted in this very ambiguity, which allowed a Marxist to believe that the Bolshevik victory was an extension of Marx's thought, and a Revolutionary Syndicalist and anarchist to believe that it was the achievement of his own non-Marxian ambitions. Indeed, if many European Socialists joined the Comintern in the name of the postulates of Marx, many Revolutionary Syndicalists and Anarcho-Syndicalists saw in the Bolshevik triumph a supreme realization of some of the ideas of their masters, who had been Marx's enemies, men like Proudhon, Bakunin, and Kropotkin. But since in most West European countries it was Marx's ideas that had prevailed over those of his adversaries, and since the political and labor organizations claiming to be Marxist were much stronger than the Revolutionary Syndicalist and Anarcho-Syndicalist groups, the latter in joining the Comintern could not bring any significant segment of the working class to the cause of Communism, only small active minorities. The one exception was Spain.

The struggles that pitted Marx against Bakunin, and which dragged on between the Socialists and anarchists during the first years of the Second International, ended everywhere in Europe with the victory of the Marxists over the Anarcho-Syndicalists, save in Spain, where at the beginning of the twentieth century the Anarcho-Syndicalists were more important and powerful than the Socialists. At the December 1919 congress of the Confederación Nacional del Trabajo (CNT) ["National Confederation of Labor"], which claimed a membership of 700,000, a motion made in the presence of 450 delegates to join the Communist International was adopted by acclamation, and a delegation was sent to Moscow for the Second World Congress; however, only one of its members, Angel Pestaña, succeeded in actually getting there, after an eventful three-month journey. The CNT's joining the Comintern reflected that misunderstanding so typical of many who affiliated initially with the Third International. The Communist neophytes attributed their own ideas (or passions) to Lenin instead of trying to learn what his political doctrine and practice really were. The resolution of the CNT congress represented an extreme case, pro-

claiming, as it did, the support of the Spanish Anarcho-Syndicalists for both Bakunin and Lenin: "Summing up the ideas set forth
by the different speakers who have addressed us here today, the
Central Committee proposes: first, that the CNT of Spain declare
itself a firm defender of the principles of the First International
backed by Bakunin; and second, that it declare its provisional
support for the Communist International because of its revolutionary character, but that simultaneously the CNT of Spain should
organize and convene a universal workers' congress that will determine the bases on which a true International of Workers shall
act." [23]

One of the Spanish anarchists most strongly impressed by the
October Revolution and its aftermath, Manuel Buenacasa, Secretary-General of the CNT in 1918-19, described ten years later—
when he had become an opponent of Communism—the influence
exerted by the Russian Revolution on the Spanish anarchists:
"The Russian Revolution gave still greater strength to the subver-
sive, Socialist, and libertarian spirit of the Spanish anarchists. . . .
For many of us, indeed for most of us, the Russian Bolshevik was
a demigod, bearer of the freedom of the common weal. . . . Who in
Spain, being an anarchist, was not proud to call himself a Bolshevik? " [24] In the same vein another witness to the events wrote:
"During the final weeks of 1917 the news of the Bolshevik triumph
reached Spain. The masses of workers did not know the details
and were none too familiar, either, with the victors' ideology. But
the certain knowledge that in one great nation capitalism had
collapsed, and that henceforth the workers would be governing
there, produced indescribable enthusiasm. . . ." [25]

It was only later that a political justification was found, the
anarchists believing that they had discovered elements of their
own ideas in the words and deeds of Lenin. One of the pioneers in
this Spanish support for Communism, Joaquín Maurín, attributed
the sudden new confraternity with the Bolsheviks to three key
factors—agrarian revolution, unconditional peace, and the institution of the Soviets: "The Spanish anarchists had grasped the peasant problem much earlier than had the Socialists. . . . What mainly
attracted Anarcho-Syndicalist elements to the Bolshevik Revolution was agrarian reform and the promise to end the war. The
Bolshevik slogan "peace, bread, land" seemed to have been bor-

rowed from the Anarcho-Syndicalists. . . . The myth of the soviet [workers' council] was very close to the role envisaged for the 'syndicate,' and the Anarcho-Syndicalists made it their own." [26]

BOLSHEVISM'S UNIVERSAL MESSAGE

Compared to the twentieth-century influence of Bolshevism, Marx's messianic message in the nineteenth century was necessarily limited, both sociologically and geographically. He had addressed himself to a single social class, the industrial proletariat, product of a single economic order, capitalism. He belonged and referred to but a single region of the earth, the West. He exploited neither nationalism nor the peasantry for the sake of the revolution. Lenin's message was quite different. His revisionism consisted in his taking a world view. Instead of addressing himself only to the working class, he would appeal to all exploited classes. Instead of singling out capitalist society, he would frame his message to cover pre-capitalist, feudal society as well. Instead of beaming his ideas only at the West, he would broadcast them worldwide. Instead of combating nationalism and scorning the peasants, he would draw strength from both of those gigantic forces.

In March 1919 the program of Russia's Communist (Bolshevik) Party, drawn up by Bukharin and Lenin and adopted at the Party's Eighth Congress, affirmed at the outset: "The era of the Communist Proletarian Revolution has begun throughout the world. This revolution is the inevitable outcome of the development of capitalism, at present dominant in most civilized countries." [27] That same month, at the First Congress of the Communist International, and the next year at the Second Congress, this belief in a world Communist revolution was the prime substance of everything that Lenin and his colleagues had the two congresses adopt. Such a five-continent revolution was not a part of either Karl Marx's ideology or the Socialist International's program. Until Lenin's victory in Petrograd and the establishment of the Communist International, every major historical event (war or revolution) and every political organization had had only a regional or at the most a continental effect, and never a worldwide one. The French Revolution was confined to Europe, its techniques and the existing communications of the time not allowing for its universalization. The First and the Second Internationals did not go beyond the Western world, and when Marx and Engels and their disciples launched the call "Proletarians of all countries, unite" it was obvious that they were appealing only to the workers of the industrial countries. Even World War I saw battles only on the European continent, while the battlefield of the world revolution passed within a few years from Europe to China and Indonesia and shortly thereafter reached the Latin American continent.

Whereas Marx reduced the history of the Western world to a single dominant antagonism, Lenin built his revolutionary policy around the exploitation of a multitude of antagonisms, emphasizing first one, then another, depending on which seemed most useful at the moment. In Hegelian dialectics, contradiction was the source of all progress; in Lenin's policies it became the prerequisite of all success. In the worldwide political war that he waged against his enemies Lenin was never embarrassed if his exploitation of this or that alleged contradiction seemed momentarily in conflict with his doctrine. He also benefited from the fact that when planning worldwide exploitation of a specific contradiction through the agency of the Communist International, he could draw on his own experience in Russia with the Bolshevik Party and the multinational empire. Having succeeded in Russia, he was sure that he would be no less successful in the world at large.

With Lenin, Communism on the plane of revolutionary strategy became identified with the exploitation of all contradictions, and on the plane of revolutionary organization it became the great haven for the disaffected. There did not exist in Russia (or in any other country in which Communists later seized power) a solid base for the development of a movement according to Marx's views—that is, the existence of a large working class created by the industrialization of a country; yet there certainly existed a solid base for the development of a movement according to Lenin's views, namely the reality of a deep dissatisfaction, in a majority of cases more of national, pacifist, and racial origin than of social discontent. Although dissatisfaction has always existed in all societies, Lenin's Communism was the first modern political movement which learned how to manipulate it in various ways: technically (by channelling it into appropriate organizational molds), ideologically (by offering a global vision of an all-encompassing social change), and tactically (by its ability to profit from any circumstances, without being embarrassed by doctrinal and moral scruples). The essential thing for Communism was to become that social force capable of capturing the existing dissatisfactions that might propel it to power. Lenin, the ex-member of the Socialist International, succeeded in doing this in Petrograd in November 1917 (but another ex-member of that same International, Mussolini, was no less successful in Rome, five years later).

The main contradiction that Lenin had been able to exploit within Russia so as to transform his tiny party into a mass movement was that between war and peace. He had only scorn for pacifism. But once he realized that his call to civil war did not go down well with the masses while a plea for peace won their deepest approval, he did not hesitate to give peace top billing. He explained his turnabout with unabashed frankness at a confidential meeting with foreign Communists on July 11, 1921 (though the text of his statement was not made public until 1958):

> At the beginning of the war we, the Bolsheviks, held to only one slogan: ruthless civil war. We branded everyone a traitor who was not for civil war. But when we returned to Russia in March 1917, we changed our position completely. On returning and talking with the peasants and workers, we realized that they all favored defending the fatherland, but naturally in a completely different sense than was meant by the Mensheviks. . . . At our April 22 conference the left wing demanded the immediate overthrow of the government. The Central Committee, on the other hand, was against the slogan calling for civil war, and we instructed all agitators in the provinces to denounce the shameless lie that the Bolsheviks wanted civil war. [28]

It was in 1917 also that Lenin moved to exploit pacifist feeling in the world at large. When he had a statement drawn up and signed by eleven European internationalists willing to endorse his trip across the Kaiser's Germany, six of these signatories were Scandinavian Socialists profoundly imbued with pacifist ideas. When he took power in Petrograd, his first public decree pertained to peace, and it went beyond the confines of the Russo-German war: "The [Workers' and Peasants'] Government proposes to all the governments and peoples of all the belligerent countries that they

conclude an armistice immediately."[29] Indeed, among the senti-
ments that led many of the young intellectuals in Europe and
America to rally to the cause of Soviet Russia and the Third
International, pacifism was certainly not the least influential with
some of those in leading positions, such as Georges Pioch, the
secretary of the most important organization in the French Communist Party immediately after its founding, the Federation of the
Seine. These pacifists, of course, were all completely unaware that
Lenin's opposition to the World War did not remotely mean that
he was against war in general, as the 1919 Bolshevik program made
clear: "All of this leads inevitably to the planning not only of civil
wars within different countries, but of revolutionary wars both by
proletarian states obliged to defend themselves and by oppressed
peoples in order to shake off the yoke of imperialist powers."[30]
The Western pacifists were probably unaware of the role which the
war in the Bolshevik view played for the cause of Communism:
instead of waiting for the realization of Socialism through a maximally developed capitalism, the Bolsheviks expected to seize power through the maximally developed consequences of the war. This
is what Zinoviev declared in all bluntness at the end of the first
year of his presidency of the Communist International: "The
world revolution will be born from the world war. This is directly
related to the fact that the revolution started in the most backward countries. It is also the world war to which the first proletarian revolution is indebted for the truce which was so benefici-
ent. . . . Victory of Communism is as inevitable as the return of the
day after the night."*

Communism could achieve decisive successes through the exploitation of two key ideas, peace and nationalism, and through
the mobilization of two key social forces, youth and the peasantry, which built the bulk of Communist troops first in Russia
and then in the other countries where the Communist revolution
triumphed. The synthesis of these four factors operated first in the

*L 'Internationale Communiste, No. 6, October 1919, pp. 827-28. Ten years
later, writing for the last time and as a simple publicist in the same review,
Zinoviev repeated a similar thought: "The Communist International is born
from the world war, and it is in a new war that her destiny will again be
decided." "Dix années de lutte pour le révolution mondiale," ibid., March
1929, p. 204.

Bolshevik victory in Russia and then in the establishment of the Communist movement throughout the world.* Every time the Communist movement succeeded in identifying itself in the eyes of the masses (above all in the eyes of the youth and the peasantry) with the claims of peace or with the service of a national interest, its chances of political victory were powerfully enhanced. Every time another political movement preempted pacifist and nationalist feelings, the political task of the Communists was rendered much more difficult. And every time the Communist movement could be branded as an enemy of peace and nationalism and thus be deprived of popular support, it suffered a severe setback.

From the outset, the Communist International tended to identify itself in Europe if not with the interests of all nations at least with those of the vanquished ones. "Bolshevism is a sickness of defeated peoples," [31] said Jenő Varga in 1919, attributing that definition to the "champions of the bourgeoisie." It is true that the revolutionary or supposedly revolutionary acts of 1919-20 were on a larger scale in the countries defeated in the war—Germany, Austria-Hungary, and even Italy (regarded as cheated out of the fruits of victory)—than in the victor countries. Then came the fight against the Treaty of Versailles, the Russo-German Rapallo Accord, the Comintern's action against the very existence of certain countries (such as Yugoslavia)—all of which tended to bring the defeated countries closer to Moscow.

Although Lenin was initially thinking in terms of the West, as soon as the Communist International was founded he had to address himself simultaneously to the peoples of Europe (primarily the defeated ones) and to the oppressed peoples of Asia. In his report to the Second All-Russian Congress of the Communist Organizations of Eastern Peoples, held in November 1919, he mentioned first the civil war in Germany, then the social revolution in Western Europe, and lastly the revolution in the East: "It goes without saying that only the proletariat of all the world's advanced countries can win final victory. We Russians are beginning the

*It goes without saying that a skillful exploitation of the pacifist feelings existing among the masses did not rule out—in fact it complemented—an effective use of armed force in the service of the Party. The first Communist victory, that of November 7, 1917 in Petrograd, was the proof of such a combination.

work which will strengthen the English, French or German proletariat. But they cannot triumph without the help of the toiling masses of all the oppressed colonial peoples, especially those of the East." [32] These oppressed colonial peoples, having already had a fictitious representation at the Comintern's founding congress, were to play a considerable role, which they certainly did not play at the congresses of the Second International, at which prior to 1914 no Negro (African or American) or Arab was ever seen on the speakers' platform, and from which only one Asian ever spoke, the Japanese, Katayama, who no longer lived in his homeland. By contrast, at the early congresses of the Communist International one saw a whole parade of Negroes, Arabs, and Asians. Among the latter, the most numerous were militants from two great Asian countries, both lacking a modern economy: India without national independence and China without national unity.

In the accelerated rush of history after World War I, Lenin's ideology was snapped up by the revolutionary movement in the East, just as in the preceding century Marx's ideology had been seized by the revolutionary movement in Russia. When he was elaborating his theory concerning the inevitable fall of capitalism and the no less inevitable advent of the proletarian revolution, Marx certainly did not have Russia primarily in mind, but this did not prevent many young Russian intellectuals from deriving their faith from Marxism, nor Lenin from waging his revolution in the name of Marxism. And later on, when Lenin after 1917 was elaborating his own conception of world revolution, he certainly did not have primarily the East in mind, particularly because in China and India the majority of the intellectuals were under the dominant influence of Sun Yat-sen and Gandhi. But this did not prevent the more radical young semi-intellectual Asian militants from deriving their faith from Bolshevism, nor from working for revolution in Asia first.

As Marxism had arrived in Russia at just the right moment, in the 1880s, to supply a Weltanschauung to a revolution-minded youth ready to fight but in need of a "scientific" political formula, so in the 1920s Lenin's Communism came to Asia to furnish a Weltanschauung to those young militants who needed political, moral, and material support for the revolution that they envisaged. As Lenin had taken from Marx what suited his temperament and will to battle, so the young revolutionaries of the East who rallied to Lenin and the Comintern took from them what they lacked to implement their designs. The idea was a simple one, which reconciled the struggles for two different ideals, one nationalist (independence) and the other revolutionary (social justice), through a system of political organization of which they had scant knowledge, using a new political technique the more readily because they had never been systematically exposed to the Marxism of Marx nor had any experience with the Socialist movement of the Second International. Lenin's Communism struck them as a weapon which they needed in order to gain power and achieve the national and social liberation of their peoples.

In 1919 and 1920, between Lenin and the Comintern on the one hand and the first Asian Communist militants on the other there was a difference of opinion as to the best Communist world strategy. Believing revolution imminent in the West, the Comintern leaders did not hesitate to assert at Eastern congresses that the West took priority, as Lenin stated in his report in November 1919, a thesis which the Comintern delegation repeated to the first congress of Eastern peoples at Baku in September 1920 through the person of Pavlovich-Weltmann, an ex-Menshevik who had gone over to Bolshevism and become an expert of Eastern affairs: "One must not forget this very simple truth: that the peoples of the East could not achieve their freedom without joining forces with the [Western] proletariat."[33] But at the very moment Lenin was preaching the priority of revolution in the West, a young Oriental, Sultan-Galiev, was criticizing this Bolshevik point of view: "From the tactical standpoint, however, the revolution has been misdirected. What might appear important when seen in isolation (the Spartacist movement in Germany, the Hungarian revolution, etc.) are but secondary phenomena when viewed in the total context. This stems from the fact that the revolutionary leaders' attention was riveted on the West. . . . Orienting the international Socialist revolution exclusively toward the West was a mistake."[34]

What attracted the first young Asian intellectuals and semi-intellectuals to the Communist International was their own certainty that they could bring about a triumph of Communism directly and immediately without having to wait for capitalism to develop in their respective countries, or for the victory of Socialist revolution in Europe. Two young nationalist militants from different regions who espoused the new faith offer a good illustration of this conversion to Communism. One was M. N. Roy, born in India, the heart of Asia; the other was Ho Chi Minh, born in Indochina, at Asia's southeast tip. Before October 1917 neither knew anything at all about Russian Bolshevism, and both were outside the Second International and unfamiliar with Marx's theory. But when he came to the Second Comintern Congress in 1920, Roy was already a believer in the possibility of direct and immediate social revolution more in the East than in the West: "What I learned during my several months' stay in Germany about the conditions in Europe and their immediate perspective fostered in me the feeling that the proletariat in the metropolitan countries would not succeed in their heroic endeavour to capture power unless Imperialism was weakened by the revolt of the colonial peoples ... I wondered why the revolution should not spread eastward, and resolved to rush to the exciting task of opening the second front of the World Revolution." [35] The next year, in 1921, young Nguyen Ai Quac (the future Ho Chi Minh), newly converted to Communism, would profess the same faith: "Is the Communist system applicable to Asia in general and Indochina in particular? This is the question that interests us today. Our answer is yes." [36]

The Russian Revolution and the Communist International thus became the instrument of a great long-range historic mutation. Anton Pannekoek, the Dutch Marxist philosopher who was still a supporter of that revolution and International when he wrote in April 1920, highlighted the twofold aspect of that mutation. First, Russia was in the process of becoming "the center of the new Communist world order," a phenomenon which he placed in its historical context in these terms: "Certainly this will not be the first time in the history of the world when, as man switches to a new mode of production or is passing through one of its phases, the center of power shifts to other regions. In antiquity it moved from the Near East to Southern Europe, in the Middle Ages from Southern to Western Europe. With the creation of colonial and mercantile capital, first Spain, then Holland and England, and with the rise of industry, England alone, became the leading country."[37] Secondly, this great new historic role now devolving upon Russia as the center of world Communism was to make itself felt, according to Pannekoek, more in Asia than in Europe:

> We fail to see this world revolution in its full universal significance if we view it only from the standpoint of Western Europe. Russia is not only the eastern part of Europe but—not merely geographically but economically as well—much more the western part of Asia.... The Russian revolution is the beginning of Asia's great revolt against the West-European concentration of capital in England. One generally looks only at their effect on Western Europe, where the Russian revolutionaries, owing to their advanced theoretical training, have become teachers of the proletariat striving upward to Communism. But even more important is their influence on the East.[38]

During four centuries of expansion, Western Europe had imposed its domination on other continents by dint of its superior technological and industrial capabilities. Its technology and industry, so long as they remained solely in European hands, had sustained European domination for ages, the sole exception being that they happened to be assimilated by one people of color, the Japanese. But now it had been learned that these weapons with which Europe had been able to impose its will could be turned against Europeans, as Japanese industry demonstrated to European capitalism, and as the war of 1904-5 had proved to the Russians. But this case was atypical; Europe's material strength had been copied, but its political ideology had not. Until then none of its great political ideas—neither those of the French Revolution, nor nineteenth-century nationalism, nor parliamentary democracy, nor the utopian or Marxist socialisms—had had any repercussions in mass movements on the continents inhabited by people of color (except to a certain extent, during the 1911 Chinese revolution).

With the victory of the Bolshevik revolution and the founding of the Communist International, the underdeveloped continents encountered for the first time a political ideology from the West that was readily transferable to the East. Like Lenin, who had russified Western Marxism and called for revolution against capitalism, the Communists of the underdeveloped countries would easternize Russian Bolshevism and call for holy war against capitalism *and* the West (the two for them being the same). Ever since the Industrial Revolution the history of the West had been synonymous with the history of the world, the only actors on the scene being Westerners. But with the advent of the Bolshevik revolution and founding of the Communist International, the non-Western peoples and continents were invited onto the stage of world history, an invitation the local Communist militants promptly accepted despite their initially small numbers and often divergent views.

On two occasions during his life as a revolutionary, Lenin felt that his hour had struck on history's great clock, and each time he acted accordingly. The first was in the autumn of 1917, when he recognized that he could seize power in Petrograd. The second was when he realized that it was possible to wage an effective fight against Western colonialism in Asia and elsewhere. A single night had sufficed to assure the Communist victory in Petrograd, but it was going to take decades to light the fires of battle among the peoples of color. Lenin, the Russian revolution, and the Communist International opened the first breach for this historic development.

—6—

Lenin and the Left Communists

Forty years after the Communist International's Second World Congress, a Soviet writer, Lev Nikulin, recalling the role that Lenin had played on that occasion, had this to say: "One must remember that Lenin was the Christopher Columbus of Socialism in action, and that he led the world revolutionary movement down unexplored paths."[1] Even before being true of world Communism, this was true of Russian Communism. At the decisive moments of the year 1917—to go no farther back into the history of Bolshevism—Lenin, like Columbus, was leading the Bolshevik Party "down unexplored paths," giving it a direction which, without him, it surely would not have taken. In April 1917 he pushed his Party to the "left" just as it was drifting to the "right." In July he counseled prudence while Bolshevik "hotheads" were calling for revolution. By September he was insisting on urgent preparations for a forcible seizure of power, which Zinoviev and Kamenev vigorously opposed right up to the eve of the action.* At the beginning of 1918 he fought the left majority of the Central Committee in order to force acceptance of his own views on the peace of Brest-Litovsk.

Just as Bolshevism would have deviated from its "right line" without Lenin, without him European Communism would have taken an entirely different turn. After the revolutionary setbacks of 1919 Europe's Communist militants veered sharply to the "left," at the very moment Lenin was writing his definitive work against that tendency. Between the two diametrically opposed

---

*In a personal letter written from his "prison" in Berlin on October 29,1919, and not intended for publication, Radek said on this subject: "Nine out of ten of all the Party intellectuals, the best of them, Zinoviev, Kamenev, Rykov and Nogin, were solidly against Lenin when he, that calculating stormer, cooly announced: 'The time has come.' " In Max Barthel, *Kein Bedarf an Weltgeschichte—Geschichte eines Lebens* [No need for world history—a story of a life]. Wiesbaden, 1950, p. 59.

political courses, it was Lenin's that won. It triumphed in the International as it had earlier in the Bolshevik Party.

"LEFT COMMUNISM" IN GERMANY

The first large European country to have a significant Communist party, Germany, was also the first to experience the surge of a strong trend to the left. Even at the founding of the party, in the final days of December 1918, in the presence of Rosa Luxemburg, Leo Jogiches, and Paul Levi, who held the opposite view, the majority of the delegates had rejected any participation by the party in the parliamentary elections, an unmistakable symptom of the "leftist disorder." Even Liebknecht, as he confided to Radek, could not make up his mind: "Liebknecht told me that, when he wakes up in the morning, he is against taking part in the elections, but that by evening he is for it again."[2]

With the collapse of the uprisings of January, March, and April of 1919, and after the death of Rosa Luxemburg and Leo Jogiches, followed by disarray within the party, which was then forced underground, the leftist tendency gained an increasingly stronger hold in several of the country's larger cities, like Hamburg and Berlin. At two important party meetings, the first in Berlin on June 14 and 15, 1919, the second a national conference held in Frankfurt am Main from August 16 to 18, the Central Committee—particularly the party chairman, Paul Levi—and the leftists clashed over the issues of Syndicalism and parliamentarianism, though a final test of strength was avoided. But as early as September 9, at the conference of the Berlin organization, the Central Committee's motion on "the need for revolutionary parliamentarianism" was voted down by the majority of the delegates, and that same month one of the two heads of the Hamburg organization, Heinrich Laufenberg, published a pamphlet entitled *Zwischen der ersten and zweiten Revolution* (Between the First and Second Revolutions), in which he advocated a relentless fight against parliamentarianism and the trade unions. Finally, from October 20 to 22 the Second Congress of the German Communist Party met in Heidelberg and vicinity, where the first item on the agenda was Paul Levi's general report on the political situation, followed by a statement of "theses on Communist principles and tactics." The last thesis was the key one: "Members of the German Communist Party who do not share these views as to the Party's nature, organization and action, and/or who contravene or have contravened them orally or in writing, must leave the Party."[3] In the final vote, the "theses" were approved and adopted, with thirty-one delegates voting for, eighteen against. That same day, October 21, the leaders of Hamburg's left opposition, Laufenberg and Wolffheim, walked out of the congress, while most of the rest of the opposition decided to return to the next day's session. But after all the tumult that had occurred, Paul Levi asked them to leave the room, and when they refused announced that the next day's session would be held at a place whose address would be revealed only to those supporting the majority position. The congress thus continued without the opposition.

On that occasion, possibly for the first time since Radek had been in Berlin, there was disagreement between him and Levi. On October 15, from his residence under police surveillance, Radek wrote in a letter to Levi: "In both cases strongly advise against splitting tactic. The differences within the party are not unbridgeable. . . . We cannot afford a split. . . . Strongly advise trying to split the Hamburg crowd."[4] So while Radek was proposing to split not the Communist Party but the left, Levi was pushing hard to split the party. On this point he soon collided with Lenin, whose opinion, though there had been no exchange of views, was identical with Radek's.

Actually the German Communist Party did split, and without any interference from Moscow, owing to the break in communications caused by the blockade, the *cordon sanitaire*, and the civil war. It was not until October 28 that Lenin learned of the event, from a radio news broadcast. Gravely upset, that same day he wrote two messages to the German Communists, the purpose of both being obviously the same: to prevent the rupture from becoming irreparable. In the first letter, to the German Communist Party's Central Committee, addressed specifically "To Comrades Paul Levi, Clara Zetkin, and Eberlein," Lenin said:

> I can hardly believe the news just heard on the radio that, on the basis of a vote of 25 to 18, you have expelled the minority group from the party, with the result that they have now reportedly formed their own party. I know very little about this opposition group that has broken

away; I have seen but a few issues of the Berlin *Rote Fahne* [Red Flag]. My impression is that these are young, inexperienced, very talented agitators, in their youth and inexperience somewhat like our own 'left' Communists of 1918. So long as there is agreement on the *essential* point (power of the soviets as against bourgeois parliamentarianism), an alliance with them strikes me as feasible and necessary, just as it is equally necessary to break with the Kautskyites. If the split was unavoidable, one must try not to widen it; the Executive Committee of the Third International should be asked to mediate. . . . From the international standpoint, restoring unity to the German Communist Party is both possible and essential.[5]

In his message to the left Communists, sent to the Central Committee with a request that it be delivered to "those departing," Lenin again pleaded for restoration of unity and proposed mediation by the Comintern:

It is my conviction that Communists who agree on the fundamentals—on the fight for dictatorship of the proletariat and power in the hands of the soviets, and being implacable foes of the Scheidemanites and Kautskyites in every country—could and should act together. It is my belief that the differences of opinion on minor issues can and will be ironed out, a result necessitated by the logic of our common struggle against a truly formidable enemy: the bourgeoisie and their confessed lackeys (the Scheidemanites) and secret handmaidens (the Kautskyites). . . . While I am not a member of the Executive Committee of the Third International, I feel certain that it will offer its services to the German Communists in the interest of restoring unity to German Communism.*

Some of Lenin's important traits are revealed in these two texts: his habit, almost a conditioned reflex, of comparing what

---

*V. I. Lenin, *Polnoe sobranie sochinenii*, 5th ed., vol. 39, Moscow, 1963, p. 255. It is characteristic that the leadership of the German Communist Party, specifically Paul Levi, who alone dared to act in such a manner, did not hesitate in early 1920 to censor Lenin's open letter of October 10, 1919, to the Italian, French, and German Communists by cutting out a sentence praising one of the two Hamburg leaders. The excised sentence read: "Heinrich Laufenberg, in his excellent pamphlet *Between the First and Second Revolutions*, demonstrated and proved this [the betrayal of Scheidemann and Kautsky] with remarkable force, vividness, alacrity, and conviction." This was probably the first and last time that a foreign party had the temerity to "censor" Lenin. Cf. *Der Weg der Revolution* ["The Path of Revolution"], published by the German Communist Party (Spartacus League), n.d., p. 4, and V. I. Lenin, *Polnoe sobranie sochinenii*, 5th ed., vol. 39, p. 214.

was going on in Europe with what had happened in Russia (left communism); his concern that no useful combat troops, whether leftist or not, be lost to Communism, and that Europe's nascent Communist parties not be reduced to closed little circles cut off from the masses; and finally, his readiness to intervene in the internal affairs of the German Communist Party and to speak in the name of the Communist International without even, technically speaking, being a member of its Executive Committee.

While it is not known at what precise moment these two Lenin messages reached their intended recipients—Thomas's W.E.S. having just started to operate in Berlin—nor what the reactions were of the Central Committee and of the "leftists," the fact is that during the next five or six months neither side pushed the issue to the point of open warfare. (This was not true, though, of the Hamburg group, which by now was headed toward "national Bolshevism," and would soon desert the International, the German Communist Party, and finally even the party that the "leftists" were about to found.) Nevertheless, while provoking no open conflict, both sides continued to make life uncomfortable for each other. Thus on December 19, 1919, a general meeting of the German Communist Party's Berlin staff came within six votes of a unanimous resolution not to consider itself bound by the decisions of a Central Committee selected by a "rump conference." At that party's Third Congress on February 25 and 26, 1920, August Thalheimer, in the name of the Central Committee and the W.E.S., informed his listeners that "the Moscow Executive Committee requests two representatives of the opposition to come to Moscow for a face-to-face exchange of views."[6]

THE GERMAN COMMUNISTS AND THE KAPP-LÜTTWITZ PUTSCH

The putsch by Kapp and Lüttwitz, an attempt by Junkers and militarists to get rid of the parliamentary system and Social-Democratic rule, turned the debate between the "leftists" and the official German Communist Party leadership into a tactically vital issue for the entire German labor movement.

The problem that arose was the more difficult to solve because it had not been predicted by the accepted theory. At the very first congress of the Communist International, when Lenin had formulated his theses on bourgeois democracy and the dictatorship of the proletariat, his fundamental assumption had been that apart from those two systems there was nothing else; no third way existed. But in the Germany of March 1920 a third way was presenting itself: the overthrow of bourgeois democracy and government by Social Democrats and the substitution of a dictatorship of Junkers and militarists. So what was one to do now? Had he been present on the scene, Lenin would have had a ready answer, recalling once again the experience of the Russian revolution, in which, when confronted by the threat of a Kornilov putsch, the Bolsheviks had fought in defense of bourgeois and Socialist democracy, which proved more useful to them than to Kerensky. So the German Communists, facing a similar situation, should have reacted in the same way. But Lenin was not there; he was no longer even in touch with the leaders of the German Communist Party, whose chief, Paul Levi, was then in prison. The result was that, when the critical moment came, the German Communist Party was completely disoriented and, to use the Communist terminology, went from ultra-leftist deviation to rightist opportunistic deviation.

The ultra-leftist deviation showed itself on the very day, March 13, on which the putschists seized the government buildings in Berlin and the Braun-Noske administration fled the capital. The Central Committee of the German Communist Party—or, more precisely, those of its members who were in Berlin and in touch with the Berlin organization, the overwhelming majority of which had "leftist" tendencies—published a manifesto stating: "It will not lift a finger for the democratic republic, which was but a threadbare mask for the dictatorship of the bourgeoisie. . . . The working class, even yesterday still in the chains laid upon them by the Ebert-Noske crowd, weaponless and under the severest pressure from their employers, is for the moment incapable of action. We consider it our duty to state this clearly."[7]

That this policy was wrong from the standpoint of Bolshevik tactics, and that the assumed inability of the working class to act was a misjudgment, would promptly be demonstrated. The labor unions came out immediately for a general strike, which was supported by the masses and joined by two Socialist parties, with the result that by March 17 Kapp was brought to his knees. During these troubled days, and those that followed, the German Communist Party leaders committed one blunder after another, issuing contradictory declarations which were never translated into action. The party published on March 15 a second manifesto in which it approved the general strike but demanded as its outcome the replacement of bourgeois democracy with a Soviet republic and the disbanding of the army, the police force, and the Volunteer Corps, with a Red Workers' Army to take their place—all empty words which came to nothing and were ignored, even by Communist militants. On March 17 the German Communist Party's Berlin organization, a bastion of left opposition still within the party, distinguished itself by calling for the formation of a Red Army in Berlin, of which Broński, Moscow's eye in Berlin (along with Thomas), was to say a little later: "Recruiting offices were opened and posters were put up inviting individual workers to come in and join the Red Army. As was to be expected, these recruiting offices, which were not intended seriously, were closed down by the Baltic troops."[8]

After these "leftist" errors came a rightist deviation expressed in the Central Committee's declaration of March 21: "The German Communist Party sees in the formation of a Socialist government containing no bourgeois-capitalist parties a desirable situation for spontaneous action by the proletarian masses and for their maturing to the point where they can exercise proletarian dictatorship. The party will behave toward that government as a loyal opposition."[9] This statement stirred up the left, and the Central Committee was split. Several days later a group headed by Brandler and Thalheimer put to a vote of the Central Committee a resolution roundly condemning the March 21 declaration, but only eight members supported it. Then another resolution, still hostile to the March 21 text but more moderately worded, was proposed by Eberlein, E. Meyer, and Friesland (Reuter); it was adopted by a vote of 12 to 7.

All this occurred while Paul Levi was in prison, from where on March 16 he wrote to the Central Committee, having just learned of the first "leftist" declaration of March 13: "I have just read your proclamation. My opinion is that the German Communist Party is headed for moral and political bankruptcy. I am unable to

understand how in such a situation one can write such things as
'the working class . . . is for the moment incapable of action. We
consider it our duty to state this clearly.'" [10]

THE COMINTERN AND THE KAPP-LÜTTWITZ PUTSCH

Four personages directly or indirectly involved in the affairs of the
German Communist Party, at four different levels of the Comintern hierarchy, expressed their opinions concerning that party's
attitude during the Kapp-Lüttwitz episode. Taking them in the
ascending order of rank within the Comintern, we start with
Broński, who after Radek's departure had stayed on in Berlin as
Comintern representative and close collaborator of Thomas. We
then quote Radek, who immediately after the putsch declared that
"a certain responsibility falls upon me for the political line of the
German Communist Party," which was both a euphemism and a
display of false modesty, for during the years 1920-23 he enjoyed
at the Kremlin the same power of decision with regard to Germany that Trotsky then had with regard to France. Next we hear
from Zinoviev, president of the Communist International, and
finally from Lenin, the possessor of the supreme power in both
the Comintern and the Bolshevik Party.

Broński's opinion was expressed in a long letter originally published in *Communist International* under the pen name Spartacus,
with a mention that the author was "a very influential German
Communist militant." The text was later published as a pamphlet
under the pen name M. Braun. The author pronounced the argument of the Berlin organization, contained in the March 13 appeal,
to be absurd, but at least he tried to account for it: "That leaflet
reflected the momentary mood of the workers in Germany and
particularly in Berlin, where the Noske regime was especially
hated. . . . People were congratulating each other on the
putsch." [11] Broński did display some understanding, though, of
the March 21 declaration concerning "loyal opposition":

If the purely Socialist government is faithful in its dealings with our
"loyal opposition," if it continues the struggle against the counterrevolutionary bourgeoisie and reactionary Junkerdom with all means at
its command, and does not throw roadblocks in the path of the workers, we ought not only function as a loyal opposition but more than

that: the German Communist Party would be obligated to support such a government, for its struggle is our struggle. . . . The declaration of the German Communist Party's Central Committee rendered a historical service. If politically it never amounted to anything, if no purely Socialist government came into being, the fault is not that of the German Communist Party. [12]

Karl Radek, writing from Moscow, did not share Broński's views, and even publicly attacked them: "If Braun [Broński] asserts in his pamphlet that the call to battle on March 13 was psychologically impossible because the workers rejoiced at Noske's downfall, he reveals himself as an unreliable observer. How else are we to explain that, twenty-four hours later, Berlin was gripped by a general strike? It is not that the masses were incapable of action but that those comrades from the Central Committee then in Berlin were laboring under a completely false attitude toward putschism." [13] Unlike Broński, Radek had no extenuating word to say about the Central Committee and nothing but censure for the March 13 appeal (as did Paul Levi in his prison): "I would never for an instant have believed that in the forefront of the German proletariat, in that part that had been raised and steeled in battle, the struggle against putschism could have yielded such fruit as the March 13 appeal of the Central Committee." [14] He was no less hard on the deviationists in the opposite direction and their March 21 appeal: "It stems also from the fact that, confronted with a phantom of a workers' government, the Communist Party forsakes its revolutionary posture in declaring that it will function as a loyal opposition vis-à-vis that government, meaning that, qua loyal opposition, it will make no preparations to overthrow the regime or perform its obvious duty to agitate politically for its goals and slogans."*

Zinoviev took a very different view of the Kapp affair. The main factor helping Radek to see the matter clearly, his intimate knowledge of the situation in Germany, was lacking for Zinoviev when on March 25, immediately after the German events, he af-

*K. Radek, "Die K.P.D. während der Kapptage," *Die Kommunistische Internationale*, No. 12, 1920, p. 169. This criticism of Radek's, written in June of 1920 and published in July, reflected his view of the situation in Germany in 1919-20 and leaned heavily on the ideas set forth in Lenin's book *"Left-Wing" Communism, an Infantile Disorder*, which had just come out.

fixed his signature as Chairman of the Executive Committee of the
Communist International to its appeal "regarding the civil war in
Germany." Zinoviev's revolutionary zeal was in direct proportion
to his distance from the theater of battle; it was the easier for him
to urge a revolutionary offensive in Germany for he was safe in
Petrograd at the time. Sticking with the Leninist formulae of
1919, he did not see that the problem of Germany in March 1920
was quite different: "What does the counterrevolutionary attempt
in Berlin prove in the eyes of the workers of the world? It demon-
strates once again how right the Communist International was in
its repeated assertion that, during the period of civil war that is
upon us, only two types of dictatorship are possible. Either that of
the proletariat, which frees mankind and rebuilds social life on the
foundations of Communism, or that of the most savage bourgeois
and military reaction, which throws its noose around men's throats
and drags them into new wars. Either the one or the other; there is
no middle ground." [15]

Having made a wrong diagnosis, Zinoviev naturally gave the
wrong advice to the German Communists: "*German proletarians,
arm yourselves! Form workers' councils [soviets]! . . . Assemble
your Red Army! . . . .*Continue your offensive." [16] This is exactly
what had been attempted in Berlin and what Braun (Broński), who
was there on the scene, did not hesitate to label absurd. Radek was
more outspoken yet: "At the moment when establishment of an
out-and-out Junker regime was compelling even Social-Democratic
workers to enter the fray, the attitude of the Central Committee
was one of anti-putschist cretinism." [17]

As for Lenin, in his *"Left-Wing" Communism, an Infantile Disorder*, he had occasion to express himself, not on the first appeal
of March 13 (which undoubtedly he would have roundly damned)
but on the second, that of March 21. He approved it in principle
but criticized it on important tactical grounds: "This statement is
quite correct both in its basic premise and in its practical conclusions. . . . Undoubtedly, such tactics are mostly right. But while it
is not worth harping on trifling errors in wording, we cannot refrain from saying that a government of social traitors should not
be described (in an official statement of the Communist Party) as
a "Socialist" government, and that one cannot speak of excluding
"bourgeois-capitalist" parties" when the parties both of

Scheidemann and of Messrs. Kautsky and Crispien are petty-bourgeois democratic parties." [18]

What happened next was what always happened when Lenin took one view of a problem after Zinoviev had already expressed a different one: the president of the International did an about-face, lined up with Lenin, and became the leading champion of the position that was not his own. The Levi viewpoint, as soon as it was made known in Moscow, met with Lenin's approval, and against Levi's wishes (on the insistence of Zinoviev) was published in the official organ of the International. Levi would reveal this on May 4, 1921, at the moment of his break with the Comintern, before the Central Committee of the German Communist Party lined up against him, and no one stood up to say him nay: "You know that at the time the letter was published in the *Communist International* against my wishes. When in Petersburg I learned of its intended publication, I immediately objected, pointing out that it was not intended for public consumption. It was Zinoviev who maintained that when a party commits such catastrophic blunders as the German party had during the Kapp putsch, criticism of it ceases to be a private affair." [19] As Levi tells it, the Central Committee of the German Communist Party blocked publication of that issue of the *Communist International* in Berlin for three months, until the Executive Committee decided to bring it out on its own.

So the Kapp-Lüttwitz putsch had sown grave discord within the leadership of the German Communist Party, discord exacerbated by personal resentment against Paul Levi. Moscow would subsequently exploit this in the matter of the "March action," in 1921, which was to end with Levi's breaking with the Comintern.

THE SPREAD OF LEFT-WING COMMUNISM IN EUROPE

Three weeks after the Kapp-Lüttwitz putsch the left-wing Communist opposition decided to make official its break with the German Communist Party. The founding congress of the dissident party convened on April 4 and 5, 1920, and the new party took the name Kommunistische Arbeiter Partei Deutschlands, KAPD [Communist Workers' Party of Germany]. A detailed report on its creation was published some twenty days later in the newspaper to be known thereafter as the *Kommunistische Arbeiterzeitung* ["Communist Workers' Newspaper"]. According to that report, the twenty-four delegates from the provinces and eleven delegates from Berlin, representing a total of 38,000 party members, unanimously condemned the opportunism of the German Communist Party in the presence of a delegate from the Central European Bureau of the Third International. (This was later denied by Moscow, which in no way rules out the possible presence of an envoy from either the Vienna Southeastern Bureau or the Amsterdam Bureau, both of which had been won over to left-wing Communist ideas.)

The founding congress, while breaking with the German Communist Party, did not intend to break with the Communist International, as emphasized insistently by the speaker addressing himself to the first item on the agenda, namely "Our Attitude toward the Third International." He said: "[We] *support the decisions of the Third International. . . . We must therefore carry on our fight against the Spartacus League within the Third International. . . . Hence we do not have to apply for admission of our party to the Third International; we have only to declare it a member.*"[20] This statement was ample proof that the leaders of the new party knew nothing whatever about Bolshevism and the Third International. They were hostile to Communist participation in parliaments and trade unions, which they saw as parts of the bourgeois-capitalist system. They branded the German Communist Party opportunist and equated Levi, its chairman, with Ebert, the leader of the official Socialist party, and with Kautsky, the ideologue of the Independent Socialists. A pamphlet written by Otto Rühle and published in early June of 1920 under the auspices of the KAPD went even farther by rejecting lock, stock, and barrel all political parties, including the German Communist Party: "With the dominance of the bourgeoisie came parliamentarianism. With parliamentarianism came political parties. . . . Even the German Communist Party has become a political party. . . . It has become a parliamentary party like all the others. A party of compromise, opportunism, criticism, a party that fignts with words."[21] Still, despite opinions in such flagrant opposition to the line of the Third International, the founders of the KAPD believed their party would automatically become a full-fledged member of the International!

Germany, though, was far from being the only country to experience a surge of left-wing Communism. In most of the countries of Central and Western Europe the same leftist ideas surfaced almost simultaneously around the start of 1920. In Holland the Communist leadership nucleus, composed of several prominent figures from the Socialist movement and some of Europe's leading Marxist thinkers, had been deeply split ever since the appearance of left-wing Communism, as evidenced by their attitude at the Amsterdam conference in February 1920. On one side was the group that had formed around the two Communist deputies, David Wijnkoop and Willem Van Ravesteyn, and on the other were the two Marxist intellectuals, Hermann Gorter and Anton Pannekoek, with Henriette Roland-Holst vacillating in between. Despite their mutual hostility, both groups adopted most of the left-wing Communist position, the Gorter-Pannekoek tandem being the farther left.

When in June 1920 a delegation of the Dutch Communist Party (which at that time had 61 sections with a total of 2,431 members) left for the Second Congress of the Communist International, it was composed entirely of Wijnkoop people, accompanied by three other militants, of whom one was J. Proost, traveling under the assumed name Jansen, who was to stay on in Moscow as Dutch representative to the Executive Committee. On arriving in Moscow, they learned that Lenin was about to publish a book against left-wing Communism in which he criticized the Dutch left, specifically on the parliamentary question. Indeed, referring to the Amsterdam Bureau's *Bulletin*, Lenin minced no words, denouncing its arguments as "sheer rot." "The Dutch," Lenin wrote, "and the 'leftists' in general argue like doctrinaire revolutionaries who have never taken part in a real revolution or who have never deeply pondered the history of revolutions, or who naïvely mistake the subjective 'rejection' of a certain reactionary institution for its actual demolition through a combination of objective factors." [22] Lenin made a copy of his book available to the Dutch delegation before it was published in translation in the different European languages.

In the wake of that gesture, Wijnkoop wrote a letter to him in which he was at pains to make a clear distinction between the Dutch Communist Party, which he headed, and the Gorter-Pannekoek group, which he too made a point of condemning.

Lenin added this letter as an appendix to his book: "We must protest against your holding the Communist Party responsible for their conduct [i.e., that of some members of the Dutch Communist Party]. That is quite wrong. It is also unfair, for those members of the Dutch Communist Party have had little or no part in the party's present work, and directly and indirectly they are trying to palm off as Communist Party slogans statements of position which the Communist Party of Holland and all of its agencies have been solidly against and still solidly oppose."[23] Lenin paid only partial heed to this correction. In the next edition of his book, he replaced the term "the Dutch Tribunists," which took in the entire staff of the party newspaper, with the phrase "certain members of the Dutch Communist Party," which seemed, without saying so, to confine his criticism to the Gorter-Pannekoek group alone. But in his speech of July 30, 1920, to the Second Congress of the Comintern he said of Wijnkoop that the latter "shared almost all of Pannekoek's errors."

In Italy left-wing Communism made its appearance on the initiative of Amadeo Bordiga. In Naples he founded the newspaper *Il Sovieto*, in which he espoused from the outset the cause of the Bolshevik revolution while opposing participation in parliamentary contests; he called his group "Abstentionist Communists." On this point Bordiga's position was exactly opposite that of Lenin, with whose views at the time he was not too well acquainted, while on another major point, namely the break with the Reformist Socialists of the Turati-Treves stripe, he stood foursquare against the opinion of the Socialist Party's real head, Serrati, who preferred to stall and compromise. Like other spokesmen of European left-wing Communism who were to journey to Moscow in 1920, Bordiga took an active part there in the activities of the Second Comintern Congress, at which he presented a report that he had co-authored and his theses on parliamentarianism, to which he reaffirmed his categorical opposition: "In the present period of history . . . there is no possible way in which the parliamentary rostrum can be used to advance the revolutionary task of the Communists."[24]

In Great Britain, left-wing Communism first appeared in early 1920, directing its fire against two tactics that Lenin particularly favored: parliamentary participation and penetration of the

Labour Party. The Workers' Socialist Federation, headed by Sylvia Pankhurst, swiftly announced its support for the Communist International yet opposed its basic tactical ideas. The Shop Stewards' and Workers' Committees movement was also dead set against operating within the Labour Party, as was the Scottish Workers' Committee, one of whose prominent militants was a young laborer, William Gallacher, a member of the Shop Stewards' delegation to the Second Comintern Congress.

In Switzerland a Communist Party was set up on the initiative of Jakob Herzog, expelled on October 1, 1918, from the Swiss Social-Democratic Party because of his ultra-leftist views. This Communist Party established contact with both the Comintern's Amsterdam Bureau (whose February 1920 conference Herzog attended) and the Vienna Bureau, for whose revue *Kommunismus* he wrote several articles in favor of workers' soviets and an armed insurrection in Switzerland. In April 1920, at the very moment when Lenin was writing his *"Left-Wing" Communism*, that Swiss Party showed typical characteristics of a leftist "disorder," for its fourth national conference adopted a resolution on parliamentarianism which began in the following way: "The Swiss Communist Party rejects any participation in bourgeois parliaments." [25]

In Austria the Communist Party was dominated by the left-wing Communists even after the failure of Dr. Bettelheim's putsch. The arrival of the leaders of Soviet Hungary, who had fled to Austria, was to reinforce this trend. The weekly *Kommunismus* became its mouthpiece. Thus in March 1920 the journal published an article by György Lukács, a former commissar under the Hungarian Soviet Republic, which criticized parliamentary participation by Communists. This state of mind led the Austrian Communist Party in August 1920 to come out in favor of boycotting the parliamentary elections, as described by a witness present when the decision was made: "Toward the end of August the Communist Party started preparing its campaign for the legislative elections to be held in October. Carried away by his sectarian temperament, Koritschoner adopted the 'abstentionist' position of Bordiga. To everybody's surprise, his order not to participate was supported by Toman, whose opportunist propensities were well-known. But, conscious of the party's weakness, Toman wanted to keep it a secret. The Koritschoner-Toman coalition won out handily over the few realistic militants like Joseph Strasser, then director of the *Rote Fahne*, who favored participation." [26]

In France left-wing Communism was weaker than elsewhere. It had no roots within the great mass of workers, as the KAPD in Germany did; it had no Marxist theoreticians, as the Dutch group did; it had no international ties with the Comintern Bureaus in Amsterdam, Vienna, or Berlin, as all the other "leftist" groups did; nor did it have any contact with Moscow, unlike all the other Communist parties. In France this trend, linked to the name of Raymond Péricat, recruited its handful of supporters from among the Revolutionary Syndicalists and anarchists, and not from Socialist or Marxist ranks. In February 1919 Péricat launched the weekly publication *L'Internationale*, which was transformed into another short-lived journal, *Le Communiste*. The "Communist Party" proclaimed in April 1919 and said to be linked to the Third International soon became known as the "Federation of Soviets." These developments involved only a small number of members. [27]

"LEFT-WING COMMUNISM"—AN INTERNATIONAL FACTION

In the first half of 1920 left-wing Communism seemed, if not stronger, at least noisier than the Communism of strict Leninist obedience. In Germany thirty to fifty per cent of the membership had left the Communist Party to join the KAPD. Italy's Bordiga Communist group was already gaining ground, and at the Socialist party congress in Bologna in October 1919 its presence as a distinct political fraction was felt. Elsewhere the left-wing Communists did not appear to be playing so important a role. In Holland, with two deputies in the legislature and 2,000 members, or in Switzerland with the isolated Herzog group numbering some 1,200, they certainly did not have enough weight to exert any revolutionary influence, the same being true of the tiny Communist groups in England and of Péricat in France with his fictional "soviets" in scattered parts of Paris and its suburbs. The threat posed by this left-wing Communism was more to the Communist movement itself than to capitalist order: the Communist idea was in danger of being monopolized by sectarian groups cut off from the masses, which would have resulted in the workers' staying with the Socialism of the right or center. Thus in Germany, in the trade-union movement, on the one hand there was the powerful center directed by Karl Legien and other reformers with a registered membership of seven million, and on the other the Arbeiterunion, run by the left-wing Communists with a membership of about 100,000.

Left-wing Communism posed another threat once it started forging international ties and behaving like a faction embracing all of Europe. At the beginning of 1920, of the three branch offices of the Comintern in Western Europe—Berlin, Amsterdam, and Vienna—Amsterdam and Vienna were serving the left-wing Communist cause. The ties that Amsterdam and Vienna were forging with foreign Communists equaled if not exceeded in scope and importance those forged by the W.E.S. under Thomas and his people in the German Communist Party. True, the W.E.S. had the double advantage of being the only bureau to adhere faithfully to Lenin's tactics and the only one to be in regular communication with Moscow, which in the long run was to prove decisive, though this was not immediately apparent. Amsterdam had established contact in many of the countries of Western Europe and even with the American Communists. Vienna had financial resources that enabled it to publish the important weekly *Kommunismus*, which in the course of 1920 mustered many of the left-wing Communists from all over Europe (with the exception of France). The Austrian Communist movement was represented in its pages by contributions from Gerhart Eisler (the managing editor), Karl Frank, Paul Friedländer, Franz Koritschoner; Hungary by Béla Kun, György Lukács, Jenő Varga, Béla Szántó, József Révai; the Communist Youth International by Willi Münzenberg and Richard Schüller; the Italian left by Bordiga; the Dutch group by Anton Pannekoek; the German left by Paul Frölich and Arkadi Maslow. The Comintern, on the other hand, was not represented by a single article from the pen of its president, Zinoviev, though several pieces by Lenin and Radek were published in it, and one article more than a year and a half old from the journal *Kommunist*, the organ of Moscow's left-wing Communists!

Béla Kun, who had left Budapest wearing the halo of true leader of the Hungarian revolution, and who from the first issue of Vienna's revue *Kommunismus* became one of its principal collaborators, did not hesitate to express some harsh opinions about the German Communist Party in the wake of the Kapp-Lüttwitz putsch. Himself a leftist, Kun believed in 1920 that the revolution was imminent in Europe, and above all in Germany, as he concluded in an article devoted to the events in that country: "There is no doubt that for every Communist the axiomatic starting point is that *we live in an era of revolution. . . . The revolutionary readiness means . . . the constant disposition for battle, from which follows at the same time the building of the organization, and then the propensity to be armed at any moment.*"[28] Not only did he criticize the German Communist Party declaration concerning "a loyal opposition" but he completely rejected the USPD, with which the Comintern was in the process of forging contacts in order to draw it, at least partially, into its orbit. Early in 1920 Lenin was very poorly informed about what was happening in European Communist circles, and he complained of the "fragmentary news that we sometimes get from abroad."[29] But with his unerring ability to sniff out deviation, and even more any factionalism, he was not to be misled as to the real danger of the leftist phenomenon, and he would respond accordingly.

Thus by the end of March 1920 Lenin had decided to strike back in three ways: first through the Comintern, by the measures it could take; second, by publishing his pamphlet *"Left-Wing" Communism, an Infantile Disorder*; and lastly by having the leaders of the European left come to the Comintern's Second Congress, scheduled to convene in July 1920. Up to the spring of that year left-wing Communism had not been proscribed by the Comintern, but once Lenin stepped in, matters took a different turn. It was in April that he wrote his book against left-wing Communism, and it was surely no coincidence that the date on which he completed it, April 27, was the day after the Comintern had resolved to abolish the leftist Amsterdam Bureau. A similar fate befell the Comintern journal *Communist International*. Its tenth issue, published in May 1920, opened with an article by Hermann Gorter, which appeared ahead of articles by Lenin and Trotsky. Its eleventh issue, which appeared the following month, carried a report by J. Herzog, a Swiss left-wing Communist. Likewise, starting with the sixth issue (Russian edition) the cover carried a list of the contributors, which included six prominent Dutch Communists:

Roland-Holst, Pannekoek, Gorter, Wijnkoop, Rutgers, and Van Ravesteyn. But the names of Gorter and Pannekoek appeared in the journal for the last time in the tenth issue, dated May 11, 1920. A pamphlet by Pannekoek published under the pseudonym K. Horner, on world revolution and Communist tactics, which set forth views very different from those that Lenin had just developed in his book against left-wing Communism, went to press in May and came out in Petrograd in early June. This was the last time that the foreign left-wing Communists enjoyed the right to publish freely in Soviet Russia.

Lenin acted henceforth either on his own, as in his writing of *"Left-Wing" Communism*, or with the double authority of his name and that of the Comintern, as when on June 12, 1920, he published in the eleventh issue of *Communist International* an article very critical of the Viennese left-wing Communist journal *Kommunismus*. He singled out two of its contributors, Béla Kun and György Lukács, as typical cases of the Communist "infantile disorder," specifically in their views on parliamentarianism. As was his custom in polemical strife, he minced no words: "This article by G. L. is very leftist and very bad. His Marxism is purely verbal. The distinction made between 'offensive' and 'defensive' tactics is entirely imaginary." [30] In another instance Lenin used the authority of the Comintern to impose overnight on the Austrian Communist Party an about face in the matter of electoral tactics, a fact which party spokesman Gerhart Eisler did not hesitate to publicize in these terms: "This change of plan did not stem from any sudden change of mind by the majority about participating in the parliamentary elections. That did not happen at all. No, it resulted from a decision of the Executive Committee of the Third International instructing the Austrian Communist Party to take part in the elections." [31]

DISPUTES OVER TACTICS: LENIN VERSUS LEFT-WING COMMUNISM

While the first move to counter left-wing Communism had been undertaken by Lenin through the agency and authority of the Comintern, the second was a personal act—the writing of *"Left-Wing" Communism, an Infantile Disorder*, in April 1920. The pamphlet appeared first in Russian in early June, but then the

Comintern had it translated into German, French, and English, and those translations were published in July. Lenin personally supervised its printing and did everything he could to have its translations into the principal languages ready so that the text could be distributed to the delegates coming to attend the Second Comintern Congress. (It was not until later that the pamphlet was published in the West. The W.E.S. brought out the German edition at the end of July 1920, while the French edition was not published in Paris until November.)

Rarely has a work so slender in its number of pages had so profound and lasting effect upon the international workers' movement. During the decades that followed *"Left-Wing" Communism* played the inspirational role earlier played by the Marx-Engels *Communist Manifesto*. Just as Marx and Engels had brought some trenchant new thinking into the European Socialist movement, Lenin too brought a new creative approach to the matter of revolutionary strategy and tactics.

When Lenin's lieutenants stressed the importance of that little book, they were not simply flattering Lenin; it was indeed immensely important. Zinoviev, in a speech in Petrograd shortly after Lenin's death, was to say about it: "Take Lenin's little pamphlet *'Left-Wing' Communism, an Infantile Disorder* into your hands. Is it not a Bible for the entire working class? . . . For the tactics of the Communist Party this work is no less important than Marx's *Das Kapital* for Marxist theory." [32] A. Andreev, a member of the Bolshevik Central Committee and the Bolshevik delegation to the Second Comintern congress, declared that the book had become a guide for Communists in all countries. [33] Lenin's "Bible" was of major importance not only for having introduced the Communist movement to the unexplored terrain of strategy and tactics but for best expressing the true spirit of Leninist Communism. To grasp the essence of Leninism, one did not really have to read Lenin's pseudo-philosophical writings (*Materialism and Empirio-Criticism*, or his theoretical writings (e.g., *The State and Revolution*), or even his economic analyses (*Imperialism, the Highest Stage of Capitalism*). One had only to read *"Left-Wing" Communism, an Infantile Disorder*, a thin little pamphlet, yet a far weightier document than the texts that had preceded it. Pitted against the left-wing Communists on the subject of revolutionary strategy and tactics, Lenin was like Clausewitz debating military art with armchair strategists.

It is not surprising therefore that his arguments quite literally demolished the positions of the left-wing Communists on tactical matters, as, for example, their refusal to compromise, their abstention from parliamentary life, and their rejection of any participation in the trade-union organizations. In language that was often brutal—"out-and-out idiocy," "muddle-headedness," "monumental humbug," "utter ineptitude," "ignorance of the ABCs of Marxism," "empty phrases," "ridiculous childishness"—Lenin implacably demonstrated the true sickness of left-wing Communism: its lack of political perspicacity. His words were acrimonious, his candor unprecedented in the history of the international labor movement. He had officially and publicly consecrated the immorality of his policies: everything that served the Communist cause was ipso facto moral. It was in this spirit that he defined the necessity for resorting to special methods to penetrate mass-membership organizations such as trade unions: "We must be able to withstand all this, to agree to any sacrifice, and even—if need be—resort to all sorts of stratagems, artifices, illegal methods, to evasions and subterfuges, only so as to get into the trade unions, to remain in them, and carry on Communist work within them at all costs."[34] And to persuade the left-wing Communists in England to infiltrate the Labour Party and help it to achieve power at the expense of the Conservatives and Liberals, he used this argument: "I wanted with my vote to support Henderson in the same way as a rope supports a hanged man. . . . The impending establishment of a Henderson government will prove that I am right, will bring the masses over to my side, will accelerate the political death of the Hendersons and the Snowdens, just as was the case with their confrères in Russia and Germany."[35]

Throughout his book Lenin set forth his own conceptions of the history and the science of politics. The history consisted in the example of the Bolshevik Party, for it alone had seized and retained power in Europe, whence it followed that its tactics, if not perfect, were at least better than what anyone else had to offer. Within the framework of these tactics compromises were not at all ruled out:

The German "Leftists" should know that the entire history of Bolshevism, both before and after the October Revolution, is jam-packed with instances of maneuvering, temporizing, and compromising with other

parties (including bourgeois parties)! ... The victory of the Bolsheviks
over the Mensheviks necessitated the use of tactical maneuvers, accom-
modations, and compromises not only before but also after the 1917
October Revolution, but, needless to say, only such maneuvers and
compromises as would help, advance, unify, and strengthen the Bolsheviks at the expense of the Mensheviks. [36]

Fortified by that experience, Lenin definitively concluded: "To
reject compromise 'on principle,' to deny the admissibility of any
compromises at all, regardless of what kind, is a form of childishness that one had difficulty taking seriously." [37] The question of
compromises was but one element in a much larger picture. Revolutionary strategy and tactics, the real political war, must result
first in the conquest of power, then in its retention and consolidation: "Strictest loyalty to the ideas of Communism must be combined with an ability to make all necessary practical compromises,
to maneuver, conclude agreements, zigzag, retreat, etc., so as to
hasten the day of seizing power and the consequent toppling from
power of the Hendersons ... and in order to choose the right
moment, when the decay of these 'pillars of the holy right of
private property' is at its peak, for a determined onslaught by the
proletariat to overthrow them and seize political power." [38]

Zinoviev was right in calling the book a "Bible" for Communists,
for from it they learned the real meaning, in application to political warfare, of concepts that until then had been deemed relevant
only to military science. They got from it, too, ideas entirely new
for them, such as the necessity for combining legal with illegal
activities, for iron discipline within the party organization, for
assigning priorities to different problems and solving them in
stages. They learned from it also that the Communist movement
must avoid at all costs being isolated from its allies, even temporary ones, and that it must never fail to exploit divisions among its
enemies: "To wage a war for the overthrow of the international
bourgeoisie, a war a hundred times harder, longer, and more complicated than the most stubborn of ordinary wars between countries, and to refuse in advance to maneuver, to exploit conflicts of
interest (however temporary) among one's enemies, to refuse to
deal or compromise with potential allies, no matter how fleeting,
unstable, vacillating and reluctant,—is this not folly in the extreme? " [39]

Lenin had very rightly seen that the danger in left-wing Communism lay mainly in its sectarianism: the refusal to participate in institutions and organizations such as parliaments and trade unions which were dominated by a bourgeois, petty-bourgeois, and Socialist-reformist mentality. The left-wing Communists were cutting themselves off from the masses and were doomed to remain a tiny sect with no political influence. To nip this danger in the bud, Lenin excoriated the left-wing Communists for their empty phrases, telling them quite flatly: "As long as you are unable physically to disperse the bourgeois parliaments and all other reactionary institutions, you *must* work *in* and *with* them, precisely because *there* you will still find workers who are stupefied by the priests and the dreariness of rural life; otherwise you risk becoming mere babblers." [40] It was not merely a question of parliaments and trade unions but of all mass-membership institutions, and Lenin kept hammering this home: "You must be capable of any sacrifice, of overcoming the greatest obstacles in order to agitate and propagandize systematically, with perseverance, persistence, patience, and in those *very* institutions, societies, associations (even the most reactionary) where proletarian or quasi-proletarian masses are to be found." [41]

This whole line of argument had two weaknesses that Lenin preferred not to notice. The first was that left-wing Communism had been fathered by Lenin himself and his Bolsheviks—an illegitimate child perhaps, but nevertheless his. Lenin the doctrinaire had made left-wing Communism possible; Lenin the politician wanted to repudiate and crush it. Had not he himself thundered against "parliamentary cretinism" and the "trade-union bureaucracy"? Was it not he who had pilloried the entire Socialist International, belonging always to its extremist wing? The left-wing Communists were merely translating these views from ideology and propaganda into action and tactics—which brought them into direct collision with Lenin, now the tactician, no longer the doctrinaire.

The second weakness was that his preachments on tactics, to be effectively applied, depended on two prerequisites. One was that the left-wing Communists cease being leftists and become just plain Communists and follow the line laid down by Lenin. The other was that the mass-membership democratic organizations behave in conformity with Lenin's predictions—that is, submit to being penetrated and manipulated by the Communists. The first condition was realized at the Comintern's Second Congress, owing

mainly to Lenin, but the second was not; in 1920 the British
Labour Party and the trade unions took a hostile attitude toward
Communist penetration, and by the end of 1921 all the Socialist
parties rejected Moscow's proposals for a united front.

THE HISTORICO-POLITICAL DISPUTE:
LEFT-WING COMMUNISM VERSUS THE COMINTERN

Beyond crucial problems of tactics, which Lenin handled thoroughly, the left-wing Communist phenomenon embraced also a whole
complex of historical and political questions which the spokesmen
for the left had raised and which Lenin had made little or no reply to.
So the dispute between him and them developed on two different
planes—on the tactical, where his answer was crushing, and on that
of the "objective" course of political history, where the left's main
criticisms were passed over in silence. While history had proven
Lenin right about tactics (with the important exception of the
Labour Party, which had not behaved as he had expected), it was
to support the criticisms and fears of the left on other major
issues, such as the Bolshevik vision of revolution in Europe, the
relationship between the Soviet state and the Communist International, and the corrupting dictatorial power of the Executive
Committee of the Comintern, entirely in the hands of the Bolsheviks.

Two of the leading ideologues of left-wing Communism, the
Dutchmen Hermann Gorter and Anton Pannekoek, who had been
the first Marxists in Western Europe to rally to Lenin before his
victory in Petrograd, also were among the first to bring home to
him the essential contradictions of the policy that he was imposing
on the Comintern. Actually, Gorter and Pannekoek, in accord
with Henriette Roland-Holst (who attended the Zimmerwald conference in 1915 but did not join the "Zimmerwald Left" on that
occasion) did join that Left shortly after the Zimmerwald conference. When this Dutch group brought out the first issue of the
journal *Vorbote* in January 1916, Trotsky refused to sit on the
editorial committee, though Lenin and Zinoviev were members of
it and contributed articles. In 1916-17, a time when Lenin was
heaping obloquy on most of Marxism's recognized theoreticians,
starting with Kautsky, and was attacking even the ideas of Rosa

Luxemburg, as expressed in her pamphlet signed "Junius," he had only flattering and respectful things to say about the theoretical works of Gorter and Pannekoek. In 1916, Lenin characterized as "excellent" Gorter's pamphlet on imperialism, war, and the Social-Democrats; in 1917, in his book *The State and Revolution*, he supported Pannekoek against Kautsky: "In this debate it is Pannekoek who represents Marxism against Kautsky."[42] In 1918, cut off from the outside world, in his message to the Soviet ambassador in Bern, Berzin, Lenin sent regular greetings to only two Europeans, Guilbeaux and Gorter.

In 1920 Gorter came to Moscow, where he had talks with Lenin. He addressed the Executive Committee of the Comintern and published his *Reply to Lenin on Communism's Infantile Disorder*. In April of that year Pannekoek wrote his pamphlet *World Revolution and Communist Tactics*, which Lenin took notice of and which the Viennese revue *Kommunismus* published in full. Gorter and Pannekoek were thus the first Communist theoreticians to question publicly the identity of the revolution consummated in Russia and the one expected in Europe. In place of an identity, they detected a certain contradiction. In 1919-20 Lenin firmly believed that he had drawn up the plan for world revolution. The Russian model would inexorably become the model for all of Europe, and from the first lines of his *"Left-Wing" Communism* he treated as axiomatic "the historic inevitability of the repetition, on the international scale, of what happened in our country."[43] But Gorter in his *Reply to Lenin*, written in July 1920 and published in August in the official organ of the KAPD, stressed that this much touted parallel did not in fact exist. Throughout his pamphlet Gorter kept coming back to this argument, addressing himself to Lenin personally: "I think you are wrong about the parallels between Western European revolution and the Russian revolution, about the preconditions for revolution in Western Europe. . . . There is an enormous difference between Russia and Western Europe. In general, the importance of the impoverished peasantry as a revolutionary factor diminishes as one moves from East to West. . . . You reason as a Russian, not as an international Communist acquainted with true capitalism, Western capitalism."[44]

Gorter had put his finger on a key nerve in the life of the Communist International, as the years ahead were to confirm ever more dramatically. But the Bolshevik leaders did not deign to make any serious reply. They responded either with polemics, like Trotsky and Zinoviev, or with scornful silence, like Lenin and, later, Stalin. When in 1920 Gorter came to Moscow to express his ideas to the Executive Committee, Trotsky—in Lenin's absence— simply turned his argument around, declaring ironically:

> Comrade Gorter didn't express the views of his own particular tendency. He excoriated and lectured us, poor orphans of Eastern Europe, purportedly in the name of Western Europe. Unfortunately I haven't seen Gorter's mandate, so I can't tell whether he was really delegated by Western Europe to give us his edifying lecture. . . . Had I wanted to emulate Comrade Gorter in undertaking an evaluation of revolutionary political views along cultural-national lines, I might have begun by saying that Comrade Gorter reasons not so much after the Western-European manner as after the manner of the Dutch. He speaks not in the name of France or Germany or England, with their rich experience of proletarian struggles, but primarily in the name of a section of a small Dutch party.[45]

Pannekoek, for his part, went farther than Gorter. Not stopping at the differences between Russian and Western ways of looking at things, he harped on the increasing contradiction between two agencies both in the hands of the same people, the Soviet government and the Communist International. At the very moment, in April 1920, when ·Lenin was writing *"Left-Wing" Communism*, Pannekoek was writing his own pamphlet on the future of world revolution and the most suitable Communist tactics. He analyzed the nascent contradiction between Soviet Russia, obliged as a national state to strive for understanding and coexistence with the capitalist world, and the Third International, created to destroy that capitalism. This contradiction was exacerbated by the fact that Russia was still the only Communist country, and the Comintern depended more and more on it. The incompatibility between the national policies of Soviet Russia and the revolutionary vocation of the Communist International was fully brought out by Pannekoek:

> Hence the Russian Soviet Republic finds itself forced by the slowness of revolutionary developments in Western Europe to seek a modus vivendi with the capitalist world. The Third International . . . has no

formal connection with the government policies of the Russian Republic and should pursue its own business in complete independence of it. Actually, though, this separation does not exist. The Communist Party being the backbone of the Soviet Republic, through the persons of its members the Executive Committee is intimately involved with the government of the Soviet Republic and thus becomes a tool by which that government intervenes in Western European politics. So it becomes understandable that the tactics of the Third International . . . are determined not only by the needs of Communist propaganda in those countries but also by the political requirements of Soviet Russia.[46]

What Gorter and Pannekoek were saying in a general way, the militants of the KAPD, who were in more direct contact with the policies of Moscow, were simultaneously asserting more specifically, mincing no words about the Comintern's meddling in the internal affairs of their party and about the role of Moscow's emissaries and the money they were spreading around. At the German Communist Party congress in October 1919, before the split, a spokesman for the left-wing Communists demanded that the money issue be taken up before the vote on the party's platform: "We demand an explanation of the uses being made of party funds, and I therefore move that the acceptance of the theses be put off until after the financial and auditor's report has been heard."[47] At the close of the debate, Laufenberg made a motion to this effect, which brought him a reply from Paul Levi, who wanted to rid the congress of the leftists, particularly of Wolffheim and Laufenberg (which did happen the next day). Levi shot back: "The accounts will be audited only by Communists. The matter of finances has nothing whatever to do with acceptance or rejection of the platform."*

At the founding congress of the KAPD, in April 1920, another basic question about the functioning of the Communist International was raised. It concerned the role of the Moscow emissaries installed in Berlin since the autumn of 1919 under the

---

*Bericht über den 2. Parteitag der K.P.D., p. 38. When it finally clashed with the KAPD majority and went over to "national Bolshevism," the Hamburg group became still more explicit on this subject, passing in July 1920 a resolution which said of the German Communist Party: "Financed with funds supplied by the Russian government, its agents consider it their job to promote Russian policies in Germany." *Kommunistische Arbeiterzeitung*, Berlin, No. 112, July 1920.

mantle of the W.E.S. "How did this Western European Secretariat come into being? " asked the speaker on the first item of the agenda, immediately answering the question himself: "Representatives were sent from Moscow to tell us of the Russian experience so that we might profit from it. Actually we all gained the impression that these Russian representatives not only failed to advance the cause of world revolution but positively impeded it. We who were in a position to observe the doings of these persons at close hand were often astonished at how little they knew of the realities and true situation in Germany, and at how little they bothered to familiarize themselves with the German scene." [48]

A few weeks later the same criticism was leveled not only at the role of Moscow's representatives in Berlin but at the top leadership of the Comintern, as set forth in a statement of principles by the heads of the KAPD left: "There is not and could not be any special tactic of or by the International, a tactic independent of the doings of the different Communist parties, for it is up to the proletarians in each country, and not to any little circle, to determine the tactics to be followed in that country. If the Communist International believes that specific Russian tactics are mandatory and can be imposed on all countries by Muscovite decree, it thereby merely reveals what it means by an 'international' policy." [49]

Thus in the dispute between Lenin and the left-wing Communists, history sided with Lenin in the short run and with the leftists in the long. Lenin was right in moving vigorously to crush sectarianism but wrong in believing that Europe would follow the Russian path of revolution. He was even more mistaken in deeming it inevitable that Europe's Socialist parties of the right and center would ultimately be compromised and defeated (as happened with the Social Revolutionaries and Mensheviks in Russia), and that the political demise of the Hendersons would be followed in England and elsewhere by Communist victory.

On the other hand, the left-wing Communists were wrong in the short run, for their policies could only isolate Communists from the masses of workers, and they were wrong in regarding Lenin's book as "opportunism," a charge which Gorter made publicly: "It [the book] leads us back into that swamp into which Scheidemann, Renaudel, Kautsky, MacDonald, Longuet, Vandervelde, Branting, and Troelstra had taken us. . . . Such a book is for the revolutionary Communist proletariat what Bernstein's book was for the pre-revolutionary proletariat."[50] In the long run, though, the objections raised by the left proved justified, not only in their historical perspective of the growing contradiction between the Soviet state and the Comintern, and the corrupting role of Moscow's money and emissaries, but even on the very points on which Lenin was right in the short run, such as those concerning parliamentarianism and the trade unions. Lenin's reasoning in trade-union and parliamentary matters rested above all on the experience of the Bolshevik party, while the reasoning of Gorter and Pannekoek (as well as of the other leftists who would attend the Second Comintern Congress) rested on the experience of the workers' movement in the West. There existed, besides an essential politico-social difference between the two milieus, another difference with respect to the duration of their political and trade-union experiences. The Bolshevik experience covered barely fifteen years: only since 1905 had the trade-union organizations in Russia been allowed to function legally, and not until 1907 did the Bolsheviks first take part in a parliamentary campaign, for the second Duma. On the contrary, for over half a century trade-union and parliamentary activities had unfolded fully in the countries of Western Europe. On the basis of his fifteen-year Russian experience Lenin could argue in favor of his tactics, but Gorter, Pannekoek, and others could invoke the outcome of a much longer historical process unfolding in the West: the growing role of the trade-union bureaucracy and of the "parliamentary cretinism" in the workers' movement. What guarantees did there exist that at the end of another half-century the same process would not appear in the Communist movement too?

Lenin himself, always concerned with the verdict of history, was later to acknowledge indirectly that some of the main theses of the left opposition were well-founded (after that opposition had been expelled from the Comintern). He obviously could not submit for public discussion the problem of the growing conflict of interests between the Soviet state and the objectives of the Communist International, just as he could not renounce the policy of imposing Bolshevik practice on all of the Comintern. But by the beginning of 1921 Lenin could no longer overlook the evidence that most of Europe's workers were not flocking to Communism and that the course of events there was not following the Russian model. That is when he decided to do an about-face, which his united front ploy was designed to accomplish. He came to realize, too, that the Russian scheme of things had too much permeated the entire Comintern, as the left had asserted in 1920, and he did not hesitate to say so in his last speech to the Comintern at its Fourth Congress in 1922. Finally, Lenin's last article, *Better We Do Less but Do It Better*, published in 1923, contained an idea that immediately became an integral part of the Comintern's credo: "The outcome of the struggle will depend in the end on the fact that Russia, India, China, etc. comprise the immense majority of the earth's population. And it is just that majority that for several years now has been swept up with incredible speed into the battle for its liberation. There can be no shadow of doubt as to the final outcome of this world struggle. The ultimate victory of Socialism is absolutely and totally assured." [51]

In April 1920, when Lenin's eyes were still riveted on the expected revolution in Europe and not at all on Asia, Pannekoek put forth the ideas that Lenin would repeat almost verbatim in 1923: "This world revolution is not seen in its full universal meaning when viewed only from the Western European standpoint. . . . Asia's cause is actually that of all mankind. In Russia, China, and India . . . live some 800,000,000 people, more than half the earth's entire population. . . . So, perhaps sooner than presently expected from outward appearances, will Asia's national freedom movements, on the firm material basis of a class struggle of the workers and peasants against the barbarous oppression of world capitalism, adopt a Communist ideology and program." [52]

The Second World Congress and Negotiations
with the European Delegations

The Second Congress of the Communist International was actually the first authentic international meeting of the new organization's members and supporters, its founding congress in 1919 having been merely improvised, both in the manner of its preparation and in the way in which it was conducted. At the second one, too, Lenin went all out. Never before or after did he plunge so deeply into the work of a Comintern congress, churning out so many important documents and personally contacting so many people. It is true that at the founding congress he had presided over or inaugurated nearly all of its sessions, but the "theses" on democracy and the dictatorship of the proletariat which he composed were little better than a routine agitprop tract. At the Third Congress, in 1921, he took an active part on only two issues, Russian policy and Comintern tactics in the wake of the "March action" in Germany. But in the preparations for the Second Congress he played a key role and then plunged deeply into the work of its plenary sessions and committees, participating in all the backroom jockeying before, during, and after. The Second World Congress was the apogee of the Lenin presence, physical and political, in the Comintern.

LENIN'S STATE OF MIND AND THE CLIMATE
AT THE SECOND WORLD CONGRESS

To understand fully and evaluate properly the important decisions taken at the Second Congress, as well as those made by the congresses of 1919 and 1921, one must have some idea of Lenin's state of mind at the time. In 1919 it was because he believed that the world revolution had already begun, and the collapse of the Second International was an accomplished fact, that he rammed through the decision to set up the Communist International immediately. Firmly convinced that the year 1920 would see Russia's revolution spread to Europe, he directed all the work of the Second Congress toward that event, dictating its decisions accordingly. Similarly, because by 1921 he no longer believed that revolution imminent, at the Third Congress in June he condemned the "theory of the offensive" and in December imposed upon the Comintern the United Front tactic.

In March 1919 Lenin had believed it essential to set up the Communist International immediately in spite of two major obstacles: the nonexistence in Europe of mass Communist parties of any kind, and the opposition of Eberlein, the only important delegate, representing the German Communist Party. In the weeks preceding the Second Congress, just a little over a year after the initial founding one, Lenin did not lack arguments showing that events had proved him right on one major point. If in 1919 no mass Socialist party had been represented at the Moscow congress, the same would not be true at this Second Congress, for Europe's four leading Socialist parties were sending delegates. From Germany would come the USPD, from France the SFIO, from Italy its Socialist Party, and from Czechoslovakia the Social Democratic Party, all represented by their top leaders. If in March 1919 the Third International seemed little more than a figment of propaganda, by 1920 it was well on its way to becoming a powerful bloc of mass parties—and very "fashionable," as Lenin would put it.

Since, in the months following the International's founding, events had proved him right on this point, he was all the more convinced that the other part of his prediction—that the revolution would spread across Europe—would also come true. Just as he had correctly foreseen the decay of the Socialist parties and their evolution from the Second to the Third International, he now firmly believed in the predicted imminent collapse of bourgeois democracy, installed everywhere in Europe right after the war, and in the heralded advent of the so-called proletarian revolution. He voiced this conviction repeatedly in the months preceding the Second World Congress, writing at the end of his book *"Left-Wing" Communism, an Infantile Disorder* that "most workers with any awareness . . . are ready to die for the revolution," and that "the ruling classes are experiencing a governmental crisis," concluding that "we thus clearly note the presence of those two pre-requisites for a successful proletarian revolution." [1]

A few days before the opening session, held in Petrograd on July 19, this belief had become a certainty for Lenin, for it now rested on a solid fact: the advance of Russia's Red Army into Poland had begun on July 4, 1920, with the capture of Rovno, and was proceeding effectively. That advance prompted Lenin to wage war on Poland, not to conquer that country for the sake of conquest, but by overrunning it to unleash revolution and—his main purpose—speed its spread to Germany. When Lord Curzon submitted to the Soviet government precise proposals for a Russo-Polish armistice on July 11, Lenin's reaction was negative, as evidenced by his telephone message the next day to Stalin, then in Kharkov: "Personally, I think this is all a hoax . . . they want to snatch the victory out of our hands with deceitful promises." [2]

On July 16, convinced that he was right, Lenin called a full meeting of the Central Committee and imposed his will on them: "The plenum of the Central Committee have decided to reject British mediation in negotiations between the Soviet Republic and Poland, and have given orders and taken steps to continue and step up the offensive." [3] So, having been the main opponent of revolutionary war against Germany in 1918, Lenin was the chief advocate of revolutionary war against Poland in 1920. Both times he made the Central Committee go along with him. But while in 1918 he had had to put up a bitter fight within the party against the proponents of a revolutionary war, a fight that went on for weeks, placing him at one point on the minority side in the Central Committee, in 1920 he won that body over on the first day.

Although events in 1918 had quickly proved him right in not wishing to wage revolutionary war against Germany, events in 1920 were headed toward proving him wrong in the action in Poland. Again it was the advice against war that was right. Those opposed had good reasons for their disapproval, each having intimate knowledge of one of the vital ingredients of Lenin's hoped-for success in that offensive. First there was Trotsky, the commander-in-chief of the Red Army and thus in the best position to know what it was militarily capable of: "It was I perhaps who wanted that war least of all, for I saw only too well how hard it would be for us to fight it after three years of incessant civil

strife. . . . On my return to Moscow, I found those in charge resolved to fight to the finish."[4] Then there was Radek; on October
12, 1920, Lenin said to Clara Zetkin about his hopes earlier that
summer for a revolution in Poland: "Radek predicted how it
would turn out. He warned us. I was very angry with him, and
accused him of 'defeatism.' But he was right in his main conten-
tion. He knows affairs outside Russia, and particularly in the West,
better than we do, and he is talented. He is very useful to us. We
were reconciled a short while ago."[5] Finally there was the group
of Polish Communist leaders, whose state of mind has been reported by Trotsky: "There was one unknown: What was the attitude of the Polish workers and peasants? Some of our Polish
comrades, like the late J. Marchlewski, a friend and supporter of
Rosa Luxemburg, viewed the matter with considerable pessimism.
Marchlewski's assessment was a big factor in my wish to get out of
that war as quickly as possible."[6]

These reservations notwithstanding, in keeping with Bolshevik
practice all the leaders were obliged to support the decision of the
Central Committee (actually Lenin's). This was true of Trotsky,
who had to order the Red Army to march on Warsaw; of the
Polish Communists, who joined the Red Army, even setting up a
provisional government (headed by Marchlewski); and finally of
Radek, who, when the Second Congress was over, left for the
Polish front.* Their opposition had not dented Lenin's resolve.

---

*Before sending Radek to the Russian-Polish front, Lenin decided to take
another measure which could only displease Radek: he removed him from the
post of secretary of the Communist International. Alfred Rosmer, a member
of the Comintern's Executive Committee, relates what was taking place at the
ECCI meeting of August 7, in the presence of Lenin: "The reelection of
Zinoviev to the presidency [of the Comintern] did not raise any problem, but
it was very different when the problem of the secretariat was discussed: the
Russian delegation requested the elimination of Radek" (*Moscou sous
Lénine*, Paris 1953, p. 116). The Russian delegation succeeded in replacing
Radek by Kobetsky, without giving an open justification for that measure,
and also without Rosmer—judging by his autobiography—understanding the
real motive of the elimination. In fact, Lenin, furious over Radek's opposition
(as he later admitted to Clara Zetkin), undertook a double punitive action
against Radek: he removed him from a leading position within the Comintern
and he sent him to the front to implement a political line with which he
disagreed. (This replacement of Radek by Kobetsky, a man without experience and without authority in Comintern circles, proved to be short lived: at
the next Comintern congress Kobetsky lost the post.)

Both as to revolutionary offensives (as in Petrograd in November 1917) and tactical retreats (as at Brest-Litovsk), events had so often proved him right that he was sure they would do so again. It was in this frame of mind that he arrived in Petrograd, three days after the full meeting of the Central Committee, to attend the opening of the Second World Congress on July 19, and meet the delegates coming in from Europe, particularly Germany, and steer and shape the work and decisions of that congress.

Back in Moscow, where the congress moved after July 23, Lenin received "Thomas," the head of the Berlin W.E.S., and questioned him at length on the situation in Germany, though he had made up his mind in advance about what was going to happen there, as Thomas later reported: "He was convinced that we were making giant strides toward social revolution in Germany."[7] On July 28 he received at the Kremlin the French Socialist delegation, consisting of Louis-Oscar Frossard and Marcel Cachin. The victorious advance of the Red Army was resuming, the revolutionary government of the Socialist Republic of Poland was being set up at Bialystok, and on August 1 Brest-Litovsk was captured. In his talks with the French visitors Lenin was euphoric: "Yes, the Soviets are in Warsaw. Soon Germany will be ours, Hungary reconquered; the Balkans will revolt against capitalism; Italy will shake. Bourgeois Europe is cracking at every seam in the hurricane."[8]

Lenin's euphoria was contagious, engulfing all who attended the Second Congress, thanks to careful staging by the Bolsheviks, who knew the art well. In the congress hall hung a huge map, with every day the same ritual, as noted by Angelica Balabanova: "During the three weeks the congress was in session every meeting opened with a reading of the news from the front announcing Russian victories. I translated those bulletins into the various languages of the delegates; their enthusiasm was reflected in their speeches and in the way they discussed and dealt with other problems."[9] After the victory announcements had been read, the Red Army advances were pinpointed on the big map with red flags, to the great joy of all. Speeches and resolutions expressed great optimism. It was widely believed that the military campaign in Poland was already won, and that the Communist revolution in Germany was imminent. For example, during a single session on July 30, while discussing the conditions of admission to the Comintern, several speakers mentioned the revolutionary situation in Germany as an accomplished fact. Serrati declared: "I know that the situation in Germany is revolutionary," but he added the same concerning Italy: "The situation is genuinely revolutionary, both from the economic and the psychological standpoint." [10] Ernst Däumig exclaimed: "Every kilometer which the Red Army covers represents an incentive to the revolution, is a step forward toward revolution in Germany." [11] Walter Stoecker asserted: "We shall soon, perhaps in a few weeks, face new revolutionary battles in Germany." [12] The same viewpoint was expressed in Zinoviev's concluding speech at the congress: "It is possible that in Germany the working class will face decisive battles even in the next months." [13]

But concerning the hope of any immediate revolution in Poland, with Germany following suit, Lenin found a different appraisal at the very Comintern summit: he did not receive the expected reply from the man whose opinion he certainly valued most, Paul Levi. It was the first time that the leader of the Bolsheviks and the Spartacist chief had met since 1917 in Switzerland. The congress had no sooner opened in Petrograd than Lenin spoke to Levi of the main problem on his mind, revolution in Germany. After returning to Berlin, Levi addressed the German Communist Party Central Committee on August 25, explaining in veiled terms that he indeed had not given Lenin the expected reply: "On my first day in Russia Comrade Lenin asked me: 'What if we reach the German border? Will the German proletariat revolt?'* I told him my feeling was that that would be determined not only by external considerations but by internal factors also." [14] Angelica Balabanova, who claims to have been present at the conversation, has supplied a somewhat dramatized version: "Levi replied calmly, 'In three months or maybe three weeks. Or maybe there will be no revolution at all.' The 'at all' ended the conversation. Nodding, Lenin rose and left." [15] In any case, Levi again sided with Radek, as he had during the year 1919, and differed with Lenin as to the chances of revolution. That Paul Levi had doubts about the

---

*It appears that the date of the coming revolution in Europe was at that time Lenin's standard question, asked even of the non-Communists, according to the testimony of H. G. Wells, who visited Moscow in September 1920: "When will the social revolution break out in England? Indeed, Lenin, Zinoviev, Zorin, and many others candidly asked me that question." *La Russie telle que je viens de la voir,* Paris, 1921, p. 84.

success of a revolution in Germany appears evident from the very prudent formulations he used in his speech on July 30, in contrast to the certainty of the other speakers: "The situation for Germany will be difficult and tragic. Once again comes the moment when the destiny of the world revolution will be put for months, maybe for years, into the hands of the German proletariat. When the conflict between the Entente and Russia sharpens and when the collision occurs, then the position of the German proletariat will be decisive." [16]

Despite Levi's doubts, the foreign delegates found themselves submerged in a sea of contagious enthusiasm, which seemed all the more dazzling as they were generally unfamiliar with the country, did not know its language, and were allowed no contact with the debris of the still surviving Socialist and trade-union opposition. This aura of enthusiasm and its effect upon the foreign delegates were described both immediately after the congress and a number of years later always in the same general terms by numerous witnesses, Communist, non-Communist and ex-Communist.

Mrs. Snowden, the wife of the Labour Party leader and like her husband hostile to Bolshevism, wrote an account of a demonstration that erupted when Trotsky appeared in a Petrograd theater just before the Second Congress: "As soon as the great audience caught a glimpse of Trotsky, it rose as one man and with wild enthusiasm applauded its hero again and again. Naturally we rose with the rest to pay our respects to the man who was leading in his country's battles and winning all the time. The cheers redoubled and trebled. People shouted themselves hoarse. It was the most spontaneous thing I have ever seen. It was wonderful! " [17]

J. T. Murphy, who for years remained in positions of leadership within the British Communist movement and the Comintern, before he broke with Communism in 1932, described in his autobiography the climate of the Second Congress: "The congress closed on August 7, 1920, amidst scenes of tremendous enthusiasm. . . . There would be another world congress in a year's time, and who knew how far the revolution would have swept the world by then? " [18] Marcel Cachin, a convert to Bolshevism but until the end of his life a Politburo member of the French Communist party, exclaimed at the congress of Tours: "Soviet Russia is in deep distress; we did not close our eyes to that. But the faith, enthusiasm, and belief in the future there are nevertheless admirable and touching. We witnessed a spectacle that moved us to the very marrow of our old Socialist bones." [19]

Ten years later, at a time when he was still an orthodox Communist, Willi Münzenberg, who had come from Berlin on behalf of the Communist Youth International, wrote in his memoirs: "All the delegates had gone to Leningrad for the opening of the congress of the Communist International. The welcome extended us by the Leningrad proletariat and our days in Leningrad made an unforgettable impression on me." [20] According to Angelica Balabanova, the Italian delegation got an especially warm reception: "I have seen many huge gatherings and mass demonstrations in Russia, with beautiful banners, parades of the youth and military forces, manifestations of joy and mourning, but none so spontaneous and unanimous as those attending the arrival of the Italian delegation in Petrograd. There were demonstrations every evening until we left for Moscow." [21]

What this careful staging accomplished at the outset would be enhanced and reinforced by the foreign delegates' personal contacts with Lenin, and secondarily with Zinoviev. In an attempt to win converts to Bolshevism, invitations had been sent to many Socialists, regardless of their pasts, and left-wing Communists, notwithstanding their tactics, which Lenin of course considered wrong. But this Second Congress was to be a healing one which would thereby gain the support of the masses, a support conspicuous by its absence at the time of the First Congress. If in 1919 pilgrimages to Soviet Russia were few and far between, by 1920 there seemed to be almost too many of them. Whether they were dyed-in-the-wool, old Socialist chieftains or members of the militant youth newly attracted to Communism, they shared an almost total ignorance of what Bolshevism really was and meant. The words of Bohumír Šmeral, who had come to Soviet Russia in the spring of 1920, applied to almost all the other foreigners in Russia at that time: "I did not know a word of Russian, had read hardly any of the Bolshevik literature, but the October Revolution had greatly impressed me." [22]

LENIN'S ACTIVITIES AT THE SECOND CONGRESS

Throughout the Second Congress Lenin believed himself armed with a great triple truth. He had read world capitalism's future, mastered the law of revolution, and knew when the revolution would come. Capitalism's future was collapse, followed by world revolution. The law of that revolution was to be universalized application of the Bolshevik model. Its coming was bound to be soon, as augured by the Red Army advance in Poland. At the previous congress, in March 1919, he could project his perspective, but lacking contacts with Europe and any existing Communist parties he could not extend his Bolshevik truth to the whole of the international movement. Also, with no Red Army advancing on Europe, there was no reliable force able to carry the revolution abroad. But by the time of the Second Congress these two lacunae had been filled, and he did his best to maximize the effects.

The congress agenda faithfully reflected Lenin's concerns and thinking. The chapters of his *"Left-Wing" Communism. . . .* (Parliamentarianism, Role of the Communist Party, Trade Unions, Policy toward the Labour Party) became agenda items and subjects scheduled for debate. The only important issue not dealt with in the book was the agrarian question—an issue, however, not new to Lenin, who had been concerned with it from his earliest days in politics.

Preparatory work for the opening of the Second World Congress corresponded to a line of conduct typical for the majority of Comintern proceedings. It was characterized by three successive stages mirroring the three echelons of the real hierarchy of that organization (and irrespective of its official, statutory setup). The highest echelon of the hierarchy was Lenin himself; once his ideas were fully grown and his intentions fixed, he transmitted them to the next echelon, the Politburo of the Bolshevik Party. The Politburo busied itself effectively at three of its sessions (those of June 1 and 18 and July 16) with the forthcoming work at the Comintern congress. Finally came the third echelon: the Executive Committee of the Comintern, whose task was to implement what Lenin had conceived and the Politburo had approved.

Once the congress was under way, Lenin's line of action followed a tight pattern. The drafts of theses were elaborated in advance, then paraphrased in the reports. A committee was set up for each agenda item, and the debates always ended with adoption of the proposed theses, which then became the law. All the theses were either authored by Lenin or directly inspired by him. When he himself was not the main committee speaker, some other Bolshe-

vik leader (Zinoviev, Bukharin, or Radek) was. The exception was
the committee on the agrarian question. Though Lenin did write
the original draft of its theses, it was Marchlewski, a Pole, long
known to Lenin and the Bolsheviks, who was assigned the role of
main speaker on the issue. The theses on all the agenda items were,
of course, merely generalized recitals of Bolshevik experience,
hitherto axiomatic for the Bolshevik party and now to be holy
writ for the Communist International. Lenin's introductory statement on the first item, entitled "The International Situation and
the Basic Tasks of the Communist International," applied equally
to every question that the congress was to consider: "The theses
on the questions concerning the basic tasks of the Communist
International have been published in every language, and contain
(especially for the Russian Comrades) nothing very new, since
mainly they just extend to the different Western countries, specifically to Western Europe, some key aspects of our own revolutionary experience and lessons learned from our revolutionary movement."[23]

When Lenin undertook a task that he regarded as important, he
threw himself into it totally. There were no half measures. He
interested himself directly in almost all the theses that the Second
Congress was to adopt, either personally writing their original
texts (as on the national and colonial issues, the agrarian question,
the basic tasks of the Second Congress, conditions for admission
to the International) or overseeing their writing (as on parliamentarianism and Syndicalism). He also took part directly in the work
of many of the congress committees, such as those on the national
and colonial issue, the agrarian question, the conditions for admission to the International, world situation and the tasks of the
Comintern. He also made numerous speeches at the plenary sessions. At the first session, on July 19, he presented his report on
the world situation and the tasks of the Communist International.
On July 23, at the second session, he gave a speech on the role of
the Communist Party. On July 26 he delivered the report of the
committee on the national and colonial issue. On July 30 he discussed the terms and conditions for admission to the Comintern.
On August 2 he spoke on parliamentarianism, and on August 6 on
whether British Communists should join the Labour Party. Besides
making speeches at the public sessions of the congress, Lenin took

an active part in the discussions behind closed doors of the committees of the congress.[24] Before, during, and after the congress he had more talks with foreign delegations than he had ever had or would ever have again. After the congress, he personally received the leaders of even the tiniest Communist groups, men like Queeland of the Irish party, Van Overstraeten of the Belgian party, and Rheiland of Luxembourg. But he always knew how to assign priorities to problems and parties. It became evident at the congress that he concerned himself mainly with the affairs of only five parties, four important to him as European mass movements and the fifth as a problem in tactics. The four, whose leaders he received more than once, were those of Germany, France, Italy, and Czechoslovakia. And they were the only parties whose chiefs he would still receive at the next two Comintern congresses (when he was no longer speaking to the heads of small parties). The fifth delegation in which for reasons of tactics he took an active interest, both at the congress and in private talks, was that of the British leftist groups. The problem that they posed was that of finding a way to have a single independent Communist party while at the same time, for tactical purposes, maintaining membership in the Labour Party so as to penetrate and honeycomb it with one's own people. It was to those five parties that Lenin would address himself in his various writings during the period from 1920 to 1922, demanding to see their publications and keeping abreast of their affairs.

Despite all his work at the congress, Lenin knew perfectly well that it was not enough merely to compose theses and make speeches. The job of persuasion had to be backed up by another more important one: organizing. For him organizing a congress, ever since the split at the Brussels-London congress of 1903, meant first assuring himself of the support of a nucleus of reliable delegates, preferably the majority, even if that involved using questionable methods to inflate the number of his supporters. At the First Comintern Congress he had simply manufactured delegates; at the Second Congress, where the Bolsheviks were confronted with two international "deviations," left-wing Communism and centrism, his problem was to capture the majority, which is why the assigned voting strength was distributed so differently at the two congresses. In 1919 the committee on credentials made the magnanimous gesture of giving one German delegate five votes, with only five votes also going to the entire Bolshevik delegation, which included Lenin, Zinoviev, Trotsky, and Bukharin. At the Second Congress the German Communist Party delegation, headed by the party chairman, again was allotted five votes, but this time the Bolshevik delegation appropriated 64. Of the 169 deliberative votes to be cast at the congress, Lenin wanted to be sure of a safe absolute majority, which he comfortably guaranteed himself by bestowing votes on European political refugees in Russia (from Georgia, the Baltic countries, Finland, Yugoslavia) and on Communist parties having special ties with the Bolshevik party (as those of Azerbaijan and Eastern Galicia); he also gave votes to selected trusted Bolshevik agents, who were suddenly proclaimed delegates from foreign Communist movements (for example, the Bulgarian professional revolutionary S. Mineff, under the assumed name Vanini, was appointed to the agrarian committee as a French representative).

During the summer of 1920 Lenin still believed, even more than in 1919, that the Communist revolution would spread to Europe, though his attitude toward foreign Communist leaders had profoundly altered in the interim. When in January 1919 the document was drafted that was to convene the conference at which the Communist International would be born, Lenin and his colleagues were still unaware of the death of Rosa Luxemburg and Karl Liebknecht, and when the congress took place at the beginning of March, the third Spartacist leader, Leo Jogiches, was still alive. But by 1920 not one of three top leaders of Germany's revolutionary movement was left. The man who considered himself their spiritual and political heir, Paul Levi, carried much less weight in Bolshevik eyes, and a few months later he would break with Moscow. Thus the beheading of the Spartacus League had rid Lenin of the one team of European Communist leaders that could have challenged Bolshevik hegemony in the Comintern.

Left to face Lenin and his Bolsheviks were but two shaky groups, which had no hope of standing up to Moscow: the left-wing Communists, mostly youngsters with no international prestige or political experience, and the turncoats from centrist Socialism. The former were slated to be educated by Lenin, the latter re-educated, and both were to be bent to Bolshevik iron discipline. Typically, at the very moment at which he was preparing to welcome Europe's Socialists, he was tightening the screws on Russia's Socialists in Moscow and Petrograd. The friendly hand extended to the former was accompanied by the mailed fist directed against the latter. In March 1920, on learning that the censor at the Commissariat of Foreign Affairs had let by a letter from the Menshevik leader, Rafael Abramovich, addressed to Dr. Rudolf Hilferding, a leader in the USPD, he sent word to the Bolshevik Party Politburo demanding a merciless investigation, in which he requested Dzerzhinsky's aid, suggesting that the Commissariat of Foreign Affairs be purged. [25] When in May 1920 the foreign Socialist delegations began to arrive in Moscow, the Bolsheviks took special care to see that they had no contact with Menshevik Socialists and Social Revolutionaries, who were still at liberty in Russia, though under constant surveillance. They succeeded in all cases except that of the British delegation: "The British resisted these measures most vigorously. They tried to get around the obstacles placed in their path, being desirous of learning the true situation in Russia. They visited representatives of opposition parties, attended forbidden meetings, and gathered up all the documents that certain organizations were able to smuggle to them. True, their ignorance of the Russian language largely did prevent their studying and fully understanding conditions in Russia, but they at least tried to get along without the official interpreters, relying instead on certain American anarchists." [26] When the Second Congress opened, the Menshevik leader Martov, whose home was being watched and periodically visited by GPU agents, wrote a letter protesting the government's refusal to grant him and his comrade Abramovich exit visas, the upshot being that the Bolsheviks prudently changed their minds and did let them leave for Germany. [27] When the French Socialist delegation appeared before the Comintern Executive Committee in Lenin's presence, he gave his one stock recipe for taking care of Social Democrats:" 'You shoot them,' he said several times." [28]

THE BRITISH LABOUR DELEGATION

The first foreign delegation to arrive in Soviet Russia, the British, did not attend the Second Congress and was the only one to return home with an irrevocably negative attitude toward joining the Communist International. It was made up of three representatives from the Trade Union Congress, four delegates from the Labour Party (headed by Ben Turner), and two leaders of the Independent Labour Party (ILP), not counting two observers, one of whom was Bertrand Russell. Of these three components (Trade Unions, Labour Party, and ILP), only the third was worthy in Bolshevik eyes, for it had opposed the World War, though more out of pacifism than revolutionary ideology, and it had been against foreign intervention in the civil war in Russia. Yet the ILP remained hostile to the Communist International, as evidenced by the vote taken in April 1920 at the annual party conference. The motion to join the Communist International went down to defeat 472 to 206, and instead a declaration was adopted stating merely that the party favored consultation with Moscow and the left Socialist parties in Europe.

Nevertheless, Lenin attributed great importance to the arrival of this delegation, as we learn from A. Lozovsky:

> I clearly remember his great interest in the visit of a delegation of British trade unionists. The Central Council of Russian Trade Unions had assigned me the task of welcoming the delegates. Before going over to meet them in Petrograd, I had a talk with Lenin. . . . After I met and welcomed them, from Petrograd I telephoned to Lenin back in Moscow to let him know my first impressions. He questioned me at length concerning each delegate, on their respective reactions to different events, on what struck them most, what they were saying about Soviet Russia, etc. Did their statements merely reflect a "European" politeness, or were they actually sincere? I described to him in detail my initial contact with them, and he kept asking me more and more questions. After accompanying our foreign visitors on a trip along the Volga, I talked with Lenin again.[29]

In addition to these two conversations with Lozovsky, the first on May 12 and the second in June, Lenin received the British in a body, then had a talk with Clifford Allen of the ILP, and during the Second World Congress received Bertrand Russell.

When he received the British delegation on May 26, he must already have known from Lozovsky of their disapproving attitude. For his part, he had already made up his mind about Communist activities in England, having just then finished writing his book *"Left-Wing" Communism, an Infantile Disorder*, which made clear that he was not counting too heavily on the Independent Labour Party to set up any future Communist party, but more on other groups (the British Socialist Party, the Socialist Labour Party, and the Workers' Socialist Federation) and on militants such as William Gallacher and Sylvia Pankhurst. Still, he had spelled out for the British Communists what future tactic they should follow: form a unified party and penetrate the Labour Party. The positions of the two sides having thus hardened, nothing much could come of the conversation, as Mrs. Snowden later confirmed: "He showed a surprising lack of knowledge of the British Labour Movement. He gave to conscious and intelligent Communism a far larger place in British politics than can truly be accorded to it. . . . Lenin believes that a very tiny Communist group, working upon a mass of inflammable human beings, suffering from unemployment and hunger, can make the revolution necessary to establish a new order of society. . . . He appears to think that the British revolution is imminent." [30]

Once the British delegation was deemed lost to the Communist cause, the Bolshevik leaders accepted the fact and behaved accordingly, as the attitude of the Comintern's Executive Committee made clear. The leaders of the International showed no further eagerness to receive the British delegation or answer its questions about the terms and qualifications for admission to the Comintern. On returning to England, R. C. Wallhead, the chairman of the ILP, noted in his report to the party: "Your delegation experienced some difficulty in obtaining an interview with the Executive of the Third International. Time after time I pressed for an appointment, but it seemed almost impossible to arrange matters satisfactorily. The business methods at the headquarters of the Third International were extremely dilatory." [31] When he finally did get an appointment, he could not help observing that "at the time the interview took place, the Third International was an entirely ad hoc body." [32] In actual fact, its Executive Committee was a tight little Bolshevik team consisting of Radek, Bukharin, Balabanova and a few supernumeraries from the countries bordering Soviet Russia (such as Latvia and Finland), none of whom uttered a word during the discussion. Wallhead also remarked after the interview how prone the Russians were to look at the international problems of the labor movement through Russian spectacles: "It was very difficult to discuss matters with the leaders of the Third International, owing to the strong nationalist direction they adopt. Every question is deeply coloured with ideas peculiarly Russian. I think it understandable, but certainly the very pontifical attitude they adopt does not make discussion easy."[33]

After making quite clear that they had not come to "beg for admission to the Third International," the British delegates concluded their discussion with the Executive Committee by submitting a detailed questionnaire of twelve points on which they requested information before presenting the matter to their party. According to Wallhead's report, made the following year to the ILP congress, the Executive Committee's reply did not reach him until June 21, an hour before his departure from Moscow: "The reply is long and rambling, and does not answer clearly several of the points raised. It is incorrect in places historically, and it judges the British situation from a purely Russian point of view."[34]

Two of the delegation members did not leave Moscow with their colleagues but stayed on for a time in Russia. One was Robert Williams, from the Labour Party, the other A. A. Purcell, a trade union representative. On June 15 and 16 they had a conference with Zinoviev in the presence of the Italian Syndicalist leaders concerning formation of a trade union international. But as the ILP declined to join the Comintern, so the following year the trade unions declined to join the Profintern.

Having failed to capture any of the three components of the British delegation, the Bolsheviks spared no effort to recruit at least one of its members. Their choice fell on Clifford Allen, another ILP member, for according to A. Balabanova "Allen was the only one who was definitely sympathetic to the Soviets."[35] He therefore received special care and attention. His party colleague, Wallhead, got to talk with Lenin only once, in the presence of the entire delegation, while Allen (according to the letter that he wrote to his party) could boast of "several conversations with Lenin." But he was against revolutionary violence and in favor of all-out internationalism, so he was not convinced by the conversations, as he himself reported: "The chief difficulty I experienced in discussion with its [the Third International's] leaders was its very definitely nationalist colouring. . . . I should not be making a fair or accurate report if I did not emphasize this point [Bolshevik insistence on revolutionary violence]. I might add that in the several conversations that I had with Lenin this point of view was clearly emphasized."[36] So the efforts to win over Allen also failed. He did not participate in the Southport congress in March 1921, where the motion to join the Comintern went down to defeat, with 97 votes in favor and 521 against; but at the next national conference, in April 1922, he was elected ILP treasurer.

LENIN AND THE CZECH SOCIAL DEMOCRATIC LEADER, BOHUMÍR ŠMERAL

With rare exceptions, the leaders of Europe's Socialist movement knew very little about Lenin's ideas, not to mention the man himself. It was not until the eve of the Second Congress and in the course of its sessions that many had their first opportunity to take a close look at him and get to know some of his traits. In 1920, among the other European Socialist delegates in Russia, were two whose behavior during the First World War constituted what Lenin had branded as Socialism's high treason, Bohumír Šmeral and Marcel Cachin. But during their stay in Russia these two leaders were converted to Bolshevism and helped bring their respective Socialist parties into the Third International; they personally remained Comintern members for life, while almost all Europe's other Communist leaders of the 1919-21 period gradually broke with Moscow. Lenin played no small part in getting these two "Socialist opportunists" to join, the weight of his personal authority being liberally used to silence the voices raised against allowing "social patriots" into the Comintern.

The problem as to whether to overlook the past records of some of Europe's Socialist leaders who had come to Moscow was of particular concern to those who had defended the internationalist and pacifist cause at a time when these "social patriots" were practicing their nationalism. The Italian delegation was a case in point. Serrati, the party chief and head of its delegation to the Second Congress, whose own anti-militarist internationalist past was impeccable, resolutely opposed letting such people in, and he did not hesitate to say so openly in Moscow and write the same when he got back to Italy: "No concession or extra favors for those who during the war shamefully betrayed the interests of the working class, who, after indulging their nationalist madness, now cheerfully announce their eagerness to submit to all the rigors of Muscovite discipline. Tomorrow they will betray us again." [37] But it was permissible to assume the opposite, at least in the cases of Šmeral and Cachin. Precisely because of their pasts, they would be less demanding and more obedient than certain others whose records were clean. A politican's quondam compromisings can be a better guarantee of his future tractability than the record of a battle well fought. And so it was with Šmeral and Cachin.

Šmeral heard Lenin speak at the Ninth Congress of the Russian Communist Party on April 3. By April 10 Šmeral's signature appeared among those of the members of the Communist International's Executive Committee, though Czechoslovakia had no Communist party and Šmeral had not been appointed by anyone to join the Third International. On April 23 he addressed a meeting held in honor of Lenin's fiftieth birthday in Petrograd, but it was not until May 5 that he had his first direct contact with the Soviet chief. The interview started in this rather typical manner: "I wanted to tell him the story of my life. Lenin interrupted me: 'I am familiar with your past, your evolution. There is no point in discussing it.' He had the delicacy not to mention my Social Democratic activity." [38] This was somewhat disingenuous, since Lenin would have been less concerned with his Social Democratic past than with his "social patriotism" in the service of Austria-Hungary and the Habsburg dynasty during the war. Šmeral was invited to have a second talk with Lenin on May 22, less than a week after Lenin's interview with the British delegation. Lenin was much nicer to him than to the Englishmen: "This time he talked to me in detail about setting up a Communist party in Czechoslovakia. He advised me on how to attract to the Third International as many as possible of the left-oriented members of the Social Democratic Party and to found a Communist party without losing touch with the majority of workers belonging to the Social Democratic Party. When I returned from Moscow, I was a new man. I set out sincerely, loyally, along the path of Communism, of Bolshevism." [39]

While Šmeral may have felt himself miraculously transformed by this lightning revelation of a new faith, Lenin was more down to earth in his appraisal of the conversation, as Trotsky later intimated in the portrait that he drew of Šmeral: "Czechoslovakia was born, and the Austro-Hungarian, Šmeral, was up a political blind alley. Where was he to go? Many were those initially intoxicated by Czechoslovak statism. Still more numerous were the ones whose hearts beat for the Russia of the October Revolution. But not a soul was shedding tears after the Austro-Hungarian Empire. It was in this context that Šmeral made his pilgrimage to Moscow. I remember explaining to Lenin the psychological mechanism of Šmeral's Bolshevism. With a smile that spoke volumes Lenin replied: 'Probably so. Yes, probably you are right. Many like that will come to us now. We must keep our eyes open. They must be watched at every step.' "[40] After the return of Šmeral, a delegation was sent from Prague to attend the Second Congress; it included the three militants B. Hula, A. Zapotocký, and M. Vaněk, the latter chosen by Šmeral personally "for the express purpose of keeping an eye on Zapotocký so he wouldn't promise Lenin a revolution in Czechoslovakia."[41]

THE FROSSARD-CACHIN MISSION TO THE SECOND CONGRESS

While the other important European delegations (such as the German and Italian) encompassed the top leaders of both the Socialist centrist and Communist tendencies, the French delegation was composed only of two prominent centrists: Frossard and Cachin; the Communist-leaning Committee for the Third International could not send its representatives to Moscow, for its three secretaries and some of its other top militants were in jail at that time. Thus the political talks in Moscow were reduced to negotiations with Frossard and Cachin, with Lenin playing a determining role. The essential factor in Lenin's judgment first of Šmeral, then of the two Frenchmen, was his awareness of their political and sentimental attachment to the cause of Soviet Russia and the Comintern, a frame of mind which he wanted to nurture and strengthen. Cachin and Frossard (the latter replacing Jean Longuet, who was a grandson of Karl Marx and had originally been appointed a member of the mission to Soviet Russia) left for Russia intimately determined to join the Third International, provided nothing was done to make it impossible. As Frossard said later in his speech to the congress of Tours: "When we went to Russia, to me only one course seemed possible and desirable: joining the Third International. It was with the fixed intention of smoothing the French party's way into it that I left Paris for Moscow with Cachin. . . . Everybody knows this."[42] Lenin and his colleagues would know it also, and act accordingly.

Naturally the Bolsheviks were willing to forget the past of these two Socialists once they learned of their interest in joining the Comintern. Cachin had been guilty not only of "social patriotism" in France during the war but of certain suspicious involvements abroad, such as his contacts with Mussolini's dissident Socialists in Italy and his trip to Russia in April and May of 1917 to try to discourage its government from leaving the war. More recently, in July 1918, at a banquet in Paris in honor of Kerensky (organized by a newspaper of which Cachin was a director) he publicly said to Kerensky, whom Lenin had overthrown and banished: "They have snatched your people away from you by appealing to their despair. Scorn these unjust attacks! We know of your burning sincerity and invincible faith in the face of this immense misfortune."[43] As for Frossard, as late as February 1920 (the month of the Strasbourg congress of the SFIO, where the mood in favor of joining the Third International was growing), he had written: "Hewing purely and simply to the Moscow line would be vain and short-lived; vain because in joining the International the French Socialist Party would not be taking with it the other elements of the nation; short-lived because the mentality of the French proletariat, of France's Socialist troops, would not change with this 'change of address.' "[44]

By the time they left Russia, they were more sympathetic to the Comintern, though they still knew virtually nothing about it. Neither spoke any language but French; neither had ever had any contacts or dealings with Russian Bolsheviks. When they left Paris on May 31, they did not even know that the Second Comintern Congress was about to be held, and it was only twenty-four hours later, while they were underway and in Reval, that they learned about the convocation of that congress.

Consequently, their mandate did not authorize them either to take an active part in the Second Congress or to apply for membership in the Third International. It was only after the June 19 meeting of the Comintern's Executive Committee that Frossard and Cachin asked the Socialist Party leadership to accredit them as delegates to the congress, and the request was granted. But if they followed their instructions in this procedural matter, in the more fundamental one—the nature of their mission—they did not. The Strasbourg congress and the party's Administrative Committee (the CAP) had directed them to try to arrange for an international conference in which two distinct groups would participate: the Communists of the Third International and the Socialist parties that had broken with the Second International. This was exactly what Lenin did *not* want. It was not that he was unwilling to consort with Socialists of the center, but he refused to deal with them as any recognized international unit. He did want "centrist" representatives from Britain, France, Germany, and elsewhere to come to Russia, not for any meeting between the Communist International and a centrist coalition but rather for contact between the Communist International and each centrist party separately. He also wanted to take advantage of the divisions *within* each centrist party, between the leftists and the others, trusting the leftists to provoke the split and then join the militants already won over to Communism to set up a unified Communist party in each country. This was one of his chief projects during 1920, and it was very largely successful.

Frossard and Cachin threw aside the task assigned them by their party and worked to promote the policy laid down by Lenin—that is, to make it possible for the SFIO to join the Third International. Lenin's statement to the Executive Committee concerning the French matter on June 19 (before the Second Congress started), his first talk with Frossard and Cachin on July 7 (again, before the congress began), and his second talk with them on July 28 cemented the agreement. In the days following the June 19 meeting of the Executive Committee, Frossard was approached confidentially by several persons who had spoken with Lenin on the subject: first Kamenev (sent by Lenin to ask Frossard and Cachin to stay on for the congress), then Radek, and then the French Communists Jacques Sadoul and Lucien Deslinières, who were received by Lenin on June 23. They all said virtually the same thing: "He [Lenin] strongly favors the agreement. . . . You can say that Lenin wants the agreement. . . . Lenin has confidence in your good faith, but he would like you to remain on here for a while . . . to get rid of your opportunism." [45] The role of the Comintern Executive Committee was to translate Lenin's will in this matter into fact.

This policy, incidentally, did not enjoy the approval of the foreign Communists arriving in Moscow for the Second Congress. Wijnkoop, the head of the Dutch delegation, protested vigorously against the presence of Frossard and Cachin, as did others, like Willi Münzenberg, the head of the Communist Youth International, who said: "We were especially furious to see at the congress the French Socialist Party delegation headed by Frossard, and to note the immediate arrival of the German Independent Socialist delegation, which included Arthur Crispien and Dittmann. We strenuously opposed letting those parties in, and in my speech I attacked them." [44] Serrati, the head of the Italian delegation and one of the presiding officers at the Second Congress, was also against the French delegation and against letting the SFIO attend the congress.

But the Bolsheviks, ignoring them all, were moved by a higher consideration: implementing the pre-established plan of Lenin and his colleagues to create a revolutionary Communist party in France by uniting the two forces of the left already supporting the Comintern—the Committee for the Third International and the revolutionary Syndicalists—with the SFIO center. The center had had a majority of the Socialist party membership since 1918, and controlled its administrative apparatus, including the secretariat and the newspaper *Humanité*. This is why the Bolshevik leaders were determined to push ahead. As Frossard and Cachin reported, they were immediately taken in hand by the Bolshevik delegation, which in the circumstances they called the "permanent bureau of the International": "The day after our arrival in Moscow on June 16, we were in touch with the permanent bureau of the Communist International, that is with citizens Zinoviev, Radek, Kamenev, and Bukharin." [47] At the Executive Committee meeting on June 19 they were questioned by many of the Soviet leaders, starting with Lenin. Later they had another meeting with the Bolshevik leaders, at which no other foreigners were present.

While Lenin's statement to the Executive Committee on June 19 pertained exclusively to the French problem, it was indicative in many ways of his general thinking on the activities of foreign Communists. Thus, when the problem of the relationship between the SFIO and the trade unions, which were acting separately, was posed by Lenin at that meeting, he proposed a typically Russian solution: "As with the trade union organizations, there must be no compromise. Yet the French party is always compromising. There again it is mistaken. Organized labor in Russia was against the Bolsheviks in 1917. We beat them in an open fight against their leadership by planting organized Communist cells inside the trade unions."[48] On the situation in France involving relations between the party and the peasants, Lenin referred again to Russia: "The French comrades object that their peasants are presently hostile. In Russia the peasants had no opinion."[49]

When first stated, Lenin's ideas on revolutionary tactics were quite unknown in the European labor movement. But as they kept being repeated, and Lenin never tired of repeating them, they lost their original character, showing more and more of their Russian-ness. Sometimes, too, there was an obvious disparity between a measure's actual effectiveness and the effectiveness that Lenin attributed to it, agitprop being an example. Lenin fervently believed that the toiling masses would flock inexorably to the banner of Communism once it was finally unfurled—that is, when they had been properly worked up by agitation and propaganda. This is why he believed that preparation for the revolution must start with well-conducted agitation and propaganda from within the central party apparatus. Thus, heading his criticisms of the SFIO on June 19 was his axiom that the groundwork for revolution is laid by the party newspaper, as noted by Frossard: "Lenin is not asking us to bring about the revolution immediately. He does not know exactly when this can be done, and that is not what concerns him. What does matter is getting ready for it. *L'Humanité* is not doing that. (Often it does just the opposite.) *Le Populaire* is not doing it either. The Executive Committee of the Third International does have a stab at it from time to time."[50] Several months later, on November 4, 1920, writing to and about the Italian Socialist Party, which was then disobeying Moscow and threatening a split, Lenin used the same argument: "The propaganda currently being made by the Milan publication *Avanti!*, under the direction of Serrati, instead of preparing the proletariat for combat spreads confusion and disarray among them."[51] Evidently, according to Lenin's logic, every party in Europe before staging its November 7 had to have its *Iskra* and its *Pravda*.

As for Frossard and Cachin, they were subjected to "self-criticism"—a key tool in the Bolshevik chest, then still unknown to Western Socialism. That was their first taste of Bolshevik methods. Once Lenin and his colleagues realized that Frossard and Cachin were ready to pay a price to get into the Comintern, they did not fail to press their advantage, and the two received rough treatment. Alfred Rosmer, a member of the Comintern Executive Committee and one of the presiding officers at the Second Congress, later repeated the remarks of a Bolshevik who attended that Executive Committee meeting: "A pity you weren't there yesterday when your Cachin and Frossard appeared before the party's Central Committee. Bukharin reminded them of their chauvinism, their wartime treason. It was quite touching. Cachin was in tears."[52] In the statement read by Cachin on June 29, at the second meeting at which the French problem was discussed, their "self-criticism" was explicit: "But you are right in reproaching us for not having acted more vigorously. Aware now of your sufferings and prolonged privations, we understand your annoyance and complaints. To help you in your resistance, we should have dared acts of boldness, but did not."[53]

Always ready to exploit any difference in opinion (or character) among their interlocutors, the Bolsheviks saw the difference between Frossard and Cachin. Of the two, Frossard should have been politically the less suspect and closer to the Bolsheviks. He had sided fairly early with the pacifist "centrist" element in the SFIO, while Cachin had remained a "social patriot." However, it was not merely a question of political ideas but of human beings, and the Bolsheviks quickly perceived that Cachin was the more malleable. Whenever any decision had to be made, from the first (to remain at the Comintern congress) to the last (their final conversation with Zinoviev before they returned to France), Cachin favored whatever Moscow wanted. Faced with the solidarity between Cachin and the Bolsheviks, Frossard ended up by giving in, which he himself later acknowledged in a single sentence of regret: "I am sorry now that I did not offer Cachin more resistance."[54] The

Bolshevik leaders did not fail to note this fact, as evident from the first speech at the end of the Second Congress delivered before the Petrograd Soviet by Zinoviev in his dual capacity as chairman of that Soviet and presiding officer of the Communist International. All his praise was reserved for Cachin: "Marcel Cachin and Frossard represented the French Socialist Party. The former is editor of the official party organ, the latter party secretary. Cachin was among those who at the start of the Russian Revolution favored prolonging the war and was for the offensive desired by Kerensky, but today he is sincerely repentant. He is a true friend of the working class, a man completely devoid of selfish interests. . . . Even before the congress, he had openly confessed his errors to a meeting of the Moscow Soviet, and in the name of his friends had asked the Russian proletariat for forgiveness. He said literally: 'I beg your pardon.' " [55] The Bolshevik leaders had not erred in their judgment. Within Comintern ruling circles Cachin might be known as a "political weather vane," as Lenin dubbed him, or as a man who "made a profession of siding with the majority," as Manuilsky, the Comintern representative in France, had charged to his face, yet he would not desert the ranks of the French Communist Party or the Communist International.

This high-handed treatment, which the Bolshevik leaders did not dare try on the British or Germans, or on the Italian delegation, apparently worked well in the case of the two Frenchmen. An incident that occurred at the beginning of July, fifteen days before the congress opened, shows to what extent the Soviet leaders were confident of being able to make the two French penitents dance to their tune. On July 4, Frossard and Cachin had sent a telegram to the Socialist Party's National Council stating that "The Executive Committee of the International urgently invites us to participate in the congress, without any implied commitment as to what attitude our party will ultimately adopt." [56] But two days later, on July 6, while Frossard and Cachin were off on an excursion along the Volga, Zinoviev and Radek sent another telegram to that same National Council announcing the adherence of the two French representatives to the principles of the Communist International: "The Executive Committee of the Communist International suggested to Cachin and Frossard that they stay on for the Congress. . . . They have consented, making a fairly explicit statement about recognizing the principles of the Communist International." [57] When questioned about this by the party's Administrative Committee on his return, Frossard declared: "That telegram was sent without our knowledge. We did not learn of it until we got back." [58]

THE NEGOTIATIONS WITH THE USPD DELEGATION

On the eve of the opening of the Second World Congress, Germany had no less than four workers' parties calling themselves Marxist: the official Socialist Party, the Independent Socialist Party of Germany (USPD), the Communist Party (Spartacus League-Communist Party of Germany), and the Communist Workers' Party of Germany (KAPD). Their respective attitudes toward the Communist International differed widely. The Socialist Party under Ebert, Scheidemann, and Noske was bitterly hostile to the Comintern. The Communist Party was a member of the Comintern by right, and the Communist Workers' Party was going to be allowed to join in a fellow-traveler status. The position of the USPD was less certain, for its members could not agree.

Born of internationalist pacifist Socialism of the center, at odds with the official Socialist Party, the USPD was drifting more and more to the left, closer to the Comintern, as evidenced by its program adopted at the congresses of Berlin in March 1919 and of Leipzig on November 30 to December 6, 1919. The resolution approved by unanimous vote at Leipzig was nearer to what Lenin and the International were calling for than were the resolutions passed by the Communist Party (Spartacus League), which had been badly split by the Leftists. It contained three statements on principle and tactics very dear to Lenin: the adoption of the system of soviets; the acknowledgment of dictatorship of the proletariat as the principal means for destroying the class society; and working for revolution within trade unions and parliaments.

But unanimous agreement on their revolutionary program did not prevent USPD members from disagreeing about the attitude they should adopt toward the Third International. At that same extraordinary Leipzig congress three different resolutions were proposed, the first by Rudolf Hilferding, the second by Georg Ledebour, the third by Walter Stoecker. The first two, presented by two leaders who opposed the official Social Democrats and had been against the war (Ledebour was at Zimmerwald), did not call for direct entry into the Third International; the third, submitted by a militant who in 1914 had been guilty of "social chauvinism," did propose joining the Comintern immediately: "Since the Independent Social Democratic Party of Germany agrees with the principles of the Third International, seeing in it the nucleus of a truly revolutionary International, the party congress calls upon the Central Committee to take our party into the Third International." [59] When put to a vote, the resolution lost 170 to 111.

Having no direct contact with Europe, Lenin was unable to assess properly this USPD drift toward Communism. In his article "Heroes of the Bern International," written on May 28, 1919, less than four months after that conference in the Swiss capital and three months after the founding of the Comintern, he was not stingy in the abuse that he heaped on the whole USPD leadership—not only on Kautsky, whom he saw as a symbol of treason, and on Hilferding and Haase, the party chairman, but on the representative of its leftist faction, Ernst Däumig, whom he characterized as a "philistine," "lackey," and "liar." In January 1920, following a USPD proposition to open negotiations in view of its admission to the Communist International, Lenin drafted a response which he submitted for approval to the Bolshevik Politburo on January 20. In that text he virulently attacked the USPD as a whole, without mentioning its leftist trend, which was sympathetic to the Bolshevik theses. His verdict was unequivocal: "In the opinion of the Russian Communist Party, there is no place for such a party in the Communist International." [60]

But Lenin was not insensitive to new facts of life, and when they became clear to him he was ready to modify his tactics accordingly. He did so several times on the eve of and during the Second Congress—and his first accomodation involved the USPD itself. In all probability the common stand of Karl Radek and Paul Levi toward cleavages within the USPD contributed to Lenin's softening of attitude. Unlike Lenin, Radek did not believe that all of the USPD leaders were concealed Mensheviks. Having lived in Berlin

throughout 1919, he made a sharp distinction between the two
wings of German Independent Socialists, and in this connection he
offered in October 1919 the following advice in a letter addressed
to the second congress of the German Communist Party (Spartacists): "The anarcho-syndicalist obscurity and confusion [within
the German Communist Party] must be overcome, and the Party
must join the forthcoming struggles on a united and determined
front. Only then will it be able to attract the left wing of the
USPD."[61] Paul Levi, an even warmer and more long-time advocate
of rapprochement with the USPD leftists, took charge of the operation. He was instrumental in effecting (contrary to Radek's advice) the total split with the anarcho-syndicalists within the German party at the same congress, and he actively fostered a policy
aiming at fusion of the German Communists with the USPD's left
wing. When Radek returned to Moscow in January 1920, he advocated a new political conduct toward the USPD, the one he and
Levi were pursuing in Berlin. That his words did not fall on deaf
ears was evident when on January 20 the Bolshevik Politburo
discussed Lenin's draft response to the USPD, and Lenin himself
was nominated to the commission charged with writing a definitive answer.[62] When published on February 5 under Zinoviev's
signature, that answer was not only much longer than the initial
Lenin version but also appreciably modified. While Lenin's draft
had rejected the admission of the USPD into the Comintern as a
party, the final document closed the doors only to its right-wing
tendency: "We categorically refuse any collaboration with the
rightist independent leaders and the Longuetites who pull the
movement backward toward the bourgeois marshland of the yellow International."[63]

    Lenin's readiness to modify his original intransigeance toward
the USPD as a whole, was soon confirmed by other acts in accord
with the Radek-Levi line. Thus, through the office of the Western
European Secretariat in Berlin, negotiations began between the
USPD and the Presidium of the Comintern which led to an official
invitation to the USPD to send delegates to the next Comintern
congress. Moreover, in the supplement to his *"Left-Wing" Communism*, written on May 12, 1920, Lenin stated that "a compromise
between the Communists and the left wing of the [German] In-

dependent [Socialists] is indispensable and useful to the cause of Communism, although it will not be easy to realize."*

When the USPD delegation arrived in Moscow, Lenin saw that his likening of that party to Martov's Mensheviks was wrong, and that again Radek's and Levi's assessment of the situation in Germany was more accurate than the impression gained of it in Moscow, which had no direct contact and lacked information. Actually, the USPD delegation arrived already split; Crispien and Dittmann were very reluctant to join the Third International then, but Däumig and Stoecker had secretly decided to jump right in, even if it did mean splitting their party. This divergence of views became evident on the very day of their arrival in Moscow, July 21, when they appeared before the Comintern Executive Committee. Lenin was not there, but Zinoviev, Radek, Paul Levi, Ernst Meyer, Serrati, Frossard, Cachin, and Wijnkoop were.Wijnkoop protested against the presence of this delegation, as he had against that of the French delegation. They were subjected to merciless interrogation by Radek, Levi, Meyer, and Serrati, which dragged on through a second session, at which Trotsky was the chief accuser. The split was obvious, as Frossard noted afterwards: "The Germans are split. Stoecker had been won over to the Third International. Däumig wants to join, too."[64] Ernst Meyer also made clear to the Bolsheviks that they must exploit this "internal contradiction" in the German Socialist delegation: "Can't you see that Däumig and Stoecker remain silent, while only Crispien and Dittmann do the talking. Does it not dawn on you that this delega-

---

Polnoe sobranie sochinenii, 5th edition, vol. 41, Moscow 1963, p. 94. There are other examples of Lenin's willingness to rectify his position at the time of the Second Comintern Congress; two will suffice. First, when on the eve of the congress M. N. Roy informed him of certain new aspects of the colonial issue, Lenin had him draw up some additional theses (for details see Chapter Nine of this volume). Second, with regard to the situation in France, Lenin changed his mind about the tactics of the pro-Communist elements still within the Socialist party. The switch followed a talk with Alfred Rosmer, who had just arrived in Moscow and informed Lenin that the Left stood a good chance of capturing the majority of the SFIO, which Lenin had not realized. This information caused him to redraft the theses in which he had advised the Left to break immediately with the Socialist party. (See Alfred Rosmer *Moscou sous Lénine—les origines du communisme*, Paris, 1953, pp. 69-70.)

tion is divided, that the USPD has two wings, which have split apart, the one belonging not at all to the other? "[65]

The discord became manifest at the delegation's first appearance before the Executive Committee and remained evident throughout the congress. Thus it was that when the USPD delegates had to submit written replies to the questions asked them at the Executive Committee meeting, they agreed on their answers to all the questions except the first and most important, put to them by Radek, concerning the division between left and right within the USPD: "Stoecker wanted to give an answer that would bring out the fact that he and Däumig did not concur in our answer to the Executive Committee. . . . The upshot was that we could not agree on the reply. The discussion within the delegation came to naught."[66] The four USPD representatives sat on the committee concerned with terms and conditions for admission to the Comintern. On July 25 and 26 part of the debate was devoted to the USPD, and Lenin, Trotsky, Zinoviev, and Radek participated. According to E. Meyer, it was at those two meetings that Crispien and Dittmann did the talking while the other two kept silent, which on the second day prompted Crispien to say to Stoecker: "I am convinced that you are working against us, behind our backs even."[67]

Crispien's accusation about things going on "behind our backs" could only have come from someone ignorant of the Bolshevik device known as "factional work," because as of then a "pro-Comintern faction" was working away inside what was still nominally a single party, though the outsiders of course did not know this. In his confidential report presented on August 25 to the Central Committee of the German Communist Party after his return from Moscow, Paul Levi stated that this "factional work" had been engineered in Moscow: "In special conversations held with these two comrades (and this is not for the agitprop or public consumption) it was further agreed that they promised to take very definite steps to form and organize a left wing within the USPD."[68]

Moscow's tactic appears then in complete clarity. It would admit the left wing with Däumig and Stoecker to the Comintern, and keep Dittmann and Crispien out. Lenin confirmed this at the congress on July 30 when he spoke in reply to Serrati, who had insisted that no one possessed a "sincerometer" (an instrument for gauging revolutionary sincerity). This was an allusion to Dittmann and Crispien in particular. If, according to Lenin, the Bolsheviks did not yet have such a gauge, they nevertheless did know enough about measuring sincerity to tell which way the wind was blowing: "So one can say, even without possessing a 'sincerometer' . . . that Crispien's orientation does not coincide with that of the Comintern. When we say this, it will be a guideline for the entire Communist International." [69] *Roma locuta, causa finita!* It was one of the first acts of excommunication that the "new Rome" undertook on Lenin's authority in the European labor movement. He was merely putting into effect what he had written on February 14, 1920 and published in the official organ of the Comintern: "Leaders of this stamp [French Longuetites], and like those of the Independent Socialist Party of Germany and the Independent Labour Party of England, are not needed by the proletariat." [70] The "proletariat" of course was identified with the organization that he had wrought and had the supreme power and right to think for. He decreed Crispien's exclusion from the International, as he did several months later that of Longuet. The same would have befallen the British Independent Labour Party, the ILP, had its leaders applied for admission.

Lenin's intransigeance was the more significant as Crispien, in his speech to the congress, had accepted nearly all of the terms and conditions for admission to the Comintern, only meekly demurring at the name "Communist" (instead of Socialist) and at combining illegal activities with legal. Even the final statement submitted by both Crispien and Dittmann at the end of the debate on the conditions for admission, made clear their wish to find a satisfactory formula that would enable them to join the Comintern: "The further negotiations with our party, which the congress has authorized the Executive Committee to undertake, will then eventuate all the sooner in the desired results." [71] The statement by Däumig and Stoecker was more outspokenly in favor of joining the Comintern.

But when the divided delegation tried to draft a joint statement, Dittmann rushed up, saying that all the conditions that had been rendered more acceptable and less onerous, to facilitate the USPD delegation's joining, not only had been taken out but new and different ones had been added. E. Meyer briefly informed the congress of the changes; Zinoviev then called for a vote. There was no further discussion. Which is why Crispien, in his report after the congress, acidly complained: "These so-called formal terms are a very effective tool in the hands of the Russian comrades with which to rob us of will, render us helpless, and make us submit to a tactic which we must resist, because it is solely and merely Russian. . . . It is particularly regrettable that the congress decided the last minute to throw in some new, more stringent conditions after we had managed, in committee, to hammer out a workable compromise."[72] Another last-minute maneuver would be launched several months later at the French Socialist Party congress in Tours, this time against Jean Longuet, in order to split the party and keep Longuet out of the Comintern. It was Zinoviev's famous "pistol shot," though Lenin was the one who pulled the trigger.

THE TWO KAPD DELEGATIONS

During May, June, and July of 1920 negotiations were being conducted simultaneously with representatives of Europe's major Socialist parties on the one hand, and with delegates who had come to explain the left-wing Communist point of view on the other. The latter included very diverse elements, some having already broken with the Communist parties officially recognized by Moscow and set up dissident Communist parties of their own. So it was with the KAPD. Others, like the British delegates, had not yet managed to form their own Communist party but had already been won over to left-wing Communism. Also present were representatives of Revolutionary Syndicalism, who supported the Bolshevik revolution and even the Third International but were opposed to joining the Communist Party.

Of all these leftist groups, politically and numerically the most important was the KAPD: politically because it operated in Germany, the country that concerned Lenin most; and numerically because at the time of its founding, in early April 1920, it boasted a membership of 38,000, or half the total German Communist Party membership before the split. When the KAPD leaders first found themselves in conflict with the official German Communist Party leadership, particularly with Paul Levi, they had not yet any quarrel with Moscow. On the contrary, the day after its founding the KAPD took pains to emphasize its devotion to the cause of the Third International: "Since its founding, the KAPD has been in the camp of the Third International. Despite all efforts of the KPD bureaucrats to block our path to the Executive Committee in Moscow, we have managed to establish relations with it and to tell it about ourselves. We are hoping that the forthcoming congress of the Third International, whose decisions we recognize, will admit our party to membership."[73] According to an eyewitness, it was Lenin himself, ever concerned to gain and hold the revolutionary worker element, who dictated the affirmative decision: "A delegation from the [German] Communist Workers' Party came to Moscow and got the Comintern's Executive Committee to admit it to membership as a fellow-traveler party. The decision was Lenin's of course. He was told of the large number of revolutionary workers that belonged to this party. Then the two long talks that he had with Hermann Gorter, a member of its delegation, offset all the bad things that Radek had said about it."[74]

While actually Gorter was not officially a member of that first KAPD delegation, not being German, he nevertheless carried considerable influence with Lenin, whom he had known since long before the October Revolution. The delegation itself had only two members, Jan Appel and Franz Jung, a writer. Setting out at the end of April 1920, it arrived in Moscow in May and took part in two meetings of the Executive Committee attended by Lenin, Zinoviev, Radek, and Bukharin (the only names that Appel mentioned in his report after his return). At those meetings the stumbling block was the ideas of the KAPD theoreticians Fritz Wolffheim and Heinrich Laufenberg, on the one hand, and Otto Rühle on the other. When they arrived in Moscow, Appel and Jung had not seen the pamphlet by Wolffheim and Laufenberg, *Kommunismus gegen Spartakismus* ("Communism versus Spartacism"), and they were unaware of the position that Otto Rühle had taken concerning the existence of any Communist party at all. The pamphlet by the two Hamburg theoreticians immediately landed the delegation in hot water. Excerpts from it were read at the Executive Committee meeting. The thoughts expressed by its authors represented a far graver crime than mere deviation on parliamentarianism and Syndicalism, for now they were moving away even from left-wing Communism and gravitating toward a "national Bolshevism." That is why Appel, on his return, wrote:

"We attempted to defend our point of view in the matter of parliamentarianism and the trade unions. . . . But this was made extremely difficult, if not forthwith impossible, when at the beginning of the meeting excerpts were read from a pamphlet we had never heard of, entitled *Kommunismus gegen Spartakismus*."[75] Called upon to make known their opinions on what the pamphlet had to say, and on Rühle's ideas, Appel and Jung disowned the authors: "We said that we would do our best to have such elements eliminated from our party. . . . In that connection, we were shown a resolution of comrade Rühle's . . . directed against party unity, which made the Executive Committee wonder even more whether we really are a single coherent organization. . . . [We said] that we considered these party-destroying elements to be in violation of our own party program and that we would do our best to purge the party of them."[76]

Thus Appel and Jung came to endorse that fundamental Bolshevik tool, then being introduced into the Comintern—the Moscow-ordered purge. The delegation also had a chance to read Lenin's book *"Left-Wing" Communism*, and in general reacted favorably to Lenin's advice and ideas. But when it came to German problems, "we declared that in principle we agreed with the guidelines set forth in the book, and we conceded that our own tactics may have become somewhat rigid. But where it criticized conditions in Germany, we did not hesitate to point out its errors."[77]

The outcome of these talks became known through an "open letter" to the members of the KAPD dated June 2, 1920, and signed by Zinoviev. It was another Bolshevik device being transplanted to the Comintern: it assumed that the toiling masses and the militants would be on the side of the Comintern, and that leaders were out to prevent any contact between the two, so that one had to go over the heads of the leaders and appeal to the masses and militants directly. The "open letter" of June 2 ended with four concrete proposals, of which the first was that Wolffheim, Laufenberg, and Rühle be immediately expelled from the party. The other three were: unconditional submission to the decisions of the Second World Congress; appointment of a committee of reconciliation to bring the two German Communist parties back together, to be chaired by a representative from Moscow; and thirdly, the dispatching of a delegation to the Second Congress, scheduled to start on July 15.

Meanwhile a second KAPD delegation had left for Moscow before the first one returned home. The KAPD was completely befuddled in its behavior and policy toward the Comintern. The first delegation had left without knowing the latest position taken by Wolffheim and Laufenberg on the one hand and by Rühle on the other. The second delegation arrived at the congress not knowing what the first had said and agreed to, and without having seen Zinoviev's "open letter." That explains why the new delegation, made up of two members, happened to be headed by Otto Rühle. It explains also the terms of the second delegation's report: "If the content of this 'fraternal' letter had been known to the KAPD Central Committee before our departure, it would never have sent delegates to Moscow to attend the congress. . . . We learned all these things only after arriving in Moscow, and thus found ourselves hopelessly boxed in from every side." [78]

The Bolshevik team had made up its mind to rake this second delegation over the coals. But things were not that easy; Otto Rühle was no newcomer to politics. While he did not know much about Bolshevism, he knew a great deal about Marxism and the European labor movement. And though he did not know the Bolshevik leaders, he did know Radek quite well, which gave him some idea of the methods in use at the congress: "Every effort was being made to commit all the parties belonging to the Third International to implementation of the social revolution by what we have designated as the 'Eastern method'—tightly centralized organization, parliamentarianism, and a 'revolutionary' trade union policy being its key features. To secure its adoption at the congress, Radek had been agitating for weeks in every possible way among the arriving delegates. Knowing Radek, we know what this means." [79]

Toward this second delegation the Comintern leaders, including Lenin, behaved according to a well-laid plan, which encompassed not only their immediate goals but predicted how their opponent would react. All went well so long as the operation went "according to plan," but the minute the other side departed from the script, the whole play was wrecked. And so it was with the drama of Rühle and his colleague, A. Merges. The Moscow calculation was that they would confess their guilt, accept humiliation, and

beg forgiveness. But they didn't. After long discussions with
Lenin, Zinoviev, Radek, and Bukharin they announced their decision, on July 18, the night before the congress opened, not to take
part in it, to retract the announcement that the KAPD would join
the Comintern, and to refuse the voting rights that they had been
offered. The effect produced by this was stunning. The Bolshevik
leaders were forced to an abrupt change of tactics, as the KAPD
delegation reported on its return: "Our decision had an astonish-
ing effect. Until then we had been treated like naughty children
whose misdoings had worried and annoyed their poor parents, and
who therefore needed to be soundly spanked. But now suddenly
they started to court us. . . . There was no further mention of any
'preconditions' for letting us into the Third International. . . . It
would be enough if later the KAPD would just clarify its relations
with Wolffheim and Laufenberg. The expulsion of Rühle from the
party was dropped. . . . Several days later we even got another
explicit invitation to attend the congress, and were informed that
the Executive Committee had granted us full voting rights." [80]

But Rühle and his colleague fired off a curt note to the Executive Committee flatly refusing to participate in the congress, and
repeating that they would not have come to Moscow at all if they
had known beforehand of that "open letter." They concluded
with an assurance that they were not taken in by the privilege,
now so suddenly conferred upon them, of being able to vote at the
congress: "That the Executive Committee is now ready to grant us
the right to vote at the congress, even though the KAPD has
neither fulfilled nor promised to fulfill any of the stringent requirements so emphatically laid down in their 'open letter,' is but
one more proof that we were right in our initial evaluation of the
nature and purpose of those requirements." [81] Moscow's unexpected decision to grant voting rights to the KAPD delegation not
only failed to change that delegation's mind about leaving the
congress but also infuriated the official German Communist Party
delegation.

THE BICKERING WITH THE
GERMAN COMMUNIST PARTY DELEGATION

While no delegation representing industrial Europe had attended
the Comintern's founding congress, there were two such delega-

tions, the German and Italian, at the Second Congress. The German Communist Party chief, Paul Levi, headed his Party's delegation and Giacinto Serrati led that of the Italian Socialist Party. In that capacity they were elected, along with Lenin and Zinoviev, to preside over the congress (as was Rosmer, who came from France but without any delegation, since he had merely been appointed by the Committee for the Third International). Recent events seemed to justify the assumption that agreement would be quick and easy between the Bolshevik leaders and the German and Italian parties, which had joined the Comintern immediately and voluntarily and had recently taken positions very close to Bolshevism. The Spartacus League was the first mass Communist party to be established in Western Europe, and the Italian Socialist Party had remained solidly pacifist and anti-militarist throughout the war. But the assumption proved unfounded and disagreements erupted, though they differed in nature from those with the Socialist delegations that had come for negotiation. These two distinguished leaders of the European labor movement, Levi and Serrati, who were in Moscow for the first time (though this was not their first contact with the Bolsheviks, whose acquaintance they had made in Switzerland during the war), clashed almost immediately with Lenin and his entourage. The main cause was the thorny problem of the relationship between the Bolshevik party and the other member parties of the Comintern. It was clearly Lenin's intention to run the Comintern with the same iron hand with which he ran the Bolshevik Party and later the Soviet state. But neither Levi nor Serrati was a man to knuckle under and they bucked the Bolsheviks on many points.

Unlike Serrati, who publicly disagreed with Lenin during the debate on the theses presented by the Bolshevik leader and his collaborators, Levi condemned less the political and tactical ideas of the Bolsheviks than their methods of operation and command. And while the official minutes of the congress do contain a partial record of the differences with Serrati, there is no mention of the conflict between the Russians and Paul Levi, which produced the most important incident that occurred. Lenin surely regarded the fight with Levi as more serious than the differences of opinion with Serrati, for while events, time, and persuasion could change an opponent's mind on matters of policy and tactics, they were less likely to do so where organization was concerned. Here the

Bolshevik viewpoint confronted every Communist leader, and especially Levi, who headed the most important section, with a simple inescapable choice: to accept or reject what the Russians called "the guiding role of the Bolshevik party"—or "dictation from Moscow," as their Socialist adversaries phrased it. Levi and his delegation considered the problem especially serious, for they were the only foreigners who had been familiar with Bolshevik methods since before the revolution.

Ernst Meyer, who had accompanied Paul Levi to Moscow, would explain on his return, to the assembled congress of the German Communist Party, that this mutual mistrust between Bolsheviks and Spartacists stemmed from many years before the revolution, as well as from some recent events (at the First and Second Comintern Congresses). Of the period before the revolution, he noted: "The Russian comrades said that they had the impression that the German party, owing to its traditional attitude toward the Russian party, which was based on that of comrades Rosa Luxemburg and Leo Jogiches, still harbored a certain reserve toward the Russian Party." [82] Another exacerbating factor was that just as Eberlein had threatened to walk out of the First Congress if the decision were made to set up a Communist International immediately, the German delegation at the Second Congress tendered a similar threat in writing. Meyer has referred to the Bolsheviks' unhappiness: "Both the earlier behavior of comrade Eberlein and the announced walkout from this congress put our Russian comrades in a disagreeable mood, and caused them to display some irritation with the German delegation." [83]

This incident at the Second Congress followed in the wake of the unilateral decision of the Russian Communist Party Central Committee to grant voting rights to the KAPD delegation. Under the Comintern bylaws the Central Committee of the Russian Party had no such authority, which was vested solely in the Executive Committee of the Comintern. But the Central Committee was Lenin himself, who behaved like the Comintern's real master, which angered the German delegation and especially Paul Levi. The Germans made no public show of resistance at the open sessions of the congress, which was already under way and proceeding with its work, but they did put up a fight on two other levels. They went directly to the Russian Communist Party Central Committee, and they unleashed a debate before the Executive Committee of the Comintern.

When Paul Levi learned that the Russians were planning to grant voting rights to the KAPD delegation, on the next day, July 22, he drafted an official letter which he submitted in the name of his party to the Russian Communist Party Central Committee. In it he raised two objections. First, as to the political and tactical wisdom of the decision, he drew attention to the rapid weakening of the KAPD: "So this, our own policy . . . has had the result that almost all the workers in the KAPD by now have left it. Most of them have come back to us. Admittedly, others are still politically apathetic, but we shall win them back, too. During these last weeks the KAPD has been reduced to a collection of elements essentially unsuited for a political organization." [84] He then pointed out that while the Comintern was busy stiffening the admission requirements for foreign organizations, it was flatly contradicting itself in the case of the German dissidents: "The KAPD has not met a single one of the requirements for admission to the Third International." [85] After ticking off all the requirements unfulfilled, he concluded with a brief promise of what would happen if the KAPD were admitted: "If that happens, we shall leave the congress and go home." [86]

The move was unprecedented in the history of the Comintern.* A discussion before the Executive Committee followed, and Levi used the same line of argument as in his letter of July 22, stressing the contradiction in letting the French Socialists and the USPD attend the congress, which he approved, and then granting the same privilege to the KAPD delegation, which he categorically objected to. L.-O. Frossard, who was present at the debate and who "with pen in hand followed all the deliberations of the International," some months later, after he had become Secretary General of the French Communist Party and Paul Levi was on the verge of breaking with Moscow, would report: "It was Paul Levi who led the opposition. He struck us that night as most lucid, a precise subtle speaker, a man of firm principle." [87] Frossard noted

---

*A similar threat would be made at the Fourth Comintern Congress in 1922, but by a less important party, the Yugoslav, and then only by the majority faction within the delegation, and not by the delegation's totality.

also the remarks of Zinoviev, who "replied in vehement terms," and of Bukharin, who made "a concise statement," as well as the speeches of the Italian Socialist chief, Serrati, and the leader of the Italian "leftists" Bordiga, both of whom agreed with Levi. When the vote was taken, the Russian position won 25 to 5. The no votes included those of Levi, Serrati, and Marchlewski, who a few days later was appointed to head the Polish provisional government at Bialystok.

The conflict was temporarily defused only by the KAPD delegation's stubborn refusal to go along, as Levi himself, after his return, reported to his Party's Central Committee on August 25: "The conflict, which was threatening to grow more serious, was resolved by the KAPD itself when Rühle and Merges said they would not take part in the congress and disappeared from Russia illegally." [88] But according to Frossard deep scars remained: "The KAPD will be admitted. But the decision is meaningless, since Rühle will not return, and discord has been sown between Paul Levi and the Executive Committee, discord that will rapidly worsen." [89] Levi could not express himself quite so openly before the entire party membership, but at the Fifth Congress of the German Communist Party in early November 1920, he would not hide his bitter feelings: "I tell you quite frankly, Comrades, that what led to our relatively harsh tone in Moscow was a form of behavior on the part of our Russian comrades about which I can only say: I would have expected something better from Communists." [90]

Confronted with Levi's critical attitude the Russians did not sit idly by hoping to change his mind through patient argument. On the subject of opposition, whether at a congress or within a party, the Bolsheviks were experts, having practiced it themselves in the Russian Social Democratic movement and the Socialist International. So, immediately after the Second Congress and in the months that followed, they methodically laid the groundwork for settling their score with Levi, using Radek in particular, who from this time on no longer sided with Levi but worked against him. Three main devices were employed.

First, disunity was sown within the German Communist Party delegation. Its decision to leave the congress if the KAPD was granted voting rights had been unanimous, but the next day another delegate, Jakob Walcher, belatedly declared "that he could not go along with such a step on the part of the German delegation."[91] According to E. Meyer, this new opposition, plus the KAPD delegation's refusal to participate in the congress anyway, prompted the German Communist Party delegation to rescind their original decision. Second, a faction loyal to Moscow was formed within the ranks of the official leadership to isolate the titular head, or at least crowd him into a minority position. During the Second Congress an anti-Levi, pro-Soviet faction sprouted within the German Central Committee: "For this reason, even during the congress Radek and the Comintern's other full-time officials, Zinoviev and Bukharin, attempted to construct within the German delegation a 'left wing' around Ernst Meyer. They even contacted individual members of the Leftist USPD in an attempt, before the merger, to interest them also in forming an anti-Levi wing within the future united party."[92] Third, they plotted to pit the party's rank and file against its "summit," to organize the left-oriented subsections of the German Communist Party against Paul Levi at the top, who would be branded a "rightist." The Berlin organization was their prime target.

When Levi, obviously aware that the Russians were trying to undermine him, took steps to thwart them, he automatically became guilty of "factionalism," the name of any and every form of the crime of resisting the Comintern. This grave charge was levied against him by Heinrich Brandler, who belonged to the pro-Soviet faction, and succeeded Levi as party head in 1921: "No further proof is required that, ever since his return from the Second Congress in Moscow, Levi has been trying to organize an opposition conspiracy."[93]

THE ITALIAN DELEGATION

The Italian case at the Second Comintern Congress had some similarities to the German, for the Italians also felt the sting of the Bolshevik methods. The Italian delegation too was badly split, which made it much easier for the Bolsheviks, by exploiting the internal dissension, to set up a faction loyal to them. Alfred Rosmer, an eyewitness, reported: "The Italian Socialist Party was so deeply split that it is scarcely an exaggeration to say that each of its delegates stood for something different. Isolated within this delegation, Serrati tried single-handedly to hold all these diverse elements together, but in vain."[94] A situation made to order for the Bolsheviks! Balabanova tells in her memoirs what Zinoviev asked of her shortly after the delegation arrived: "A few days after the arrival of the delegation in Petrograd I received a message from Zinoviev asking me to come to his office and to bring with me some of the Italian Socialists whom I considered 'the most radical.' At the time this request aroused in me no particular suspicion but as soon as I repeated the invitation to Serrati, he seemed to understand what it meant."[95] She then relates how the Bolsheviks in this way recruited two of the delegation members, Bombacci and Graziadei, whom they persuaded to remain in Moscow after the rest of the delegation had left. For the short run the choice was a good one, for Bombacci and Graziadei were solidly in favor of splitting the Socialist party and establishing a Communist party, but it proved less felicitous in the long run, because Bombacci migrated from Communism to Fascism and Graziadei took it upon himself to revise Marxian economics and was expelled from the party in 1929 (though he was readmitted later).

On June 19, a month before the Second Congress opened, the Italian delegation was received at the Kremlin by the highest agency of the Soviet state, the All-Russian Executive Committee of Soviets. (At that time the Bolsheviks were not bothering to distinguish too carefully between the Soviet government and the Communist International.) Serrati submitted to it a report strongly emphasizing the solidarity of his party with revolutionary Russia, but asking also that the Executive Committee please trust the Italian Party: "The Executive Committee of the Communist International should have confidence in our Party, which has voluntarily marched at its side, through Zimmerwald and Kienthal, until now we stand together in the Third International, toward which we of the Italian Party have conscientiously done our duty."[96] But at this same moment Bombacci was in Moscow writing a different report, published immediately after Serrati's in the official Comintern organ, in which the language was very different from Serrati's, calling for an immediate split of the Socialist Party: "The Italian Socialist Party should get rid of those who both in theory and in practice are openly hostile to the dictatorship of the proletariat."[97]

In addition to the delegation's being split, the Bolsheviks had another trump that they could play. As in Germany, where the Berlin party organization was at odds with the Central Committee and its chief, Paul Levi, in Italy also the official leadership of the Socialist party was being criticized by two organizations whose influence reached far beyond their home cities. In Naples, Amadeo Bordiga had formed his "abstentionist" group, and in Turin a circle of young intellectuals clustered around the weekly *Ordine Nuovo*, were expressing views very close to those of the Comintern's Executive Committee. Bordiga attended the Second Congress and was appointed co-speaker on the issue of parliamentarianism. While the *Ordine Nuovo* group was "out of sight," not directly represented, it was not "out of mind." On the eve of the Second Congress the official organ of the Comintern praised it in its introduction to a published statement of principle: "In his theses, printed here, Comrade Lenin has already shown that the authors of that document, the militants of Turin, are completely right in their criticism of the present Socialist party. The Communist International must leave no stone unturned to have the reformers thrown out of that party so that it can enter upon the path of Communism."[98] On July 4, two weeks before the congress opened, in his theses on the main tasks confronting the International, Lenin indeed had stated, in item 17, that "the concrete proposals submitted to the National Council of the Italian Socialist party in the name of its Turin section . . . coincide with all the basic principles of the Third International."[99]

So, in the days preceding the opening of the congress, Lenin—and through him the Communist International—had already embarked on a policy bound to clash with Serrati's. This would become evident and more pronounced as the congress progressed. Serrati frequently opposed the theses and positions of the Bolsheviks, and of all the foreign leaders there he won the prize for resisting Moscow. Lenin's decision to crush the Italian Socialist party and set up a Communist party was probably an outgrowth of the negotiations and discussions at the Second Congress, just as Serrati's intention not to knuckle under to Lenin was strengthened by the decisions of that congress. Serrati wrote as much on his return from Moscow: "So the results of the Third International's Second Congress have to be considered in the light of these organizational premises (which are not without importance), and we see that these results must be revised. . . . All the decisions of the congress . . . are founded on the delusion that it is possible to create a 'new' state of affairs in all countries at the same time." [100] Now, if there was anything on earth that Lenin considered sacred and absolutely immune from the slightest revision, it was those decisions of the Second World Congress, on which he had lavished the sum total of his revolutionary, tactical, and organizational certainties. And here was Serrati, the very day after their adoption, clamoring for revision of these great truths. The power of Lenin's wrath would soon make itself felt.

THE ANARCHO-SYNDICALISTS

The Anarcho-Syndicalist delegates who had come from the various European countries to attend the Second Congress were to the left of the "left-wing Communists." While the latter at least accepted the idea of having a Communist party and did claim to be followers of Marx, the former roundly rejected both. If at the congress Lenin and his Bolshevik colleagues did manage to woo back some of left-wing Communism's proponents and bring them into the Comintern fold, with their Anarcho-Syndicalist guests their success was zero.* An example was Angel Pestaña, a representative of Spain's Confederación Nacional del Trabajo. Others who manifested resistance were Augustin Souchy, from Germany, and Italy's Armando Borghi; both were more immune to Bolshevik theory and Soviet reality than any and all of the other delegations. One reason was that the Anarcho-Syndicalists were better informed about conditions in Russia than the other delegations (except for the British) because of their contacts with Russian anarchist militants still surviving in the country, such as the old apostle of anarchism, Pyotr Kropotkin; or young militants like Victor Kibalchich-Serge, who had returned to Russia after political activity in Spain and France; or the two militants from the United States, Alexander Berkman and Emma Goldman. Thus, for exam-

---

*An exception was Alfred Rosmer, a prominent militant of French revolutionary syndicalism who did not take part in the leftist doings at the Second Congress because of his friendship and respect for Trotsky.

ple, "shortly after arriving in Petrograd and installing himself at the Hotel International, Pestaña received an unexpected visit from an old fellow warrior and friend, Victor Serge. . . . In private conversations the latter told him about the negative aspects of the revolution, showing him, so to speak, the dark side of the moon." [101]

Pestaña, who was granted a vote at the congress, made three speeches at it on the alleged necessity for the existence of a Communist party. One drew a sharp reply from Trotsky. He voted for the resolution calling for creation of a Red Trade Union International and signed the manifesto published at the end of the congress. When the congress was over, he was received by Lenin. Starting on subjects already amply discussed at the congress, "dictatorship of the proletariat," "democratic centralism," the "proletarian revolution," and so on, the conversation suddenly took an unexpected turn. Asked by Lenin what impression the congress delegates had made on him, Pestaña replied with a long monologue in which he characterized them all, with few exceptions, as fundamentally bourgeois, not because of their statements during the congress but because of their private behavior:

> I refer to the contradiction between the speeches that they made at the congress and their daily lives at the hotel. . . . How do you expect us, Lenin, to believe in the revolutionary, altruistic, liberating sentiments of most of these delegates, who in their everyday lives behave not one jot differently from the most inveterate bourgeois? They grumble and curse about the mediocre and insufficient food, forgetting that we foreign delegates enjoy an unfair advantage. . . . By what right do they speak of brotherhood, they who talk down their noses to the servants in the hotel, heaping insults and abuse on them, because they are not always there on the spot to gratify their smallest whims. . . ? And the haughtiness and scorn with which they treat those who have no connections in the Soviet government or Communist International is quite sad and disgusting. [102]

This twist of the conversation having nothing to do with the issues dealt with at the congress or the problems raised in the endless debates and negotiations, Lenin cut it short and took quick leave of Pestaña, who never joined the Communist movement and never again set foot in Russia.

With Armando Borghi the Comintern seemed to have more of a chance during his stay in Moscow. Arriving at the end of the Second Congress, Borghi was invited to meet the Bolshevik party and Comintern leaders and to attend the meetings of the latter's Executive Committee immediately after the congress. Thus it was that on August 25, in Borghi's presence and after prolonged discussion, the Executive Committee unanimously adopted the following resolution: "On the basis of the decisions of the Second Congress concerning the policy to be followed toward the revolutionary wing of the Syndicalists, anarchists, and members of the Shop Stewards and of the IWW, and in recognition of the declaration by the representative of the Unione Sindicale Italiana, Comrade Borghi, that he accepts the decisions of the Second Congress, the Executive Committee herewith resolves to admit the Unione Sindicale Italiana to membership in the Third International." [103]

But this resolution turned out to have little meaning. The Unione Sindicale Italiana never became a full-fledged member of the Communist International, and despite the fact that its two delegates, Vecchi and Mari, did attend the founding congress of the Profintern in July of 1921, and approved the decisions adopted and signed a pact with the representatives of the Italian Communist Party to coordinate their activities within the country, no effective cooperation ever developed with either the Italian Communist Party, the Comintern, or the Profintern. The very next month, on August 13, 1921, the seven members of the Presidium of the Comintern's Executive Committee, watching from afar what was happening in that Italian organization, decreed: "It will be the duty of Comrade Gennari to keep the Executive Committee informed about the congress of the Unione Sindicale and to let us know when it will be. It is the job of our Italian representative to keep an eye on things." [104]

Relations between the Comintern and Borghi continued to deteriorate rapidly. In 1921 Borghi launched a campaign against the Comintern and the Profintern, and the general council of his organization, meeting in November of that year, expressed many reservations concerning those organizations. When the congress of the Unione Sindicale Italiana convened in Rome in early 1922, the anti-Bolshevik element, led by Borghi, won out, and a resolution was passed spurning any collaboration with the Communist International. The latter reacted by condemning Borghi and his movement for their counterrevolutionary, anti-Bolshevik attitude, and the Profintern followed suit, addressing an open letter to the members of the Unione Sindicale Italiana in hopes of luring them away from Borghi's negative influence. [105]

The Debates at the Second World Congress

As in other respects, the Second Congress differed from the preceding one, and those that would follow, in the tenor of its debates. At the First Congress there had been really only one spirited debate, that concerning the most propitious time for setting up a Communist International. At later congresses, delegations of individual parties (German, Italian, Yugoslav, etc.) would raise points pertaining to their respective countries without touching upon the Comintern as such. But at the Second Congress it was the Comintern itself, in its every aspect—its basic ideology, tactics, and organization—that was the subject of acrimonious debate, often followed by votes showing substantial minorities not in favor of its ideas.

The existence of such a central core of ideas was something new only for the non-Russian members of the International; to the Russians it was merely a transplanting of Lenin's political ideas from the Bolshevik context to that of the Comintern. In this regard, as we saw in the previous chapter, the Second Congress was a veritable Lenin festival, manipulated by him personally through carefully selected Bolshevik intermediaries. All the reports prepared for the congress shared two characteristics: the ideas in them were but summaries of Lenin's thinking, and the people presenting them were either Bolshevik Party leaders of long standing, men like Zinoviev and Bukharin, or revolutionary militants from the days of Tsarist Russia by then safely absorbed into the Bolshevized Soviet system, men like Radek and Marchlewski. The only report entrusted to a foreign Communist was the one on the Comintern's bylaws. Though presented by a Bulgarian, Kabakchiev, the Bolsheviks had written it, as was confirmed at the end of the session, for it was not Kabakchiev who had the last word but Zinoviev, the official spokesman of the bylaws committee.

FORM OVER SUBSTANCE: HOW THE PARTY WAS SHAPED

A. Lozovsky, a Bolshevik delegate and one of the speakers at the Second World Congress, recalls in his memoirs the decisive role that Lenin played in the proceedings:

> When one stops to consider that Lenin wrote the resolution on the international situation and basic problems confronting the Comintern, and the one on the national and colonial question; that he wrote the 21 conditions [for admission] and three quarters of the resolution on the role of the Communist parties; that he participated in the work of all the committees, then delivered their reports to the congress—it becomes quite obvious that Vladimir Ilich, from the first day to the last, saturated that congress with Communist ideas. He strove to show the delegates who had recently joined the Comintern, people with great revolutionary gusto but no Marxian consciousness, what Bolshevik tactics meant and were, and the approach that had to be taken to solving the problems facing the international labor movement.*

Lozovsky was right, except about the foreign delegates' ignorance of Marxism. What they were ignorant of was Bolshevism.

Among the elementary Bolshevik truths that Lenin sought to hammer into the foreign delegates attending the congress was the importance of tactics and organization, which took absolute priority over those pertaining to program and doctrine. This had always been characteristic of Lenin's political behavior. His first original published work, *What Is To Be Done?*, written in 1902, was devoted solely to organization and tactics, which underlay, too, the split that he provoked at the London congress the following year. It had nothing to do with the Party's program, which had been approved by Bolsheviks and Mensheviks alike. After the founding of the Comintern in March 1919, Lenin wrote but a single work

*S. A. Lozovsky, "Iz vospominanii o V. I. Lenine," *Voprosy istorii KPSS*, no. 7, 1966, p. 109. Concerning the conditions for admission, it should be noted that Zinoviev was the appointed speaker on the subject at the congress, and that shortly after Lenin's death he wrote: "They [the 21 conditions] were drafted by me but, to the last detail, inspired by Lenin." (*Die Kommunistische Internationale*, no. 31-32, 1924, p. 13). In Lenin's *Polnoe sobranie sochinenii* (5th ed., vol. 41, Moscow, 1965, pp. 204-12) the 21 conditions are published and Lenin is named as their author.

on the problems of the international Communist movement, his *"Left-Wing" Communism, An Infantile Disorder*, which was again devoted to tactical matters, not to doctrine. In the debates at the Second Congress, six of the questions discussed pertained to tactics: the national and colonial issue, parliamentarianism, the trade unions, the agrarian problem, the establishment of soviets, and the entry of Communists into the British Labour Party. Five concerned organization: the role and structure of the Communist party, the conditions for admission to the Comintern, its bylaws, the selection of its home city, and the representation of the different parties on its Executive Committee. Two questions had to do with current political events: the world situation and basic tasks facing the International, and the situation in Poland. Program and doctrine did not figure in the debates at all.

The five organizational matters were of personal concern to Lenin and Zinoviev. The debates on them were designed to enlighten the foreign delegates and soften them up for ultimate inevitable adoption of the Bolshevik viewpoint. Zinoviev's address on "The Role and Structure of the Communist Party" was aimed principally at the leftist elements in attendance (such as the Shop Stewards, the revolutionary Syndicalists from the Latin countries, Germany's KAPD), to make them see the need for a party organized on the Bolshevik model. The report on "The Conditions for Admission to the Communist International," also delivered by Zinoviev, was directed at the centrists (such as the USPD, the SFIO, the Italians), to make them understand the true nature of a Bolshevik-type party, which they would have to accept if they wanted to belong to the Comintern. The report on the bylaws of the Communist International, presented by Kabakchiev, spelled out the fundamental laws that were to govern the life of the organization. The decision as to where the Comintern would have its permanent headquarters put the official seal on their de facto location in Moscow. The final apportionment of the different parties' representation on the Executive Committee formalized another de facto situation: the disproportionate distribution of power.

When Lenin first disclosed his thinking on organizational matters in the early days of the present century, he was proposing a solution only for the Socialist movement in Tsarist Russia, with whose leaders (Plekhanov, Axelrod, Martov, Rosa Luxemburg, Trotsky) he immediately collided. But when he founded the Communist International in Moscow, that earlier state of affairs was reversed. Offering his same old ideas on organization—this time for universal, not merely Russian adoption—he encountered not a single opponent of any stature within the Comintern.. The Second International had flowered during the period when Russian Socialism was in the process of being Westernized, increasingly suffused with Western Socialist thought. The rise of the Third International, however, was characterized from the beginning by a reverse development, the gradual Russification of the Western labor movement, with Bolshevik ideas becoming mandatory dogma for non-Russian as well as Russian Communists. In the days of the Second International the Russian Socialists tried to be Marxian in the Western manner. Under the Third International it was the Westerners who struggled to be Communist in the Russian manner. But the originality or uniqueness of Russian Communism lay more in the domain of tactics and organization than in that of theory or ideology. The simple reason was that, where the latter were concerned, Lenin undoubtedly had derived much of his own thinking from Marx and Engels, and even from Kautsky and Plekhanov, whereas in the realm of tactics and organization he was entirely his own man, owing nothing to any Western Marxist from the old Internationals. This had an important consequence for the Communist International from its very inception: a Marxist, if he belonged to the Communist party, and even more so if he was against it, could disagree with Lenin's interpretation of Marxism, but no one anywhere could contest his interpretation of Bolshevism, for Bolshevism and Lenin were one.

On the first of the five organizational questions dealt with at the Second Congress, that of the party's role and structure, Zinoviev concluded his report with the words: "I believe, Comrades, that I can now conclude and summarize by saying again that, if we are to profit from the experience gained in the Russian Revolution, we must adhere to this one idea above all others: we need a communist party, a centralized party, one with iron discipline. . . . For the progressive Russian worker the party is sacred, the highest

Being, dearer than anything—his lodestar. And in this the working class of the rest of the world should follow the Russian example."[1]

Ten days later another organizational issue, the Comintern bylaws, came up for discussion, the appointed speaker being Kabakchiev, who began by saying: "The Communist Party of Russia can serve as prototype and paragon, to be imitated not only in the direction and lucidity of its policies and rigorously Marxian behavior but in its strict organization and iron discipline."[2] In being proclaimed the sole model for the international Communist movement, the Bolshevik party gained irreversible permanent advantages. Its spokesmen at that congress, and at those which followed, were free to lavish criticism on any and all other parties in the Comintern, while not one of those more than sixty other parties dared to criticize the Bolsheviks. A. Crispien, who spoke at the congress, mentioned the fact in his address: "Only the Russian Communists were not criticized. Not one of the other member parties was spared."[3] This state of affairs seemed perfectly logical and natural to the delegates. The many who had failed to set up a real Communist party and pull off a Communist revolution had no right to criticize the few, the Bolsheviks, who had successfully done both. The Russian party was thus permanently forearmed against committing blunders in running its affairs. And so it came to pass that, while the Bolshevik Party was in charge of everything and had all the say, and naturally took credit for all successes, the failures were always blamed on someone else.

After the Second Congress, first for non-Russian Communists, then for the outside world, the word *party* began to take on a new meaning, though retaining the old spelling and pronunciation. Until that time, for the Marxists of the Second International, their *party* was a political organization, regarded as somewhat more important perhaps than their trade unions, cooperatives, parliamentary activities, and so on, but a political entity nonetheless. After the Second Congress, however, for Communists of the entire world the *party* became what it had earlier come to be for Russian Communists, a synonym and surrogate for History, the Army, the Church. The party was equated with History because it was seen as the instrument of an unstoppable process leading inexorably first to world revolution and then to a Socialist world order—an enterprise without precedent in human annals. It was equated with the Army because to wage a successful revolutionary war one had to have a high command (the party Politburo and Comintern Executive Committee or Presidium), soldiers (the party rank and file), officers (party cadres), battle plans (revolutionary strategy and tactics), discipline ("democratic centralism"), and of course, as in any army, deserters (party renegades). It was equated with the Church because one needed a faith and gospel (Marxism according to the Bolsheviks), saints (Marx and Engels), a pope (Lenin), canons (the Comintern's decisions, resolutions, theses), and, to complete the tableau, heretics and excommunications (the party's dissidents and purges). This total concept of *the party* naturally eventuated in party totalitarianism. In delivering his report on the party's role and structure on July 23, Zinoviev conjured up a series of images to explain the party's essence to the foreign delegations: "And the party is the brain of the working class. . . . At such a time we need a general staff, a centralized party. . . . What we must do is organize the vanguard of the working class so that it can truly lead the masses in this struggle. . . . The Communist party, according to the Marxist definition, is an organization that affects, touches, all aspects of the labor movement—without exception. Its spirit must be the governing one in the soviets, trade unions, schools, cooperatives, in all organizations in which the working class participates. That is real Marxism."[4] The description fitted the Bolshevik model well, but this was not "real Marxism," being rather Marxism as revised by the Bolsheviks.

During that same session Lenin also made a speech, clarifying the Bolshevik conception of *the party*, specifically the party's proper, most effective relationship with the masses. He conceded that the party could muster no more than a minority of the working class in the capitalist countries: "A political party can embrace only a minority of a class, just as the class-conscious workers in any capitalist society comprise but a minority of all working people. So we have to admit that the great mass of workers can be guided and led only by the enlightened minority."[5] Secondly, it was the party's duty and mission to sweep the masses along with it: "We need parties that are in true constant touch with the

masses, and know how to lead them."[6] It was this alliance between the party militants and the masses outside the party framework that furnished the "subjective" ingredient so essential for the
revolution's victory, in addition to the "objective" ingredient, that
is, the historical process found to be operating by and according to
the laws of Marxism.

The distinctive basic feature of the new kind of party that
Lenin was proposing to the foreign delegations attending the
Second Congress was "democratic centralism" (or simply "centralism"). When this term was first used, at the 1906 Stockholm
congress of reconciliation and reunification of Bolsheviks with
Mensheviks, in the second paragraph of the bylaws, the Mensheviks, who were in the majority, accepted it without a murmur,
doubtless attributing to it a meaning very different from Lenin's.
When the foreign delegates to the Second Comintern Congress
heard it spoken there, they too could have had no inkling of the
sense in which Lenin used it. So he undertook to explain it to
them. In his theses on the party, after setting forth the reasons
(item 13) that Communist parties had to be built "upon a foundation of iron proletarian centralism," and had to maintain within
their ranks "an iron military-type law and order," he went on to
define "democratic centralism": "The Communist party must be
built upon a foundation of democratic centralism. The main principle of democratic centralism consists in election of the top party
leaders from below, the essential and unconditional obligation to
obey all orders and regulations from above, and the existence of a
strong centralized party administration whose authority shall be
generally recognized and respected during the period between
party congresses."[7]

In the theses on the conditions for admission to the Comintern
(item 12), he returned to his definition of democratic centralism.
This time, however, of the three aforementioned attributes, one
was significantly missing—election of the top party leaders from
below: "The parties belonging to the Communist International
must be built upon a foundation of democratic centralism. In
these times of intensifying civil war, the Communist party will be
able to do its duty only if its organization is as centralized as
possible, if it maintains iron discipline internally, and if its central
administration, fortified by the confidence of the party members,
is equipped with all necessary powers and authority."[8]

The "democratic centralism" practiced within the Communist parties had logically to be complemented by its implantation in the Comintern. As a local party organization had to abide by the decisions of the national party leadership, so a member party in the Comintern had to submit to the governance of the latter's Executive Committee. In his closing speech after the debates on the party's role and structure, Zinoviev declared on July 24: "We must be a single Communist party, with subdivisions in different countries. That is the meaning of the Communist International."[9] On July 29, in the debates on the conditions for admission to the Comintern, reminding his listeners that the Second International had properly been termed a mere "post office box," the president of the Third International gave emphatic assurances that the Third was not going to be just "a bigger, better P.O. box painted red. This the Communist International will never be! "[10] On August 4, during the debates on the Comintern bylaws, he struck another blow for "absolute centralism": "We are a united international party with branches in different countries."[11] The principal speaker on the bylaws, Kabakchiev, hammered away at the same idea: "The experience of the Second International has taught us that the Communist International, in order to accomplish its tasks and attain its goal, must be a rigorously disciplined, tightly centralized organization, and must supervise and harmonize the revolutionary activities of the proletariat in all countries."[12]

The natural corollary of the Comintern's "absolute centralism" was the absolute eradication of any shred of autonomy on the part of the foreign member parties. To a British delegate who asserted that whether the British Communists decided to join the Labour Party was essentially their own business, Lenin replied tartly: "Comrade Ramsay says 'it is the business of us British Communists to decide the matter.' Now, just what kind of International would that be if every little section could come and say 'some of us are for, some against; so let every man decide for himself.' What need would we have for an International, congresses, debates? "[13] Zinoviev, too, vetoed the idea of any independence within the Comintern, roundly castigating an Italian Socialist leader, whose party was already a member: "Treves favors joining the Communist International immediately, but on condition that one is not necessarily committed to anything, and that no specific political line of action will be prescribed for any individual country. What he means is that, sure, he is for jumping right in, but without obligation, with the 'freedom' for people to keep on doing just whatever they were doing before." [14] While the Comintern's non-Russian sections enjoyed no autonomy at all within the organization, the Russian section had full power over each and every one of them, including the power to expel them. The power of expulsion was vested in the Executive Committee, which had been controlled by the Bolsheviks from the inception of the Comintern. In fact, article 9 of the ECCI bylaws stipulated: "The Executive Committee of the Communist International has the right to demand, of the parties belonging to it, the expulsion of groups and/or individuals who violate international discipline, and to expel from the Communist International parties that contravene the decisions of the World Congress." [15]

The justification for these organizing principles, which were entirely new to the European Communists, rested on the dual postulate that the Bolshevik Party alone had succeeded in seizing political power and in winning its civil war, and that the European proletariat was now on the verge of its own struggle for power, which likewise would eventuate in civil war. The concept of a Communist party was bound like a Siamese twin to this idea of revolutionary struggle for power and civil war. That was explicitly stated in the resolution on the party's role and structure and on the Comintern bylaws. In article 5 of the first of these two resolutions it was declared that: "Every class struggle is a political struggle. The goal of the struggle, which inevitably is transformed into a civil war, is to seize political power. Political power cannot be seized, organized, and wielded other than by a political party." [16] The second resolution, on the bylaws, reaffirmed this: "The Communist International sets itself the goal of fighting by every means, even by force of arms, for the overthrow of the international bourgeoisie and for the creation of an international Soviet republic—as a stage in the transition to complete annihilation of the State." [17]

Of the Second International, Kautsky had said that it was a peacetime instrument. To the Bolsheviks, the Third International was a weapon of war, whether civil or international. To accomplish their historic mission, the Communist parties needed the promise and taste of success (the Bolshevik enterprise in Russia) and a monitory example of failure (the Socialist movement in the West). The extent to which the Bolshevik leaders were unwilling to take account of the diversity within the Western labor movement, and to allow for certain specifically Western features of that phenomenon, is amply illustrated by two events that occurred during the debates at the Second World Congress. The first concerned the relations between political parties and the trade union movement, for which in the West varying compromise solutions had been arrived at. In some countries trade union members were regarded as automatically belonging to the labor party, as in Great Britain and Norway (the Norwegian Labor Party having affiliated with the Comintern). In other countries there was close cooperation between the trade unions and the Socialist parties, as in Germany and Italy (the Italian Socialist Party having joined the Comintern as early as 1919). In still other cases the trade union movement and Socialist parties went their separate ways, as in France, or coexisted in enmity, as in Spain and the United States. But the solution proposed by the Bolsheviks, and adopted by the Second Congress, for the Communist movement of the entire world was simply the Bolshevik formula as practiced in Soviet Russia.

The second instance of the obstinate Bolshevik refusal to allow for the peculiarly Western aspects of certain problems involved the presence of Freemasons in the Comintern. On July 23, immediately after Zinoviev had presented his report on the role and structure of the Communist party, Serrati, who headed the Italian delegation, spoke briefly in support of the Zinoviev theses but then proposed, by way of clarification: "In that case the congress must take up also the matter of Communists' joining Masonic lodges, which typify organizations dominated by a spirit of petit-bourgeois radicalism and political opportunism. We ask that the congress forbid Communists to join such organizations." [18] Serrati was followed on the rostrum by Lenin and Trotsky, who replied to the objections and arguments raised by the preceding speakers. Neither, however, deigned to utter a word about Serrati's proposal. Two years later Trotsky explained why: "When Serrati at the Second Congress made the demand that the twenty-one conditions be supplemented by another one breaking with Freemasonry, it appeared to us as if he were joking, as if he were suggesting something similar to withdrawal from some order of

Jesuits."[19] Six days later, on July 29, Zinoviev delivered another report on organizational matters, this one on the conditions for admission to the Comintern. As soon as he had finished, Angelica Balabanova, the secretary of the Comintern since its founding, took the floor to propose again that Freemasons be excluded: "The parties belonging to the Communist International are called upon to exclude from their ranks any members of the Freemasons, a petit-bourgeois organization, and to forbid comrades belonging to the Communist International, particularly in the West, to join or belong to any Freemason lodge."[20] During that same session another Italian speaker, Professor Graziadei, recalled the decision taken by the Socialist party in 1914 on the incompatibility of being a Socialist and Freemason at the same time, and he called for an amendment, to that same effect, of the conditions for admission to the Third International, though stressing that the importance of the problem was not the same in all countries: "The matter is of little interest to the Russians, but is of great moment in the Romanic countries, and in England and America, where Freemasonry is quite influential."[21] At the evening session that same day Bombacci, another spokesman for the Italian delegation, which was badly split on many issues but apparently unified where Freemasonry was concerned, delivered a speech in which he, too, in his closing remarks, demanded that party membership be decreed incompatible with being a Freemason. But all the Bolshevik speakers—Zinoviev, Radek, Lozovsky, Rakovsky and Lenin—completely ignored the Italian delegation's proposal in their own discussion of the conditions for admission, though it was their custom to reject or support proposals and arguments presented by foreign speakers. What made this the more surprising was that these Bolshevik leaders who had lived for many years in Europe (particularly Rakovsky and Lozovsky who had lived in France) had observed at close hand and even participated in the labor movement of the countries in which they resided, and they should have known that Freemasonry did play a certain part in Europe's Social Democratic movement, and even in the parties that were applying for admission to the Comintern. So Graziadei had hit the nail on the head. Having little reason to be concerned about Freemasonry themselves, the Russians neglected the issue or assumed that the Western Europeans were only superficially concerned with it.*

Conversely, whenever a problem—and even more so its solution—was a product of Russian experience, it was generalized to cosmic validity and became Comintern writ and basic law. An example was the universalization of the Moscow style of penetrating non-Communist organizations. In the half-century of its active life, the European labor movement had evolved very diverse organizational forms: political parties, trade unions, cultural societies, athletic clubs, cooperatives of various kinds, workers' schools and colleges. But never had it dreamed of attempting to infiltrate the middle-class political parties, Christian trade unions, and nonpolitical cultural societies or athletic clubs for the purpose of taking them over or influencing their leaders from within. In the Third International, however, all of this would be reversed. On July 4, two weeks before the opening of the Second Congress, Lenin wrote in his Theses on the Tasks Facing the Second Congress (article 9):

> In every last organization, league, union, association, society or what have you—first those of the proletarian, then those of the nonproletarian toiling and exploited masses—whether political, professional, military, cooperative, educational, athletic, or whatever, in nature—Communist groups or cells must be planted, preferably openly, but also secretly, which will be necessary whenever they are in danger of being broken up, arrested, or expelled by bourgeois elements. These cells must be tightly bound together, with one another and with party headquarters, trading information and experiences, carrying on agitation,

---

*Not until two years later did Trotsky finally perceive the importance of the Freemasonry problem in the French Communist Party, and the Fourth Comintern Congress passed a resolution devoted in part to Freemasonry, which exhumed the arguments of Graziadei and Serrati, and even went so far as to assert that a separate resolution, passed unanimously at the Second Congress, had ruled Communism and Freemasonry incompatible (see *Protokoll des vierten Kongresses der kommunistischen Internationale*, Hamburg, 1923, p. 990). However, that alleged resolution does not appear among the documents of the Second Congress. Moreover, if it had existed at that time it would have been known to foreign Communists; yet a year and a half after the congress one of the top French Communist leaders, Albert Treint, expressed his astonishment at the absence of an anti-Freemasonry rule (see "Maçonnerie et communisme," *Cahiers Communistes*, Paris, December 7, 1921, p. 51).

spreading propaganda, organizing, plunging into every corner of social existence, into every nook and cranny of the mass of toiling workers. Through their all-embracing efforts, they must systematically educate themselves, the party, their class, the mass. [22]

This same root concept is found again in the theses on the party's role, which extended the duty to infiltrate even to reactionary organizations: "By no means are Communists to shun mass worker-organizations whose policies are at variance with those of the party. If need be, they shall not hesitate to join and make use of even those that are out-and-out reactionary in character (yellow trade-union associations, Christian societies, etc.)." [23]

The foreign delegations thus found themselves, without being at all prepared for it, undergoing an actual pre-Bolshevization, distinct from the formal and actual Bolshevization that they would suffer later on, in 1924. Some of the speakers from Western Europe did not fail to object. As soon as the initial report on organization, the one on the role and structure of the Communist party, had been presented by Zinoviev, four speakers—three Revolutionary Syndicalists and one Communist—drew attention to two negative and disquieting aspects of this Bolshevik tissue that the Comintern was proposing to graft onto the young body of the West's Communist movement, namely Moscow's misconceptions of events and affairs in other countries, and the hasty attempt to universalize a uniquely Russian experience.

The first to speak was David Ramsay, a representative of Britain's Shop Stewards Committees, who began by saying: "I regret to note that the Communist International, all reports and documents notwithstanding, seems not too well-informed about what the Shop Stewards movement really is." [24] Angel Pestaña, speaking in the name of Spain's Revolutionary Syndicalists, undertook to refute Zinoviev's allegation to the effect that the Revolutionary Syndicalists' hostile attitude toward the idea of political parties was due to the sly influence of the bourgeoisie: "It has been alleged that one of the reasons that the workers want nothing to do with political parties is traceable to the influence of the bourgeoisie. It is an oversimplification to believe that revolutionary movements, like the Syndicalist, can be blandly dismissed as reactionary. That is an error. It is also not true that the leaders of the trade unions say they want to stay out of politics."[25] Jack Tanner, another representative of the Shop Stewards, spoke next, emphasizing the dubiousness of any forced universalization of purely Russian experiences: "What has happened in Russia cannot serve as model and prototype for all countries. The present situation in England, for instance, is generally quite different from that in pre-Revolutionary Russia. . . . I ask the Russians and other delegates whether they too cannot learn something from others, from the economic struggles and revolutionary movements in other countries, instead of playing only the role of teacher."[26] He was followed to the rostrum by David Wijnkoop, a spokesman for the Dutch Communist Party, who concluded his remarks in a similar vein: "We must not follow the Russian example blindly. We must learn from the Russian Revolution, but we cannot simply hammer conditions in Western Europe and America to the shape of the Russian model. Comrade Tanner has said that we must not be dogmatic but a little flexible, supple. That is the only way that we can have an International capable of bringing the truly revolutionary groups together, as it must."[27] A few days later, when Zinoviev delivered his next report on organizational matters, this one on the conditions for admission to the Comintern, another speaker, Walter Stoecker, who all his life was to hew to the Moscow line, nevertheless did protest that "one cannot just mechanically apply the Russian methods to the countries of Western Europe."[28]

The ideas that were to shape the organization of the Communist party and Third International, as expounded by Lenin and Zinoviev at that congress, also drew fire from Western speakers. In the face of the patently dominant trend toward "centralization," Ernst Däumig, who three months later was to become one of the two chairmen of the united German Communist Party, recalled the unhappy experience with that phenomenon in Germany's labor movement: "When we were the opposition in the old party, we saw how the party leaders, the Scheidemanns and Eberts, set themselves up as dictators, got control of the party funds and newspapers, and resorted to every kind of coercive measure, until finally many of Germany's progressive workers started to loathe the party leaders and the command structure. The upshot was that the USPD became strongly decentralized. . . . And now we are being told by Moscow that we can get rid of our decentralization, in fact must get rid of it." [29] When the matter of the Comintern bylaws came up for discussion, a speaker from the United States, Alexander Bilan, warned against overgeneralization of the rule about recourse to civil war, that is, against any attempt to apply it blindly to every country: "If we set up armed combat as a general rule to be followed without exception, failing to take account of the special conditions in each country, and this no matter whether the situation is ripe enough, and whether such an armed struggle is really necessary and can actually be pulled off, it may happen that in some countries, in which such a struggle would not yet be possible, the call for armed conflict could provoke a crushing reaction." [30]

Generally speaking, the delegates to the Second World Congress adopted two different attitudes toward the organizational ideas of the Bolsheviks—one immediately, the other after a period of second thoughts. Their immediate reaction was to raise objections during the congress debates, but in the end they voted with the Bolsheviks on every issue. Three dominant currents ran through the delegations from Northern, Central, and Western Europe. The first was that of the left-wing Communists (overwhelmingly the young militants), who seized the opportunity during the debates on the conditions for admission to the Comintern to express their disagreement with the Lenin-Zinoviev draft, which they criticized not for overharshness but for not being harsh enough. This was the gist of the speeches by Jakob Herzog from Switzerland, M. Goldenberg from France, Amadeo Bordiga from Italy, David Wijnkoop from Holland, and Willi Münzenberg from Germany. The second current was evident among the delegations whose members had remained, consciously or unconsciously, impregnated by Western-style (as opposed to Bolshevik-style) Marxism—for example, Italy's Socialist Party, the SFIO and USPD, Sweden's Left Socialists, the Norwegian Labor Party—and even, to some extent, the Communist Party of Germany. They, too, had objections to Bolshevik ideas on organization, some expressing them in open session, like the USPD spokesmen, and others like Frossard and Levi doing so in the closed committee meetings. The third current comprised the Revolutionary Syndicalists (sometimes tainted with anarchism), whose speakers minced no words in criticizing the

Bolshevik views on organization as soon as Zinoviev first presented them in his report on the party's role and structure.

Nevertheless, the striking fact was that every time the theses and resolutions on organization were put to a vote, they were unanimously adopted. The preceding attacks and criticisms that peppered the debates did not prevent the attackers and critics from supporting the Bolshevik viewpoint when the crucial test came. When Zinoviev, who had been appointed to draft the final text of the theses on the party's role and structure on behalf of the committee, presented them on July 24, they passed unanimously. When on July 30, after three debates in plenary session, another committee submitted the final text of the conditions for admission to the Comintern, their adoption fell only two votes short of being unanimous. When, finally, on August 4 the Comintern by-laws were voted on, they too got a unanimous yes vote.

So, for the immediate present, the Bolshevik formulae were ruled universal and triumphed over all resistance at the congress, despite the extreme diversity of situations and circumstances within the labor movement throughout the capitalist world and the root heterogeneity of the assorted delegations attending the congress. To the two enduring factors that helped to shape the life of the Comintern—the existence of the Bolshevik regime as the world's only revolutionary power, and the influence of Lenin as the Comintern's towering personality—were added temporary factors arising from the situation of the moment, which accounted for this contradictory performance at the Second Congress: the hope, following the military victories in Poland, of imminent revolution in Europe, the sense of euphoria with which it suffused the congress, and the total ignorance on the part of the European delegations of the true nature of Bolshevism. A few short months later, while the enduring factors continued to influence the Comintern's existence, the temporary ones had begun to evaporate. This is why the attitude displayed by the delegates and parties at the Second Congress was to change so markedly once it was over. Some, like certain representatives of Revolutionary Syndicalism such as Angel Pestaña and Augustin Souchy, would break with the Comintern immediately, refusing then and there to join the organization. Others, like the representatives of European Socialism, would make their break a little later; the only two Socialist parties to join the Comintern as parties, the Italian and the Norwegian, would sever the ties during Lenin's lifetime. The third group, who broke away only much later, included many of the left-wing Communists in attendance at the Second Congress, who did not start their fight with the Comintern until the years after Lenin's death in January 1924. In all three cases, the Comintern used against the non-Russian leaders of the break-away factions that guillotine which they themselves had helped erect with their speeches and votes at the Second Congress.

THE DEBATES ON PARLIAMENTARIANISM

The business of educating and re-educating which was begun with the writing of *"Left-Wing" Communism* was to be continued at the Second Congress through the debates on each of the agenda items. Where parliamentarianism was concerned, the Bolsheviks had to fight two conflicting "sicknesses," that of the "leftists" and that of the ex-"centrists." The deviation of the former consisted in their radical anti-parliamentarianism, their firm opposition to any participation by Communists in that "bourgeois" institution. The deviation of the latter was the opposite sin of pro-parliamentarianism or "opportunist parliamentarianism," as the Bolsheviks called it. The main speaker on this question, Bukharin, took pains to make clear in presenting the theses that the Bolshevik leaders made a sharp distinction between the two: "This radical anti-parliamentarianism is much more to our liking than opportunist pro-parliamentarianism." [31] The obvious reason was that, while the left-wing Communists in their zeal had gone one step farther than Bolshevik tactics required, the ex-centrists had not yet rid themselves of the practices from the past. So the former had to be kept from moving too far too fast, and the latter had to be nudged along to keep them from lagging behind.

In October 1919, well before writing his chapter on parliamentary tactics in *"Left-Wing" Communism*, Lenin had published his thoughts on parliamentarianism in an open letter to the Italian, French, and German Communists—the three movements that he regarded as most important in the Comintern. In it he held that, to attain power, one could not rely on "parliamentary cretinism"; "Only scoundrels and fools can believe that the proletariat must wait to capture a majority in elections, held under the thumb of the bourgeoisie, in the vise of wage slavery, before seizing power. That is the height of stupidity or hypocrisy. . . . The parliamentary cretins and modern Louis Blancs insist upon elections, staged and run by the bourgeoisie, in order to find out how the majority feels. But that is the view of pedants, political corpses, or wily tricksters."[32] Even so, Communists must still participate in the parliamentary process so as to have access to the masses, in order to influence them: "Our fight against the betrayers of Socialism, the Scheidemanns and Kautskyites, must be a merciless one, but we must not fight it by participating in bourgeois parliaments, reactionary trade unions, and so on—or by boycotting those organizations. That would be an error . . . we must see to it that the party does participate in bourgeois parliaments, reactionary trade unions, and in the factory councils, deformed and castrated by the Scheidemanns. The party must be everywhere that the workers are, where it can speak to them and influence them."[33]

That Bukharin was chosen to be main speaker on the issue of parliamentarianism was further evidence of Lenin's guiding role and power. Bukharin knew little about matters of this kind. In the past he had taken no interest in the battles on this front, and tactics did not much interest him either. With Lenin, however, tactics was a passion. Even before the revolution he had fought the leftist deviation within the Bolshevik party (the "Otzovists"), and one of his favorite pastimes was excoriating the opportunist deviations of all of Western Europe's Socialist parties. The theses presented at the Second Congress reflected his experiences and conclusions: all that Bukharin had to do was paraphrase Lenin and Zinoviev (the latter had signed a supplement to the theses that was published in the Comintern organ the day before the congress started), and that is what he did from his very first sentence: "In considering a problem, we must always start by evaluating its historical setting. Here we are confronted with a fundamental difference between the earlier period, one of peaceful development, and the present period . . . one of civil wars and proletarian dictatorships."[34]

As adopted in final form by the congress, the theses were something distinctly new in Socialist theory and practice with respect to parliamentary life in the Western countries: "For Communists, no parliament today can remotely serve as the arena of a struggle for reform or betterment of the situation of the working class, as parliaments sometimes did in the past. . . . Communism refuses therefore to regard parliamentarianism as one of the possible future forms of society. It refuses to see it as a conceivable form of dictatorship of the proletarian class. It denies the possibility of any lasting take-over of parliaments. It adopts as one of its aims the abolition of parliamentarianism. It consents to make use of bourgeois governing institutions only for the purpose of destroying them."[35] To this end, the theses laid down the role that Communists should play in parliaments in the form of several axioms: since the class struggle was a struggle for political power, mass action and civil war must be its chief weapon; parliamentary action was but a secondary instrument in that struggle; the parliamentary rostrum was to be used for agitation and revolutionary propaganda; the Central Committee of the Communist Party had absolute power to select the candidates and control every word and act of Communist members of parliament, including the right of veto and purge; every Communist member of parliament had the duty, on instructions from the Central Committee, to engage in both legal and illegal activities; every Communist member of parliament was answerable not to the people who elected him but to the Communist party. These iron formulae and a few others like them combined to produce the result that Lenin wanted—to plant within the parliaments a force having no respect for the rules of political fair play in a democracy. Parliamentary governments were thereupon confronted with a new problem: should they, in the name of freedom, grant full and equal rights to a party which publicly proclaimed its intention of exploiting democratic institutions solely in order to destroy them? Should they, in the name of and out of respect for the principles of democracy, allow total freedom of action to a party which flouted the democratic process and which, in 1920, represented a completely isolated case among all the political movements which participated in the elections and in the parliamentary life in Europe?

But this was not the question that Lenin would have to answer. He and his colleagues were faced with a different problem: how were they to persuade the left-wing Communist militants of the correctness of the Bolshevik tactic, both in the committee meetings and at the plenary sessions of the congress? The debates at the committee meetings were not made public, but one of the participants, Willi Münzenberg, has reported on them in his memoirs: "At the committee meetings, along with Jakob Herzog, Bordiga, and Gallacher, I ardently defended the anti-parliamentary position of our former Heidelberg group. Generally speaking, I belonged to the left wing of the congress, and that prompted Lenin to say to me jokingly 'I am sure you will die a leftist.' "[36]

The confrontation that developed at the plenary session between Bukharin, Radek, and Lenin on the one hand, backed by several foreign Communists, and Bordiga, Herzog, and Gallacher on the other, was characteristic in two respects. First, the speakers who disagreed with Lenin did not beat around the bush but stated their positions forthrightly. It was an open collision of conflicting views, a free exchange of argument and counterargument without ulterior motive, without stage effects or pressure by the Bolsheviks, except of course the indirect moral pressure exerted by the sheer weight of their revolutionary prestige and Lenin's personal authority. Second, everyone wound up reaching general conclusions based on his particular experience in his own country. Lenin and Bukharin cited the example of Russia, Gallacher that of England, and Bordiga that of Italy, with only Shablin offering the case of Bulgaria in support of Lenin's view. But while Lenin and his comrades did judge all problems in the light of Russian experience, at least they had some knowledge about the Socialist and Communist movements in the West. Most of those on the other side, apart from the situation in their own countries, knew little about the movement in the other Western countries and still less about the realities of the Russian revolution. The remark by J. T. Murphy, a delegate and speaker at the congress, was well-founded: "When a general or principal question was under consideration, every delegation approached it from the angle of his or her own particular country. Only the Russians showed any real knowledge and sense of internationalism, though frequently they wore Russian spectacles when looking through the international window."[37]

Of all the adversaries of parliamentarianism, the most important one to speak was Amadeo Bordiga, the future founder and head of the Italian Communist Party. He denied that parliaments had any value whatever for the revolutionary cause, and he pointed out the danger of trying to impose the Russian model on Europe as a whole: "The tactical experiences characteristic of the Russian revolution cannot be transferred to other countries. . . . Also, we are unable to envisage just what kind of destructive activity Communists could carry on in parliaments. . . . This is pure dreaming. . . ." [38] Bordiga then presented his own theses, which gave Lenin a chance to reply. He started by noting: "Comrade Bordiga . . . has nevertheless failed to answer any of the arguments which other Marxists have offered here in favor of participation in parliaments." [39] But Lenin himself had little to add, merely repeating his well-known views. The final text of the theses, read by Bukharin, in the end was adopted almost unanimously, with seven votes against and three votes for Bordiga's theses.

On August 7, the day the congress ended, Lenin attended the first meeting of the Executive Committee and forced through a new decision in support of his theses on parliamentarianism. His purpose was to change the mind of the Austrian Communist Party, which had voted overwhelmingly to boycott its country's parliamentary elections. In the name of the theses that had just been adopted by the congress, and under the new bylaws empowering the Comintern to step in and reverse the decisions of any of its sections, Lenin imposed on the Austrians a change of tactics, but not without vigorous protest from the Austrian delegation (to which Steinhardt-Gruber again belonged). According to Paul Levi, "After the congress, at the first meeting of the Executive Committee, it was decided, over the spirited protests of the Austrians, that the Austrian Party must participate in the elections to be held that September [1920] ." [40] On August 15 Lenin sent a letter to the Austrian Communists refuting the argument against their taking part in those elections. On August 31 the letter was published in *Die Rote Fahne*, the organ of the Austrian Communist Party, and at the party's national conference the next day the decision to boycott the elections was rescinded, and it was ruled that the party would participate. The result was a disaster. The Communists received only 22,000 votes, the Social Democrats 1,072,000.

Lenin's meddling in the affairs of the Austrian party was a spectacular demonstration both of his personal authority and of the party's lack of appeal among the workers. So the Lenin view on exploiting parliaments for revolutionary purposes, which had become the law of the Comintern, did not automatically solve the problem. On the contrary, it opened the door to two new dangers for the foreign Communist parties. The first was that of seeing the theses on parliamentarianism remain a dead letter because there were no Communist members in parliaments. That was the case in most Western countries, which were the only ones that had parliaments at the time. It was true of large nations like the United States, England, smaller ones like Austria, Holland, Denmark, and others, not to mention those whose governments had outlawed Communists, making their election to parliament impossible. But there was another, longer-term danger. The theses threatened to become a dead letter not merely because no Communists could get elected to parliament but because if any significant number of them did get elected, that might push the whole Communist movement into "parliamentary cretinism." Neither Lenin nor Bukharin, confident of the effectiveness of Bolshevik methods, worried about this danger during the debates, unlike one of the leftist speakers, the Swiss Communist Herzog, who pointed to the example of the German Social Democrats: "The Social Democrats in Germany, old Wilhelm Liebknecht and Bebel, also declared: 'We are going into parliament only to use this forum for revolutionary purposes.' But their revolutionary activity very quickly turned to opportunism and reformism."[41] And indeed, by the second decade of the Comintern's existence the Communist fractions in the various parliaments, while completely obedient to the party, displayed no revolutionary zeal, as later illustrated by the confusion and surrender of the two strongest parliamentary groups that the International had in Europe: the one in Germany in 1933, at the time of Hitler's arrival to power, and the one in France in 1939, which at the beginning of the war was outlawed.

THE TRADE UNION ISSUE

The role of trade unions preoccupied the Bolshevik leaders in 1920 and 1921 at both the domestic and international levels. On the domestic level, it was the period of the famous debate about the trade unions, begun at the Ninth Bolshevik Party Congress in March 1920 with the publication of various theses, including those of Zinoviev and Tomsky, head of the Soviet trade unions, and resumed at the fifth trade union congress in November 1920. At a party central committee meeting in early December, the Trotsky-Bukharin position triumphed over Lenin's by a vote of eight to seven, only to be beaten at the Tenth Party Congress in March 1921 by Lenin, whose "Platform of Ten" included among its signatories Zinoviev, Tomsky, and Lozovsky, the future secretary general of the Red Trade Union International, to be known as Profintern. This long-flaming controversy had to do with the role of the trade unions in the Soviet state, which officially was governed by the proletariat, and with their relations with the Communist party.

If the Bolshevik leaders were not in full agreement in 1920 about the role of the trade unions *after* the Communist seizure of power, they were in full agreement about that role *before* the Communist victory. Once again the ideas prefabricated by Lenin were to become sacred doctrine and law for the Communist International. In May 1920 the Comintern's official organ,*Communist International*, which was published simultaneously in Russian, German, French, and English, ran in its tenth issue an article by Lenin entitled "Should Revolutionaries be Politically Active in Reactionary Trade Unions? " (Actually, this was chapter six of his forthcoming book on left-wing Communism, but it was published as an ordinary article with no mention of the book.) Two months later, during the first week of the deliberations of the Second Congress and before that body had had a chance to debate the trade union question, those attending had at their disposal issue number twelve of that journal, which bore the date of July 30, and whose second article under the heading "Theses Presented by the Executive Committee of the Communist International" represented the official position which Moscow intended to have prevail in the debates about to begin. Included were the theses on the trade-union movement. Like all the other theses set forth in that issue and the preceding one, they bore no individual signatures but were presented as the collective official voice of the Comintern's Executive Committee.

These theses answered clearly and categorically three main questions being asked by Communists and non-Communist trade unionists who had come to the Second Congress from Europe and America:

One: Should it be mandatory for Communists to participate in trade union organizations even if the latter were reformist, opportunist, and reactionary? The answer, a categorical yes, was to be found in point four of the first part of the theses: "In view of the clearly pronounced tendency of the great mass of workers to join trade unions and the objective revolutionary character of the struggle that these masses are carrying on in spite of the trade union bureaucracy, it is important for Communists of all countries to join the trade unions and work to make them conscious instruments in the battle for the overthrow of the capitalist system and the establishment of Communism."[42] Complementing this thesis was point six, which sought to spell out the task of the U.S. Communists in the face of the existence of "opportunistic trade unions," like the American Federation of Labor, and of revolution-oriented but non-Communist trade unions, like the Industrial Workers of the World:

> Where a split has already occurred between the opportunistic and revolutionary wings of the trade union movement, or where alongside opportunistic trade unions there are revolution-oriented ones, non-Communist though they may be, as in America, it is the duty of Communists to help the revolutionary trade unions, to assist them in freeing themselves of trade union prejudices and in adopting the Communist program, which is the only reliable compass pointing the way through the maze of complex issues involved in the economic struggle. But helping revolutionary trade unions does not mean that Communists should withdraw from opportunistic trade unions, which are in a state of political turbulence and are slowly moving toward the class struggle.[43]

Two: Was the autonomy, not to say the independence, of trade unions to be respected, or should they be under the complete control of the Communist party? Here again the answer was unequivocal, as emerged at the end from point seven: "This tactic prompts Communists to establish the most perfect union between the trade unions and the Communist party and to place the trade unions under the actual leadership of the party, the avant-garde of the workers' revolution. To this end, Communists must organize Communist groups in all the trade unions and, through them, seize political control of the entire trade union movement and run it." [44]

Three: Was it the duty of Communists in every case to split existing trade union organizations, as they were then doing to the Socialist parties? Here the answer was less clear and categorical, the principle being admitted but not its automatic and general application: "In their political activities inside the trade union movement Communists should not hesitate to split those organizations if that should be necessary for them to keep from abandoning their revolutionary action inside the trade unions and from giving up their efforts to make them a weapon in the revolutionary struggle." [45] In the next sentence this idea was rendered more explicit: If such a split did become absolutely necessary, it should not be allowed to occur under circumstances in which the Communists would find themselves isolated from the great mass of workers remaining loyal to the old organization.

Despite the long bitter battle over procedure and amendments provoked by these theses at the Second Congress, when all was said and done, no element of this Bolshevik "holy trinity" had in any way been modified. All survived intact and were reaffirmed in the final decisions of the congress. But the battle over procedure and amendments was long and bitter for two reasons. First, attending that congress were many delegates who for years had been active in the trade union movements of their respective countries, and who, having a wealth of experience of their own, took positions different from those of the Comintern theses. Lenin's ideas, for instance, on the duty of Communists to participate in bourgeois parliaments actually affected only the very small number of Communist leaders elected, or ever likely to be elected, to any parliament (the German Communist Party then had only two deputies in the Reichstag). But the Lenin directive requiring Communists to work inside so-called reactionary trade unions affected almost all Communist activists, and in any case all Communists who were workers. It also affected many delegates who were not members of the Communist party but who worked body and soul in and for the trade union movement, such as several of the revolutionary Syndicalists from continental Europe and most of the British delegation. Secondly, while on all the other items of the congress agenda Lenin had spoken his mind during the committee discussions and at the congress, either as main or supporting speaker (or had at least revised the theses, as on the question of the peasants), when it came to the trade union issue, he let Zinoviev and Radek run the show. The upshot was that his staying in the background left the field open to the opposition, who found it easier to stand up to Zinoviev and Radek, as W. Gallacher made clear in the open debates on the subject: "When I got to Russia, to Petrograd, I was handed a copy of Comrade Lenin's pamphlet on the 'infantile disorder' of the left-Communists, in which I found my own name and a description of my activities. I accepted the rebuke as a child accepts a reprimand from his father. But now comes Comrade Radek, who also sets himself up as our teacher. He will not succeed." [46] To top matters off, when the debates concerned the best tactic to follow with regard to the United States labor unions, the only two Bolshevik leaders present who had ever lived in the United States, Trotsky and Bukharin, kept silent, and the defense of the Bolshevik viewpoint was left to three other Bolsheviks, Radek, Zinoviev, and Lozovsky, none of whom had ever taken a serious interest in the U.S. labor movement or even visited the country; at least two of the three knew no English.

This battle over the trade union question began before the congress started and continued during it. There were preliminary discussions beforehand, particularly with the British delegation, as Lozovsky later reported during the debates at the plenary session: "We discussed the matter with our British comrades for six whole days and nights." [47] The committee on the trade union question was appointed on July 24 though the issue was not due to be debated until August 3. The committee meetings were quite long, as Zinoviev later told the congress: "The committee had six meetings, each lasting five hours." [48] One committee member, Alfred Rosmer, tells of its work in these terms:

> When I joined the committee, it had already had several meetings, though you might have thought it was the first. . . . Radek, only half listening to the discussion, was searching hurriedly through big piles of newspapers being brought to him by Comintern couriers. When he had finished, the meeting was adjourned until such time as might suit his fancy to reconvene it. Once during a plenary session of the congress we were informed that the committee was to meet as soon as that session

was over. They usually ended around midnight. Our discussion was resumed and went on until two or three o'clock in the morning, when everyone finally went to bed, knowing perfectly well that the time had been wasted.[49]

The trade union question was dealt with at the plenary sessions of the congress in the same special way in which it had been handled in committee. When at the third session, on July 24, the committees were appointed for the different items on the agenda, the procedure was exactly the same for each. First the selected main speaker would present the official theses to the plenary session. Then came the discussion or debate, followed immediately by a final vote for adoption of the theses or, in some cases, for returning them to committee for amendments, also to be voted on. The trade union issue was an exception. There were five votes taken on it, two on procedure, three on substance. The first came at the beginning of the July 23 session, held in Moscow and presided over by Lenin. (Actually that was the first working session of the congress. The only preceding one, convened in Petrograd, had been more for ceremony and propaganda purposes.) As soon as the congress agenda became known, John Reed, speaking on behalf of twenty-nine delegates, got up to propose that it be changed, that the trade union question be moved from second place on the agenda to third. The reason he gave was: "We must discuss the trade union question thoroughly and have time to translate and study carefully all the materials on it. I move that, in the discussion of this question, English be admitted as working language."[50] According to the official minutes, his motion was defeated by fourteen votes, but the exact number voting for and against was not stated. This little incident was doubly revealing. It showed that, on the trade union issue, an opposition group had formed, its members being mainly the Anglo-Saxon delegates with John Reed as their spokesman. It showed also that the Russians were unwilling to grant even the smallest seeming concession to that opposition. (Meanwhile, because of the lengthy debates in the committee, the trade union question was not given second place on the agenda, as the Russians wanted, or third as Reed suggested, but wound up in fifth place.)

First came the debates on the role and structure of the Communist party, on the national and colonial issue, on the conditions for admission to the Comintern, and finally, on parliamentarianism. Only then, on August 3, did the matter of the trade unions come up for discussion. Karl Radek was the appointed lead-off speaker. He started by drawing attention to the extraordinary increase in the number of trade unions that had occurred since the end of the war. The number of unionized workers in the big Western countries such as Germany, France, Italy, England, and even the United States, had anywhere from doubled to quintupled, depending on the country. He also pointed out that in the most industrialized countries, the masses of workers were not joining the revolutionary unions but those more interested in reform: "It is characteristic that in all the countries in which the revolutionary unions have shown little or no growth, examples being the IWW in America and the Syndicalists in Germany (which have grown some numerically but relatively hardly at all), the great mass of workers go straight into the big reformist unions."[51] He made another observation too, unrelated to social reality, rather a little piece of Communist theory: "The general situation of the working class is such that any thought of a reformist tactic, of gradually raising the real wages of the working class and improving their standard of living, is an out-and-out opportunistic delusion. Even to dream of such a thing is reactionary utopianism."[52] From this analysis Radek drew the necessary conclusion about the attitude that Communists had to take toward so-called opportunistic reformist trade unions: "So, as a general rule, we are out to take over the unions."[53] And to make quite clear that it was a general rule, he began by calling upon the American Communists to join the American Federation of Labor: "But there is no tactical advantage in our stubbornly refusing to join the A.F. of L. Our job is to work inside it."[54]

After the spokesman for the majority viewpoint had delivered his report and recommendations, it was customary to give the floor to an opposition speaker, as had been done the day before in the debate on parliamentarianism, when Bordiga was permitted to give a dissenting speech. Since at the July 23 meeting John Reed had spoken up on behalf of a group of twenty-nine delegates especially interested in the trade union question, and since he was the only one of the Anglo-American group who understood both the trade union problem in the West and Comintern affairs in

Russia, it was logical to expect him to be chosen opposition speaker from the trade union committee, of which he was a member. But that is not what happened. Two other English-speaking delegates mounted the rostrum, one the American Louis Fraina, who was not even a member of the trade union committee, the other the Englishman Jack Tanner, who was on the committee. Both began their remarks by declaring that essentially they agreed with Radek and the officially blessed trade union theses. Fraina, the first to speak, started by saying: "After our discussions at the trade-union committee meetings it turns out that we are more in agreement than expected. The differences of opinion that still exist concern the importance of individual points and certain matters of procedure, not substance." [55] Speaking next, Tanner said much the same: "Comrade Radek's speech has made it clear that there can be no fundamental differences of opinion. I would like to re-emphasize this." [56] After that, the two speakers did express some minor reservations about Radek's report, Fraina about working inside the A.F. of L., Tanner on the attitude of the Shop Stewards toward reformist trade unionism.

The second plenary session devoted to the trade union issue was held that same day, the evening of August 3. There were three other speakers. Jakob Walcher, a German Spartacist, and A. Lozovsky, a Russian Communist, upheld the official Comintern viewpoint, while the third, Nicola Bombacci, opposed it, his one argument being: "I deny utterly that trade unions have any revolutionary function whatsoever." [57] On the surface this second plenary session started out with the debates proceeding in the usual way, like the debates over the other agenda items, when suddenly an incident occurred that changed the plans of the Russian delegation.

At the first session the Bolsheviks had had no difficulty in executing their opening maneuver, that of defusing the opposition by silencing its one real spokesman and replacing him with two "softer" speakers. When that succeeded, they were ready for their second maneuver, namely turning off the debate altogether at the second session and keeping the adversary from speaking at all, which Zinoviev personally undertook. Immediately after Lozovsky finished, he announced: "The Presidium moves that the debate be closed and the vote be taken. Sixteen speakers have registered to

speak." [58] While the first maneuver had succeeded without protest, this second one raised a storm. John Reed grabbed the floor,
taking issue with Zinoviev: "They are shutting off debate deliberately so they won't have to discuss the matter with the British and
American delegations." [59]

Three British delegates, MacLaine, Gallacher, and Tanner, sided
vocally with Reed, while Zinoviev and Radek each spoke twice in
counterattack before the vote was taken on whether to shut off
debate. It was the second vote on the trade union question, again
on a procedural matter, not a substantive one. According to Zinoviev, fifty hands went up in favor of ending debate, twenty-five
against. The total came to less than half of the 169 castable votes.
According to the official minutes, John Reed again grabbed the
floor to make the terse announcement: "On behalf of the American delegation I would like to inform you that we refuse to vote
on these theses." [60] He was immediately backed up by Tanner in
the name of the British delegation, by Wijnkoop, the Dutch representative, and Pestaña, the only Spanish delegate. All abstained
from the vote. The brief statements attributed to them in the
official minutes were not what they actually said in their speeches,
to judge from this reply by Zinoviev to a threat (not reported in
the minutes): "I would merely like to say that one should be
careful about threatening to walk out of the congress, because,
first of all, no one is afraid of threats, and secondly because they
are quite out of place at a Communist congress." [61] Anyway,
Zinoviev finally brought the theses to a vote, with the one concession that the text to be voted on was only "a basis" and that the
committee would review it again, with the problem being resub-
mitted to the plenary session if the committee could not unanimously agree. When at last the vote came (it was the third chronologically but the first on the substance of the theses), there were
sixty-four in favor and thirteen declared abstentions. Again, the
majority did not vote.*

Two days later, on August 5, after the trade union committee
had finished its work, the problem was again brought to the plen-

*This result is given in the German edition, *Der zweite Kongress der Kom-
munistischen Internationale*, Hamburg, 1921, p. 526, but in the English
edition, *The Second Congress of the Communist International*, Moscow,
1920, p. 338, a different result is given, namely 84 to 18.

ary session, with Radek once more being the principal speaker. His speech made clear from the outset that the committee had been unable to reach unanimous agreement. He blamed the Americans, accused them of trying to "kill the theses by amending them to death," and of attempting to "pull a fast one on us in the resolution." [62] Declaring flatly that any retreat, any compromise with the Americans was impossible, he set out to demolish their position by a strange and devious method, namely reading out selected excerpts from the amendments that the American delegation had proposed. Not only were these not disclosed in full to the plenary session, but even the excerpts quoted by Radek were not recorded in the official minutes. And when in support of their position the American delegation brought out a letter received only two months before from the Comintern Executive Committee sanctioning their present view, Radek rejected the argument on the thin grounds that the letter in question had not been approved by all the Executive Committee members and that anyway it was in error. The text of the letter, which Radek read off, was deleted from the minutes, too. With the Americans thus disposed of, Radek did deign to present four minor amendments, each only a sentence or two long, which somewhat lengthened the original text without changing at all its basic orientation.

Again it was John Reed who spoke up for the committee minority and for the entire American delegation. Rejecting Radek's charge that the opposition was engaged in sabotage, he urged that points four, five, six, and seven of the theses be thrown out and replaced by the American amended version (that text, too, is missing from the account of Reed's speech in the official minutes). After Reed, a British speaker, William Gallacher, voiced his support for the American position, insisting on the right of British and American Communists to stay out of the official reformist opportunistic trade unions and carry on the good fight in their own way from the outside. As soon as Gallacher had finished, Zinoviev got up and declared that "we are not going to make a single concession to our British Comrades here, because what they want means the destruction of the Communist International." [63] After the speech by Fraina, who again was conciliatory, expressing surprise that Zinoviev and Radek were so "excited," and minimizing the disagreement, which he hoped would be followed by agreement at the next congress, a fourth vote on the theses was taken. The minutes do not tell how many voted for, how many against, or by what margin the theses were adopted. They merely report laconically: "Vote taken on Radek theses, which were adopted." [64] But since Reed had also demanded a vote on the amendments proposed by the Americans, a fifth vote was taken. Here the official minutes break all previous records for cryptic brevity. Without a hint as to the outcome, they report: "Vote taken."*

This final battle must have been a hot one, to judge from the many glaring gaps in the official minutes. A. Rosmer later reported: "When the resolution was put to the congress, John Reed sought me out. He was very disturbed. 'We can't go back to America carrying a decision like that,' he told me. The only friends the Communist International has in labor union circles are the Industrial Workers of the World, and here you are sending us into the arms of the A.F. of L., in which it has nothing but implacable enemies." [65] Reed did not give up. Despite all the votes at the congress, several weeks afterwards he wrote to Communist friends in America: "At the next congress these theses will have to be changed." [66] But on October 17, 1920, he died in Moscow and the theses remained unchanged.

As was often to happen during the life of the Comintern, in the impassioned controversy over the trade unions both sides were right in their critical analysis, both wrong in the solutions they proposed. The Americans and the English-speaking delegates in general were right to insist that it was impossible to transform their countries' official reformist trade unions into instruments of revolution, while Radek and Zinoviev were right to point out the numerical weakness of the revolution-oriented trade unions and the fact that the most workers belonged to the official reform-oriented ones. But the British and Americans were mistaken in believing they could form a strong revolutionary trade-union movement outside and despite the big official unions. The Bolsheviks, Lenin first among them, were equally mistaken in believing that they could take over the so-called reactionary trade unions from within and turn them into an arm of the revolution.

The decision taken at the Second Congress obliging American

*Der zweite Kongress. . . ., p. 636. Another source, published by order of the Communist Party of Austria, gives the outcome of the vote as 57 against Reed, 8 for. Cf. *Der zweite Kongress der Kommunistischen Internationale*, Vienna, 1920, p. 98.

Communists to join and work inside the American Federation of Labor, a decision imposed on them against their will, and the congress' other decision forcing British Communists into the Labour Party, were ample proof of the decisive moral and political authority wielded by the Bolsheviks at that assemblage. This did not prove, however, that Lenin's policy was right. It was only *praxis* (the Marxian magic word) that could demonstrate the truth and rightness of a social or political idea—except, alas, in this case, for as it turned out neither of those hard-fought decisions ever got translated into *praxis*.

THE AGRARIAN QUESTION

All the items on the agenda of the Second Congress had been formulated and decided in advance by Lenin in his *"Left-Wing" Communism*, with one exception: the agrarian question. The omission did not mean, though, that Lenin took no interest in the matter. For twenty of the years that he had belonged to the Russian revolutionary movement (1897-1917) Lenin had been literally obsessed by the key questions of how to put together a revolutionary party, gain allies, and seize power. He believed that the answer lay in the answer to another question: in a huge, preponderantly peasant country like Russia, how does one go about winning over, or at least neutralizing, the peasantry during the struggle for power? His views on this varied with events, but always in function of that master imperative: assuring the support of the peasantry. In 1903 he had written the agrarian plank in the party platform, making very modest demands on behalf of the peasants, but by 1905, a year of revolution, he was sponsoring much more radical proposals, calling for confiscation of the large estates for the benefit of the peasants, and these were presented in April of that year to the Third Congress, held in London. In 1917, before the Revolution, the Bolshevik program envisaged "nationalization of all land by the State," "organized collective agriculture" and the creation of "model farms." [67] But when the revolution actually came, Lenin junked his own program and grabbed that of his political adversaries, the Social Revolutionaries, which called for dividing up the big estates and leaving the small and medium holdings intact. Since this had won the Bolsheviks the support of many peasants, Lenin was consequently convinced that he had found the permanent formula for winning over the peasants to the Communist revolution. He admitted as much to the foreign Communists in an article published by the Comintern organ shortly before the Second Congress: "The victorious Bolsheviks wrote into their land decree not a single word of their own true thoughts but copied letter for letter the demands on behalf of the peasants printed in the newspapers of the Social Revolutionaries." [68]

Lenin tried to go back to his own, collectivist program in February 1919 when the All-Russian Central Executive Committee promulgated the law instituting "communes,"—the Socialist agricultural administrative units. In his report of March 1919 to the Eighth Party Congress he declared: "We are encouraging communes, but they have to be set up in such a way as to win the peasant's confidence." [69] Despite Lenin's high hopes and exhortations, the experiment with the communes was a failure, and he switched again to a moderate position by introducing the New Economic Policy. At the Third Comintern Congress in 1921 he attempted to explain to foreign Communists—many of whom still were clamoring for "offensive tactics"—the "flexibility" of Bolshevik policy, reminding them of his about-face on the agrarian question during the Revolution: "Within a few short weeks we managed to win over nine tenths of the peasantry by reviving and implementing not our own program but that of the Socialist Revolutionaries." [70]

While that policy was no doubt clever and effective, it was clearly not Marxist. Everyone knew that the Socialist Revolutionaries were at the opposite pole from Marxism on the agrarian issue. The USPD, whose ranks included German Marxism's leading authorities, such as Kautsky and Hilferding, did not fail to hammer away at Lenin's abandonment of Marxism in its public exchange of letters with the Comintern on the eve of the Second Congress. The party spokesman Crispien stressed the point to the Congress itself:

> As for the agrarian question, to our astonishment we note that the Executive Committee is recommending to Germany's revolutionary proletariat methods which are a direct throwback to petty-bourgeois attitudes, which we ourselves have long since transcended. We are

urged, for instance, to make clear to the small peasants that the proletariat, once it has taken power in the state, will immediately improve
their situation at the expense of the dispossessed big landowners, will
free them from the latters' yoke, will treat them as a special class and
give them large tracts of land, will rid them of debt, etc. This whole
idea is an out-and-out rejection of our Marxist tenet whereby the big
estates are to be immediately socialized, that is, made the property of
society as a whole and operated as public utilities.[71]

Crispien unfolded these arguments at the session on the evening of
July 29, and Lenin replied the next day—not in the name of
Marxism but in that of political expediency: "That is a pedantic
point of view. . . . We shall always find, and should make it a point
to find, some portion of these vast holdings that can be parceled
out to the small peasants, perhaps not as an outright gift but under
some lease arrangement, so that the small peasant will tangibly
gain from the act of confiscation. Otherwise he will fail to see any
difference between dictatorship by the Soviets and the one that
preceded it. If the proletarian government does not adopt this
policy, it cannot survive."[72] In plainer words, power seized in the
name of Marxism could only be held with a program contrary to
Marxism, just as Russia's revolution had been staged and waged in
the name of Marx but could not have been won by strict application of his teachings.

The Russian experience with the agrarian problem had led
Lenin to two axioms. One was that in Eastern Europe (not to
mention Asia and all other industrially underdeveloped regions)
Communist victory would be impossible without the help of the
peasants; the other was that, to gain the help of the peasants, they
had to be kept in the dark as to Communism's ultimate agrarian
aims. At the Second Congress these two axioms would become law
for the entire Comintern, and the theses on the agrarian question
would so state.

Lenin shared the job of drafting the theses with the Polish
Communist leader Marchlewski, who in May 1920 wrote an article
entitled "The Agrarian Question and World Revolution" as a preliminary report on the agrarian issue to be discussed at the Second
Congress. In early June, before being published in the Comintern
organ, a copy was shown to Lenin, who, on reading it, immediately drafted his own version of the theses, which he handed to

Marchlewski on June 7, who looked it over and returned it to Lenin with his comments on June 23. The agrarian committee of the congress was informed of the Lenin draft, but "unfortunately Comintern files have preserved no record of the committee's deliberation."[73] At the congress, Lenin was chairman of the agrarian committee and Marchlewski was its principal speaker until July 30, when he had to leave for Bialystok and the Polish front, having been made head of the revolutionary provisional Polish government. So when the agrarian question came up for public debate on August 4, he was not there. He was quickly replaced by Ernst Meyer, a member of the German delegation.

Marchlewski's article and the Lenin version of the theses approached the agrarian problem very differently. The first was based on the peasants' geographical distribution, the second on their social stratification. Marchlewski viewed the problem only in the European context, while Lenin already had his eye on Asia (he was drafting then, too, the theses on the national and colonial questions). Marchlewski started by dividing Europe in two: first there was Central Europe, "the territory encompassing the geographic zone extending from about the Dnieper in the East to the Elbe in the West, and from the Baltic Sea to the Balkans."[74] Western Europe took in the rest of the old continent. Concerning Central Europe, he wrote: "The main thing is that, in this zone, big landholdings play an important role in the economic life, comprising in places from thirty to fifty per cent of the total land area, and sometimes more."[75] From this Marchlewski drew two conclusions, one about the Communist program, the other about Communist action. Concerning the program, he was against distributing land to the peasants, proposing instead a solution akin to the one attempted by the Soviet regime in Hungary in 1919: "Breaking up the large rural enterprises, which in all those countries are operated more or less efficiently and economically, would be bound in the end to lower the yield of the soil. . . . Things being as they are in those countries, dividing up the big estates would not significantly benefit the great mass of the poor, because there are just too many of them."[76] As for Communist action, knowing full well that the peasants would not be enthusiastic about keeping the large estates intact, their ownership merely transferred from the feudal aristocracy to the government, Marchlewski deduced that the peasants could not be looked upon to support the revolution: "It follows that it is not peasant support of the Communist program that we should strive for; it is enough to neutralize the peasants until after the decisive battle that the proletariat is waging against capitalism." [77]

Europe's other half, as Marchlewski saw it, presented a different picture: "To the west of Central Europe starts a territory where big estates play almost no role, where the agrarian system is entirely one of small bourgeois landholders with a rural economy to match." [78] Any chance of capturing those peasants for the Communist cause was slighter still: "To hope to involve them in revolutionary action is vanity. . . . Even to dream of converting them to the cause of proletarian revolution is idle. The problem reduces to neutralizing them and keeping them indifferent with compromises." [79]

After complimenting Marchlewski for having so "perfectly stated the theoretical bases of the Communist International's agrarian program," [80] Lenin spelled out the tactical considerations. His conclusions were quite different from Marchlewski's. While the latter had expressed skepticism, if not pessimism, about getting the peasants in either Eastern or Western Europe to support the Communist cause, Lenin believed—on the strength of the Russian example—that their support could be had. In Europe and Asia both, all one needed was a gimmick, some way to "hook" them.

Instead of classifying Europe's peasants geographically, Lenin broke them down into social categories, which he saw as being mainly three, each characterized by a special function. At the bottom were the working peasants, whose support of the Communist revolution had to be won at all costs. In the middle were the peasants of moderate means, who were to be neutralized. On top sat the wealthy peasants, whom the party and Communist revolution must destroy.

The bottom class or working peasants consisted in turn of three subclasses: landless farm proletariat; semiproletariat (peasants who worked in various agricultural or industrial enterprises but farmed their own little plots, which they either owned or rented); and, lastly, the small landowners or small-scale farmers. Lenin believed that each of these subclasses could be won over to Communism: "Taken together, these three elements of the rural population make up the majority of the inhabitants of all capitalist countries. The success of a proletarian coup d'état, both in the cities and villages, can therefore be considered an absolute certainty." [81] He was as sure as he was frank. The frankness was his unashamed use of the term "proletarian coup d'état" as a synonym for the so-called proletarian revolution, for a coup d'état is precisely what the seizure of power in Petrograd had been. He generalized it again a few sentences later in invoking "the truth, perfectly demonstrated by theoretical Marxism and sufficiently proved experimentally by Russia's proletarian revolution." [82] No less remarkable was his utter certainty. He hadn't the slightest doubt that what had happened in Russia could be reproduced in the capitalist countries, notwithstanding Marchlewski's view that the small peasants were "the most conservative and even most reactionary element in the population."

Just above the working peasants stood the "middle peasants," the Communist policy toward whom Lenin defined thus: "For the immediate future and throughout the initial stage of its dictatorship the revolutionary proletariat cannot take on the task of politically conquering this rural element but must confine itself to neutralizing it until after the battle being fought between the proletariat and bourgeoisie." [83] But the "working peasants" were to be won over and the "middle peasants" neutralized by the same formula that the Bolsheviks had used in Russia in November 1917, and which directly violated the true Communist program, namely preserving the institution of private property: "However, in most capitalist countries the proletarian authorities must not immediately abolish completely the right of private property, and certainly will not take from the poor peasants, and those in modest circumstances, their landholdings, whose area an effort will be made to increase." [84]

Lastly there was the top layer, the rich peasants, on whom Lenin declared merciless war: "This stratum of the rural population is numerous and represents the most inveterate foe of the revolutionary proletariat. All political work of Communist parties in rural areas must be concentrated on the fight against this element." [85] He also prescribed what form the battle should take: "The revolutionary proletariat must confiscate instantly and unreservedly all the land belonging to these big landowners." [86]

Up to this point everything that Lenin had written in his draft of the theses was adopted without change, except for a few unimportant words here and there. It was not until they reached point six of the draft that the committee was provoked into a debate. The result was that that point was considerably modified. The issue was what should be done with the big estates after the Communists confiscated them. Should they be kept and collectivized in the name of the revolution, or should they be broken up and parceled out?

Marchlewski in his article had distinguished between countries in which small landholdings predominated and those in which big estates were preponderant, and he favored breaking up and distributing the big estates in the former, where they were not a major factor in the rural economy, but was against it in the latter, where they were. Lenin, though, was much less categorical on this point. His sense of the realities and power relationships, and his better knowledge of the disappointing experiment with the collectivist "communes" set up by the Soviet government, made him more cautious in attempting to apply the pure Communist doctrine. He wrote: "But it would be a big mistake to carry this rule too far [i.e., collectivization of the big estates] and never permit *any* of the land expropriated from the expropriators to be doled out to the small and sometimes middle peasants in the region."[87] In other words, the Russian model was absolute law when it came to organizing a true Communist party anywhere, but the Russian answer to the agrarian question must not be slavishly copied. Lenin cautioned against blind imitation of Russia's collectivist example, which meant that by 1920 he was already skeptical about the commune experiment even in Russia. A short time later he abandoned it.

So here Lenin disagreed with the foreign Communists, who were more Catholic than the Bolshevik Pope. As V. Kolarov reported, "After long debate. . . Lenin consented to some changes in the wording of point six so as to emphasize that 'in the advanced capitalist countries' one must 'preferably preserve intact the large agricultural enterprises,' while keeping one's options open regarding any exceptions that might have to be made as 'the surest way to attract the peasants to the cause of the revolution.'"[88] Thus, while Lenin's original version had contained a brief section advocating "communes," followed by three much longer sections warning against slavishly imitating the Soviet model, the final version was much closer to Marchlewski's than to Lenin's position. The three long paragraphs of reservations were removed, with still greater stress laid on the need to establish "communes" as opposed to dividing up the big estates: "Keeping the large agricultural units intact is more in the interest of the revolutionary elements of the population, especially of the farm workers who have no land of their own, and of the semiproletariat and small landowners, who often live from their labor in the large enterprises. Also, nationalizing the large estates makes the urban population less dependent on the countryside for food." [89]

Yet Lenin did manage to stick in one exception to this collectivization rule, convinced that it was tactically essential to assure himself the support of the peasants and not turn them against the Communists: "In countries where big estates are few and where many small tenant farmers are clamoring for land, breaking up the big estates and parceling them out may be one sure way of winning peasant support for the revolution, whereas keeping those few estates intact would have little or no effect on the urban food situation." [90]

The final text was presented by the German Communist leader, Ernst Meyer, to the session of August 4. He confined himself to amplifying the theses, reporting that the most important change was the one made in item six, as Vasil Kolarov tells us: "The speaker, whose report of the committee's deliberations, incidentally, was not entirely accurate, declared among other things: 'The greatest change was made in item six. The first version stressed an exception to the rule that the confiscated estates must not be broken up. The committee eliminated that section, substituting another stipulating that the large agrarian production units must be kept intact' [which is not what really happened—V. Kolarov.]" [91]

When the issue came up for open debate, some spoke up in support of the theses, men like Shablin (Bulgarian), Grigori Sokolnikov (Russian), and Raymond Lefebvre (French), while two Italian speakers, whose political views in other ways differed, expressed reservations. As Kolarov further tells us, the Italian delegation, though the most representative of Western Europe politically

and numerically, took no part in the agrarian committee's deliberations: "Despite the congress' decision, the Italian party was not
represented on this committee, because the split Italian delegation
had been unable to agree on a candidate." [92] At the public debates
at the congress itself, the first Italian speaker, Professor Graziadei,
remarked: "One notes a striking similarity between Comrade
Lenin's theses on the national and colonial question and those on
the agrarian question. . . . It is the same method that has been used
with regard to other issues; it consists in sizing up one's opponents, then making them such concessions as they or the moment
may demand." [93] Still, he was willing, he said, to vote for the
theses, which the changes had made acceptable. The second Italian
speaker,Serrati, who was even more critical, announced that he
would abstain from voting. He began by insisting that discussion
like this was out of place at that congress: "In my opinion the
matter does not concern this congress, which is a congress of
comrades who, coming from industrial countries, do not really
know what the issue involves." [94] He was especially critical of the
concessions made in the theses: "Like the theses on the national
and colonial question, these on the agrarian issue show no awareness that the concessions now being made to various social strata
in order to gain their sympathy, or at least neutralize them, may
prove very dangerous for the proletariat when the revolutionary
showdown finally comes, and may steer them onto an ever more
opportunistic path of more and more concessions." [95]

The congress overrode Serrati's objections, and the theses were
adopted without a single dissenting vote. Just as the decisions
adopted on parliamentarianism and the trade unions would become law for the entire international Communist movement, the
agrarian theses too fixed the behavior pattern for all Communist
parties. Henceforth they were committed to a three-phase policy:
(1) during the struggle for power, they must promise land to the
landless peasants (agrarian reform) while guaranteeing the property of the landed peasants; (2) during the initial period after
taking power, they must actually carry out the promised reform
and honor the property guarantee; (3) once their power is consolidated, they will take the land away from the peasants and collec-
tivize it, by force if necessary. This, then, was the new "general

line" followed first in Soviet Russia and later in Eastern Europe and China, even after the Comintern had ceased to exist.

SHOULD COMMUNISTS JOIN THE LABOUR PARTY?

Unlike the issues of parliamentarianism and the trade unions, discussed first in *"Left-Wing" Communism* and then made part of the agenda of the Second Congress, another problem which Lenin had tackled authoritatively, even passionately, in that book was not on the agenda announced in the invitational letter to the Second Congress signed by Zinoviev and Radek. It concerned the policy, or rather tactic, to be adopted by the British Communists, who had not yet founded a party of their own, toward Britain's Labour Party. The omission did not mean that the Second Congress would not deal with that problem or would fail to endorse the position already laid down by Lenin. In his first draft of the theses on the basic tasks of the Communist International, completed on July 4, two weeks before the congress opened, he had already firmly stipulated what tactics the British Communists were to follow, which dovetailed with the other ideas expressed in the book: "At the same time, the Second Congress of the Third International is bound to pronounce itself in favor of the adherence of the Communist groups and organizations, and/or those sympathetic to Communism, to the British Labour Party, even though the latter has not yet left the Second International." [96]

This directive of Lenin's set forth "concretely" what he regarded as a key problem, but one that had been more or less unknown to the foreign delegations, namely Communist penetration of non-Communist political organizations. It caused something of a stir at the congress, as Paul Levi reported on returning from Moscow: "The matter of Communist participation in non-Communist organizations became particularly acute in connection with the question by the British comrades as to whether the British Socialist Party should have anything to do with the Labour Party.... In Moscow the Russian comrades, including Lenin, were strongly in favor of Communists' remaining in such a party so long as there was any chance of making effective propaganda. But if such organizations tried to tie our hands or shut us up, then of course we should get out." [97]

While not previously on the agenda, the matter of the appropriate Communist tactics in England was discussed on two occasions at plenary sessions, and at Lenin's suggestion a special committee was set up to consider it during the interval between sessions. Careful scrutiny was the more necessary as the majority of the six-member British delegation (S. Pankhurst, Gallacher, Tanner, and Ramsay) were leftists, hence opposed to dealings of any kind with the Labour Party. This attitude was supported not only by the leftists there from other countries but even by individuals who denied being leftists (like Wijnkoop), or were suspected of the opposite deviation, "opportunism" (like Serrati). Together they made a fair number. When the vote was taken, more voted against the Lenin position than in any other controversy.

At the July 23 session, after Zinoviev's report on the role and structure of Communist parties, Ramsay, who represented the Shop Stewards' Committees, made a statement , whereupon Mac-Laine, representing the British Socialist Party (BSP), requested the floor to speak in support of Lenin: "In England we have a large workers' party, the Labour Party, which is not at all Communist and contains various Communist parties within it. Among England's parties a discussion is in progress over whether the Communist parties in the Labour Party, which itself is neither Socialist nor Communist, should stay in it or associate with it. The BSP's answer is yes." [98] After the debate, a rift developed between the opponents and proponents of the tactic recommended by the Bolsheviks. Wijnkoop, again disagreeing with Bolshevism's leaders, spoke against the MacLaine amendment calling for adoption of the tactic, and he cited the opinion of the British delegates who opposed it. Paul Levi, in the name of the Comintern's Western European Secretariat, announced his disagreement with Wijnkoop, whom he referred to as the spokesman for the Amsterdam Bureau. Serrati, in turn, sided with Ramsay, raising the question as to whether the tactic would not promote opportunism: "By allowing Communists to remain in such an organization, we again open wide the door to Possibilism." [99]

After these speeches, most of them in opposition to his tactic, Lenin took the floor, again demonstrating his unique mode of thought and argument. Like a great teacher about to reveal to his pupils the essence and profundity of a science of which they were completely ignorant, Lenin explained to his listeners that joining the Labour Party did not involve automatically the sin of "opportunism." To the foreign Communists, who did not yet know what Bolshevik organization was and meant, he explained that what he was proposing was merely a tactic, but a key tactic: infiltration. Military men called it the tactic of the Trojan horse; naturalists knew it as "termite work"; in other words, mixing with the enemy in order more easily to defeat him. In his theses on the basic tasks of the Communist International this had been made perfectly clear:

> So long as the Labour Party continues to leave its member organizations free to criticize, act, make propaganda, agitate, and organize on behalf of the dictatorship of the proletariat, and on behalf of Soviet power . . . Communists should make every effort and be willing to accept certain compromises in order to have the chance of influencing the great mass of workers, of denouncing their opportunist leaders in public forums, where the masses can see and hear them, of hastening the transfer of political power from the hands of direct representatives of the bourgeoisie to those of "worker lieutenants of the capitalist class," so as to rid the masses as soon as possible of their last illusions on the subject.[100]

In his speech to the congress Lenin hammered at this central theme with still greater force than in the theses: "The Communist party may associate with the Labour Party so long as it retains its freedom to criticize and pursue its own policies. That is the main thing."[101] This precept was to govern the Communists' behavior whenever they entered any other, larger organization. They must keep their freedom of action, and operate as a group apart within the large body.

A further point was Lenin's certainty, still unshaken in 1920, that if the Communist party just did its job well, that alone would bring the masses ultimately into the Communist camp. In this he had that same quasi-religious conviction, couched in scientific terms, that once inspired Russia's Narodniks, who believed that to bring light and truth to the benighted peasants one only had to walk among them and spread the good word. It did not occur to Lenin, in 1920, that the Communists might follow his instructions to the last letter and that the masses might still not respond. At the Second Congress he infected others with his faith, as J. T. Murphy, one who favored Lenin's tactic, confirms: "A year, perhaps two years, at the outside three years would, we thought, see the masses of the British labor movement deserting the opportunist leaders and following the Communist party." [102] The relationship between the avant-garde—that is, the party—and the great mass of workers Lenin defined thus: "The British Socialist Party is free to call Henderson a traitor and yet stay in the Labour Party. This is the avant-garde of the working class collaborating with the backward workers, the rear guard. This is so important for the entire movement that we absolutely insist that the British Communists become a link between the party, that is, the minority of the working class, and the remaining mass of workers." [103]

Convinced that he was always right, even when the majority of other Communists did not agree with him, Lenin did not put much stock in majority rule. He had made this a point of law in the Bolshevik Party and was doing the same in the Comintern: "Now, comrades Tanner and Ramsay come and tell us: But the majority of the British Communists will not accept that. Must we then absolutely agree with the majority? By no means. . . . If the majority is against us, then we must organize the minority separately. That will teach them a lesson." [104]

Lenin proposed forming a special committee to study the question, but the minutes give no hint of the work of that committee, and report only sketchily the ensuing debate at the plenary session of August 6, the last of the congress. The address by the committee's principal speaker, Alfred Rosmer, who was also its chairman, is not mentioned in any of the official records—a significant detail. Lenin was introducing here another rule that he had used in the Bolshevik Party. In the name of "discipline," Lenin would request a person who opposed an idea or tactic of his to advocate it in public, as if it were the opponent's own view. So it was with Rosmer, as he later revealed: "Lenin obviously had a majority of the committee with him, but, sensing that there was still serious opposition to his views, he wanted the matter brought before the congress and, even though I had spoken against that point, he asked me to present the committee's report at the plenary session." [105]

The official record mentions speeches by only two opponents, Pankhurst and Gallacher, and two proponents, MacLaine and Lenin, who spoke last. He hit from another angle the point that he made in the preceding debate: no individual party in the Comintern had a right to determine its own tactics, that power belonging solely to the International itself, which was the supreme central body; having Communists join the Labour Party was merely a form of infiltration and in no way obliged them to cease working against the Labour Party leaders; Communists who did join the Labour Party were to enlighten the masses of backward workers, and so on. He tossed in only one new argument, namely that a party made up mostly of workers and run mainly by leaders of working-class origin (as the Labour Party was) was not by his standards a workers' party, while a party consisting mostly of professional revolutionaries and run mainly by intellectuals (like the Bolshevik Party) indeed was one. He told his audience: "But whether a party is or is not a true workers' party depends not only on whether its members are workers but also on who leads them, and on what they do and what political tactics they adopt. . . . Judged by this standard, which is the only correct one, the Labour Party is completely bourgeois." [106]

After his speech, when the vote was taken, his directive to the British Communists to rejoin the Labour Party carried by 58 to 24, with two abstaining. Never again would history witness so many delegates voting against the Bolshevik leaders at a Comintern congress. In the end, the British Communists were forced to adopt the Lenin view. When the congress was over, even Gallacher, who had opposed it until the very last session, agreed to work for what Lenin wanted, as he reports in his memoirs:

> Before I left Moscow, I had an interview with Lenin, during which he asked me three questions.
>
> "Do you admit that you were wrong on the issue of parliamentarianism and affiliation with the Labour Party?
>
> "Will you join the Communist Party of Great Britain when you return? (A telegram had arrived several days earlier informing us of the party's formation.)
>
> "Will you do your best to persuade your Scottish comrades to join it? "
>
> To each of those questions I answered yes.[107]

The new-born British Communist Party hewed faithfully to the line laid down by Lenin. On August 10, 1920, its leaders sent a letter to the Executive Committee of the Labour Party requesting affiliation. Their request was turned down on September 11 in a letter signed by the Labour Party Secretary, one of the "traitors" whom Lenin was promising the rope of the hanged as a reward for a socialist-communist alliance, Arthur Henderson, who informed the Communists of the irreversible verdict: "After full consideration of the resolution and your request, it was resolved that the application for affiliation be declined, and I was instructed to inform you that the basis of affiliation to the Labour Party is the acceptance of its constitution, principles, and program, with which the objects of the Communist Party do not appear to be in accord." [108]

The Leninist dogma remained in force nevertheless, and, in the years that followed, the British Communists kept reapplying, even as late as 1935, after the Seventh Comintern Congress. Unfailingly, the Labour Party turned them down.

The Lenin tactic, defended through thick and thin, remained a dead letter for a simple reason, which did not occur to Lenin in 1920: Communist infiltration could be real and effective only if the non-Communist "partner" consented to play the role that Lenin had written for him, that of victim and dupe. But if the partner, here the Labour Party, refused to play along, the tactic naturally failed.

The National and Colonial Questions and the Comintern's Initial Policy in the East

Lenin concerned himself very early with the national problem for the same reason that he took an interest in the peasantry. In the one case he wanted to bring into the revolutionary struggle a discontented social class (the peasantry), in the second case a discontented national category (the non-Russian peoples of the Tsarist empire). Again his originality lay not in his theory but in his strategy. The victory of the revolution depended less on gathering together all the true believers than on corralling all the malcontents, including many who didn't have any interest in Marxian theory. This same thread ran all through Lenin's thinking, from his days as a young Marxist until his death as ruler of Soviet Russia. As early as 1897, in his tract *The Tasks Facing Russia's Social Democrats*, he was already urging the necessity for lending temporary support to non-Socialist forces:

> Such support neither assumes nor requires our compromising in any way with non-Social Democratic programs and principles. It is merely the support of an ally against a determined enemy. In lending such support, the Social Democrats speed the downfall of the common foe. . . . Social Democrats support any revolutionary movement against the existing social system, any oppressed national or ethnic group, any persecuted religion, any humiliated social class, and so on, in their struggle for equal rights. . . . While demonstrating the solidarity that binds this or that opposition group to the workers, Social Democrats always put the workers and their interests first. They are always careful to make clear that the alliance is only temporary and conditional, ever stressing that the proletariat is a class apart, which tomorrow may be opposing its allies of today.[1]

This idea, which he formulated during his exile in Siberia, of a necessary alliance with the oppressed national minorities living within the confines of Tsarist Russia was still very much alive when he became master of Russia, only by then its aim was not restricted to his native land but embraced the entire planet, as he acknowledged in his report to the Second All-Russian Congress of Communist Organizations of Eastern Peoples, on November 22, 1919: "So the Socialist revolution will not be only, or mainly, a struggle of the revolutionary proletariat of each country against its own bourgeoisie. No, it will be a struggle of all the colonies and all countries oppressed by imperialism, and all dependent countries, against international imperialism."[2]

Such a basic and constant preoccupation had other significant manifestations. The 1903 congress of the Russian Social Democratic Labor Party, despite the protest of the Polish Social Democratic delegation, inserted in the party program the recognition of the right of nations to self-determination. Later, and in particular after 1913, the nationality problem became one of Lenin's major concerns,[3] but his theories in that field did not obtain definitive expression until the publication of several of his writings of early 1916. The best known of these was his pamphlet *Imperialism, the Highest Stage of Capitalism*, in which Lenin described what he believed to be inexorable laws of history determining the destiny of twentieth-century capitalism. Written in cautious language because of censorship (Lenin wanted his pamphlet to be published legally in Russia), he did not spell out the outcome of the situation he depicted, though his diagnosis of imperialism being the highest and the last stage of "moribund" capitalism clearly implied that the outcome would be revolutionary. He left unspecified whether the revolution would start in the exploiting or the exploited countries or parts of the world.

Though Lenin's ideas about imperialism were hardly original (his main sources were the British liberal writer J. A. Hobson and the Austrian Marxist Rudolf Hilferding), a by-product of the main theme—his views on the national question—pitted him against other prominent Marxists, such as Rosa Luxemburg, Karl Radek, and Hermann Gorter. In particular, he did not share their doctrinal views that in the epoch of imperialism there can be no more national wars (Luxemburg), or that the argument of self-determination fosters the idea that it is a duty of Social Democracy to support every struggle for independence (Radek). In an article written in March of 1916, entitled "The Socialist Revolution and the Right of Nations to Self-Determination," he put forward several theses which would become hallmarks of Leninism. He postulated, from the outset, that "victorious socialism must achieve complete democracy and, consequently, not only bring about the complete equality of nations, but also give effect to the right of oppressed nations to self-determination, that is, the right to free political secession." He warned, however, that the aim of socialism was not to reduce the present division of mankind to yet smaller states; the aim was to bring nations closer to each other, to merge them: "Just as mankind can achieve the abolition of classes only by passing through the transition period of the dictatorship of the oppressed class, so mankind can achieve the inevitable merging of nations only by passing through the transition period of complete liberation of all the oppressed nations, that is, their freedom to secede." Necessarily then, "the proletariat cannot but fight against the forcible retention of the oppressed nations within the boundaries of a given state, . . . [and] must demand the right of political secession for the colonies and for the nations that 'its own' nation oppresses." At the same time—and the point is of crucial importance—"the Socialists of the oppressed nations . . . must particularly fight for and maintain complete, absolute unity (also organizational) between the workers of the oppressed nation and the workers of the oppressing nation."

These fundamental principles being established, Lenin divided the world into three categories: first, the advanced capitalist countries of Western Europe and the United States of America, in which the bourgeois, progressive, national movements came to an end long ago and where the task of the proletariat was to liberate the oppressed, both in the colonies and within its own country; second, the countries of Eastern Europe, including Russia, with their developed bourgeois-democratic national movements, in which the task of the proletariat was to merge the class struggle of the workers of the oppressing nations with the class struggle of the workers of the oppressed nations; and third, the semi-colonial countries (China, Persia, Turkey) and all the colonies, in which the Socialists must render determined support to the more revolutionary elements in the bourgeois-democratic movements for national liberation. For Russia, where according to Lenin 57 per cent of the population belonged to oppressed nations, "the recognition of the right of nations oppressed by Tsarism to free secession from Russia was absolutely obligatory for Social Democracy in the interests of its democratic and Socialist tasks."[4]

These ideas became singularly relevant after the Bolshevik accession to power in October 1917. Until then Lenin had made a battleground out of the problem of the national minorities within the Russian state, a battleground which he subsequently broadened to include the entire world colonial problem. Here again his own ideas were to become those of the Communist International, notwithstanding a certain amount of internal opposition, just as his earlier thesis about Russia's national minorities had met with some resistance from Marxist Social Democrats in Russia and elsewhere.

THE NATIONAL AND COLONIAL PROBLEM FROM NOVEMBER 7, 1917, UNTIL THE SECOND COMINTERN CONGRESS

Just as Lenin and his colleagues had not awaited the formal founding of the Communist International, in March 1919, before starting their activities in the international labor movement, they did not wait either to formalize their policy before taking action in the matter of the national minorities and colonialism. The theses on the subject were not adopted until the Second World Congress, in July and August of 1920. After seizing power in Petrograd, the Bolsheviks had envisaged their effort in this area as being directed at two main targets: the European peoples living in Western Russia, such as the Balts and Poles, and the Eastern peoples who were Russia's neighbors in Asia, such as the Turks and Persians. The policies framed at this time for the Bolshevik Party and Soviet government were to become those of the Communist International, and the first trusted key men then chosen by the Soviet government would later emerge as the leading figures in the different Communist parties and in high positions in the Comintern. Thus, shortly after the Bolshevik victory on November 7, 1917, Lenin and Stalin appointed the first commissars for the various national groups. They included Peter Stuchka, one of the founders of the Latvian Communist Party; Vikenti Mickievicz-Kapsukas, the co-founder of the Lithuanian Communist Party; Julian Leński-Leszczyński, later the secretary-general of the Polish Communist Party; Mustafa Subhi, the founder of Turkey's Communist Party and the only Turkish representative at the Comintern's founding congress; Sultan-Zade, the founder of the Iranian Communist Party; and Pak Chin-sun, the secretary-general of the Korean Socialist Party, founded in Soviet Russia in June 1918. All these commissars (with the exception of Subhi) later became members of the Comintern's Executive Committee, and Leszczyński even became a member of its Presidium. This continuity in the personnel selected to implement the policy toward different nationalities, and with regard to colonialism, was also characteristic of the ideas that they were supposed to put into practice.

Two of the earliest rulings of the new Soviet government, the Decree on Land and the Declaration of the Rights of the Peoples of Russia, adopted respectively on November 8 and 15, 1917, were of the highest theoretical as well as practical interest. The Declaration, signed by Lenin as chairman of the Council of People's Commissars, and Stalin, as People's Commissar of Nationality Affairs, solemnly proclaimed "the right of the peoples of Russia to free self-determination, even to the point of separation and the formation of an independent state."[5] By making such a promise the Bolsheviks put themselves immediately in a special political position vis-à-vis the non-Russians, and appeared as the only predominantly Russian party championing the non-Russians' claims to independence.[6] It was indeed the opening of a completely different perspective for the non-Russian nationalities living on both Russia's western and eastern confines, this promise of liberation from what many resented as the Russian "Prison of Nations." In accordance with the November 15 Declaration, separate national commissariats were gradually created uner the People's Commissariat of Nationality Affairs (Narkomnats) and their official role was to put into effect the principle of self-determination. In fact, if not legally, there existed two groups of national commissariats: those of the borderland nations of the West and those of the internal nationalities of Great Russia. In both instances these commissariats created bigger problems than anticipated.

The Western group was created first and from the outset played a more important role. The first national commissariats of that group—Polish, Latvian, Estonian, and Lithuanian—covered the countries more developed than Central Russia, with a more numerous industrial working class and the more experienced Social Democratic parties. The entire region, moreover, was considered, in accordance with the classical Marxist theory, as a link with the coming revolution in Central and Western Europe. The new commissars therefore—the Latvian Stuchka, the Lithuanian Kapsukas, and the Pole Leszczyński—persisted in their Marxist-Luxemburgist views and had difficulty accepting Lenin's ideas on the national and peasant questions.*

The Luxemburgist anti-national and cosmopolitan line of the "proletarian" Western national commissariats' leaders did not correspond to the general attitude of the majority of the inhabitants of Russia's "Western confines," who regarded favorably the principle of self-determination and aspired to separate themselves from their "foster-mother" country. To capitalize on such feelings, and despite opposition from Western national commissars, Stalin ordered on November 15, 1917 (old style) a "nationalization" of the army which he called "the free gathering of the fighters on the

---

*When Stalin proposed Leszczyński's nomination as the Polish Commissar at the People's commissars' meeting on November 24, 1917, Lenin objected on the ground of his "Luxemburgist" opinions (see *Leninskii Sbornik*, vol. 21, Moscow, 1933, p. 95, note 2; this document is not included in the fifth edition of Lenin's *Polnoe sobranie sochinenii*). In his book *Piat' mesiatsev sotsialisticheskoi sovetskoi Latvii* (Five Months of Socialist Soviet Latvia), published in 1919, Stuchka revealed that on doctrinal grounds he categorically refused to "self-determine" during the Brest-Litovsk negotiations; he complied, very reluctantly, only after the German defeat in the fall of 1918 (pp. 5-6 and 21). Kapsukas' general attitude was very similar—see his articles published during the year 1930 in the Polish Communist publication *Z Pola Walki* (From the Battlefield) which at that time was published in Moscow. Stalin's deputy People's Commissar, Pestkowski, also a Polish "Luxemburgist", publicly criticized (in May 1918, at the second conference of the Polish and Lithuanian Socialist groups in Russia) the theory of national self-determination, calling it "disastrous for the revolution and contrary to the principles of Marxism". In the reminiscences of his work, published in *Proletarskaia revoliutsia* (Moscow, No. 6, June 1930, pp. 130-31), Pestkowski wrote that at the meetings of the Commissariat's ruling body, he several times opposed official Soviet national politics "although I knew perfectly well that it was the line of Comrade Lenin and of the Party's Central Committee".

national principle ... within the limits of any military detachment."[7] The implication of that principle created problems, and Krylenko, who after the Bolshevik revolution assumed the supreme command of the Russian army, complained to Trotsky about the disintegrative effects of the formation of national troops, the Poles in particular. In answer, Trotsky re-emphasized the validity of the principle of national troops as an effective weapon in the struggle against the bourgeoisie, and insisted on providing "a solid and secure connection" between national regiments "in the persons of energetic and tactful commissars."[8] Still, the problem was not solved, and with the exception of the Letts, most of the national detachments did not remain faithful to the Bolshevik side.

Parallel with the Bolshevik work among the borderland nations of the West went propaganda efforts aimed at foreign Orientals. Hundreds of thousands of foreign citizens were living on Russian territory at the time of the October revolution. The most numerous were some 63,000 war prisoners, soldiers and officers of the Turkish army, scattered in different camps. Then came some fifty to sixty thousand Turkish nationals, living in the southern parts of Russia and interned for the duration of the war. Finally, there was a large number of Turkish migratory workers, especially in Turkestan. The second largest group of foreign workers was from Persia; in 1920 their number reached 100,000, mainly in Middle Asia. In the early 1920s, nearly 280,000 Chinese Moslems lived and worked in Turkestan, as did some 250,000 Koreans in the Russian Far East. "Thus, in 1917-1920 on the territory of Soviet Russia there resided no less than a million citizens from the contiguous Eastern countries."[9] These groups, like their Western counterparts (the Germans, the Austrians, the Hungarians, and the Yugoslavs), were natural targets of Bolshevik propaganda and of efforts to build Communist national organizations. Thus in July 1918 a conference of Turkish left-wing Socialists took place in Moscow, and there emerged, under the leadership of Mustafa Subhi, a central committee of the Turkish Socialists and Communists. It was the nucleus out of which a year and a half later the national Turkish Communist Party was born.[10] Iranian Communist groups were also established, in 1918 and 1919 in Astrakhan and Moscow, and in December 1918 a central committee of an All-Russian revolutionary organization of Chinese workers was set up in Moscow.* In October 1918 these groups produced a Union for the Liberation of the East, whose stated aim was to solidify a united anti-imperialist front and to head a struggle which would ultimately lead to a federal United States of Asia.[11]

But just as among the first Western Communists proclaiming their support of the Bolshevik revolution there were many who until the Second Comintern Congress had espoused political views and tactical approaches very different from those propounded by Lenin, the same was true among the first Eastern Communists. The conference of Turkish Revolutionary Socialists in 1918 was completely ignorant of the fundamental Bolshevik concepts of the struggle for national liberation and the need for a temporary alliance with the local bourgeoisie: "Underestimating the national-liberation character of the revolutionary movement in Turkey, the conference naturally rejected the idea of a temporary accomodation between the proletariat and the country's bourgeoisie designed to intensify the struggle against imperialism. The Turkish Socialist party, declared M. Subhi, had to sever its ties with capitalism and enter into no alliance with it."[12] On the other hand, these same first Eastern Communists often seemed to attach more importance to the military fact of the existence of a Red Army than to the political fact of a Communist party role in the revolutionary process. No doubt impressed by the teachings of recent history, namely that the most spectacular Bolshevik successes were primarily military, like the seizure of power in Petrograd on November 7 and the 1918 civil war victories, these Eastern Communists drew the obvious conclusion: the Red Army could do the same thing in their country and put the Communists in power.

*M. A. Persits, "Vostochnye internatsionalisty v Rossii i nekotorye voprosy natsionalno-osvoboditelnogo dvizheniia," in *Komintern i Vostok*, Moscow, 1969, p. 61. According to the author, "Not only Chinese, but also Soviet historians of the Chinese Communist Party, do not take sufficiently into account this circumstance when describing the initial stage of the Communist movement in China. Invariably they point to the fact that the first Chinese Communist groups appeared besides China also in Japan and in France, but do not mention the forming and active work of Chinese Communist cells in Soviet Russia." *Ibid.*, pp. 77-78.

This is why, as we learn from information from Comintern archives that came to light only in 1969, the Turkish delegation to
the First All-Russian Congress of Communist Organizations of
Eastern Peoples in November 1918 (known also as the first congress of the Moslem Communists) advocated forming Red Army
units, made up of Turkish Communists and former prisoners of
war, whose mission would be to concentrate first on the southern
front and then bring about a revolution in Turkey. [13]

Even while this first congress was in session, from November 4
to 12, 1918, a complete identity of views did not exist at the
Bolshevik Party summit either. In those days Lenin was entirely
preoccupied with his hope for an outbreak of revolution in Germany and Austria-Hungary. His time was so taken up that he did
not put in a single appearance at this First Congress of Communist
Organizations of Eastern Peoples, though he did manage, while it
was going on, to rush around and give speeches all over Moscow—
for example, at the sixth special congress of Soviets, at the official
trade union conference, at a workers' meeting at the old Michelson
factory, at the unveiling of a monument in memory of Marx and
Engels, at a general meeting of Cheka personnel, and at a conference of delegates representing impoverished peasants. Stalin, however, did attend that first congress, giving proof that, unlike Lenin
and the other Bolshevik Politburo members, his gaze was not fixed
solely on the expected revolution in the West. While the congress
was in session, in the first issue of *Zhizn natsionalnostei*, the official weekly paper of Narkomnats, dated November 9, 1918, he
wrote an editorial (a slightly different version of which was published in *Pravda* of November 6 and 19) in which under the heading "The Worldwide Significance of the October Upheaval" he
declared: "The October revolution is the first revolution in world
history to break the age-old sleep of the laboring masses of the
oppressed peoples of the East and to draw them into the fight
against world imperialism. The formation of workers' and peasants' soviets in Persia, China, and India, modelled on the soviets in
Russia, is sufficiently convincing evidence of this." [14] A few weeks
later, on December 1, in an editorial in the same paper, entitled
"Don't Forget the East," he was even more explicit: "At the time
when the revolutionary movement is rising in Europe . . . the eyes

of all are naturally turned to the West. . . . At such a moment one
'involuntarily' tends to lose sight of, to forget, the far-off East,
with its hundreds of millions of inhabitants enslaved by imperialism. Yet the East should not be forgotten for a single moment, if
only because it represents the 'inexhaustible' reserve and 'most
reliable' rear of world imperialism. . . . For the truth must be
grasped once and for all that whoever desires the triumph of
Socialism must not forget the East."*

When he addressed the First Congress of the Communist Organizations of Eastern Peoples on November 11, 1918, Stalin emphasized above all the absolute necessity of a united front between
the revolution in the West and the Eastern revolution: "Our duty
is to build a bridge between the peoples of the West and of the
East and, having created the united front of the revolution, to
break the ring of imperialism which encircles us. However, nobody
would be able to complete this greatest of historical tasks easier
and with less pain than you, the Moslem Communists. Nobody
will be able to build a bridge between West and East so easily and
so quickly as you, because the gates of Persia, and India, Afghanistan, and China are open for you." On behalf of the Central
Committee he then advised the congress that in order to achieve
"the greatest closeness of our forces" all the Moslem Communist
organizations must be united into a "unique section of the Russian
Communist Party with the Section's Bureau at the head."[15]

The First All-Russian Congress of Communist Organizations of
Eastern Peoples had in fact a twofold aim: to implement in practice the principle of democratic centralism with respect to the
deviationist-prone Moslem Communists and to enable them more
effectively to spread revolutionary ideas among the peoples of the
East. The first purpose was served by electing a Central Bureau of
the Moslem Organizations of the Russian Communist Party under
the leadership of Stalin himself. The former Department of Inter-

*Zhizn natsionalnostei, No. 3, November 24, 1918. Also in Stalin's Works,
vol. 4, Moscow, 1953, pp. 174 and 176. In the same vein Stalin wrote an
editorial under the significant title "Light from the East," published simultaneously on December 15, in both Zhizn natsionalnostei and Pravda, cf.
Works, vol. 4, pp. 181 and 185-86. In this article he put at the opposite poles
"the West with its imperialist cannibals . . . a breeding ground of darkness and
slavery" and "the light . . . coming from the East."

national Propaganda for the Eastern Peoples was reorganized, with Mustafa Subhi* in charge, as the Bureau's specialized propaganda vehicle. In order to carry out its activities (its aim was explained as "gradually bringing the revolutionary masses to an understanding of the idea of world communism") the Department was divided into twelve sections: Arab, Persian, Turkish, Azerbaijani, Bukharan, Kirghiz, (Caucasus) Mountaineers', Kalmuk, Chinese, Korean, Japanese, and Indian. For all these sections one headquarters, with one common office, was foreseen.†

The holding of the first congress of Moslem Communists came shortly before a more significant political reorganization which took place during the preparations for the founding congress of the Communist International, and was sanctioned by the Eighth Congress of the Bolshevik party. During the preparatory sessions for this congress, at which the setting up of the Third International was treated (according to an editorial in *Zhizn natsionalnostei* of February 2, 1919), the problem of the organizational structure of the Russian party arose in connection with the existence of several "national," domestic and foreign, "groups" and "sections" which had been created inside the Russian party and were supposed to take part in the Eighth Congress. It was decided to accomplish a sort of a division of labor, passing all the foreign groups over to a new international organization. Thus the new Central Bureau of Communist Organizations of Eastern Peoples was

---

*The necessity for the reorganization of the Moslem Communist work was explained in the congress' resolution by the incompetence of the former leaders who "led the Moslem proletariat to Communism unskillfully and without a definite plan." *Zhizn natsionalnostei*, No. 3, November 24, 1918. In 1921, after Subhi's death, Sultan-Galiev indicated in an article that Subhi in 1918-19 had to work under adverse political conditions: "For a long time, he was obliged to work in an atmosphere of mistrust and suspicion. This terribly depressed him." "Mustafa Subhi and his Work," *Ibid.*, No. 14 (112), July 16, 1921. As the future would show what Sultan-Galiev wrote about Subhi could also have been an anticipated autobiographical note!

†*Zhizn natsionalnostei*, No. 5 (13), February 16, 1919. The official report of the Central Bureau of the Moslem Organizations, submitted to the Eighth Congress of the Bolshevik Party, in March 1919, mentions ten sections of the Department of International Propaganda—the nine sections mentioned above, minus the Japanese and Indian, but plus the Tatar. *Vos'moi s"ezd RKP(b)*, Moscow, 1959, p. 498.

established absorbing also the previously existing Union for the Liberation of the East. Some of its representatives had been admitted (with a few votes) to the First Comintern Congress. They were divided into two groups, the "domestic" and the "foreign." The former, officially called the United Group of the Eastern Tribes of Russia, composed of Yalimov, Bekentayev, Altimirov, Mansurov, and Kasimov, represented the Bashkirs, the Kirghizians, the Tatars, and the Caucasians, and were given jointly one deliberative vote. The latter, representing the sections of the Central Bureau of the Eastern Peoples—Subhi, Shgenti, Bagirow, and Husseinow, in the name of the Turkish, Georgian, Azerbaijan, and Persian Communists—had consultative votes only. The congress also admitted, with a consultative vote each, a representative of the Chinese Socialist Labor Party and the Korean Workers' League, though Chicherin, the chairman of the credentials committee at the congress, explained that the Chinese and Korean delegates belonged to the émigré groups of Chinese and Korean workers living on Russian soil. [16]

All these delegates played a minimal role at the congress, although Yalimov and Subhi made use of the occasion to deliver brief speeches insisting on the necessity of "building revolutionary centers among the peoples of the East." [17] The main thrust of the congress' manifesto, drafted by Trotsky, was contained in the following sentences which clearly indicated the Comintern's initial "Western orientation": "The liberation of the colonies is possible only in conjunction with the liberation of the metropolitan working class. The workers and peasants not only of Annam, Algiers, and Bengal, but also of Persia and Armenia, will gain their opportunity of independent existence only when the workers of England and France have overthrown Lloyd George and Clemenceau and taken state power into their own hands. . . . Colonial slaves of Africa and Asia! The hour of proletarian dictatorship in Europe will also be the hour of your own liberation!" [18]

This subordination of the East to the West was also visible in the establishment of the first Comintern leadership: none of the Eastern representatives were taken into the Executive Committee of the International. On the other hand, Subhi submitted to the congress a "Short Report of the Central Bureau of Communist Organizations of Eastern Peoples." It was said in the report that the Bureau represented the non-Russian Communists of Turkestan, Bashkiria, the Volga-Tatar region, Kirghizia, and the Caucasus, as well as the Communist émigré groups from Turkey, Persia, Azerbaijan, Bukhara and Georgia. The Bureau was publishing fifteen newspapers in different languages and considered "the awakening of the peoples of the East" its main task.[19]

Deliberations and decisions of the Eighth Bolshevik Congress (March 18-23, 1919) had another important aspect: they represented a definite break with the religious (Moslem) organizational basis. From that time on, no difference between the Moslem and non-Moslem "peoples of the East" was tolerated: "Any mentioning of Islam was henceforth prohibited. Even the principle of *Moslem unity*, the very basis of Sultan-Galiev's doctrine, was indicted."[20]

As all these meetings and reorganizations took place, revolutionary attempts in Berlin and Munich failed, the Hungarian Soviet Republic collapsed, the soviet regimes in several countries formerly members of the Tsarist empire, such as Finland and the Baltic states, were liquidated, and nowhere else did revolutionary attempts show any promise of success. All this did not lead Lenin to abandon the idea of the coming revolution in the West, but it certainly moved him to consider the revolutionary potential which the East offered. Consequently, he showed an increasing interest in Soviet Eastern policy. He drafted the decision to send in October 1919 a special Turkestan Commission to Tashkent and he addressed a special message to the Communists of Turkestan. He played a major role at the Second All-Russian Congress of Communist Organizations of Eastern Peoples (Moscow, November 22-December 3, 1919), gave an important speech at that occasion, and crossed swords with a particularly qualified spokesman for the Eastern revolutionary approach, Sultan-Galiev.*

*Mizra Sultan-Galiev, born in the 1880s, was a Volga Tatar by origin and had been a Communist since the end of 1917. In the second half of 1918 he became a close collaborator of Stalin in the Commissariat of Nationality Affairs; in December of the same year he was promoted to the post of chairman of the Commissariat's Central Moslem Military College. This and other official functions made him at that time the most prominent Moslem in the entire Soviet hierarchy. Some of his ideas, however, at first supported by Moscow, later led him into conflict with the Bolshevik leadership. Thus, Sultan-Galiev favored political autonomy for Moslem Communists, advocated the establishment of a separate Moslem Red Army, and worked toward the creation of a large Soviet Moslem autonomous republic in the Volga-Ural region. (On March 22, 1918, the Commissariat of Nation-

No verbatim proceedings or detailed reports on the debates at this congress were published, and in general it was not given great publicity. The Moscow press, for example, wrote much more about the conference on the work in the countryside than on the Moslem Communist congress. *Zhizn natsionalnostei*, on the other hand, devoted a considerable amount of space to the congress, particularly in its issues of December 7 and 21, but its reporting showed a tendency to be extremely cautious in revealing any controversy at the congress debates. That such a controversy existed was obvious from a *Pravda* editorial of November 26, in which the Moslem communists were rebuked for being preoccupied with "establishing at home autonomous republics on the national-territorial" principle instead of concentrating on their international tasks. The congress was opened on November 22 by Stalin in the presence of some 80 to 100 delegates, and began under the chairmanship of Sultan-Galiev.† Lenin delivered his report at the first session, drawing a general picture of the situation and balancing his older and primary concern for a victorious revolution in the

ality Affairs, at Stalin's recommendation, published a decree which announced the forthcoming founding of a Tatar-Bashkir soviet republic; it never became a reality, but it indicated an early disposition of Russian Bolsheviks to play a national-autonomist, "Moslem," game.) Moreover, as just mentioned, Sultan-Galiev did not see eye to eye with Lenin on the matter of the Comintern's revolutionary strategy, and later, in 1921, he even advocated the creation of a Colonial International to counterbalance what he saw as the Comintern's Western orientation. Early in 1923 he was arrested, and in June of the same year, at a special conference of representatives of minorities convened in Moscow, he was accused by Stalin himself of various nationalist-Moslem deviations. Despite his official repentance, he was expelled from the Communist party and disappeared in 1930. See Richard Pipes, *The Formation of the Soviet Union. Communism and Nationalism. 1917-1923*. Revised edition, New York, 1968, pp. 168-170; 260-262. See also Serge A. Zenkovsky, *Pan Turkism and Islam in Russia*, Cambridge, Mass., 1960, p. 176 and chapter XII; Alexandre Bennigsen and Chantal Quelquejay, *Les mouvements nationaux chez les Musulmans de Russie. Le "Sultangalievisme" au Tatarstan*, Paris-The Hague, 1960, especially chapters II and III of the second part.

† According to an article in *Zhizn natsionalnostei* of December 7, the congress was attended by "about 100 delegates representing the organized Moslem proletariat in the ranks of the Russian Communist Party, consisting of some 60,000 members." Later, the number of delegates was reduced to 80 (cf. Stalin, *Works*, vol. 4, p. 446, note 79) or "71 delegates with decisive and 11 with consultative vote" (cf. Lenin, *Polnoe sobranie sochinenii*, 5th ed., vol. 39, p. 515, note 118).

West by adding an Eastern component. [21] He restated his well known viewpoint that "we are witnessing in Western Europe the decomposition of imperialism. . . . Everyone knows that the social revolution is maturing in Western Europe by leaps and bounds, and that the same thing is happening in America and in Britain." The novelty, this time, was Lenin's elaboration on the theme of the struggle of "backward peoples of the East" and the coordination of the "pure-proletarian movement with revolutionizing the backward peasant masses." He stressed the "colossal and global significance for all the peoples of the East" of the accomplishments of the Red Army, but he warned his listeners of the peculiarities of Communist work in the East and the necessity to adapt the general theory of Communism to "conditions in which the majority of the population are peasants, and in which the task is to wage a struggle not against capitalism but against medieval relics." Justifying the awakening of bourgeois nationalism in backward countries and urging those in the attendance to "base yourselves on bourgeois nationalism" while preparing the masses for the future victory of the international revolution, Lenin concluded: "It goes without saying that only the proletariat of all the world's advanced countries can win final victory. . . . But they cannot triumph without the help of the toiling masses of all the oppressed colonial peoples, especially those of the East." [22]

Lenin, however, met a strategic challenge at the same congress in the person and through the arguments of Sultan-Galiev. Galiev, in opposition to what was then the official Bolshevik party and Comintern line, insisted that the East would play the leading role in the world revolutionary process, declaring: "The East is a revolutionary cauldron capable of putting a revolutionary torch to all of Western Europe." [23] On November 27, in the dispute over the primacy of "East or West," the congress passed a compromise resolution purporting to grant equal importance to both, holding that "the Third International is obliged to proclaim that the national liberation movement in the East and the social revolution [going on in the West] are presently pursuing the same common goal, namely that of throwing off the yoke of the capitalist imperialists." [24]

Lenin also took part in other controversies of the congress

which were carefully hidden at that time. S. Said-Galiev,* in
1925, revealed that there were "not unimportant differences of
opinion among the participants of the congress, the Tatars and
Bashkirs in particular," and that the resolution on the Tatar-
Bashkir Republic, once more proposed by Sultan-Galiev, regardless of the attitude of the preparatory conference and *Pravda's*
editorial, was adopted by "an insignificant majority." According
to Said-Galiev, the differences among the congress' members had
been transferred to a special meeting of a group of congress
delegates with the members of the Russian Communist Party
Central Committee, with Lenin at its chair. "The nationalist
speakers" spoke fervently and at length; Lenin intervened for
the sake of the minority, and, on Stalin's proposal, the meeting
decided to revoke the decree of March 22, 1918, on which the
congress resolution was based.†

The conflict between the Tatars and the Bashkirs was not the
last one to disturb the congress. The problem of relations of the
Communist organizations of "non-Russian tongue" to the general
Russian organizational setup was also discussed during the four-
day sessions of the congress, and the articles by Al-Harizi in *Zhizn
natsionalnostei*, "On the Results of the Congress of the Peoples of
the East," [25] clearly indicated, despite the author's cautious ex-
pressions, that all the delegates did not see eye to eye on this
subject. The core of the problem was the method of establishing
"national" Communist centers: either their members should be
elected from the bottom, that is locally, or nominated from the
top by central party authorities. The latter method, proposed by
the Bolshevik Central Committee, was criticized by Al-Harizi as
being "bureaucratic" and sapping the confidence in the party in

---

*Not to be confused with Sultan-Galiev, S. Said-Galiev was in 1918 the
head of the leftist faction of Tatar Communists, and after the establishment of the Tatar Autonomous Socialist Soviet Republic in September
1920, he became the chairman of the Tatar Council of People's Commissars. He lost his life in 1939, during Stalin's purges.

†*Proletarskaia revoliutsia*, No. 9, 1925, p. 111. The problem was finally
solved by the creation, in the fall of 1920, of the separate Tatar and Bashkir Autonomous Socialist Soviet Republics. The dream of a large, national-
ly autonomous, Moslem-dominated state in the Volga-Ural region was definitively buried, and replaced by a very different concept of "Soviet
autonomy" in the increasingly centripetal Bolshevik practice.

the eyes of Communists of different nationalities. Fearing that "the most undesirable results" could follow, Al-Harizi went on to emphasize the importance and peculiarities of the East:

> The majority of humanity lives in the East and they are still little touched by capitalism. . . . To start in the East an agitation on behalf of the Russian Communist Party would be to condemn ourselves in advance to failure. Our enemies will immediately present us as Russian imperialists of the old type, from former times. The unique possibility of approaching them is via the Communists among the peoples of the East or Moslems. . . . The Tatar Communists who are numerous enough, and Moslem comrades from the Baku region should be used in maximal number. . . . It is a pity that, until today, the Third Communist International does not have a good Eastern division, and still waits for its workers. It will be necessary to concentrate all the work in the Central Bureau of the Eastern Peoples.[26]

Immediate organization of the revolutionary forces of colonies and semi-colonial capitalist states was strongly urged in two separate resolutions, both connected with Lenin's report and drafted by Sultan-Galiev.[27] Among the second resolution's ten theses, the most important one concerned the establishment of Communist parties in the Eastern countries as sections of the Third International, and the necessity to "assist until a certain moment the Eastern national movement which aims to abolish the power of Western European imperialism." Still, thesis number six stated that "all the revolutionary work in the East must be performed in the already existing and in the future soviet republics of the Eastern peoples." The building up of an Eastern Red Army and the training of Red commanders among the proletarians of the Eastern peoples were advocated.* The congress closed on December 3, after having elected a Central Bureau of seven members and seven deputy members, including Sultan-Galiev.

---

*According to the Soviet historian M. A. Persits, Lenin was "resolutely opposed" to the idea of a Moslem army. Persits quotes M. V. Frunze, the chief commander of the Red Army in Turkestan in January 1920, who had discussed that topic with Lenin, with the latter's conclusion that "one cannot even talk about it." *Loc. cit.*, p. 95.

LENIN AND THE ELABORATION OF THESES
ON THE NATIONAL AND COLONIAL QUESTIONS

Although there is no doubt that Lenin watched carefully the complex evolution of national-colonial problems after the fall of 1919, in the first half of 1920 he seldom intervened in these problems directly. On February 2, in his more than twenty-page report on the activities of the Soviet government to the Central Executive Committee of Soviets, less than one page was devoted to the question of the East. Moreover, he stated that "our policy in the East must be still more cautious and patient, for here we are dealing with nations that are much more backward; they are under the oppressive influence of religious fanatics and imbued with the greatest distrust of the Russian people."[28] On February 18, answering the questions of a Berlin correspondent for an American information agency, Lenin spoke about the "awakening of Asia" and stressed that the Soviet plans in Asia were the same as in Europe: "Peaceful coexistence with the peoples, with the workers and peasants of all nations that are awakening to a new life, a life without exploitation, without landlords, without capitalists, without merchants."[29] On March 1, in a speech at a congress of "toiling Kozaks," Lenin treated the question of imperialism and said: "The number of our allies in all countries is growing, though much slower than we would wish but growing just the same. . . . In every country, even in India where 300 millions live in British bondage, an awakening of political consciousness and the revolutionary movement grows from day to day. All these peoples have their eyes fixed on one star: the star of the Soviet Republic."[30]

However, in his speech at the first anniversary celebration of the Comintern, on March 6, Lenin did not mention explicitly the question of revolution in the East but repeated his old belief in revolution unfolding in the West: "Europe is going to the revolution not in the way we have gone, but as a matter of fact Europe is doing the same."[31] Neither the prospects of revolution in the East nor the national-colonial question in general had been extensively treated at the Ninth Congress of the Bolshevik Party (March 29 to April 5). However, after that congress, in May and June, spectacular developments took place in the East—the occupation by the Red Army of Baku and Enzeli, the proclamation of the

Azerbaijani and Kuchuk Soviet governments, and British military and diplomatic retreat; in the West the Red Army's offensive began and Kiev was reached by the middle of June. Thus, the question of the East in particular, and the national-colonial question in general, became of the greatest importance, as illustrated by the works of the Second Comintern Congress.

The process of elaboration and adoption of the theses on the national and colonial questions stretched over the months of June and July 1920 and was accomplished in several phases. In the first, Lenin drafted the theses and circulated his draft to various individuals whose opinion he valued. In the second, he decided,after his discussion with M. N. Roy, to have him draw up some additional theses, which he, Lenin, would then review and edit. In the third, Lenin, at the congress, chaired the committee on the national and colonial questions and steered its debates. In the final phase, when the theses came up for discussion at the plenary session of the congress, he appeared on the platform personally as the first and main speaker in their support.

After making a few notes and roughing out a draft, in one sitting on June 5 he dashed off the entire initial version of the theses, which consisted of twelve main points, divided into three categories. Category one, covering the first three points, was devoted to refuting the claims of bourgeois democracy and its lies and hypocrisy concerning the national question. Category two, embracing the next five points, presented the solution to the problem, the one conceived and being proposed by the Bolshevik party. Category three, taking in the final four points and which took up more space than the first two categories put together, laid down the ideas and policies that were to guide Communist action with regard to the whole business. As Lenin wrote, "It is also necessary, first, to demonstrate ceaselessly that the Soviet system alone can effectively ensure equality among nations . . . and, second, that all Communist parties must give direct aid to the revolutionary movements in the dependent countries or among peoples not enjoying equal rights (for example, the Irish, the American Negroes, etc.), and in the colonies." [32] Farther on, at the end of point eleven, he listed among the requirements for Communist action: "The Communist International must conclude a temporary alliance with the bourgeois democrats in the colonies and backward countries, yet must not merge with them or fail firmly to maintain proletarian freedom of action, however rudimentary."[33] This simple sentence at the end of the theses was to become, the very next month, the official creed that would guide the acts of all sections of the Comintern until its administrative death and even after its technical burial.

That same day Lenin sent his draft around to certain other of the Communist leaders, asking for their views and suggested improvements. Not until forty-three years later, when the fifth edition of his complete works was published, did we learn the names of those individuals. His choice of "advisers" was doubly characteristic. First, only one foreign Communist was included, the Bulgarian Nedelkov-Shablin, partly because by June 5 the foreign delegates had not yet arrived for the Second World Congress, though many Polish, Baltic, and other non-Russian Communists keenly interested in the problem but suspect in Lenin's eyes of "Luxemburgism" were in Russia at the time. Second, virtually none of the old or new Bolsheviks consulted belonged to the Comintern apparatus, holding instead positions in the party and government hierarchy: G. Chicherin, N. Krestinsky, J. Stalin, M. Rafes, E. Preobrazhensky, S. Lapiński, and several leaders from Bashkiria, Kirghizia, and Turkestan.[34] From the very sparse information made available in 1963 and 1968 it would appear that three of the most important Bolsheviks consulted, Chicherin, Stalin, and Preobrazhensky, did not hesitate to express their disagreement. Chicherin objected to the thesis obliging Communists to support national liberation movements and make alliances with the local bourgeoisie in the backward countries. He wrote: "Making an alliance with the local bourgeoisie is perfectly all right, but only among oppressed peoples faced with the task of eliminating a home-grown feudalism supported by the bayonets of an oppressor nation, as in Persia. Especially among the Persians is it appropriate for the workers and bourgeoisie to join forces to rid themselves of the unbearable yoke of their feudal lords, who have sold out to the British."[35] Preobrazhensky also attacked the Lenin theses laying down the Communist policy to be followed in the colonial countries. After pointing out that "it is wrong to exaggerate the revolutionary importance of the nationalist uprisings in the colonies," he drew a historical parallel: "The commerce-oriented bourgeoisie and intellectual upper crust in the economically backward countries inevitably aspire to solve the national problem in pretty much the same framework that the big bourgeois powers used in setting up their nation states."[36] From this theoretical parallel he drew a practical conclusion concerning the future relationship between the Socialist Europe about to be born and the colonial and dependent countries: "If the possibility of economic agreement with the leading nationalist groups gets ruled out, repression by force and forced annexation of the important economic regions into the Union of European Republics will become inevitable until the workers among several of the peoples, liberated from their bourgeois masters, bring to the fore a group capable of holding power on a basis of federation with Europe."[37] In support of this idea, Preobrazhensky suggested that Lenin modify point eleven of his theses; like Chicherin, he got nowhere. Finally, Stalin had a word to say in opposition to article seven, which spoke of a federation (albeit transitory, only to solve the national problem) involving relations between Soviet Russia and the other independent Soviet republics (Finland, Hungary, Latvia, and the Ukraine) and those between Russia and the autonomous republics within its borders (Bashkiria, Tatary, and others). In his reply to Lenin on June 12, Stalin declared that actually this difference between the independent republics and the autonomous republics, supposedly representing two distinct types of federation, "either does not exist at all, or is so small as to equal zero."[38] Again, Lenin was not moved. (When Stalin advanced the same idea two years later, Lenin criticized it both in a published article and in a letter to members of the Politburo.)

But if Lenin ignored the objections raised by some of his long-time companions and members of the Bolshevik Central Committee, he did listen a few days later to criticisms offered by a man whom he had just met, M. N. Roy, a new convert to Marxism who knew next to nothing about Bolshevism. When Lenin had encountered opposition within Tsarist Russia (from the Bund, Polish Marxists, and others) concerning his ideas on the national problem, he had yielded nothing to his gainsayers, convinced that he understood the problem far better than they did. But in the person of this young Indian, Roy, Lenin found himself confronted not with a critic on the national issue but on the colonial question, an area in which he lacked the personal knowledge that he had about affairs in Russia and Europe in general. He admitted this to

Roy at their first meeting, when he handed him the draft of his theses: "Lenin . . . proceeded to plead his ignorance of the conditions in the colonial countries. Therefore, he needed my cooperation in the preparation of a document which was destined to be a landmark in the history of the revolutionary movement." [39] The Lenin-Roy meeting had two direct consequences for the theses to be presented to the congress. Firstly, the Theses on the National and Colonial Questions, as they were entitled on the congress agenda, became only the Theses on the Colonial Question. The national question was dropped both from Roy's supplementary theses and from the subsequent committee discussions and debates at the plenary session. Throughout those debates an important aspect of the national question was passed over in silence, namely what the Communist policy would be in Europe's multi-national countries (such as Czechoslovakia, Yugoslavia, and Poland), a problem that was to plague the Comintern in the years ahead. Secondly, in contrast to what happened with the other theses (such as those on the role of the party, parliamentarianism, the trade unions, and the agrarian issue, to which no amendments were accepted by the congress despite the criticism voiced by many delegates), when it came to the Theses on the National and Colonial Questions, Lenin first offered to Roy the privilege of drafting the complementary theses and getting them accepted by the congress—something without a precedent and without a repetition in other Comintern congresses of Lenin's era.

As in the case of Sultan-Galiev's disagreement with Lenin seven months earlier, Roy—another spokesman for the Eastern cause and strategy—after having read Lenin's theses, and after his first conversation with the Bolshevik leader in July 1920, immediately put his finger on the main point of difference:

I disagreed with his view that the nationalist bourgeoisie played a historically revolutionary role and therefore should be supported by the Communists. The Polish Communists of the Luxemburg school used to remark in jest that I was a true Communist, while Lenin was a nationalist. . . . In the capitalist countries, there were Communist parties which could be helped with the confidence that they were dedicated to the cause of social revolution. But in the colonial countries similar instruments for revolution were absent. How then could the Communist

International develop the national liberation movement there as part of the world proletarian revolution?

Lenin's answer to my question appeared to me to be based on ignorance of the relation of social forces in the colonial countries. In our first discussion, he frankly admitted his ignorance of facts, but took his stand on theoretical grounds. . . . Historically, the national liberation movement had the significance of the bourgeois democratic revolution. Every stage of social evolution being historically determined, the colonial countries must have their bourgeois democratic revolution before they could enter the stage of the proletarian revolution. [40]

Lenin and Roy had several private discussions together, which culminated in Lenin's inviting Roy to draft an alternative set of theses for the committee on national and colonial questions, to which Roy responded with a counteroffer: "I agreed to formulate my critical notes and positive ideas in a document, which, I insisted, should be presented not as alternative but as supplementary theses. Lenin agreed, remarking that we were exploring new ground and should withhold final judgement pending practical experience." [41]

After Roy drafted his theses, of which he had only two copies, he kept one for himself and the next day took the other to Lenin, who made some deletions, specifically where Roy's hostility toward bourgeois nationalism in colonial countries got the better of him. In article four of his theses, Roy had stressed the need for the Comintern to establish close relations with the revolutionary forces in the economically and politically oppressed countries, maintaining that the ultimate success of the world revolution depended on common action by East and West (which was in line with the thesis adopted at the Second All-Russian Congress of Communist Organizations of the Eastern Peoples). But in the next article he elaborated a point of view of his own, which conflicted with Lenin's: "This alliance of the Communist International with the revolutionary movement in the oppressed countries does not signify support for the doctrine of nationalism." [42] Lenin simply struck this out. Roy's seventh thesis was the key one, for in it he exposed—as Lenin had not—the paradox of having two different movements in the colonial countries, one bourgeois nationalist, the other revolutionary Socialist, with the first seeking and gaining control over the second. Roy not only opposed this control, as did

Lenin, but he opposed virtually any joint action by Communists and nationalists: "The Communist International must not seek among the bourgeois nationalist elements any aid or support for the revolutionary movements in the colonies. The mass movement there is growing up independently of the nationalist movement."[43] That, too, Lenin struck out, as he did Roy's two final theses, ten and eleven, one of which depicted the national democratic bourgeoisie and the mass of peasants and workers as two hostile forces that could never work together. This last deletion cut the Roy theses from the original eleven down to nine.

That done, the private debate between Lenin and Roy ended, but a new controversy flared between them before the committee on national and colonial questions, of which Lenin was chairman and Maring (Sneevliet) secretary. On July 25 the committee met from morning until night, and witnessed again differences between Lenin and Roy, notwithstanding the supplementary theses drafted by Roy and "edited" by Lenin. At the meeting Roy gave a report about India (which he had been away from since 1914), but he went beyond purely Indian problems and threw in some remarks that rekindled his dispute with Lenin concerning the role of the national bourgeoisie. First, concerning India he said: "India has the ingredients necessary for the formation of a strong Communist party. But the revolutionary movement there, insofar as the broad masses of the people are concerned, has nothing in common with the national-liberation movement."[44] He urged the necessity for eliminating from Lenin's eleventh thesis the paragraph proclaiming it essential for all Communist parties to assist the bourgeois democratic liberation movement in the Eastern countries. Finally, he took issue with the Western perspective of the world revolution and offered an Eastern one in its place. As it was reported in the committee proceedings: "Comrade Roy maintains that the revolution in Europe depends utterly on the course of the revolution in the East. Unless revolution triumphs in the Eastern countries, the Communist movement in the West may fall apart. World capitalism draws its main resources and income from the colonies, primarily from Asia. . . . It is therefore essential to fuel the revolutionary movement in the East, and adopt as a fundamental thesis that the fate of world Communism depends on the victory of Communism in the East."[45]

This viewpoint was firmly resisted by Lenin, who replied: "The

Hindu Communists must support the bourgeois democratic movement without merging with it. Comrade Roy goes too far when he says that the fate of the West depends entirely on the development and strength of the revolutionary movement in the Eastern countries. Though India has five million proletarians and thirty-seven million landless peasants, the Hindu Communists still haven't succeeded in forming a Communist party in that country, a fact which by itself cuts much of the ground from under Comrade Roy's opinions." [46]

Again, it was not the Lenin theses that were changed, but the supplementary theses offered by Roy. His points 3, 4, 7, and 8 were edited into line with the views expressed by Lenin in his version. On July 26, as main speaker and spokesman for the committee on national and colonial questions, Lenin mounted the rostrum to deliver to the congress his address on the subject, which he began with this statement: "Our committee has unanimously adopted the original theses, with the amendments and supplementary theses. In this way we have arrived at complete unanimity on all the important questions." [47] He obviously had no wish to have displayed there at the plenary session the persisting differences of opinion, or to spark any resumption of the controversy.

THE NATIONAL AND COLONIAL QUESTIONS
AT THE SECOND COMINTERN CONGRESS

Taken globally, the contingent of Eastern and colonial representatives, both domestic and foreign, at the Second Comintern Congress, was far from impressive. Out of a total of 218 delegates attending the congress (169 with full votes, and 49 with consultative votes) there were 25 "Easterners." Eight regions and countries, with 17 representatives, had full votes: Azerbaijan, Armenia, Georgia, Turkey, Persia, Korea, the Dutch East Indies, and Mexico.* Five regions and countries, with eight representatives, had

---

*The inclusion of Mexico among the Eastern countries is to be explained by the role M. N. Roy played at the Second Comintern Congress as a delegate of the Mexican Communist Party. In fact, Roy had settled in Mexico in 1917, where he later met Mikhail Borodin, the first Comintern emissary in North America. Roy took part in the founding of the Mexican Communist Party in September 1919, and the next year he and his wife went to Soviet Russia by the way of Berlin.

consultative votes: Bukhara, Persia, India, China, and Mexico. The
strongest single national delegation was the Russian one, with 69
members (64 with full votes). [48] The commission on national and
colonial questions had 20 members, six of whom came from Eastern or colonial countries: Maring (Dutch East Indies), Roy (Mexico), Allen (India), Sultan-Zade (Persia), Slavucky (Turkey), Lan
Sin-dzan (China), and Pak Chin-sun (Korea). The Western orientation of the Comintern was also obvious from the reports of Communist activities submitted to the congress: 30 reports dealt with
the European countries, two with the American continent (reports
on the United States and on Argentina), and five with Asia (Dutch
East Indies, Japan, China, Korea, and Armenia). [49]

This "Western" preoccupation of the congress was corrected,
however, by Lenin's analyses contained in his report on the international situation and the fundamental tasks of the Communist
International, offered on July 19, and in his report of the commission on national and colonial questions, delivered on July 26. The
first report presented a global picture of the maturing world revolution. Repeating his well-known views about the expansion and
contradictions of imperialism, and quoting profusely from Keynes'
The Economic Consequences of Peace as proof that after the
Peace of Versailles Europe and the world were headed for bankruptcy, Lenin claimed that 1,250 million persons, or 70 per cent
of the world's population, were living under colonial subjugation,
with only 250 million benefiting from that state of affairs. He
described the "staggering national debts" in the victor countries,
the "incredible impoverishment of the masses," and the "enormous disparities between wages and prices," and concluded that
the "mechanism of world capitalism is falling apart." He justified
the calling of the congress a "world" congress because it was attended by representatives of the revolutionary movements in the
colonial and backward countries. Their participation was "only a
small beginning," but Lenin saw its importance as the sign of a
"union between revolutionary proletarians of the capitalist, advanced countries, and the revolutionary masses of those countries
where there is no or hardly any proletariat, that is, the oppressed
masses of colonial, Eastern countries." He added that "one of the
most important tasks now confronting us is to consider how the
foundation-stone of the organization of the Soviet movement can

be laid in the *non*-capitalist countries." He ended his report insisting once again that "we are more and more becoming representatives and genuine defenders of this 70 per cent of the world's population, this mass of working and exploited people."[50]

Such was the general framework of the world situation into which Lenin inserted his report of the commission on national and colonial questions. He began by stating that the "cardinal idea" underlying these theses was the "distinction between oppressed and oppressor nations." The second basic idea was that the most important political reality in the world was "the struggle waged by a small group of imperialist nations against the Soviet movement and the Soviet states headed by Soviet Russia." Thirdly, he emphasized the question of the "bourgeois-democratic movement in backward countries" and stated that by the commission's unanimous decision instead of a "bourgeois-democratic" movement in these countries one should speak of the "national-revolutionary" movements. He explained the change of terminology by an essential political consideration: "We, as Communists, should and will support bourgeois-liberation movements in the colonies only when they are genuinely revolutionary, and when their exponents do not hinder our work of educating and organizing in a revolutionary spirit the peasantry and the masses of the exploited."[51]

Lenin's commission report then turned to the question of Communist tactics and policy in countries with pre-capitalist conditions, with no industrial proletariat and no purely proletarian movement. Taking as an example the Russian Communists' work in Turkestan, Lenin explained that the idea of peasants' soviets was applicable to feudal and semi-feudal conditions and that "the backward countries can emerge from their present stage of development when the victorious proletariat of the Soviet Republics extends a helping hand to these masses and is in a position to give them support." The essential conclusion of the commission was that the backward peoples must not inevitably go through the capitalist stage of development. Therefore, "The Communist International should advance the proposition, with the appropriate theoretical grounding, that with the aid of the proletariat of the advanced countries, backward countries can go over to the Soviet system and, through certain stages of development, to Communism, without having to pass through the capitalist stage."[52] After the modifications made first by Lenin and then by the commission, Roy's supplementary theses contained nothing that contradicted Lenin's, though their emphasis was more pronouncedly Eastern and revolutionary. He insisted on coordination between the proletarian revolution in the home country and the revolutionary forces in the colonies in order to secure the final success of the world revolution. More sharply than Lenin, Roy distinguished between "the national aspirations of the native bourgeoisie" and the "mass action of the poor and ignorant peasants and workers for their liberation." Espousing the Soviet idea, his theses warned, however, against revolutionary over-zealousness: "The revolution in the colonies is not going to be in its first stages a Communist revolution . . . [but] must be carried on with a program which will include many petty bourgeois reform clauses, such as division of land, etc." [53]

Despite that apparent identity of views in the Lenin and Roy reports, several speakers during the general debate at the congress alluded to divergencies between Lenin and Roy, but since Roy could agree with the general thrust of Lenin's argumentation, Lenin did not find it necessary to enter into public debate with Roy over nuances. He must have been satisfied with both his substantively revolutionary and tactically flexible formula, applicable in alternative situations. In the case of a speedy revolution in the West, backward countries could easily be transformed into Soviet Republics, and the revolutionary mass struggle could be divorced from the bourgeois-nationalist movement. In the contrary case, if the revolution in the West would fail to materialize, an anti-imperialist struggle in the East could continue, and the tactics for the Communists would then be to support the most radical elements within the nationalist bourgeoisie of the backward nation. [54] It appeared that all the participants in the congress had perceived and approved the main lines of Lenin's approach, with one exception which for a brief moment shattered the near-unanimity of the congress.

SERRATI'S OPPOSITION TO LENIN'S LINE
ON NATIONAL AND COLONIAL QUESTIONS

The two-day debate on the national and colonial questions at the plenary meetings of the Second Congress (on July 26 and 28) proceeded without controversy until the end of the second day. The first discussant, John Reed, dealt with the revolutionary potential of the Negro question in the United States, emphasizing both its racial and social sides. Following Reed, another American, Louis Fraina, spoke of a "gigantic revolutionary movement embracing the whole of the Americas" and stated that the "destruction of the United States imperialism" must be a "fundamental task of the Communist International."[55] Radek followed on the rostrum with a discussion of British colonial vulnerability and the contradictions existing within the Labour party. He fully supported Lenin's position and arguments. After Radek's speech, the chairman of the meeting, Serrati, proposed to close the list of speakers, but was overruled.

The next day's debate began with the intervention of Sultan-Zade.* He expressed his satisfaction with Lenin's theses, in particular with the adaptation of the Soviet system to the conditions of backward countries, but had doubts concerning the theses of Roy and "a number of comrades in Turkestan" that "the triumph of Communism in the rest of the world depends upon the success of the social revolution in the East." In his view an Eastern revolution could not succeed "without the support of a simultaneous revolutionary movement in England and in the rest of Europe." He was also not enthusiastic about Communist cooperation with the "bourgeois-democratic movements," particularly in the more advanced countries such as Persia, where according to him it was necessary to "create a purely Communist movement in opposition to the bourgeois-democratic movement."[56] The Italian Antonio Graziadei accepted Lenin's distinctions between the "exploited" and "exploiting" nations, but had a reservation on another score; he feared that the "heroic efforts of our comrades in Russia in their struggle against so many enemies contain in themselves the danger of a kind of opportunism of the left which the Third International should strive to avoid." He proposed also to introduce some changes in the eleventh Lenin thesis concerning Communist policy in the Eastern countries, giving more leeway to the

*He emigrated from Persia to the Russian Caucasus in 1907 and joined the Bolsheviks in 1912. At the time of the Second Comintern Congress he was living in Tashkent, where he devoted his life to political work among the émigrés from Persia and other Eastern countries.

local Communists and replacing the word "support" with "active interest" in regard to non-Communist revolutionary movements. [57]

Then the two representatives of the Far East were given the floor. Lao Si-tao reported on the complicated political situation in China and affirmed that "the soil in China is prepared for revolutionary propaganda" while "the support of the Chinese Revolution is important not only for China, but also for the revolutionary movement of the whole world." [58] After him a Korean, Pak Chin-sun, described the situation of Korea under Japanese occupation and concluded that the Korean Communist Party "will be one of the principal factors in converting oppressed Korea into one of the members of the World Federation of Soviet Republics." [59] In further debates the speakers did not touch upon the colonial problem but spoke about Ireland or the Jewish problem. The Turkish representative, in turn, called pan-Islamism and pan-Turkism imperialist slogans. After his speech the German delegate Walcher proposed that debate be closed, arguing that further discussion could not bring any positive results. Maring objected and finally Lozovsky's proposal was adopted, which was to give the floor only to representatives of countries which had not yet been heard. Stressing his seven years of close collaboration with the revolutionary movement in the Dutch East Indies, Maring declared the national and colonial question was of the greatest importance for the further development of the world revolution. He saw no difference between Lenin's and Roy's theses and insisted on the necessity of training better revolutionary cadres in the East. He proposed that the Third International give the leaders of the Far Eastern revolutionary movement the opportunity of staying for half a year in Soviet Russia in order to acquire a proper understanding of what was taking place there: "Moscow and Petrograd have become a new Mecca for the East and we must give the Eastern Communists the opportunity to get a theoretical education in Communism so as to help make the Far East an active member of the Communist International." [60]

After this and a few supplementary but non-essential interventions, Zinoviev proposed to close the discussions and pass on to the final vote on Lenin's and Roy's draft theses. At that moment the unexpected arrived, for Serrati, a member of the congress presidium, declared that he would not vote for either set of theses; in his opinion, they contained "not only some contradictions but also a grave danger for the Communist proletariat of the advanced countries, for the proletariat which should be constantly opposed to every class compromise, especially in the pre-revolutionary period." In Serrati's view the definition of "backward countries" was "too vague and too indefinite not to be confused with the chauvinistic interpretation of the term." He denied revolutionary meaning to any sort of struggle for national liberation carried on by the democratic bourgeoisie: "Only by means of a proletarian revolution and through the Soviet regime can the subjected nations obtain their freedom. This cannot be done by temporary alliances of the Communists with the bourgeois parties called nationalist-revolutionaries." He concluded: "The lack of clarity in the theses may serve as a weapon in the hands of the chauvinist pseudo-revolutionaries of Western Europe against Communist International activity. For these reasons I shall have to abstain from the vote." [61]

This first open opposition to the theses unanimously approved by the commission, made not by a speaker in the debates but in the formal declaration of a presidium member, produced great shock: "What we just heard is unprecedented! " exclaimed Wijnkoop, who violently objected to Serrati's declaration and accused him of giving ammunition to the bourgeoisie by asserting that the entire Comintern colonial policy was counter-revolutionary. Serrati retorted that his declaration was based on the special political situation in Italy (he probably had in mind the Fascist movement, which was also "revolutionary" and thus according to the theses was to be supported by the Communists): "For six years I have fought in my country against the nationalist movement and if I were to vote in favor of such a resolution a contradiction would appear between my position in Italy and my voting here." [62] To this Zinoviev reacted by calling Serrati's statement "very uncomradely" and objected to his "official declaration against us." A counter-declaration was therefore in order: "We are being accused of allegedly supporting bourgeois-revolutionary movements. We do not want to support them. What has been said here is this: the Communists support every revolutionary movement. I do not know what specific struggles are taking place in

Italy. We have experiences from many countries and have found that we as Communists must give support to every revolutionary movement."[63] Roy's reaction was even stronger: "The one who regards it reactionary to aid these people in their national struggle is himself a reactionary and sides with imperialism." He proposed that Serrati's declaration not be included in the official proceedings of the congress. This proposal was supported by Wijnkoop, who argued that Serrati had first to submit his ideas to the congress of the Italian party.

Serrati's rejoinder was sharp. He protested against the proposal to eliminate his declaration from the proceedings and said ironically that he himself could propose to strike from the proceedings "all the stupidities which were uttered at the congress." He maintained that Roy did not understand his objections and reminded Zinoviev that he was always speaking "plainly and straight" and that he intended to introduce a different resolution, the outline of which he then stated. Its gist was once again that the Communist movement must not support the bourgeoisie even in backward countries because of the danger of losing one's class position and class consciousness.[64] When Wijnkoop tried to reply, Zinoviev interrupted him and declared that Serrati had the right to demand that his opinions be included in the proceedings. On Paul Levi's proposal the debate was then closed. Before passing to the final vote on the draft theses Bombacci declared that he did not share Serrati's opinion. Graziadei stated that he would vote for the theses. The Spaniard Pestaña declared that he would not take part in the vote. Zinoviev then read the theses on the national and colonial questions again, and the congress voted unanimously to approve them, with three abstentions.[65]

THE BAKU CONGRESS, SEPTEMBER 1-7, 1920

In his report at the first meeting of the Baku congress, Zinoviev stated that it was "the complement, the second part, the second half of the work of the congress which recently had concluded its labors in Moscow,"[66] that is, the Second Comintern Congress. The decision to call a congress in Baku had been reached by the Executive Committee of the Comintern in June 1920, before the opening of the Second Congress. On July 3, the Moscow *Izvestiia* published an appeal entitled "To the Enslaved Masses of Persia, Armenia, and Turkey," signed by Zinoviev and Radek on behalf of the Executive Committee and by fourteen different Communist parties and groups. The date of the congress was not clearly indicated in the appeal; at the beginning August 15 was mentioned, and at the end September 1 or 2. The language used in the appeal was inflammatory, and it called upon the workers and peasants of Persia, Armenia, and Turkey to associate with the workers and peasants of Europe and America in order to "accelerate the upheaval of world capitalism . . . and assure the liberation of the workers and peasants in the whole world." The appeal further stated that "everywhere in Europe and everywhere in America the workers are rising with weapons in their hands against the capitalists in blood-stained fights." It explained in the following terms the purpose of the forthcoming gathering:

> Workers and peasants of the Near East! If you will organize yourselves, will form your own workers' and peasants' power, if you will arm yourselves and unite with the Russian Workers' and Peasants' Red Army then you will defeat the English, French, and American capitalists, will liberate yourselves from the oppressors, will gain freedom and will be able to create the free world republic of the toilers. . . .
>
> About all this we wish to talk with you at the congress. The Executive Committee of the Communist International as the representative of the English, French, American, German, and Italian workers will come to Baku in order to discuss with you how to join the efforts of the European proletariat with your efforts for the struggle against the common enemy.[67]

The launching of such an appeal at such a time was certainly prompted by a conjunction of several foreign and domestic events. In Persia the "Kuchuk Khan government" had just been formed in Gilan province and it intended to advance southward toward Teheran. In Turkey, Chicherin had just agreed to exchange diplomatic missions with Kemal Pasha. Despite a formal treaty with Armenia and Georgia, recognized as independent states by Soviet Russia, violent propaganda was waged against the ruling Armenian and Georgian Mensheviks and in favor of Soviet power in both countries. The situation in Turkestan was still uncertain, and in interior Russia the organization of the autonomous Tatar republic had met several difficulties. On the other hand, the counter-offensive of the Red Army on the Polish front unfolded favorably and the Red Army was near Warsaw by mid-August.

This new situation found the Comintern without an appropriate apparatus to cope with it. It did not have a special section for the East. The propaganda and organizational work in the Eastern countries was not centralized in one institution. In the first half of 1920 it was mostly concentrated in Tashkent, where the émigrés from the adjacent countries were assembled. On April 14 a conference of the Persian left-wing party "Adalet" was held in Tashkent under the leadership of Sultan-Zade. Khivan and Bukharian Communist organizations were also set up in Tashkent along with a small Turkish organization. Afghan and Indian revolutionary groups were also there. The Department of International Propaganda, reorganized at the First All-Russian Congress of Communist Organizations of Eastern Peoples in November 1918, did not develop beyond agitation and propaganda work and its official communiqué published in the summer of 1920 mentioned only a "preparatory stage toward the organization of the Third International's Eastern division." The communiqué stressed the necessity for the Executive Committee of the International to "assume leadership over this organization, which has every chance of becoming its middle-Asian division in the nearest future."[68] It is quite probable that when this last request came to the debates of the Comintern Executive Committee, it was decided to transfer the whole apparatus on Communist work "in adjacent countries" from Tashkent in Turkestan to Baku in the Caucasus and to hold there the "congress of the peoples of the East."

No rules on the election of delegates to this congress were published. The invitation "to come to Baku in the greatest possible numbers" was made in the same way as invitations to pilgrimages "to the Holy places." Thus, any good-willed worker or peasant "of the Near East" would be welcomed, as would "representatives of the peoples' masses who are living further away." Supervising the preparatory organizational work for the congress were Elena Stasova, a former secretary of the Bolshevik Central Committee (until March 1920) and G. K. Ordzhonikidze, who was the party Central Committee representative for the Caucasian front. Stasova was nominated secretary of the party's Trans-

Caucasian Bureau. In Baku, on Ordzhonikidze's proposal, A. Mikoyan, Nariman Narimanov, and Said-Galiev were co-opted into the organizational committee of the congress.[69] After Stasova's report on the agenda and time of the congress the committee decided to admit in total 3280 delegates from several countries. There were six topics on the agenda: tasks of the congress of the peoples of the East; the international situation and the tasks of the toiling masses of the East; the national and colonial question; the agrarian question; the question of the structure of the Soviets in the East; and organizational questions. In addition it was decided to organize during the congress' session a military parade and a funeral for the 26 "Baku commissars" shot in Turkestan in 1919 (their remains had been moved to Baku).[70] No credentials committee work was mentioned in the congress proceedings; there was no published list of either the "delegates" or the organizations they were supposed to represent.

According to the statistical data contained in the original proceedings of the congress, a total of 1891 persons of 37 nationalities were in attendance, with 1273 Communists among them. The most numerous ethnic group were the Turks, followed by the Persians, Armenians, and Russians.* The total number of "delegates" at the congress was as uncertain as their credentials and nationality. Enver Pasha, who arrived at the congress with formal credentials from "the Union of Revolutionary Organizations of Morocco, Algeria, Tunisia, Tripolitania, Egypt, Arabia, and Hindustan," was not considered a delegate at the congress.[71] But who was entitled to decide who was and who was not a delegate? Probably the Comintern's organizational committee, Stasova and the others. There is no doubt that they did recognize as "delegates" most of the people who were transferred recently from Turkestan to Baku; these were, at least, politically sure. That this was not the case with many other "delegates" comes out clearly

*Pervyi s"ezd narodov Vostoka. Baku, 1-8 sent. 1920. Stenograficheskie otchety. Petrograd, 1920, p.5. In a recent publication a Soviet author contests the data of the proceedings. According to him "not less than 2050 delegates" took part in the congress, with 1071 Communists. The most numerous delegation came from Azerbaijan, the North Caucasus and Turkestan. In general about 80 percent of the congress' participants were Soviet "domestic" Orientals. G.K. Sorkin, Pervyi s"ezd narodov Vostoka, Moscow, 1961, pp. 21-22.

from Stasova's reminiscences: "It will be sufficient to say that among the delegates were several khans and beys who had decided to profit from the journey to Baku in order to conclude different business transactions: sell carpets, leather goods, etc. The speculation was so evident, and some people so out of place, that undoubtedly they should have been arrested; however to do this in Baku would have compromised the congress. Thus it was decided to let them leave Baku."[72] According to another source, during the Baku meeting "several delegates said prayers on small rugs and some members of the Presidium were carrying rosaries all the time in their hands."[73]

Officially the congress was divided into two factions: the Communists and the non-party delegates. Even before the opening of the congress on September 1, two separate slates of candidates for the congress Presidum were presented on behalf of these factions. They were combined and received "an almost unanimous vote" by the congress.[74] In fact neither of these factions, nor even the congress' full Presidium could say much about the congress proceedings: everything was decided beforehand by the Comintern organizers and by Zinoviev, who was also elected chairman of the congress.

Before the official inauguration of the congress, its organizers and delegates took part in the night session of a joint meeting of the Baku Soviet and the Azerbaijan Trade Union Congress. Successive speakers were Narimanov, Zinoviev, Radek, Béla Kun, Thomas Quelch, John Reed, and Karl Steinhardt (Austria). All of them stressed the importance of the East in general and Baku in particular in the global struggle, and Zinoviev and Radek drew some parallels between Baku and Warsaw, both of which had been great industrial cities of the former Russian Empire. According to Zinoviev:

> Every old revolutionary knows that in our strikes, demonstrations, and risings, in the revolutionary struggle, we usually name after Petrograd and Moscow, Baku, Warsaw, and Riga. . . . I mentioned Warsaw. At the present moment the white banner is still floating in the air over Warsaw . . . but we can say: it will not be months but weeks before our Red Army will again stretch its red hand for Warsaw. . . .

The war of the RSFSR against White Poland is not only the war of the Western proletariat but also of the toiling nations of the East against our subjugators!

The Communist International wishes to unite under its banner the people speaking in all languages. The Communist International is sure that under its banner will come not only the European proletariat but also the heavy mass of our reserve, our infantry—hundreds of thousands of peasants inhabiting Asia, our Near and Far East.[75]

After Zinoviev, Radek spoke glorifying revolutionary Baku, saying that at this congress of the nations of the East, Soviet Russia, or rather the world proletariat which she represented, had "one sword more—the indignation of the peoples who used to live under the oppression of world capitalism, primarily English."[76]

The language problem was a very difficult one during the congress: the speeches were translated or summarized in two or three Eastern languages. This greatly prolonged the debates. As a result, not all the speeches of the Westerners were delivered at the congress; most of them were published in the press and included in the proceedings. From the fourth meeting on, only three languages became official: Russian, Turko-Azerbaijan, and Persian. Zinoviev was in the chair at all the meetings except the first, at which he had delivered his main report; Narimanov was then the presiding officer. Most of the meetings were held late in the evening or at night. On September 3, a Friday and a Moslem holiday, there was no congress meeting but a military street parade. In all, seven plenary meetings were held by the congress between September 1-7; on September 8 the ceremonial funeral of the 26 "Baku commissars" took place.

At the first meeting of the congress, after the election of the 32-person Presidium (18 from the Communist faction and 14 from the non-party faction), Zinoviev delivered the main report on the principal aims and tasks of the congress. Substantively, it was a series of variations on the main themes on the national and colonial questions developed by Lenin at the Second Comintern Congress. Tactically, it was an application of the new Comintern general line with regard to the revolutionary potential of the East. Emotionally, Zinoviev was above all trying to develop in the audience the frenzy of a "genuine holy war against English and French capitalists." At the same time he stressed strongly that the message of congress was not exclusively directed to Communists and explained: "We do not ask: 'To what party do you belong? ' We ask only one thing: 'Are you a worker? ' " Likewise, he stated that "the first task of our congress is to wake up millions of peasants," while "the task of the more civilized . . . workers of Europe and America is . . . to teach them to use arms against the civilized beasts who are sitting in London and Paris offices." He then asked "Why cannot the peasants of Turkey, Persia, India, China, and Armenia do what the Russian peasant, who was a serf not long ago, was able to do? " He explained that the Soviet government was ready to "assist any revolutionary struggle against the English government," but delineated clearly the differences and similarities between the Communist and nationalist movements: "Their [the nationalists'] task is to assist the East to liberate itself from English imperialism. We, however, have another task, not less important—to assist the toilers of the East in the struggle against the rich men, to assist them to build their Communist organizations." He pictured the rising of "dozens and hundreds of millions of peasants [able to] set up a Red Army in the East . . . to organize an insurrection in the rear guard of the English, to set fire to the robbers, to make the life of any impudent English officer, who is domineering in Turkey, Persia, India, and China, impossible." [77]

After Zinoviev's report the floor was given to Radek to deliver his report on the international situation and the tasks of the toiling masses of the East. The tone and arguments used by Radek were similar to those of Zinoviev, and if possible even more inflammatory and anti-British. In Radek's eyes world imperialism was "suffocating in the process of a huge crisis" and Italy was "literally on the eve of revolution." The victory of the rising peoples of the East depended on their unity with Soviet Russia. The struggle was total and pitiless: "It is impossible for Soviet Workers' and Peasants' Russia to exist for a long time side by side with capitalist countries. . . . Temporarily the Russian worker can seek peace and accord with them, can seek a peace during which the revolution in other countries will grow stronger, but permanent peace between the country of labor and the countries of exploitation is impossible. . . . We are linked with you by fate: either we will unite with the peoples of the East and will promote the victory of the Western European proletariat, or we will perish and you will stay in slavery." Appealing, in turn, to a holy war against the Allies he went so far as to allude to the old, historical invasions: "We appeal, comrades, to the feeling of struggle which used to inspire the peoples of the East at the time when these peoples, led by their great conquerors, went against Europe. We know, comrades, that our opponents will say that we are appealing to the memory of Genghis Khan and to the memory of the conquerors of the Khalifs of Islam. But we are sure that yesterday you have shown your daggers and revolvers not for the aims of conquering, not to make a cemetery of Europe; you have taken them in order to create jointly with the workers of the whole world a new culture— the culture of the free toiler." [78]

After Radek's report the joint debate on the two main reports was opened. The Presidium limited the number of speakers to six. They spoke different tongues and, when their speeches were translated, there was some confusion because the audience did not always know when a speaker was expressing his own opinions and when he was translating somebody else's speech. After three speakers who described the situation in several countries of the Middle East, four committees of the congress were established to debate the agrarian question, the national and colonial question, the Soviet structure, and organizational problems.

At the third meeting of the congress, on September 4, the debate was continued and a representative from the non-party faction, Narbutabekov from Turkestan, delivered a long and rather curious speech, a mixture of praise and criticism of the Soviet authorities. He declared that "our Moslem peoples and the peoples of the East do not wish any other power but Soviet," and that they wholeheartedly supported the Bolshevik slogan of self-determination, having full confidence in Russian ideological leaders. He stressed, however, that "the East is completely different, its interests are different from those in the West; that is why the direct application of the Communist idea will meet resistance there." The particularities of Eastern peoples had therefore to be recognized and "the steps taken by the Soviet power in this direction [must] be made not on paper but in reality." He then ap-

pealed directly to the supreme Bolshevik leaders to be aware of
and to correct acts of usurpation and "Red imperialism" in Turkestan:

> We, the Turkestanians, are saying that we have never seen comrade
> Zinoviev or comrade Radek or any other leader of the revolution. They
> should come and see what is happening here, that the local authorities
> are definitely establishing a policy that drives the toiling masses away
> from Soviet power. . . . In order that the Turkestan story be not re-
> peated in other parts of the Moslem world, I am warning our authorities
> that we know all the defects of the policy which was applied there for
> three years, and we are saying: remove all your counter-revolutionaries,
> remove your carpetbaggers who spread national conflicts, remove your
> colonizers who work now under the mask of Communism! . . .
> Moslems are coming and saying that our beliefs are trodden upon, we
> are not allowed to pray or to bury our dead according to our customs
> and religion.[79]

Narbutabekov's speech made a great impression on the audience
and was translated into five Eastern languages. On the other hand,
he was criticized by a speaker from Daghestan who reproached
him for dealing with domestic trivialities when the much more
important issue of the world revolution was on the agenda.[80]
Among the other non-conventional speeches which aroused quite a
stir at the congress was a declaration by Enver Pasha (read by
Ostrovsky in Russian), who regretted having been forced to make
war on the side of German imperialism but who professed a new
faith in a "trusted and genuine ally—the Third International."[81]
In the same spirit, a representative of the Ankara government
spoke enthusiastically about the devotion of the Anatolian peasants to the idea of an international revolution and friendship
toward the Soviet Union.[82] These declarations and the subsequently adopted draft resolution, submitted by Zinoviev, to give
support to "those national revolutionary movements which are
aiming to liberate the oppressed peoples of the East from foreign
imperialist yoke," met with some disapproval and showed the lack
of unanimity of the congress on this touchy issue.

The next lengthy report on the national and colonial questions
was submitted by Mikhail Pavlovich-Weltmann. He developed
some of the familiar Lenin theses on these problems, and also
emphasized the theme of a "holy war" against the "world bourgeoisie." He declared that "the whole East is saturated with the

bacteria of revolution," and indirectly answering the critic from Turkestan, he described in lyrical terms the glowing future of Eastern peoples under a Soviet regime: "Two or three decades will pass and we will see . . . new great works of new talented poets and novelists coming from the workers' and peasants' midst. Tatar, Bashkir, and Kirghiz poetry and literature, which are now just awakening, will blossom in full glory . . . will glitter with unseen, incomparable beauty, which neither classic Hellenism . . . nor the civilization of the Middle Ages nor capitalist epochs was able to produce. . . . Yes, all this will be." [83] Two final reports were then read at the congress: Béla Kun's on the building of Soviets in the East, and Skachko's on the agrarian question. They were followed by the presentation of the draft theses which, having been approved by the Presidium, were voted upon by the congress without debate.

The seventh and last meeting of the congress was the most important, because it dealt with the organizational setup of the entire revolutionary movement in the East. The Comintern's intentions were clearly formulated by Zinoviev, who stated at the opening of the meeting:

> We wish that, after the congress disperses, an organ will stay on which will continue the work so perfectly started by our historic congress. . . . We will gather congresses of the peoples of the East not less than once a year, and in order that during the lapses of time between congresses the work of revolutionary propaganda, agitation, and liberation struggle in the East continues, we propose that the First Congress of the Peoples of the East set up a permanent Council of Propaganda and Action of the Peoples of the East . . . composed of 47 persons.

> The Council . . . will organize the propaganda in the whole East, publish a journal, *The Peoples of the East*, in three tongues . . . and organize a university of social sciences for the people working in the East. The plenary sessions of the Council . . . will be held not less than once every three months in Baku . . . a presidium of seven persons . . . a division in Tashkent and other centers where necessary. The work of the Council will be under the leadership and control of Comintern's Executive Committee, which will designate two (out of seven) members of the Council's presidium with the right to 'veto.' [84]

After a brief discussion, Ostrovsky read a draft list of the members of the Council, 35 of whom belonged to the Communist faction and 13 to the non-party faction (the list contained, thus, one person more than Zinoviev previously had stated). Among the Communists, six persons—Pavlovich, Kirov, Ordzhonikidze, Stasova, Yeleyeva, and Skachko—were designated as representatives of the Communist International.[85] When Zinoviev put this list en bloc to a vote, there were some protests from the audience and shouts of "Not fair," from the Persian group, but Zinoviev quieted the audience and proclaimed that the Council had been elected fairly. He made also the closing speech of the congress, whipping up once more the anti-Western feelings of his audience. He paid particular attention to the grievances of Turkestanians and promised solemnly, in the name of the Soviet government and the Communist International, that "those elements which adhere to the Communist party but who are behaving in such a way that they dishonor the Communist name and are baiting one part of the population against another" shall be "exterminated." He went on to praise "the rising star" of the peoples of the East, while affirming that "the Allies are disintegrating before our eyes. . . . The Council of Action is already stronger in the East than the bourgeois council of ministers in England or any other council of ministers." And he concluded, after invoking again the "holy war against the robbers and the capitalists": "Seventy years ago our common teacher, Karl Marx, issued his appeal 'Proletarians of all countries, unite!' We, the disciples of Karl Marx, continuers of his work, have the opportunity to develop this formula, to amplify it, broaden it and say 'Proletarians of all countries and *oppressed peoples of the entire world, unite!*' "[86]

THE AFTERMATH OF THE BAKU CONGRESS

From the propaganda point of view the Baku congress was a great success; it had an influence on the imagination of the world and its symbolic, revolutionary name became and remained famous. Its actual work and achievements, however, were something quite different. The Georgians and the Armenians, who watched the Baku congress very carefully from behind their precarious borders, called it from the very beginning the "purest mise en scène." Contemporary Soviet writers have ridiculed this opinion,[87] but in the long run the Georgians and the Armenians were right. The general political situation in the world changed radically in the months after the congress and the work begun at Baku was suddenly abandoned. Despite Zinoviev's categorical statement that similar congresses would be gathered "no less than once a year" the Baku congress was never repeated in the same form, and its organ, the Council of Propaganda and Action, was dissolved early in 1922, after a year of formal existence.

Initially the Council started to work with great energy. On September 8, 1920, its first meeting was held; it was decided to nominate a presidium of nine persons (not seven, as Zinoviev had proposed to the congress), with Stasova as secretary, to publish the proceedings of the congress and its four-language organ, *The Peoples of the East*, and two manifestoes or appeals of the congress "To the Peoples of the East" and "To the Workers of Europe, America, and Japan," to organize six-week "shock courses" for activists, etc. In general, the Council considered itself the supreme leader of the whole revolutionary movement in the East, the chief Eastern Comintern instrument. In order to be in close contact with the Comintern leadership, a delegation of forty persons was sent from Baku to Moscow.

The general line of the Council's policy at that time was expressed in its appeal "To the Peoples of the East" published on behalf of the congress. It claimed to speak as the representative of the toiling peoples of the East (over twenty-five peoples and countries were mentioned) who, having united among themselves and with the revolutionary workers of the West, were calling for "the first genuine holy war under the red banner of the Communist International." The common foe, "imperialist England," was singled out for attack in most vehement terms. [88]

This general line was then fully approved by the Comintern Executive Committee. At its plenary session of September 20, in Moscow, Zinoviev presented a detailed report on the Baku congress. According to excerpts of what he said—and in contrast with the later published proceedings of the Baku congress—he affirmed that the non-party faction "was much more numerous than the Communist faction" and actually included representatives of "bourgeois parties" who wanted "from us nothing but arms." [89] He mentioned his talks with Enver Pasha and affirmed that the "average level of consciousness of the delegates to the congress was rather high" and that the most characteristic trait of the congress was that it was "an expression of the spontaneous strength of the masses." Zinoviev revealed that among the members of the congress presidium there were differences of opinion about the character and tasks of the permanent organ planned by the congress; some people wanted it to be a kind of "super-government" of all the Eastern Soviet states. This idea was rejected and the congress set up the Council of Propaganda and Action. The Executive Committee approved Zinoviev's report and confirmed the appointment of Stasova and Pavlovich-Weltmann as Comintern representatives in the Council of Propaganda and Action. In October 1920 the first issue of *The Peoples of the East* appeared in Russian and Turkish; the Arabic and Persian editions were delayed. On November 2, the "shock courses" began. Political economy, the building of Soviets, geography, the origins of the earth and man, were studied in these courses. [90]

Very soon, however, it became obvious that the Council and its members were far from representing a homogeneous political body. On November 28, at a plenary meeting of the Comintern's Executive Committee, Pavlovich and Sultan-Zade reported on the work of the Council of Propaganda and Action. In his lengthy theses on the development of the communist movement and the tactics of the imperialist bourgeoisie in the East, Zade contested the accepted opinion that social revolution in the colonial and semi-colonial countries must be preceded by a national-democratic revolution. He foresaw a "sharp crisis" in the relations between the national liberation movement in the colonial and semi-colonial countries and Soviet Russia, with the result that the national bourgeoisie would either "pass over to the counterrevolutionary camp, as in Persia," or "at the first opportunity reach an agreement with capitalist Europe, as in Turkey." He also feared that the Eastern countries could become "La Vendée of the worldwide revolution," where the frightened Western bourgeoisie could transfer its capitals. Implicitly criticizing Lenin's fundamental thesis in this matter, he argued that Eastern Communists should direct the revolutionary movement against both the international and local bourgeoisie, and that the illusory concept that the bourgeoisie of the backward nations was still capable of fighting on the side of the national-democratic revolution must be abandoned forever. [91]

This conclusion was in open contradiction to the general line of the Baku congress and must have stirred quite a controversy at the November 28 meeting. The same was probably true with the organizational question. Although the official account of that meeting was silent on this score,[92] the monopolistic leading role of the Baku Council of Propaganda and Action in Eastern revolutionary work was contested in several quarters. Thus an article in *Zhizn natsionalnostei* of December 15, 1920, entitled "The Comintern and the East," openly criticized the Council and stated that in its three months of existence it had shown that neither the Council itself nor its presidium were "able to embrace in their work the whole Near East, and by no means the Far East, which because of its distance is practically not included in the Baku union of the peoples of the East." Even Tashkent, to which some of the members of the Council had been delegated, did not feel it necessary to maintain contact with Baku and worked "almost independently"; it preferred to deal directly with Moscow. In this connection the article revealed that the above-mentioned Baku Council delegation, sent to Moscow, submitted in October 1920 a memorandum to the Comintern suggesting that it set up not one but three centers for work in the East: in Baku for Turkey, Arabia, Syria, Egypt, Armenia, Georgia, Persia, Azerbaijan, Daghestan, and the Terek region; in Tashkent for India, Afghanistan, Turkestan, Kirghizia, Bashkiria, Chinese Western Turkestan, Kashmir, and Atlay; and in Irkutsk for China, Korea, Mongolia, Manchuria, Siberia, and Japan. "The necessity to organize these three councils," argued the memorandum, "is dictated mainly by the impossibility of embracing the whole East from one center, for geographical and other reasons," but the work of the new councils should be supervised directly from Moscow by a special Eastern section which the Comintern should set up.

The fate of the Council of Propaganda and Action was certainly influenced by Stalin's visit to the Caucasus and Baku in the early fall of 1920. He was apparently not impressed by the Council's work, because shortly after his return to Moscow, Stasova was suddenly recalled from her post in Baku. In her reminiscences she wrote:

> By the end of October, J.V. Stalin arrived in Baku. I reported to him on the entire work, because his authority on all national questions, since the time of our underground work, was for me undisputable. I asked him whether our line of work and methods were right. He answered positively. . . .

Once in the evening, when I intended to go to a meeting, a cipher was brought from the Party's C.C. It instructed me to pass over to comrade Pavlovich-Weltmann all the matters of the Council of Propaganda and Action and on Armenia and to go as a member of the C.C. Bureau to Rostov on the Don, where Frumkin was working. N. N. Narimanov wanted to keep me in Baku in the Secretariat of the C.P. I was obliged to refuse and to go to Moscow. What had happened then I do not even know exactly. Obviously, I asked Moscow to inform me about this. If I had made any mistakes, I said, I should be informed in order to avoid repeating them. However, I got no answer. Zinoviev was instructed to inform me that it was not a question of mistrust.[93]

The exact date of Stasova's removal is not known; it took place in December 1920, after the Comintern's Executive Committee meeting of November 28. On December 10, Ordzhonikidze was designated to replace Stasova as the Comintern representative in the Baku Council's presidium. He had plenty of other work to do, however—military, Soviet, and party tasks to strengthen Soviet authorities in Transcaucasia—and consequently he was not able to give proper attention to the work in the presidium of the Council of Propaganda and Action.[94] But his ineffective leadership was not the only reason for the presidium's sagging performance.

In its report to the Comintern of April 1921, the Baku council stressed that the lack of proper workers and the frequent changes in its leadership impeded its work in the East. According to Sorkin:

The insufficient activity and the final liquidation of the Council were caused by the overestimate of the Council of Propaganda and Action of the status of the struggle for liberation in the countries of the East, by its overestimate of its own forces and possibilities. . . . This was unrealistic and incorrect. It was incorrect to think that it was possible to lead the national-liberation movement from one center. Only political parties acting in each country are able to perform such a task. This was the main reason for the insufficient activity of the Council of Propaganda and Action, and this is why it was liquidated by the Communist International.[95]

While all this was certainly true, another factor must be added to the list of causes of the Council's disintegration. As early as January 14, 1921, in his report on the Eastern question presented at the Comintern's Executive Committee meeting, [96] Sokolnikov pointed out the inconsistency in the sympathies of the bourgeois-landowner class in the East toward Soviet Russia and the fact that at the first opportunity "our military allies in the East were concluding agreements with our military enemy—the Entente." Sokolnikov then mentioned the extreme diversity of conditions in individual Eastern countries and the necessity for Communists to "take carefully into consideration all the particularities of each individual country and to avoid any routine." To adopt diversified tactics was obviously a retreat from the general line of the Baku congress, which had proclaimed a global "holy war" of all the Eastern peoples under the Red Banner of Communism. Such a call was not favorably received by the Moslems of the foreign countries, nor did it correspond any longer to Soviet international policy.

The crucial element in the new situation was that the attitude toward Soviet Russia taken by those Eastern countries which never belonged to the former Russian Empire was quite different from their attitude toward the Communist movement in general. Whereas they were willing to maintain the most friendly relations with Russia (and to receive from her any material assistance, arms over all), they were more or less openly hostile toward local Communists. There were, however, certain variations in the general situation in each individual country. There were practically no local Communists in Afghanistan, whose new revolutionary regime of Ammanoullah had friendly relations with Moscow, which found expression in the formal treaty concluded with Soviet Russia on February 28, 1921.

In Persia the situation was more complicated. Local and émigré Communists (from Russia) had done their best to influence the Kuchuk Khan movement and its revolutionary government. Since this government was quite openly supported by Moscow, the Teheran government was unfriendly to both the Communists and Moscow and maintained friendly relations with Great Britain. With Britain's assistance, Teheran made it practically impossible for genuine Persian delegates to go to the Baku congress and persecuted local Communists. However, by the end of 1920 the Kuchuk Khan forces were practically destroyed and a Soviet writer at that time drew the following conclusion from that event: "The overestimation of the real relations between the powers may lead to a dangerous gamble, profitable to international imperialism. An example of this is the assistance given to Kuchuk Khan, a feudal prince from Gilan, in 1920 in Persia." [97] The new Persian government of Reza Khan, which in February 1921 occupied Teheran, annulled the former Anglo-Persian treaty and on February 26 concluded a treaty with Soviet Russia. The new Persian government, like the one of Afghanistan, was friendly toward Russia but unfriendly toward local Persian Communists.

A similar though much more complicated situation occurred in Turkey. The revolutionary government of Kemal Pasha, a victor over the Allies, represented by Greek troops, was soliciting Russia's friendship and used some of the Bolshevik methods and slogans, but it was hostile toward all the agitators and organizers of the Turkish Communist Party which had been imported from Russia. Instead it was willing to tolerate the local, national Turkish Communist Party which, with some success, had been organized on Turkish soil and which published its own journal. [98] The relationship between the Moscow-supported Turkish Communist movement organized and led by Mustafa Subhi since 1918 among the former Turkish prisoners of war and the improvised domestic Communists was most unfriendly. The prisoners were indoctrinated with Communist ideas in the Soviet Union and were sent to Turkey for political or military work; some Red Turkish detachments had been organized in the Crimea, Turkestan, and the Caucasus in order to be moved to Turkey. Although, for obvious political reasons, Subhi's name was not mentioned in connection with the Baku congress and the activities of the Council of Propaganda and Action, there is no doubt that he was active behind the scene. When the first "shock courses" of the Baku Council were completed, on January 16, 1921, at the graduation ceremony the "first scouts of the Council" were created and were enjoined to go to different Asian countries to "bring with them the light of revolutionary consciousness and . . . direct the toiling masses onto the path of the decisive struggle with world imperialism." [99] There were fifteen Turks among the graduates who, led by Subhi, went to work in Anatolia. Formally tolerated by the Turkish authorities, they were badly received by the local population, stoned in several towns and villages, and finally under suspicious circumstances drowned in the Black Sea near Trabzon, where Subhi had been born some 35 years before. The massacre of these Turkish Communists had taken place just as the Ankara government was negotiating simultaneously with Moscow and London. Despite the Trabzon event, the Russian-Turkish treaty was signed in Moscow on March 16, 1921. Whatever the feelings of the Bolshevik leaders might have been, the signing of the treaty was explained by the supreme interests of the international revolution: "To start a fight with Turkey," stated an article in *Zhizn natsionalnostei*, "would mean to lose the revolution and the struggle against English imperialism in the whole East and, obviously, Soviet Russia will never do this."[100] After the signing of the treaty, formal relations between the Turkish state and Soviet Russia were correct and even friendly; however, the Turkish government did not change its hostile attitude toward non-local Communists. The Communists tried a comeback, and after the Third Congress of the Comintern its Little Bureau formed a special committee for "the reorganization of the Turkish Communist Party and a new registration of its members."[101] This was the formal end of the Subhi incident. However, the most intransigeant Turkish elements did not adapt themselves to the new situation. Enver Pasha and his followers did not accept the Turkish-Soviet rapprochement; completely disappointed with the Soviet foreign political line, they joined the Turkestan rebels and were massacred by a detachment of the Red Army in 1922.

The formal normalization of the relations between Soviet Russia and its Eastern neighbors early in 1921 had its counterpart in the West, where the armistice and peace treaty with Poland were signed respectively on October 12, 1920, and March 18, 1921.[102] They were both symptoms of the new Soviet policy of peaceful co-existence with the capitalist world. The essence, never put in writing, of the new situation was the implicit agreement that the Soviet government would have a free hand within territories it controlled, but would not go beyond their borders. On their part, the Western Powers would end intervention in Russian domestic affairs provided that Soviet Russia gave up further expansion of the revolution by means of the Red Army. In the summer of 1920, during the successful push of the Red Army westward, the Soviet government was reluctant to accept these

terms; however, after the defeat on Vistula, in mid-August, the
policy of an interim breathing spell was finally adopted. The
domestic troubles of the early spring of 1921 (the peasant and
Kronstadt revolts) forced the Soviet leaders to abandon the former
war policy and to adopt the New Economic Policy, which made
necessary a radical change in Soviet Russia's foreign relations.

The repercussions of that policy on the Comintern's Asian
Bureaus were both immediate and drastic: shortly after their
establishment they were liquidated, following the pattern of the
Comintern European branches. The Baku office, as already indicated, saw the end of its political effectiveness in the departure of
Elena Stasova. The life span of the Tashkent Bureau was equally
brief. It was established one month after the congress and after the
birth of the Baku Bureau, in October 1920. Again the staff was
predominantly Russian, two of its three members being Russian
Bolsheviks, as reported by the third, M. N. Roy: "Sokolnikov,
Safarov, and myself were to constitute the Central Asiatic Bureau
of the Communist International. Sokolnikov then held a high military position; he was Commander of the Red Army in Central
Asia, on the Turkish front. He was also Chairman of the Turkestan
Commission of the Central Soviet Government." [103] Roy had an
ambitious plan of revolutionary action for that Bureau, which he
revealed to Lenin before leaving for Asia: "My plan was to raise,
equip, and train such an army in Afghanistan. Using the frontier
territories as the base of operation and with the mercenary support of the tribesmen, the liberation army would march into India
and occupy some territory, where a civil government would be
established as soon as possible.... The requirements for implementing the plan were obvious: a sufficiently large quantity of
arms, field equipment, training personnel, and plenty of money.
The last item was sanctioned by the Council of People's Commissars on the recommendation of the Communist Party [of Rus-
sia]." [104]

Roy left for Tashkent in November 1920, but once he got there
he found that his grandiose revolutionary scheme would not be
easy to implement. Three months later Roy left Tashkent, invited
to Moscow to participate in the Third Comintern Congress, where
he was to give a report on the activities of the Tashkent Bureau. In
Moscow, on submitting an outline of his report to Lenin, he was

more than surprised to learn that at this congress, in contrast to the previous one, the colonial question was to be treated as a "poor relation." He was allowed to speak only five minutes, which he used not to make his report but to protest against the "opportunistic manner in which the Eastern question has been treated at this congress." [105] His protest in no way altered the decision of the Bolsheviks to close down the Tashkent Bureau, and a short time later Roy himself wrote: "After the Third Congress, it was decided to abolish the Turkestan Bureau of the Communist International and to open an Eastern Section with headquarters in Moscow to take charge of promoting and guiding the revolutionary movement in the colonial world." [106] Roy's former colleague at the Tashkent Bureau, Georgi Safarov, was soon put in charge of that section.

The Comintern's third Asian branch, established outside Moscow but on Soviet soil, at Irkutsk, was similarly short-lived. That Bureau came into being in July and August 1920, first as the Section of Oriental Peoples within the Siberian Delegation of the Bolshevik Central Committee, to be transformed in January 1921 into the Comintern Secretariat for the Far East. Among its directors was B. Shumiatsky, later rector of the Communist University of the Toilers of the East—KUTV (a school for training Comintern cadres), who was in charge of publishing the *Bulletin of the Far Eastern Secretariat of the Comintern*, the first issue of which appeared on February 27, 1921, and the last in May of that year. [107] It was roughly at this time that the Bureau ceased its activities; Shumiatsky was taken up with his work in Mongolia, where he remained until February 1922. In the course of its brief existence the Irkutsk Bureau undertook to establish the first contacts with China, as evidenced by a visit to that city, in the spring of 1921, of the Chinese Communist, Chang Tai-lei, en route from China to Moscow as the first authentic Chinese Communist delegate to take part in a Comintern congress. At the same time, another of the future leaders of the Chinese Communist Party, Liu Shao-chi, also arrived in Russia, as he confirmed forty years later; [108] on his way there he probably passed through Irkutsk. A third among the pioneers of Chinese Communism, Chü Chiu-pai (alias Tsiu Tsiu-po, Tsiu Wito, and Strakhov), the secretary-general of the Chinese party in 1927, was already at that time in Moscow, from whence he sent an article that appeared in the first issue of the Irkutsk bulletin. [109]

The first revolutionary Sturm and Drang period of Comintern activities in the East came to an end with the closing of its Asian bureaus. The slogan of a general, anti-imperialist holy war was simultaneously abandoned. Instead, a different, everyday political and propaganda work emerged, consisting of building a Communist party in each country that would be supervised directly by Moscow.

— 10 —

The Split in the European Socialist Parties

There had been only a few delegates and no foreign delegations at the First Congress of the Communist International. Between the First and the Second Congress there had been no breaks within the Socialist parties on the issue of joining the new International. At the Second Congress, however, there would be representative foreign delegations, and numerous rifts were to develop immediately afterwards in the various Socialist parties.

As soon as it came into being, the Communist International launched an appeal for new members, and those on the far left in the Socialist parties who had been won over to the Communist idea began to examine their consciences. In the months following the birth of the International, votes were taken in many Socialist parties, with widely varying results. In some instances a majority favored going along with Moscow, with only a minority opposed; in others the reverse was true. Either way, when the voting was over, the proponents and opponents of embracing the new International went on living together in the same parties. Soon, however, it became obvious that such a state of affairs could not last.

THE EUROPEAN SOCIALIST PARTIES
AFTER THE FOUNDING OF THE COMINTERN

Europe's first large Socialist party to take a stand on the issue immediately after the founding of the Comintern was Italy's. Its executive committee, meeting in Milan on March 19,1919, at the suggestion of Gennari, Serrati, and Bombacci, passed a resolution (by a vote of ten to three) which concluded with the words: "The Party therefore resolves to resign from the [Socialist] International Bureau and affiliate with the new revolutionary Socialist

417

International, founded on the principles of our Russian Communist comrades."[1] After this decision the minority, which included men like Constantino Lazzari, the party secretary from 1912 to 1919, remained in the party and continued to hold positions of responsibility. The majority, led by Serrati, never dreamed of taking disciplinary or punitive action against them.

The following month, at the special congress of the French Socialist Party (SFIO) held in Paris from April 20 to 22, three motions were made calling for clarification of the party's position with regard to the old Socialist International and the new Communist International. One made by Jean Longuet expressing the "centrist" point of view got 894 votes. Another by Barthélemy Mayéras representing the "right" received 757. A third by Fernand Loriot, who spoke for the far left favorable to the Comintern, received only 270, and the motion to join that body was defeated. Even so, the far left stayed in the party and the majority took no action against them. That same month, April 1919, the Social Democratic Labor Party of Norway announced its readiness to join the Comintern, and reaffirmed this position at its conference on June 8. The vote taken concerning adoption of the Soviet system in Norway showed clearly the numerical strength of the proponents and opponents of the Moscow line; 275 voted in favor, and 63 against. Here again, the minority was not expelled from the party, nor did they themselves break with it. On June 14, by a vote of 186 to 22, the national conference of Sweden's Social Democratic Left resolved to join the Comintern, and no attempt was made to evict the defeated minority from that party either.

Two left Socialist parties that had broken with their official Social Democratic parties did wind up in the Communist camp. At its congress on November 16 and 17, 1918, the Social Democratic Party of Holland changed its name to Communist Party of Holland, imitating the Bolsheviks, who had made the same change at their own congress in March 1918. At their congress of May 25 to 27, 1919, the Bulgarian "narrow" Socialist party renamed itself the Communist Party of Bulgaria and joined the Comintern.

The Swiss Socialist Party, at its congress in Basel in March 1919, after resolving almost unanimously to break with the Second International, voted 318 to 147 to join the Communist International. But the decision had to be ratified in a party-wide referendum organized by the membership at large, and in this it was reversed: only 8,600 voted to join the Comintern whereas 14,364 voted against. But once again these two conflicting votes, with the party rank and file overruling their leaders, did not split the party.

The opposite occurred in the Socialist Party of Greece. Its national council decided in May 1919 to sever ties with the Second International but voted against joining the Third International; yet the party congress, convening in Athens on April 5, 1920, voted almost unanimously in favor of joining the Comintern. At the congress of unification of the Socialist Workers' Party of Yugoslavia (Communists), held in Belgrade from April 20 to 23, 1919, and attended by Communists from different regions of the country but also by centrist Socialists from the old Serbian Social Democratic Party, the majority voted to break with the Second International and join the Third International. The special congress of Germany's Independent Socialist Party (USPD), held in Leipzig from November 30 to December 6, 1919, saw another clash of centrist Socialists with Socialists favoring the Comintern. The motion made by Walter Stoecker on behalf of the far left, calling for immediate affiliation with the Comintern was defeated, 170 to 111; again the two factions did not split but remained in the same party. At its congress in December 1919 Spain's Socialist party, by a vote of 14,000 to 12,500, rejected immediate affiliation with the Communist International.

The significant fact that these divisions within Europe's Socialist parties were not deep enough to split them pointed to another truth, no less important: pro-Comintern sentiment was not predominant in Central and Western Europe, where labor parties and trade union movements were strongest. Except in the case of Italy, Europe's Socialist parties—including those controlled by centrists, such as the SFIO, the USPD, and the Austrian Socialist Party— voted solidly against involvement with the Comintern. And of course those parties led by former "social-patriots" (as in Germany, Belgium, and England) showed no inclination whatever in that direction. Even when a Socialist party was not yet divided into these disputing factions, it was nevertheless cool toward Comintern beckonings. On January 15, 1919, the 25-member executive committee of the Czechoslovak Social Democratic Party passed the following resolution: "Our party has nothing in common and wants nothing to do with the tactics of the Russian Bolsheviks and German Spartacists, which can only lead the nation and the working class to ruin and spill the workers' blood in fratricidal battles. Anyone in favor of establishing an independent Bolshevik party is an enemy of social democracy."[2] One would have to wait another year, for the months after the Second World Congress, to see cleavages develop in Europe's large Socialist parties.

LENIN, PROPHET AND SPLITTER

Shortly after the Comintern's Second Congress Lenin saw his grand dream come true: the final break in Western Europe between reformist Socialism and revolutionary Socialism, a repetition on the international stage of what had happened in Russia—the splitting of Menshevism from Bolshevism. The events ahead would confirm what Lenin had long foreseen. Again, to those around him, he was the infallible prophet, a demiurge of history, which he seemed to mold at will. That several years might have to lapse between a Lenin prediction and its faithful fulfillment did not matter, for it is a prophet's duty to foresee things before others think them possible. But to his disciples Lenin was no ordinary prophet; he was a Marxist prophet and therefore a scientist, with a genius for foreknowing the revolutionary future.

The first case in which his clairvoyance had disclosed horizons undreamed of by other Marxists, including Bolsheviks, was when he succeeded in splitting Russia's Social Democrats in 1903. At first none of the leading Russian Social Democrats would follow him, and even among Bolsheviks there were misgivings about the savage fury of his attack, later characterized by Stalin as a "tornado in a teacup." But Lenin did not swerve. The split, consummated in fact in 1903, became official and final in 1912, but it was not until after November 7, 1917, that its immense historical impact would be felt. Another lag between a Lenin prediction and its subsequent fulfillment followed his proclamation in 1914 of the need to break with the Second International and create a Third. It was then only a statement of principle which he had no power to implement. Again it was November 7, 1917, at Petrograd that made possible the translation of the word into the deed—the founding of the Third International in March 1919.

But Lenin had predicted one more great event: the sundering of the Western Socialist parties. Ever since 1917 he had been calling upon Socialists to transcend the spirit of Zimmerwald and set up revolutionary Marxist parties distinct from "centrism" and "opportunism," even if this meant breaking up the existing parties. The big Socialist parties paid little heed before the creation of the Comintern, and even for a year afterwards. It was not until the second half of 1920 and the beginning of 1921 that Lenin's idea began to become political reality, destined to help shape Europe's labor movement for decades to come.

The exact chronology of events or how long it might take for them to happen mattered little to the prophet once he was firmly convinced that he had prophesied aright and that history would be his proof. In Russia, instead of waiting for economic conditions to ripen and fit the Marxist mold before triggering his revolution, he unleashed it forthwith, leaving worries about economics for later. In the international Communist movement, instead of biding his time until mass Communist parties could be set up in the major Western countries, he simply conjured the Comintern into existence, pulling it, so to speak, out of an empty hat, so as to have a tool with which to hasten the creation of national Communist parties. For Lenin, force was midwife to the Communist revolution, and the Comintern was midwife to the Communist parties.

Convinced that he was ahead of history, Lenin kept his eye peeled for the unfolding of it. When he saw it coming, he acted instantly, stepping on or brushing aside any around him who failed to see it too. In Russia in April 1917 he was aware that his closest companions, assembled in party conference, had not yet perceived that it was possible to jump from a so-called bourgeois republican revolution straight to a proletarian Socialist one. By October he sensed that the party, notwithstanding its vacillation and doubts, could successfully seize power. By March 1919 he believed the time had come to found the Comintern, regardless of what the Germans thought. By 1920 he saw that Europe's large Socialist parties could be split.

Choosing the right moment was always the key factor in the execution of Lenin's grand schemes. Concerning November 7, 1917, at Petrograd, many Bolshevik leaders have since said and written that if they had not seized power at that exact moment they never would have been able to. Likewise, had Moscow not succeeded in splitting Western Europe's large Socialist parties in late 1920 and early 1921, it would have had much less success in the same endeavor in the second half of 1921, and it is not certain that the split-at-any-price operation would have taken place at all if it were attempted in 1922. Until late 1920 the right moment had not yet come, as evidenced by the lack of significant splits in 1919 and early 1920. After that, the right moment had passed. Actually, the rifts completed or begun in the months immediately following the Second Comintern Congress, which ended on August 7, 1920, proved very advantageous for the Communists, while those that came in 1921 were much less so, some even proving detrimental. In the first instance, the Comintern followers could claim a majority of the membership of the workers' organization being split; in the second, they remained a minority. The congresses of the German USPD, the French SFIO, and the left wing of the Social Democratic Party of Czechoslovakia, all held between the end of September and end of December of 1920, brought victory to the Comintern supporters, while the congresses of the Italian Socialist Party and French CGT in 1921 left them a vanquished minority. These ups and downs were reflected within the parties themselves, depending on when their "temperature" was taken. In the Spanish Socialist Party, for example, at its second special congress on June 19, 1920, the faction in favor of the Third International won a majority (which it had not had at the first congress in December 1919), with 8,269 voting for, 5,016 against, and 1,615 abstentions. But by the time of its third congress, in April 1921, the number of Comintern supporters, as shown by the vote, had dropped to 6,025 and the number of its opponents had jumped to 8,808.

These very different voting results during the second half of 1920 as compared with 1921 were in no way due to the aftermath of World War I, whose devastating effects and painful memories were surely more influential in 1919 and early 1920 than later in 1920, when these cleavages took shape. The difference cannot be explained either by the social or economic condition of the working class. There is no discernible correlation between a plight of the working class in 1920 that would have pushed it toward Moscow's revolutionary Socialism and a betterment of its condition in 1921 that would have turned it away. Nor is the explanation to be found in the mere fact of the Comintern's existence. Between the First and Second World Congresses that body never ceased calling for a clean break between Communists and Socialists and beating the drums for formation of Communist parties in the different European countries, though with small effect.

The only factor that can account for the rifts that Moscow succeeded in producing during the second half of 1920 was Soviet Russia's political and military successes at that time. Communism's decisive victories in Russia and elsewhere came when its militants, armed to the teeth, seized power in Petrograd, or when its "Red soldiers" were advancing. The second half of 1920 was marked by two spectacular triumphs by the Soviet Red Army. While thrashing the Whites in the civil war, it trounced the Polish Army and marched to the gates of Warsaw. But in the first months of 1921 hope disappeared that it would resume its advance on Western Europe. Then came the "tactical retreat" represented by the NEP, which eclipsed the civil war victories. A Soviet Russia marching steadily westward and building up its strength at home — and this was the outside world's impression during the large part of 1920—could not help impressing many Socialist militants. This same Russia, forced to backtrack militarily and then retreat in major domestic and foreign policies, as it did in 1921, could not wield the same influence. The first Communist groups had sprung into being in the afterglow of the Bolshevik victory of November 1917. The first mass Communist parties in Europe were born in the wake of the Soviet gains in 1920. Since there were no more spectacular Soviet military victories after that, there was also no further spectacular Communist thrust in Europe.* And beginning in the latter half of 1921, this turnabout, accepted by Lenin for Soviet Russia, would be extended to the Comintern.

But at the time of the Comintern's Second Congress, and immediately after, Lenin was still far from foreseeing his imminent "tactical retreat." He was still wholly on the offensive, both with his Red Army and the Communist International. Having picked the moment at which to cleave Europe's large Socialist parties, he also picked the cleaver with which the job was to be done. It was he who drew the line of demarcation within those parties, barring certain Socialist leaders despite their willingness to accept the

*Likewise, when Soviet soldiers made their deepest penetration into Europe in 1945, all the European Communist parties reached the peak of their numerical and electoral strength.

Comintern framework. And it was the Comintern, actually Lenin and Zinoviev, who handpicked the Moscow emissaries sent to implement the rifts. Some were to play a public role and make speeches at congresses that would cause a big stir—for example, Zinoviev at Halle, Clara Zetkin at Tours, and Kabakchiev at Leghorn (backed up by Rákosi, the second delegate). While the former two had a certain international prestige and knew the language of the country, the third had neither political prestige nor any knowledge of Italian, which helped to produce the failure at Leghorn. But paralleling the activities of these delegates, who were the official Comintern spokesmen, were those of its secret emissaries, who worked within the three big parties for many weeks, even months, before the congresses at which the actual rifts occurred. This was the function of Radek in Germany, Zalewski and Degot in France, and Degot and Liubarsky ("Carlo") in Italy, whose job was to hammer into Moscow's supporters the rudiments of those two complementary tactics long used by the Bolsheviks in Russia and which were now to be introduced on the international stage: first penetrating a target organization and honeycombing it with one's own people, then splitting it. These were the field officers, dispatched to execute a maneuver planned by the Moscow general staff, which is to say by Lenin.

He alone had the authority to name his allies and enemies on the spot. He could slam the Comintern door in the face of anyone whose present or recent past attitude obviously qualified him for membership (men like Longuet and Serrati), as he could throw open that door to other Socialist leaders whose recent positions ought logically to have disqualified them (for example, Cachin and Šmeral). In 1920, Lenin supplemented this indulgence on the right with an indulgence on the left. Despite the criticism that he was being too hard on "leftism," he was eager to retain in the Comintern not only the leaders of left-wing Communism, like Bordiga, but even those on the far non-Communist left, such as the supporters of revolutionary syndicalism and anarcho-syndicalism. This double indulgence stemmed from a single major concern: to have within the Comintern those Western labor leaders who had the ear of the masses and were deemed "salvageable" notwithstanding their pasts, or assimilable despite their current politics.

SPLITTING THE USPD AT HALLE

Of Europe's major countries, Germany was the first to have an important Communist party and the first to see its "centrist" Socialist movement internally split. These two developments could not help strengthening the Kremlin conviction that Germany was the European country farthest advanced toward Communist revolution.

On their return to Germany from the Second Comintern Congress, Stoecker and Däumig, won over to the Comintern cause, began beating the propaganda drums in favor of joining, while two other delegates, Dittmann and Crispien, began agitating for the opposite. A national conference of district Party representatives was called for September 1 to 3, 1920, to hear the delegation's conflicting reports. According to USPD historian Eugen Prager: "Though no actual decisions were made at the conference, the words of Crispien and Dittmann made so deep an impression that one could safely assume that an overwhelming majority of the representatives would have voted against accepting the conditions. Stoecker and Däumig fell completely flat."[3]

But Moscow's partisans succeeded in turning the tide, partly owing to their own efforts but also because of direct personal intervention by three leading Comintern lights: Lenin, Radek, and Zinoviev. Thus, the battle erupting on German soil between those for and against the USPD's joining the Comintern grew into a public fracas between Germany's Independent Socialists, who were opposed, and the Comintern chiefs.

Lenin zeroed in on two articles by Dittmann, published at the time of the national conference in the official organ of the USPD, which described the disappointment of German workers who had gone to help "build Socialism" in Soviet Russia, and which had made a profound impression in USPD circles and on German public opinion as a whole, producing waves even in London and New York. On September 8, to a telegram on the subject sent him by a British journalist, Lenin made a typical reply. Without touching at all upon the articles' substance, he attacked their author personally, blackballing him in advance from Comintern membership, even before the USPD congress had had a chance to make up its mind:

> It is natural that Kautskyites of the Crispien and Dittmann stripe should
> be displeased with Bolshevism. It would be a sad thing if people like
> that did like us. It is natural that such petit-bourgeois democrats—which
> is what Dittmann|is—should be exactly like our Mensheviks, and in the
> decisive struggle between the proletariat and bourgeoisie be often on
> the side of the enemy. Dittmann is all steamed up about our having to
> shoot a few people, but it is natural in these cases that the revolu-
> tionary workers should shoot Mensheviks, and that Dittmann might not
> particularly like it. It will be a dark day when the Communist Interna-
> tional ever lets in any Dittmanns (of the German, French, or any other
> model).[4]

Not long after, on September 24, in a letter to the French and German workers, Lenin again took issue with Dittmann and Crispien, proclaiming that he had no choice but to break with them.

As for Radek, he wrote a pamphlet, *Die Masken sind gefallen* ("The Masks Are Off"), against Dittmann, Crispien, and Hilferding, but more important he came to Germany secretly a short time before the split. The public never knew this, but Radek himself confirmed it several years later in his autobiography: "In October 1920 I went to Germany secretly to help organize the congress, during which we were to bring about unification of the left Independents and Spartacists."[*] The USPD congress did take place at Halle between October 12 and 17, and the German Communist Party congress, expected to endorse the unification, began on November 1, the actual congress of unification running from December 4 to 7, 1920, and Radek was in Germany the whole time. He was quite in his element there, because unifying the USPD left with the German Communist Party had been one of Paul Levi's chief goals since 1919. Levi had established regular secret contacts

---

Entsiklopedicheskii slovar', Institut Granat, Moscow, 1926 [?], vol. 41, part II, p. 168. In fact Radek arrived in Germany in September—not in October as he wrote in 1926—as may be seen from an article he wrote in March 1923: "It was at the moment of our defeat in the war against Poland, at a time when the negotiations of Riga began. I was about to leave Russia and to see Lenin. . . ." The Riga negotiations started on September 11, 1920. Cf. Radek's article on Lenin, *La Correspondance Internationale*, March 14, 1923, p. 152.

with that left (as revealed at the USPD congress in Leipzig, held from November 30 to December 6, 1919). Radek, who was of the same mind, wrote in September 1919 while still interned in Germany: "With the USPD as a whole, so long as it is headed by people like Haase, Dittmann, and Hilferding, there can be no union or even alliance. . . . In any mass action a prime aim must be to reach an accord with the independent masses of workers, and for that we cannot bypass the Independent leftist leaders."[5]

Zinoviev was picked to be the principal Comintern speaker at the Halle congress, which he was to attend in the company of Bukharin, who was replaced at the last moment, however, by Lozovsky. But the Comintern president was not to be the only Russian speaker, for Yurii Martov, the Menshevik leader and former friend of Lenin's, showed up too, having come all the way from Russia to contradict Zinoviev and plead with the USPD not to join the Comintern. Nothing better symbolized the triumph of Bolshevism and the bankruptcy of Menshevism than the presence of those two personalities in Halle. While Martov stood head and shoulders over Zinoviev as a man, Zinoviev was politically far stronger owing to the prestige of the Bolshevik revolution and to recent events in Russia.

Zinoviev came to Halle on October 12. It was the first and last time that the President of the International had a chance to visit Europe in that capacity. He did so under particularly favorable circumstances, Moscow's supporters being assured in advance of a majority at the congress, a fact which the Comintern President did not fail to learn of as soon as he set foot on German soil at Stettin: "The first question that we asked comrade Curt Geyer was: 'Who are in the majority at the congress, we or they, the leftists or the rightists? ' 'The majority are with us,' said comrade Geyer, 'and those supporting us are standing firm, like a rock.' "[6] Zinoviev's position was the stronger for he had the better role to play, that of demagogue and polemicist, at which he was a past master. On the congress rostrum he gave free rein to his talent, delivering a four-and-a-half-hour speech, by his own account the longest he had ever given. It was a superb performance, as acknowledged even by Eugen Prager, the USPD historian, who had little sympathy for the Comintern: "Zinoviev's report was undoubedly a major oratorical feat. . . . He had complete mastery of the spirit of the German language, even if he did occasionally have to feel around for an expression, but that only gave his speech an appealing added flavor. He was characterized at that time as one of the greatest demagogues of the century. And that was certainly doing him no injustice. . . . His speech made an enormous impression on his followers."[7]

The Zinoviev speech was more of an exercise in mob manipulation than in political analysis. He was more interested in stirring up his audience than in explaining to them the problems facing the labor movement in Germany and the world. For Zinoviev, Lenin's faithful mouthpiece, the issue was completely clear: "You must choose. Are you for Menshevism or Bolshevism?"[8] The line laid down in that way reflected the outlook prevailing at the Second Congress in the summer of 1920, an outlook that Lenin himself would begin to revise only a few weeks after the Halle congress, having begun to believe it wrong. It consisted in a series of axioms, much in vogue in 1919 and 1920, the main one being that the situation in general was now ripe for Communist revolution, which had not yet occurred solely because of the treachery of the Social Democratic leaders and trade unionists. "The situation is this. The working class is already strong enough to knock over the bourgeoisie by, say, tomorrow morning—if we all stand together and firmly support Communism. If the workers are still slaves, the only reason is that we have not yet shaken off the accursed legacy of that foul ideology within our own ranks. . . . Every day that passes you can see how the so-called Trade Union International is nothing but a weapon in the hands of the international bourgeoisie, indeed the sharpest and deadliest of their weapons and, one might add, the only serious weapon that they have left to use against us."[9]

With that viewpoint, Zinoviev saw everywhere the stirrings of revolution, despite the treachery of the Social Democratic leaders and trade unionists: "Look at the situation as it really is. Have you not noticed that in Italy, for the past several weeks, we have a budding revolution, a budding proletarian revolution?! . . . Among British workers we are witnessing upheavals of worldwide, historic import. . . . The Balkans, too, are dead ripe for proletarian revolution."[10] Having just returned from the Baku congress, Zinoviev naturally included the Orient in his cosmic panorama of imminent revolution: "The mullahs of Chiva naturally aren't Communists. . . . If you want world revolution, if you want to free the proletariat from the fetters of capitalism, you must not think only of Europe but must turn your eyes toward Asia too. . . . So we say to you . . . that a proletarian revolution without Asia would not be a world revolution."[11] Addressing himself in conclusion to the German Socialists ready to embrace Communism, Zinoviev obviously sought to reassure them: "We do not ask you to start a new war or pull off the revolution tomorrow morning! What we do ask is that you get ready and systematically make propaganda not against Communism, but for it. Not against the revolution, but for it. That is the only real condition."[12]

The most detailed reply from opponents of joining the Cominern came from Rudolf Hilferding, who set out to refute point by point everything that the President of the International had said. Stressing that Zinoviev had studiedly avoided any mention whatever of many of the major problems (such as the true meaning of the twenty-one conditions for admission), he hammered away, both at the beginning and end of his speech, at the specifically Russian character of the Comintern, and at the fact that it was completely tied to Moscow:

> It is most characteristic how Zinoviev . . . equates world conditions with conditions in Russia, how he sees all party relationships in the Russian context. . . . I believe that we are entitled to say that the founders of the Communist Party of Germany [an allusion to Rosa Luxemburg, Karl Liebknecht, and Leo Jogiches] would not sign the twenty-one conditions. Their true meaning is that the European labor movement, as well as that in the East, is to be . . . turned into a tool of the Moscow Executive Committee's power politics. And their Central Committee is nothing more or less than the Central Committee of the Russian Communist Party. Everything they tell us about representatives of other countries cannot for an instant close our eyes to the plain fact that these so-called representatives are actually under the thumb of the Russian Communists.[13]

Hilferding also refuted Zinoviev's optimistic predictions of early revolution in the Balkans and elsewhere:

> One should not make such prophesies; Zinoviev should not make them

.... Tactics like that are little more than a game of chance, an all-or-nothing gamble, on which no party can base its policies. . . . Why, in England and France the Communist movement is completely without influence. As things are, even to dream of uniting the workers and bringing them into the revolutionary camp merely by organizational means, by founding new parties and writing bylaws, is quite utopian .... I fully understand how Russian comrades, vested with authority to govern in their own country—and who thus have an effective, extraordinarily rigorous, and far-reaching power—how these comrades might seriously overestimate the power situation even in countries in which the proletariat does technically have the power to govern, as in Italy. The course that this revolutionary development will follow cannot be decreed from without, but depends on economic and social power-relationships between and among the classes in the individual countries, and it is utopian to believe that it can be hurried along by any solution or command concocted or issued from the outside. [14]

Hilferding also strongly criticized Zinoviev's thesis on revolution in Asia: "What the Communist International is doing in the East cannot be called a socialist policy in any sense of the word. It is rather power politics in the interest of the Russian Soviet Republic, which is engaged in a struggle with England, a power struggle in which the Russian authorities must naturally ally themselves with the mighty, and those mighty are not the workers in their tiny splinter organizations but the representatives of the nationalistic middle-class movement." [15]

Yet, despite all this criticism, Hilferding was not in principle opposed to joining the Comintern. What he condemned was Moscow's desire to split the USPD and the way in which the Comintern was organized, with a single party (Russia's) having already appointed itself master and all the others its subordinates: "We are being split from without over the issue as to whether we should join the Third International, a thing that we all want to do."*

*Protokoll über die Verhandlungen des ausserordentlichen Parteitages in Halle, Berlin, n.d., p. 185. A position similar to Hilferding's—in favor of joining the Third International but against splitting the Socialist party, which was ready and willing to join, and against knuckling under to the Bolsheviks—would produce a similar cleavage in the SFIO in December and in the Italian Socialist Party in January 1921, the Comintern's Russian leaders having already firmly made up their minds to bar from the future International any and all who criticized or questioned its internal organizational structure. To

Hilferding was not deceived as to what Zinoviev and his followers were really after at Halle. The split had been plotted in advance; the pro-Bolshevik wing of the USPD, the leaders of the German Communist Party, and the Comintern general staff had collaborated closely in the execution of the plan, a prime element of which was selecting the exact line of fissure that the split was to follow. The decision to join or not to join the Comintern was not to depend on the opinions expressed by USPD militants themselves but on a line of demarcation pre-drawn by Moscow. The fact that the German Communist Party was the most important foreign party in the Comintern and was run by the headstrong veteran leader, Paul Levi, was part of the reason that this demarcation line was drawn only after consultation and agreement with German Communist leaders, which constituted an exceptional privilege conceded by Moscow, when one remembers that the decision to admit the two French "centrist" Socialist leaders, Frossard and Cachin, had been made unilaterally by the Soviet chiefs. This did not happen in the case of the USPD, as Paul Levi was to note shortly before his break with Moscow: "When it comes to splitting parties not organizationally bound to us, one can do as we Communists did and make the noose wider or narrower. In Germany, for example, the Executive Committee drew the Comintern line so as to satisfy the wish of us Germans to keep out the Ledebour people and bring in everyone to the left of Ledebour and Rosenfeld."*

When the congress voted on October 16, 1920, the Däumig-Stoecker motion to join the Third International got 237 votes, and

Lenin and Zinoviev, acceptance of the idea of a dictatorship by the proletariat (of which Hilferding expressed approval in his speech) was less important than acceptance of the Bolshevik scheme of organization (which Hilferding flatly rejected and which, as he made a point of stressing, Rosa Luxemburg had turned down as far back as 1904). Hilferding's attitude infuriated Zinoviev, who after the speech characterized him as a "petty shopkeeper" having "the mind of a worm." G. Zinoviev, *Dvenadtsat dnei v Germanii*, Petersburg, 1920, p. 22.

**Der Beginn der Krise in der KP Deutschlands*, Remschied, n.d., p. 19. Levi added a remark about Zinoviev's behavior in Halle which highlighted the latter's typical volatility: "When comrade Zinoviev came to Germany—and this was not only my impression—he was completely different, and we, whom in Moscow he had regarded as more or less semi-independent, had to keep hold of his coattails so that he wouldn't run too far." *Ibid.*, p. 19.

there were 156 votes against it. The split was thus consummated, and the left wing remained in session without the right wing, in the presence of Zinoviev, who welcomed the result and set the winners the following task: to bring all the revolutionary elements together into a single Communist party. The left elected the new leaders of its own, since of the twelve on the Central Committee only four had voted to join the Comintern. Their first appeal, signed by the two new chairmen, Ernst Däumig and Adolf Hoffmann, announced the vote of the ex-USPD membership as follows: "237 delegates out of 395 decided in favor of the Third International, the balance of votes showing that 144,000 had voted for, 91,000 against."[16] Returning to Petrograd in a euphoric state, Zinoviev provided even more glowing figures, asserting: "It is obvious that of the simple party members, the workers, at least nine tenths support the (USPD) left. The weeks and months to come will show whether this is really so."[17] As for the future Communist party, to consist of this left united with the Spartacists, Zinoviev foresaw a "workers' party that will wind up with seven to eight hundred thousand members."[18]

With Radek secretly on the scene, steps were immediately taken to effect the preplanned union. A joint appeal signed by Zinoviev, the Central Committee of the German Communist Party, and the Central Committee of the (Left) USPD was published on October 30, 1920, and on November 3, in his report to the Comintern Executive Committee, Zinoviev declared unification in Germany to be imminent. It was just at this time, from November 1 to 3, that the German (Spartacist) Communist Party held its fifth and last congress in Berlin, attended by seventy delegates representing the 78,715 members. The congress of unification was held from December 4 to 7, and the new party took the name Vereinigte Kommunistische Partei Deutschlands (United Communist Party of Germany) or VKPD for short, with Paul Levi and Ernst Däumig as co-chairmen.

But the weeks and months ahead were to disappoint Zinoviev. By 1921 the majority of delegates who attended the Halle congress were still unable to boast of having brought in with them either a majority of the USPD voters or a majority of its members. As for the voters, in the 1920-21 winter elections for deputies to seven state diets (Landtage), they gave more of their votes to the

Halle USPD minority, which, continuing under the USPD emblem, got 1,481,000, than they did to the United Party comprised of the USPD left and the Spartacists, who received 1,440,000 (while the official Social Democratic Party walked off with 5,309,000). On February 24, 1921, the day after these elections, VKPD Chairman Paul Levi was forced to conclude: "I have the feeling that as many ex-USPD voters switched to the Socialists as to us."[19] As for the former USPD members, the VKPD report presented at their congress in August 1921 admitted: "It is probably true, though, that many workers in the USPD who had originally voted to join the Third International did not join the VKPD."[20]

SPLITTING THE SFIO

During World War I the labor movement in France had no equivalent of the Spartacus League, nor was there any split in the official Social Democratic Party—two political phenomena experienced by the Germans even before the November 1917 coup at Petrograd. The divergencies that began in Germany during the war and produced three different labor parties—the SPD, the USPD, and the KPD—occurred in France within the SFIO, the country's only labor party. But in the SFIO the process followed the USPD pattern, proceeding in three successive phases. In the first, during 1919 and early 1920, the party majority was against immediately or directly joining the Comintern. During the second, which spanned the latter half of 1920, the majority of delegates to its congress favored joining. In the third and final phase, during 1921 and 1922, the majority of the voters no longer sided with the Communists but with those who had remained Socialist.

The two factors largely responsible for producing the extreme leftist trend among Socialists, opposition to the war and admiration of the Bolshevik victory at Petrograd, were influential in the French Socialist labor movement also, but later than in other countries. The reason was that opposition to the war and support for the Third International proved strongest in defeated countries like Germany, Bulgaria, and Hungary; the next strongest in countries in which some of the population believed themselves "cheated," despite being technically on the winning side (for example, Italy and parts of Yugoslavia); then in countries that had remained neutral (like Sweden, Norway, Holland, and Switzerland); and was weakest in victor countries such as France, Belgium, Czechoslovakia, and England. The extreme leftist trend was nonexistent in the SFIO when the war broke out in 1914, and was still very feeble immediately after the Bolshevik revolution, and even when the war ended in 1918. At the SFIO congress in April 1919 only 14 per cent of the voting delegates favored joining the Communist International, though some of the Socialist parties, like the Italian and Norwegian, were then voting almost unanimously to join, while others, like the Yugoslav party, had a heavy majority in favor. Ten months later, at the congress that opened in Strasbourg on February 25, 1920, the extreme leftists who advocated joining the Comintern immediately obtained 34 per cent of the votes, yet by the end of the year, at the congress in Tours, 75 per cent voted to join it.

During World War I opposition on the far left did not become an important movement until the October revolution. Even after that, the Communists had to survive in power and consolidate their hold on Russia before the far left abroad could pick up any significant new strength. If the Bolshevik seizure of power had turned into another Paris Commune, there would have been little impetus toward a strong Communist movement in other countries. But Bolshevik power, firmly in the saddle with the end of foreign intervention and having won the civil war and moving westward in Poland, began to exert a fascination even upon people who, shortly before, were refusing to have any truck with Moscow.

Suddenly this same regime in Russia, governed by the same men, was viewed in a different light by the same French Socialist militants. In January 1918 Charles Rappoport, who would become one of the leaders of the French Communist Party (as a member of its Comité Directeur) after its creation at Tours, stigmatized Lenin and his Bolshevism in these terms: "By an act of force, Lenin has just overthrown not only the Constituent Assembly but also and, above all, his own doctrine, the international Socialist program. The Lenin-Trotsky Red Guard have just shot Karl Marx, whom they are always hailing as their patron saint against the militarist opportunists. It is a mad dash for the abyss! Blanquism with Tartar sauce! The suicide of the Revolution. One does not toy like that with the basic laws of a free country."[21]

Marcel Cachin, who in 1920 would play a leading role in getting Socialists to join the Comintern and who from the outset until his death in 1958 would be a member of the Central Committee of the French Communist Party, hurled some equally heavy charges at the Bolsheviks only six months later: "We are not Bolsheviks, and no more than Merrheim do we want to sign, as they did, a new treaty of Brest-Litovsk. Since Mirbach's execution, the Bolsheviks have become so chummy with the German government that the latter takes them openly under its wing. Revolutionaries everywhere are watching in bewilderment the Bolshevik police doing Berlin's chores in hunting down and shooting Socialists who rid their country of the usurper."[22]

When in February 1920, at the Strasbourg congress, the motion of the Committee for Reconstruction of the [Second] International, inspired by Marx's grandson, Jean Longuet, carried with more than 49 per cent of the votes (against 34 per cent for the pro-Communists), the draft resolution bore the signatures of twenty-four leading lights on that Committee. But by December some of the signatories had switched their support from reconstruction of the old International and wound up as members of the Comité Directeur of the new Communist party: Amédée Dunois, Louis-Oscar Frossard, Henri Gourdeaux, Lucie Leiciague, Paul Louis, Daniel Renoult, Joseph Tommasi, and Raoul Verfeuil.* The leader of the group, Jean Longuet, was missing. As in Germany, where the Bolshevik leaders had opened the Comintern gates to Walter Stoecker, who soon moved up to head the German Communist Party, and who in 1914 had been a "social patriot" and "social chauvinist," while closing them to Otto Rühle, who during the war was the first Social Democratic deputy to follow Karl Liebknecht, so in France in 1920 the Bolshevik leaders let in Marcel Cachin, a well-known "social-chauvinist" during the war, but kept Jean Longuet out. This happened notwithstanding the praise given Longuet as late as February 1920 by the official organ of the Communist International under the signature of V. Taratuta-Kemerer, who was in charge of problems of the movement in France and resided in the Kremlin itself, and who, writing about

*Tommasi and Verfeuil were elected members of the Comité Directeur of the French Communist Party at its second congress, held in Marseilles in December 1921.

Longuet and the editorial policy of *Populaire*, emphasized that
"here in Russia we all recognize the valuable services that the
Populaire rendered to the Soviet Republic with its editorial campaign. He . . . was the first to raise his voice in defense of Russia's
workers and peasants then fighting for Communism."[23]

For an entire year, from the end of 1919 until the end of 1920,
the Longuet problem preoccupied Lenin, Trotsky, and Zinoviev.
In the meantime, at the Second Comintern Congress one point was
firmly established concerning the founding of the future French
party: Frossard and Cachin were to be let in, the former as secretary, since his was the highest administrative rank in the SFIO, and
the latter as director of *Humanité*, the party's top propaganda
post. To forge a mass Communist party in France, the Bolsheviks
had to amalgamate two elements which until then had been separate and often hostile: the Committee for the Third International
and the ex-reconstructionists, who wanted to resuscitate the old
Second International and whose two spokesmen in Moscow were
Frossard and Cachin. In Germany the goal had been to fuse the
Spartacists and the left wing of the USPD in order to split that
party; in France the fusion would be between the Committee for
the Third International and the SFIO center, again for the purpose
of producing a split. There was a special reason for letting in the
ex-centrists. The leaders of the Committee for the Third International had all been in jail since March 1920, waiting for a trial
whose outcome threatened to put them out of circulation for
some time. The Bolshevik chieftains, aware of the true situation
and knowing where the strength lay, could not expect to have a
strong Communist party in France if the leaders of the Communist
far left were in prison and the centrist leaders all blackballed. But
letting Frossard and Cachin into the Comintern of course required
that they accept the invitation, that they consent to step inside
when Moscow opened the door. Two decisions taken by Moscow
could make it hard for them to do this, or to bring any of their
Paris friends in with them: the barring of Jean Longuet and the
gist of the twenty-one conditions for Comintern admission. This
explains the skillful and seemingly moderate tactic employed
against the SFIO. It would not do to rush things with Cachin and
Frossard still in Moscow, for too categorical a demand that the

SFIO break with Longuet and jump unconditionally into the Comintern would have immediately alienated the centrist majority and its leaders. On the other hand, letting Longuet in and waiving the twenty-one admission requirements just for the French would have meant Lenin's abandoning two of his root ideas. So Lenin decided on a third course. He would let the French swallow gradually, in small doses, the bitter double pill: the excommunication of Longuet and submission to the twenty-one conditions.

Longuet symbolized for Lenin what Kautsky and Hilferding had in Germany. There was not therefore the slightest chance of Lenin's admitting him to the Comintern, though Longuet's thinking was much closer to Lenin's than that of many others who would be let in. On receiving a letter from Fernand Loriot and the Committee for the Third International at a time when ties with France (and Europe generally) were very tenuous, Lenin in his reply, dated October 28, 1919, named only one Socialist politician who had to be fought: "You of course still have a long fight ahead of you against French opportunism, a particularly subtle form of which is the mentality of Longuet."[24] At almost the same time Trotsky published an article attacking Longuet in the official organ of the Communist International (the issue of November-December 1919), and in a letter to his friends in France he demanded that they dump him: "Putting an end to Longuet-ism is an urgent requirement for political health."[25] Despite these attacks, Longuet continued to seek to reach an accomodation with Moscow. He sent a personal letter to Lenin on the eve of the Strasbourg congress, along with the text of the draft resolution drawn up by the Committee for Reconstruction of the [Second] International. From February 8 to 14, 1920, Lenin wrote out his objections to the resolution, publishing an article on the subject in the March issue of the Comintern organ in which he was very harsh toward Longuet, his resolution, and his entire attitude: "With leaders like that [Longuet-ists] the proletariat will never be able to achieve its dictatorship."[26] On February 28 Lenin wrote Longuet a letter in answer to the one that he had received from him. A few days later, Longuet was again at the center of the dialogue between Moscow and Paris: "On March 9, 1920, the Administrative Committee appointed citizens Marcel Cachin and

Jean Longuet to go to Russia on a mission of inquiry and negotiation."[27] But when the time came for them to leave, "citizen
Longuet, who was busy and could not get away, was replaced by
citizen Frossard."[28] In Moscow, despite his absence, Longuet was
once more under discussion. On July 29, in a declaration signed by
Frossard and Cachin, and read by the latter, it was stated: "We are
convinced that if our friend Longuet were here, after some reflection he would have the same opinion as we."[29] Frossard, who
supported Longuet's position, reported on his return: "There
never was or has been any Longuet policy. His policy is that of a
group within the party who think and feel as he does. We accepted
responsibility for it with him. We would have dishonored ourselves, had we for one moment even dreamed of abandoning the man
with whom we had stood for so long in the interest of a common
cause. . . . That was our attitude [in Moscow]. We were totally
united, and finally wrung from Zinoviev an assurance that they
would not insist on barring Longuet."[30] Yet the seventh of
Lenin's twenty-one admission requirements stipulated the opposite: "The Communist International cannot accept that notorious
opportunists, as they are now represented by Turati, Modigliani,
Kautsky, Hilferding, Hillquit, Longuet, MacDonald and others,
should have the right to figure as members of the Communist
International. This could only lead the Communist International
to resemble strongly the wrecked Second International."[31]

Between Zinoviev's promise to Frossard and the attitude
adopted by Lenin there was no possibility of compromise. In the
months that followed the Second Congress it did seem that Zinoviev's promise was becoming the official Comintern line with regard to relations between Moscow and Longuet. In October 1920,
at the Halle congress, the Comintern President had occasion to
converse with a "Longuet-ist" delegation consisting of . Longuet
himself and Daniel Renoult. The chat between Zinoviev and
Longuet was quite friendly, as Longuet later recalled at Tours: "In
Halle I had a chance to talk with Zinoviev. . . . At the time he did
not regard me as a social traitor."[32] At Tours, the second participant in the conversation, Renoult, confirmed this in a remark to
Longuet: "You remember how, in Halle, Zinoviev greeted you
with brotherly courtesy."[33] At Halle, Longuet had publicly dis-
sociated himself from the speech by Martov, a fact which Zinoviev
himself was pleased to stress: "Longuet deemed it his duty to

protest, directly from the speaker's platform, against the attacks on Soviet Russia made by Martov in his speech."[34] This amicable contact between the Comintern President and the Longuet delegation at Halle led several days later to the signing, in Berlin, by Zinoviev and Renoult, of a statement to this effect: "The exception provided in article 20 [of the admission requirements] regarding the exclusion of 'centrists' shall apply to Longuet, Paul Faure, and the members of their group. If after the vote of the next congress they are still in the party and are willing to accept its decisions as well as the theses and conditions of the Communist International, their admission under those conditions will then become final, subject to ratification by the Comintern's Executive Committee.[35]

Returning to Petrograd at the end of October 1920, Zinoviev went on to Moscow to attend the regular weekly meeting of the Bolshevik Politburo and Comintern Executive Committee, the latter to be held on November 3. Fortified by his success at Halle, he did secure ratification of all that he had agreed to in Germany, including even the accord with the Longuet group. But he did not reckon with Lenin, who within twenty-four hours set forth his "objections to the untimeliness of this measure [admitting Longuet], giving his principal arguments for his decision [*not* to admit him]."[36] Lenin's proposal amounted to a veto, for his opinion alone carried more weight than the decision of the Comintern's entire Executive Committee. Longuet's fate was thus sealed, and the job of carrying out the decision against him was assigned, naturally, to Zinoviev—in line with Lenin's customary method of having a policy implemented by one who had disapproved it but had to be bent to discipline.

The Lenin veto was not disclosed at the time. The first evidence of his intention did not come to light until 1963, in the fifth edition of his collected works, and even then without reproduction of the text. In 1920, nobody in France had any inkling of what was afoot, which is why Zinoviev's famous "pistol shot" telegram—countersigned by the Comintern Executive Committee, headed by Lenin, Trotsky, and Bukharin—caused a sensation when it was learned of on December 28 by those attending the congress at Tours. The ax had finally fallen on Longuet and his friends: "The draft resolution signed by Longuet and Paul Faure shows that Longuet and his group have no intention of being exceptions in the reformist camp. They have been and still are determined agents of bourgeois influence on the proletariat. . . . The Communist International can have nothing in common with the authors of such resolutions." [37] But the resolution, irrevocably damned by the Bolsheviks, proclaimed that "the first duty of party members is at all times and all places to go to the defense of the Soviet Republic," and it recommended that the party "apply for admission to the Communist International," though adding that "the party has the duty to say in all loyalty that a certain number of these conditions are, in its judgment, against the interests as well as the tradition of the French Socialist movement and impossible to apply or inadvisable. It expressly takes exception to the conditions touching on its own internal setup." [38]

The Bolshevik tactic, which consisted in exploiting if not provoking conflicts in the enemy camp, had entirely succeeded in this case. The leader, Longuet, found himself cut off from his friends and supporters. Even Frossard did not stick to the protestations of solidarity with Longuet that he had uttered several weeks earlier. As for the reason given for keeping Longuet out, namely his reservations concerning the internal party setup called for in the decisions of the Second Congress, a number of those were shared by Frossard and his friends, who were let into the Comintern, and were held also by the Committee for the Third International.

Regarding the conditions for admission to the Comintern, a misunderstanding between Moscow and Paris had arisen at the Second Congress. It stemmed from the fact that on July 26 the congress, in the Executive Committee's appeal to members of the French Socialist Party, had stated only nine conditions for admission, whereas Zinoviev as the appointed main speaker on the subject at the session of July 29 had laid down nineteen conditions, to which he then added a twentieth, stipulated by Lenin. The difference between the two sets of conditions was significant, for those beamed at the French sidestepped some important points—such as revolutionary agitation within the armed forces, activities among the farm population, the fight against the Amsterdam Trade Union International, democratic centralism, periodic purges, and the requirement that two thirds of the new central committee be partisans of the Comintern. The difference enabled Frossard to use a double line of argument. On the one hand, he could claim that the Comintern had laid down only nine conditions to the French Socialists, since the rest were unknown to him and Cachin while in Moscow, which obviously was untrue, for at the plenary session on July 29 Cachin read a statement on behalf of the French delegation in which he referred to the twenty conditions that Zinoviev had mentioned in his speech, and he consented to them. Frossard used this argument in the polemics preceding the congress at Tours, in his public dispute with his former centrist colleague, Mayéras, who was against going along with Moscow, and in his writings after the break (as well as in his memoirs). Yet at the time of his joining the Comintern, he raised another argument, expressing some reservations about conditions not included among the nine formally presented to the French, as in his speech at Tours, where he voiced misgivings about the Bolshevik position on the trade union issue, on the question of national defense, and on the expulsions that Moscow was demanding. Even the motion for affiliation to the Comintern, signed in common by the Committee for the Third International and by Frossard, Cachin, and their friends (published in the *Bulletin Communiste* on November 4, 1920), contained many reservations with regard to the twenty-one conditions of admission. Thus condition number three, concerning illegal political work, was omitted from the text presented to the congress of Tours, as was condition number four, pertaining to revolutionary activities in the army. Condition number seven, demanding a total break with the reformists and specifically vetoing the entry of Jean Longuet into the Communist International, was modified in such a fashion that the word "break" and the enumeration of Socialist leaders proscribed by Moscow were omitted. Condition number nine, which spoke of the "subordination" of trade unions to the Communist party, was altered so that instead of "subordination" the words "coordination" and "cooperation" were used to describe the relationship between the party and the trade unions. Finally, the seventeenth condition, which made it obligatory for every new Comintern section to adopt the official designation "Communist party of. . ." appeared differently in the motion presented at Tours: that motion proposed a "temporary acceptance" of a new party name, such as "Socialist Party, French Section of the Communist International."*

These many reservations, expressed at two levels—by Frossard, on the one hand, and by the Committee for the Third International on the other—were accompanied by another obstacle initially confronting the Comintern. While Moscow had sent to the congress at Halle its titular chief, Zinoviev, and its man responsible for Germany, Radek, it had no one of comparable stature to perform the same function at Tours. In Moscow, during the Second World Congress, Trotsky was still preoccupied with the civil war and the hostilities against Poland, and had not yet taken charge of Communist affairs in France. Those entrusted with them in 1920 had no political authority comparable to Trotsky's, Zinoviev's, or Radek's. They were Taratuta, a member of the Russian delegation at the Second Congress, Abramovich-Zalewski and "Vanini", members of the French delegation, and Degot, Moscow's fourth emissary, who arrived in Moscow only after the congress was over. Of the four, Abramovich-Zalewski was the only one to come to France on the eve of the congress at Tours, where he played the role of a grey eminence. This prompted a Longuet supporter, André le Troquer, to protest to the congress from the rostrum: "I shall violate no secret, but I do find it annoying that our party is deliberating under conditions such as these. While I do wish to join the Third International, I am not willing to put up with the clandestine surveillance that is going on, surveillance even of this congress." [39]

In addition to this secret representative, whose presence gave birth to the term "the eye of Moscow," there was another one who was there openly, Clara Zetkin. Apart from the speech that she was to make at the congress, she was drawn into the Bolshevik game, which here only Zalewski knew about and was actively playing: conspiracy with respect to the class enemy and honeycombing the target party with one's own people. The conspiracy was actually a staged show. On the morning of December 28, Clara Zetkin announced that she found it "impossible to take part in the congress and carry out the mandate entrusted to me by the Executive Committee of the Third International," yet that afternoon she

---

*Boris Souvarine was the author of this motion for affiliation to the Comintern, except for the part concerning the relations between the party and the trade unions which was drafted by Amédée Dunois.

appeared on the rostrum, made a speech to the congress, then immediately vanished, the lights in the room suddenly going out. This touch of showmanship was Zalewski's doing, and did not sit well with Clara Zetkin, as she wrote to Paul Levi a few days later: "The melodrama was not to my taste . . . but I had to go along with what our friends wanted."[40] The honeycombing of the party about to be formed, that is, the separation of the Communists deemed reliable from those considered less so or not at all, also began in Tours while Clara Zetkin was there. Since Frossard refused to have anything to do with Zalewski, the latter being the moving spirit of the "reliable" Communist nucleus, the pro-Moscow faction, according to Clara Zetkin's letter, included the following: "I had two meetings with C [achin], Vaillant [-Couturier], Renoult, Renand [René Reynaud], Rappoport, and A[bramovich-Albrecht-Zalewski-Alexander] before attending the congress, and I regard those two meetings as having constituted the most important part of my work."[41]

As for the public debates at the congress, it was a case of the deaf debating the deaf. To begin with, since everything had been rigged in advance, everyone knew how the vote would go, and the colorful speeches from the platform had little chance of influencing what the delegates were going to do. Then too, there was no forthright confrontation on the problem that had actually split the SFIO, as there had been none in the USPD, namely on those twenty-one conditions for admission to the International—in other words, on the organizational as opposed to the ideological aspect. Earlier, at Halle, Hilferding had noted that Zinoviev glossed over this problem, even though its bearing on the Comintern's future was fundamental. At Tours the situation of those who advocated joining the International was the same. Some, like Frossard, themselves expressed reservations about the twenty-one conditions, while others, like Clara Zetkin and Marcel Cachin, avoided the subject, so that no serious analysis favorable to the twenty-one admission requirements was undertaken, though they were at the very heart of the criticisms raised in the speeches of Paul Faure, Jean Longuet, and Léon Blum.

Longuet, the best versed of the three in the affairs of the Socialist International up to 1919, including Russian Socialism, subjected the Comintern to a withering critique similar to Hilferding's at Halle, emphasizing in particular that "the [Second] Congress of the Third International took place at a time when our Russian comrades were particularly elated by their victories over Poland. Convinced that the Red Army was irresistible, in that euphoric state, at that tragic moment, they begat an International which is not an International of the proletariat of all countries, but a specifically Russian one with Russian ideas and Russian discipline, and which cannot be adapted to other countries."[42] Recalling Zinoviev's telegram, read to them the night before, Longuet exclaimed: "If you want us to stay in—and I am tied to the movement with every fiber of my being—the air must be breathable. Yesterday we received from Moscow an outrageous, provocative message. . . . The time has come to decide whether you are ready to submit to the lash. For myself, I am not."[43]

Léon Blum, the spokesman for a group more to the right than that of Longuet and Faure, criticized both the organizing principle, as Faure did, and the Bolsheviks' ideas concerning the International itself, as Longuet had. The future head of the SFIO put his finger on the three key features of the Communist International. First, though, he queried his colleagues on their ideology: "You are in the presence of an aggregate, a doctrinal whole. This being so, the question that you face is: Do you or do you not accept this doctrinal package that has been formulated for you by the congress of the Communist International? And by 'accept'— and on this I hope we all agree—I mean accept in one's mind, in one's heart, in one's will. I mean accept with the resolve henceforth to adhere in thought and deed to this new doctrine."[44]

Blum then attacked the new essence that Bolshevism was introducing into the international Socialist movement: "But what we have here is not merely a revision or readaptation. I shall endeavor to show you—and it is at the very core of my demonstration—that this is a new Socialism, new in all its essentials: its concepts of organization, of the interrelationship of the political and economic systems, of revolution, and of dictatorship of the proletariat." [45] In conclusion, Blum turned to the Bolshevization of the Comintern: "[This new Socialism] rests, on the other hand, on a kind of vast factual error, which has consisted in attempting to generalize for the whole of international Socialism a handful of notions drawn from a particular local event, that of the revolution in Russia, and to set up as a necessary and universal rule for all

Socialism the alleged experience post-distilled from the actual facts by those who gave life and reality to the revolution in Russia."[46]

This new International, according to Blum, was proposing to scrap numerous ideas dear to the SFIO, such as proportional representation for the different viewpoints within the central committee and freedom of discussion, and seeking to impose other ideas foreign to the SFIO and typical of Bolshevism, such as a centralized system requiring that every internal unit be subordinated to one hierarchically above it, secret agencies, purges, with ultimate supreme power in the hands not of the national party but exclusively in those of the Comintern Executive Committee: "In the final analysis, it is that Executive Committee that will have the ultimate power over you, that will have the right to bar groups and individuals, that will centralize all political action. It will have its own office in every country, an office reporting exclusively to it. It will reserve unto itself the right to set up secret organizations to be imposed upon you."[47]

But, as to be expected in a dialogue between the deaf, the unanswerable arguments were met with unanswering silence by the Comintern's supporters. In the absence of Loriot and Souvarine—the two real leaders of the movement favoring joining the Third International who perhaps could have taken up the challenge and given an effective reply—the main Communist speakers at the congress in Tours (Marcel Cachin for the former centrists who had gone over to the Comintern and Paul Vaillant-Couturier for the left) made no attempt at all to meet this critical objection. As for Frossard, in his many speeches and talks at the congress he expressed some doubts and disagreement with aspects of the Comintern line, as immediately after the speech by Clara Zetkin, when he spoke up against the exclusions being demanded by Moscow: "I speak here in the name of a united majority: no exclusions! "[48] In his last address at the congress, Frossard again voiced disagreement with Moscow's attack on Longuet: "Had I been able to yesterday, I would have said then what I am saying to you tonight, distinctly, clearly: I do not agree with Zinoviev. I do not regard you as handmaidens of the bourgeoisie."[49]

The final vote, to distinguish the supporters from the opponents, gave the supporters an overwhelming majority: 3,208 voted for the joint resolution of the Committee for the Third International and the Frossard-Cachin group; 1,022 for that of the (Longuet-Faure) Committee for Reconstruction of the International; the motion by the Committee of Socialist Resistance (Blum) having been withdrawn, there were 397 abstentions from Léon Blum friends. Finally, the Pressemane motion received only 60 votes.

Moscow's satisfaction, however, did not match the size of the vote. If the numerical outcome seemed to justify a feeling of triumph, the decisions taken at the congress had a different effect. So it was not surprising that the Executive Committee, meeting in Moscow after the affair in Tours and discussing the matter at length, confined itself to sending, on January 10, 1921, a message clearly indicating that it still regarded the problem of French membership as far from settled: "The Executive Committee of the Communist International warmly congratulates the French proletarians on their victory at Tours. . . . The Executive Committee of the Third International requests you to send a representative to it in order to settle, once and for all, the question of your affiliation."[50]

Thus, the French Communist Party was no sooner born than its relationship with Moscow became a problem, one that would grow in importance as the years went by, becoming ultimately the Comintern's number one problem. From the beginning, a phenomenon began to emerge in France similar to the one experienced by the USPD in Germany, in that neither the members of, nor the voters for, the old SFIO would be represented in the new Communist Party in proportions equal to their relative strength at the time of the Tours congress. The Communist Party never regained the nearly 75 per cent of the former SFIO voters that it had with it at the moment of the split in Tours. The municipal by-elections in April and July 1921 in the main centers of labor strength such as Paris, Marseilles, Lyon, and the Paris suburbs (Colombes), as well as the legislative elections in the Oise Department, showed everywhere the same pattern: Socialist candidates running ahead of the Communist candidates. Their percentile strengths at the congress of Tours were reversed by the voters in 1921, when the SFIO captured a majority, going from 55 to 70 per cent, leaving the Communists a minority. The same trend began to be reflected in the membership figures of the two parties, though another year or two would have to go by before the numerical ratio was reversed here also.

THE SPLIT IN THE ITALIAN SOCIALIST PARTY

Lenin's decision to close the Comintern door on the leaders of centrist Socialism dominated not only the Second Comintern Congress but the congresses of Halle and Tours as well. It had rougher sailing, however, in the case of the Italian Socialist Party. Unlike the barred Germans and Frenchmen—Dittmann, Crispien, Longuet, and their supporters—the head of both the Italian Socialist Party and its centrist faction, Giacinto Serrati, had a seat in the presidium of the Second Congress alongside Lenin and Zinoviev. Yet only three months later, this same Serrati came under violent attack by Lenin and Zinoviev. In less than six months after the Second Congress, Moscow and Serrati had broken. The break, which took place at the congress of Leghorn in January 1921, was different in two ways from those that had preceded it at Halle and Tours. In Germany and France the split had occurred in Socialist parties not previously belonging to the Communist International, whereas at Leghorn the eruption occurred in a party which as early as 1919, first in March through its directing committee and then in October at its congress in Bologna, had voted overwhelmingly to join. But unlike the congresses at Halle and Tours, where the majority voted to enter the Comintern, at Leghorn the majority voted to leave it. The consequences of what happened at Leghorn had a greater impact internationally. There were profound reverberations within the leadership of the German Communist Party, which accelerated the crisis in that most important section of the Comintern.

Whereas the French Socialists in 1920 joined the Communist International in a state of ambiguity, the Italians had joined it in 1919 in a state of ignorance and frivolity. That it was an act of frivolity was confirmed by some of the Italian leaders, like G. E. Modigliani, who let fall some remarks to Longuet which were reported shortly thereafter to the Executive Committee of the Comintern by Zinoviev himself: "Here is how, in a conversation with Longuet, he [Modigliani] urged the leader of the French 'independents' to join the Third International: 'Friend Longuet,' he said in effect, 'why don't we join the Third International? What does it commit us to, after all? Actually it involves nothing more than sending in, every couple of weeks or so, a pretty picture postcard.'"[51] These carefree words of Modigliani's enraged the Bolshevik leaders, who remembered all too well their own characterization of the Second International as a mere "post office box." They could not tolerate such things being said about the Third. As to Italian ignorance of things Bolshevik, one need only note that the two cornerstones of Lenin's theoretical edifice, the dictatorship of the proletariat and the system of Soviets, received at best a whimsical interpretation at the hands of the Italian Socialists. Concerning the first, the delegate of the Swiss Socialist Party, Graber, saw this well in October 1919 when he attended the congress in Bologna. On questioning the representatives of Italy's official party, Graber was constrained to observe "that not one of the comrades whom I asked gave me a definition of dictatorship of the proletariat even resembling the definition given by the comrade whom I had asked just before." [52] As for the system of Soviets, the party's national council, meeting in Florence in January 1920, had decided upon a makeup of the Soviets which led to various interpretations within the party, starting with that of its secretary, Egidio Gennari, who wanted to abandon the idea of setting up a Soviet system throughout Italy and concentrate instead on creating a model Soviet in just one locality. The national council at its next meeting, in Milan in April 1920, reaffirmed "the need for Soviets" and called upon the leadership to produce them. "So that the leaders will not flag in their accomplishment of this task, we are providing them a charter for the Soviets, in which in a few dozen articles everything is spelled out. All we need now is for the Soviets to be created."[53]

Their contacts with the Italian delegation at the Second World Congress only strengthened the conviction of Lenin and his colleagues that the men and affairs of the Italian Socialist Party were in need of being straightened out. Apart from well-known reformists such as Ludovico d'Aragona, almost every one of the other delegates represented a different viewpoint within the party, including those who had finally come over to Communism, men like Amadeo Bordiga, Nicola Bombacci, and Antonio Graziadei. But the most serious case was that of Serrati, who in his speeches (and sometimes with his votes) opposed many Comintern dicta—as on the national and colonial question, on the agrarian issue (he was the only delegate to vote against the theses), on proposed immediate exclusion of Turati,* on the strict enforcement of the twenty-one admission conditions, on the need for the British Communists to join the Labour Party, and on the merits of the Comintern decision to admit the KAPD to the Second Congress. All these Comintern decisions, theses, and directives were the work of Lenin himself; he had poured into them his deepest thoughts on tactics and organization; and now Serrati had the temerity to reject them outright. It was therefore probably around this time that Lenin decided that there was no room in the Comintern for Serrati. It was Serrati he had in mind when, during a discussion in Moscow, he remarked: "We must simply tell our Italian comrades that the policy of the Communist International is the one being followed by the members of the *Ordine Nuovo* group, not that of the present majority of Socialist Party leaders and their faction in parliament." [54]

The first public hint of the position that Moscow was preparing to take on the Italian question was an appeal addressed to the central committee of the Socialist Party, all the party members and the entire revolutionary proletariat of Italy, an appeal drafted by Bukharin, edited and supplemented by Zinoviev, under Lenin's supervisory eye. On learning of it, the Italian delegation in Moscow discussed it with some heat and expressed their disapproval. Serrati in particular was dead against it. But the Comintern overrode the opposition, and while the Italian delegation was touring the Ukraine, the appeal, dated August 21, 1920, was published over the signatures of Zinoviev, Bukharin, and Lenin.

The appeal contained two central ideas. The first was that Italy was ripe for revolution: "The working class in Italy is suffused with admirable unanimity. To a man, the Italian proletariat is for

---

*Serrati was not opposed in principle to the exclusion of Turati and the other reformists, but only to Moscow's procedure in this case. At the meeting of the Executive Committee of the Comintern, on August 11—that is, after the end of the Second Congress—the problem of the purge of Italian reformists was discussed in the following fashion: "Nobody opposed the exclusion from the party of people like Turati, Modigliani, d'Aragona, etc.; but the Italian comrade (Serrati) insisted that the exclusion should be done in a way that would not alienate the masses." *L'Internationale communiste*, September 1920, p. 2593.

revolution. The Italian bourgeoisie cannot rely on its regular troops, for at the decisive moment they will join the insurrection-aries. The farm workers are for the revolution. Most of the peas-ants are for the revolution. . . . All the prime prerequisites for a grand victorious proletarian revolution encompassing the whole people are now present in Italy. . . . The Third International so concludes."[55] The second thought was that a purge of the Italian party was becoming urgently necessary if the revolution were to be a success: "The very presence within your party of Modiglianis, Turatis, and others of their stripe is a negation of any serious proletarian discipline. The enemy sits in your own house."[56]

Less than ten days later, on August 30, the workers at the Romeo plant in Turin, after finishing work that evening, refused to leave and stayed on to occupy the factory; on the following day, some 280 metal-working plants in Milan were seized by their workers; and then this movement spread to nearly all of Italy within a bare forty-eight hours, with "workers' committees" and "red guards" springing up everywhere. The news could be inter-preted in Moscow in only one way: the imminent revolution in Italy foreseen by the Comintern was now beginning. Once again, in the eyes of the Bolsheviks, Lenin had been proved right. When this development in Italy continued on into September, the Com-intern decided that the time had come to transform the takeover of factories into a revolutionary coup aimed at seizing power, and on September 22, in the name of the Executive Committee, Zino-viev addressed the Italian proletariat in these terms: "You cannot win merely by grabbing a few factories and mills. . . . Our conclu-sion is that you must broaden your takeover, make it general, indeed nationwide. In other words, you must expand the move-ment into a general uprising aimed at ousting the bourgeoisie, seizure of power by the working class, and establishment of a dictatorship of the proletariat."[57]

But by this time the movement was already losing its steam, and four days later, on September 26, it petered out into a com-promise, which did not, however, prevent Lenin and Zinoviev from continuing to insist that Italy was in a state of revolution. On October 25, as he was about to leave Germany, Zinoviev sent another public letter to the Italian Communists affirming: "All the necessary prerequisites for victory of a proletarian revolution exist in Italy. All that is needed is for the working class to be properly organized." [58] Unable to grasp the fact that the first revolutionary wave had washed out to sea, he drew the classic Bolshevik conclusion that its failure was due to treachery by the Italian "Mensheviks." Then, under the signature of the Comintern's Executive Committee, he wrote: "Supported by the reformists and trade union bureaucracy, d'Aragona and his henchmen thwarted the workers' will. *The Italian capitalists were rescued by d'Aragona, Turati, Modigliani, Dugoni, and other capitalist agents.*" [59] It was in the autumn of 1920 also that Serrati's fate was sealed, as confirmed by Longuet's report of a discussion that he had with Zinoviev at Halle that October: "I was saying to Zinoviev: 'But the Italian movement is headed by men whose thinking is closest to your own. They were raised, grew up in the very atmosphere of your movement, and Serrati, a member of the Moscow Executive Committee, has told you that it is not possible to bring off a revolution in Italy at the moment.' Zinoviev's reply was typical of a mentality which I leave to you to judge: 'Then Serrati,' he said, 'is a traitor too.'" [60]

The conception held by the Bolshevik leaders, in the fall of 1920, of what was going on in Italy was perfectly consistent with their general outlook but totally at variance with the facts. There was no treachery by Serrati that autumn, neither physical (since he did not get back to Italy until September 15, when the workers' flareup was beginning to decline) nor political (his attitude being neither more nor less "defeatist" or "opportunist" than that of the local Communist leaders, who several months later were to found the Italian Communist Party). The policy of these Communist leaders was far from one of promoting any immediate revolution, if reports from Italian and foreign Communist sources are to be believed. Angelo Tasca, a leader of the Turin group that had launched the *Ordine Nuovo*, recalled the reluctance of that city's Communist leaders to hazard any attempt at revolution: "Even in Turin, where there is, after all, a bold avant-garde, better armed than elsewhere, the Communist leaders are refraining from any initiative in that direction, and are holding back the elements at the Fiat works who had their trucks all warmed up, ready to sally forth." [61] A leader of the Italian Communist Youth, Ignazio Silone, has described the attitude of one of the Communist Party founders, a spokesman for that same Turin group, whose thinking

was supposed to be closest to that of Moscow: "My most tenacious political recollection is of the appointment of Terracini, of
the Turin Socialist delegation, along with Turati and others, to the
committee that was to draft a law on the workers' control." [62]
Anyway, there was nothing unusual about this state of affairs for
Italy, as Serrati pointed out in his comments concerning one of
the many manifestoes of the Comintern Executive Committee
addressed to the Italian Socialists and syndicalists: "It is quite true
that representatives of the organizations have begun talks with the
government, but this is something that everybody does, the reformists as well as the purest Communists. Did not Bombacci
negotiate with the government ministers during the railroad
strike?" [63] Several months later, at the Comintern's Third
World Congress, Clara Zetkin was to question publicly the official
version of what was going on in Italy: "Comrade Terracini has told
us here that the party committee debated two days over the question as to whether they should or should not launch a revolution.
Still, I cannot put all the blame on Serrati for the fact that they
decided not to. Serrati wasn't even in Italy at the time. He was on
his way home from Moscow. And I even think that we cannot
blame only the Serrati-ites, since the maximalists were then in the
majority on the committee." [64]

Once war had been declared on Serrati, Lenin had but a single
goal: to win that war by isolating Serrati from his friends, as was
being done in France with Longuet. Starting in October and November, an avalanche of manifestoes, open letters, appeals, and
newspaper articles rained down upon the Italian Socialists from
Moscow. They were signed either by the Executive Committee, by
Zinoviev, or by Lenin, who on November 4 wrote an article on
"The Struggle within the Italian Socialist Party," which was published on November 7 in *Pravda* and reprinted the following
month in *Communist International*. In it Lenin hit at two main
points. The first was the revolution-ripeness of the crisis in Italy
and the battle-readiness of the Italian proletariat: "Everyone sees
and admits that the revolutionary crisis is becoming nationwide.
By its actions the proletariat has shown itself capable of rising
spontaneously and of uplifting the masses into a powerful revolutionary movement." [65] The second concerned the formation of a
Communist party and the exclusion from it of the centrist Socialist leaders: "Today it is essential, utterly indispensable, for victory

of the revolution in Italy that a wholly Communist party, incapable of hesitation and weakness at the decisive moment, become the true avant-garde of the revolutionary proletariat. . . . Excluding [the reformist leaders] will not weaken but strengthen that party, for 'leaders' of this type can only lose the revolution 'in the bourgeois manner,' even if they do remain loyal." [66]

Once the decision was taken, it remained only to implement it on the spot. Lenin knew better than anyone in the Comintern that agitprop was not enough unless supported by an efficient local apparatus doing the necessary factional groundwork. Since the Italian Communists knew nothing of this technique, one had to send them "teachers" from Moscow. Thus it was that two Russian militants were secretly in Italy during the months preceding the party split.

The first was Vladimir Degot, who had spent time in Italy on a secret mission for the Comintern at the end of 1919 and in early 1920. On returning to Russia, he was received by Lenin, who questioned him at length on his work in Italy: "I talked a lot about Serrati," wrote Degot in his memoirs. [67] By the autumn of 1920 he was back in Italy, where he would spend the months preceding the Leghorn congress. The second "teacher" had arrived in Italy at the end of 1919. It was N. M. Liubarsky, whose name remained unknown even to the Italian Communist leaders. They knew him only as "Comrade Carlo," though he wrote in the Italian Communist press under the pen name "G. Niccolini." On arriving in Italy, where he had once lived as a political exile, he cooperated closely with Serrati. Together they launched the publication *Il Communismo—Rivista della Terza Internazionale*, to which Serrati lent his political authority, Niccolini contributing the moral support (and probably money) of the Comintern. In the course of 1920, even before the Second Comintern Congress, their cooperation stalled, and "Niccolini" made contact with the *Ordine Nuovo* in Turin. When open war was declared on Serrati, two emissaries from Moscow participated on the Communist side, if they did not actually run the show. Three weeks before the Leghorn congress, Serrati would learn, and publicly reveal, the role of these emissaries:

The Executive Committee of the Communist International sends its own representatives to every country, individuals whom it selects from among Russian comrades whom its members know and trust. The Executive Committee alone judges whether these representatives possess the qualities needed for fulfillment of their appointed missions. And it is to the Executive Committee alone that these gray eminences send their private reports, reports whose contents may be totally unknown to those heading the parties in the countries in which these "informants" do their work. The information that they send is not subject to criticism or control. They report whatever they please, and that is that. And they don't tell you, let you know, give you any chance at all for discussion. And don't ask either what means the informant uses in the pursuit of his task. And, of course, please don't inquire whether such a state of affairs might not lead to corruption. . . . We had the naïveté to express these misgivings to Moscow and propose some practical remedies to preclude the dangers mentioned. The effort failed.[68]

The activities of "Comrade Carlo" in Italy were judged differently by different Communist leaders, depending on their respective viewpoints. On returning from Leghorn, Mátyás Rákosi had only good to say about him to the German Communist Party leaders: "A representative of the Communist International has also been in Italy for a year, and he is well-informed about everything that is going on in the party."[69] But Paul Levi, when he returned from Leghorn, wrote from Berlin to the Executive Committee in Moscow in order to attract its attention to the growing personal animosity between "Comrade Carlo" and Serrati.*

In addition to these secret emissaries, in Leghorn as at Halle and Tours, there were publicly acknowledged Comintern delegates who were to speak at the congress. The original plan was for Moscow's first team, Zinoviev and Bukharin, to attend, but in the end they were unable to and were replaced by two delegates not even members of the Comintern Executive Committee, the Bulgarian Khristo Kabakchiev and the Hungarian Rákosi. Kabakchiev had been a secret Comintern agent in Italy during the weeks preceding the Leghorn congress, before assuming his new role as an official speaker at the congress. His official biography states: "After the congress at Halle, he went to Italy, where on orders from the Executive Committee of the Communist International he helped prepare for the Socialist Party congress and helped unify the 'internationalist group' and Communist left in their fight against the

*For a most significant excerpt from this letter, see Chapter Four, p. 163.

reformists."[70] While entrusting a Comintern mandate to these two militants who enjoyed no international authority and were completely unknown in the movement in Italy, Zinoviev refused to grant one to Paul Levi, who possessed all the qualities lacked by the other two, for he knew the country and could speak its language, enjoyed great prestige in the international Communist movement and belonged to the Comintern Executive Committee elected at the Second World Congress. As the Italian congress drew near, Levi was asked by Clara Zetkin to go to Leghorn: "My dear Paul, please do arrange to come to Leghorn. Just your presence there is bound to have a good effect. The development of our party has made a very great impression abroad."[71] But Zinoviev was not of that opinion, as Levi later reported to his own party's Executive Committee: "The Executive Committee, that is, Comrade Zinoviev, refused to send me as a representative to Italy."[72] Nevertheless, Levi did go to Leghorn, accompanied by a second delegate from the German Communist Party, Paul Böttcher, who belonged to the anti-Levi group; but it was Levi who spoke for his party's central committee.

The mission entrusted to Kabakchiev and Rákosi, and the position that Levi planned to defend, conflicted irreconcilably on one key point: the attitude to be adopted toward Serrati. Kabakchiev and Rákosi had instructions from Moscow to pronounce excommunication upon the Italian leader, while Levi had come to Leghorn to try to prevent any break between Serrati and the Comintern. The Kabakchiev-Rákosi team worked busily against Serrati before and during the congress, without ever having any contact with him. In fact, Serrati was not even aware of their presence, though he was still theoretically a member of the Executive Committee that had sent them. This sufficiently telling fact about the methods that Moscow used against Serrati was reported by Levi in the memorandum that he sent on January 20 to the Executive Committee of the Comintern: "Comrade Serrati appeared and said that he had reported my conversation with him to his comrades, and informed me that his comrades wanted to talk with me. He asked whether I were willing. I replied that I would be happy to, but asked whether they wished to have a representative of the Executive Committee present also, which I favored. Astonished, Comrade Serrati then inquired whether a representative of the

Executive Committee were there. Taken aback by his question, I did not know whether I had jumped the gun in letting him know of the presence of an Executive Committee representative, so I replied evasively. Anyway, Serrati agreed, which I reported to Comrades Kabakchiev and Rákosi." *

Levi's position, approved by Radek, who had secretly been in Germany since September, and by the Central Committee of the KPD, was described in these terms by Levi himself: "I left early Wednesday morning, having spent the night before, from eight until one in the morning, in a discussion with the Executive Committee representative, who was then in Berlin, and we went into the Italian matter in some detail. I read him the important passages from Comrade Zetkin's letter, which I had received that morning, and he agreed that we should work in that direction, namely to try to retain Serrati but definitely insist that he throw out the Turati crowd.... The Central Committee [of the KPD] was aware that this course might not run parallel in all respects to the Executive Committee line." [73]

Once at the congress, which started on January 15, Levi's efforts were of no avail against the strict orders that had been given the two Moscow delegates, as became obvious from his hour-and-a-half-long conversation with them and Serrati. The very next morning Kabakchiev mounted the rostrum and, in the name of the Executive Committee, read off a statement drawn up in collusion with Moscow, the main point of which was Serrati's excommunication. It was delivered in the form of a Russian-style indictment, an exposé constructed of long "theses," little suited to an Italian audience, a fact which Levi pointed out in his report to the Executive Committee: "I feel I must say that the statement did not

*"Bericht des Genossen Levi an das Exekutivkomitee der III. Internationale über den italienischen Parteitag," January 20, 1921. (Document in the possession of the authors.) It is to be noted that Levi's report described the parts played by all the protagonists in the Leghorn drama, those both on the Comintern side (Rákosi and Kabakchiev) and on the Italian side (Serrati, Bordiga, Bombacci, Graziadei); but Levi's report did not say that Antonio Gramsci was present at these negotiations, at which the fate of the Italian Party was decided. ("Gramsci himself played a very small role at the Congress of Livorno. He delivered no speeches, and he rarely participated in the discussions." John M. Cammett, *Antonio Gramsci and the Origins of Italian Communism*, Stanford, 1967, p. 154.) As for Palmiro Togliatti, he was not even a delegate to the Leghorn congress.

make a favorable impression, on structural grounds alone. It was twenty-six typed pages long, much too long to be read off at a congress, let alone an Italian congress, with any hope of its being at all effective. Another mistake was that the entire lengthy statement was devoted solely to an attack upon Serrati, which profoundly upset the assemblage, which after all did constitute a majority of the congress, where the Serrati supporters outnumbered the others at least three to one."[74] This Russian-style pronouncement was greeted by the audience in the Italian style, which at the Third World Congress Zinoviev stigmatized as follows: "It [the Leghorn congress] was literally transformed into a circus. When Kabakchiev got up to speak, they shouted 'long live the Pope! ' Someone released a dove, and there were unheard-of displays of chauvinism. Then everyone blamed Kabakchiev."[75]

Levi's apprehensions about a break between Serrati and Moscow were well-founded, as was his assessment of Serrati's superior strength at the congress, which he had pointed out on January 20 in his report to the Executive Committee; at the election consecrating the split which took place the following day, the Communists got 58,753 votes against 14,695 for the revisionist Socialists (led by Turati), while an absolute majority, 98,023, voted for Serrati and his group.

Moscow's decision was thus "translated into action" with immediately detrimental effect. On January 10, 1921, in her letter to Paul Levi, sent ten days before the split and five days before the congress started, Clara Zetkin diagnosed Moscow's psychological error: "Our Moscow friends have done their best to dampen Serrati's love for the party, to force him to the right instead of luring him to the left. They have not yet learned that while the fist often is a necessary instrument, striking people in the face has been out of fashion in the West since the Middle Ages. One must stroke their beards gently, with kid gloves."[76]

Her use of the term "our Moscow friends" raises the question as to who was actually responsible for the Leghorn split. The responsibility and initiative were certainly not Radek's, for he was in Berlin when suddenly notified of Moscow's decision, and had to do an abrupt about-face, abandoning the position that he had shared with Levi, as Levi later explained to the Party leaders: "On Sunday a telegram arrived from Moscow which the Executive

Committee representative interpreted to mean that the Executive Committee's latest decision was all-out war against Serrati. So their representative—and Comrade Däumig here was a witness—wanted a similar telegram sent to me so that I would know about the new policy. The telegram was sent off from here on Sunday, but because that was the day I left Leghorn, it didn't reach me." [77] Even if the telegram had reached him in Leghorn, it is not certain that it would have made him change his stand, as Radek did. The two were thereafter at odds on the Italian question.

The initiative behind Serrati's excommunication was not Zinoviev's, nor did it originate with the Executive Committee, the entity statutorily empowered to author such decisions. It was Lenin's. Radek admitted this quite frankly to the Central Committee of the German Communist Party at a closed meeting on January 28, 1921: "The Executive Committee was hesitant about sending the telegram. Zinoviev wanted to wait, but Lenin forced the decision through." [78] So Lenin's will had prevailed, just as it had shortly before in the case of Longuet, again against the advice of Zinoviev, who would have been crushed in any contest with Lenin, for the vote would have been taken not by the Executive Committee of the Comintern but by the Bolshevik Party Politbureau. As Paul Levi reported to the leaders of the German party: "I'm not at all sure that our Russian friends agree among themselves. According to reports that I have received, Zinoviev took a different stand but was voted down." [79]

In a message dated January 25, 1921, Lenin and the other Comintern leaders expressed their complete solidarity with the Italian Communists. Lenin in particular stuck to his guns concerning Serrati. Two months after Leghorn he received letters from Clara Zetkin and Paul Levi about the March action in Germany; in his reply of April 16 he accepted most of their objections concerning it, but added that they were wrong on the Italian question—"Regarding Serrati, I consider your tactic wrong." [80] But events would soon prove that it was Lenin's tactic that was wrong, indeed triply wrong.

To begin with, he was wrong about the true strength of the newly formed Italian Communist Party. In their message of greeting of January 25, the Comintern's Bolshevik leaders said: "We are deeply convinced that the awakened workers of your country will join you in increasing numbers every day. . . . The future belongs to you and not to those who, in one way or another, want to make peace with the bourgeoisie through the reformists." [81] But the Bolshevik emissaries to the West, observing the Italian situation at first hand, were less optimistic. On January 28, only a week after the birth of the Italian Communist Party, Radek frankly admitted to the German Party's Central Committee: "I am convinced that the cleavage in Italy has greatly worsened the prospects for revolution there in the immediate future. Our having a Communist party in Italy is an illusion. . . . We must expect that party to be weak for a long time to come." [82] Degot, recalling in his memoirs the climate in Italy on the eve of the Leghorn congress, had to concede:

> There were no reliable leaders to head up the future Communist party. Bombacci, who enjoyed wide popularity, was a romantic, unstable though devoted to the revolution. . . . Gennari is unquestionably a Marxist of great talent, but lacks initiative. Gramsci is a much deeper thinker than the others. He has a better understanding of the Russian revolution, but no power of attraction for the masses, first because he is not much of a speaker, and second because he is too young, too short, and hunchbacked, which makes the audience uncomfortable. Taken together, all this made it seem likely that, with leaders like these, the Italian Communist Party would be less influential than Serrati. [83]

Lenin made another mistake, both political and psychological, in dismissing as hypocrisy Serrati's many protestations of good faith and repeated insistence that he did want to stay in the Comintern. Serrati was saying this at a meeting with the KPD leaders, on October 28, 1920, during a visit to Berlin, at the very moment Moscow was launching its offensive against him. He said it, too, on the occasion of the split in Leghorn, as Levi reported in his memorandum to the Comintern Executive Committee: "Serrati told me again what he had already said. . .namely that he had no intention of going to Vienna to embrace the Second-and-a-Half International, that he and his group were and would remain Communists. If the Third International refused to accept them, then he would 'remain at the Third International's door, on bended knees, if need be,' but he would have nothing to do with the Second International." [84] And immediately after Leghorn, on his return visit to

Berlin, he repeated the same, as Curt Geyer, the German representative on the Executive Committee, reported at the meeting of
February 22, 1921: "Serrati came to Germany and approached
the Central Committee. No official session was held with him.
Some of the comrades on the Central Committee asked him what
he was going to do now. He said he felt as though he were a
member of the Third International. When someone remarked that
that did not seem to be the case, however, he replied that, yes,
they were still waiting in front of the church."[85] Actually, less
than six months later the Comintern had to yield to Serrati's will
to belong to it, and it reopened negotiations which led to his
re-affiliation.

These first two mistakes of Lenin's, concerning Italy's labor
and Communist movements, were supplemented by a third regarding Italy as a whole and the international labor movement in general. His argument that the advance of proletarian revolution in
Italy urgently required the establishment of a Communist party
and a definitive split with Serrati soon was refuted by events. In
the fall of 1920, the Comintern tactic in Italy was similar to that
proclaimed by the German Communist Party the previous March,
at the time of the Kapp-Lüttwitz putsch; the difference was that
the Comintern had condemned the German party for using that
same tactic, whereas now it was urging the Italian party to adopt
it. In both cases its diagnosis of the identity of the Communist
movement's principal enemy was wrong. The Bolsheviks believed
that the imminent death struggle was to be between the Communist proletarian revolution and capitalist society (including capitalism's supposed arch-henchmen, the Social Democrats), whereas
the real battle shaping up was between parliamentary democracy,
which safeguarded the existence of all parties, including even the
Communist (and which often did need the active support of Social
Democrats), and a Fascist dictatorship out to destroy all parties,
starting with the Communists and finishing with the liberals and
Catholics, after knocking off the Social Democrats in between. At
the time of the Kapp-Lüttwitz putsch the German Communist
Party had not grasped this, but the consequences were not tragic,
because the two other major workers' parties had grasped it and
were able to thwart the putsch. But in Italy the two leading workers' parties, the Serrati Socialists and the Communists, did not see

the real danger, and the Comintern contributed nothing toward helping them understand that after 1921 the real enemy was not the parliament-oriented bourgeoisie but Mussolini and his movement. The Leghorn split weakened the Italian labor movement, making impossible any cooperation among the country's democratic forces (Catholics, liberals, and Socialist reformists) to block Mussolini's victory. Serrati, still resolved to get into the Comintern, imitated its error. In October 1922, at the Socialist Party congress, on the eve of his ultimate admission to the Comintern fold, he addressed himself to his party's reformist wing, which was about to split off: "You seek an alliance with Democracy, and you say that Socialism too is democratic. But Socialism is proletarian democracy, that is, true democracy, while the other is bourgeois democracy, a falsification of true democracy. . . . Let all who want to work for the revolution march with us, and those who want to prevent the revolution go with the bourgeoisie." [86]

A month later, in early November of 1922, Serrati was again in Moscow to attend the Fourth Comintern Congress; in Rome, instead of the heralded proletarian revolution it was the Mussolini counterrevolution that had won the field. As Lenin and Serrati were making their peace in Moscow, Fascism was spreading its blanket over Italy. Thus the far left helped lift Mussolini to power in 1922, as it would help Hitler ten years later.

SPLITTING THE CZECHOSLOVAK SOCIAL DEMOCRATS

There were only two countries in Europe of which the Comintern could boast that, after splitting the Socialist parties and setting up a united Communist party, the Communist party attained a membership numbering several hundred thousand: these were Germany and Czechoslovakia, in which Social Democratic parties, among Europe's first, had been established in the nineteenth century.

The cleavage process in Czechoslovakia occurred in the same stages as in two other countries, Germany and France, in which the majority of the USPD and the SFIO delegates assembled in congress had declared itself in favor of the Moscow position. In the beginning, in 1918 and 1919, the far left was a very weak minority, and its power was diminished further because with the proclamation of the Czechoslovak state on October 25, 1918, a

coalition government was formed which gave some of the power
to the Social Democrats. In June 1919 it was a Social Democrat,
Tusar, who became head of the coalition government (at the very
moment at which the SFIO and USPD had just opted for the
opposition). At the Twelfth Congress of the Czechoslovak Social
Democratic Workers' Party, held from December 27 to 30, 1918,
the far left, a feeble minority, ran a candidate for the executive
committee, A. Zapotocký, who received only 126 votes out of a
total of 644. When in June 1919 the Czechoslovak government
took part in the intervention against Soviet Hungary, the left was
still weak, as the party head Bohumil Jílek admitted to the Comintern's enlarged Executive Committee: "By June the bourgeoisie
was already strong enough, with the help of the Social Democrats,
to launch an attack on the Hungarian Soviet Republic, and dealt it
a mortal blow. The resistance of the party's left wing to that
attack was small." [87] At the Social Democratic Party's national
conference, which opened on October 5, 1919, the far left was
present as an autonomous united faction, but its statement of
principle in favor of Communism was rejected by the majority 65
to 36, which indicated that by the end of 1919 the far left was
gaining ground.

From then on, the far left asserted itself as a "fractionist"
organization within the Social Democratic Party, and scheduled
its first national conference for December 7, 1919. One of the
decisions taken at that meeting proclaimed the need to sever relations with the Second International and join the Third. The next
conference of the "Marxist left" took place on March 7, 1920.
Two months later its leader, Bohumír Šmeral, in the absence of
Alois Muna, who was in prison, traveled to Moscow, where he
talked with Lenin. Another delegation of the "Marxist left" went
to Russia to participate in the Second World Congress. It included
the three militants Břetislav Hula, Antonín Zapotocký, and Miloš
Vaněk; they were joined by Ivan Olbracht, who had been in Moscow since Šmeral's arrival. Šmeral did not attend the Second Congress.

When the delegation returned to Czechoslovakia, the campaign
in favor of joining the Comintern and setting up a Communist
party gained vigor and popularity. When the thirteenth party congress was announced for September 26, advance pollings of the

delegates showed a majority for Communism and the Comintern. The official leadership decided to postpone the congress until December but the partisans of the "Marxist left" assembled on the original date, claiming the support of 321 of the total of 464 elected delegates, which represented 68 per cent of the Social Democratic Party membership. The congress was held in Prague, and Šmeral and Zapotocký were among the main speakers. It took no important step toward Communism, however, nor did it vote to set up a Communist party or to join the Comintern. A few days later at Karlsbad, on October 3, at the congress of Czechoslovakia's German Social Democratic Party, the majority voted down the Communist left's motion 295 to 144.

In December 1920 there were disturbances in Czechoslovakia which for a while created a tense situation in the country. On December 9, by government order, police occupied the headquarters of the Social Democratic party—which initially had been forcibly taken by the leftist faction against the will of the official Social Democratic leadership—and also seized the editorial offices and printing plant of the party's main newspaper, as well as its administrative offices. The left responded by calling a general strike, but the government proclaimed a state of siege, set up special tribunals, arrested about three thousand people, and the strike collapsed, not from weariness or through compromise, as it had in Italy a few weeks earlier, but under the pressure of the police and army, who were assisted by the nationalist Sokol organization. On December 19, Zinoviev sent greetings to the Czechoslovak workers, phrased in the usual style, forecasting inevitable revolution and citing the example of Russia: "The Communist International calls upon all Czechoslovak workers and soldiers to turn their bayonets against their oppressors. . . To the workers of Czechoslovakia we say: courage, Comrades! After July, Russia had its October. You will have yours." [88]

In early 1921 the Communist left in Czechoslovakia resumed its agitation for official establishment of a Communist party outside the Social Democratic Party, but for several reasons the effort did not immediately succeed. One was the ethnic structure of the new state. In an ethnically heterogeneous country like Czechoslovakia, unifying the different groups favoring Communism was more difficult than in ethnically homogeneous countries. From the outset the Communists had to contend with this ethnic factor, though they refused to admit it publicly. The three ethnic groups that had come together to form the new Czechoslovak state acted separately and independently to set up their own Communist organizations. On January 16 and 17, 1921, 149 delegates of "the revolutionary class of Slovakia and Sub-Carpathian Russia" met first at Lubochna, then at Ruzomberok. Among them were 88 Slovaks, 36 Hungarians, 15 Germans, 6 Ukranians and 4 representatives of the Jewish movement Poale Zion. They accepted unanimously the 21 conditions for admission to the Comintern, with one exception. The vote on condition 17, requiring that the party's name be changed to Communist Party of Czechoslovakia, was postponed until the congress of unification and the creation of a single revolutionary party for all Czechoslovakia.

After Slovakia, it was the turn of the Sudeten region, the home of Czechoslovakia's Germans. Barred from the Sudeten Social Democratic Party at its Karlsbad congress in January 1921, the elements of the far left, led by Karel Kreibich, met on March 12, 1921, at Liberec (Reichenberg); they voted to accept the 21 conditions for admission, and proclaimed formation of a German section of the future Czechoslovak Communist Party. Gyula Alpári, the Hungarian Communist leader who had fled to Czechoslovakia after the débâcle of the Hungarian Soviet Republic, and who was soon to hold an important job in the Comintern propaganda apparatus, attended the meeting, at which he played a significant role, as Kreibich reported: "We always acted in agreement with Comrade Alpári. It was with him in particular that I worked out the stand that we would take at the party congress in Karlsbad [January 1921], and what I was to say concerning the report of the first speaker [at Liberec]."[89]

This left the main ethnic group, the Czechs, who had not yet established any Communist organization. That irritated Moscow, to judge from the criticisms leveled by Zinoviev at Bohumír Šmeral, whom he charged with "vacillation" in his report of mid-March 1921 to the Tenth Bolshevik Party Congress.[90] It was not until May 14 through 16, 1921, that the left in Bohemia and Moravia finally got together in a municipal hall in Prague. The 569 delegates claimed to represent more than 350,000 members, not only Czechs but also Slovaks and Hungarians (representatives of the Communist Party's German Section were there as guests). Just before the congress opened the Comintern Executive Committee sent a letter calling urgently for the immediate creation of a Communist Party of Czechoslovakia: "The Communist International sends its fraternal greetings to your party congress in the hope that it will become the founding congress of the Communist Party of Czechoslovakia. Two and one half years have passed since Czechoslovakia became an independent state. . . . We hope that the party congress will not only adopt the name of Communist Party, to set itself clearly apart from the Social Democrats, soiled by their coalition with the bourgeoisie, but that it will also clearly and unmistakably declare its acceptance of the principles and tactics of the Communist International." [91] The letter warned those attending the congress of the dangers of nationalist deviation and insisted upon the necessity for the Comintern to have a single, strongly centralized Communist party within the framework of the Czechoslovak state.

The main speaker at the congress was Šmeral, and two important resolutions were adopted unanimously. The first declared that the congress of the left of Czechoslovakia's Social Democratic movement favored joining the Third International unconditionally, and changing its name from Social Democratic left to Communist party. The second laid down the procedure for establishing a Communist party for all of Czechoslovakia, stipulating: "The Executive Committee is instructed to delegate from among its members comrades who, jointly with delegates of the Party's German section, shall comprise an action committee. It will be the duty and function of the action committee to complete preparations for unification of the regional parties, specifically: (1) to work out a joint set of organizational bylaws; (2) to draw up a program of action; (3) to lay the groundwork for a joint party congress." [92]

So instead of immediately setting up a single Communist party for the entire country, it was necessary to initiate a fusion process between two Communist movements, a process that would take several months. Knowing that this would not please Moscow, those attending the congress felt obliged to send the Comintern a letter of reassurance: "We can assure you, comrades, that the creation of a unified Communist Party of Czechoslovakia as a section of the Third International has become, from this day, merely a problem of organizational procedure, a problem that will be solved in the immediate future." [93]

The Comintern's Third World Congress, to be held from June 22 to July 12, 1921, would not be able to boast of having a single Communist Party for all of Czechoslovakia. This constituted an almost unique exception in the general panorama of the European Communist movement at that juncture. The Comintern subsequently sent one of its emissaries N. M. Liubarsky, "Comrade Carlo," who had proved his mettle in Italy, to implement its directives concerning the immediate establishment of a Communist party. Undoubtedly he did play an important role, to judge from the report that B. Jílek, the head of the Czechoslovak Communist Party, made to the Comintern's enlarged Executive Committee (but which was not published in the Comintern press): "The committee of the six [whose task it was to unify the Czechoslovak Communists] worked in close touch with the Executive Committee's representative, Comrade Carlo."*

The majority that the Communist left had picked up by September 1920 began to melt away just as the Czechoslovak Communists were finally unified in the fall of 1921. The same decline of influence had set in a few months earlier in Germany and then in France. In June 1922 party spokesman Jílek, addressing the enlarged Executive Committee, confessed that "the party has fewer members now than it had at its birth." [94] The statistics for that year confirm this; its registered membership dropped from 350,000 in 1921 to 170,000 in 1922.

THE SPLITTING OF THE OTHER SOCIALIST PARTIES

Splits within the Socialist parties and the formation of Communist parties everywhere in Europe and in the few non-European countries were regarded by the Comintern as an irreversible process

---

*Report of Comrade B. Jílek to the enlarged second plenum, June 1922, page 6. It was at its meeting of July 16, 1921, that the "little bureau" of the Executive Committee had decided to send an emissary to Czechoslovakia, but the assumed name "Comrade Carlo," and of course the identity of the assumer, remained secret.

leading to a final Communist worldwide victory. In fact, instead of the assumed irreversibility, splits proved to be two-way streets, bringing to local Communist parties and to the Comintern some huge initial successes and far fewer long-lasting political benefits, but registering also many drawbacks even where everything at the beginning seemed to be promising. Striking cases in this respect were those of the only two large Western European Socialist parties—the Italian and the Norwegian—which in 1919 joined the Communist International en bloc, without internal split. Soon, however, that unanimity began to disintegrate: splits which occurred it Italy in 1921 and in Norway in 1923 left only a minority of former Socialist party members in the Comintern camp. In Italy, that minority was moderately substantial, and this enabled the Communists to play a certain role in the country's political life. In Norway it was relatively much smaller. Of the 105,000 who in 1919 belonged to the old Labor Party, which joined the Comintern, only 15,000 were left after the break in 1923, which stripped the Norwegian Communists of any political significance.

The Socialist splits in three of Europe's most advanced countries—Germany, France, and Czechoslovakia—initially favored the Comintern cause and brought to the new Communist parties temporary majorities; but in the following months these successes were considerably eroded. The Socialist splits in other countries followed in main lines an identical pattern: Socialist parties in Europe's unindustrialized regions favored joining the Comintern much more eagerly than those in the industrialized regions. The more industrially developed a country or region was, especially if it had a deep-rooted trade union organization and a well-established reformist Socialist party, the less support it gave to the Comintern cause.

The strongest support for the Comintern came from a region that in 1914 was Europe's most backward from the standpoint of industrialization and in terms of entrenched trade union and Socialist party strength: the Balkans. In Bulgaria the "broad" (reformist) Socialist Party was stronger than the "narrow" (revolutionary) Socialist Party before 1914, but after October 1917, and the founding of the Comintern, the narrow party became far stronger and a serious political factor in the country. In Rumania the Socialist Party at its congress on May 9, 1921, accepted the 21

conditions for admission to the Comintern by a vote of 432 to
111, but the Communist party there never managed to become a
mass party. Communism in Greece got off to roughly the same
start. At the second congress of the Greek Socialist Labor Party,
held in Athens on April 5, 1920, the vote went almost unanimously for joining the Comintern, but again the Communist party, born
of a weak Socialist party, failed both at its foundation and during
the first decade of its existence to become a numerically and
electorally strong party. In Yugoslavia, an ethnically heterogenous
country with a very mixed economy, an effort was made in 1919
to unify the parties and affiliate with the Comintern. The Socialists in the regions least developed industrially—Serbia, Bosnia, and
Dalmatia—were almost unanimous for unification and joining. In
Slovenia, the country's most industrialized region, on the other
hand, the Socialist Party had existed since 1896; it had refused to
join the Comintern, as did the Social Democratic Party of Croatia
and Slavonia, founded in 1894. Equally characteristic was the fact
that the first two men to serve as secretary-general of the Yugoslav
Communist Party were Filip Filipović, won over to Socialist ideas
during his thirteen-year stay in Petrograd at the beginning of the
century, and Sima Marković, who advocated a Serbian version of
revolutionary syndicalism before 1917. Also typical was the fact
that in the legislative elections of 1920 the Communist party got
its heaviest vote in Montenegro and Macedonia, which before 1914
had had neither a Socialist party nor any trade union movement.

At the two geographical ends of Europe, Finland and Spain,
countries that still lacked much industry immediately after World
War I, important segments of the Socialist parties rallied to the
Comintern. In Finland the party had been founded in Soviet Russia in 1918 by the exiled Socialists Manner and Kuusinen, and
could count on exerting a certain influence in the labor movement. The Spanish Socialist Party at its congress in April 1921
went back on its earlier decision to join the Comintern, the proposal this time being finally defeated by a small majority (8,808 to
6,025), so that the Communist party did have some influence in
Socialist circles; but the majority of the previously registered
membership of the Socialist Party, more than 50,000, refused to
switch to the Communist party.

Wherever Europe's Socialist parties did not split, or wherever the cleavage was not deep, Communist parties remained insignificant or nonexistent. The weakness of the Communist parties was merely a reflection of the strength of a country's Socialist party and trade-union organizations. In Sweden, apart from its official Social Democratic party, there was the left-wing Socialist party, which supported the Comintern. In March 1921 it split over the 21 admission requirements. Afterwards the number of Comintern adherents dropped from 25,000 (in 1920) to 14,000. In Denmark in 1921 the Social Democratic party had 115,000 members, of which the Communist party picked up only 1,200; the splinter groups of the far left never succeeded in shaking the bastions of the official Social Democrats. Britain's large Labour Party escaped the Communist dissension altogether, and even the smaller Independent Labour Party, at its congress of March 1921, refused to join the Comintern by a strong vote of 521 to 97. In 1921 the numerical strengths of the different British labor parties were: the Labour Party 4,417,000 registered members; Independent Labour Party 35,000; the Communist Party 10,000. In Austria, too, the powerful Socialist party remained intact and united around its leaders, with 491,000 members, while the Communists had 14,000. An equally solid disproportion prevailed in Belgium, where the Socialist party had 718,000 members, the Communist 1,100. In Holland in 1919 the reformist Social Democrats had some 42,000 members; the Communists had 500. In Switzerland, after the January 1921 referendum which went against the Comintern by a vote of 25,475 to 8,777, the Socialist party had 54,000 members, the Communists 6,000. Even in the United States, it was over the issue of joining the Comintern that the Socialist party split, the first time at the party congress in Chicago on August 30, 1919. The left walked out and met separately the next day. The second time was when at its congress in May 1920, the "centrist" motion calling for conditional affiliation with the Comintern got 1,339 votes, against 1,301 for unconditional affiliation. The chief result of all the bickering was that Socialist party membership, up to 104,822 in 1919, dropped to 26,766 in 1920, taking a further plunge to 11,019 in 1921. The Communists did not profit from this; their own membership declined from 15,000 in 1920 to 12,000 in 1921.

Comintern and the March 1921 Action in Germany

In both 1919 and 1920 Germany's Communist militants had engaged in insurrection: in January 1919 in Berlin, in April in Munich; and in March 1920 in the Rhineland, Westphalia and Saxony, paralleling the general strike that followed the Kapp-Lüttwitz putsch. But in neither year had the official leadership of the German Communist Party deliberately triggered or effectively conducted the insurrectionary clashes, and the Comintern, the next higher echelon over the German Central Committee, had had nothing to do with them at all. Insurrectionary flareups occurred again in March 1921, particularly in Central Germany, only this time leaders of the German Communist Party and the Comintern were involved; more than that, it was they who started it all, as they would again in October 1923.

In its hall of martyrs the Comintern first enshrined Rosa Luxemburg and Karl Liebknecht, the two principal victims of the fighting in January 1919, and glorified the leaders of the Soviet republic in Munich. Later the Comintern exalted the armed clashes of October 1923, although they were modest, in order to weave out of whole cloth the mythic cult of party leader Ernst Thälmann. But it maintained a stony silence concerning the actions of March 1921. Actually, the magnitude of the fighting, measured in terms of lives lost, was far greater in March 1921 than in January 1919 in Berlin or October 1923 in Hamburg. According to the records of the German authorities, in March of 1921 some 3,470 Communist militants were arrested, 145 killed, and the number of wounded or otherwise injured, though unknown, must have greatly exceeded the number killed.* In contrast, when on January 25,

*Walter Drobnig, *Der mitteldeutsche Aufstand 1921. Seine Bekämpfung durch die Polizei*, Lübeck, 1923, appendix 13. To the repression by the police during the March action was added the subsequent repression by the courts,

1919, the funerals were held of the Communists who had fallen in the recent fighting, there were only thirty-two coffins. And immediately after the clashes of October 1923 in Hamburg, when the Communists reported the events in the official organ of the Comintern, they listed only six killed and a handful of wounded.[1] But the Comintern made no attempt to glorify those killed in the March 1921 episode; it even denied having fathered that misadventure.

THE GERMAN COMMUNIST PARTY BEFORE THE MARCH ACTION

The victory over the USPD at the Halle congress in October 1920, followed by the congress uniting the USPD left with the Communist party (Spartacus League) in early December, had given a feeling of confidence both to the leaders of the newly united German party and to Zinoviev, who had been the main speaker at Halle. This feeling of confidence was based on their appraisal of the state of mind of the masses. Wasn't Lenin always saying that without the masses no revolutionary action was possible? And did not this key word "masses" endlessly recur in the writings of Rosa Luxemburg, including the articles written on the eve of her assassination? While the support of these masses was precisely and most sorely what the Spartacists had lacked, the situation was now transformed by the creation of the United German Communist Party, known as the VKPD—or so it was euphorically assumed. Just as soon as the masses had been won over and annexed to this new party, the scene would be set for revolution. This mass Communist party would differ from a mass Socialist party primarily in its ability to lure, drag, and push the proletarian masses into revolution. The resolution on the subject passed at the congress of unification hammered away at this theme: "The old Communist party could not launch any mass action because it did not have the masses behind it. . . . The new United Communist Party is strong enough, when events permit or require, to initiate actions on its own. . . . Small, without influence on the broad masses or workers,

described in Moscow two months later as follows: "Ten thousand proletarians were thrown into prison. Forty special courts, set up by President Ebert, the Social Democrat, dispensed summary justice, sending workers to their death, sentencing others to long years at hard labor." *Moscou*, a French-language newspaper published in the Soviet capital, May 28, 1921, article "La défaite de mars," p. 2.

the old Communist party struggled bravely for the idea of revolution. Now large and buttressed by broad mass support, it will continue the good fight. It cannot do otherwise, for the hour of the revolution's victory nears."[2]

From then on the chronic dilemma that had haunted the old Spartacist Communist party—whether to assume an offensive or a defensive position—was categorically resolved, and the word *offensive* started to replace the somewhat vague term *action*, so much in vogue and favor at the congress of unification. The following month, on January 28, 1921, at a meeting of the Central Committee of the United Communist Party, Karl Radek had an argument with Paul Levi in which he vigorously insisted on the brightness of the prospects for an early new revolutionary offensive: "The Red Army is not being demobilized. It is being made more flexible, and is being shifted to the southwestern and western borders. We shall not make war in the winter. . . . I can tell you that the thought of an aggressive foreign policy is more in our minds than it used to be."[3] This statement by Radek lagged several months behind the drift of Lenin's thinking, for when Radek had taken leave of Lenin in September 1920 events were about to dampen Lenin's hopes and confirm Radek's warnings; thus in January 1921, when Radek defended what had been Lenin's opinion in the fall of 1920, Lenin was just coming around to the Radek viewpoint, which until then he had opposed.

Nevertheless, two of the most lucid leaders of Communist affairs in Germany, Radek and Levi, did come out at this time for taking the offensive. In fact, after Radek, Levi declared on February 24 to the assembled Central Committee: "I tell you that at least in the present situation the tactic of the Communist International has in any case to be an aggressive one."[4] At the same time, on February 22, two other important leaders were telling the Comintern Executive Committee in Moscow exactly the same thing. One was Curt Geyer, the Moscow representative of the VKPD, the other Guralsky, a Comintern envoy to Germany. To Zinoviev, Radek, Béla Kun, and several other of the committee members Geyer said: "The party's political activity has had to be based on the actually existing general situation in Germany. Briefly, that situation is that the objective prerequisites for a revolution, for a decisive action, are at hand. . . . It is the view of the VKPD that establishing a linkage with those already organized is the road that can lead to an offensive against the bourgeoisie in Germany, and can lead that offensive to success. . . . The possibility of sharp and heavy fighting is a thing of the near future."[5] Guralsky, who from 1920 to 1924 was to shuttle regularly between Moscow and Berlin, added that the proper perspective was that Germany was passing through a period of revolution and that the VKPD therefore must engage in revolutionary action.[6]

It was no coincidence that Geyer, who was pressing for a revolutionary offensive, came from the USPD left, for the ex-leftists of the USPD often displayed a fire-breathing impatience not shared by the Spartacists. Even back in the days of January 1919 it was they, starting with Georg Ledebour, who had manifested "putschist-Blanquist tendencies," as Radek wrote in September of that year.[7] After the unification, the USPD's ex-leftists stuck to their old ways, and this to the very eve of the March episode, as Y. S. Reich—"Thomas," a qualified witness, recalled: "The members of that party were more inclined to hazardous undertakings than were the old Spartacists. The latter were better grounded in Marxism. Former members of the Independents, like Däumig, became fervent proponents of insurrection. Whenever at a Central Committee meeting anyone proposed taking up arms, it was always an ex-Independent."[8]

But during the period from December 1920 to early March 1921 the "line" of the German Communist Party, and of the Comintern as well, was not solidly in favor of a revolutionary offensive. Actually, the topmost echelons of the party and the Comintern were of two minds. The first was that they should strike now while the iron was hot, with the masses being won over and a strong party in the making. The second was that the masses were not really won over but were still outside the VKPD, and that the new united party was not remotely equal to the task of waging an offensive. Curiously enough, this latter view was held simultaneously or alternately even by those who were plumping for an offensive, including Radek and Levi. In the same month in which Radek urged aggressive tactics on the German Communist Party's leadership, he had written only three weeks before, in agreement and collaboration with Levi, the famous "Open Letter" published on January 8, 1921, in the Communist daily *Rote Fahne* and addressed to the four trade union organizations and three labor parties, the SPD, the USPD, and the KAPD. The letter proposed a program of common action in the area of social and economic demands. Bearing no resemblance to any "revolutionary offensive," the proposal was indirect evidence that the Communist leaders realized that most of the workers were not with them, which required them to appeal to the other workers' organizations. If the "masses" assembled at the congress of unification in early December 1920 had been numerous and strong enough, there would have been no need a bare month later to call upon the "masses" affiliated with those other organizations. The open letter was a tacit admission that the expected rush into the Communist camp had failed to materialize.

More direct proof came in the weeks following the congress. When the compiling of the new VKPD membership list was completed, it was clear the USPD militants had paid little attention to the decision of their delegates to the Halle congress, since the percentage of those members switching over to the VKPD was smaller than that of the delegates voting for the Comintern at the Halle congress. Similarly, the local parliamentary elections of February 1921 for seats in the Prussian Landtag (provincial diet) showed that most of the former USPD voters were not following their leaders into the Communist camp, and that a strong majority of the working class was remaining loyal to the Socialist Party of Ebert, Scheidemann, and Noske. The Communists got only 1,156,000 votes, while the USPD, whose majority at Halle had opted for Communism, pulled in almost as many votes as the VKPD (1,087,000). The SPD drew 4,171,000. This outcome prompted Paul Levi, several weeks later, to write that "for the moment the Communists constitute about one fifth of the proletariat."*

That the masses remained cool to VKPD influence was a serious enough handicap, but there was yet another. The general condition of the VKPD itself was found nowhere near up to scratch by

---

*Paul Levi, *Unser Weg. Wider den Putschismus*, Berlin, 1921, p. 15. The same argument was later used by Trotsky: "In the March days—and I say this quite openly—we did not have behind us one-fifth or even one-sixth of the working class and we suffered a defeat." *The First Five Years of the Communist International*, vol. I, New York, 1945, p. 304.

the man in Moscow primarily responsible for its affairs, Karl Radek. Returning from Germany in early February 1921, at the February 22 Executive Committee meeting he stated flatly: "I tell you that, as of now, the majority of organized workers are still with Scheidemann." He continued with a merciless critique of the German party: "If we want that party to move ahead, we have to accept the fact that its present state is poor, that it's making a thousand mistakes, and that this new amalgam with USPDers and Spartacists is showing certain tendencies which we have to fight."[9] His concluding sentence, falling like a headsman's axe, was: "I hope that developments in Italy and Germany have made clear that in Germany we don't have a Communist party, only a hydro- cephalic child on rickety legs, and that the Executive Committee must intervene in the German situation with the utmost vigor."[10] Guralsky in his speech a few minutes later summarized Moscow's conclusion in similar terms.[11]

THE KPD-COMINTERN CLASH PRECEDING THE MARCH ACTION

Since November 1920, when the Comintern decided to let the KAPD join as a "fellow-traveler" party, against the advice of the leaders of the German Communist Party and its chief, Paul Levi, relations between Moscow and the German party had gotten worse and worse. Paul Levi was at the hub of the conflict. His disagreement with Moscow was an all-pervasive feature of his per- sonal political drama, which consisted in three major riddles: how to sustain effective Communist action in a country four-fifths of whose proletariat eluded the party's influence and remained loyal to the two Socialist parties; how to run his party effectively when at every important juncture (January 1919, March 1920, and soon March 1921) its executive committee proved consistently unequal to the job at hand; and how to lead the German Communist Party on any kind of autonomous basis in the face of Moscow's constant meddling.

Even before relations between them started to deteriorate, Levi had succinctly acknowledged the situation to be unsalvageable: "One simply cannot work with the Russians."[12] He saw only one way out: a complete break. Radek recalled Levi's behavior at the time of the Second World Congress: "It suffices to note that on

the night on which the Executive Committee voted overwhelmingly to let the KAPD join, Levi announced that he was leaving the
congress. I restrained him and asked: 'Where do you think you're
going—politically speaking?' " [13] Since November 1920 Levi's
fights with the Executive Committee in Moscow and, through
Moscow's connivance, with other leaders of his party, had become
more and more frequent. Until then he had agonizingly refrained
from mentioning them in public or discussing them in the Communist press, but from that point on he was determined to air the
whole business.

The Executive Committee decision in November 1920 to let the
KAPD join the Comintern as a "fellow-traveler" party, despite the
friction at the Second World Congress and undiminished opposition of the leaders of the United German Communist Party,
was what provoked the first clash with Moscow. When the German
party lodged an official protest, it received in reply the following
telegram: "The Executive Committee has instructed the Little
Bureau to publish a letter addressed to the workers of Germany,
explaining the reasons for its decision." [14] But on February 24,
1921, Levi reported: "That letter has so far not arrived."[15] The
second collision was over the structure of the new Red Trade Union
International. It was followed a few weeks later, at the end of
January, by a third falling-out over the split engineered at the
Italian Socialist Party congress in Leghorn. This was what finally
blew the lid off the kettle and blasted the crisis into public view.
On returning from Leghorn, Levi found Karl Radek still in Berlin.
On Lenin's orders, Radek had done an overnight about-face on the
matter of how to handle Serrati, and was now attacking Levi for
opinions that he himself had held and expressed only the week
before. The party's central committee met at Radek's request, and
it was there that the dispute between the two men became violent.
Declaring that he had come to discuss matters, not to listen to
insults, Levi walked out. The next day Radek sent a letter of apol-
ogy, retracting his charges against Levi. [16]

Just as Radek was leaving Berlin for Moscow, another emissary,
Rákosi, arrived from Leghorn, also en route to Moscow. He, too,
convoked a meeting of the German party's central committee, at
which there was a veritable storm of motions and resolutions,

some approving the Comintern posture at Leghorn (as Rákosi wanted), others lambasting it (as Levi wished). Moscow's increased moral authority plus the already nearly completed "taming" of the German party's apparatus tipped the scales in Rákosi's favor. The meeting lasted from February 22 to February 24, and his motion won out over Levi's by a vote of 28 to 23. Levi immediately resigned as party chairman, and four other leaders followed suit. One was Clara Zetkin, who reported several months later at the Third World Congress, by which time she had broken with Levi: "Regarding that decision of the central committee, the thing that prompted my own resignation from the German Communist Party leadership was the meddling of Comrade Rákosi, the Comintern representative in Italy, in our debate." [17]

Even before the meeting, the hassle over the Italian affair had broken into public print, because, during his stay in Berlin, Radek published three articles on the subject, which he signed with the initials "P. B." Paul Levi fired back with two articles of his own entitled "We and the Executive Committee," in which he reiterated all his objections. Some were of a technical nature, such as his criticisms of the faulty communication between Moscow and Western Europe and the slowness with which information was transmitted. Others pertained to policy, such as the handling of the Italian matter. But the main issue was one of principle—the difference in perspective between Russian and Western Communists: "Our Russian comrades assess the situation from a vantage point very different from that of the rest of us. They assess it as the already established rulers of a country." [18]

These public spats and the February resignations of the most eminent party leaders spoke eloquently enough of the unhealthy state of affairs, but there were still other symptoms. Levi had hardly begun his fight with the Comintern when he entered a verbal duel with a leftist group whose principal spokesmen were Ernst Reuter (Friesland), Arkadi Maslow, and Ruth Fischer. At the Executive Committee meeting on February 22, Guralsky, the Comintern emissary to Germany, bluntly assailed Levi (still the official head of the German party) while supporting the leftists: "[The United German Communist] Party has entered into sharp collision with the Executive Committee. . . . The party is healthy, but its leadership is ill. There exists a left wing within the party. It is weak, and was born last year at the party congress on December 6 . . . but it is truly revolutionary. Levi is wrong [in attacking that wing], and struggle against him and against the tendency he represents is mandatory. . . . The current perspective is that Germany must go through a revolutionary period, and that the United German Communist Party must engage in revolutionary action. . . . Anti-putschism must be eradicated, the left wing must be well protected, and persons in the leadership who have committed serious blunders must be eliminated without pity."* [19]

Unlike the earlier left within the German party, which had broken away to form the KAPD and had grown increasingly hostile toward Moscow, this new left pursued the opposite course. It went out of its way to stay in the Party and to be friendly with Moscow, a policy which helped its spokesman, Friesland, to become first a member of the central committee and then secretary-general of the party, all within the year 1921, and all thanks to Lenin, as Clara Zetkin revealed in her memoirs. Later, in 1923, that same policy carried two other leftist leaders, Ruth Fischer and A. Maslow, to the party's peak positions—this time thanks to Zinoviev.

The pretext for the clash between Levi and the Berlin left was the watchword that Levi had coined on February 24 about "an alliance between Germany and Soviet Russia," which he explained thus: "We were of the opinion that there is no motto more likely to catch the interest of the proletariat and involve it actively in our foreign policy than 'alliance with Soviet Russia.' " [20] But the Berlin organization, in the hands of the leftists since February 10, condemned that view in its resolution: "Most reprehensible of all is the motto calling for an 'alliance' of capitalist Germany with Soviet Russia 'to save the nation.' " [21] The counter-watchword of the Berliners was expressed by Ruth Fischer in her opposing argument: "For us there is no such thing as a nation! " [22]

During the first days of March the party leadership, with Heinrich Brandler and Walter Stoecker having replaced Paul Levi and

---

*Guralsky's advocacy of "eradicating anti-putschism," i.e. combatting Paul Levi, should be understood as a prologue to the "putschist" March action that the German Communist Party launched four weeks later.

Ernst Däumig as titular chairmen, veered closer and closer to the position of the Berlin left. On March 4 the central committee broadcast an appeal to the German proletariat, the theme of which was: "The only thing that can help the German working class is direct battle—the overthrow of Germany's bourgeois government."[23] The following day Paul Levi wrote a letter to the central committee about that manifesto, expressing his disagreement with it: "I regard the central committee's policy as a disastrous error."[24]

On March 8 there was a joint meeting of the central committee and the Communist deputies in the Reichstag, hence attended by Levi and Clara Zetkin, at which Paul Frölich, a leading advocate of the new direction that had taken office after Levi and Däumig resigned, maintained that in the event of any action the battle cry should be "overthrow the government and elect workers' councils." At this juncture Béla Kun, who had already arrived in Berlin, stepped in and took over.

THE CRUX: MOSCOW'S ROLE

When Radek and Levi fought it out behind closed doors in the presence of the German Communist Party leaders on January 28, they did manage to see eye to eye on one point. Both considered the nature of the relationship between Moscow and the Communist movement in the West to be the root of the problem. Radek reported his exchange with Levi in these terms, which the latter never denied: "When I asked him to spell out just what he thought the relationship of the Executive Committee to Europe should be, he replied: 'It makes no difference what anyone does or says, you can never get anywhere with them.'"[25] Speaking next, Levi went straight to the marrow: "While my relations with Zinoviev have improved somewhat since his visit to Germany, I must still say that we are looked upon with some mistrust, and any attempt to resist the error will be seen as an attempt to oppose the Communist International. That is the farthest thing from my mind. The Third International must continue to be headquartered in Moscow. But I tell you, the little altercation has reopened my eyes."[26]

480 Lenin and the Comintern

Levi was immediately to learn that, even when one had been chairman of the Comintern's most important foreign member-party the very night before, one could not oppose Moscow and stay in the Comintern. Several days after their spat, when Levi informed Radek that he was going to publish in *Rote Fahne* his unfavorable opinion of the behavior of the Comintern delegation in Leghorn, and would include a critical analysis of the problem of Moscow's role, Radek, speaking for Moscow, warned him: "With that article you set off a deliberate campaign against the Executive Committee. But we shall be one jump ahead of you, and draw our sword against you." [27]

The truth was that before returning to Moscow Radek had put together in Berlin an anti-Levi faction, to which the party management was entrusted, first in fact and later in name too, just as Levi and his friends were stepping out. With the help of this ruling faction, Radek managed to isolate Levi. That was the prelude to the standard Bolshevik coup de grâce: political liquidation. As emerges from a Radek letter dated March 14, 1921, this group consisted of the following trusted persons: Brandler, who had become party chairman; Thalheimer, his mouthpiece and chief ideologue; Frölich, a personal friend of Radek's, who had not been a Spartacist; Ernst Meyer, a veteran Spartacist; Paul Böttcher, who had come over from the USPD; and "Felix" [Felix Wolf], a Moscow man of confidence in the German party. When he got back to Moscow at the beginning of February, even before Levi had resigned as party chairman, Radek sent a letter to the anti-Levi faction, which began with a declaration of war on Levi: "What Levi did after my departure with regard to the Italian matter is proof that he wants a fight with the Executive Committee. . . . Seeing this, the Executive Committee will come out publicly against him and expose the rudderless vacillation of the central committee. This will give the comrades who don't want the VKPD to become another party of the Serrati stripe a clear chance to take open political action against Levi and the Levi-ites. In that fight the Executive Committee will give you strong support." [28] Several days later this conflict became less secret. An open declaration of hostilities against Levi was made public in Moscow and Berlin simultaneously: the Comintern Executive Committee met on February 22 to discuss the situation in the VKPD, and the

VKPD's central committee began a meeting on that same day to consider its internal affairs and the drift of its relations with Moscow.

In Moscow the opening shot against Levi was fired by Radek, who had suddenly become the most resolute opponent of a policy he had strongly favored only the month before; he was picked for the job of finishing off Levi precisely because he had been so close to him from 1917 to 1921. After twice accusing Levi of being "a proponent of these opportunistic tendencies"—a charge which at the end of 1923 would be leveled at Radek himself and two of his principal Levi-liquidators in 1921, Brandler and Thalheimer— Radek hurled a threat: "A word now on relations between the German party and the Executive Committee of the Third International. I am convinced that, if it should come to a fight between Moscow and Berlin, the German party leadership would be in ashes and in its grave within two months, for the masses would go over its head and side with Moscow." [29] Radek thus enunciated one of the main elements in the Bolshevik creed with regard to the Comintern. It was also a profound political truth, boiling down to this: whenever Moscow and the leadership of a foreign Communist party had any kind of falling out, Moscow would be the winner, pulling "the masses" over to its side (and of course the party apparatus), thereby isolating the opposition leaders, who were then expelled from the Comintern and the party.

The charge of "opportunism" was supplemented by one of "factionalism," or attempting to generate an organized opposition to the Comintern. After the Leghorn congress Serrati had gone to Berlin and met with several leaders of the German Communist Party, some of whom had made trips to neighboring countries and discussed the situation with Communists there. This drew from Radek the accusation that Levi was trying to set up a second Executive Committee in Berlin. The site predominantly favored at the founding congress in 1919 had now, by February 1921, become an emblem of heresy: "If the German party were insane enough to try, with Serrati, to form an Executive Committee to lead the revolution, the revolution itself would send them straight to hell. When I talked with our German comrades about the German party's influencing the Executive Committee, I told them it was their right to seek to influence the Committee, but not by dispatching Stoecker to Switzerland and Vienna and having him say that he brings greetings from the German party." [30]

Levi knew that the Executive Committee was busily stirring up a pro-Soviet faction against him. (He had seen the contents of some of Radek's confidential letters.) At the end of his speech of February 24 he alerted his friends on the central committee: "But to start up factionalism in this young party, to embark again upon that course whose inexorable outcome is so well known to us, is a thing that I would like to warn our members against." [31] Levi's own prognosis of the end result of any direct clash between the pro-Soviet faction and himself, supported by his friends, differed from Radek's. The latter prophesied Moscow's victory, and events would prove him right, while Levi mistakenly predicted the death of the party: "For I tell you, Comrades, Communism in Germany cannot survive another split." [32]

By early March preparations had been completed for Levi's "liquidation." On March 14 Radek wrote to the members of his faction in Berlin: "Levi will soon go under. We must do everything possible to keep Däumig and Zetkin from going down with him." [33] On March 16 before the entire Bolshevik Party congress, and in a report to be circulated that same day throughout Europe, Zinoviev made the war against Levi official: "But each day we realized more and more that Comrade Levi was leaning in the direction of opportunism. So today there is not the slightest doubt or difference of opinion among us as to the absolute necessity of a struggle against that comrade." [34] The same day, in Levi's absence, the German Communist Party central committee met and the next day, at the instigation of Béla Kun, decided to go ahead with their March action.

THE COMINTERN'S ROLE IN THE BIG DECISION

The insurrection triggered in March 1921 was the first such undertaking in Europe (and the world) attempted at the instigation of and under the leadership of a team specially sent from Moscow and consisting of important figures in the Comintern. All the previous revolutionary episodes had occurred either before the Comintern's birth or without the participation of any consultants sent from Moscow to call the shots.

Béla Kun, the top member of this particular team, was then undoubtedly Europe's most famous Bolshevik. He had taken part in the Russian revolution and headed Soviet Hungary, a combination of exploits that no other European Communist leader could match. Also, both in rank and in function he stood at the summit of the Comintern hierarchy. At the time of his departure for Germany he was a member of its two governing entities, the Secretariat of the Executive Committee and the Little Bureau (which to the Comintern Executive Committee was what the Politburo was to the Bolshevik Party central committee). That in February 1921, before leaving for Berlin, he had a powerful voice in the running of the Comintern's affairs was strikingly confirmed indirectly, in another connection, by Radek, who in a letter that he sent in mid-February to his "pro-Soviet faction" in Berlin shortly after returning to Moscow, summarized under point five the thinking of the Comintern Executive Committee, of whose members he mentioned, besides himself, only Lenin, Zinoviev, Bukharin, and Béla Kun.

Two of Kun's lieutenants also had imposing credentials. The first was Guralsky, who in 1920, even before the Second World Congress, became the Comintern's delegate to the German Communist Party. In that capacity he attended the Executive Committee meeting of February 1921 devoted to the situation in Germany. The second was József Pógany, a Hungarian ex-Socialist, who had joined up with the Communists and after the collapse of the Soviet regime in Hungary had become a member of the Comintern's secret apparatus. (In this capacity he ultimately left for the United States under the pseudonym "Pepper.")

There are two indications that this threesome was not a Comintern "delegation" in the usual sense, sent to Germany only for inspection purposes. In the first place, a permanent Comintern delegation of the customary type was already on the scene, staffed with important personages from the Soviet apparatus, people like Felix Wolf who had already been active in Germany for two years, and Y. S. Reich-"Thomas," who had been heading up the W.E.S. for the past year and a half. Both these men knew Germany well and spoke the language like natives, while the three new special Comintern emissaries spoke German with a heavy foreign accent, and two had never been in the country before. Secondly, this particular threesome certainly did not represent the whole of that unusual Comintern delegation, as we learn from *Pravda* forty-five years after the event: "F. Münnich was one of the military leaders of the workers' uprising in Germany in 1921." [35] The reference is to Ferenz Münnich, another Hungarian, who had embraced Bolshevism while in Russia in 1917 and who ended his political career as prime minister of the Hungarian Communist government and a member of the Hungarian Politburo. The one thing that these four individuals prominent in the March affair had in common was not any special knowledge of Germany, which they lacked, but their familiarity with the Russian revolution and Russian-style civil war.

The action that Béla Kun was about to trigger in Germany dovetailed nicely with his personal views about what should be done in that country. Although he had never been politically active in Germany, he had a ready-made set of opinions concerning the situation there. In April 1920, immediately after the Kapp-Lüttwitz putsch, he wrote in *Kommunismus*, the Comintern journal published in Vienna: "Germany is objectively completely ready for a dictatorship of the proletariat, but subjectively the prerequisites for that dictatorship are not present. This means that the great mass of the proletariat are not yet consciously fighting for a proletarian dictatorship." [36] When shortly after the Spartacists merged with the left wing of the USPD the first voices were heard proclaiming the need for a "revolutionary offensive," Béla Kun from his post in Moscow made himself their champion. Alfred Rosmer, then in the Soviet capital as a member of the Executive Committee, recalled: "At the beginning of the year [1921] Trotsky had a visit from Béla Kun, who had come to discuss with him tactics which, according to him, the International ought to adopt. It was an absolute and urgent necessity, he said, to plunge into a systematic offensive, with full use of all the resources the Soviet Republic could muster. The bourgeois governments were still weak. Now was the time to hit them, again and again, with a chain of uprisings, strikes, insurrections. Later would be too late. This was his thesis. Trotsky threw cold water on it, aghast at the very idea." [37]

So it was not surprising that Germany was selected to be the testing ground for Kun's theory of the offensive. According to Communist doctrine, Germany was the first country in the world in order of revolutionary importance, and was also of course the cradle and original home of Marxism itself. Hence the two elements deemed essential by Marxist Communists, the theoretical aspect plus the objective situation, were now in perfect conjunction; all the stars were in the right places. The mystery about the whole affair, though, which Moscow did its utmost to keep a mystery, especially after its failure, was this: why were Béla Kun and his group sent to Germany at that moment to foment this revolutionary outburst, and who sent them? And when they got there did they or did they not exceed the authority they had been given?

The Executive Committee's role in the affair is amply documented by materials from the Comintern's secret files and by the testimony of members of its Executive Committee at the time. All flatly agree on one thing: the Executive Committee, the sole entity empowered under the bylaws to make political decisions for the Comintern, took no explicit decision calling for the action in question. In fact, it was not consulted when the decision to dispatch Béla Kun was made, nor was it informed when Kun launched his operation. The confidential minutes of the February 22 meeting substantiate this. The Executive Committee usually met once a week, on the day that Zinoviev came to Moscow to attend Politburo meetings. February 22 was the last time the Committee met before Kun left for Berlin. His departure could not have been later than February 27 or 28. The first item on the agenda at that February 22 meeting was the situation in Germany. Participating in the discussion were Geyer, a German Communist Party representative on the Executive Committee, who gave a report; Radek, who had returned from Berlin in early February; Goldstein, a KAPD representative on the Executive Committee; and Guralsky, a Comintern delegate to Germany. In the course of the meeting which lasted four hours and was devoted solely to German affairs, there was no reference or allusion made to the Béla Kun enterprise. That the Executive Committee was kept completely in the dark on this occasion—as it would be later prior to other attempted putsches, such as that in Tallinn in 1924—is confirmed by two of its members, Curt Geyer and Alfred Rosmer.[38]

Another entity, smaller and more intimate than the Executive

Committee, the Little Bureau (the future Presidium of the Executive Committee), does not appear to have discussed the matter either. Between the end of the Second Congress in August 1920 and the start of the Third in July 1921, its meetings were scarcely more frequent than those of the Executive Committee. The latter met thirty-four times during that period, the former thirty-nine times. Moreover, between those two congresses the composition of the Little Bureau was such as to make it more of an ad hoc committee than a general decision-making body. When the Second Congress was over, it was still an all-Bolshevik entity, consisting then of Zinoviev, Bukharin, and Kobetsky, who was promoted to Secretary of the Comintern. Later they were joined by Endre Rudnyánszky, a Hungarian who had embraced the Bolshevik cause and stayed on in Russia instead of returning to Hungary in 1918 with Béla Kun and the others. Finally there was Ernst Meyer, a German communist leader whose election was strictly symbolic, since he left Moscow immediately after the congress. In the time between the Second and the Third congress four new members were co-opted to the Little Bureau: Béla Kun, the prime mover behind the March action in Germany; Alfred Rosmer, who swore that he had no advance knowledge of the affair; Karl Radek, who joined after his return from Berlin; and Wilhelm Koenen, who served as a German representative but did not reach Moscow until shortly after the March episode. By elimination, then, only Zinoviev, Béla Kun, Radek and Bukharin could have been involved.

LENIN, KUN, AND LEVI

Lenin did not attend the Executive Committee's February 22 meeting. (Officially, he did not even belong to the Little Bureau, and since the Second Congress had been listed as only an acting member of the Executive Committee itself.) Though in the early months of 1921 he was indeed occupied with extremely grave and urgent domestic problems, he never turned his attention from the Comintern's prime concern, Germany. At the beginning of the year he had had an opportunity to talk with two of Moscow's principal agents in Berlin, Victor Kopp and Karl Radek, who had both recently returned to the Bolshevik capital. Kopp represented the Soviet government vis-à-vis German government circles (Socialist and bourgeois) and, secondarily, vis-à-vis German Communists.

Radek represented the Comintern, primarily in Germany's Communist circles, secondarily in official circles. Kopp was given an audience with Lenin on January 27, and Radek was received by Lenin on February 12, having just spent several months in Germany. Apart from them, the only foreign Communist leader with whom Lenin had frequent contact in February 1921 was Béla Kun. On February 9 he talked with Kun, who had come in his capacity as Secretary of the Comintern's Executive Committee. On February 15 Lenin signed and returned to him a letter of invitation addressed to the Czechoslovak "left," and on February 26 had another hour-long talk with him. This last was on the eve of Kun's departure for Germany and shortly before his elevation to membership in the Comintern's Little Bureau, news of which was announced by the German Communist Party organ *Rote Fahne* on March 2. Until now nothing has been published concerning the substance of that conversation, even though, ever since the Twentieth Congress of the Communist Party of the Soviet Union in February 1956, it has been the policy of both Moscow and Budapest to emphasize the close friendly relations between the two men. The possible official reasons for this silence are understandable. One would naturally wish to quell any suspicion that Lenin could have been involved in the March affair. Hence the chronology of his daily activities, detailed in the fifth edition of his collected works, omits all mention of his having received, around the time of this episode, two important German Communist Party delegations. One had left Berlin before the event, the other immediately after it. Wilhelm Koenen, a member of the first, has recounted their conversation with Lenin, which has been published even in Russian (Moscow, 1960). Fritz Heckert has done the same for the second delegation, and his account has been published in Moscow several times (1935, 1939, and 1959).

Certainly these few facts, and silences, do not in themselves prove that Lenin knew about and had given his blessing to Kun's mission to Germany. But one is entitled to wonder how likely it is that he would have talked with Lenin for an hour on the eve of his departure for Berlin without once mentioning his trip and its purpose, in view of Lenin's supreme role in major Comintern affairs and given the close relationship between the two men. Measured by the number of contacts and personal conversations, the relations between the chief of the Russian revolution and ex-head of

Soviet Hungary were by far the most intimate that any foreign Communist leader had with Lenin from 1918 to 1922. Which is why, in a message from Budapest in June 1919, Kun could dare to say to Lenin: "I am proud to consider myself one of your most fervent disciples, but I believe that in one point I have surpassed you: in the question of *mala fides*." [39]

Lenin's attitude toward Kun was a mixture of affection and annoyance. He liked him because of his exemplary revolutionary past and total loyalty (to Lenin),* but some of his actions angered him—which helps explain the remarkable ups and downs of Kun's career in the Comintern. In 1920, arriving in Moscow just as the Second World Congress was ending, he was received by Lenin on August 14 and appointed a Comintern representative, along with Zinoviev and Radek, to the Congress of Eastern Peoples to convene in Baku on September 1, after which he was named a member of the Revolutionary Council of the Red Army troops warring against Wrangel in the Crimea. It was there that he did something that made Lenin furious. Despite his firm promise not to harm any Whites taken prisoners by the Reds, in November of 1920 he had several thousand of them slaughtered. As punishment, Lenin sent him to remote Turkestan, which throughout 1919-20 was the scene of curious events, a mixture of abuses and brutalities perpetrated alternately by local Communists and emissaries dispatched from Moscow. In the end a special term was coined in the Soviet capital to designate this particular breed of Communist: "Turkestantsy." Interestingly, some of these people, after their exile in Turkestan, were elevated to the Comintern. Thus on March 24, 1920, Lenin sent a note to the Bolshevik Politburo: "Get Heller and Broïdo out of there immediately." [40] Heller became the Comintern's principal emissary to Italy, where he called himself "Niccolini"; Broïdo became founder and director of the first Comintern cadre school, known as the Communist University of the Toilers of the East (KUTV). Béla Kun got his promotion, too, landing back in Moscow in February 1921 at the Comintern

*This protective attitude that Lenin displayed toward Kun, reserving to himself alone the right to criticize him while denying the privilege to all others, was not unlike his behavior toward such men as V. Taratuta, J. Hanecki, and H. Guilbeaux, whom, once he reached the pinnacle of power, he fondly protected in spite of their dubious reputations because of services that they had rendered to him in former times of need.

summit, a member of its two main governing bodies, the Secretariat and Little Bureau. (This is why Levi, who knew the Comintern inside out, could not resist including in his pamphlet on the March action a little quip about the "Turkestantsy" that Moscow was sending to Europe.)

When Kun returned from Berlin after his March venture flopped, he was punished again by being shipped off in May to the Urals. But Lenin continued to protect his person while condemning his ideas, as he did at the Third World Congress, at which Kun reappeared. As a leading advocate of the March action, Kun was literally felled by Lenin's criticisms, which hit him like a shaft of lightning. Some said that he went straight into hysterics; others reported that he had a heart attack.* In any case, he had to go to a sanatorium for treatment. On July 19 Lenin wrote to his own physician, L. G. Levin: "Please give me a brief report on the state of Comrade Kun's health, and how long he will require care, and what kind of care you plan for him."[41] For about a month Kun had to stay away from any political activities.†

While Lenin valued Kun's political loyalty though putting little stock in his political intelligence, he rated Paul Levi high on both counts. On the subject of his political loyalty, even after the final break with him, Lenin wrote to the German Communists on August 14, 1921: "I must explain to you, Comrades, the reasons for my long defense of Paul Levi at the Third Congress. In the first place, I became acquainted with him through Radek in Switzerland in 1915 or 1916. At that time he was already a Bolshevik. I cannot help feeling somewhat suspicious of those who embraced Bolshevism only after its victory in Russia and after its string of triumphs in the international arena."[42] As for Levi's political lucidity, Lenin supported his initiatives and ideas throughout the

*His having had "an attack of hysterics" is reported by Ernö Bettelheim in *Die Krise in der KP Ungarns*, Vienna, 1922, p. 19. We are told by "Thomas" in *Contribution à l'histoire du Comintern*, p. 26, that it was instead a "heart attack."

†Though elected one of the seven members of the Executive Committee's Little Bureau (Presidium) at its founding meeting on July 13, he was absent from its meetings because of his illness until August 13, when he assumed his seat on the Committee and began his effective tenure as a member of the Presidium. See *Die Tätigkeit der Exekutive und des Präsidiums des Exekutivkomitees der Kommunistischen Internationale vom 13. July 1921 bis. 1. Februar 1922*, Petrograd, 1922, pp. 5-7 and 86.

entire crucial year 1921. The first initiative, undertaken by Levi and Radek jointly, was the Open Letter of January 8, to which Lenin gave his approval as soon as he learned of it from Radek on the latter's return, as Radek later reported to his friends in Berlin: "Lenin gave me his complete backing and support." [43]

When the German Communist Party's central committee split in February 1921, the two rival factions each sent representatives to Moscow. Both delegations were in the Soviet capital at the time of the March episode, and were received by Lenin, as Koenen, the spokesman for the anti-Levi faction, relates: "During those tense March days Lenin was heavily overburdened with work, and he frankly told us so. Nevertheless, he listened very closely to our report of the dissension within Germany's Communist Party. . . . Since I had consistently and firmly spoken out against the Serrati-Levi line, I was sent to Moscow to present that point of view. Otto Brass defended the other approach. Lenin attentively heard us out, asked a few questions on matters of interest to him, but expressed no definite opinion on the split in our party's central committee. He left no doubt, though, that Serrati's policies had to be vigorously opposed." [44]

Lenin's determination to declare war on Serrati but not on Levi was further strengthened on March 27, when Levi sent him a long letter explaining the March episode and beseeching him personally to put matters right: "Because I regard the situation of the Communist party as not only difficult but conceivably disastrous, because I believe its very life to be in danger, I am appealing to you personally, not knowing how familiar you may be with details of Comintern policies. I ask that you look into the situation yourself and take such action as you deem necessary." [45] Levi's request did not go unheeded. Lenin did thenceforth concern himself personally with the results of the March débâcle, which he roundly condemned. But in the end he condemned Levi, too.

While refusing to make any public mention of the March episode—apart from a covert allusion to the failure of the strike, made on April 11 in his address to the Communist members of the Central Trade-Union Council—Lenin continued to hope for the best where Levi was concerned (unlike Zinoviev and Radek, who already had declared war on him), and to be increasingly sharper in his criticism of what had happened in Germany; but he spoke this way only in high inner circles, never publicly. On April 7, when Lenin had just received Levi's letter but had not yet had a chance to talk with Béla Kun, Radek wrote to the German party's central committee, describing Lenin's feelings about Levi: "The old man still hopes these people will come to their senses."[46]

Several days later, on April 16, replying to the letters from Levi and Clara Zetkin, Lenin reaffirmed his approval of the famous Open Letter: "I consider that to have been a *completely correct* tactic (I condemned the contrary opinion of our 'leftists,' who were against it)."[47] He also accepted Levi's version of the March affair, conceding that Béla Kun had indeed represented the Executive Committee and had committed a serious error: "I can well believe that the Executive Committee's representative did advocate a stupid tactic, one too far to the left. 'Let us strike immediately in order to help the Russians! ' Yes, this particular gentleman has often 'struck' too far to the left. In my opinion, you should not back down in such cases but protest and bring the matter at once to the official attention of the [Comintern's] entire Executive Bureau."[48]

A month later, in May, Fritz Heckert, another representative of the German central committee, showed up in Moscow in the company of Mátyás Rákosi, his mission being to defend both the March action and the "theory of the offensive." The two were not well received by Lenin, as Heckert reports in his memoirs:

Lenin, inviting me in German to sit down, in a slightly ironic tone said: "Well now, Comrade Heckert, tell me all about your heroic exploits in Central Germany." Requiring no urging, I unburdened myself. He commented: "But they say you were beaten." "On the contrary! " I protested, setting out to prove to him that this was definitely not the case. "Quite the opposite! " I insisted: "Since those events our party has steadily fattened and battened! " "Ho, ho! " he retorted: "I would love to see your proof of that." Rákosi tried to back me up. Lenin jumped on him,* then said to me: "Can't you see that you were deliberately goaded, tricked, and that you fell for it? For which the party will pay dearly."[49]

---

*In his earlier version of this conversation (1935) Heckert quotes Lenin as saying to Rákosi: "So you, too, babble asininities and shoot your mouth off without thinking." *L'Internationale communiste*, No. 3, 1935, p. 212.

Most probably Lenin knew in advance about Kun's trip to Germany, since the two met and talked the very day before Kun left. Also, in his reply to Levi, Lenin acknowledged that Kun was in fact an authorized Comintern representative and had acted in that capacity. Finally, at the Third World Congress, Lenin consistently refused to discuss the nature of Kun's role and parried all questions about it. Still, this does not fully explain his attitude toward Kun at the time of the latter's departure for Germany. In the absence of hard facts, one might reasonably assume that Lenin was aware that a secret delegation, or at least a special one, headed by Béla Kun, was being sent to Germany—which would account for his refusal to discuss in public the nature of its mission or the extent of its authority—but that he was not consulted in advance about the action the delegation would take after reaching Germany, which would explain why he felt free to criticize it privately.*

THE ROLE OF ZINOVIEV AND RADEK

Zinoviev's role is much clearer. Béla Kun could have left for Berlin without any formal instructions from Lenin, but it is inconceivable that he could have gone there, as an accredited Comintern representative, without Zinoviev's approval. Since neither the Little Bureau nor the Executive Committee had given Kun any such instructions, only Zinoviev could have done so. The one remaining question is whether Zinoviev would have dared to attempt so serious an enterprise, particularly in Germany, without first consulting Lenin. The answer depends upon which period of time the question refers to. It would definitely be no for the years 1919 and 1920. The memory of Zinoviev's "desertion" in October 1917

---

*Contrary to the case of Lenin, it is not difficult to establish the role of Trotsky in that affair: during his conversations with Boris Souvarine in the second half of 1921, Trotsky insisted that he did not know anything about the action planned in Germany, and it is highly probable that this was so. But from the fact that Lenin never mentioned that action to him, Trotsky deduced that Lenin himself was not acquainted with the action, which is much more doubtful. The mission of Béla Kun went back to February 1921, just after a grave crisis within the Bolshevik party (on the trade union question) when Trotsky opposed Lenin, and before another serious crisis (Kronstadt and NEP) during which Trotsky sided with Lenin. It is not certain, therefore, that at the end of February 1921 the Lenin-Trotsky "alliance" was already sealed, as it would be somewhat later.

was still too fresh, and Lenin's personal interest in the momentarily expected European revolution, especially in Germany, was still too great. For 1923 the answer would clearly be yes. In that year on two occasions, September in Bulgaria and October in Germany, Zinoviev did light the revolutionary match without bothering to clear the matter with Lenin, who was already gravely ill. For 1922, the situation is cloudier. Zinoviev might at that time have gone ahead on his own,without advance authorization from Lenin, who was sick even then and devoting himself mainly to domestic affairs, having given up hope of any Communist revolution in Europe. As for early 1921, the absence of documentary evidence and the testimony of witnesses makes it difficult to make any categorical affirmation.

The least one can say is that Zinoviev could hardly have sent an important, secret mission to Germany, a country in which the Kremlin took so keen an interest, without first informing Lenin and the Politburo, if only to cover himself. As it happened, the full Bolshevik Party central committee met on February 24, only two days before Lenin received Béla Kun, devoting its morning deliberations entirely to domestic affairs. A precise list of the agenda items is included in the chronology in Lenin's *Complete Works*. The afternoon session was given over to international affairs. But as to the actual afternoon agenda that same chronology is silent, disposing of the subject with the customary formula: "Lenin took part in the meeting of the full Central Committee, at which the oil concessions and other matters were discussed." [50] We can only guess what the other matters were.

In February and March of 1921, while Lenin was staggering under a huge load of domestic problems, receiving bad news from all sides, Zinoviev was having his own troubles in Petrograd, whose soviet he was chairman of, especially with the strike that erupted there in February—a prelude to the insurrection at Kronstadt that flared up on March 2, when Béla Kun was already in Berlin. In the latter part of February, Zinoviev spent several days in Moscow. On February 22 he chaired an Executive Committee meeting devoted to Germany, though neither he nor Béla Kun said a word, and on February 24 and 25 he attended the meeting of the full Bolshevik Party central committee. These chores done, he returned to Petrograd, and Kun was received by Lenin, leaving immediately afterwards for Berlin.

When the March venture failed, Zinoviev, unlike Lenin, has-
tened to give it his blessing. The Executive Committee manifesto
dated April 6, 1921, addressed to "the revolutionary workers of
Germany," after saluting their action as the first conscious effort
to "end domination by the exploiters," frankly emphasized that
the whole thing had been a Communist initiative of which the
Comintern completely approved: "This first organized assault by
Germany's revolutionary proletariat was not crowned with success, thanks to the infamous betrayal of proletarian interests by
the SPD. . . . The Communist International tells you: You did
right! You have opened a new page in the history of the German
working class. Arm yourselves for your future battles. Learn from
your past ones." [51] When Lenin began criticizing Béla Kun more
and more harshly before and during the Third World Congress,
Zinoviev did not follow suit. More deeply involved in the affair
than Lenin, hence more compromised by its failure, and having
less authority, Zinoviev doubtless did not feel as free to dump it
all at Kun's doorstep and play Pontius Pilate. He had to resort to
another expedient: try to bury the whole incident as quickly as
possible.

As for Radek, he lacked the authority to entrust such a mission
to Béla Kun. He, like Kun, was a Comintern delegate to Germany; they were of equal rank, too, in that both were members of
the Comintern's Little Bureau (Presidium). The only question
about Radek was whether he knew in advance what Kun was
supposed to do in Germany, but it is certain that Radek had no
power to thwart Kun's mission. On March 14, by which time Kun
had already been in Berlin for nearly two weeks, Radek wrote a
confidential letter to his "faction" among the German party leaders. In it he discussed three subjects which he then deemed serious: the difficulties in Soviet Russia; the struggle to get rid of
Levi; the potential imminent complications inherent in the international situation. Foreseeing the possibility of some act of revolution in Germany, he did not predict any early date for it and made
no allusion to the Béla Kun mission. On March 25, he published an
article in *Pravda*, under the title "Signs of Storm in Germany," in
which, without enthusing as Zinoviev did in the Executive Committee manifesto of April 6, he made a point of stressing that

Germany was on the threshold of a new revolutionary offensive: "From the very first day of its existence as a united party, it [the VKPD] set itself the goal of action, of going on the offensive. . . . We do not know how soon events will break there, or how far they will go, but it is obvious that *we are witnessing in Germany a rising new wave of revolution.*" [52] Five days later, on April 1, he wrote a confidential letter to the German party's central committee (to which Levi and his supporters no longer belonged), admitting from the outset his uncertainty as to the nature and meaning of what had really happened: "As of this writing, I have heard only news from Nauen. From those reports I can't figure out whether the present action has occurred spontaneously or is something that the party is behind. The fact that it all started in the district in Central Germany where we happen to be strongest, and that the second outbreak has come in Hamburg, inclines me to assume that the party is behind it."*

THE WHYS AND WHEREFORES OF THE MARCH ACTION

Two aspects of the episode left to be explored are Moscow's motives in dispatching Béla Kun to Germany, and then Kun's own behavior. Our information concerning the first is relatively certain; regarding the second, one can only hypothesize. Confidential writings from the period, and even some that have been published, make it clear that Moscow had two complementary motives, or hopes, in setting off the little powder keg in Germany: the grave plight of Soviet Russia at that time, and a sincere belief that a new war was about to break out between the "imperialist" powers. The first was rooted in the concept of "proletarian revolutionary solidarity." Since November 1917 Soviet Russia had borne the brunt of imperialist capitalist pressure, thereby aiding the cause of Europe's proletariat; now it was Europe's turn to make a sacrifice for Russia as it struggled through a particularly difficult time. The second motive sprang from that supreme experience of the Russian Communists, their success in seizing and holding power as they saw it,

*Letter from Radek to the German Communist Party's central committee dated April 1, 1921. This letter was first published in Paul Levi's journal *Unser Weg (Sowjet)*, no. 8/9, August 1921, pp. 248-51.

by dint of their enemies' "imperialist contradictions" in the most aggravated form: war. The recent imperialist-capitalist war had been the instrument and avenue of the Russian Bolsheviks' success. Logically, therefore, the next imperialist-capitalist war, thought to be imminent, would perform the same service for the German Communists, the second strongest link in the Comintern chain. These two threads of reasoning run through all the writings from March and April of 1921, starting with those of Radek, the Bolshevik in most frequent touch with the German Communist Party leaders.

In his letter of March 14, when Béla Kun was already busy in Berlin, Radek wrote of Russia's difficult situation: "Situation as follows: big concessions to peasants necessary, which means temporary economic strengthening of capitalist elements. . . . Spring and summer will be very hard. Help from abroad to raise morale of the masses here essential." [53] This succinct summary addressed to the German party leaders, who several days later would launch their great uprising, was repeated, with more candor if less skill, in Kun's remarks of March 10 to Clara Zetkin and March 14 to Levi. Levi, assuming that Lenin was aware of Kun's arrival in Berlin, sent him a report of what Kun had said:

> You know that four weeks ago a comrade was sent to Germany by the Comintern. It was not until ten days ago that I myself, for the first and so far the only time, had a chance to talk with him. Prior to that, he had spoken with central committee members. I do not know what he told them but can only guess from what he said to Comrade Clara nine days before my talk with him.* The gist of what he said to me, and to Comrade Clara, who immediately reported it to me, was the following. He said that Russia was in an extremely bad situation, and that it was absolutely necessary to take some pressure off of her through actions of various kinds in the West, and that for this reason the German party had to do something right away. [54]

*The confusion concerning the exact days of these meetings stems from Paul Levi himself. In fact the difference between the talks Béla Kun had with Clara Zetkin and Paul Levi was not nine days (as Levi wrote to Lenin), but four. Levi himself verified the discrepancy, and in a speech he had delivered before the leaders of the German Communist Party on May 4, 1921, he stated that Béla Kun met Clara Zetkin on March 10, and that he had a discussion with Kun on March 14. Cf. Paul Levi, *Was ist das Verbrechen? Die Märzaktion oder die Kritik daran?* Berlin, 1921, p. 8.

Even after the collapse of the March venture, August Thalheimer, the brains behind the new drift in Germany, reporting in a letter to Radek on April 14, was still arguing the necessity for initiatives in Europe to cover the tactical retreat going on in Russia: "I have never believed that your concessions to the peasants pose any serious danger. There is every indication that the movement in Central and Western Europe is picking up steam."[55]

But this argument, which in the eyes of Radek, Kun, and Thalheimer had force enough to justify the action taken in Germany, became high treason when aired by Paul Levi at the April 7 meeting convened for party officials and functionaries: "For this reason I merely want to say—and it does have to be said—that the central committee's decision of March 17 was preceded by negotiations concerning an operation to be undertaken. And you will remember that in Russia at the time there was that little trouble in Kronstadt. [*Booing from the audience.*] Is one not supposed to say that? [*Shouts of no!*] You see, ladies and gentlemen comrades, how very serious our situation is when this extremely cautious remark is met with booing."[56] The indignation of the Communist apparatchiks at this statement by their former party chairman was understandable. To announce publicly what leaders in Moscow were whispering in secret, namely that the March "offensive" in Germany had been fathered by a Russian decision dictated by Bolshevik needs to cope with an internal Russian problem, was a naked admission that the most important foreign party in the Comintern was actually "under Moscow's thumb"—which is exactly what the Socialists had been claiming for some time—and that the Comintern was indeed but an obedient appendage of the Russian government. In 1921 it was impossible to acknowledge this, and it grew increasingly so as Germany and other countries in subsequent years experienced more of these abortive "arranged revolutions."

If the men of Moscow were accurate in their analyses of the Soviet Union's plight, the conclusion that they drew from it—that an insurrectionary act staged in Germany would alleviate it—was highly inaccurate. But their second motivating belief, that another murderous imperialist-capitalist war was imminent, was even quicker to prove itself a chimera. Radek used it repeatedly, before and after the March fiasco. In his confidential letter of March 14 he foresaw war with Poland and told the German party leaders what their task would be in that event: "Everything depends on the world political situation. If the rift between Germany and the Entente widens, and war breaks out with Poland, then we shall have something to say. Because these things may very well happen, you must do everything in your power to mobilize the party. . . . If war does come, our thought must be not of peace or protest but of getting arms." [57] In an article published in *Pravda* on March 25 he referred again to the "general conflict between Germany and the Entente" and to the expected attempt by the Polish bourgeoisie, freed of their worry in the East, to resort to armed force in Upper Silesia; he concluded that this in turn would weaken the power of the German bourgeoisie to resist any action by the workers. In a confidential letter to the German party's central committee on April 1, when the abortive March uprising was in its death throes (which Radek could not then have known), he was still using the old war argument: "I'm afraid you may have made your move a couple of weeks too soon. I fear that a tactical error has been made in that you didn't wait for hostilities between Germany and Poland." [58]

The same rationale that Radek expounded in his March 14 letter to the pro-Soviet "faction" was put forth that same day in the conversation that Levi had with Béla Kun, the only difference being that the ex-chief of Soviet Hungary, who didn't believe in halfway ப.ories, predicted an imperialist war between America and England, too. This intriguing possibility was evoked again three days later by the German party's new chairman, Brandler. Levi wrote: "Then on March 14 I had a talk with that same comrade, in the course of which he not only repeated to me what Comrade Zetkin told me he had said to her, but—and I am sorry to have to deprive the comrades who made those statements at the March 17 meeting of any prize for originality—he also repeated to me verbatim those passages of which I have published excerpts from the central committee's minutes, except for the reference to a likely war between England and America." [59]

At the March 17 meeting of the central committee, which had decided to adopt as its own the Kun view that an "offensive" act was urgently necessary, Brandler, speaking for the central committee, based his case on the dual foundation of the German-Polish war foreseen by Radek and the Anglo-American war previsioned by Kun: "Concerning Lenin's choice, one can only say what Levi did say at the conference four weeks earlier, except that the antagonism between America and England has meanwhile grown. Unless a revolution intervenes to change the course of events, we shall soon be witnessing an Anglo-American war. . . . On March 20 the sanctions will be stepped up, and on that same day we have the plebiscite in Upper Silesia, which will probably result in a fight between the Polish and German bourgeoisie. . . . It is ninety percent certain that there'll be armed clashes."[60]

This leaves for analysis the last of the motives behind the March débâcle, that unforeseen something which prompted Béla Kun to seize the initiative, even if it did mean exceeding his credentials. As it happened, two unexpected events occurred after Kun left Moscow for Berlin. The first was the Kronstadt insurrection, the second the decision of Karl Severing, the Socialist minister of the interior in the Prussian government, and his Socialist colleague Otto Hörsing, the Oberpräsident of the state of Saxony, to send police detachments into Central Germany's industrial heartland.

On learning of the March episode, Radek wrote openly to *Pravda* about a possible connection between events in Germany and the Kronstadt uprising: "The news of recent counterrevolutionary flareups in Russia obviously aroused German workers."[61] Actually, the Kronstadt insurrection began on March 2, just as Béla Kun arrived in Berlin, and was extinguished by March 18; the action in Germany did not begin until March 21. Consequently, when he left Moscow at the end of February, Béla Kun could not have known anything about the Commune of Kronstadt; on the contrary, during the week when he succeeded in urging the plan for insurrectionary action on the German Communist Party, and especially upon the Party's Central Committee on March 16-17, the events at Kronstadt were in full swing and could have been easily taken into account by Kun in his political machinations.

Unlike Radek, Levi presented, in his final letter to the presidium of the Third Comintern Congress on May 31, a well-documented, carefully thought-out defense of his views, conceding only that he should not have equated the instructions that Kun may have received from the Executive Committee in Moscow with what he actually did after arriving in Germany:

And I must stick to what I said about the Executive Committee's influence, though in the Committee's favor I should perhaps mention the fact, which I have not yet adequately stressed in public, that the Executive Committee—unlike its representatives in Germany, who ran away with the ball—merely made some *suggestions*, which it assumed would be weighed,, modified as necessary, or even rejected by persons on the scene able and willing to exercise independent judgment. It apparently did not reckon with the possibility that the VKPD leaders would close their eyes and swallow everything spooned out to them in the Executive Committee's name.[62]

While the news from Soviet Russia did help to trigger the March episode, specific provocative acts advanced the date of its outbreak. There was premeditation on both sides, by the Communists and the Social Democrats. On the Communist side it involved a scheme of Béla Kun's, which he revealed first to Clara Zetkin and then to Levi; it left both of them aghast.[63] It was picked up by the central committee's spokesman, Paul Frölich, who declared: "We must see to it that the outbreak occurs, even if it means our deliberately provoking the local police."[64] The other provocative act, in Communist eyes, was supplied by the Socialists. On March 16, the very day that the Communist Party's central committee had its meeting, Otto Hörsing announced his intention to send police reinforcements into the Eisleben-Mansfeld district, the only area where Communists outnumbered Socialists. On March 17 representatives of that district's police conferred with Hörsing and Severing. Whether the Socialist authorities were aware of the Communists' preparations and had decided to thwart them by acting first, or whether their countermeasures simply happened to coincide with the planned Communist move, the outcome was the same. The Communists reacted instantly. Thus, in violation of Lenin's teaching that one must never be sucked into combat at a time and place of the enemy's choosing, the Communist leaders advanced the date of their planned assault from March 27-28, right after Easter, to March 21-22, and the battle was joined. After their defeat, Brandler wrote: "Were we supposed to back down in the face of this provocation by Hörsing? I say no! It was our duty to summon the German proletariat into battle against it. And that is what we did."[65] Later, especially after Lenin began to call the shots, the action taken by Governor Hörsing was systematically inflated and declared solely responsible for what had happened, while the Communist contribution, including Eberlein's role as the central committee's representative, was not mentioned.*

THE ROLE OF BÉLA KUN IN BERLIN

As far as promoting any revolution was concerned, Béla Kun's actions were a disaster. They confirmed the absence of both an "objective" revolutionary situation in Germany and a "subjective" political intelligence in the revolution's would-be authors and instigators. But seen from the perspective of the Comintern hierarchy, these blunders had one redeeming feature. For the first time the Comintern's most important foreign member party—or at least its leaders, cadres, and other functionaries—subordinated themselves completely to a Moscow emissary and did exactly what, in Moscow's name, he had ordered them to do. This cementing of Moscow's prestige, accompanied by the obvious taming of the German party, added up to an enormous plus. The lesson would be remembered on future occasions when Moscow would again decide out of the blue to have the German Communists or the entire Comintern adopt this or that policy instantly.

Initially, Kun and his putschist ideas were not received with general approval in Berlin. Though he managed to sell his plan to the German party's central committee, some other leading European Communists to whom he presented it in Berlin, Germans included, greeted it with considerable hostility. The cleavage

---

*Concerning the role of Hugo Eberlein, who decided to heat up the insurrection by strategically pouring oil on the fire, we have the first-hand testimony of Lenick and Bowitzki, who were the Communists' top military and political figures, respectively, in Mansfeld, where most of the action occurred. In their report of April 12 to the party's central committee they wrote: "On Tuesday, the 22, Comrade Hugo showed up from Berlin as the central committee's representative to take charge of the operation in Central Germany and keep it moving. . . . He gave official orders to blow up the munition depot in Seesen, and then a few hours later, to make it appear that the authorities were reacting, he ordered the dynamiting of the building just bought by the producer cooperative. . . . He had us blow up all kinds of things, including the Class-Struggle Building." (*Vorwärts*, November 25 and 26, 1921. Taken from documents that Clara Zetkin was carrying with her to the Third World Congress. On July 8 they were confiscated at the border by the German police and later published in the Socialist press.)

was fairly clear-cut. Those who had been to Moscow, recently or earlier, and who were at all close to the Bolshevik leaders opposed Kun and his ideas; those on the central committee, who had taken office after Levi and his friends had left, were all in favor.

Among the German Communists, Clara Zetkin and Paul Levi expressed total disapproval of Béla Kun and his plans. Zetkin's feelings about Kun were so strong that she announced that she "would in the future refuse even to talk to him unless witnesses were present."[66] The Comintern's permanent Berlin representative, "Thomas," who like Zetkin and Levi had conferred with Lenin in 1920, likewise utterly opposed the Kun venture and vainly tried to warn Moscow: "Of course I informed Moscow. I protested violently and demanded that Kun be recalled. I sent them proof that the preconditions necessary for any uprising simply did not exist in Germany. Moscow remained silent. One had the impression they were playing a waiting game. If the insurrection succeeded, they would take credit for it. If it failed, they would disown it."[67] Kun had occasion to divulge his schemes to two old Polish Socialist militants who had gone over to Bolshevism, Adolf Warski and Stanisław Lapiński. They, too, refused to take part: "The conversation after several hours degenerated into a heated argument. Again Kun did not spell out his plans, but their drift was plain enough. Warski and Lapiński were both dead against an attempted uprising or any other wild ventures. Kun berated them angrily: 'You have the guts of chickens. You don't look at things with Bolshevik eyes.'"[68]

Another secret Comintern emissary to the German Party was Felix Wolf, whose job it was to oversee clandestine operations. Close to Radek and a member of his "faction," he too had come up through the school of the Russian revolution and knew the Bolshevik leaders well. Joining the others in opposing the March venture, he was immediately subjected to violent attacks. One of his attackers was Eberlein, who demanded he be kicked out of the party: "Comrade Wolf, who is close to Comrade Walcher, was in Erfurt, where he forced the district secretary to sign a statement [against the action]. This is unheard of! That bunch must be thrown out of the party."[69] At the next meeting of party functionaries, on April 10, chairman Brandler announced that Wolf had been excluded. Levi complained about it in a letter to the presidium of the

Third Comintern Congress, attributing this purge to "a direct order from another Executive Committee representative" [Rákosi]. He added: "On that day [April 10] proceedings were begun to expel two comrades [R. Müller and F. Wolf]."[70] This disciplinary reprisal assumed far-reaching importance. It was henceforth impossible to hold a party job without sharing, or at least pretending to share, the opinions of the bosses, a situation which party apparatchiks in Germany and in the Comintern bureaucracy, quickly grasped.

In addition to these German and non-German critics in Berlin, Kun had a bone to pick with other Communist luminaries especially invited to Germany to represent Europe's parties at the scene of the big revolutionary action. This feature of the operation was kept even more secret than Kun's own presence. He himself quickly became known in high Berlin Communist circles for the fame of his exploits in Hungary and for what he was now proposing. The other foreign visitors, however, remained deep in the shadows during, and especially after, the event. The reason was simple and highly compelling. The fact that foreign Communist parties had been invited to send delegates to witness the show was proof positive that the performance had been scheduled in advance by planners at the Comintern summit, which reduced to ashes the emergency fabrication *ex post fiasco*, that the whole thing had been a spontaneous outburst by an enraged German working class in response to a vile provocation by Hörsing. So it was necessary of course, after the deed had aborted, to keep the presence of the foreign audience an airtight secret. It was mainly Levi who "leaked" the presence of the emissaries from Moscow, which was not the least of the reasons for his being expelled from the party and Comintern. But at the time, and for the most part thereafter, the secret was kept about the witnesses invited from the "fraternal parties."

The summoning of these foreign viewers was dictated by the accepted reasoning that the Communist revolution was fundamentally an international phenomenon. The Bolsheviks had always maintained that the primary reason for the defeat of the 1905 Russian revolution was the absence of a propitious international climate, and that the revolution of 1917 had succeeded because the conflict and contradictions between the two imperialist-capitalist camps had made the necessary changes in that climate. According to the same reasoning the collapse of Soviet Hungary was due in part to the absence of the appropriate "international revolutionary conjunction," essential to its success.

So naturally, for a succesful revolution in Germany one needed the collaboration, in various forms, of the proletariat of the neighboring countries; this is why the foreign guests were on hand (and were present again in Moscow in 1923 when new preparations were afoot for the "German October.") In March 1921 the guests included Communist representatives from the Entente countries: France, England, Czechoslovakia, Luxembourg, and possibly Belgium. There for France was Victor Méric, a member of the French party's directing committee, to which he had been elected two months earlier at the congress in Tours. From England came Tom Bell. Representing Czechoslovakia, where the different national Communist groups had not yet united, was Skalak for the Czechs and Karel Kreibich (or A. Neurath) for the Sudeten Germans. The Luxembourg party sent its chief, E. Rheiland. Attached to the group as interpreter was L. Revo, a Berlin correspondent for *L'Humanité*.

Communists who remained faithful to their party for life have avoided speaking of their stay in Berlin in March 1921, as well as about their relations with the leadership of the German Communist Party and the delegation of the Comintern. In contrast, Victor Méric, who broke with the party, revealed the whole story. For him it began one evening at the editorial offices of *L'Humanité,* when Frossard and Cachin said to him: "Tomorrow morning you take the train for Berlin. A revolutionary uprising, a big 'putsch' is being planned there. It is essential that the French party be represented." [71] As soon as he got to Berlin, on the morning of March 23, Méric went to see Revo, *L'Humanité* correspondent there; within a few minutes Revo received a telephone call from Stoecker, Däumig's replacement as VKPD chairman. Stoecker wanted to know whether the French delegate had arrived yet, after which the two left for the VKPD offices, where they met other foreign delegates. The foreign visitors spent the day with Kun and several German party leaders waiting for news of the start of the "revolution." When it came, as Méric relates in his memoirs, Kun found it highly reassuring and full of promise: "I looked at Béla Kun. He was jubilant. He was shaking his head and rubbing his hands, like a new man. A second emissary appeared, then a third. More details. In one section of Berlin there was a pitched battle between proletarians and soldiers. Many corpses. Kun was still rubbing his hands, laughing his head off." [72]

In the face of "these successes of the revolution in Germany" Kun explained to Méric why it was necessary to have a French party representative on hand to witness the armed uprising in Germany: "You must now immediately proclaim a general strike in France, to demonstrate your solidarity with the German revolution, and to keep the French troops stationed in the Rhineland from intervening." [73] Méric later wrote that he listened to these words in alarm, just as Clara Zetkin and Levi had listened when Kun spoke to them in this vein about Germany. Méric paid no attention to Kun's instructions, which made the latter furious, as he would demonstrate several months later, when he filed charges against Méric with the Comintern's Executive Committee, on the eve of the Third World Congress.

The German party's central committee, on the other hand, offered Kun virtually no resistance. Arriving in Berlin in early March, he went straight to work, and by March 16 or 17 he had lined up the party's entire official leadership in support of his views. During the discussions the most prominent proponents of the new drift held the floor, each in turn siding with Kun and repeating his arguments. Party chairman Brandler, the old Spartacist Ernst Meyer, Radek's friend Paul Frölich, and Friesland (Ernst Reuter), the head of the Berlin left, spoke one after another, each stressing his wholehearted approval. This unanimity fathered a resolution, which opened with the call: "The workers are herewith summoned forth into battle, for the following purposes: (1) to overthrow the government. . . ; (2) to forge an alliance, for defense and offense, with Soviet Russia; (3) to disarm the counterrevolutionaries and arm the workers." [74]

At that moment the party's propaganda engines began to grind. On March 18 the party daily *Rote Fahne* began publishing appeals for revolution and an offensive push. A typical appeal, entitled "A Clear Answer," closed with the statement: "A worker tells the law to go to hell and gets himself a gun wherever he can find one. . . .

Every counterrevolutionary is armed. The workers should make just as good revolutionaries as those others make counterrevolutionaries."[75]

These appeals for action continued, and action there finally was. On March 21 and 22 the strike and insurrection began. They ended in total disaster. Wherever the Communists essayed an attack, as in Central Germany and Hamburg, they were crushed.[76] The fiasco changed the picture for everybody: for Paul Levi, the former party chairman, whose conflict with Moscow now became irreversible; for the German party's central committee, who sought to conceal their retreat with an elaborate verbal display featuring a complex "theory of the offensive"; for the Comintern emissaries; and, last but not least, for the Comintern itself.

LEVI'S REBELLION

Though Levi knew what Kun was planning in and for Germany, he had no hand in the preparations. This suited the German party leaders, who were obviously eager to escape his control. They gave him permission to leave Berlin, as he explained afterwards at a meeting of party functionaries: "When I talked with them and we spoke of the coming action, I asked when exactly it was likely to be. Certainly not before Easter, I was told. I then asked if there would be any objections to my taking a trip. Assured that there would not, I took off and was already out of the country—though not in Italy; I didn't get that far."[77] The first news of the outbreak reached him in Vienna. He came straight back to Berlin, and on March 27, while the fighting was still going on, wrote Lenin a seven-page letter which contained this gloomy prediction: "This act not only dooms the perhaps genuine partial uprising (in the best sense of the term) in Central Germany, but in my view also destroys the fruits of a two-year struggle, a two-year effort by the Communist Party of Germany.... Two or three more such episodes, actions which the proletariat feels to be against its own interests ... and the Communist Party will be in ashes. And we shall have to start all over again, under far more difficult circumstances, and try to rebuild what we now have."[78]

He concluded the letter with an assurance that he had no desire to raise the banner of revolt against the Comintern, saying that he was thinking merely of writing a pamphlet on the subject: "Personally I have no intention of setting myself against the Communist International's policies in Germany. I have already told the Executive Committee's representative, to whom I explained my position, that I would do nothing to interfere with the operation. . . . And even now I shall do nothing more than perhaps write a little pamphlet setting forth my views." [79]

Three days later, on the night of March 31, the German party leaders halted the insurrection. On April 1 they published an announcement to this effect, and the fighting was over. On April 3 and 4 Levi wrote his pamphlet, which he entitled *Unser Weg. Wider den Putschismus* ("Our Way. Against Putschism"). Even before it appeared on April 12, the official party leadership, speaking through party chairman Brandler, and Berlin's left opposition, represented by Ruth Fischer, branded Levi a traitor, not because of his attitude toward the German party or the March débâcle but because of his attitude toward Moscow. Ruth Fischer told him to his face: "Comrade Brandler has already said that all those who go around writing that Moscow needs corpses are not only critics but betrayers of the revolution. . . . This [is a] fairy tale about Moscow needing corpses, to which even Comrade Levi has cautiously lent his voice by saying that Russia was in trouble and there was a revolt in Kronstadt. . . ." [80]

Thus battle was joined, with Levi and his friends on the one side and the official party leadership, supported by the left opposition, on the other. The issue went far beyond the March fiasco itself. At its core were two problems that were to haunt the Comintern throughout its life. The first was a moral one: was it right to use unfair methods in internal fights with fellow Communists? Was the lie an admissible weapon not only against the external class enemy but also against intra-party Communist dissenters? The second was political: could the relationship between Moscow and its foreign "fraternal parties" be on no basis other than that of subordination of the latter to the former? Levi, in rebelling, gave an answer to these questions that was very different from the one that Moscow finally gave.

When he undertook his critique of the March affair, Levi threw into it the passion of a man torn by inner conflicts, for he could not fail to see what the result would be; but he tackled the job with the thoroughness of a serious lawyer. In his analysis, published as a pamphlet, the final and most important part was devoted to the problem of a national party's relationship to the Comintern Executive Committee. During the two years from the assassination of Leo Jogiches in March 1919 until he resigned as party chairman in February 1921, Levi had been the number one Communist in both Germany and the Comintern (not counting the Russians, of course). In presenting his grievances against the Executive Committee, he could, and did, speak as one who knew whereof he spoke.

He accused the Executive Committee of going over the head of the official German party leadership during the time that he was its chairman, giving as a characteristic example the indigestible propaganda that Moscow tried to circulate in Germany: "We recall a case in which the German Central Committee unanimously vetoed publishing a certain tract, declaring it unsuitable, but which was then published over our heads anyway." [81]

He criticized the Comintern's top leaders, pronouncing them unequal to their jobs. While he did not mention names, insiders knew that he meant Zinoviev and Radek. What he said was: "We believe that there is a strong feeling, not only here in Germany but everywhere, that the Executive Committee's leadership is not up to par. This is not only because it is not headed by a Marx, as the First International was, or by a Lenin, but because of the great technical difficulties involved." [82] In his criticism of Zinoviev, the president of the Communist International, he went so far, in his second pamphlet, *Was ist das Verbrechen?* ("What Is the Crime?"), as to dredge up the latter's attitude at the time of the seizure of power in Petrograd on November 7, 1917. The argument was rather neat: Zinoviev had publicly, and in advance, disapproved of the insurrection in Russia that would succeed some ten days later, while Levi had publicly, but only afterwards, condemned the attempted insurrection in Germany, which failed. Tactically, however, the argument was weak, because by bringing up a subject that was absolutely taboo in Comintern circles, it merely strengthened Zinoviev's resolve to sink Levi as quickly and utterly as possible, though Lenin, for his part, was still hoping that the situation would smooth itself out and that a final break with Levi could be avoided. As for Radek, Clara Zetkin advised Levi to "limit your polemics against Radek. The fellow is not worth it. The less you say about him, the better." [83] But Levi went ahead anyway.

He also attacked the Moscow practice of sending out secret emissaries. Alluding to Béla Kun's sojourn in Turkestan, he wrote: "Russia is in no position at present to send out its best people. They have jobs in Russia in which they are irreplaceable. . . . So Western Europe and Germany have been selected as a training ground for a string of second-raters, who apparently come here to learn to read and write. I have nothing against these 'Turkestantsy' and wish them all the best. I do think, though, that they and their little tricks would do less harm in Turkestan." [84]

After dissecting the behavior of Rákosi in Berlin, following the latter's exploit in Leghorn, Levi criticized the comportment of these emissaries in general: "I refer to these delegates' direct and secret communication with Moscow. To our knowledge, in virtually every country in which such emissaries are at work the dissatisfaction with them is the same. . . . They never work with, but always behind the backs of, and quite frequently against, the domestic party's central committee. Moscow listens only to them." [85]

He next criticized the Executive Committee itself: "The Executive Committee functions like an arm of the Bolshevik secret police stretching out beyond Russia's borders. An impossible state of affairs." [86] He concluded his analysis by fixing the blame for the German party's catastrophic situation squarely on the Comintern Executive Committee: "Thanks to the Executive Committee and its role, the existence of the German Communist Party, hitherto Europe's only Communist-led mass party, is in grave danger." [87]

Levi drew answering fire from the Comintern, and particularly from its president, Zinoviev, who called him "an infamous liar." This time a group of German Communist leaders, Clara Zetkin among them, who at that point felt as Levi did, sprang to his immediate defense. They issued a statement: "We hold that the Executive Committee has no right to pass judgment without full knowledge of the facts, or to brand as liars comrades who happen to think as we do. We shall give our answer to Comrade Zinoviev's unproved, and unprovable, allegations before the forum of the

International." [88] Levi's own ironic reply to Zinoviev's insult was:
"Since I assume that the Executive Committee chairman does
know the true facts, this public insult is taken as proof of a high
degree of confidence in my rectitude and sense of duty as a Communist." [89]

After this multi-barreled attack on the March action and its
architect, Béla Kun, on the official leadership of the VKPD, and
on the Comintern's two top figures, Zinoviev, its president, and
Radek, its proconsul in Germany, Levi found himself at war with
an array of adversaries consumed by one thought: to crush him.
Wilhelm Pieck, who would hardly win any prizes for intelligence,
nevertheless managed to comprehend that in order to hang on to
his job he had better know which side his bread was buttered on;
he said in April about Levi: "But the worst thing is that he has
sown mistrust of the central committee and of the Executive Committee's representatives." [90] Replying to Pieck in his speech of
May 4 to the central committee, Levi confessed ironically: "Yes, I
certainly did that, and I do plead guilty to this particular variety
of lese majesty." [91]

In acknowledging this "crime" Levi seemed, or pretended, to
believe that it would not entail capital punishment. His precise and
lucid analysis of the German party's situation, which he rightly
termed disastrous, did not lead him to similar conclusions about
his own situation. Like any Communist leader rebelling against
Moscow, he believed that he was being true to Communism, which
he accused the others of perverting. In this sense his was the first
case of its kind (not counting Serrati's), but it would be repeated
many times.

The first delusion that Paul Levi nurtured from March to June
of 1921 was that it was possible to criticize the Comintern
publicly and still stay in it. His March 27 letter to Lenin, his May 5
statement indicting Zinoviev, and his letter of May 31 to the Third
Congress presidium, made clear that he continued to regard himself as a Communist and had no wish to break with the International. Clara Zetkin had warned him on April 11 that such a
position was unrealistic: "I have read your pamphlet from beginning to end very carefully. It is absolutely excellent. But make no
mistake, it will get you thrown out." [92] This happened a few days

later. While Lenin lived, so long as dissent was merely about Comintern tactics with regard to bourgeois parliaments or trade unions, or only involved spats with left-wing Communists, as at the Second World Congress, or revolved about such issues as defensive versus aggressive policies, as at the Third Congress, the Bolshevik leaders could afford to look upon the "deviationists" as salvageable, and they tried to keep them in the Comintern and leave them in the positions of leadership that they held in their parties. But once a foreign Communist chief dared to criticize the way in which the Comintern was run, calling into question not mere tactical concepts but the discipline, internal structure, and very functioning of the institution, he was beyond the pale. To disagree about tactics, so long as one knuckled under and accepted the Comintern's ultimate decision, was not "high treason." But to disagree and then violate discipline, by refusing to accept that decision, definitely and automatically was. This was Levi's crime.

His second delusion was his belief that in Moscow his cause was not lost simply because, as he wrote to a friend on the eve of the Third World Congress, his analysis had been correct and his views were even shared by Lenin and Trotsky: "In Moscow, Lenin, Trotsky, and many others believe exactly as I do, but they cannot forgive me for knocking one of the jewels out of the Executive Committee's crown."[93] He did not yet fully realize, as he later would, that Lenin (for it was he who so decided) could put up with almost anything, including the imbecility of which he would accuse Rákosi and Kun, and the ignominy of Radek with his barefaced lie that Moscow had had no hand in the March affair, but that he could not afford to forgive a breach of discipline like Levi's. So long as one served the cause, one's stupid or shameful deeds could be pardoned and even defended. But a breach of discipline, never. There could be no pardon for that, even when the rebel proved right.

At the time of his rebellion Levi suffered from a third delusion. He believed that because he was right in his analysis of the situation in Germany and elsewhere, Moscow in the end would bow to the evidence, not only about the March fiasco but about Soviet perspectives in general concerning Europe's Communist movement. Shortly before the Third World Congress he wrote:

It's the same old nonsense that Moscow always wants to believe, namely that a Soviet-type revolution would have occurred by now if there
weren't a Serrati in Italy or a Levi in Germany standing in the way. The
Muscovites completely overlook the fact that conditions in Western
Europe are utterly different from those in Russia. There you had an
agrarian revolution with some 95 per cent of the population in favor. In
Italy the revolutionary role of the peasants is much smaller. In Germany the peasants are counterrevolutionary. In Western Europe the
proletariat is tightly organized; in Russia the masses were not organized.
These are some of the differences that Moscow one day will have to try
to grasp.[94]

But what happened was the opposite. Instead of trying to grasp
them, the men in Moscow more resolutely ignored them.

The Levi rebellion far transcended the man himself, the March
débâcle, or even the German party. It was a turning point in the
internal history of the Comintern. The Levi case supplied crushing
proof that Radek's warning of February 1921, that any national
party leadership resisting Moscow would be ground to ashes, was
no idle threat. Levi's downfall demonstrated the point, and in view
of his stature it was a major Moscow victory. He was Rosa Luxemburg's spiritual heir, the head of Europe's most important Communist party; he had been close to Lenin before October 1917; and in
December of 1920 he was still so prestigious within the party that,
according to Malzahn and Radek, Heckert and Brandler had to beg
him to accept the VKPD chairmanship, his acceptance having been
made the subject of an ultimatum by the ex-USPD.[95] But his
illustrious past, titles and prestige were of little avail when he
collided with Moscow. When the collision finally came, the members of his party and its central committee stuck with Moscow, and
nearly everybody, including Clara Zetkin, deserted him. From
then on, whenever any foreign party's leadership or chief had a
falling-out with Moscow, there was only one choice: give in or
get out. The Radek axiom became a universal theorem, which
would ultimately prove valid against even Radek, and against the
Brandler-Thalheimer tandem that he put in charge of the German
party.

In the three months that the Levi affair lasted the Comintern
paid a smaller price for its victory than it had in the Serrati case,

which in Italy in January 1921 cost the Italian party most of its members and produced a troublesome backwash in the German party, the Comintern's most important foreign section. Levi's downfall in Germany made no such waves. Article 13 of the Comintern bylaws, adopted at the Second Congress, had frozen into law Moscow's resolve to block any further intercourse between the foreign parties themselves except through the agency of the Executive Committee, so that each member party knew about the others only what Moscow saw fit to divulge. The desired upshot was that each knew less and less about what was happening in the others, and grew more and more isolated from them. This explains why the German party's former chairman, who had also been a presiding chairman at the Second World Congress and was a member of the Executive Committee, could break with the Comintern, and why later, in 1923, the entire Norwegian Labor Party could pull out, without provoking ruptures in other sections of the Comintern. This system of "insulation" was perfected in use against the opposition within the Comintern before it was later turned against opponents within the Bolshevik Party.

The Levi rebellion afforded the Comintern an opportunity to bring into play another weapon, which could be called the dialectic of betrayal. When confronted with a foreign Communist leader who was resisting Moscow's ukases, the Bolsheviks employed a method which consisted in first labeling the offender as belonging to the camp of the "class enemy" (usually the Socialists) and then actually forcing him into that camp. Since every attempt by any foreign leader to create a Communist movement of his own, outside the Moscow orbit, ended in failure, there were only two courses open to him: either to leave politics (which is what Radek, in his letter of April 7, 1921, to the central committee, predicted for Levi); or to join, or rejoin, some other political movement, generally a Socialist one. So every foreign Communist leader had an option, which Moscow envisaged for him with equanimity, but which often enough the man himself did not comprehend until much later: he could either knuckle under and do as he was told, and keep his job and titles, or he could resist Moscow's demands and thereupon cease being a Communist leader, and then cease being a Communist. Each of the foreign Communist chiefs who

entered the Comintern while Lenin lived was given a choice between two kinds of betrayal, "subjective" or "objective." Those
who wanted to remain faithful to their idea of Communism from
the beginning had to break with Moscow, where they found an
increasingly deformed image of their ideal; thus in order not to
betray themselves they had to betray the Comintern and Moscow.
That was the case of the majority of the founders of the Communist parties. Inversely, many of the leaders who succeeded the
generation of founders behaved differently: they betrayed the
ideal of their youth but remained faithful to Moscow.

The Levi rebellion was a model of a clash whose origins were
obvious, though systematically denied by Moscow: the collision
between Bolshevik policies and management of the Comintern, on
the one hand, and the policies and interests of a foreign Communist party on the other. It was also a classical instance in which
those claiming to be the most faithful and purest Marxists—the
Bolsheviks—declined to apply Marxist standards and reasoning to
themselves.

On many occasions Marx had pointed out how, in class societies, the ruling class usually defends its interests in the name of
lofty general principles, refusing even to acknowledge the existence
of any class antagonisms. The Bolshevik leaders fell into this same
behavior pattern when confronted with the conflict of interests
between Soviet Russia as a nation state and the Comintern as an
international organization for Communist revolution, but run by
the same small group of Russians. Brandishing vague lofty principles of "world revolution" and "proletarian internationalism,"
they consistently denied that such a conflict existed. But conflict
there was, between the dominant concentrated power of the Russians at the helm and the dominated scattered force of the foreign
Communist parties making up the Comintern membership. As
with most other conflicts, only a fight could resolve it.

Marx and Engels had made it an axiom of their historical materialism and conception of politics that the history of all societies
was but the history of class struggle. Stretching this formula slightly, one can say that the entire internal history of the Communist
International was a kind of class struggle, with Moscow in the role
of the ruling class and the foreign parties as the exploited proletariat. One of the first casualties in this battle was Paul Levi.

FROM OFFENSIVE ACTION TO THE THEORY OF OFFENSIVE

By the time of the March action the German party's rallying cry had become "seize the offensive! " Even when the strike and insurrection were disintegrating, Paul Frölich wrote in the party review *Die Internationale*: "There has been no time during these past two years when the government was as weak as it is now. . . . Under these circumstances the VKPD decided to seize the offensive." [96] Several days later, on learning of the defeat, Radek assessed the situation realistically in a confidential letter to the central committee: "The fact is, too, we are all convinced that, now that the offensive has failed, we are going to suffer a setback." [97]

Yet it was immediately after the March failure, that this same "offensivist" cry—which Lenin was about to scuttle (a decision not yet relayed to Berlin)—received the German party's formal blessing, becoming simultaneously its general political line and its official doctrine. It became its political line when, after being proposed by the central committee, it was adopted by that body and by the assembled party officials and cadres. It became its official doctrine when the central committee published a collection of articles to justify the new line.

The central committee met on April 7 and 8, a week after the March offensive had collapsed and was abandoned. The party officials and cadres assembled on April 7 and 10. At the first meeting a motion was made to give the floor to Levi so that he could present his critique of the recent action, but this was voted down twice in a row. He was given the right to address only the assembled officials and cadres on April 7, but was interrupted by the audience, which had been conveniently rigged, as it was again on May 4, when he spoke for the last time, then to the central committee.

The central committee meeting on April 7 and 8, with Levi absent, was a festival honoring the late fiasco and the theory of the offensive in general. Those in favor had no need to say anything, having already made their case at the meeting of March 16 and 17, before the attempted uprising. When the theses on the subject were put to a vote on April 8, and it was requested that the recent course of action and its continuation in the spirit of the theory of the offensive be approved, the leadership won by a comfortable majority of 26 to 14. The theses were a reiterated plea for offensive action: "The decisive battle for power can be fought by the working class only in the context of a broad, mighty offensive. . . . The VKPD must eliminate the organizational and tactical shortcomings that thwarted the first attempt. If it is to fulfill its historic mission, the party must stick to that revolutionary-offensive line on which the March action was based, and with determination and confidence push onward along the same path." [98]

At the meeting of the party officials and cadres, the left opposition, through the voices of its three leaders, Reuter (Friesland), Maslow, and Ruth Fischer, expressed total agreement with the official party line. Reuter, preceding Levi to the rostrum, concluded his remarks with a glorification of the offensive policy: "We do not confine ourselves to mere propaganda and agitation . . . the Communist party exists not only on paper and at party congresses but is in raw reality the fighting avant-garde of the proletariat, an avant-garde which, by staying on the offensive, deepens the capitalist crisis to such an extent that victory of the working class, of the proletariat, becomes assured."[99]

Speaking on April 10, at the second meeting of this assemblage, Maslow also ended his speech with a eulogy of the offensive, and a demand that Paul Levi (whom he did not name) be expelled: "Our party was defense-minded and thereby lost its meaning as a Communist party. A defense-minded party is, by definition, Social-Democratic. If it intends to be a Communist party, it has to be offensive-minded. . . . We have had a meeting of the central committee at which portentous decisions have been made. They not only reaffirm the policy of the offensive but demand that that policy be carried out. Anyone not supporting it does not belong in the Communist party and must be gotten rid of." [100] When the party officials had finished their deliberations and the time came to close the meeting, Ruth Fischer made the final speech, replacing Reuter, who was absent. She did not forget to extol what she obviously believed to be a positive aspect of the March fiasco: "All of us favor a policy of the offensive. . . . Why, we were in serious danger of becoming a mere Socialist party, in a wrapper labeled 'Communist.' But the defeat saved us." [101]

While these spokesmen of the central committee and Berlin's left opposition were busy expressing their joint approval of the new offensive line, Béla Kun, still hanging around the German capital, continued to carry on in theory what had failed in practice. His two lieutenants in this enterprise were August Thalheimer and Paul Frölich, who each contributed articles to the symposium on the tactics and organization of a revolutionary offensive, published by the VKPD central committee. (Two months later Kun and Thalheimer drafted some theses on Comintern tactics, their intention being to extend their theory of the offensive from the confines of Germany to the broad international plane, but Lenin silenced them.)

In the very introduction, which was not signed but was obviously the brainchild of Kun and Thalheimer, the offensive was stressed as the prime mission for the future:

> The purpose of these articles is to orient the party toward the policy of a revolutionary offensive, tactically and organizationally. . . . We cannot win by defending ourselves. . . . The Communist Party must seize the initiative. . . . Our adversaries are right when they say that what the party did in March, if left as an isolated act, would be a crime against the proletariat. But as the first in a series of such actions, each more powerful than the last, the March offensive becomes a liberating deed. The activity of the party creates, by itself, new situations, widens the battle ground, and, by itself, forces the offensive into an ever larger scope. It conquers the masses and leads them to victory.[102]

In the first of the two articles Thalheimer, who from then until the end of 1923 figured as the party's leading theoretician, explained that what had happened in March was necessary to shake the masses out of their passivity: "While the Open Letter and the agitation for an alliance with Soviet Russia did meet with the masses' approval, neither succeeded in breaking through their wall of passivity. In view of the over-all situation, the VKPD had to take it upon itself to smash through that wall."[103] In his second article Thalheimer described the March action as the beginning of the final struggle for a revolutionary seizure of power: "And so these March battles are the prelude to a general offensive by the working classes, thus to a general offensive of Communism in Germany."[104]

The symposium was published in late April 1921, its theme

becoming automatically "required thinking" for the entire party and its press. In it the central committee, after declaring approval of the policies and tactics of the leadership, said in its "Guidelines Concerning the March Action": "Outwardly this revolutionary offensive ended in a defeat for the VKPD, which is now temporarily isolated from much of the working class. Actually, however, the defeat holds the fruit-bearing seeds of new, broader revolutionary acts." [105] This was further confirmation that Levi was right in asserting that the party, having become putsch-oriented, had lost touch with the masses. But the Berlin Communists clung stubbornly to their view (quite alien to Lenin's own perspective). On June 1 Maslow wrote in the party's theoretical review: "If one asks what it was that was new in the March action, the answer must be: the very thing that our adversaries criticize it for, namely that the party went into battle without giving a damn about who would follow." [106] Be that as it may, the essential elements of the German party's line were now known. The resolutions of its governing organs and the public elaboration of its "theory of the offensive" made everything clear. Only one thing was left to learn: Moscow's reaction. It was not long in coming.

MOSCOW'S ANSWER

After the March fiasco and Levi's rebellion, it was incumbent upon the Comintern to make some public statement. It could easily do so with regard to Levi and the other leaders who had disapproved of the action in Germany, but commenting on the action itself was a more complex operation. The crisis in the German party, which had been steadily worsening since January, was resolved overnight after the March action, which burst the abcess that Levi constituted in Comintern eyes. His expulsion was decided upon with breath-taking speed, given the still serious difficulties that plagued communications between Moscow and Berlin. His pamphlet *Unser Weg* came out on April 12. On April 29, with a document bearing the signatures of Lenin, Trotsky, Zinoviev, Bukharin, and Radek, the Executive Committee promulgated his excommunication. This incidentally was one of the last occasions on which all five Bolshevik leaders co-signed an official public Executive Committee text, which indicates how important they considered the matter to be. The statement did not beat around the bush. Its first sentence declared: "Paul Levi is a traitor. That was everyone's opinion." [107] From the outset it made much of the pamphlet that Levi had just published, which, according to the Committee's resolution, had aroused the indignation of all the Committee members. It would appear that after receiving, during the preceding month, the many reports on what had happened, including the letters from Levi and Clara Zetkin, and after his initial talks with the Communists from Berlin, Lenin personally supervised the drafting of the resolution, for two of its points closely matched the things that he did and said during the ensuing months, up to the beginning of the Third World Congress. First, he refused to extend the excommunication of Levi to all the others who had opposed the March venture. His aim was to keep those leaders in the party, especially Clara Zetkin, while isolating Levi, thereby rendering him less dangerous. Consequently, there was not a word against Clara Zetkin, who then still sided with Levi, and Lenin compelled Zinoviev and Radek to leave her alone. Secondly, unlike the Executive Committee statement of April 6, the one telling the German Communists "you did right! " this one contained no expression of approval. In fact, it even seemed to imply that Levi had been right, which Lenin frankly admitted on several later occasions: "Even if Levi was right in his over-all appraisal of the March events, he still had to be kicked out of the party because of his serious breach of party discipline. By his behavior at such a moment he literally stabbed the party in the back." [108]

The Executive Committee decision of April 29, expelling Levi, thus confirmed the one taken on April 15 by the German party's central committee. But others were purged at the same time from the party and Comintern apparatus in Berlin. In this Zinoviev and Radek had a free hand; Lenin did not concern himself with such trifling matters. One of those excised was Felix Wolf, alias Krebs, alias Rakov (his German and Russian pseudonyms), who was Moscow's secret emissary at German party headquarters. In May 1921 he was replaced by Elena Stasova, the new watchdog over the German party's underground activities.

As soon as Levi was thrown out, his case became a prototype in another respect. The technique of massive accusation and polemic, which Moscow increasingly unleashed against him in artillery-like barrages, was to become a familiar weapon in the arsenal of Comintern methods. As weapons go, it had the advantage of simplicity, consisting of only three parts, which the Bolsheviks had been using for years to eliminate domestic opponents but which were new on the European Socialist scene.

The first was the establishment of guilt by chronological association, for which the formula was always the same: "At the very moment at which, etc." It consisted in wiring together simultaneous but unrelated events. Event one was usually an accredited "class enemy" busy attacking the Communists, while the coinciding event two would be a Communist leader in the act of making criticisms, which, though entirely unconnected to the substance of event one, were automatically judged helpful to the "class enemy." In Levi's case the proof was easy. One had only to show that here was Levi publishing a pamphlet against the action in March "at the very moment" at which the working class was fighting under the party's banner, and "at the very moment" at which the party was being exposed to the White terror, to reach the self-evident conclusion that Levi was a traitor. The first argument was advanced by Pieck in his speech of May 4 to the central committee. Replying to this charge in his own speech later that day, Levi proved that, by the time he had started writing his pamphlet, all fighting had ceased, the central committee having by then already thrown in the towel. Pieck sat mute.[109] The second barrage in the accusation of complicity with the enemy was the Executive Committee's resolution, which made so much of the fact that Levi had published his pamphlet "at such a moment." In his answering letter of May 31 to the Third Comintern Congress presidium, he set forth detailed evidence that there was no connection between the pamphlet and the reprisals of the German authorities, and that the latter had made no use of what he had written.[110]

The procedure's second element was the old-fashioned false equation: showing that what a Communist critic was saying was identical to what the enemies of Communism were saying, the simple logic being that, since Comrade X was expressing the same views as the Socialist and bourgeois class enemy, Comrade X had necessarily become an enemy. This peculiarly Bolshevik twist of reasoning, it should be said, had never been turned against the Bolsheviks by their foes. Lenin and the Tsarist secret police, for instance, shared an intent to split Russia's Social Democrats, yet it never occurred to any Russian or European Social Democrat to accuse Lenin of being in the service of the Tsar's secret police. Similarly, Liebknecht and Clemenceau both wanted, and worked for, the overthrow of Kaiser Wilhelm II, but no European Socialist would have deemed either to be "objectively" serving the other's cause. With the Bolsheviks, considerations of fair play were jettisoned. In his own pamphlet against Levi, Radek pointed out: "The fact that he charges the Communist party with the very things that people like Hilferding give as their reasons for not joining it—sectarianism, putschism à la Bakunin, dictation from Moscow—proves that he shares the outlook of our enemies, and thinks like a Centrist." [111] Levi, in his "farewell letter" to the Comintern, after citing this type of argument, which he characterized as a "deceitful ploy," concluded: "So the question now is not whether we are using Hilferding's arguments, but rather whether the VKPD's March action fits our conception of Communism or the Hilferding caricature of Communism. If only one answer to this question is possible, that is not my fault." [112]

The third and final element consisted in sidestepping the actual substance of a Communist opponent's views and attacking the man himself, for which purpose his political past was ransacked for semblances of "incriminating" evidence, a procedure which gave birth to the new science of rehistoriography, by which ordinary history may be renovated, remodeled, and rewritten to taste and convenience. And so it was that Radek, Brandler, and the others immediately began making discoveries about Levi and his past, which turned out to be full of artifacts pointing to an almost congenital hostility on his part toward Moscow, his behavior at the Second World Congress in 1920, then previously at the Heidelberg congress in October 1919, being cited as two examples.

While the Comintern could sweep Levi under the rug very quickly, the March fiasco and its embarrassing offspring, the "theory of the offensive," were not that easy to dispose of. The process dragged on until the Third Congress, when Lenin was finally ready to impose his solution. The Comintern meanwhile was in a bind. It could not go on glorifying the débâcle, as Zinoviev had done on April 6, for Lenin's own attitude was becoming more and more critical. Neither could it publicly acknowledge the role played by Béla Kun, not to mention the Zinoviev contribution, which would have substantiated the Levi criticisms and been a heavy blow to the Comintern's prestige. Nor was it free to dump the responsibility at the doorstep of the German party leaders, whom the Comintern and Radek had themselves just handpicked and enthroned. While the agony of the situation was naturally not allowed to show in public, its painful presence was attested to by Radek's confidential letter of April 7 to the central committee: "We passed two resolutions, one for the eyes of the leadership and central committee, the other for public consumption. But, just before he left, Zinoviev asked me to treat as secret, for the time being, even the one to be published." [113]

Immediately after the March action and Levi episode the Comintern Executive Committee, and particularly Zinoviev and Radek, who were directly responsible for German affairs, had to execute a violent change of course. Under the circumstances they were compelled to deny that the Comintern had played even the remotest part in the disaster. The Committee's April 29 resolution against Levi declared at the outset: "In the name of the Little Bureau of the full Executive Committee, Zinoviev branded as an infamous lie the allegation that the Committee or representatives thereof had instigated the March action. The German counterrevolutionaries, whom Levi had thrown in with, need this fable." [114] The Zinoviev statement was followed by one from Radek, dated May 10: "Needless to say, the Soviet government and Comintern Executive Committee knew nothing about the March events until news of them was broadcast to the world by the Berlin radio stations." [115] This was not only a political but a technological lie, designed to give the impression that the only channel that the Committee had for receiving hot news from Berlin was the German radio. Yet in his confidential letter to the central committee a month earlier, concerning the resolution that Zinoviev was hesitant to publish (probably because of Lenin), Radek had written: "If we do decide to publish resolution B, I shall telegraph." [116] Brandler, promoted into Levi's place, felt it his duty to follow the Zinoviev-Radek lead. After the March effort had collapsed, he published a pamphlet of his own categorically denying any Comintern involvement:

Levi really takes the cake with his allegation, which he obviously got straight from *Freiheit* and merely reworded a little, that the action was the work not of [our party's] central committee but of the [Comintern] Executive Committee, or of "Turkestantsy" as he calls them, and that the central committee were only puppets dancing to Moscow's tune. This is the slyest, dirtiest piece of slander in Levi's whole pamphlet, and he will have to produce proof, unless he is willing to admit that he was lied to, or lied himself. I here declare most explicitly that neither I nor, to my knowledge, any central committee member was requested orally or in writing by the [Comintern] Executive Committee, or persons close to it, to undertake any particular action, or specifically, the March action.[117]

EPILOGUE

The March affair and Levi's expulsion made obvious that Moscow deemed it more important to have foreign Communist leaders obedient to its orders, even at the price of their suffering defeats and losses in their own countries, than to have others who saw clearly and turned out to be right but broke Comintern discipline. This is why the wrongheadedness of the German Communist leaders about the March action and about the "theory of the offensive" was condemned at the Third World Congress but they themselves were allowed to retain their positions in the German party, whereas although Levi's ideas finally prevailed he himself was declared a renegade. To be right, in politics, has never been a guarantee of victory. This was all the truer in the Comintern, where the Bolsheviks' convenient definition of "discipline" was the ruling concept. Rarely in Comintern annals had an errant leader been pilloried so harshly while having his ideas so speedily adopted.

First at the Second World Congress in the summer of 1920, and then again in November of 1920, Levi had protested admitting the KAPD as a fellow traveler party, showing the sterility and danger of such an act. A year later the Comintern had to bow to the evidence and sever ties with the KAPD. In January 1921 Levi had vigorously criticized the expulsion of Serrati, and this had been largely responsible for turning Moscow against him. In April of that year, in his polite reply to Levi and Clara Zetkin about the March affair and Kun's role in it, Lenin was inclined to agree with their criticism, while insisting and even "proving" to them that they had been wrong (and he right) about Serrati: "Your tactic in

the Serrati matter I consider to have been mistaken. Any defense
or even semi-defense of that man was an error." [118] Yet by the
summer of 1921, at the Third World Congress, a delegation from
Serrati's party showed up, and at the next congress., in November
1922, Serrati and his friends were welcomed back into the Comintern. Finally, Levi had condemned the March action and "theory
of the offensive." The Comintern soon buried the former in silence and killed the latter at the Third World Congress.

Lenin had a high regard for Levi's political acumen, and he
publicly displayed his esteem, sometimes directly borrowing his
ideas. At the time of the Kapp-Lüttwitz putsch, in 1920, he sided
with Levi against the German party's central committee. In January 1921, when Radek and Levi drafted the Open Letter, Lenin
steadfastly stood behind them, and in his speech on Comintern
tactics at the Third Congress had further praise for it: "The 'Open
Letter' was a brilliant political move." [119] When in early June 1921
Radek submitted to him the draft of the theses on Comintern
tactics, co-authored by Kun and Thalheimer, Lenin not only flatly
rejected them but, addressing Zinoviev, began his reply with the
comment: "The fact is that, in many respects, Levi is *politically
right*. Unfortunately, he has committed some breaches of discipline, and for that the party has expelled him." [120]

When Lenin was not paying homage to Levi's ideas explicitly,
he was often doing so implicitly, and, by embracing them, giving
them the ultimate consecration. The following are two examples.
On February 2, 1921, Levi, still the VKPD chairman, made a
speech in the Reichstag in which he demanded "an alliance between
Germany and Soviet Russia," and he proposed it as a Communist
watchword. His words produced a furor among German party leaders. The pro-Soviet faction, made up of Radek and the left opposition, who were against anything and everything Levi said and did,
vied with each other in anti-Levi outbursts and harangues, both
within the central committee and in the Communist press. At a
secret central committee meeting Paul Frölich declared: "We
must say that we were disappointed with Comrade Levi's
speech." [121] At this juncture he was interrupted by Maslow,
who could get out only one word about it: "Scandalous! " A

motion was made to censure Levi for his attitude. Lenin was obviously unaware of the interlude, for on April 16 he wrote: "Unfortunately, I've been so busy and overworked these past weeks that I've had almost no chance at all to keep up with the German press. I saw only the Open Letter."[122] But in his last missive to Lenin, on March 27, Levi took pains to explain the tactical significance of his call for a German-Soviet alliance. Several days after receiving it, on April 11, Lenin made a speech to the Communist members of the Soviet trade unions. (It was not published until 1932.) He himself supported Levi's idea: "For Russia an alliance with Germany holds enormous economic promise, regardless of whether the revolution there is soon victorious. We can work things out even with Germany's bourgeois government, because the Treaty of Versailles condemns that country to a hopeless situation, while allying herself with Russia would open entirely new doors."[123]

Soon after his expulsion, another idea dear to Levi became a Lenin preoccupation. In his speech of February 24, 1921, to the German party's central committee, in the face of the optimism associated with the new drift, which took it for granted that the masses were now solidly behind the VKPD, Levi had concluded with a plea to his comrades not to cut themselves off from the masses or move in a direction different from theirs: "Between Communists and the masses there must be no parting of the ways."[124] In his letter to Lenin he also explained his own purpose in calling for the alliance (and in publishing the Open Letter)—"to draw into the movement, too, those masses in Germany who do not belong directly to the Communist party." [125] As it happened, this idea of moving closer to the masses became the chief slogan and main directive that Lenin, at the Third Congress, broadcast to Communists the world over, and when in December 1921 the policy of the United Front was approved and adopted, its link to the past was that Open Letter of January 8, which was its first concrete manifestation.

Lenin also adopted the Levi view that the "theory of the offensive" was sterile and harmful, as evidenced by his attacks on it at the Third Congress. But even before that, Moscow's sword had fallen, and the book on it published by the German party's central

committee was proscribed. P. Neumann, a spokesman for the pro-
Levi opposition at the Third Congress, announced: "Comrade
Thalheimer, theoretician, has published a symposium. The Executive Committee has forbidden its circulation."[126] Thus the chronological sequence in which Lenin removed the two eyesores was
the reverse of that in which the German central committee had
spawned them. The latter had staged its offensive in March, and
begat a covering theory in April. But Lenin strangled the theory
first, leaving the offensive to be buried later.

The German Communist Party was bound to suffer from the
rude blows that it sustained during the first half of 1921. Just
prior to the March fiasco, the new united Communist party, according to its promoters' estimates, had some 500,000 members;
this was the figure advanced by Curt Geyer at the Executive Committee meeting on February 22 and by Béla Kun in his conversations in Berlin. The official records show that by August, when the
congress at Jena was held, its membership had dropped to
359,613, and it dropped to 224,389 by the second quarter of
1922.[127] In the elections for the Prussian Diet in February, before the débâcle, in the constituency of Greater Berlin the VKPD
drew 233,000 votes. For the elections of October 16, the list kept
by Reuter, who had been promoted to party secretary general,
showed only 160,000.

The darkest aspect of the March action—the exact role of Moscow, which remained a forbidden subject throughout 1921, and
before, during and after the Third World Congress—was the last to
be exposed to the light of truth. In January 1924, reviewing the
first five years of the Comintern's existence, with Lenin recently
dead and the old leadership of the German party all but gone,
Zinoviev, perhaps profiting from the absence of these restraints,
decided to assign sole blame for the March fiasco to the German
party. This at least was a step forward, in which a half-truth replaced the total lie, forced on the Third World Congress, that it
had all been strictly a defensive operation. Zinoviev now said: "In
March 1921 the German Communist Party organized the so-called
March rebellion, which ended in a severe defeat."[128] In 1926,
when Zinoviev's days of power in the Comintern were on the
wane, Béla Kun was apparently feeling a little freer, too. In his
"official biography," published in the biographical dictionary of

the some two hundred leading figures in Russia and the October revolution (in which he and Rakovsky were the only two of non-Russian birth to be included), he had this statement inserted: "In 1921 the Comintern sent him on a mission to Germany, where he directed the March action taken by the proletariat."* The truth could hardly have been put more succinctly, provided that one does not forget that in the Bolshevik vocabulary the word "proletariat" was identical to "Communist Party."

Granat, Entsiklopedicheskii slovar russkogo bibliograficheskogo instituta, vol. 41, part I, p. 251. One should add that in early 1922 (in *Die Internationale*, January 1922, pp. 9-10) Radek made reference to the March affair, saying that the party had committed "the error of armed rebellion." Obviously at that time he could not implicate the Comintern, or Zinoviev and Kun, but only the German Communist Party.

1921—The Change of Course

As a master of revolutionary strategy and tactics, with an almost infallible instinct for knowing exactly when to take the offensive and administer the coup de grâce, Lenin also knew when to retreat and make temporary concessions. The Brest-Litovsk peace was a typical example. It had split the party and led to the open formation of a leftist faction within it, and Lenin even found himself in a minority of the central committee. Similarly, the first hints of the change of course in 1921 also stirred up currents of resistance. The Soviet government had published its decree on the foreign concessions on November 23, 1920, and in a speech on December 21, Lenin had to admit: "According to our information, the concessions that we have granted have caused widespread concern and unrest, not only in party circles and among the working masses but among many of the peasants too."[1] In the debate on the trade union question, which was raging during the same month, he was again outvoted in the central committee and the committee divided temporarily into two groups of almost equal number. On one side were Lenin, Zinoviev, Kamenev, and Stalin, and on the other Trotsky, Bukharin, and several others, including the committee's three secretaries, Krestinsky, Preobrazhensky, and Serebryakov. But again Lenin won out, and with regard to both the treaty concessions and the trade unions, his own policies were adopted.

The change of course in 1921 differed from the preceding ones in its unparalleled scope. Whereas the switches in tactics of April and October 1917 (before the seizure of power) affected only the Bolshevik Party, and those after November 7 (for example, the peace of Brest-Litovsk) involved the Bolshevik Party and Soviet state, the change of course in 1921 had profound effects on three fronts: the Bolshevik Party, the Soviet state, and the Comintern. The consequences for the Comintern were more significant than for Soviet Russia, for several reasons. In deciding to switch from the offensive to the defensive inside Russia and to replace War Communism with the New Economic Policy, Lenin was seeking of course to gain time in the face of an obviously receding revolutionary wave; as he was fond of saying, to win time is to win all. He was prepared to yield a little in the economic sphere if he did not have to surrender any political gains. He could afford to fall back on his absolute power within Russia, and wait for a new revolutionary surge, whether in Soviet Russia or the capitalist world. But when he imposed this new defensive tactic on the Comintern in 1921, the Communist parties in the capitalist countries had no similar stronghold to retreat to. Nowhere were they in power, and nowhere did they represent a majority of the working class.

Since in Lenin's eyes a switch to the defensive had been made necessary by objective circumstances, the new policy would inevitably bring to the fore a basic contradiction that was to haunt the Comintern to the end of its days. The Bolshevik Party, acting through the same group of leaders—technically the Politburo in the Kremlin, but actually Lenin (and later Stalin)—governed Soviet Russia and ran the Comintern, functioning both as the party in power in one country and as the driving spirit behind a world revolution. This dichotomy dated, of course, from the Comintern's birth in Moscow, but its effect was felt less in 1919 and 1920 than in 1921 and after. Lenin had acted initially on the assumption of imminent revolution in Europe; later he acted on the opposite assumption, having lost faith in the advent of that revolution. At first, Soviet Russia's position as Europe's only Communist country and ruler of the Comintern was seen as only temporary; later it was accepted as permanent, and the Comintern had to tailor its policies to fit events in Russia—the NEP, famine, the re-establishment of relations with capitalist countries, and a little later the bitter struggle between Lenin's would-be successors. The relationship between Soviet Russia and the Comintern changed. Instead of Soviet Russia's being at the disposal of the international Communist movement, as Lenin believed it should in 1919 and 1920, it was the international Communist movement that henceforth would have to shape its actions to serve the interests of Russia. Though officially Soviet Russia remained the avant-garde country of Communist world revolution, in truth the international Communist movement became the tail of the Russian dog. From then on, as in any war, the subordinate Comintern would be under the orders of the Russian general staff, which would always take care not to endanger its best troops (the Russian Bolshevik Party and Soviet power) in wasteful attempts to rescue any expendable sections of the Comintern threatened with annihilation. After 1921, unqualified support of Soviet Russia became the number one public and official duty of all foreign Communist parties— with no reciprocal obligation on the part of Russia, however. This was made explicit at the Third Comintern Congress, held in June and July of 1921, where it was proclaimed in the theses on Comintern tactics: "Unqualified support of Soviet Russia remains, as before, the prime duty of Communists in all countries."[2] This was a complete reversal of the position which Lenin had formulated himself at the Second Comintern Congress, when he advanced the thesis that the country in which the revolution had already triumphed (Russia) had to accept the greatest sacrifices in order to support international Communist movement. He wrote at that time: "Proletarian internationalism requires, first, the subordination of the interests of the proletarian struggle in one country to the interests of that struggle on a universal scale; and second, the capacity and the readiness of nations which are in the process of defeating the bourgeoisie to accept the greatest sacrifices in order to overthrow international capital."[3]

After 1921, as the probability of revolution in Europe grew smaller every day and the Soviet regime continued to strengthen its hold on Russia, two irreversible processes began in the Comintern. On the one hand, all the non-Russian sections became increasingly dependent on the policies and decisions of the dominant Russians. On the other, the incompatibility of Soviet Russia's national interests with the interests of the international Communist movement deepened. As long as a wave of revolution seemed to be sweeping over Europe, this incompatibility was not felt to exist, not even by so lucid a European Communist leader as Paul Levi; at a closed meeting of the German Communist Party's central committee on August 25, 1920, after his return from the Second World Congress, he rejected the very thought of any conflict of interest between the Comintern and the Soviet government: "That danger, conceivable in theory, I cannot imagine ever actually materializing. My own feeling is that it cannot possibly exist in practice, because the identity of interests between the Communist International and Russian Soviet Republic . . . is so great that no such clash can develop."[4] Barely six months later, when this same Paul Levi was engaged in public battle with Moscow, the underlying cause of his break with the Russian leaders was that the "impossible" had happened after all. The interests of the German Communists had collided with those of the Kremlin.

The general conflict of interest between the Soviet government and the Comintern was to be augmented after 1921 by a set of particular conflicts between the national sections and the Comintern. Most of the big Communist parties had come into being after the Second World Congress in 1920, whose decisions were predicated upon the assumption of an inevitable international civil war. Not only had these parties failed in their attempts to foment revolution; with two or three exceptions, they had stopped trying. Organized to operate as revolutionary movements—with secret networks, professional revolutionaries, iron discipline, and insurrectionary techniques—they were now condemned to function without recourse to any major revolutionary act. Thus after 1921 the Western Communist parties were to exist in a kind of vacuum, without a real prospect of revolution or civil war. They began to resemble what they had reproached the pre-1914 Socialist parties with being: revolutionary in word, reformist in deed. But the Communist parties would not lapse into the "opportunism" of the Socialist parties, for two reasons. First, unlike the old Socialist International, whose structure and organization were democratic, the national sections of the Communist International became gradually patterned on the Bolshevik model. Secondly, after 1921, the Comintern's growing dependence on Soviet Russia, the first and only Communist state, and on its Bolshevik Party, whose leadership had to be followed by all the foreign parties, would restrain the foreign parties from wallowing in the sins that Lenin laid at the door of the Second International: reformism, pacifism, "parliamentary cretinism," ministerialism, class collaboration, and all the rest. After 1921 Moscow would steer the foreign parties more and more toward a Bolshevik-type organization, and this produced another paradox: as the prospects for revolution diminished, the popular basis of Western Communist parties contracted, but their apparatus broadened; in other words, party members and voters

grew less numerous, but the number of full-time party functionaries increased.

REASONS FOR THE CHANGE OF COURSE

The change of course in 1921 did not occur all at once or simultaneously in all areas of Bolshevik policy. In the foreign policy of
Soviet Russia it began after the Red Army's defeat in Poland,
starting with such measures as the decree of November 23, 1920,
regarding foreign concessions, and continued into early 1921 with
the signing of the first treaties of friendship with countries in the
Middle East (Persia, Afghanistan, and Turkey) and the conclusion of
the first commercial treaty with an "imperialist" Western power
(Great Britain) on March 16. The new direction was made evident
economically with the introduction of the NEP, inaugurated at the
Bolshevik Party's Tenth Congress in March 1921. Within the party
it was reflected, again at the Tenth Congress, first in the forbidding of intra-party factions, and then in a massive purge which
resulted in the expulsion of 24 per cent of party members.

It was in the policies of the Comintern that the change occurred
last and most slowly—because of the priority that Lenin gave to
Russian domestic affairs and also because the Kremlin did not yet
have the Comintern firmly in hand. In Soviet domestic affairs
there was a lag, generally, of only a few weeks between the final
recognition that the new situation called for a defensive strategy
and the actual implementation of a new policy, while in the
Comintern the process took an entire year and was completed in
four phases. The first phase came in November and December of
1920, when Lenin at last realized that revolution in Europe was
less imminent than had been supposed, a fact which he began to
acknowledge in public speeches. The second came after the collapse of the uprising in Germany, in March 1921, when Lenin
criticized that action directly, if privately, to a number of leaders
who were responsible for it. The third began when he had the
"theory of the offensive" openly condemned at the Third Comintern Congress, in June and July of 1921, over the opposition of
several important European Communist parties. The fourth began
in November and December of that year, when he conceived his

United Front tactic and had it adopted by the Comintern leadership (though he himself did not take part in the meetings of the top-level Comintern agencies, leaving it to Zinoviev, Radek, Bukharin, and Trotsky to defend the new policy).

Lenin's greatest political talent was his ability to take the pulse of a political environment into which he had just moved. This explains why he would draw different conclusions about the same problem, depending on whether he was a political refugee in Zurich or a Bolshevik leader in Petrograd, or whether he was in hiding beyond the Finnish frontier or presiding as chairman over the Council of People's Commissars. In 1914, as a refugee in Switzerland, and out of touch with events in Russia, he called for transforming the imperialist war into a civil war, but by April 1917, newly returned to Petrograd, he realized that that course would harm the Bolshevik cause. Also, while a refugee in Switzerland when the so-called bourgeois revolution broke out in February and March of 1917, he did not believe that it could be converted directly into what he called a Socialist proletarian revolution, yet after his arrival in Petrograd he proclaimed that very thing as his party's objective. Just as he knew how to read the stars in Russia's revolutionary atmosphere of 1917, he was later able to read them in another environment, one entirely new to him—the domain of Soviet power, where again he matured rapidly, as illustrated by his handling of the treaty of Brest-Litovsk. Leo Jogiches, a man who knew Lenin well but was not especially predisposed to favor his views, remarked to Clara Zetkin after the first year and a half of his reign: "The revolution has educated Lenin. He has learned much, indeed an enormous amount. Look what he has become! Who among us would have dreamed it? ! The revolution has forged out of the Bolsheviks that leadership-giving party that it needed. We can well believe that this party has experienced some powerful inner process. The Mensheviks and SRs put great faith in formulae and slogans, but behind it all they lost touch with the lifeblood of the revolution . . . . The Bolsheviks have grasped what the present situation requires."[5]

Thus, generally, Lenin could size up a political situation immediately and correctly gauge the strengths of the opposing forces if he was there and could observe it in person. But if it was far off, he needed time to study it. This explains why he was able between

1918 and 1920 to make realistic decisions about Russian affairs while being so wrong in his analyses of events in the West. Cut off from Europe's labor movement, he could not personally take its pulse. He was not wrong, of course, in judging it impossible for Soviet Russia to guarantee the survival of Soviet Finland in 1918 and Soviet Hungary in 1919, but he badly overestimated the chances of revolution in Europe, and particularly in Germany. He was right in ceasing by the summer of 1920 to regard it as a function of the Soviet government to make revolutionary propaganda, a task which he had expressly assigned it in 1918. When Kamenev, chosen to head the Soviet delegation in political negotiations with the British government, told Lenin that he intended to conduct the affair "in the spirit of the broadest possible agitation," Lenin immediately advised against it: "In this situation any unmasking [of British imperialists] could be harmful. This is not 1918. We have the Comintern for such purposes."[6] But Lenin was not right in believing that the Red Army's advance into Poland would trigger a Communist revolution, first in that country and then in Germany.*

The Second Comintern Congress had finished its work on August 7, 1920, in an atmosphere of euphoria generated by the Red Army's advance on Warsaw. Lenin did his best to keep in touch with the front. On August 3, for instance, he telegraphed the military commanders Smilga and Tukhachevsky to "do everything possible to broadcast throughout Poland the Polish Revolutionary Committee's manifesto, using our aircraft for the purpose."[7] In a telegram on August 9 he admonished the heads of the Polish Revolutionary Committee, Dzerzhinsky and Marchlewski: "Your reports are too laconic. We very urgently need detailed information on the mood of the farm laborers and Warsaw workers, also on the political outlook in general. Please reply today if possible."[8] Despite the scarcity of news from the front, on August 14, as the Soviet advance was about to be halted in the commencing battle for Warsaw, which lasted from August 14 through 17, Lenin cabled Kamenev in London: "We have almost no news from

*See in this connection the section of Chapter Seven of this volume, entitled "Lenin's State of Mind and the Climate at the Second World Congress," pp. 271-78.

Poland. What news there is supports our conclusion, shared by the entire central committee: a little extra vigilance and victory should be ours! "[9]

Lenin had assigned top priority to the Polish affair; he had sent there the Red Army's best troops, its ablest commanders, and even his War Commissar, Trotsky; and he had drawn some trusted veterans from the Polish revolutionary movement who were now exercizing the highest functions either in the Soviet state (such as Dzerzhinsky) or in the Comintern (Radek), and had integrated them into the Polish Revolutionary Committee that was to serve as a provisional Communist Polish government. As late as August 19, the day after the Red Army had begun its retreat (the extent of which Lenin did not yet realize), he sent Radek a telegram demanding a firm policy of liquidation of the big estates and kulaks, and effective aid to the poor peasants.[10] The first brigade of Germans was then being formed at Minsk, to be commanded by Melcher, an Austrian Communist who had taken part in the Russian revolution. Arvid, a Baltic Communist, was to be its political commissar.[11] What Lenin's Polish policy amounted to and what hopes it elicited in Moscow at the time, was later privately described by Radek to the leaders of the German Communist Party:

> During the war in Poland the Executive Committee believed that the movements in Western Europe were coming to a head, and that the Red Army's westward thrust would have the effect not of introducing Bolshevism there by force but merely of breaking through the crust of the ruling class's military power, the assumption being that sufficient internal forces had been unleashed in Germany to sustain the initiative .... The Executive Committee thought that the situation in Germany was reaching a point at which it would be possible to seize political power. Their belief was that once we got to Warsaw there would be no further need for us to march on Germany.[12]

The hopes came to naught. Defeated outside Warsaw, the Red Army started to fall back on August 17. Brest-Litovsk was abandoned on August 21, and the eastward retreat became general along the entire front. Peace talks at Riga began on September 11. Lenin had to recognize that he had been wrong about Poland. He did not say so publicly, though he did in private, in a conversation with Clara Zetkin on October 12.* In that conversation Lenin also acknowledged that the Polish workers had behaved as anything but allies: "And in the Red Army the Poles [Polish peasants and lower middle-classes] saw enemies, not brothers and liberators. They felt, thought and acted not in a social, revolutionary way, but as nationalists, as imperialists. The revolution in Poland on which we counted did not take place. The workers and peasants, deceived by the adherents of Piłsudski and Daszyński, defended their class enemy, let our brave Red soldiers starve, ambushed them and beat them to death."[13]

Though admitting that he had been wrong about Poland, he was not yet revising his outlook regarding the overall prospects for revolution. The setback in Poland he viewed initially as more of an episode than a turning point, an episode in the sense that the forward march of the revolution was bound to have its ups and downs, as he had often written (most recently in *"Left-Wing" Communism*). Thus, the Polish campaign should not be considered as an event that would terminate one phase of the revolution (the offensive) and inaugurate another (the defensive). In late August, on the eve of the peace talks between Soviet Russia and Poland in Riga, he summarized in a Communist journal the prospects opened up by the Second World Congress: "The revolution of the proletariat, the throwing off of capitalism's yoke, is coming and will come in all countries of the world."[14]

On September 22, he reaffirmed his conviction that the war against Poland had nearly toppled imperialism and had profoundly influenced Germany: "Poland, the last bulwark against the Bolsheviks, being entirely in the hands of the Entente, is so much of a keystone in their system that when the Red Army threatened it, the whole structure began to totter. . . . The advance of our troops on Warsaw threw all Germany into an uproar. The scene there resembled the one in our country in 1905."[15] A few days later, on October 15, the preliminary peace treaty with Poland having been signed on October 12, he reiterated: "We see it confirmed that our Russian revolution is but one link in the chain of international revolution, and that our cause stands firm and invincible, for the cause of revolution is on the march throughout the world,

*See the full quote, Chapter Seven, p. 274.

and the economic situation is so evolving as to weaken our enemies and make us stronger every day. That this is no exaggeration, idle boast, or wishful thinking has now been proved to you again by the Polish war."[16]

That he had not immediately recognized that the revolutionary wave in Europe was beginning to ebb after the Soviet setback in Poland was partly due to the fact that, two weeks after the defeat outside Warsaw, revolution seemed to be brewing in another major country: Italy. The seizing of factories by workers, which had begun in Milan on August 31 and was spreading to many other places, came at just the right moment to distract attention from Poland, and it appeared to confirm Kremlin expectations of an early revolution in Italy. Even during the Polish campaign there were those on the Executive Committee who, according to Radek, kept insisting that the main revolutionary thrust should be directed against Italy: "Another view held by some Executive Committee members, by those favoring the so-called southeastern gambit, was that the main stab should be aimed not at Germany but along an entirely different front, namely through the countries sitting on an agrarian powder keg (Eastern Galicia, Rumania, Hungary), the idea being that, once we reached Drava and the Sava, this would speed up revolution in the Balkans, thereby creating the necessary agrarian hinterland for revolution in Italy." [17]

It was at this juncture that the Bolshevik leaders drafted an appeal to the Italian Socialist Party and to Italy's "revolutionary proletariat." Written by Bukharin, expanded by Zinoviev, and cosigned by Lenin on August 27, its aim was to produce an immediate break with the Turati "right." When the disorders erupted in Italy several days later, they seemed to confirm the correctness of the Lenin diagnosis that Italy was ripe for revolution. When the wave of strikes subsided, Lenin saw that as confirming another of his axioms, namely the inevitable treachery of the right-wing Socialists and centrists. On September 24 he wrote to the German and French workers: "Events in Italy should open the eyes of even the most stubborn of those maintaining that there is no harm in 'unity' and 'peace' with the Crispiens and Dittmanns. Italy's Crispiens and Dittmanns (Turati, Prampolini, d'Aragona) began to *thwart* the revolution there the very instant it showed promise of becoming *real*. And real revolution, sooner or later, is what there is going to be, all over Europe, all over the world—whatever the cost in agony and suffering."[18] On November 4 he wrote a long article on the problems facing the Italian Socialist Party. Having nobody who could explain to him the situation in Italy, as Radek was able to do for Germany, and knowing even less about the movement in Italy than the one in Poland or Germany, he stuck to his delusions about "the impending decisive battle of Italy's working class against the bourgeoisie for control of the State."[19] Again, the only danger he could see was the one allegedly posed by the reformist leaders: "If vacillating leaders desert the field at a time like this, it will not weaken but actually strengthen the party, the labor movement, and the revolution. In Italy now such a time is at hand. That the revolutionary crisis there is engulfing the entire nation is seen and acknowledged by all."[20]

He published this article on November 7, the anniversary of the Bolshevik revolution, perhaps intending it as a symbol of devotion to the revolutionary cause in Europe, where militant actions by workers were being reported nearly every week from all corners. But as in Italy, these ended in failure. On October 23 a general strike began in Rumania, and led to repressive measures by the government; by October 28 it had been crushed. On November 2 the miners in Belgium walked off their jobs, staying out until November 15, when they finally capitulated to the government. On December 1 Norway's railway workers struck, but that strike too collapsed. On December 8 another strike was called at the Czech industrial center of Kladno, and it threatened to sweep the country when most Bohemian and Moravian workers went on strike on December 13. On December 14 the Czech government struck back, smashing the strike and arresting many of the leaders. On December 30 a general strike was proclaimed in Yugoslavia. Again the authorities responded vigorously, snuffing out the strike by January 3 and using it as a pretext to crack down on the Communists.

The list of countries in which the offensive-minded labor movement had been crushed, and those in which it had not dared to take the offensive, was long. It included the five nations deemed by Lenin most essential to Europe's revolutionary cause. In two of them, Italy and Czechoslovakia, the radical spirit of the labor movement had been flattened. In the other three, no spontaneous mass action had occurred. Poland had not wavered under the Soviet onslaught, nor had Germany been swayed. The militancy in France was nipped in the bud with the breaking of the strike of May 1920, following which the Communist and syndicalist leaders were arrested, even before the SFIO was split. Lenin could not fail to react to this avalanche of disappointments and defeats, all coming within less than five months after the end of the Second Congress. From 1918 until late 1920 his speeches and writings referred often and emphatically to the imminence of world revolution. But once he realized and admitted to himself that it was perhaps not so imminent, his assertions of its inevitability (in even the more distant future) grew rarer.

On November 6, 1920, in celebration of the Bolshevik revolution's third anniversary, Lenin spoke—possibly for the last time—of the coming international revolution in Europe. He admitted that the Bolsheviks would never have dared to seize power in Russia had they not been firmly convinced that a world revolution would follow: "We knew at the time [in 1917] that our victory would be secure only if our cause triumphed throughout the world; in fact we initiated our work counting entirely on the world revolution." [21] He saw the Russian revolution as merely the prelude to revolution in the more developed countries: "We have always known and must never forget that our cause is an international one. Until the old order has been toppled in all countries, including the richest and most civilized ones, we have only won half the game, perhaps less than half." [22] But revolution was "due" in Europe, notwithstanding temporary setbacks:

> You probably already have a fair idea of what is happening in one of the countries [Germany] now readiest and ripest for revolution. But the same is going on in all countries. Communism has developed, gained strength, forged itself into a party in all the advanced nations. During this time, of course, the international revolutionary cause has suffered minor defeats in a few small countries where robber-barons have moved in and helped crush the movement, as Germany, for instance, helped smash the Finnish revolution, and those colossi of capitalism—England, France, and Austria—snuffed out the revolution in Hungary. But in so doing, they only strengthened a thousandfold the forces of revolution in their own lands. [23]

Two weeks later Lenin was retreating from this position. Though still clinging to the thesis that consolidation of the Bolshevik revolution was inconceivable without a subsequent revolution in the highly developed countries—"For our victory to be secure and lasting, we must achieve victory for the proletarian revolution in all, or at least a few, of the main capitalist countries "[24] —he acknowledged that his earlier predictions of imminent revolution in the West had not come true: "We have seen that neither side has yet really won or lost, neither the Soviet Russian Republic nor the capitalist rest of the world. And we have seen that, even though not all of our predictions have been literally and quickly fulfilled, enough of them have to give us the important thing, the chance and ability to keep the proletariat in power and the Soviet Republic alive, even if Socialist revolution has been delayed in the rest of the world."[25]

By the end of 1920 Lenin had abandoned his hope of seeing the revolution engulf the capitalist world. He replaced it with the more modest aim of securing Soviet Russia's coexistence with the capitalist countries, as he confessed a little farther along in his speech of November 21: "Though we have not yet won a world victory (the only kind that can be secure and lasting for us), we have fought our way into a position where we can coexist with the capitalist powers, who now are forced to have trade relations with us."[26] On December 6 he told Bolshevik militants in Moscow: "But the speed, the tempo, at which revolution is developing in the capitalist countries is far slower than it was in our country . . . which is why we cannot keep relying on guesses about the future, or count at present on that tempo's speeding up."[27] A fortnight later, on December 21, at the Eighth All-Russian Congress of Soviets, he brought the subject up again, still in connection with the concessions, but this time omitted any mention at all of world revolution or the presumed speed of its approach. In his second report, the following day, he gave birth to another distinction, thereafter to be de rigueur in Russia: speaking of the activities of the Council of People's Commissars, he pointedly no longer lumped together the policies of the Soviet government (which he was reviewing) and the doings of the Communist International, concerning which he again said not a word about the prospects for revolution abroad.

From this time forward, if he spoke of world revolution at all it was merely to say that it would not occur in the near future. On March 15, 1921, at the Tenth Bolshevik Party Congress, after he had just completed the change of course in domestic policy and introduced the NEP, he was discussing the payment of taxes in kind, when he suddenly threw in, in passing, as an axiom apparently requiring no further elaboration, this statement: "So long as there is no revolution in other countries, it would take us decades to extricate ourselves . . . . Basically the situation is this: we must satisfy the middle peasantry economically and go over to free exchange; otherwise it will be impossible . . . in view of the delay in the world revolution, to preserve the rule of the proletariat in Russia."[28] In his closing speech, on March 16, he did promise that, once certain differences were overcome, the party would "march on to ever more decisive international victories." But the promise was perfunctory and vague. A month later, on April 25, he again referred to world revolution, saying only that it had been postponed, which in turn had compelled the Bolshevik Party to make some concessions within Russia: "for, if the workers' revolution has been delayed in other countries, then we shall have to make certain sacrifices, if only to bring about a rapid, even immediate improvement in the situation of our own workers and peasants."[29]

Lenin's loss of hope for revolution in the West later became firmly rooted in his mind. At the 1920 celebration of the third anniversary of November 7, 1917, the first two thirds of his speech had dealt with world revolution and only the final third with the Russian revolution. In his 1921 speech his brief remarks pertained solely to problems of the Russian revolution; world revolution was not mentioned at all. Similarly, in an article that he wrote at the time, there was only one reference to international revolution: "We began the job. Exactly when the proletarians of this or that nation will finish it is unimportant. The important thing is that the ice has been broken, the way opened, the path marked."[30]

In abandoning his hope of revolution in the West in the near future, Lenin was not only sacrificing a key element of his revolutionary credo since November 7, 1917, but was reaching a conclusion held by his worst enemies, Kautsky and Hilferding. In August

1918 Karl Kautsky wrote in his critique of Bolshevism, *Die Diktatur des Proletariats*: "The Bolshevik revolution was founded upon the assumption that it would serve as the trigger for a general European revolution, that Russia's bold initiative would inspire the proletarians of all Europe to rise up . . . . All very logical and learnedly substantiated, provided one accepted the premise that the Russian revolution indeed would spark a European revolution. But what if it didn't? So far it hasn't."[31]

In his reply to Kautsky, written in October and November of 1918, Lenin rejected this line of argument, accusing Kautsky of bad faith and of betraying Marxism:

> Kautsky has confused the tactic which counts on a European revolution at a more or less close range but at an unspecified date, and the tactic which counts on the same revolution at a fixed date. A neat little trick, very neat!

> The second tactic is a stupidity. The first is *a must* for a Marxist, for any revolutionary proletarian and internationalist—*a must* because it alone, according to Marxist theory, correctly takes into account the objective situation engendered by the war in all European countries; it alone does justice to the international tasks facing the proletariat. . . . A renegade in politics, when it comes to theory, Kautsky *is not even able to phrase the question* about the objective premise of a revolutionary tactic. . . .

> For a Marxist, relying on European revolution is a must provided of course a *revolutionary situation* is present.[32]

Zinoviev was fond of repeating Lenin's revolutionary credo, and did so right up to the minute that Lenin revised it. At the Halle congress, on October 14, 1920, Zinoviev drew a basic line of division between Germany's Independent Socialist leaders (like Rudolf Hilferding) and the Communist leaders, accusing the former of not believing in world revolution and extolling the latter for being so firmly convinced of it, and he urged the former to confess their heresy publicly: "Of course it is no crime for you to be persuaded that world revolution is impossible at present, but in that case you should clearly and honestly say so."[33] On November 13, after returning from Halle, he made the same accusation: "[This Hilferding] is a skeptic through and through. He is convinced that the revolutionary movement has passed its peak and that today Germany and all Europe are merely experiencing the death throes of an ebbing revolutionary wave."[34] A month later Lenin himself, though hardly a "skeptic through and through," was to say virtually the same thing.

But if he joined Kautsky and Hilferding in abandoning hope for revolution in Europe, Lenin did not cease hoping for revolution in general. At the end of June 1919, with a wave of revolution rolling over Europe, with Russia living under War Communism, he wrote a piece in support of the "Communist Saturdays,"* which contained the following simile: "If, to help mankind conquer syphilis, a Japanese scientist has had the patience to test 605 preparations before finally hitting upon the 606th, which met all the key requirements, then those of us working on the much harder problem of defeating capitalism ought to have the perseverance to test, if necessary, hundreds and thousands of ways, means, and devices for use in the good fight, so that we may perfect the best of them."[35] And once he realized that revolution in Europe was not imminent or even visible on the horizon, he began looking for some of the ways and means he had spoken of. He came up with two. He found one, the United Front tactic, the year after initiating his change of course, and at the end of 1921 he imposed it on the Communist parties in the capitalist world. He found the other at the outset of his change of course, when he commenced shifting his hopes for revolution from the industrialized capitalist West to the underdeveloped, colonial Near and Far East.† In so doing, he was simultaneously revising both classical Marxist theory and the Bolshevik version of it as formulated at the beginning of the November revolution. In the sphere of revolutionary action, he helped open up a vast and fertile field for future revolutionary movements.

The switching from a Western-oriented to an Eastern-oriented revolutionary strategy did not come for Lenin as a global, overnight change of orientation; it evolved relatively slowly as he

---

*"Communist Saturdays" were introduced by a decision of the Bolshevik Central Committee in May 1919. In order to enhance production the workers were asked to lengthen their working day by one hour, accumulate these extra hours, and put in six extra hours of manual labor on Saturdays.

†In the second volume of this work, separate chapters are devoted to the United Front tactics, and to the early Comintern work in the Far East, especially China.

realized that the proletariat in the West was not about to follow a
Bolshevik course. His key public pronouncements between the end
of 1919 and the middle of 1921 will illustrate these points. Addressing the Second All-Russian Congress of Communist Organizations of Eastern Peoples, on November 22, 1919, he said that the
Socialist revolution was not merely or even mainly a struggle of
the revolutionary proletariat of each country against its own bourgeoisie but of all countries oppressed by imperialism. He concluded by defining three different roles, to which he assigned
different degrees of historical importance. One was that played by
the Russians, who had been first to undertake a revolution.
Another, obviously the most important, was that of the Western
proletariat, who would assure ultimate victory for the Socialist
cause. The third, and least significant, was the function of the
colonial peoples, whose job it was to aid in the general assault
upon the capitalist-imperialist world: "It goes without saying that
only the proletariat of all the world's advanced countries can win
final victory. We Russians are beginning the work which will strength-
en the English, French or German proletariat. But they cannot triumph without the help of the toiling masses of all the oppressed
colonial peoples, especially those of the East."[36]   In his speech to
the Second Comintern Congress on June 30, 1920, Lenin stated as
a self-evident truth: "Speaking generally, in the world-historic
sense, it is fair to say that a Chinese coolie in a backward country
cannot by himself wage a revolution."[37]   Four days earlier at the
same congress he had condemned the idea, already expressed by
some Communists (and which he himself would later accept in
large part), "that the fate [of the revolution] in the West would
depend entirely on the progress and strength of the revolutionary
movement in the Eastern countries."[38]

Once his hopes for imminent revolution in the West began to
fade, the view that he expressed in July 1920 had to be revised. It
was no coincidence that in his speech of December 6 that year, to
the members of the Moscow section of the Bolshevik Party, he
acknowledged for the first time that the "revolutionary tempo" in
capitalist countries was different from that in the Russia of 1917,
and that the basic Marxist slogan had had to be amended accordingly: "The Communist International has published and addressed
to the peoples of the East the slogan 'Proletarians of all countries

and oppressed peoples, unite!' One comrade has asked me 'But when did the Executive Committee order the wording of the slogans to be changed?' To tell you the truth, I don't remember. Of course this new slogan doesn't entirely stick to the letter of the 'Communist Manifesto,' but that document was written under very different circumstances. In the context of today's political situation, this new slogan is the right one."* But that was merely one step in the evolution of Lenin's strategic and tactical thinking, and it was not his habit to go only halfway. A few months later, in his speech closing the Bolshevik Party's Tenth National Conference on May 28, 1921, he spoke of the decay of capitalism, stressing not the revolutionary actions of the industrial proletariat in the West but the stirrings of the oppressed colonial peoples:

> Of course, when we set out to fashion a policy that we intend to have last for years, we must not for a minute forget that the international revolution, the speed and circumstances of its coming, may change everything. For the moment a kind of temporary, unstable, yet functioning equilibrium has been established, one in which the imperialist powers, despite their hatred of the Soviet Union and desire to strangle it, have given up the idea because the capitalist world is progressively decaying and increasingly disunited, and the pressures exerted on it by the oppressed colonial peoples, whose numbers total more than a billion souls, grow greater every year, every month, every week. [39]

Finally, when Lenin presented his report on Russian Communist Party tactics to the Third World Congress on July 5, 1921, he said: "And it is clear that the movement of the majority of the earth's population, aimed originally at national liberation, may play a much larger role in the coming decisive battles of the world revolution against capitalism and imperialism than we all had expected." [40]

Polnoe sobranie sochinenii, 5th ed., vol. 42, pp. 71-72. The new version of the slogan, whose origin Lenin could not recall, made its first public appearance three months earlier, on September 7, in the speech by Zinoviev closing the Baku congress. He had concluded it with the statement: "Seventy years ago our common teacher, Karl Marx, issued his appeal 'Proletarians of all countries, unite! ' We, the disciples of Karl Marx, continuers of his work, have the opportunity to develop this formula, to amplify it, broaden it and say 'Proletarians of all countries and *oppressed peoples of the entire world, unite!* " *(Pervyi s'ezd narodov Vostoka,* Baku, 1-8, sent. 1920. Stenograficheskie otchety, Petrograd, 1920, p. 232. Emphasis in the text.) Cf. Chapter Nine of this work, p. 406.

DIRECTION AND EFFECTS OF THE CHANGE OF COURSE

The two changes of course, one in the policies of Soviet Russia, the other in the tactics of the Comintern, were so closely interwoven that it is difficult to separate them, either in time or in substance. As it gradually dawned on Lenin that there would be no revolution in Poland, Germany, Italy, or anywhere else, the need to change course, in both Soviet Russia and the Comintern, began to haunt his thoughts. But in early 1921 the dangers that he saw menacing Russia's Soviet regime from within required that top priority go to domestic affairs; a revision of Comintern policies could wait. A short time later, at the Third Comintern Congress, where his main contribution was to have been a report on the tactics of the Russian Communist Party, he found that this subject was no longer controversial. The number one problem had become the tactics of the Comintern, so he had to deal with that instead.

Lenin saw his dual change of course as a single integrated fallback executed on two different battlefields in the same war. Once embarked on the new course, which included granting concessions to foreigners and engaging in trade negotiations with capitalists, he was at pains to emphasize that the new tactic constituted neither opportunistic desertion of Communist principle nor any peace treaty with the capitalist world. In that same speech on December 6, 1920, he denied any resemblance between his tactics and those of the opportunistic Socialists, reminding his listeners of Brest-Litovsk: "One hears talk, among other things, of opportunism. Opportunism is sacrificing one's fundamental interests for paltry short-term gains. That is the essence of its theoretical definition. And that is where many have gone astray. In the negotiations at Brest-Litovsk, for instance, we did sacrifice some Russian interests, as one defines 'interests' from the standpoint of patriotism, but from the Socialist standpoint they were minor interests. So, yes, we did sacrifice a great deal, but everything we sacrificed was minor."[41] On December 21 he rejected the allegation that having contacts with capitalists meant making peace with capitalism: "It would be a big mistake to assume that just making a peace treaty granting concessions [to capitalists] means making peace with capitalism. The treaty was about a war; it was the lesser evil for us, and for the workers and peasants, less evil than being pulverized by tanks and artillery."[42] On April 11, 1921, in his closing speech on the foreign concessions (kept secret until 1932) he again drew for the Bolshevik members of the Soviet trade unions his favorite analogy comparing the concessions of 1921 to the 1918 Brest-Litovsk negotiations, vigorously insisting that both were mere ruses of war intended solely to trick the enemy: "Remember the treaty of Brest-Litovsk. Why was the job so ticklish? Why the result so hard to defend? When I was asked [at the time] whether I was hoping or planning to trick the Germans, officially I had to say no. But now the treaty is history . . . . As we know, Comrade Ioffe, our ambassador to the German government, was expelled from Germany on the eve of the revolution there. So who can say who was tricking whom? We cannot tell the exact number of days that will elapse between the signing of an initial treaty of concessions and the outbreak of the first major European revolution."[43] Finally, in his speech of October 17, devoted to the NEP, he returned to the theme, but this time the key word was not *trick* but *beat*: "That is what this whole war boils down to: who is going to win; who will get to the trough first . . . . In short, who will beat whom? If the capitalists get organized first, they will drive out the Communists, and that will be that. One must look at these things soberly: who will crush whom?"[44]

Conceived in such a neo-Machiavellian way, the change of course would have important consequences, one of which would survive Lenin and become a permanent feature of Bolshevik practice on both the domestic and international fronts: the disappearance of candor, a quality which, until then, Lenin had liberally displayed. If his doctrinal and political thinking did not change, what he said publicly most distinctly did. He had been in the habit of expressing openly, often brutally, not only his formal thoughts but even his informal ulterior motives, sometimes to the consternation of foreign Communists, as when in the spring of 1920 he wrote in *"Left-Wing" Communism* that one should freely lie, tell whatever falsehoods might be necessary, to worm one's way into the reformist trade unions, and also that the British Communists should support the Labour Party "as a rope supports a hanged man."

But after the change of course, while perhaps retaining his candor in private, his ulterior motives were no longer paraded in public. If occasionally he did lapse into his old brutal openness, it was only in reference to Russian affairs, which were firmly under the party's control, not to international matters affecting the interests of capitalist governments with which he was seeking to establish contacts. On December 6, 1920, he made a second speech to Moscow's Bolshevik militants devoted to the foreign concessions, second chronologically but first in political importance. It was published in an abridged form in *Krasnaia gazeta*. Three years later, in 1923, it was exhumed from the party archives and republished, but again not in full, as explained in the accompanying editor's note in Lenin's *Collected Works*, first edition: "The editors have deleted several passages whose publication would be inappropriate today."[45] Lenin's next speech on the subject was delivered on December 21 to the Bolshevik fraction of the Eighth All-Russian Congress of Soviets (the few Socialist delegates to the congress being excluded). It was given behind closed doors and not published until 1930, with no indication whether deletions may have been made. (By 1930 the concern for textual accuracy, even where Lenin's writings were concerned, had fallen far below what it had been in 1923.) Another example of the new policy of not divulging what was said in inner Bolshevik circles was the decision of the Tenth Party Congress, in March 1921, not to publish point seven of the resolution on party unity, written by Lenin personally, which spelled out the methods of ejecting from the party any and all members found guilty of sowing dissent or violating discipline. Still another Lenin speech, delivered and recorded on April 25, 1921, on those same concessions to foreign capitalists in Russia, was not published until 1924, after his death. Some statements that he made to Bolshevik members of the Central Trade Union Council on April 11, 1921, did not appear in print until 1932. Lenin himself had warned on that occasion against publishing everything that Communists said in confidence to one another: "Here, the trade union people and party leaders must exercise some discretion about what can and should be told to the press, for the Russian press is read by many capitalists. At the time of the Brest-Litovsk negotiations, for instance, we did not tip off the world about what instructions we were giving to Comrade Ioffe."[46]

The Bolshevik Party leaders did not permit publication of everything that Lenin said and wrote in 1921-22, which would have thrown more light on the true direction of his change of course.* But certain texts, though never published in the U.S.S.R., were nevertheless filed away in the party archives. One was a note that Lenin wrote in March 1921, which later, in February 1924, shortly after his death, happened to be copied by Yurii P. Annenkov, an artist officially appointed to look over the photographs of Lenin, as well as his printed articles and manuscripts, in the collection of the V. I. Lenin Institute. (Annenkov's job was to prepare artistic material for books being written about Lenin.) The note that he copied said:

> From my own observations during my years as an émigré, I must say that the so-called educated strata in Western Europe and America are incapable of comprehending the present state of affairs, the real balance of power. Those elements should be regarded as deaf-mutes and treated accordingly . . . . A revolution never develops in a straight line, in a process of uninterrupted growth, but in a zigzag of ups and downs, forward thrusts and temporary lulls, during which the forces of revolution wax gradually stronger, in preparation for the day of final victory.
>
> This being so, and in view of the time needed for the Socialist world revolution to mature, we must take special steps to speed our victory over the capitalist countries.
>
> First, to soothe the fears of the deaf-mutes, we must proclaim a separation (fictional though it be) of our government and its agencies (the Council of People's Commissars, and so on) from the party and Politburo and especially from the Comintern. We must declare that the latter entities are independent political organizations merely tolerated on Soviet soil. Mark my word, the deaf-mutes will swallow it.

---

*A discussion held at the Historical Institute of the Soviet Academy of Sciences, on June 17 and 18, 1964, at a time of the relatively liberalized regime of Khrushchev, confirmed that Deposit No. Two of the Soviet archives, devoted entirely to the personality and work of Lenin, was still inaccessible to Soviet historians. Cf. *Kultura*, Paris, No. 5, May 1965, pp. 122-28.

Second, we must declare our wish for immediate resumption of diplomatic relations with the capitalist countries—on a basis of complete
noninterference in their internal affairs. The deaf-mutes will swallow
this too. In fact, they will even be delighted and will throw open their
doors to us—and in will march the emissaries of the Comintern and
Party intelligence agents to infiltrate their countries, dressed up as diplomatic, cultural, and trade representatives*

In any case, after the change of course the Soviet government
and particularly its diplomats did start behaving as Lenin had recommended in his private memos of 1921. On August 31 and September 1 of that year, for instance, he wrote two notes to Jenö
Varga (not published until 1965) about setting up a West Europe-
based institute for collecting information on the international
labor movement (Berlin, Vienna, Copenhagen, and Christiania-
Oslo were mentioned as possible seats of the planned institute). To
implement the project, Varga stayed in touch with Lenin and
Zinoviev, and Moscow agreed to supply the necessaries (money,
personnel, and so on), but from the outset Lenin admonished
Varga to avoid any contact whatever with official Soviet agencies
in the West: "The Institute must not communicate at all with
Russian embassies." [47] Its link to the Comintern was, of course, to
be kept secret. On September 6, at Lenin's behest, the Executive Committee presidium formally did establish the institute,
but the official minutes of the meeting made no mention of
the matter.[48] A few weeks later, on September 27, in response to
charges by Lord Curzon, the British Minister of Foreign Affairs,
that the Soviet Union was violating the Russo-British treaty by
disseminating Communist and Soviet propaganda in Britain's Asian
territories, Assistant Commissar for Foreign Affairs Litvinov

---

*Novyi zhurnal, New York, 1961, No. 65, pp.146-47. The text was printed
verbatim in the Bulletin of the Institute for the Study of the USSR, Munich,
May 1962. There are three reasons for assuming it authentic: (1) it faithfully
reflects Lenin's spirit and style; (2) Annenkov could not conceivably have
invented it, an act which would have been utterly inconsistent with his
known moral attributes (apart from the fact that he completely lacked the
necessary political knowledge); (3) it has been pronounced authentic by Boris
Souvarine, who from 1921 to 1925 lived in Moscow in constant close touch
with the top Bolshevik Party and Comintern leaders.

drafted a denial directed at the gullibility so confidently assumed by Lenin in his disquisition on "deaf-mutes:"

The Russian government wishes to take this opportunity to stress once again, as it has many times before, that merely because the Third International has for obvious reasons chosen Russia as the seat of its Executive Committee—Russia being the only country that permits completely free dissemination of Communist ideas and grants Communists personal freedom—and merely because some members of the Russian government belong to the Executive Committee in their capacity as private citizens, this does not warrant identifying the Third International with the Russian government any more than equating the Second International (which is based in Brussels and includes among the members of its Executive Committee men like Monsieur Vandervelde, a Belgian government minister, and Mr. Henderson, a British cabinet officer) with the Belgian or British government. Moreover, the Executive Committee of the Third International has thirty-one members, only five of whom are Russian, and only two of those five hold positions in the Russian government.[49]

After the change of course in 1921 all official and public connection between the Soviet government, and especially its Commissariat of Foreign Affairs, and the Communist International was to be scrupulously avoided. Until then no effort had been made to conceal the ties between them. One instance of this was the contacts maintained by Chicherin and his ambassadors with the foreign Communist leaders, which did not cease but did have to be concealed. Lenin himself set the example, on May 7, 1921, when he sent a telegram to Victor Kopp, the Soviet government's official representative in Berlin, requesting him to "pass along quickly and secretly to Thomas [head of the W.E.S.] my letter to Levi and Zetkin."[50] In their confidential reports, Soviet diplomats sometimes complained of shortcomings in the foreign Communist organizations. A confidential letter from B. Souvarine, a French Communist Party representative in Moscow, to the French Communist Party headquarters in Paris, tells of the following initiative by a Soviet diplomat: "Several months ago Comrade Karakhan made a suggestion that Vaillant-Couturier forwarded to Paris . . . . I have just received another letter from Karakhan, who is now Soviet government representative in Warsaw, asking me to

expedite action on his suggestion. . . . . He wants a *Humanité* correspondent sent to Warsaw, someone who would be in close touch
with the Soviet representative and from whom he would receive
information and documents."[51] (The letter went on to discuss
whether the party would authorize the correspondent's remunera-
tion by the Soviet embassy.) Conversely, confidential complaints
were also registered about the slowness and other failings of the
Soviet diplomatic service, as when the head of the Czechoslovak
Communist Party, Bohumíl Jílek, told the Presidium of the
Comintern's Executive Committee in June 1922: "The Russian
diplomats in Prague are not very reliable . . . . For example, a
packet of documents addressed to the Executive Committee of the
Communist International, to be used for drawing up a careful
report, though delivered in Prague on the 15th, has not reached
Moscow yet. This is the quality of the Comintern Executive Committee's link with Prague. It is an intolerable state of affairs, one
which in a ticklish situation could have very disagreeable consequences for us."[52]

All of this was in perfect conformity with the first point in
Lenin's memo—the need to feign separateness of the Comintern
from the Soviet government. But then there was point two: the
promise not to meddle in the internal affairs of other countries.
Thus the diplomatic note sent by Chicherin on January 15, 1921,
to the Minister of Foreign Affairs of Rumania, concerning pending
negotiations aimed at establishing normal relations between the
two countries, contained the official assurance: "May I assure you
that, for its part, the Russian republic has no intention whatever
of interfering in Rumanian affairs or engaging in any action hostile
to Rumania. The Russian republic is firmly determined not to
permit the peaceful relations now existing between Russia and
Rumania to be disturbed."[53]

The switch in policy in 1921 produced changes in the outward
behavior of both the Soviet government and the Communist International. The Comintern's publicly visible activities began to di-
minish, but its secret operations burgeoned. Its official texts and
releases became rich in formulae, arguments, and slogans designed
to throw sand in the world's eyes, to conceal rather than reveal
what was actually going on. When the Comintern undertook a

major initiative, such as the launching of the United Front in December 1921, elaborate care was taken to hide its true origin. Also, the Comintern's financial dependence on the Russians was denied flatly and vehemently. The fact that it maintained webs of emissaries in the foreign Communist parties was shrouded in silence. The upshot was that it simply became more difficult for contemporary observers and future historians to see the Comintern's true face.

From the start of his career as a revolutionary, Lenin held to the basic belief that economics always did and always must take a back seat to politics, that voluntarism would triumph over determinism, and he saw his change of course as primarily a political act. On December 6, 1920, in explaining to Moscow's Bolshevik militants the purpose of his concessions to the foreign capitalists, he used mainly political, not economic arguments, for, as he said on that occasion, "the political factor outweighs all others." On December 21, in his report to the Bolshevik members of the Soviets about those same concessions, he said: "So, in negotiating the concessions, our own primary interests were political . . . . The economic aspect was secondary. The meat of the matter is political."[54] In explaining to the Tenth Bolshevik Party Congress the new "tax in kind," the NEP's crown jewel, he declared in the first sentence: "Replacing the assessment with a tax is first and foremost a political act."[55] His attitude was the same regarding Comintern affairs. On August 31, 1921, he wrote out for Jenő Varga his "theses" on the founding of an institute which should bear, Lenin said, the official name "Institute for Research on the Forms of Social Movements"; it was to devote no more than twenty per cent of its energies to the study of economic and social questions, and eighty per cent to political questions.[56] Finally, after the Soviet regime had surmounted the internal crisis of 1921, in reappraising that event at the Fourth Comintern Congress, he called it a purely political crisis, not an economic one, despite the famine and other economic scourges it had brought: "But in 1921, having just come through the crucial civil war, which we won, we found ourselves confronted with a new crisis, in fact the biggest internal political crisis that Soviet Russia has ever faced."[57]

Lenin's essentially political motives for his change of course had an internationalist dimension. Certainly the objective world situation, which saw no revolution in the West and the survival of Soviet Russia as the only Communist power, had profoundly influenced the new policies, but he continued to behave not merely as a Russian Communist but as an internationalist Russian Communist. Compelled to base his policies on the facts as they were, he devoted himself more to the continuing revolution in Russia than to the nonexistent ones elsewhere. The line that he laid down during the change of course, and which he preached to the Communists, was largely adopted in both the Bolshevik Party and Communist International.

Insisting that his new policy flowed inexorably from the objective situation in Russia and the world, he had the courage to admit the errors in judgment and mistaken predictions made by him and the other Bolshevik leaders. On February 28, 1921, in his remarks to the Moscow Soviet about the terrible famine, he confessed: "It was all our mistake—there's no use trying to hide the fact—just as we didn't try to hide our error in the matter of the Polish war."[58] On July 5, addressing the Third Comintern Congress, he again acknowledged: "We know for sure that we made some big mistakes."[59] The errors admitted, the important thing was to learn from them, to reshape Soviet policy and Comintern activities accordingly—and this was what Lenin was busy doing throughout 1921.

Unable to count on revolution in the West, Lenin fell back on a device which he was convinced had helped save the life of the Soviet regime immediately after November 7, 1917, and again in the Brest-Litovsk negotiations: exploiting the contradictions in the capitalist camp while at the same time lining up new allies for Soviet Russia and the international Communist movement. Setting out to explain the slowdown in world revolution and his resulting provisional economic agreements with "the capitalist sharks," he kept emphatically asserting, as in his speech of November 26, 1920: "So far we are winning out over the world bourgeoisie because they are unable to unite."[60] Ten days later, in an address to Moscow's Bolshevik militants, he expounded his entire theory about exploiting contradictions in the capitalist world:

The main thing about the concessions, from the political standpoint—

and both political and economic factors are involved here—but the main thing to remember about them from the political standpoint is that well-known rule of thumb which we have not only mastered in theory but effectively put into practice, and which for a long time to come (until Socialism finally triumphs throughout the world) will be our golden rule: to exploit the antitheses and contradictions between the two imperialisms, between the two groups of capitalist states, pitting the one against the other. Until we have conquered the entire world, we shall be economically and militarily weaker than the capitalist rest of the world. So until then we must stick to our golden rule; we must learn to exploit the contradictions and antitheses between and among imperialists. Had we not stuck to this rule in the past, we would all have been hanged long ago, each from a separate tree, and the capitalists would have cheered and celebrated.[61]

A logical corollary of this new policy became the quest for new allies, which was pursued in three domains. The first was inside Russia. Though as late as December 23, 1920, in his closing speech to the Eighth Congress of Soviets, Lenin threatened to step up the social revolution and civil war in the countryside, to eradicate the last traces of private capitalist agriculture, scarely three months later he was in full retreat, diligently introducing the opposite policy. To the Third Comintern Congress he explained: "We have made an alliance with the peasants . . . . We had to show them that we can and will change our policy quickly so as to ease their suffering at once."[62] Also, Soviet Russia's foreign policy would now be directed toward rapprochement with countries disadvantaged by the Treaty of Versailles. The purpose was to heat up their dispute with the powers that benefited from that treaty. When it came to the Comintern, Lenin imposed on its Western sections a policy of seeking political alliances with non-revolutionary forces, particularly the Social Democrats and reformist Syndicalists, just as in Russia he had switched horses and allied himself with the non-Socialist (or anti-Socialist) peasants.

Another tactical lesson that he taught the leaders of Soviet Russia and the Comintern was about the many ways in which the class enemy could be attacked. Though he had already dealt with this problem at length in the spring of 1920, in *"Left-Wing" Communism,* he was then merely teaching the rudiments applicable to the situation at that uncomplicated time, when the revolutionary wave was still rising. But having once introduced his change of course, he had to go much further. He applied his old tactical rules, but now to the new phase of revolutionary ebb. Again, what he said and did in 1921 about domestic policies in Russia were soon mirrored in the actions of the Comintern.

In October that year he told a conference of the Moscow Bolshevik Party: "We are in the position of people who have to keep retreating in order, in the end, to seize the offensive."[63] This was a rehash of the idea he had expressed to proponents of the "offensive theory" three months earlier at the Third World Congress. Citing the example of the Japanese capture of Port Arthur in their surprise attack of February 1904, he pointed out the two alternating tactics used, direct assault and siege, and drew a parallel with the new situation of the Bolshevik Party and the Communist International: "By the spring of 1921 it was clear that we had been defeated in our attempt to achieve 'by storm' our intended conversion to a Socialist system of production and distribution, that is, to bring it about by the shortest, quickest, most direct method. The political situation then prevailing made us see the wisdom of retreating to state capitalism in many sectors of the economy, in other words, of switching from a strategy of assault to one of siege."[64] He also preached that, in addition to assault and siege, there was a third tactic, namely exchanges and contacts of every kind between Communists and non-Communists, a process from which the Communists, he said, stood to gain much more than their adversaries. And when he praised that tactic to the Russians, his advice was also applicable to foreign Communists: "So why, from all our contacts with bourgeois Europe and America, is it always we who have been the gainers and not they? Why always they who have been afraid to send delegations to our country, and not we to send our delegations to theirs? And, from those they have dared to send, we have always managed to lure some of their people (however few) over to our way of thinking, despite the fact that they have mainly been Menshevik elements and individuals who came here for only a short time?"[65]

Lenin's change of course after the dual defeat in the late summer of 1920 (in August at Warsaw, in September in Italy) injected into the political war against capitalism an important new element: active opposition to the Treaty of Versailles. It was new because it represented a radical departure from the Soviet position until then, and important because it was to influence Soviet Russian foreign policy and Comintern tactics for many years to come, long after Lenin's death.

So long as the Kremlin expected capitalist Europe, both the countries that had won the war and those that had lost it, to be soon engulfed by Communist revolution, the Treaty of Versailles was considered no more than a symbol of imperialistic capitalist injustice. Attaching little significance to it, the Bolshevik chieftains at first dismissed it as a diplomatic farce being acted out by two camps of "imperialist brigands." It went without saying that the Treaty of Versailles and all its works would inevitably collapse in the revolution to come, just as the fall of Imperial Germany had erased the Treaty of Brest-Litovsk. The manifesto of the Comintern's Executive Committee on the Treaty of Versailles, published on May 13, 1919, called it "a new Brest" and while expressing its sympathy to the German working class, the manifesto equated the two imperialisms and asserted that "if the war had ended with a victory for the German imperialists they would have been as ruthless toward the defeated as their enemies now are to them". The same document did not suggest any common action against the Treaty of Versailles between the Communists and the non-Communists of the defeated countries; the only issue on the agenda for the German and Austrian workers was "to overthrow at once the government of traitors who call themselves social-democrats but who are in fact the most shameful agents of the bourgeoisie".[66] In the same spirit, the manifesto of the Second World Congress, written by Trotsky and signed by Lenin, Trotsky, Zinoviev and Bukharin, equated the vanquished imperialism of the Central Powers with the triumphant imperialism of the Entente: "The design for Europe concocted by German imperialism in the flush of its great military victories has been taken over by its vanquishers, the Entente. If the rulers of the Entente now put the defeated bandits of the German Reich in the dock, it will merely be a case of criminals trying criminals."[67] Still in the same spirit, in his *"Left-Wing" Communism, an Infantile Disorder*, Lenin did not hesitate to suggest that even a victorious German revolutionary government should temporarily accept the Treaty of Versailles: "One should understand that (if a German Soviet Republic is soon born) any tactic that would negate the obligation of a Soviet Germany to recognize for a time the Versailles peace treaty and to try to live with it, would be radically erroneous."[68]

But once the prospect of European revolution began to fade in victor and vanquished countries alike, and had to be replaced by Moscow's new policy of exploiting contradictions within the capitalist camp, the Bolshevik attitude toward the Treaty of Versailles changed. The goal now became, if not exactly common action against the victors, at least parallel or mutually supporting moves by Soviet Russia and the countries disadvantaged by the treaty. After his defeat in Poland, Lenin promptly proclaimed the interests of Soviet Russia to be compatible with those of vengeance-seeking Germany. By September 22, 1920, in his address to the Ninth Bolshevik Party Conference, convened shortly after the Polish débâcle, he was already announcing an identity of Russian and German interests in opposition to the Treaty of Versailles: "Our army's advance on Warsaw demonstrated beyond question that somewhere in that region lies the center of world imperialism's whole system, which is based on the Treaty of Versailles .... And in Germany we have witnessed the creation of the unnatural alliance between the Black Hundred and the Bolsheviks."[69] Three weeks later, on October 15, he again roasted the Treaty of Versailles, in language very similar to that later to be used by Hitler, restressing Russo-German unity of purpose in opposing it:

What is this Treaty of Versailles anyway? It is an unheard-of covenant, a peace imposed by looters, which reduces to slavery tens of millions of people, including some of the most civilized. It is not a peace at all but a list of demands dictated by brigands, knife in hand, to a defenseless victim. The treaty strips Germany of all its colonies .... And at that moment the Red Army was crossing the Polish frontier, heading for the German border. Everybody in Germany, even the Black Hundred and monarchists, was saying that the Bolsheviks would save them; everyone could see that the peace of Versailles was coming apart at the seams, and that here was a Red Army that had declared war on all capitalists.[70]

After another two months his new idea had evolved further. He now no longer spoke of the matter with reference only to the recent past (the Russo-Polish war) but as a factor to be reckoned with far into the future:

> Not counting America, Germany is the most advanced country . . . . And this is why, fettered by the Treaty of Versailles, it finds itself in an impossible position, one in which it is naturally being pushed into an alliance with Russia . . . . The Treaty of Versailles has created a situation in which Germany has no hope of relief, no hope of not being sacked, looted of its means of livelihood, with nothing left to look forward to but starvation and the extermination of its people. Obviously, the only way it can save itself is by joining hands with Russia, and that is the direction in which it is looking. [71]

When Lenin changed one of his basic political beliefs, this automatically altered his tactics too. So with his abruptly changed course in 1921, the related attack upon the Versailles treaty became a constant theme of both the Russian government and the Communist International. But the new direction was reflected first in the government's policies and only later in those of the Comintern. When it came to the latter, getting Communists to agitate against the Treaty of Versailles was naturally easier in the defeated countries than in those on the winning side. So initially the Bolsheviks concentrated their attention on Germany, but now for a new and added reason.

Before their change of course, the Bolsheviks had regarded Germany as the most important foreign country, the key to the expected general Communist revolution throughout Europe. After the change, they still considered Germany the most important country, but now in the new context of the campaign against Versailles. In the first instance they had been banking on the German Communist movement; in the second they were compelled to rely on Germany's government, politicians, financiers, and military men–all of whom, domestically, were death on Communism. So, after the change of course, Moscow pursued a two-faced policy toward Germany, one reflecting a carefully balanced political choice. On the one hand, representatives of the Soviet government, men like Victor Kopp, were negotiating initial agreements with the German authorities. On the other, agents of the Comintern (like Béla Kun) were busily trying to stir up insurrection in Germany. Sometimes the same individual was working simultaneously for both. An example was Karl Radek, who more or less secretly stayed on in Germany from early October 1920 to early February 1921, just as the change of course was being initiated.

Needless to say, these parallel activities all originated from the same source, the Politburo, which is to say with Lenin himself, but the targets were different. The target of one was the bourgeois government of the foreign country in question; the target of the other its domestic Communist party. In this three-handed game the position of each player was unique. The Bolshevik Politburo naturally knew all about these two different spheres of foreign activity abroad, since it planned and directed both itself. The bourgeois government of the foreign country, naturally aware of its own official contacts with Moscow, was not unaware of the ties between the Kremlin and the local Communist party. The third actor in the play was the local Communist party, whose members (with rare exceptions) knew nothing at all of what was going on between Moscow and their country's government. Being kept in the dark severely handicapped them. Moscow could negotiate with a bourgeois government and at the same time tell the local Communist party what to do; a bourgeois government could deal freely with Moscow and crack down on the Communist party. Caught in the middle, the party was at one and the same time unable to oppose Moscow's policy and to resist effectively the reprisals of the bourgeois government.

This policy would hamstring the Comintern till the end of its days. An early example, which turned out to be typical for the whole history of the Comintern, was the affair in Turkey. The Bolsheviks had two reasons for wanting to have friendly relations with the regime of Kemal Ataturk. First, as part of the Comintern strategy, the Communists were professing solidarity with the anti-imperialist national-liberation movements, and Ataturk's government fitted nicely into this category. Second, the aim of Soviet diplomacy, especially after the change of course, was to exploit contradictions within the capitalist world, with special attention to the defeated countries disadvantaged by the Treaty of Versailles. Turkey fitted into that category, too. Not surprisingly, the Soviet and Turkish governments found an area of common interest beyond the ordinary framework of normal diplomatic relations, as stressed in a note sent by Chicherin on June 2, 1920, to Ataturk, in reply to a letter from him, dated April 26, proposing establishment of diplomatic relations between the two nations: "The Soviet government has the honor to acknowledge receipt of the letter expressing a desire to enter into regular relations with it and to take part in a common struggle against the foreign imperialism menacing our two countries."[72] In November 1920 Ataturk appointed his diplomatic representative to Moscow and replied that same month to Chicherin's note, using in it language almost identical to that of Zinoviev, Radek, and Béla Kun in their speeches at the Baku congress two months before: "I am deeply convinced, and my conviction is shared by all our citizens, that on the day when the toilers of the West and the oppressed peoples of Asia and Africa realize that international capital is using them in order to enslave and destroy them in the interests of their masters, the capitalists, on the day when the realization of the criminality of the colonial policy reaches the hearts of the toiling masses of the world, the reign of the bourgeoisie will be over."[73]

In this game the third player, the Turkish Communist Party, was a loser, as proven by the tragic death of Mustafa Subhi and his companions.* The Turkish party could not even plead to the Comintern for a change from the sort of tactics which had led to this catastrophic result. It was also deprived of flossy propaganda campaigns in its favor, which the Comintern organized for its other sections. After this mass liquidation of an entire Communist party leadership, probably the first case of its kind in Comintern annals, the Kremlin was reluctant to launch an international propaganda campaign openly glorifying the victims or damning their executioners. Yet that same year, when a few Communists were temporarily detained in Spain and Yugoslavia, the Comintern's propaganda engines roared into action, bewailing and bemoaning these acts of repression, with a grand display of solicitude.

Less than a month after the collective assassination of Turkey's Communist party leaders, a Turkish government delegation was welcomed to Moscow to negotiate a "treaty of friendship and brotherhood," which was duly signed on March 16, 1921. Its preamble proclaimed "the brotherhood of nations," "their solidarity in the struggle against imperialism," "a desire to establish enduring and cordial relations between [the two nations] and a sincere and

*Cf., Chapter Nine, pp. 412-13.

unbreakable friendship."[74] The Turkish Communists were obviously not included in this "sincere and unbreakable friendship," for less than two months later an Ankara court sentenced several Communist leaders to up to fifteen years in prison. Not long after that, on July 27, 1921, the Turkish government banned all Communist activity. That same month the Comintern held its Third World Congress, at which the spokesman for the Turkish Communists expressed the party's loyal support for the Ataturk regime: "So long as the national movement for Turkish independence continues, we other Communists must help it along, because extermination of the Entente and imperialists will be the beginning of the world revolution that will abolish all slavery."[75] This was still the line at the next Comintern congress, in 1922, when one of the leading lights at the time, Karl Radek, said: "This is why we say to the Turkish Communists today, notwithstanding the persecution they are suffering: . . . 'Your job as defenders of the independence of Turkey, which is so very important to the revolution, is not yet finished. Protest against the persecution, but understand, too . . . that you still have a long road to travel in the company of the bourgeois revolutionaries.' "[76]

As long as the Turkish nationalist and bourgeois government pursued the policy of alliance with the Soviet government, the latter swallowed the domestic persecution of Turkish Communists, and the Comintern as well as the Turkish Communists themselves followed suit. It was only when the Turkish government appeared about to modify its policy vis-à-vis the Soviet Union that Moscow pressed the alarm button within the Comintern. Thus in an appeal to the Communists and the Turkish toiling masses, issued at the end of the Fourth Comintern Congress, it was said: "The Turkish Communist Party has always supported the bourgeois and nationalist government in the struggle of the toiling masses against imperialism. The Turkish Communist Party has even consented, in the presence of the common enemy, to sacrifice temporarily a part of its program and of its ideal . . . . The nationalist government now getting ready to ally itself with imperialism is striving to destroy your genuine representatives and to separate them from your foreign friends."[77] This appeal was revealing in a twofold sense: it confirmed the subordination of the Turkish Party to the foreign policy of Soviet Russia, and it showed how precarious was an alliance of the Soviet government with a nationalist-bourgeois regime. From the "sincere and unbreakable" friendship of March 1921, Moscow had come already in November 1922 to suspect the Turkish government because of its willingness to reach an accommodation with "imperialism" and to abandon its "foreign friends."

EFFECTS OF THE CHANGE OF COURSE
ON THE ORGANIZATIONAL PLAN

To be complete, the change of course had to go beyond mere strategy and tactics and fundamentally reorganize the Bolshevik Party, which was bound in time to affect the Communist International, which was modeled on and run by the Bolshevik Party. Lenin now had to teach the Bolshevik Party and subsequently the Comintern an important lesson, namely that whenever the party softened its external policies, it had to harden its internal discipline—discipline being more necessary in a retreat than in an advance. In this connection he proclaimed and put into practice certain principles not previously vested with the force of "law" in the Bolshevik Party: the forbidding of all internal opposition or dissent and periodic purges of the membership. At the Tenth Party Congress in March 1921, concluding his report on behalf of the central committee, he declared: "What we need now, Comrades, is not 'opposition'! Either we are for or against a thing—and will say so with our guns. But 'opposition'—no! It is the situation itself that requires this; no individual is to blame. And my belief is that this party congress will have to come to the same conclusion—that we must now have done with opposition, must clamp a lid on all of it. We have had our fill of it!"[78] To silence what opposition there was (Democratic Centralism and Workers' Opposition), he wrote his resolution on party unity, which was adopted. Strictly forbidding factionalism and ordaining the dissolution of all opposition groups, it demanded liberal use of disciplinary measures, including exclusion from the party. A vast purge began in August and September 1921; during the next twelve months some 140,000 members were expelled from the party.

Though opposition and dissent were now forbidden in the party, in 1921 they still existed in sections of the Comintern. The reason was that the party had reached, so to speak, its political maturity while the Comintern was still a child. But after the change of course an unfailing pattern became established: whatever happened in the Bolshevik Party would sooner or later happen in the Comintern. To use a formula dear to the Bolsheviks in other contexts, one could say that it was the old "law of uneven development leading to an identical outcome." During the last three years of Lenin's life, for instance, the Comintern leadership was to hold successively three different attitudes toward factionalism and dissent in the foreign sections. At first dissenters were tolerated, sometimes even negotiated with, since there was then no way to get rid of them. Next, in each foreign party Moscow began supporting the group whose position was closest to its own. Finally, when that group ultimately (and predictably) prevailed (with an assist from the Kremlin), it was proclaimed to be "the party," and all other groups were expelled or denounced. Thus, stage by stage, the purge gradually became the main tool. In his resolution on party unity, Lenin had spoken of "purging the party of unreliable nonproletarian elements." Later that year he wrote an article on "the purge," drafted a central committee circular letter on it, and wrote a letter on it to the Politburo. Those three documents served as the theoretical foundation for the ensuing vast purge. But it happened that the leadership of the Communist parties in the West and elsewhere was also packed with these so-called "nonproletarian elements." It would soon fall upon the Comintern to lay on the Lenin lash, and purge them one and all.

Another instrument of discipline introduced by Lenin in 1921 that spread from the Bolshevik Party to the Comintern was the refusal to accept a Communist leader's resignation. The only way out was to be thrown out; the option of resigning was not available. The party could force a person to take a job against his will, and then snatch the job away again and even expel the individual from the party, all with the most perfect disregard for his wishes. At the Tenth Party Congress, for example, Shliapnikov, a spokesman for the "Workers' Opposition" who had been elected to the party's new central committee, handed in his resignation. Lenin's response was vehement: "As for the announced resignation, I submit the following resolution for adoption: 'The congress calls upon all members of the disbanded group known as the Workers'

Opposition to bow to party discipline, orders them to remain at their assigned posts, and refuses to accept the resignation of Comrade Shliapnikov or anyone else.' "[79] After Shliapnikov was stripped of any right to resign, as he was on March 16, Lenin waited only until August 9 to demand, again in the name of the party, that Shliapnikov be thrown off the central committee and expelled from the party as well—a motion which fell only three votes short of the two-thirds majority required under the bylaws. Several months later, in December 1921, there was a similar case in the French Communist Party. Some members elected to the directing committee who supported the official Comintern line but found themselves in the minority at the Marseilles congress, tendered their resignations. Immediately labeling their action a political mistake, the Comintern did its best to get them reinstated. A few years later it had those same leaders (with the exception of Vaillant-Couturier) ejected from the French party.

This progressive withering away of any individual will within the Bolshevik Party and later within the Comintern was accompanied by the gradual introduction of the Great Myth: that decisions flowed not from mortal beings but from two exalted abstractions—the Party, which was always right, and the Comintern, which was infallible. When the change of course began to subject party members to harsh new restrictions, A. A. Ioffe, an important personage and once a member of the central committee, wrote Lenin a letter on March 15, two days before the Tenth Congress ended. Though never published, its tenor can be guessed from Lenin's reply: "You are wrong to keep saying (as you have a number of times) that the central committee is really just me. A thing like that could be written only by someone in a highly nervous state and under great strain. The old central committee (1919-1920) opposed me on one very important matter, as you may remember from the discussion. On questions of organization and personnel, I have been outvoted many times. You often saw examples of this when you were a member of the central committee."[80] It was true that Ioffe was in a highly nervous state, and that Lenin had sometimes been outvoted on the central committee, but Ioffe was nevertheless right in observing that in March 1921 there was an increasing tendency to equate the party with one man, a trend soon to become more pronounced. It would be even more so in the Comintern, whose foreign members felt inferior to the Russians and usually deferred to the Bolshevik Party.

The change of course in 1921 was to have another consequence for Lenin personally. More and more of his time would be taken up with Russian affairs, and less and less with those of the Comintern (which increased by default Zinoviev's role in the Comintern.) The shifted emphasis was evident in all Lenin's activities—his speeches, articles, memos, dictated letters, and interviews. During 1919 and 1920 he had avidly sought out the foreign Communists visiting Moscow, no matter how young (such as Alfred Kurella in 1919) or how politically insignificant (such as Lucien Deslinières in 1920), or even how minor or unimportant the parties they belonged to (such as E. Rheiland, the top Communist in Luxembourg), and he engaged them in long discussions, devouring all their news from Europe. But by 1921 he was growing choosier. At the Third World Congress he did not receive even delegations from parties then important, such as the Yugoslav party, a force to be reckoned with at that time.

Lenin's declining participation in the work of the top-level Comintern agencies was evident from his increasing absence from meetings of the Executive Committee, of which he was a member. During the Second World Congress he took part in some of the Committee meetings, and once after the congress ended. He attended those in June of 1921, just before the Third World Congress, but no more after that congress, not even on important occasions, as when the United Front was inaugurated in December. Nor did he participate in the first plenary session of the enlarged Executive Committee the following February. This new tendency to detach himself from the Comintern was evidenced by another incident. Shortly after the Third Congress his signature, as a member of the Comintern's Executive Committee, appeared on its manifestoes and appeals of July 17 and July 30, of August 13 and August 26. After the appeal "to the working class of England" of September 28, however, the signatures of Lenin and Trotsky no longer appeared.* That this was no accident was confirmed by the

*In the Comintern's organ *La Correspondance Internationale* of October 26, 1921 (p. 44) there appeared an appeal bearing the signatures of Lenin and Trotsky, but the date when the appeal was issued was July 17. Likewise, the publication in 1959 of some letters exchanged between Chicherin and Lenin. On October 15, 1921, the Soviet Commissar for Foreign Affairs suggested to Lenin several steps for the improvement of Soviet relations with capitalist countries. One was that Lenin and Trotsky should quietly cease to be members of the Comintern Executive Committee. Replying the next day, Lenin flatly rejected the idea: "As for Trotsky and me getting off the Executive Committee of the Communist International, that is absolutely out of the question." [81] But no longer did they sign its appeals, and the mere fact that Chicherin, who had taken active part in the preparations for the First Congress and had chaired its credentials committee (and who later withdrew from all Comintern activities himself), would even dream of suggesting that Lenin and Trotsky leave the Executive Committee was clear evidence of the Soviet government's growing desire not to be officially identified with the Comintern.

The increased importance assigned to Russian affairs at the expense of Comintern affairs was to work a triple change in the Russian personnel of the Comintern's central apparatus. At the time of the First and Second World Congresses, in 1919 and 1920, several Bolshevik leaders then serving as Soviet government officials were transferred to the Comintern. Starting in 1921, the process was reversed. Leading Bolsheviks were withdrawn from the Comintern and assigned to the Soviet diplomatic service. Of the first four secretaries of the Comintern in 1919, three had come from diplomatic posts. Berzin and Balabanova had been on the staff of the Soviet embassy in Bern. Vorovsky had been in charge of the negotiations with Finland. Also, between the First and Second World Congresses, Litvinov and Karakhan attended some Executive Committee meetings, as noted in the Committee's official report presented to the Second Congress. [82] But after the change of course, diplomats like Litvinov and Karakhan took extra care not to be mentioned in any reports on Executive Committee activities, and some of the higher-ups in the initial setup, men like Kobetsky and Hanecki, then transferred to the Soviet diplomatic service or, like Vorovsky, returned to it.

A second important change in top Comintern personnel resulted

same source carried on November 2 (p. 359) another appeal with these two signatures, but the date of its issuance was August 26, 1921.

from the infusion into it of Bolsheviks who had been downgraded immediately following the change of course. Iosif Piatnitsky, for instance, whose presence was no longer desired on the Moscow regional committee, in 1921 was appointed head of the Comintern's secret liaison and finance department (OMS). The same was true of Elena Stasova who was assigned to the Comintern secret apparatus after losing her executive position in the Bolshevik Party. A similar fate befell G. Safarov, who in 1921 engaged in a dispute with the party leadership in Turkestan. At the end of that year he was given a job as secretary to the Comintern Executive Committee. Much the same thing happened to Alexandra Kollontai, a figurehead in the Workers' Opposition, who was appointed to the Comintern central apparatus, where she worked during 1921-22, and later got a diplomatic assignment.

The third innovation resulted from the widening scope of Comintern activities, which required more and more personnel. There were not enough old Bolsheviks, so it became necessary to use the services of the more recent converts—ex-Bundists, ex-Mensheviks, and former Party dissidents, persons such as Manuilsky, Lozovsky, Borodin, Petrovsky-Bennet, Rafes, Guralsky, and a little later Martynov (who had been under attack by Lenin since the beginning of the century). These men ultimately permeated the Comintern administration.

The change of tide in 1921 made clear to Lenin that the wave of revolution and the power of attraction of Russia's example had begun to ebb. The changed attitude of the various labor parties confirmed this. In 1920 most of the important ones (such as the USPD and the SFIO) had favored joining the Comintern, while by 1921 they were registering majority votes against. In early 1921, too, the Comintern suffered its first crisis of dissidence and disobedience, which cast a menacing shadow over the very principles on which it operated and ended in the break with Paul Levi, the chairman of the German party.

So Lenin's new course, introduced on three fronts—Soviet domestic policy, Soviet foreign policy, and the tactics of the Comintern—had different results on each front. Within Russia it was successful in that the NEP did succeed in re-establishing a modicum of normality and in consolidating Bolshevik power. In the realm of foreign policy the success was only partial. Though diplomatic, economic, and other formal relationships were established with many capitalist countries, the new tactics of exploitation of contradictions within the capitalist world bore only one nourishing fruit: the treaty of Rapallo. But the new course was least successful with the Comintern. The goals that Lenin set the foreign parties from 1921 on, to capture a majority of the working class and forge a United Front with the Socialists and trade unionists, were never attained. Yet in all three areas the change of course that he launched that year had a profound influence, and one that long outlived him.

Notes

CHAPTER ONE

1. Th. Dan, *Die Sozialdemokratie Russlands nach dem Jahre 1908* (in J. Martow's *Geschichte der russischen Sozialdemokratie*), Berlin, 1926, p. 274.

2. *Ibid.*, p. 275.

3. The full text of these theses is published in *Collected Works of V. I. Lenin*, vol. XVIII ("The Imperialist War"), New York, 1930, pp. 61-64.

4. *Ibid.*, pp. 81-82.

5. V. I. Lenin, *Collected Works*, 4th ed., vol. 21, Moscow, 1964, pp. 40-41.

6. *Ibid.*, p. 171.

7. V. I. Lenin, *Polnoe sobranie sochinenii*, 5th ed., vol. 26, Moscow, 1961, pp. 161-67.

8. The full text of the Lugano conference's resolution is in Alfred Rosmer, *Le mouvement ouvrier pendant la guerre. De l'union sacrée à Zimmerwald*, Paris, 1936, pp. 183-84.

9. Nadezhda K. Krupskaya, *Memories of Lenin*, vol. II, New York, n.d., p. 160.

10. *Ibid.*, pp. 161-62.

11. R. Schüller, A. Kurella, B. Chitarow, *Geschichte der Kommunistischen Jugendinternationale* (vol. I, Richard Schüller, *Von den Anfängen der proletarischen Jugendbewegung bis zur Gründung der KJI*, Berlin, 1931, p. 105).

12. See Olga Hess Gankin and H. H. Fisher, *The Bolsheviks and the World War*, Stanford, 1940, p. 348.

13. Quoted in *Ibid.*, pp. 341-42.

14. *Ibid.*, pp. 324, 325.

15. *Ibid.*, p. 332.

16. *Ibid.*, p. 334.

17. *Ibid.*, p. 356.

18. *Ibid.*, p. 215.

19. *Ibid.*, p. 241.

20. *Ibid.*, p. 217.

21. *Ibid.*, p. 417.

22. *Contre le courant*, vol. II, Paris, 1927, p. 88. Emphasis in the text.

23. *Ibid.*, pp. 88-89.

24. *Collected Works of V. I. Lenin*, vol. XIX ("1916-1917"), New York, 1942, p. 212.

25. *Ibid.*, pp. 214-15.

26. *Ibid.*, pp. 267 *et seq.*

27. *Ibid.*, pp. 311-13.

28. V. I. Lenin, *Polnoe sobranie sochinenii*, 5th ed., vol. 49, Moscow, 1964, p. 177.

29. The full text of this letter is to be found in *Die Zimmerwalder Bewegung. Protokolle und Korrespondenz*, vol. II, The Hague-Paris, 1967, pp. 495-99.

30. V. I. Lenin, *Collected Works*, 4th ed., vol. 35, Moscow, 1966, p. 221, Emphasis in the text.

31. *Ibid.*, vol. 36, Moscow, 1966, p. 394. Emphasis in the text.

32. V. I. Lenin, *Polnoe sobranie sochinenii*, 5th ed., vol. 49, p. 330.

33. *Histoire du parti communiste russe*, Paris, 1926, p. 172.

34. *Ibid.*, pp. 172-73.

35. *Collected Works of V. I. Lenin*, vol. XIX, p. 438.

36. *Ibid.*, pp. 311-13.

37. *Ibid.*, p. 404.

38. Nadezhda K. Krupskaya, *op. cit.*, p. 197.

39. S. Grumbach, *L'erreur de Zimmerwald-Kienthal*, Paris, 1917, p. 105.

40. Full text in Frank Alfred Golder, *Documents of Russian History, 1914-1917*, Gloucester, Mass., 1964, pp. 325-26.

41. V. I. Lenin, *Polnoe sobranie sochinenii*, 5th ed., vol. 31, Moscow, 1962, p. 111.

42. *Ibid.*, p. 112.

43. Quoted in Samuel H. Baron, *Plekhanov, the Father of Russian Marxism*, Stanford, 1963, p. 347.

44. *Vospominaniia, 1914-1919*, Berlin, 1920, p. 110.

45. *Collected Works of V. I. Lenin*, vol. XX, book II, New York, 1929, pp. 380-81. Emphasis in the text.

46. *Granat*, Entsiklopedicheskii slovar' Russkogo bibliograficheskogo instituta, 7th ed., Moscow, n.d., vol. 41, part II, p. 166.

47. *Collected Works of V. I. Lenin*, vol. XX, book I ("The Revolution of 1917. From the March Revolution to the July Days"), New York, 1929, pp. 152-53.

48. *Sed'maia (aprel'skaia) vserossiiskaia konferentsiia RSDRP (bol'shevikov). Petrogradskaia obshchegorodskaia konferentsiia RSDRP (bol'shevikov)*. Moscow, 1958, pp. 18-19.

49. *Ibid.*, p. 78.

50. *Ibid.*, p. 234. Emphasis in the text.

51. *Pravda*, No. 55, May 25, 1917.

52. *Ibid.*

53. *Collected Works of V. I. Lenin*, vol. XX, book II, p. 159.

54. Quoted in *Leninskii sbornik*, vol. XXI, Moscow, 1933, pp. 58-59. Emphasis in the text.

55. *Ibid.*, vol. XIII, Moscow, 1930, pp. 277-78. Emphasis in the text.

56. *Collected Works of V. I. Lenin*, vol. XXI, book I ("Toward the Seizure of Power. The Revolution of 1917: From the July Days to the October Revolution"), New York, 1932, p. 150. Emphasis in the text.

57. *Ibid.*, vol. XXI, book II (same subtitle as above), New York, 1932, p. 92. Emphasis in the text.

58. V. I. Lenin, *Collected Works*, 4th ed., vol. 26, Moscow, 1964, p. 63.

59. *Ibid.*, p. 130.

60. *Ibid.*, p. 188.

61. *Ibid.* p. 192.

62. Frank Alfred Golder, *op cit.*, pp. 622-23.

63. *Vtoroi vserossiiskii s"ezd sovetov R.i.S.D.*, Moscow, 1928, pp. 86-87.

64. V. I. Lenin, *Collected Works*, vol. 26, pp. 291-92.

65. *Ibid.*, pp. 386-87.

66. An English version of the decree may be found in *Liberator*, New York, No. 11, January 1919, p. 23; also in *Revolutionary Radicalism*, part I, Albany, New York, 1920, p. 205.

67. *Liberator*, No. 4, June 1918, pp. 27-28.

68. *Ibid.*. No. 11, January 1919, pp. 19-20.

69. *Izvestiia*, January 30, 1918.

70. *Ibid.*, January 25, 1918.

71. *Ibid.*, January 23, 1918.

72. *Pravda*, January 31, 1918.

73. *Izvestiia*, February 15, 1918.

74. V. I. Lenin, *Collected Works*, vol. 26, p. 445.

75. *Ibid.*, p. 523.

76. *Ibid.*, vol. 27, Moscow, 1965, p. 51.

77. *Ibid.*, pp. 95, 98, 103.

78. *Ibid.*, p. 190.

79. *Liberator*, January 1919, p. 23.

80. V. I. Lenin, *Collected Works*, vol. 28, Moscow, 1965, pp. 148-49.

81. V. I. Lenin, *Polnoe sobranie sochinenii*, 5th ed., vol. 50, Moscow, 1965, pp. 194-95.

82. *Izvestiia*, December 6, 1918. Quoted in *Soviet Documents on Foreign Policy*, selected and edited by Jane Degras, London, 1951, p. 126.

83. Louis Fischer, *The Soviets in World Affairs*, London, 1930, vol. I, pp. 75-76.

84. V. I. Lenin, *Polnoe sobranie sochinenii*, 5th ed., vol. 50, p. 135.

85. *Ibid.*, p. 150.

86. *Ibid.*, p. 193.

87. *Ibid.*, p. 201.

88. *Ibid.*, vol. 36, Moscow, 1962, p. 251.

89. *Sed'moi ekstrennyi s"ezd RKP/b mart 1918 goda; stenograficheskii otchet*, Moscow, 1962, p. 171.

90. V. I. Lenin, *Polnoe sobranie sochinenii*, 5th ed., vol. 35, Moscow, 1962, p. 378.

91. V. I. Lenin, *Collected Works*, vol. 27, p. 41. Emphasis in the text.

92. *Ibid.*, p. 201.

93. *Ibid.*, vol. 28, p. 103. Emphasis in the text.

94. *Izvestiia*, April 21, 1918.

95. *Pravda*, April 25, 1918.

96. *VIII s"ezd Rossiiskoi kommunisticheskoi partii (bol'shevikov)*, Moscow, 1919, p. 386.

97. *Izvestiia*, August 30, 1918.

98. V. I. Lenin, *Polnoe sobranie sochinenii*, 5th ed., vol. 37, Moscow, 1963, p. 700.

99. V. I. Lenin, *Collected Works*, vol. 35, pp. 364-65. Emphasis in the text.

100. *Ibid.*, vol. 28, pp. 101-03.

101. *Ibid.*, vol. 35, p. 369.

102. *Ibid.*, vol. 28, pp. 292-93. Emphasis in the text.

103. *Ibid.*, p. 293. Emphasis in the text.

104. *Ibid.*, p. 105.

105. *Lénine tel qu'il fut. Souvenirs de contemporains*, vol. II, Moscow, 1959, p. 260.

106. V. I. Lenin, *Collected Works*, vol. 28, pp. 155, 160.

107. *Ibid.*, vol. 36, p. 496.

108. *Ibid.*, vol. 28, p. 337.

109. *Ibid.*, p. 206.

110. *Ibid.*, p. 416.

111. *Ibid.*, p. 114.

112. See Louis Fischer, *op. cit.*, vol. I, pp. 167-68.

113. V. I. Lenin, *Collected Works*, vol. 28, p. 113. Emphasis in the text.

CHAPTER TWO

1. *Die Kommunistische Internationale*, Nos. 31-32, 1924, p. 12.

2. *Pravda*, No. 260, November 30, 1918.

3. For the December 5 meeting, see *Izvestiia*, No. 268(532), December 7, 1918; for the December 18 meeting, *Revolutionary Radicalism*, part I, Albany, New York, 1920, pp. 421-58.

4. *Pravda*, No. 281, December 25, 1918.

5. V. I. Lenin, *Polnoe sobranie sochinenii*, 5th edition, vol. 37, Moscow 1963, p. 719.

6. *Pravda*, January 15, 1925.

7. V. I. Lenin, *op. cit.*, vol. 50, Moscow, 1965, p. 227. Emphasis in the text.

8. *Ibid.*, p. 229. Emphasis in the text.

9. J. Fineberg, "Erinnerungen an die Gründung der Kommunistischen Internationale," *Die Kommunistische Internationale*, Nos. 9, 10, 11, March 13, 1929, pp. 685-86.

10. *The Communist International, 1919-1943. Documents*. Selected and edited by Jane Degras. Volume I, 1919-1923, London-New York-Toronto, 1956, p. 5.

11. V. I. Lenin, *op. cit.*, vol. 37, p. 455.

12. *Pravda*, No. 18, January 26, 1919.

13. V. I. Lenin, *op. cit.*, vol. 37, p. 733.

14. J. Sadoul, "La fondation de la Troisième Internationale," *La Correspondance Internationale*, March 12, 1924, p. 179.

15. V. I. Lenin, *op. cit.*, vol. 37, p. 734.

16. Henri Guilbeaux, *La fin des Soviets*, Paris, 1937, p. 136.

17. M. Body, "Les groupes communistes français de Russie (1918-1921)," *Contributions à l'histoire du Comintern*, J. Freymond, editor, Geneva, 1965, p. 48.

18. V. I. Lenin, *op. cit.*, vol. 37, p. 455. Emphasis in the text.

19. H. Eberlein, "Souvenirs sur la fondation de l'Internationale communiste," *La Correspondance Internationale*, February 27, 1924, p. 154.

20. *Ibid.*

21. H. Eberlein, "Die Gründung der Komintern and der Spartakusbund," *Die Kommunistische Internationale*, Nos. 9, 10, 11, March 13, 1929, p. 676.

22. "Le récit du 'camarade Thomas' " in *Contributions à l'histoire du Comintern*, p. 8.

23. H. Eberlein, *op. cit.* (as in note 21).

24. *Ibid.*, p. 677.

25. *Ibid.*

26. G. Zinoviev, *L'Internationale communiste*, Petrograd, n.d., p. 41.

27. *Bericht über den 5. Parteitag der Kommunistischen Partei Deutschlands (Sektion der Kommunistischen Internationale) vom 1. bis 3. November 1920 in Berlin*. Berlin, 1921, p. 28.

28. J. Sadoul in *La Correspondance Internationale*, March 12, 1924, p. 179.

29. *Pravda*, March 2, 1919. Emphasis in the text.

30. *Pervyi kongress Kominterna*, Moscow, 1933, p. 256.

31. H. Eberlein, *op. cit.*, p. 677.

32. *Der I. Kongress der Kommunistischen Internationale; Protokoll der Verhandlungen in Moskau vom 2. bis 19. März 1919*, Hamburg, 1921, p. 6.

33. Tom Bell, *British Communist Party. A Short History*, London, 1937, p. 50.

34. Cf. Georges Haupt, "Lénine et la IIe Internationale," *Cahiers du monde russe et soviétique*, Paris, vol. VII, July-September 1966, p. 400.

35. For the numerical strength of the foreign Communist groups see *Vos'moi s"ezd RKP(b). Protokoly*, Moscow, 1959, pp. 501-4. For the French group, see M. Body in *Contributions à l'histoire du Comintern*.

36. Georges Haupt, editor, *Correspondance entre Lénine et Camille Huysmans, 1905-1914*, Paris-La Haye, 1963, p. 149.

37. *Pervyi kongress Kominterna*, p. 229.

38. *Le mouvement communiste international*, Petrograd, 1921, p. 149.

39. *Contributions à l'histoire du Comintern*, p. 9.

40. *Ibid.*, p. 8.

41. Karl Steinhardt, "Lebenserinnerungen eines Wiener Arbeiters," p. 195. Unpublished manuscript in Amsterdam's International Institute for Social History.

42. V. V. Vishniakova-Akimova, *Dva goda v vosstavshem Kitae, 1925-1927. Vospominania*, Moscow, 1965, p. 178.

43. S. Dzerzhinskaia, *V gody velikikh boev*, Moscow, 1964, p. 280.

44. H. Eberlein, *op. cit.*, p. 678.

45. J. Sadoul in *La Correspondance Internationale*, March 12, 1924, p. 179.

46. *Vos'moi s"ezd RKP(b). Protokoly*, Moscow, 1959, p. 141.

47. H. Eberlein in *La Correspondance Internationale*, February 27, 1924, p. 155.

48. H. Eberlein, *op. cit.*, p. 678.

49. *Der I. Kongress der Kommunistischen Internationale. . . .*, p. 7.

50. *Ibid.*, p. 8.

51. *Ibid.*, p. 98.

52. *Ibid.*, p. 99.

53. G. Zinoviev, *L'Internationale communiste*, p. 37.

54. *Der I. Kongress der Kommunistischen Internationale.* . . . , p. 99.

55. P. Orlovskii, "Rozhdenie Tret'ego Internatsionala," *Pravda*, No. 52, March 7, 1919.

56. G. Zinoviev, "Der Gründungskongress der Komintern," *Internationale Presse-Korrespondenz*, No. 12, March 22, 1924, p. 251.

57. B. Reinstein, "Auf dem Wege zum 1. Kongress der Komintern," *Die Kommunistische Internationale*, Nos. 9, 10, 11, March 13, 1929, pp. 673-74.

58. *Contributions à l'histoire du Comintern*, p. 10.

59. Karl Steinhardt, *op. cit.*, pp. 207-08.

60. J. Sadoul in *La Correspondance Internationale*, March 12, 1924, p. 179.

61. *Der I. Kongress der Kommunistischen Internationale.* . . . , pp. 131-32.

62. G. Zinoviev, *L'Internationale communiste*, pp. 42-44.

63. V. I. Lenin, *op. cit.*, vol. 38, Moscow, 1963, p. 306.

64. *Ibid.*, vol. 37, p. 511.

65. *Ibid.*, p. 514.

66. *Ibid.*, p. 520.

67. *Ibid.*, vol. 38, p. 161.

68. *Ibid.*, vol. 54, Moscow, 1965, p. 704.

69. V. I. Lenin, *Collected Works*, 4th edition, vol. 29, Moscow, 1965, p. 507.

70. *Der I. Kongress der Kommunistischen Internationale.* . . . , p. 135.

71. G. Zinoviev, "Vistas of the Proletarian Revolution," *The Communist International*, No. 1, May 1919, pp. 39-44.

72. L. Rudas, "The proletarian revolution in Hungary," *ibid.*, p. 56.

73. C. Gruber, "The Last Stage," *ibid.*, p. 63.

74. J. Sadoul, "The Third International and France," *ibid.*, p. 70.

75. H. Guilbeaux, "The Third International and the Problems of the French Proletarians," *ibid.*, pp. 75-76.

CHAPTER THREE

1. V. I. Lenin, *Polnoe sobranie sochinenii*, 5th ed., vol. 38, Moscow, 1963, p. 306.

2. *Ibid.*, vol. 35, Moscow, 1962, p. 304.

3. *Ibid.*, p. 393.

4. *Pravda*, February 1 (January 19), 1918.

5. V. I. Lenin, *op. cit.*, vol. 36, Moscow, 1962, p. 22.

6. *Lenin i mezhdunarodnoe rabochee dvizhenie*, Leningrad, 1934, p. 134.

7. *Ibid.*, p. 135.

8. O. V. Kuusinen, *Revoliutsiia v Finliandii (samokritika)*, Petrograd, 1919, p. 4.

9. *Ibid.*, p. 15.

10. *Ibid.*, p. 18.

11. *Ibid.*, pp. 4, 28.

12. *Ibid.*, p. 14.

13. *Ibid.*, p. 36.

14. S. D. Kataia, *Terror burzhuazii v Finliandii*, Petrograd, 1919, p. 1.

15. Y. Sirola, "La révolution prolétarienne en Finlande," *L'Internationale communiste*, February 1, 1928, p. 223.

16. *Ibid.*, p. 236.

17. *Bulletin communiste*, Paris, No. 10, May 20, 1920, p. 6.

18. Karl Radek, "November—Eine kleine Seite aus meinen Erinnerungen," *Archiv für Sozialgeschichte*, vol. II, Hannover, 1962, p. 132.

19. Arnold Struthahn [Karl Radek], *Die Entwicklung der deutschen Revolution und die Aufgaben der Kommunistischen Partei*, Stuttgart, 1919, p. 16.

20. *Bericht über den Gründungsparteitag der Kommunistischen Partei Deutschlands (Spartakusbund), vom 30. Dezember 1918 bis 1. Januar 1919*, Berlin, n.d., p. 8.

21. Karl Radek, *op. cit.*, p. 136.

22. *Ibid.*, pp. 137-38.

23. W. Pieck, "Erinnerungen an die Novemberrevolution und die Gründung der KPD," *Vorwärts und nicht vergessen−Erlebnisse aktiver Teilnehmer der Novemberrevolution 1918/1919*, Berlin, 1958, pp. 69-70.

24. *Illustrierte Geschichte der deutschen Revolution*, Berlin, 1929, p. 282.

25. *Bulletin communiste*, No. 6, April 22, 1920, p. 13.

26. *Die Kommunistische Internationale*, No. 17, 1921, p. 65.

27. Allan Mitchell, *Revolution in Bavaria, 1918-1919. The Eisner Regime and the Soviet Republic*, Princeton, 1965, p. 308.

28. Rosa Leviné, *Aus der Münchener Rätezeit*, Berlin, 1925, p. 8.

29. *Ibid.*, p. 13.

30. P. Werner, "Münchener Erfahrungen," *Die Internationale*, Berlin, No. 9/10, August 4, 1919, p. 6.

31. Rosa Leviné, *op. cit.*, pp. 18-19.

32. Erich Mühsam, *Von Eisner bis Leviné. Die Entstehung der bayerischen Räterepublik*, Berlin-Britz, 1929, p. 46.

33. Quoted in Helmut Neubauer, *München und Moskau, 1918/1919*, Munich, 1958, p. 54.

34. V. I. Lenin, *op. cit.*, vol. 50, Moscow, 1965, p. 277.

35. *Ibid.*

36. Quoted in Helmut Neubauer, *op. cit.*, pp. 310-11.

37. Allan Mitchell, *op. cit.*, pp. 310-11.

38. N. Zastenker, "Bavarskaia sovetskaia respublika i taktika kommunistov," *Istorik marksist*, Moscow, Nos. 4-5 (26-27), 1932, p. 247.

39. Quoted in Neubauer, *op. cit.*, p. 88.

40. Rosa Leviné, *op. cit.*, pp. 40-46.

41. Helmut Neubauer, *op. cit.*, p. 70.

42. *Ibid.*, p. 89.

43. *Ibid.*, p. 88.

44. *Ibid.*, p. 72.

45. V. I. Lenin, *op. cit.*, vol. 38, pp. 321-22.

46. Quoted in Helmut Neubauer, *op. cit.*, pp. 90-91.

47. V. I. Lenin, *op. cit.*, vol. 38, pp. 323-24.

48. "Münchener Lehren," *Die Internationale*, Nos. 10/11, June 2, 1924, p. 317.

49. "München 1919," *Die Internationale*, No. 6, middle June 1925, p. 371.

50. P. Werner, *op. cit.*, note 30, p. 8.

51. P. Werner, *ibid.*, Nos. 11/12, August 18, 1919, p. 235.

52. *Ibid.*, p. 233.

53. P. Werner, *Die Bayerische Räterepublik. Tatsachen und Kritik*, Leipzig, n.d., p. 51.

54. *Ibid.*, p. 9.

55. "Münchener Erfahrungen. II. Die Kehrseite," *Die Internationale*, Nos. 9/10, August 4, 1919, p. 13.

56. *Ibid.*

57. *Vos'moi s"ezd RKP(b), mart 1919 goda, Protokoly*, Moscow, 1959, p. 364. Emphasis in the text.

58. *Nepszava*, organ of the Hungarian Communist Party, March 25, 1919, quoted in *Vos'moi s"ezd RKP(b)*, p. 444.

59. *Communist International*, No. 1, May 1, 1919, pp. 43-44.

60. *Pravda*, April 18, 1919.

61. Béla Kun, *O Vengerskoi Sovetskoi Respublike*, Moscow, 1966, p. 163.

62. V. I. Lenin, *op. cit.*, vol. 38, pp. 384, 388.

63. *Communist International*, June 1919, No. 2, p. 201.

64. *Ibid.*, No. 1, May 1, 1919, p. 89.

65. Béla Szántó, *Klassenkämpfe und Diktatur des Proletariats in Ungarn*, Petrograd, 1920 (quoted in the preface written by Karl Radek), p. 9.

66. Paul Levi, "Die Lehren der ungarischen Revolution," *Die International-ale*, No. 24, June 24, 1920, pp. 32-33.

67. Arnold Struthahn [Radek] , *op. cit.*, p. 53.

68. Béla Kun, *op. cit.*, p. 272.

69. "Zwei Daten (21. Juli–1. August 1919)," *Die Kommunistische Inter-nationale*, Nos. 4/5, p. 73.

70. V. I. Lenin, *op. cit.*, vol. 40, Moscow, 1963, p. 131.

71. *Le mouvement communiste international. Rapports adressés au deux-ième congrès de l'Internationale communiste*. Petrograd, 1921, p. 43.

72. Béla Kun, *op. cit.*, p. 214.

73. *Ibid.*, p. 274.

74. *Ibid.*, p. 440.

75. Eugène Varga, *La dictature du proletariat (Problèmes économiques)*, Paris, 1922, p. 49.

76. Béla Kun, *op. cit.*, p. 314.

77. Eugène Varga, *op. cit.*, p. 212.

78. Béla Kun, *op. cit.*, p. 288.

79. *Die Kommunistische Internationale*, Nos. 7-8 (Nov.-Dec. 1919), p. 247.

80. *Die Internationale*, No. 24, June 24, 1920, p. 40.

81. Béla Szántó, *op. cit.*, p. 67.

82. Béla Kun, *op. cit.*, p. 237.

83. E. Bettelheim, "Die Bettelheimerei," *Kommunismus*, Vienna, August 15, 1921, p. 947.

84. Karl Radek, "Die Lehren eines Putschversuchs," *Die Kommunistische Internationale*, No. 9, 1920, p. 1325.

85. E. Bettelheim, *op. cit.*, p. 953.

86. L. Laurat, "Le Parti communiste autrichien," *Contributions à l'histoire du Comintern*, Geneva, 1965, p. 76.

87. E. Bettelheim, *op. cit.*, pp. 967-68.

88. Julius Braunthal, *Die Arbeiterräte in Deutschösterreich*, Vienna, 1919, p. 50.

89. Karl Radek, *op. cit.*, note 84, p. 1322.

90. G. Zinoviev, *Bericht des Exekutivkomitees der Kommunistischen Internationale an den zweiten Weltkongress der Kommunistischen Internationale*, Berlin, 1920, p. 21.

91. E. Bettelheim, *op. cit.*, pp. 946-47.

92. *Ibid.*

93. *L'Internationale communiste*, No. 13, September 1920, p. 2577. Letter to the editorial board of the revue by K. Steinhardt, M. Reissner, K. Toman.

94. *Bericht über die Tätigkeit des Präsidiums und der Exekutive der Kommunistischen Internationale für die Zeit vom 6. März bis 11. Juni 1922*, Hamburg, 1922, pp. 6-7.

95. V. I. Lenin, *Collected Works*, vol. 27, Moscow, 1964, p. 115.

96. *Ibid.*, pp. 184-85.

97. V. I. Lenin, *Polnoe sobranie sochinenii*, 5th ed., vol. 50, pp. 285-86.

98. *Ibid.*, vol. 51, Moscow, 1965, p. 27.

99. *Ibid.*, vol. 39, Moscow, 1963, pp. 322-23, 330.

100. Arnold Struthahn [Radek] , *op. cit.*, pp. 15, 16, 18.

101. Karl Radek, *Zur Taktik des Kommunismus*, Berlin, 1919, p. 5.

102. *Bericht über den 2. Parteitag der Kommunistischen Partei Deutschlands (Spartakusbund), vom 20. bis 24 October 1919*, n.d., p. 17.

103. V. I. Lenin, *op. cit.*, vol. 29, Moscow, 1965, p. 153.

104. Arnold Struthahn [Radek], *op. cit.*, p. 91.

CHAPTER FOUR

1. *Izvestiia*, No. 243, December 3, 1917, Quoted by L. Trotsky, *Sochineniia*, vol. III, Moscow, 1925, part I, pp. 141-42.

2. Thomas Bell, *Pioneering Days*, London, 1941, pp. 149-50.

3. *Izvestiia*, No. 259(523), November 27, 1918.

4. *Ibid.*, December 6, 1918.

5. *Der zweite Kongress der Kommunistischen Internationale*. Protokoll der Verhandlungen vom 19. Juli in Petrograd und vom 23. Juli his 7. August 1920 in Moskau, Hamburg, 1921, p. 325.

6. Cf. V. I. Lenin, *Polnoe sobranie sochinenii*, 5th edition, vol. 50, Moscow, 1965, pp. 182, 187-88.

7. *Voprosy istorii KPSS*, No. 7, July 1964, p. 109.

8. *La Fédération balkanique*, Vienna, July 1, 1927, p. 1.

9. Henri Guilbeaux, *La fin des soviets*, Paris, 1937, p. 136.

10. Rudolf L. Tökés, *Béla Kun and the Hungarian Soviet Republic*, New York, 1967, pp. 61-62.

11. M. N. Roy's *Memoirs*, Bombay, New Delhi, Calcutta, Madras, 1964, p. 200.

12. *Contributions à l'histoire du Comintern*, Geneva, 1965, pp. 11-12.

13. *Der zweite Kongress. . . .*, p. 237.

14. G. Zinoviev, *Bericht des Exekutivkomitees der Kommunistischen Internationale an den zweiten Kongress*. Herausgegeben vom Westeuropäischen Sekretariat der Kommunistischen Internationale. Berlin, 1920, p. 4.

15. *Ibid.*

16. *Der zweite Kongress. . . .*, p. 596.

17. G. Zinoviev, *op. cit.*, p. 5.

18. A. Balabanoff, *My Life as a Rebel*, New York, 1938, p. 222.

19. L. Trotsky, *L'Internationale communiste après Lénine*, Paris, 1930, p. 423. Emphasis in the text.

20. *Die Kommunistische Internationale,* No. 7-8, November-December 1919, p. 206.

21. Original letter in the authors' possession.

22. G. Zinoviev, *op. cit.,* p. 15.

23. *Der zweite Kongress. . . . ,* p. 580.

24. *Proletarskaia revoliutsiia,* Moscow, January 1930, No. 1, p. 68.

25. Photocopy of the letter in the authors' possession.

26. Cf. A. Abramovich, "Nezabyvaemye vstrechi," *Kommunist sovetskoi Latvii,* Riga, April 1961, pp. 37-41.

27. V. I. Lenin, *op. cit.,* vol. 51, Moscow, 1965, p. 239.

28. Cf. Hermann Weber, ed., *Der deutsche Kommunismus. Dokumente,* Cologne-Berlin, 1963, p. 210.

29. Copy of the letter in the authors' possession.

30. M. N. Roy, *op. cit.,* p. 274.

31. J. Maurín, "Sur le communisme en Espagne," manuscript in the authors' possession.

32. L. Trotsky, *op. cit.,* p. 409.

33. V. I. Lenin, *op. cit.,* vol. 51, pp. 217, 299.

34. Giuseppe Berti, ed., *I primi dieci anni di vita del P.C.I. Documenti inediti dell'archivio Angelo Tasca,* Milano, 1967, p. 91.

35. *Ibid.*

36. V. Degot, *Pod znamenem bol'shevizma,* Moscow, 1927, p. 131.

37. B. Souvarine in *Le Contrat Social,* Paris, September-October 1966, p. 268.

38. M. N. Roy, *op. cit.,* pp. 210-11.

39. *Contributions à l'histoire du Comintern,* pp. 17-18.

40. V. Degot, *op. cit.,* p. 130.

41. *Ibid.*

42. *Ibid.*

43. "Schlusswort des Genossen Levi" (in the authors' possession). The exact date when Levi delivered his speech, as well as the German Communist Party body before which he spoke, is not mentioned in the document. One may assume, however, from the context of his remarks, that he spoke on February 24, 1921 to the central committee of the United German Communist Party.

44. Alfred Rosmer, *Moscou sous Lénine*, Paris, 1953. p. 42.

45. Giuseppe Berti, *op. cit.*, pp. 90-91.

46. Karl Radek, "November—Eine kleine Seite aus meinen Erinnerungen," *Archiv für Sozialgeschichte*, vol. II, Hannover, 1962, p. 156.

47. Paul Levi's letter to Zinoviev (photocopy in the authors' possession).

48. *Communismo*, Rome, December 15-31, 1919, p. 6.

49. "Schlusswort des Genossen Levi."

50. Note by B. Souvarine (in the authors' possession).

51. "Séance du Présidium de l'Exécutif du vendredi 2 décembre 1921." (Minutes in the authors' possession.)

52. *L'Internationale communiste et sa section française.* (Recueil de documents), Paris, 1922, p. 18.

53. *Contributions à l'histoire du Comintern*, pp. 19-20.

54. "Bericht des Genossen Levi an das Exekutivkomitee der III. Internationale über den italienischen Parteitag," Berlin, January 20, 1921 (in the authors' possession).

55. *Stranitsy zhizni i bor'by*, Moscow, 1957 (translated into French in *Le Contrat Social*, January-February 1966, p. 47).

56. "Vstrechi s Leninym," *Istorik Marksist*, Moscow, 1935, Nos. 2-3, p. 90.

57. *Contributions à l'histoire du Comintern*, p. 12.

58. Radek, *op. cit.* note 46, p. 158.

59. Cf. *Contributions à l'histoire du Comintern*, p. 15; M. N. Roy, *op. cit.*, pp. 266, 276-77; *Der zweite Kongress....*, p. 311; W. Bringolf, *Mein Leben. Weg und Umweg eines Schweizer Sozialdemokraten*, Berne, Munich, Vienna, 1965, pp. 77, 95; J. T. Murphy's letter "An das Exekutivkomitee der K.P. in Deutschland" (in the authors' possession).

60. *Kommunistische Arbeiter-Zeitung*, Berlin, No. 90, April 23, 1920.

61. *Contributions à l'histoire du Comintern*, p. 13.

62. *Bericht über den 2. Parteitag der Kommunistischen Partei Deutschlands (Spartakusbund) vom 20. Oktober bis 24. Oktober 1919*, Berlin, n.d., pp. 35, 48.

63. *Biulleten'Kommunisticheskogo Internatsionala*, Moscow, November 26, 1920, No. 7, p. 23.

64. *Bericht über den 4. Parteitag der Kommunistischen Partei Deutschlands (Spartakusbund), am 14. und 15. April 1920*, Berlin, n.d., p. 47.

65. *Bericht über den 5. Parteitag der Kommunistischen Partei Deutschlands (Sektion der Kommunistischen Internationale), vom 1. bis 3. November 1920 in Berlin*, Berlin, 1921, p. 36.

66. *Bulletin communiste*, Paris, No. 1, March 1, 1920, pp. 14-15.

67. *Bericht über den 4. Parteitag....*, p. 46.

68. *Ibid.*, pp. 46-47.

69. *Ibid.*, p. 47.

70. *Ibid.*, p. 106.

71. Babette Gross, *Willi Münzenberg. Eine politische Biographie*, Stuttgart, 1967, p. 104. For Münzenberg's more detailed views see *Unter dem roten Banner. Bericht über den 1. Kongress der Kommunistischen Jugendinternationale*, Berlin, n.d., pp. 43-44. For Shatskin's opinions see the more complete version of his report to the same congress, published under the title *Die Aufgaben der Kommunistischen Jugendorganisationen nach der Uebernahme der Macht durch das Proletariat*, Berlin, n.d., p. 10.

72. *Bericht über die erste Sitzung des Büros der Kommunistischen Jugendinternationale*, Berlin, n.d., p. 6.

73. *Ibid.*, p. 8.

74. *Ibid.*, p. 13.

75. *Ibid.*, p. 15.

76. *Ibid.*, p. 16.

77. *Bericht über den 3. Parteitag der Kommunistischen Partei Deutschlands (Spartakusbund) am 25. und 26. Februar 1920*, Berlin, n.d., p. 85.

78. Radek's letter of October 15, 1919 (in the authors' possession).

79. Under the title "Vozzvanie Zapadno-evropeiskogo sekretariata Kommunisticheskogo Internatsionala" these theses were published in *Kommunisticheskii Internatsional*, Nos. 7-8, November-December 1919, pp. 1099-1102.

80. *Contributions à l'histoire du Comintern*, p. 15.

81. *Die Kommunistische Internationale*, No. 4/5, Berlin, 1919, p. 18.

82. *Kommunisticheskii Internatsional*, No. 12, 1920, p. 2217.

83. Cf., *Bericht über die Tätigkeit des Präsidiums und der Exekutive der Kommunistischen Internationale für die Zeit vom 6. März bis 11. Juni 1922*, Hamburg, 1922, pp. 1, 2, 3, 4.

84. V. Serge, *Mémoires d'un révolutionnaire,* Paris, 1951, p. 175. Cf. also *Contributions à l'histoire du Comintern*, pp. 15-16.

85. K. Radek, *op. cit.*, note 46, p. 158.

86. S. Rutgers, "Vstrechi s Leninym," *Istorik Marksist*, Vol. 2-3, 1935, p. 90.

87. V. I. Lenin, *op. cit.*, Vol. 51, p. 57.

88. *Ibid.*

89. *Bericht über den 3. Parteitag. . . . ,* p. 79.

90. Dr. W. Van Ravesteyn, *De Wording van het Communisme in Nederland, 1907-1925,* Amsterdam, 1948, p. 206.

91. *Ibid.*

92. *La Vie Ouvrière,* Paris, April 8, 1921.

93. S. Rutgers, *op. cit.*, p. 91.

94. *La Vie Ouvrière,* July 16, 1920.

95. J. T. Murphy, *New Horizons*, London, 1941, p. 87.

96. *Bulletin du Bureau auxiliaire d'Amsterdam de l'Internationale Communiste*, No. 2, Amsterdam, March 1920, p. 1.

97. *Ibid.*

98. *Bulletin du Bureau provisoire d'Amsterdam de l'Internationale Communiste*, No. 1, February 1920, p. 3. The difference of *Bulletin's* title should be noted: No. 1 appeared as *Bulletin du Bureau provisoire d'Amsterdam...*, and No. 2 as *Bulletin du Bureau auxiliaire d'Amsterdam....*

99. Communication of the Amsterdam Sub-Bureau of the Third International (Archives Jules Humbert-Droz, No. 0455).

100. *Bulletin du Bureau provisoire.....* No. 1, p. 7.

101. Archives Jules Humbert-Droz, No. 0461, p. vi.

102. *Bulletin du Bureau auxiliaire....*, No. 2, p. 8.

103. *Ibid.*, p. 1.

104. *Bericht über den 3. Parteitag....*, p. 81.

105. *Ibid.*, pp. 83-84.

106. *Bulletin du Bureau auxiliaire....*, No. 2, p. 8.

107. *La Vie Ouvrière*, June 25, 1920.

108. *Die Kommunistische Internationale*, No. 1, Berlin, August 1919, p. 38.

109. *Der zweite Kongress....*, pp. 583, 585.

110. *Ibid.*, pp. 584-85.

111. *Ibid.*, pp. 590; 594.

112. *Deiatel'nost' Ispolnitel'nogo Komiteta i Prezidiuma I. K. Kommunisticheskogo Internatsionala ot 13-go Iiulia 1921 g. do 1-go Fevralia 1922 g.*, Petrograd, 1922, p. 17.

113. *Bericht über die Tätigkeit des Präsidiums und der Exekutive der Kommunistischen Internationale, für die Zeit vom 6. März bis 11. Juni 1922*, Hamburg, 1922, p. 1.

114. G. Zinoviev, *op. cit.*, p. 31.

115. *L'Internationale communiste*, No. 10, May 1920, pp. 1707-8.

116. *Bericht über die erste Sitzung des Büros der Kommunistischen Jugendinternationale*, Berlin, n.d., p. 16.

117. G. Zinoviev, *op. cit.*, p. 33.

118. *Der zweite Kongress. . . .* , p. 85.

119. A. Rosmer, *op. cit.*, pp. 109-10.

120. M. Body in *Contributions à l'histoire du Comintern*, p. 52.

121. *Die Kommunistische Internationale*, No. 11, June 1920, p. 248.

122. *Manifestes, Thèses et Résolutions des quatre premiers congrès de l'Internationale communiste*, Paris, 1934, p. 47.

123. *Bericht über die Tätigkeit des Präsidiums und der Exekutive der Kommunistischen Internationale vom 13. Juli 1921 bis 1. Februar 1922*, p. 50.

124. *Bericht über die Tätigkeit des Präsidiums und der Exekutive der Kommunistischen Internationale für die Zeit vom 6. März bis 11. Juni 1922*, p. 3.

125. *Bericht über die Tätigkeit des Präsidiums und der Exekutive der Kommunistischen Internationale vom 13. Juli 1921 bis 1. Februar 1922*, p. 50.

126. *Ibid.*, p. 241.

CHAPTER FIVE

1. O. W. Kuusinen, *Die Revolution in Finnland*, Hamburg, 1921, p. 22.

2. *Lénine tel qu'il fut. Souvenirs de contemporains*, vol. II, Moscow, 1959, p. 694.

3. V. I. Lenin, *Polnoe sobranie sochinenii*, 5th edition, vol. 49, Moscow, 1964, pp. 387, 390.

4. *Ibid.*, pp. 190-91.

5. *Ibid.*, p. 383.

6. *Ce qu'il faut dire* (anarchist magazine), Paris, November 17, 1917.

7. V. I. Lenin, *op. cit.*, vol. 49, pp. 339, 341, 384, 385.

8. *Ibid.*, vol. 37, Moscow, 1963, p. 55.

9. L.-O. Frossard, *De Jaurès à Lénine. Notes et souvenirs d'un militant*, Paris, 1930, pp. 34-36.

10. *Ibid.*, p. 28.

11. *Der zweite Kongress der Kommunistischen Internationale. Protokoll der Verhandlungen vom 19. Juli in Petrograd und vom 23. Juli bis 7. August 1920 in Moskau*, Hamburg, 1921, p. 253.

12. *L'Internationale communiste et sa section française. (Recueil de documents)*, Paris, 1922, p. 14.

13. J. T. Murphy, *New Horizons*, London, 1941, p. 139.

14. Paul Levi's report (photocopy in the authors' possession).

15. Leon Trotsky, *The First Five Years of the Communist International*, vol. II, New York, 1953, p. 19.

16. Parti Socialiste, *18e congrès national tenu à Tours, Décembre 25-30, 1920. Compte rendu sténographique*, Paris, 1921, pp. 119-20.

17. *Ibid.*, pp. 139-40.

18. *L'action communiste et la crise du parti*, Paris, 1922, p. 23.

19. V. I. Lenin, *op. cit.* vol. 41, Moscow, 1963, p. 15.

20. *Ibid.*, vol. 44, Moscow, 1964, p. 90.

21. *La vie ouvrière*, April 30, 1919.

22. *The One Big Union Monthly*, (published by the IWW in Chicago), No. 7, September 1919, p. 40.

23. Joaquín Maurín, *Revolución y Contrarevolución en España*, Paris, 1966, p. 248.

24. Manuel Buenacasa, *El Movimiento Obrero Español, 1886-1926*, Barcelona, 1928, pp. 71-72.

25. J. Díaz del Moral, *Historia de las Agitaciones Campesinas Andaluzas-Cordoba*, Madrid, 1929, pp. 172-73.

26. J. Maurín, *Sur le communisme en Espagne* (manuscript in the authors' possession. This text appears in translation as an appendix in Maurín's book *Revolución y Contrarevolución en España*).

27. "Le programme communiste, 1919," *Contrat social*, Paris, September-October 1961, vol. V, no. 5, p. 290.

28. V. I. Lenin, *op. cit.*, vol. 44, pp. 57, 58-59.

29. J. Degras, editor, *Soviet Documents on Foreign Policy*, vol. 1, London, 1951, p. 2.

30. "Le programme communiste, 1919," *Contrat social*, Paris, September-October 1961, p. 291.

31. Eugène Varga, *La dictature du prolétariat*, Paris, 1922, p. 1.

32. V. I. Lenin, *op. cit.*, vol. 39, Moscow, 1963, p. 330.

33. *Pervyi s"ezd narodov Vostoka, Stenograficheskie otchety*, Petrograd, 1920, p. 145.

34. Sultan-Galiev in *Zhizn natsionalnostei*, Moscow, No. 39(47), October 12, 1919.

35. M. N. Roy, *Memoirs*, Bombay, 1964, p. 306.

36. *La revue communiste*, Paris, No. 15, May, 1921, p. 204.

37. Anton Pannekoek, *Weltrevolution und kommunistische Taktik*, Vienna, 1920, p. 40.

38. *Ibid.*, pp. 41-42.

CHAPTER SIX

1. *Lénine tel qu'il fut. Souvenirs des contemporains*, vol. II, Moscow, 1959, p. 705.

2. K. Radek, "November—Eine kleine Seite aus meinen Erinnerungen," in *Archiv für Sozialgeschichte*, vol. II, Hannover, 1962, p. 135.

3. *Bericht über den 2. Parteitag der Kommunistischen Partei Deutschlands (Spartakusbund) vom 20. bis 24. Oktober 1919*, Berlin, n.d. p. 6.

4. Radek's letter (in the authors' possession).

5. V. I. Lenin, *Polnoe sobranie sochinenii*, 5th edition, vol. 39, Moscow, 1963, pp. 253-54. Emphasis in the text.

6. *Bericht über den 3. Parteitag der Kommunistischen Partei Deutschlands (Spartakusbund) am 25. und 26. Februar 1920*, Berlin, n.d. p. 14.

7. H. Weber, editor, *Der deutsche Kommunismus—Dokumente*, Berlin, 1963, p. 139.

8. Spartakus, "Der Kapp-Lüttwitz-Putsch," *Die Kommunistische Internationale*, No. 10, Berlin, 1920, p. 155.

9. *Ibid.*, p. 161.

10. *Die Kommunistische Internationale*, No. 12, 1920, p. 147.

11. *Ibid.*, No. 10, 1920, p. 153.

12. *Ibid.*, pp. 166-67.

13. K. Radek, "Die K.P.D. während der Kapptage," *Die Kommunistische Internationale*, No. 12, 1920, p. 164.

14. *Ibid.*, p. 165.

15. *Die Kommunistische Internationale*, No. 10, pp. 230-31.

16. *Ibid.*, p. 321. Emphasis in the text.

17. K. Radek, *op. cit.*, p. 164.

18. V. I. Lenin, *op. cit.*, vol. 41, Moscow, 1963, p. 95.

19. Paul Levi, *Was ist das Verbrechen? Die Märzaktion oder die Kritik daran?*, Berlin, 1921, p. 32.

20. *Die Kommunistische Arbeiterzeitung*, Berlin, April 23, 1920, No. 90. Emphasis in the text.

21. Otto Rühle, *Die Revolution ist keine Parteisache*, Berlin, 1920, pp. 3,5,6.

22. V. I. Lenin, *op. cit.*, vol. 41, pp. 45-46.

23. *Ibid.*, p. 104.

24. *Le Phare*, Geneva, Nos. 19-20, April-May 1921, p. 438.

25. *Kommunismus*, Vienna, May 1, 1920, p. 530.

26. L. Laurat, "Le Parti communiste autrichien," *Contributions à l'histoire du Comintern*, Geneva, 1965, pp. 84-85.

27. For more detailed information of this "Party" and this "Soviet Federation," see Annie Kriegel, *Aux origines du communisme français, 1914-1920*, vol. I, Paris, 1964.

28. *Kommunismus*, Vienna, April 17, 1920, p. 410-11. Emphasis in the text.

29. V. I. Lenin, *op. cit.*, vol. 40, Moscow, 1963, p. 205.

30. *Ibid.*, vol. 41, p. 135.

31. *Kommunismus*, September 9, 1920, p. 1248.

32. *Die Kommunistische Internationale*, Nos. 31-32, 1924, p. 13.

33. *Lénine tel qu'il fut*, vol. II, p. 36.

34. V. I. Lenin, *op. cit.*, vol. 41, p. 38.

35. *Ibid.*, p. 73.

36. *Ibid.*, pp. 54, 59.

37. *Ibid.*, p. 20.

38. *Ibid.*, p. 80.

39. *Ibid.*, p. 54.

40. *Ibid.*, p. 42. Emphasis in the text.

41. *Ibid.*, pp. 36-37.

42. *Ibid.*, vol. 33, Moscow, 1962, p. 113.

43. *Ibid.*, vol. 41, p. 3.

44. Hermann Gorter, *Réponse à Lénine sur "La maladie infantile du communisme,"* Paris, 1930, pp. 7, 12, 97.

45. L. Trotsky, *The First Five Years of the Communist International*, vol. I, New York, 1945, pp. 137-38.

46. Anton Pannekoek, "Weltrevolution und kommunistische Taktik," *Probleme der Proletarischen Revolution*, Vienna, No. 2, 1920, p. 47.

47. *Bericht über den 2. Parteitag....*, p. 34.

48. *Die Kommunistische Arbeiterzeitung*, No. 90, April 23, 1920.

49. Quoted by Zinoviev, *Ce qu'a été jusqu'ici l'Internationale communiste et ce qu'elle doit être*, Petrograd, n.d., p. 12.

50. Hermann Gorter, *op. cit.*, p. 89.

51. V. I. Lenin, *op. cit.*, vol. 45, Moscow, 1964, p. 404.

52. Anton Pannekoek, *op. cit.*, pp. 41, 43, 44.

CHAPTER SEVEN

1. V: I. Lenin, *Polnoe sobranie sochinenii*, 5th edition, vol. 41, Moscow, 1963, p. 70.

2. *Ibid.*, vol. 51, Moscow, 1965, p. 238.

3. *Ibid.*, p. 440.

4. L. Trotsky, *Ma vie*, vol. III, Paris, 1930, pp. 169-70.

5. Clara Zetkin, *Reminiscences of Lenin*, London, 1929, p. 20.

6. L. Trotsky, *op. cit.*, p. 170.

7. *Contributions à l'histoire du Comintern*, Geneva, 1965, p. 19.

8. L.-O. Frossard, *De Jaurès à Lénine–Notes et souvenirs d'un militant*, Paris, 1930, p. 137.

9. Angelica Balabanoff, *Impressions of Lenin*, Ann Arbor, 1964, pp. 109-10.

10. *Der zweite Kongress der Kommunistischen Internationale*, Hamburg, 1921, pp. 342, 343.

11. *Ibid.*, p. 370.

12. *Ibid.*, p. 378.

13. *Ibid.*, p. 386.

14. Paul Levi, "Bericht über die Verhandlungen in Moskau. Rede auf der Zentralausschusssitzung am 25.8.1920" (in the authors' possession).

15. A. Balabanoff, *op. cit.*, p. 111.

16. *Der zweite Kongress.* . . . , p. 359.

17. Mrs. Philip Snowden, *Through Bolshevik Russia*, London, 1920, p. 76.

18. J. T. Murphy, *New Horizons*, London, 1941, p. 152.

19. Parti Socialiste, *18e Congrès National tenu à Tours. Compte-rendu sténographique*, Paris, 1921, pp. 185-86.

20. W. Münzenberg, *S Libknekhtom i Leninym*, Moscow, 1930, p. 191.

21. A. Balabanoff, *My Life as a Rebel*, New York, 1938, p. 262.

22. *Lénine tel qu'il fut. Souvenirs de contemporains*, vol. II, Moscow, 1959, p. 679.

23. V. I. Lenin, *op. cit.*, vol. 41, p. 215.

24. *Ibid.*, p. 521.

25. *Ibid.*, vol. 51, pp. 157, 414.

26. Boris Sokolov, *Le voyage de Cachin et de Frossard dans la Russie des Soviets (Faits et Documents)*, Paris, 1920, p. 10.

27. R. Abramovich's letter in *The New York Times*, May 10, 1962.

28. L.-O. Frossard, *op. cit.*, p. 64.

29. S. Lozovski in *Lénine tel qu'il fut*, vol. II, pp. 667-68.

30. Mrs. Philip Snowden, *op. cit.*, pp. 117-18.

31. Independent Labour Party, *Report of the 29th Annual Conference held at Southport, March 1921*, London, 1921, p. 51.

32. *Ibid.*, p. 52.

33. *Ibid.*, pp. 53-54.

34. *Ibid.*, p. 54.

35. A. Balabanoff, *op. cit.*, p. 258.

36. *Report of the 29th Annual Conference....*, pp. 58-59.

37. *Le Parti socialiste italien et l'Internationale communiste (Recueil de documents)*, Petrograd, 1921, p. 13.

38. *Lenine tel qu'il fut*, p. 682.

39. *Ibid.*, p. 684.

40. L. Trotsky, *L'Internationale communiste après Lénine (Le grand organisateur de la défaite)*, Paris, 1930, p. 406.

41. Excerpt from a letter by M. Vaněk (in the authors' possession).

42. *18e Congrès National....*, pp. 336-37.

43. *L'Heure*, July 4, 1918 (quoted in the pamphlet *Le Problème de l'Internationale*, Lille, 1920, p. 16).

44. *18e Congrès National....*, p. 121.

45. L.-O. Frossard, *op. cit.*, pp. 75-76.

46. W. Münzenberg, *op. cit.*, p. 194.

47. *Le Parti socialiste et l'Internationale*, Paris, 1920, p. 9.

48. *Ibid.*, p. 16.

49. *Ibid.*

50. *Ibid.*

51. *Le Parti socialiste italien et l'Internationale.* . . . , p. 81.

52. A. Rosmer, *Moscou sous Lénine*, Paris, 1953, pp. 60-61.

53. *Le Parti socialiste et l'Internationale*, p. 19.

54. L.-O. Frossard, *op. cit.*, p. 133.

55. *Die Kommunistische Internationale*, No. 13, Hamburg, 1920, p. 153.

56. *Le Parti socialiste et l'Internationale*, p. 17.

57. *Ibid.*, pp. 38-39.

58. *Ibid.*, p. 38.

59. Arthur Crispien, *Die Internationale. Vom Bund der Kommunisten bis zur Internationale der Weltrevolution*, Berlin, 1920, p. 42.

60. V. I. Lenin, *op. cit.*, vol. 40, Moscow, 1963, p. 61.

61. Karl Radek, *Zur Taktik des Kommunismus. Ein Schreiben an den Oktober-Parteitag der K.P.D.*, Berlin, December 1919, p. 11.

62. V. I. Lenin, *op. cit.*, vol. 40, pp. 472-73.

63. *L'Internationale communiste*, No. 9, April, 1920, p. 1446.

64. L.-O. Frossard, *op. cit.*, p. 101.

65. USPD, *Protokoll der Reichskonferenz vom 1. bis 3. September 1920*, Berlin, n.d., p. 13.

66. *Ibid.*, p. 10.

67. *Ibid.*, p. 15.

68. Paul Levi, "Bericht über die Verhandlungen in Moskau. Rede am 25-8-1920."

69. *Der zweite Kongress.* . . . , p. 351.

70. *Die Kommunistische Internationale*, No. 9, Petrograd, 1920, p. 6.

71. USPD, *Protokoll.* . . . , p. 27.

72. *Ibid.*, pp. 28, 30.

73. *Bulletin Communiste*, Paris, July 15, 1920, p. 11.

74. Henri Guilbeaux, *Du Kremlin au Cherehe-Midi*, Paris, 1933, pp. 229-30.

75. *Kommunistische Arbeiterzeitung*, No. 114, Berlin, 1920. (The exact date of the appearance of that paper was not indicated, though one may estimate it according to the material it published. Thus, Nos. 113 and 114 stem from July 1920, and the issues 133 and 136, quoted subsequently, were printed in the first half of August.)

76. *Ibid.*, No. 113.

77. *Ibid.*

78. *Ibid.*, No. 133.

79. *Ibid.*

80. *Ibid.*, No. 136.

81. *Ibid.*

82. *Bericht über den V. Parteitag der Kommunistischen Partei Deutschlands vom 1. bis 3. November 1920*, Berlin, 1921, p. 27.

83. *Ibid.*

84. "An das ZK der KPR, Moskau, 22. Juli 1920" (text in the authors' possession).

85. *Ibid.*

86. *Ibid.*

87. L.-O. Frossard, "A propos de la crise du communisme allemand," in *L'Internationale*, Paris, May 7, 1921.

88. P. Levi, "Bericht über die Verhandlungen in Moskau."

89. L.-O. Frossard in *L'Internationale*, May 7, 1921.

90. *Bericht über den V. Parteitag.* . . . , p. 36.

91. *Ibid.*, p. 27.

92. Willy Brandt and Richard Lowenthal, *Ernst Reuter—Ein Leben für die Freiheit*, Munich, 1957, p. 139.

93. Heinrich Brandler, *War die Märzaktion ein Bakunisten Putsch?*, Berlin, 1921, p. 18.

94. A. Rosmer, *op. cit.*, p. 110.

95. A. Balabanoff, *op. cit.*, p. 262.

96. *Die Kommunistische Internationale*, No. 12, Hamburg, 1920, p. 180.

97. *Ibid.*, p. 185.

98. *Ibid.*, p. 186.

99. V. I. Lenin, *op. cit.*, vol. 41, p. 199.

100. *Le Parti socialiste italien et l'Internationale*, pp. 11, 13.

101. J. Maurín, *Sur le communisme en Espagne* (manuscript in the authors' possession).

102. Angel Pestaña, *Setenta Días en Rusia. Lo que yo vi*, Barcelona, 1924, pp. 196-97.

103. *Die Kommunistische Internationale*, No. 13, 1920, p. 273.

104. *Die Tätigkeit der Exekutive und des Präsidiums der E.K. der Kommunistischen Internationale vom 13. Juli 1921 bis 1. Februar 1922*, p. 86.

105. Cf. *La Correspondance Internationale*, No. 30, April 19, 1922, articles "Ce qui se passe dans l'Union Syndicale Italienne" and "L'attitude des anarchistes italiens." In the same magazine but No. 31, April 26, 1922: "Lettre ouverte aux membres de l'Union Syndicale Italienne."

CHAPTER EIGHT

1. *Der zweite Kongress der Kommunistischen Internationale. Protokoll der Verhandlungen*, Hamburg, 1921, p. 75.

2. *Ibid.*, p. 572.

3. *Ibid.*, p. 315.

4. *Ibid.*, pp. 60, 61, 66, 73.

5. *Ibid.*, p. 87.

6. *Ibid.*, p. 88.

7. *Ibid.*, p. 123.

8. *Ibid.*, p. 392.

9. *Ibid.*, p. 111.

10. *Ibid.*, p. 239.

11. *Ibid.*, p. 597.

12. *Ibid.*, p. 572.

13. *Ibid.*, p. 89.

14. *Ibid.*, p. 239.

15. *Ibid.*, p. 604.

16. *Ibid.*, p. 116.

17. *Ibid.*, p. 601.

18. *Ibid.*, p. 87.

19. K. Radek, "Antoine Ker," *International Press Correspondence*, No. 57, 23 August 1923, p. 620.

20. *Der zweite Kongress.* . . . , p. 255.

21. *Ibid.*, p. 271.

22. V. I. Lenin, *Polnoe sobranie sochinenii*, 5th edition, vol. 41, Moscow, 1963, p. 191.

23. *Der zweite Kongress.* . . . , p. 119.

24. *Ibid.*, p. 75.

25. *Ibid.*, p. 77.

26. *Ibid.*, pp. 78, 79.

27. *Ibid.*, p. 83.

28. *Ibid.*, p. 377.

29. *Ibid.*, p. 370.

30. *Ibid.*, pp. 581-82.

31. *Ibid.*, p. 410.

32. *Der Weg der Revolution* (published by the Spartacus League), n.d., p. 8.

33. *Ibid.*, p. 10.

34. *Der zweite Kongress.* . . , p. 404.

35. *Ibid.*, pp. 468, 470.

36. W. Münzenberg, *S Libknekhtom i Leninym*, Moscow, 1930, p. 194.

37. J. T. Murphy, *New Horizons*, London, 1941, p. 150.

38. *Der zweite Kongress.* . . , pp. 422, 427.

39. *Ibid.*, p. 451.

40. Paul Levi, "Bericht über die Verhandlungen in Moskau" (in the authors' possession).

41. *Der zweite Kongress.* . . , p. 445.

42. *Die Kommunistische Internationale*, No. 12, 1920, p. 21.

43. *Ibid.*, p. 22.

44. *Ibid.*

45. *Ibid.*

46. *Der zweite Kongress.* . . , pp. 627-28.

47. *Ibid.*, p. 519.

48. *Ibid.*, p. 520.

49. Alfred Rosmer, *Moscou sous Lénine*, Paris 1953, p. 108.

50. *Der zweite Kongress.* . . , p. 58.

51. *Ibid.*, p. 484.

52. *Ibid.*, p. 486.

53. *Ibid.*, p. 492.

54. *Ibid.*, p. 491.

55. *Ibid.*, p. 501.

56. *Ibid.*, pp. 506-7.

57. *Ibid.*, p. 514.

58. *Ibid.*, p. 520.

59. *Ibid.*

60. *Ibid.*, p. 524.

61. *Ibid.*, p. 525.

62. *Ibid.*, pp. 615, 617.

63. *Ibid.*, p. 629.

64. *Ibid.*, p. 635.

65. Alfred Rosmer, *op. cit.,* p. 108.

66. Theodore Draper, *The Roots of American Communism*, New York, 1957, p. 257.

67. *Programme du Parti Social-Démocrate Ouvrier de Russie (Bolcheviki)*, Geneva, n.d., pp. 12, 13.

68. *Die Kommunistische Internationale*, Nos. 7-8, November-December 1919, p. 15.

69. N. Lénine, *Les Bolcheviks et les paysans*, Paris, 1920, p. 19.

70. *Protokoll des dritten Kongresses der Kommunistischen Internationale*, Hamburg, 1921, p. 515.

71. *Der zweite Kongress. . .* , p. 318.

72. *Ibid.*, p. 350.

73. V. Kolarov in *Die Kommunistische Internationale*, No. 9, September 1925, p. 929.

74. J. Marchlewski, "Die Agrarfrage und die Weltrevolution," in *Die Kommunistische Internationale*, No. 12, 1920, p. 91.

75. *Ibid.*, pp. 91-92.

76. *Ibid.*, pp. 92-93.

77. *Ibid.*, p. 93.

78. *Ibid.*, p. 95.

79. *Ibid.*, pp. 95-96.

80. V. I. Lenin, *op. cit.*, vol. 41, p. 169.

81. "Leitsätze des Exekutivkomitees der Kommunistischen Internationale zum II. Kongress der Kommunistischen Internationale," *Die Kommunistische Internationale*, No. 12, 1920, p. 29.

82. *Ibid.*

83. *Ibid.*, p. 30.

84. *Ibid.*, pp. 30-31.

85. *Ibid.*, p. 31.

86. *Ibid.*, p. 32.

87. V. I. Lenin, *op. cit.*, vol. 41, p. 177.

88. V. Kolarov in *Die Kommunistische Internationale*, No. 9, September 1925, pp. 930-31.

89. *Ibid.*, p. 938.

90. *Ibid.*, p. 939.

91. *Ibid.*, p. 930.

92. *Ibid.*, p. 929.

93. *Der zweite Kongress...*, p. 552.

94. *Ibid.*, p. 561.

95. *Ibid.*

96. V. I. Lenin, *op. cit.*, vol. 41, pp. 198-99.

97. Paul Levi, "Bericht über die Verhandlungen in Moskau" (in the authors' possession).

98. *Der zweite Kongress...*, p. 76.

99. *Ibid.*, p. 87.

100. *Ibid.*, pp. 763-64.

101. *Ibid.*, p. 89.

102. J. T. Murphy, *op. cit.*, p. 152.

103. *Der zweite Kongress.* . . . , p. 90.

104. *Ibid.*, pp. 90-91.

105. A. Rosmer, *op. cit.*, pp. 111-12.

106. *Der zweite Kongress.* . . . , p. 648.

107. W. Gallacher, *Revolt on the Clyde: An Autobiography*, London, 1936, p. 253.

108. Thomas Bell, *The British Communist Party: A Short History*, London, 1937, p. 65.

CHAPTER NINE

1. V. I. Lenin, *Polnoe sobranie sochinenii*, 5th edition, vol. 2, Moscow, 1958, pp. 452-53.

2. *Ibid.*, vol. 39, Moscow, 1963, p. 327.

3. Richard Pipes, *The Formation of the Soviet Union. Communism and Nationalism, 1917-1923*. Revised edition. New York, 1968, p. 35 et seq.

4. *Collected Works of V. I. Lenin*, vol. XIX, ("1916-1917"), New York 1942, pp. 47-60.

5. Quoted in *Materials for the Study of the Soviet System*, edited by James H. Meisel, Ann Arbor, 1953, p. 26.

6. Cf. Alexandre Bennigsen and Chantal Lemercier-Quelquejay, *Islam in the Soviet Union*, London, 1967, p. 67.

7. *Izvestiia*, No. 228, November 17 (old style), 1917.

8. *Ibid.*, No. 235, November 25, 1917.

9. M. A. Persits, "Vostochnye internatsionalisty v Rossii i nekotorye voprosy natsional'no-osvoboditel'nogo dvizheniia," in *Komintern i Vostok*, Moscow, 1969, p. 56.

10. *Ibid.*, pp. 70-71.

11. K. Troianovskii, *Vostok i revoliutsia*, Moscow, 1918, pp. 65-66.

12. M. A. Persits, *op. cit.*, p. 72.

13. *Ibid.*, pp. 86-87.

14. J. V. Stalin, *Works*, vol. 4, Moscow, 1953, p. 167.

15. *Zhizn natsionalnostei*, Moscow, No. 3, November 24, 1918. This speech is not included in Stalin's *Works*.

16. *Pervyi kongress Kominterna*, Moscow, 1933, p. 49.

17. *Ibid.*, p. 245.

18. *Ibid.*, p. 207.

19. *Zhizn natsionalnostei*, No. 8(16), March 9, 1919.

20. Alexandre Bennigsen et Chantal Quelquejay, *Les mouvements nationaux chez les Musulmans de Russie. Le "Sultangalievisme" au Tatarstan*, Paris-The Hague, 1960, p. 131.

21. An abstract of this report was published in *Izvestiia* of November 25, 1919, and in *Zhizn natsionalnostei* on December 7. A more complete text was printed in *Izvestiia* of December 20, and was reprinted in Lenin's *Polnoe sobranie sochinenii*, 5th ed., vol. 39, pp. 318-31. Excerpts of it in English are included in Lenin's *The National-Liberation Movement in the East*, Moscow, 1962, pp. 223-36.

22. V. I. Lenin, *op. cit.*, vol. 39, p. 330.

23. M. A. Persits, *op. cit.*, p. 96.

24. *Ibid.*, p. 100.

25. *Zhizn natsionalnostei*, Nos. 46(54), 48(56) and 1(58) of December 7 and 21, 1919 and January 4, 1920.

26. *Ibid.*, No. 46(54), December 7, 1919.

27. An abridged text was published in *Izvestiia*, No. 268(820) of November 29, 1918; a more complete one in *Zhizn natsionalnostei*, Nos. 46(54) and 47(55).

28. V. I. Lenin, *op. cit.*, 5th edition, vol. 40, Moscow, 1963, p. 98.

29. *Ibid.*, p. 145.

30. *Ibid.*, p. 177.

31. *Ibid.*, p. 209.

32. *Ibid.*, vol. 41, Moscow, 1963, p. 165.

33. *Ibid.*, p. 167.

34. *Ibid.*, p. 513.

35. Quoted in an article by A. Reznikov, "Bor'ba V. I. Lenina protiv sek-
    tantskikh izvrashchenii v natsional 'no-kolonial'nom voprose," *Kom-
    munist*, Moscow, No. 5, March 1968, p. 40.

36. *Ibid.*, p. 39.

37. *Ibid.*

38. V. I. Lenin, *op. cit.*, vol. 41, p. 513.

39. M. N. Roy, *Memoirs*, Bombay, 1964, p. 346.

40. *Ibid.*, pp. 355 and 379.

41. *Ibid.*, pp. 380-81.

42. A. Reznikov, "V. I. Lenin o natsional'no-osvoboditel'nom dvizhenii,"
    Kommunist, No. 7, May 1967, p. 92.

43. *Ibid.*, p. 93.

44. *Vestnik 2-go kongressa Kommunisticheskogo Internatsionala*, Moscow,
    No. 1, July 27, 1920, p. 1.

45. *Ibid.*

46. *Ibid.*

47. V. I. Lenin, *op. cit.* vol. 41, p. 241.

48. *Der zweite Kongress der Kommunistischen Internationale*, Hamburg,
    1921, pp. 785-87.

49. Cf. *Berichte zum zweiten Kongress der Kommunistischen Internation-
    ale*, Hamburg, 1921, table of contents.

50. V. I. Lenin, *op. cit.*, vol. 41, p. 235.

51. *Ibid.*, pp. 243-44.

52. *Ibid.*, p. 246.

53. *Der zweite Kongress.* . . , p. 149.

54. Cf. Demetrio Boersner, *The Bolsheviks and the National and Colonial Question (1917-1928)*, Geneva, 1957, p. 85.

55. *Der zweite Kongress.* . . , p. 159.

56. *Ibid.*, pp. 167-70.

57. *Ibid.*, pp. 170-73.

58. *Ibid.*, p. 176.

59. *Ibid.*, p. 180.

60. *Ibid.*, p. 196.

61. *Ibid.*, pp. 216-17.

62. *Ibid.*, p. 218.

63. *Ibid.*, pp. 218-19.

64. *Ibid.*, pp. 220-22

65. *Ibid.*, p. 232.

66. *Pervyi s"ezd narodov Vostoka*, Baku, 1-8 sent. 1920. Stenograficheskie otchety, Petrograd, 1920, p. 30.

67. *Izvestiia*, No. 144(991), July 3, 1920.

68. *Zhizn natsionalnostei*, No. 25(82), August 1, 1920.

69. G. Z. Sorkin, *Pervyi s"ezd narodov Vostoka*, Moscow, 1961, p. 16.

70. *Ibid.*, pp. 16-17.

71. *Pervyi s"ezd.* . . . , (Petrograd), p. 112.

72. E. D. Stasova, *Stranitsy zhizni i borby*, Moscow, 1957, pp. 109-10.

73. G. Z. Sorkin, *op. cit.*, p. 22.

74. *Pervyi s"ezd.* . . . , (Petrograd), p. 28-29.

75. *Ibid.*, pp. 9, 11, 12, 13.

76. *Ibid.*, p. 16.

77. *Ibid.*, pp. 30-48.

78. *Ibid.*, pp. 53-72.

79. *Ibid.*, pp. 88, 90, 91.

80. *Ibid.*, pp. 95-96.

81. *Ibid.*, p. 108.

82. *Ibid.*, pp. 112-16.

83. *Ibid.*, pp. 135-36.

84. *Ibid.*, pp. 211-12.

85. *Ibid.*, p. 219.

86. *Ibid.*, pp. 224-32.

87. Cf. M. Pavlovich in *Zhizn natsionalnostei*, No. 33(90), October 27, 1920.

88. There are some minor differences in the wording of this appeal as it was published in *Kommunisticheskii Internatsional*, No. 15, Petrograd, December 20, 1920, pp. 3141-50, and in *The Peoples of the East*, No. 1, October 1920, pp. 57-61, and reprinted in Sorkin, *op. cit.*, pp. 57-67. For example, the words "under the green banner of the Prophet," mentioned in the first source, were omitted in the latter.

89. *Kommunisticheskii Internatsional*, No. 14, November 6, 1920, pp. 2941-44.

90. *Ibid.*, No. 15, December 20, 1920, p. 3367.

91. Cf. *Zhizn natsionalnostei*, No. 41(97), December 24, 1920.

92. Cf. *Kommunisticheskii Internatsional*, No. 15, p. 3368.

93. E.D. Stasova, *op. cit.*, pp. 110-11.

94. G. Z. Sorkin, *op. cit.*, p. 44.

95. *Ibid.*, pp. 44-45.

96. *Kommunisticheskii Internatsional*, No. 16, March 31, 1921, pp. 3795-96.

97. G. Safarov, *Problemy Vostoka*, Moscow, 1922, p. 171.

98. Cf. Pavlovich-Weltmann's article on the Communist movement in Turkey, in *Kommunisticheskii Internatsional*, No. 17, June 7, 1921, pp. 4225-32.

99. *Zhizn natsionalnostei*, No. 7(105), March 17, 1921.

100. *Ibid.*, No. 6(104), March 4, 1921.

101. *Kommunisticheskii Internatsional*, No. 18, October 8, 1921, p. 4768.

102. *Dokumenty vneshnei politiki SSSR*, vol. III, Moscow, 1957, documents 131 and 350.

103. M. N. Roy, *op. cit.*, p. 392.

104. *Ibid.*, pp. 420-21.

105. *Protokoll des III. Kongresses der Kommunistischen Internationale*, Hamburg, 1921, p. 1018.

106. M. N. Roy, *op. cit.*, p. 525.

107. *Soviet Russia and the East, 1920-1927. A Documentary Survey*, by Xenia Joukoff Eudin and Robert C. North, Stanford, 1957, p. 85.

108. Liu Shao-chi, speech in Moscow's sports arena, *Pravda*, December 8, 1960.

109. *Biulleten' Dal'nevostochnogo Sekretariata Kominterna*, No. 1, 1921, p. 14.

CHAPTER TEN

1. *The Communist International*, Petrograd, No. 3, July 1, 1919, p. 370.

2. Jindřich Veselý, *Entstehung und Gründung der Kommunistischen Partei der Tschechoslowakei*, Berlin, 1955, p. 95.

3. Eugen Prager, *Geschichte der USPD*, 2nd edition, Berlin, 1922, p. 222.

4. V. I. Lenin, *Polnoe sobranie sochinenii*, 5th ed., vol. 41, Moscow, 1963, p. 277.

5. Arnold Struthahn (Karl Radek), *Die Entwicklung der deutschen Revolution und die Aufgaben der Kommunistischen Partei*, Stuttgart, 1919, pp. 52, 54.

6. G. Zinoviev, *Dvenadtsat dnei v Germanii*, Petrograd, 1920, p. 8.

7. Eugen Prager, *op. cit.*, p. 224.

8. G. Zinoviev, *Die Weltrevolution und die III. Kommunistische Internationale. Rede auf dem Parteitag der USPD in Halle am 14. Oktober 1920.* Berlin, 1920, p. 4.

9. *Ibid.* (The last sentence is incomplete in this brochure. The quotation is therefore taken from the minutes of the Halle congress: *Protokoll über die Verhandlungen des ausserordentlichen Parteitages in Halle*, Berlin, n.d., p. 151.)

10. *Ibid.*, pp. 14-16.

11. *Ibid.*, p. 29.

12. *Ibid.*, p. 54.

13. *Protokoll über die Verhandlungen des ausserordentlichen Parteitages in Halle*, pp. 180, 197.

14. *Ibid.*, pp. 184-85, 187-88.

15. *Ibid.*, p. 189.

16. *Die Rote Fahne*, Berlin, No. 211, October 19, 1920.

17. G. Zinoviev, *Dvenadtsat dnei...*, p. 15.

18. *Ibid.*, p. 113.

19. Paul Levi, *Der Beginn der Krise in der Kommunistischen Partei und Internationale*, Remscheid, 1922, p. 22.

20. *Bericht der Zentrale an den 2. Parteitag der VKPD vom 22. bis 26. August 1921 in Jena*, n.d., pp. 13-14.

21. *Journal du Peuple*, Paris, January 24, 1918.

22. *L'Humanité*, Paris, July 24, 1918.

23. A. Kemerer (V. Taratuta), "Brief an Jean Longuet und an das 'Komitee zur Wiederaufrichtung der Internationale,'" *Die Kommunistische Internationale*, No. 9, 1920, p. 1504.

24. *The Workers Dreadnought*, London, No. 41, January 3, 1920; also in V. I. Lenin, *Polnoe sobranie sochinenii*, 5th edition, vol. 39, Moscow, 1963, p. 251.

25. Leon Trotsky, *Sochineniia*, vol. 13, Moscow, 1926, p. 144.

26. V. I. Lenin, *op. cit.*, vol. 40, Moscow, 1963, p. 135.

27. L.-O. Frossard, *Le Parti socialiste et l'Internationale*. Rapport sur les négociations à Moscou, Paris, 1920, p. 5.

28. Parti socialiste, *Rapport du secrétariat au congrès national ordinaire du 25 décembre 1920*, Paris, n.d., p. 8.

29. *Der zweite Kongress der Kommunistischen Internationale*. Protokoll der Verhandlungen, Hamburg, 1921, pp. 263-64.

30. *Le problème de l'Internationale*. Controverse entre les citoyens Cachin-Frossard-Mayéras, Lille, 1920, p. 37.

31. *Der zweite Kongress...*, p. 391.

32. Parti socialiste, *18ème congrès national tenu à Tours*. Compte rendu sténographique, Paris, 1921, p. 398.

33. *Ibid.*, p. 486.

34. G. Zinoviev, *Dvenadtsat dnei...*, p. 52.

35. *Le Phare*, La Chaux-de-Fonds, No. 14, November 1920, p. 75.

36. V. I. Lenin, *op. cit.*, vol. 41, p. 686.

37. Parti socialiste, *18ème congrès national tenu à Tours*, pp. 312-13.

38. *Ibid.*, pp. 585, 583.

39. *Ibid.*, p. 447.

40. Letter from C. Zetkin to P. Levi dated January 10, 1921 (in the authors' possession).

41. *Ibid.*

42. Parti socialiste, *18ème congrès national tenu à Tours*, p. 391.

43. *Ibid.*, p. 419.

44. *Ibid.*, p. 244.

45. *Ibid.*, p. 246.

46. *Ibid.*, p. 247.

47. *Ibid.*, p. 255.

48. *Ibid.*, p. 381.

49. *Ibid.*, p. 488.

50. *Un an d'action communiste.* Rapport du secrétariat général, Cour-
bevoie, 1921, p. 37.

51. G. Zinoviev, *Ce que a été jusqu'ici l'Internationale communiste et ce
qu'elle doit être*, Petrograd, 1920, p. 15.

52. Parti socialiste, *17ème congrès national tenu à Strasbourg.* Compte rendu
sténographique, Paris, 1920, p. 286.

53. A. Rossi, *La naissance du fascisme en Italie, de 1918 à 1922*, Paris 1938,
p. 62.

54. V. I. Lenin, *Sochineniia*, 3rd edition, vol. 25, Moscow, 1929, p. 360.

55. *Die Kommunistische Internationale*, No. 13, Petrograd, 1920, pp.
289-90.

56. *Ibid.*, p. 294.

57. *L'Internationale Communiste*, No. 14, November 1920, pp. 2915-16.

58. *Le Parti socialiste italien et l'Internationale communiste* (Recueil de documents), Petrograd, 1921, p. 57.

59. *Ibid.*, p. 97 (emphasis in the text).

60. *18ème congrès national tenu à Tours*, pp. 398-99.

61. A. Rossi, *op. cit.*, p. 66.

62. *Umanità Nuova*, Rome, October 11, 1964, letter from Silone to A.
Borghi.

63. *Le Parti socialiste italien. . .* , p. 100.

64. *Bulletin du IIIe congrès de l'Internationale communiste*, Moscow, June
29, 1921, No. 6, p. 9.

65. V. I. Lenin, *Polnoe sobranie sochinenii*, 5th edition, vol. 41, p. 418.

66. *Ibid.*, pp. 418, 422.

67. V. Degot, *Pod znamenem bol'shevizma*, Moscow, 1927, p. 143.

68. *Le Parti socialiste italien. . .* , p. 113.

69. "Rede des Genossen Rákosi, Mitglied der Exekutive, am 16. Februar 1921" (in the authors' possession).

70. "Khristo Kabakchiev-Bio-bibliography" (in Bulgarian), Sofia, 1958, p. 38.

71. C. Zetkin's letter of January 10, 1921 (in the authors' possession).

72. Paul Levi, *Was ist das Verbrechen? Die Märzaktion order die Kritik daran?* Berlin, 1921, p. 42.

73. Paul Levi, *Der Beginn der Krise . . .* , pp. 15-16.

74. "Bericht des Genossen Levi an das Exekutivkomitee der III. Internationale über den italienischen Parteitag," January 20, 1921 (in the authors' possession).

75. *Bulletin du IIIe congrès. . .* , No. 4, June 25, 1921, p. 11.

76. C. Zetkin's letter of January 10, 1921.

77. Paul Levi, *Der Beginn der Krise . . .* , p. 16.

78. "Sitzung der Zentrale mit dem Vertreter des Exekutivkomitees für Deutschland, Berlin, Freitag, den 28. Januar 1921" (in the authors' possession).

79. Paul Levi, *Der Beginn der Krise . . .* , p. 22.

80. V. I. Lenin, *op. cit.*, vol. 52, Moscow, 1965, p. 149.

81. *Le Parti socialiste italien. . .* , p. 154.

82. "Sitzung der Zentrale mit dem Vertreter. . . . "

83. V. Degot, *op. cit.*, p. 146.

84. "Bericht des Genossen Levi an das Exekutivkomitee. . . ."

85. "Sitzung der Exekutive am 22. Februar 1921, Moskau" (in the authors' possession).

86. A. Rossi, *op. cit.*, p. 191.

87. "Rapport du camarade B. Jílek sur le développement et l'état du parti communiste de Tchécoslovaquie." Second enlarged plenum of the ECCI, June 1922 (in the authors' possession).

88. *Rude Pravo*, Prague, December 28, 1920. For the full text see *Kommunisticheskii Internatsional*, No. 16, 1921, pp. 3825-28.

89. *Acta Historica*, Budapest, Vol. VI, Nos. 1-2, 1959, p. 48.

90. *Kommunisticheskii Internatsional*, No. 16, 1921, pp. 3881-82.

91. *Ibid.*, No. 17, 1921, pp. 4317-20.

92. Jindřich Veselý, *op. cit.*, p. 188.

93. *Ibid.*

94. "Rapport du camarade B. Jílek...."

CHAPTER ELEVEN

1. H. Remmele, "Um den proletarischen Machtkampf in Deutschland," *Die Kommunistische Internationale*, Nos. 31-32, 1924, p. 161.

2. *Bericht über die Verhandlungen des Vereinigungsparteitages der U.S. P.D. (Linke) und der K.P.D. (Spartakusbund), abgehalten in Berlin vom 4. bis 7. Dezember 1920*, Berlin, 1921, pp. 232-33.

3. "Sitzung der Zentrale mit dem Vertreter des Exekutivkomitees für Deutschland" (Minutes in the authors' possession). The complete minutes have been published in Milorad M. Drachkovitch and Branko Lazitch, *The Comintern: Historical Highlights*, New York, 1966, pp. 285-99.

4. Paul Levi, *Der Beginn der Krise in der Kommunistischen Partei und Internationale*, Remscheid, 1921, p. 12.

5. "Sitzung der Exekutive am 22. Februar 1921, Moskau" (minutes in the authors' possession).

6. *Ibid.*

7. A. Struthahn [K. Radek], *Die Entwicklung der deutschen Revolution und die Aufgaben der Kommunistischen Partei*, Stuttgard, 1919, p. 50.

8. *Contributions à l'histoire du Comintern*, Geneva, 1965, p. 25.

9. "Sitzung der Exekutive am 22. Februar 1921."

10. *Ibid.*

11. *Ibid.*

12. *Contributions à l'histoire du Comintern*, p. 18.

13. *Die Kommunistische Internationale*, No. 17, 1921, p. 67.

14. P. Levi, *Der Beginn der Krise. . .*, p. 11.

15. *Ibid.*

16. *Ibid.*, p. 16.

17. *Bulletin des III. Kongresses der Kommunistischen Internationale*, No. 6, Moscow, July 2, 1921, p. 137.

18. *Die Rote Fahne*, Berlin, February 5, 1921.

19. "Sitzung der Exekutive am 22. Februar 1921."

20. P. Levi, *Der Beginn der Krise. . .*, p. 13.

21. *Die Rote Fahne*, February 15, 1921.

22. *Ibid.*, February 11, 1921.

23. "Exposé über die Lage der Partei, 10. März 1921" (in the authors' possession).

24. *Ibid.*

25. "Sitzung der Zentrale mit dem Vertreter des Exekutivkomitees für Deutschland."

26. *Ibid.*

27. P. Levi, *Der Beginn der Krise. . .*, p. 17.

28. "Max's" undated letter from Moscow to his faction in Berlin (probably written sometime in mid-February, in the authors' possession).

29. "Sitzung der Exekutive am 22. Februar 1921."

30. *Ibid.*

31. P. Levi, *Der Beginn der Krise. . .*, p. 24.

32. *Ibid.*, p. 22.

33. Radek's letter dated March 14, 1921 (in the authors' possession). This letter, except for the first paragraph, is reproduced in *Der deutsche Kommunismus*, edited by Hermann Weber, Cologne-Berlin, 1963, p. 210.

34. *All Power to the Workers.* Four speeches delivered at the Tenth Congress of the Russian Communist Party, Petrograd, 1921, p. 32.

35. *Pravda*, November 16, 1966.

36. B. K., "Die Ereignisse in Deutschland," *Kommunismus,* April 24, 1920, p. 440.

37. Alfred Rosmer, *Moscou sous Lénine*, Paris, 1953, p. 175.

38. Geyer confirmed this to Richard Lowenthal. (Cf. *International Communism*, edited by D. Footman, London, 1960, p. 57. Rosmer confirmed the same fact to Branko Lazitch.)

39. Béla Kun, *La République hongroise des Conseils*, Budapest, 1962, p. 209.

40. V. I. Lenin, *Polnoe sobranie sochinenii*, 5th edition, vol. 51, Moscow, 1965, p. 169.

41. *Ibid.*, vol. 53, Moscow, 1965, p. 45.

42. V. I. Lenin, *op. cit.*, vol. 44, Moscow, 1964, p. 92.

43. Radek's letter of mid-February 1921 (in the authors' possession).

44. Wilhelm Koenen, *Moi vstrechi s Leninym*, Moscow, 1960, p. 22.

45. Paul Levi's letter of March 27, 1921, to Lenin (in the authors' possession).

46. Radek's letter of April 7, 1921, to the central committee (in the authors' possession).

47. V. I. Lenin, *op. cit.*, vol. 52, Moscow, 1965, p. 149. Emphasis in the text.

48. *Ibid.*

49. *Nos rencontres avec Lénine*, Moscow, 1939, p. 18.

50. V. I. Lenin, *op. cit.*, vol. 42, Moscow, 1963, p. 592.

51. *Die Kommunistische Internationale*, No. 17, 1921, pp. 413, 415.

52. "Priznaki buri v Germanii," *Pravda*, March 25, 1921. Emphasis in the text.

53. Radek's letter of March 14, 1921 (in the authors' possession).

54. Paul Levi's letter of March 27, 1921, to Lenin.

55. Thalheimer's letter of April 14, 1921, to Radek (in the authors' possession).

56. "Funktionärsitzung der V.K.P.D. am 7. April 1921 in Kliems Festsälen, Hasenheide" (minutes in the authors' possession).

57. Radek's letter of March 14, 1921.

58. Radek's letter of April 1, 1921, to the central committee (in the authors' possession).

59. Paul Levi, *Was ist das Verbrechen? Die Märzaktion oder die Kritik daran?*, Berlin, 1921, p. 8.

60. Quoted by P. Levi in the "Funktionärsitzung der V.K.P.D. am 7. April 1921" (cf. also P. Levi, *Unser Weg. Wider den Putschismus*, p. 22).

61. *Pravda*, March 25, 1921.

62. Paul Levi, "An das Präsidium des III. Kongresses der Kommunistischen Internationale," May 31, 1921 (letter in the authors' possession).

63. Paul Levi, *Was ist das Verbrechen?* . . . , p. 8.

64. "Funktionärsitzung der V.K.P.D. am 7. April 1921. . . ."

65. "Fortsetzung der Funktionärenversammlung der V.K.P.D. in Kliems Festsälen, Hasenheide, am Sontag, den 10.4.1921," (minutes in the authors' possession).

66. Paul Levi, *Was ist das Verbrechen?* . . . , p. 8.

67. *Contributions à l'histoire du Comintern*, p. 26.

68. *Ibid.*, p. 25.

69. "Funktionärsitzung der V.K.P.D. am 7. April 1921. . . ."

70. Paul Levi, "An das Präsidium des III. Kongresses. . . ."

71. Victor Méric, *Coulisses et Tréteaux*, second series, Paris, 1931, p. 58.

72. *Ibid.*, p. 72.

73. L. Laurat, "Souvenirs" (manuscript in the authors' possession).

74. "Beschluss des Zentralausschusses vom 17. März 1921" (a photocopy of this document is in the authors' possession).

75. *Die Rote Fahne*, No. 129, March 18, 1921.

76. For a description of the "March action" see the chapter "The March

Uprising and Its Failure" in *Stillborn Revolution. The Communist Bid for Power in Germany, 1921-1923*, by Werner T. Angress, Princeton, 1963.

77. "Funktionärsitzung der V.K.P.D. am 7. April 1921. . . ."

78. Paul Levi's letter of March 27, 1921, to Lenin.

79. *Ibid.*

80. "Fortsetzung der Funktionärenversammlung der V.K.P.D. . . ."

81. Paul Levi, *Unser Weg.* . . , p. 53.

82. *Ibid.*

83. Clara Zetkin's letter of April 11, 1921 (photocopy in the authors' possession).

84. Paul Levi, *op. cit.*, p. 54.

85. *Ibid.*, p. 55.

86. *Ibid.*, p. 56.

87. *Ibid.*

88. Declaration: Otto Brass, Paul Eckert, Ernst Däumig, Curt Geyer, Adolf Hoffmann, Heinrich Malzahn, Paul Neumann, Clara Zetkin. Cf. *Bericht über die Verhandlungen des 2. Parteitages der KPD*, p. 64.

89. Paul Levi's declaration of May 5, 1921 (in the authors' possession).

90. Paul Levi, *Was ist das Verbrechen?* . . . , p. 31.

91. *Ibid.*

92. Clara Zetkin's letter of April 11, 1921.

93. From an undated Paul Levi's letter (in the authors' possession).

94. *Ibid.* This idea was further developed in his speech of May 4, 1921, before the central committee of the German Communist Party. Cf. *Was ist das Verbrechen? Die Märzaktion oder die Kritik daran?* pp. 20-21.

95. Cf. *Bulletin des III. Kongresses.* . . , No. 12, July 9, 1921, p. 275.

96. *Die Internationale*, Berlin, No. 3, 1921, p. 67.

97. Radek's letter of April 7, 1921, to the central committee.

98. *Taktik und Organisation der revolutionären Offensive. Die Lehren der März-Aktion*, Leipzig-Berlin, 1921, pp. 143-44.

99. "Funktionärsitzung der V.K.P.D. am 7. April 1921...."

100. "Fortsetzung der Funktionärenversammlung der V.K.P.D...."

101. *Ibid.*

102. *Taktik und Organisation der revolutionären Offensive* ..., pp. 3, 6.

103. *Ibid.*, p. 15.

104. *Ibid.*, p. 138.

105. *Die Internationale*, No. 4, 1921, p. 125.

106. *Ibid.*, No. 7, June 1921, p. 254.

107. *Die Kommunistische Internationale*, No. 17, 1921, p. 365.

108. *Ibid.*, p. 366.

109. Cf. Paul Levi, *Was ist das Verbrechen?* .., pp. 30-31.

110. "An das Präsidium des III. Kongresses der Kommunistischen Internationale," May 31, 1921, pp. 7-9.

111. *Ibid.*, p. 3. In this letter to the Presidium of the Third Congress of the Comintern, Levi quoted from Karl Radek's brochure entitled "Soll die V.K.P.D. eine Massenpartei der revolutionären Aktion oder eine zentristische Partei des Wartens sein? "

112. *Ibid.*, p. 4.

113. Radek's letter of April 7, 1921, to the central committee.

114. *Die Kommunistische Internationale*, No. 17, 1921, p. 365.

115. *Bulletin Communiste*, Paris, No. 24, June 9, 1921, p. 399.

116. Radek's letter of April 7, 1921, to the central committee.

117. *War die Märzaktion ein Bakunisten-Putsch?* , Berlin-Leipzig, 1921, p. 18.

118. V. I. Lenin, *op. cit.*, vol. 52, p. 149.

119. *Ibid.*, vol. 45, Moscow, 1964, p. 25.

120. *Ibid.*, vol. 52, p. 265. Emphasis in the text.

121. "Sitzung des Zentralausschusses am 22. Februar 1921" (in the authors' possession).

122. V. I. Lenin, *op. cit.*, vol. 52, p. 149.

123. *Ibid.*, vol. 43, Moscow, 1963, p. 188.

124. Paul Levi, *Der Beginn der Krise...*, p. 24.

125. Paul Levi's letter of March 27, 1921, to Lenin.

126. *Bulletin des III. Kongresses...*, No. 13, July 10, 1921, p. 293.

127. *Bericht über die Verhandlungen des 2. Parteitages der Kommunistischen Partei Deutschlands (Sektion der Kommunistischen Internationale), abgehalten in Jena vom 22. bis 26. August 1921*, Berlin, 1922, p. 13, and *Bericht über die Verhandlungen des III. (8.) Parteitages der K.P.D. (Sektion der K. I.) abgehalten in Leipzig vom 28. Januar bis 1. Februar 1923*, Berlin, 1923, p. 63.

128. *Die Kommunistische Internationale*, Nos. 31-32, 1924, p. 73.

CHAPTER TWELVE

1. V. I. Lenin, *Polnoe sobranie sochinenii*, 5th ed., vol. 42, Moscow, 1963, p. 91.

2. *Manifestes, Thèses et Résolutions des quatre premiers congrès de l'Internationale communiste, 1919-1923*, Paris, 1934, p. 104.

3. V. I. Lenin, *op. cit.*, vol. 41, Moscow, 1963, p. 166.

4. P. Levi, "Bericht über die Verhandlungen in Moskau. Rede auf der Zentralausschusssitzung am 25.8.1920" (in the authors' possession).

5. Clara Zetkin, *Roza Liuksemburg i russkaia revoliutsiia*, Moscow-Petrograd, 1924, pp. 130-31.

6. V. I. Lenin, *op. cit.*, vol. 51, Moscow, 1965, pp. 236, 438.

7. *Ibid.*, p. 248.

8. *Ibid.*, p. 252.

9. *Ibid.*, p. 260.

10. *Ibid.*, p. 264.

11. Cf. Mac Barthel, *Kein Bedarf an Weltgeschichte*, Wiesbaden, 1950, pp. 120-21.

12. "Sitzung der Zentrale mit dem Vertreter des Exekutivkomitees für Deutschland, Berlin, Freitag, den 28. Januar 1921" (in the authors' possession).

13. Clara, Zetkin, *Reminiscences of Lenin*, London, 1929, p. 20.

14. V. I. Lenin, *op. cit.*, vol. 41, p. 276.

15. *Ibid.*, p. 282.

16. *Ibid.*, pp. 348-49.

17. "Sitzung der Zentrale. . . , "

18. V. I. Lenin, *op. cit.*, vol. 41, p. 297. Emphasis in the text.

19. *Ibid.*, 416-17.

20. *Ibid.*, pp. 417-18.

21. *Ibid.*, vol. 42, p. 1.

22. *Ibid.*, p. 3.

23. *Ibid.*, pp. 3-4.

24. *Ibid.*, p. 20.

25. *Ibid.*, pp. 20-21.

26. *Ibid.*, p. 22.

27. *Ibid.*, p. 59.

28. *Ibid.*, vol. 43, Moscow, 1963, pp. 68, 70.

29. *Ibid.*, p. 248.

30. *Ibid.*, vol. 44, Moscow, 1964, p. 150.

31. Karl Kautsky, *Die Diktatur des Proletariats*, Vienna, 1918, p. 28.

32. V. I. Lenin, *op. cit.*, vol. 37, Moscow, 1963, pp. 299-300. Emphasis in the text.

33. G. Zinoviev, *Die Weltrevolution und die III. Kommunistische Internationale*, Berlin, 1920, p. 17.

34. G. Zinoviev, *Dvenadtsat dnei v Germanii*, Petrograd, 1920, p. 18.

35. V. I. Lenin, *op. cit.*, vol. 39, Moscow, 1963, p. 20.

36. *Ibid.*, p. 330.

37. *Der zweite Kongress der Kommunistischen Internationale*, Hamburg, 1921, p. 349.

38. *Vestnik 2-ogo kongressa Kommunisticheskoga Internatsionala*, Moscow, No. 1, July 27, 1920.

39. V. I. Lenin, *op. cit.*, vol. 43, pp. 340-41.

40. *Bulletin des III. Kongresses der Kommunistischen Internationale*, Moscow, July 13, 1921, p. 384.

41. V. I. Lenin, *op. cit.*, vol. 42, p. 58.

42. *Ibid.*, p. 115.

43. *Ibid.*, vol. 43, pp. 191-92.

44. *Ibid.*, vol. 44, pp. 160-61.

45. V. I. Lenin, *Sobranie sochinenii*, 1st ed., vol. 17, Moscow, 1923, p.468.

46. V. I. Lenin, *Polnoe sobranie sochinenii*, 5th ed., vol. 43, p. 195.

47. *Ibid.*, vol. 54, Moscow, 1965, p. 444.

48. Cf. *Die Tätigkeit der Exekutive der Kommunistischen Internationale vom 13. Juli 1921 bis 1. Februar 1922*, Petrograd, 1922. Meeting of the Presidium on September 6, pp. 163-68. However, *Kommunisticheskii Internatsional*, Moscow, 1969, p. 147, gives this information.

49. *Soviet Documents on Foreign Policy*, vol. I, 1917-24, London, 1951, p. 258.

50. V. I. Lenin, *op. cit.*, vol. 52, Moscow, 1965, p. 181.

51. Souvarine's letter of December 7, 1921 (in the authors' possession).

52. Jílek's report on the developments and state of the Czechoslovak Communist Party before the Presidium of the Executive Committee,

June 3, 1922 (in the authors' possession).

53. *Soviet Documents on Foreign Policy*, vol. 1, p. 229.

54. V. I. Lenin, *op. cit.*, vol. 42, pp. 95-96.

55. *Ibid.*, vol. 43, p. 57.

56. Cf. *Ibid.*, vol. 54, p. 444.

57. *Ibid.*, vol. 45, Moscow, 1964, p. 282.

58. *Ibid.*, vol. 42, p. 360.

59. *Ibid.*, vol. 44, p. 41.

60. *Ibid.*, vol. 42, p. 44.

61. *Ibid.*, p. 56.

62. *Ibid.*, vol. 44, pp. 42, 45.

63. *Ibid.*, p. 208.

64. *Ibid.*, p. 204.

65. *Ibid.*, vol. 42, p. 116.

66. Quoted in *The Communist International, 1919-1943. Documents.* Selected and edited by Jane Degras. Volume I, 1919-1923, London-New York-Toronto, 1956, p. 57.

67. *Der zweite Kongress. . . .*, p. 706.

68. V. I. Lenin, *op. cit.*, vol. 41, p. 60.

69. *Ibid.*, p. 282.

70. *Ibid.*, p. 353.

71. *Ibid.*, vol. 42, pp. 104, 105.

72. Xenia Joukoff Eudin and Robert North, *Soviet Russia and the East, 1920-27*, Stanford, 1957, p. 186.

73. *Ibid.*, p. 188.

74. *Soviet Documents on Foreign Policy*, vol. 1, p. 237.

75. *Bulletin des III. Kongresses. . .*, July 19, 1921, No. 23, pp. 519-20.

76. *Bulletin du IVe congrès de l'Internationale communiste*, Moscow, December 2, 1922, No. 20, p. 15.

77. *Ibid.*, November 27, 1922, No. 17, pp. 28-29.

78. V. I. Lenin, *op. cit.*, vol. 43, p. 43.

79. *Ibid.*, p. 111.

80. *Leninskii sbornik*, vol. 36, Moscow, 1959, p. 208.

81. V. I. Lenin, *op. cit.*, vol. 53, Moscow, 1965, pp. 273, 435.

82. Cf. *Bericht des Exekutivkomitees der Kommunistischen Internationale an den zweiten Weltkongress der Kommunistischen Internationale*, Berlin, 1920, p. 5.

Bibliographical Note

A complete bibliography, listing all the sources used in the preparation of this work, will be found at the end of the second volume.

Index